The Works of the Rev. Hugh Binning

CONTENTS

Fellowship With God (continued)

Heart-Humiliation

An Useful Case Of Conscience

A Treatise Of Christian Love.

Several Sermons Upon The Most Important Subjects Of Practical Religion.

FELLOWSHIP WITH GOD (CONTINUED)

SERMON XVI.

1 John i. 8.—"If we say that we have no sin, we deceive ourselves, and the truth is not in us."

"The night is far spent, the day is at hand," Rom. xiii. 12. This life is but as night, even to the godly. There is some light in it,—some star light, but it is mixed with much darkness of ignorance and sin, and so it will be, till the sun arise, and the morning of their translation to heaven come. But though it be called night in one sense, in regard of that perfect glorious perpetual day in heaven, yet they are called the children of light, and of the day, and are said to walk in the light, and are exhorted to walk honestly as in the day, because, though there is a mixture of darkness in them, of weakness in their judgments, and impurity in their affections, yet they are *nati ad majora*, "born to greater things," and aspiring to that perfect day. There is so much light as to discern these night-monsters, their own corruptions, and Satan's temptations,—to fight continually against them. They are about this noble work, the purifying themselves from sin and darkness, so that they lie in the middle, between the light of angels and glorified spirits, that hath no darkness in it, and the midnight of the rest of the world, who are buried in darkness and wickedness, and lie entombed in it, as the word is, 1 John v. 19, "The whole world, (κατται) lieth in wickedness: but we know that we are of God," therefore the apostle subjoins here very seasonably a caution or correction of that which was spoken about the walking in the light, and fellowship with God, which words sound out some perfection, and, to our self flattering minds, might possibly suggest some too high opinion of ourselves. If we, even we that have fellowship with God, even I, the apostle, and you believing Christians, if we say, we have no sin, no darkness in us, we do but deceive ourselves, and deny the truth. But who will say that I have no sin? Solomon gives a challenge to all the world, Prov. xx. 9, "Who can say, I have made my heart clean, I am pure from my sin?" And, indeed, there is no man so far a stranger to himself, but if he, in sobriety and calmness, retire into his own heart, the very evidence of the impurity of it will extort this confession from him. As it useth to be said of an atheist, he feels that Divine majesty within his secret thoughts and conscience which he denieth with his mouth, and he is often forced to tremble at the remembrance of him whom he will not confess.[244] So if there be any so far bewitched and enchanted into so gross and impudent a delusion, as to assert his own perfection and vacancy from sin, and freedom from obligation to any divine command (as this time is fruitful of such monsters), yet I dare be bold to say, that in the secret and quiet reflections on themselves, they find that which they will not confess. Inwardly they feel what outwardly they deny, and cannot but sometime or other be filled with horror and anguish in their consciences, by that inwardly witnessing and checking principle, when God shall give it liberty to exercise its power over them. The end of such will be, as of professed atheists. They pretend the securest contempt and most fearless disregard of God, but then, when he awakes to judgment, or declares himself in something extraordinary, they are subject to the most panic fears and terrors, because then there is a party armed within against them, which they had disarmed in security, and kept in chains. So, whensoever such men, of such high pretensions, and sublime professions, who love to speak nothing but mysteries, and presume to such glorious discoveries of new lights of spiritual mysteries; when these, I say, have flattered themselves for a season, in the monstrous exorbitant conceit of their own perfection, and immunity from sin, and, it may be, deceived some others too, when they have lived some time in this golden dream of innocency, the time will come, either when the mighty hand of God is on them here, or when they must enter eternity, that they shall awake, and find all their iniquities in battle array, mustered by the Lord of hosts, in their conscience against themselves, and then they shall be the rarest examples of fear, terror, and unbelief who pretended to the greatest confidence, clearness, and innocency. My beloved, let us establish this as an infallible rule, to discern the spirits by, and to know what religion is,—if it tend to glorify God, and abase man, to make him more humble, as well as holy,—if it give the true and perfect discovery of God to man, and of man to himself,—that is true religion and undefiled. But away with those sublime speculations, those winged and airy mysteries, those pretensions to high discoveries and new lights, if they do not increase that good old light of "humble walking with thy God" &c. If they tend to the loosing of the obligation of divine commands on thee, if they ravish man so high that he seeth not himself any more to be a poor, miserable, and darkened creature, certainly that is no fellowship with the pure light, which is not continually the discovery and further manifestation of more sin and darkness in us. For what is a man's light in the dark night of this life, but the clearing light of that darkness that is in man? And his holiness what is it, but the abhorring of himself for that? It is true, something further is attained than the knowing of this, but it is always so far short of that original pattern that the best way of expressing our conformity to it, is by how much we apprehend our distance and deformity from it.

But, my beloved, this is not all that is here meant, nor must we take it so grossly, as if this did only check the open professors of a sinless, spotless sanctity. Nay, certainly, there is another way of saying this than by the tongue and many other ways of self deceiving than that gross one, many more universal and more dangerous, because less discernible. There is something of this that even true believers may fall into, and there is something of it more common to the generality of professed Christians.

Among believers in Christ there is much difference in self judging, extreme contrarieties, both between diverse persons and in one and the same, at diverse times. You know that some are kept in the open view of their own sins and infirmities, and while they aim at holiness they are wholly disabled to that worthy endeavour by their discouragements arising from the apprehension of their own weakness and infinite short coming. Now to elevate and strengthen such spirits, that word was seasonally cast in, "and the blood of Jesus Christ cleanseth from all sin," for it properly belongs to the comfort of such fainting souls, and it is all one as if he had said, up and be doing, and the blood of Christ shall cleanse your evil doings. He goeth not about to persuade them to have better thoughts of themselves, or lower apprehensions of their sins but only to have higher and more suitable thoughts of Christ, and the virtue of his blood, and this is the only cure,—not to abate from that low esteem of ourselves, but to add to the esteem and grow in the lively apprehension of Christ. I would not counsel you to think yourselves better, but to think better of him, that all your confidence may arise from him.

Now there are others, (and it may be that same person at another time,—for the wind of temptation veers about, and is sometimes in one corner, sometimes in an other,—our adversary useth many stratagems, and will seem to flee before us, in yielding us the victory over our unbelief, that he may in his flight return and throw some other dart upon us unawares,) when they have attained any fervency of desires, and height of design after holiness and walking with God, and this is seconded with any lively endeavours, and this confirmed and strengthened with those presences of God, and accesses into the soul, that fill it with some sweetness,—then, I say, they are ready to apprehend too highly of themselves, as if they had attained, and to look below upon others with some disdain. Then there is not that present discovery of themselves, that may intermingle humble mourning with it, but a kind of unequal measuring their attainments by their desires, which in all true Christians are exceedingly mounted above themselves. Now, indeed, this is in effect, and really to say, "we have no sin." Herein is a delusion, a self deceiving fancy, that begets too much self pleasing. Let us know where our stance is,[245] infinitely below either our duty or our desire, and remind this often, that we may not be in hazard to be drunk with self love and self deceit in this particular. Besides, are there not many Christians who, having been once illuminated, and had some serious exercises in their souls, both of sorrow for sin and fear of wrath and comfort by the gospel, and being accustomed to some discharge of religious duties in private and public, sit down here, and have not mind of further progress? They think, if they keep that stance, they are well, and so have few designs or endeavours after more communion with God, or purification from sin. Now this makes them degenerate to formality. They wither and become barren, and are exposed by this to many temptations which overcome them. But, my beloved, is not this really and indeed to say, "we have no sin?" Do not your walking and the posture of your spirits import so much, as if you had no sin to wrestle with, no more holiness to aspire unto, as if ye had no further race to run to obtain the crown? Do not deceive yourselves, by thinking it sufficient to have so much honesty and grace, as in your opinion may put you over the black line, in irregeneration, as if ye would seek no more than is precisely necessary for salvation. Truly, if ye be so minded, you give a miserable hint, that you are not yet translated from the black side of darkness. I do not say that all such are unconverted, but, if you continue thus, without stirring up yourselves to a daily conversion and renovation, ye do too much to blot out the evidence of your conversion and at length it may prove to some a self destroying deceit, when they shall find themselves not passed over that line that passeth between heaven and hell, which they were studying to find out, only that they might pass so far over it, as might keep their soul and hell asunder, without earnest desires of advancement towards heaven in conformity to God. Now, for the generality of professed Christians, though there be none who have that general confession of sin oftener and more readily in their mouths, yet, I suppose, it is easy to demonstrate that there is much of this self deceit in them, which declares that the truth is not in them. You know both God and man construct[246] of men by their ways, not by their words, and the Lord may interpret your hearts by their dispositions, and raise a collection of atheism out of all together. "The fool hath said in his heart," &c. Even so say I, many pretended Christians say in their heart, "we have no sin." How prove ye that? I seek nothing else to prove it, than your own ordinary clearings and excusings of yourselves. Ye confess ye are sinners, and break all the commands, yet come to particulars, and I know not one of twenty that will cordially or seriously take with almost any sin. Yea, what you have granted in a general, you retract and deny it in all the particulars, which declares both that even that which you seem to know, you are altogether strangers to the real truth of it, and that you are over blinded with a fond love of yourselves. I know not to what purposes your general acknowledgments are, but to be a mask or shadow to deceive you, to be a blind to hide you from yourselves, since the most part of you, whensoever challenged of any particular sin, or inclination to it, justify yourselves, and whenever ye are put to a particular confession of your sins, you have all rapt up in such a bundle of confusion, that you never know one sin by another. Certainly, ye deceive yourselves, and the truth is not in you.

Let me add, moreover, another instance. Do you not so live, and walk in sin so securely, so impenitently, as if you had no sin, no fear of God's wrath? Do not the most part contentedly and peaceably live in so much ignorance of the gospel, as if they had no need of Christ, and so, by consequence, as if they had no sin? For if you did believe in the heart, and indeed consider that your hearts are sinks of iniquity and impurity, would you not think it necessary to apply to the Physician? And would you not then labour to know the Physician, and the gospel, which is the report of him? Certainly, inasmuch as you take no pains for the knowledge of a Saviour, you declare that you know not your sin, for if ye know the one, ye could not but search to know the other. What is the voice of most men's walking? Doth it not proclaim this, that they think there is no sin in them? For if there be sin in you, is there not a curse upon you, and wrath before you? And if you did really see the one, would you not see the other? And did you see it, would it not drive you to more serious thoughts? Would it not affright you? Would it not cause you often to retire into yourselves, and from the world? And, above all, how precious would the tidings of a Saviour be, that now are common and contemptible? Would you not every day wash in that blood? Would the current of repentance dry? But, forasmuch as you are not exercised this way, give no thoughts nor time for reconcilement with God, walk without any fear of hell, and without any earnest and serious study of changing your ways, and purifying your hearts, in a word, though ye confess sin in the general, yet your whole carriage of heart and ways declare so much, that you think it not a thing much to be feared, or that a man should busy himself about it, that a man may live in it, and be well here and hereafter. And is not this to deny the very nature of sin, and to deceive your own souls?

SERMON XVII.

1 John i. 9.—"If we confess our sins, he is faithful and just to forgive us our sins", &c.

The current of sin dries not up, but runs constantly while we are in this life. It is true, it is much diminished in a believer, and it runs not in such an universal flood over the whole man as it is in the unbeliever. Yet there is a living spring of sin within the godly, which is never ceasing to drop out pollution and defilement, either upon their whole persons, or, at least, to intermingle it with their good actions. Now, there is no comfort for this, but this one that there is another stream of the blood of Jesus Christ that never dries up, is never exhausted, never emptied, but flows as full and as free, as clear and fresh as ever it did, and this is so great, and of so great virtue, that it is able to swallow up the stream of our pollutions, and to take away the daily filth of a believers conversation. Now indeed, though the blood of Jesus Christ be of such infinite virtue and efficacy, that it were sufficient to cleanse the sins of the whole world, it would be an over ransom for the souls of all men, there is so much worth in it. That flood of guiltiness that hath drowned the world,—

this flood of Christ's blood that gushed out of his side, is of sufficient virtue to cleanse it perfectly away. Notwithstanding of this absolute universal sufficiency, yet certain it is, that it is not actually applied unto the cleansing of all men's sins, but yet the most part of men are still drowned in the deluge of their own wickedness, and lie entombed in darkness; therefore it concerns us to know the way of the application of this blood to the cleansing of sinners, and this way is set down in this verse, "If we confess our sins, he is just to forgive." There was something hinted at obscurely in the preceding verse, for when he shows that such as say they have no sin, who either, by the deposition of their hearts, or carriage of their ways, do by interpretation say that they want sin, such deceive themselves, and the truth is not in them, and so they have no benefit of that blood that cleanseth from all sin. And so it is imported here, that though the blood of Christ be fully sufficient to cleanse all sin, yet it is not so prostituted and basely spent upon sinners, as to be bestowed upon them who do not know their sins, and never enter into any serious and impartial examination of themselves. Such, though they say they are sinners, yet never descending into themselves to search their own hearts and ways, and so never coming to the particular knowledge of their sins, and feeling of them, they cannot at all make application of that blood to their own consciences, either seriously or pertinently. Though the river and fountain of Christ's blood run by them, in the daily preaching of the gospel, yet being destitute of this daily self-inspection and self-knowledge, being altogether ignorant of themselves, they can no more wash here than those who never heard of this blood. They being strangers to themselves, sets them at as great distance and estrangement from the blood of Christ, as if they were wholly strangers to the very preaching of this blood. Let us, then, have this first established in our hearts,—that there is no cleansing from sin, without the knowledge of sin, and there is no true knowledge of sin, without a serious soul examination of sin. These are knit together in their own nature. For how should our sins be pardoned, when we know nothing of them but in a confused generality that can never affect the heart? How should our sins not be opened and discovered before the holiness of God, when they are always covered unto us, and hid from our eyes? Certainly, the righteousness and wisdom of God require, that such a monstrous thing, so great an enemy of God's holiness, be not wholly passed away in silence without observation. If we do not observe, he will, for to what purpose should pardon be so lavished upon them who are not capable of knowing what favour and grace is in it? And certainly, that none can know without the feeling knowledge of the height and heinousness of sin. Now, I pray you, how should you know your sins, when you will not allow any time for the searching of yourselves? Many cannot say, that ever they did purposely and deliberately withdraw from the world, and separate their spirits for this business of self examination, and therefore you remain perpetually strangers to yourselves, and as great strangers to the power and virtue of this blood.

Now, in this verse, he declares it plainly in what way and method sin is pardoned by this blood. By the former verse, we have so much, that it is necessary we must search and try our ways, that so we may truly know our sins, and charge them upon ourselves, and here it is superadded, that we must confess them to him: and the promise is annexed, "he is just and faithful to forgive." Now, this confession of sin is very fitly subjoined, both to that which he declared of that great end of that gospel,—communion with God,—and that which was immediately holden forth of the remaining virtue of Christ's blood. For might a poor soul say, How shall I come to partake of that blessed society? I am a sinner, and so an enemy to God, how shall this enmity be removed? And if the answer be made, "The blood of Jesus Christ cleanseth from all sin," and so maketh access for a sinner to enter into this society, yet a question remains, and how shall the virtue of that be applied to my soul? It is sufficient, I know, for all, but what way may I have the particular benefit of it? Here it is fully satisfied, "if we confess our sins, God is just and faithful to forgive." He lieth under some obligation to pardon us. Now, many of you may think, if this be the way, and these be the terms of pardon, then we hope all shall be pardoned, for if there be no more but to confess our sins, who will not willingly do that, and who doth not daily do it? As one said, "if it be sufficient to accuse, none will be innocent," *si accusasse sufficiat, nemo innocens erit*; so you may think, *si confileri sufficiat, nemo reus erit*, "if it be sufficient to confess, none will be guilty." But, my beloved, let us not deceive ourselves with the present first apprehensions of words that occur in this kind. It is true, as ye take confession, there is nothing more ordinary, but, if it be taken in the true scripture meaning, and in the realest sense, I fear there is nothing among men so extraordinary. I desire you may but consider how you take this word in your dealings with men,—you take it certainly in a more real sense than you use it in religion. If any had done you some great wrong or injury, suppose your servant, or inferior, what acknowledgment would you take from him of his wrong? If he confessed his wrong only in general ambiguous terms, if he did it either lightly, or without any sense or sorrow for it, if he did withal excuse and extenuate his fault, and never ceased, notwithstanding of all his confession, to do the like wrong when occasion offered, would you not think this a mockery, and would it not rather provoke you than pacify you? Now, when you take words in so real and deep significations in your own matters, what gross delusion is it, that you take them in the slightest and emptiest meaning in those things that relate to God? And I am sure the most part of men's confessions are of that nature which I have described,—general, ignorant, senseless, without any particular view, or lively feeling, of the vileness and loathsomeness of sin, and their own hearts. Whenever it comes to particulars, there is a multitude of extenuations and pretences to hide and cover the sin, and generally men never cease the more from sinning. It puts no stop in their running, as the horse to the battle. Today they confess it, and tomorrow they act it again with as much delight as before. Now, of this I may say, "Offer it to thy governor, and see if he will be pleased with thee," or let another offer such an acknowledgment of wrong to thee, and see if it will please thee, and if it will not, why deceive ye yourselves with the outward visage of things in these matters that are of greatest soul-concernment? Should they not be taken in the most inward and substantial signification that can be, lest you be deceived with false appearances, and, while you give but a shadow of confession, you receive but a shadow of forgiveness, such a thing as will not carry and bear you out before God's tribunal? Therefore we must needs take it thus, that confession of sin is the work of the whole man, and not of the mouth only. It is the heart, tongue, and all that is in a man, joining together to the acknowledgment of sin, and God's righteousness, therefore it includes in it, not only a particular knowledge of our offences, and the temper of our hearts, but a sensible feeling of the loathsomeness and heinousness of these. And this is the spring that it flows from,—a broken and contrite heart that is bruised under the apprehensions of the weight of guiltiness, and is embittered with the sense of the gall of iniquity that possesseth the heart. Here, then, is the great moment of confession and repentance, what is the inward fountain it flows from? If the heart be brought to the distinct and clear view of itself and to discern the iniquity and plague of it, and so to fall down under the mighty hand of God, and before his tribunal, as guilty, as not being able or willing to open his mouth in an excuse or extenuation of sin or to plead for compassion from any consideration in himself, a soul thus placed between iniquities set in order and battle array, on the one hand, and the holy law and righteousness of God, on the other hand, the filthiness of the one filling with shame and confusion, and the dreadfulness of the other causing fear and trembling, in this posture, I say, for a soul to come and fall at the Judge's feet, and make supplication to him in his Son Christ, thus being inwardly pressed to vent and pour out our hearts before him, in the confession of our sins, and to flee unto the city of refuge,—his mercy and grace that is declared in Jesus Christ,—this, I say, is indeed to confess our sins, for then confession is an exoneration and disburdening of the heart,—it flows from the abundance of the inward contrition of it. And as this must be the spring of it, so there is another stream that will certainly flow from the ingenuous confession of our sins that is, a forsaking of them. These are the two streams that flow from one head and spring the inward fountain of contrition and sorrow for sin there is a holy indignation kindled in the heart against sin, and an engagement upon such a soul, as indeed flees to mercy, to renounce sin, and here is the complete nature of true repentance. Solomon joins them, "He that confesseth and forsaketh shall have mercy," Prov. xxviii. 13. And this is opposed to covering of sins—for "he that covereth his sins shall not prosper." And what is that to cover his sin? Confessing them in a general confused notion, without any distinct knowledge or sense of any particular guiltiness? That is a covering of sins. Or confessing sin and not forsaking of it? That is a covering of sin for to act sin over again with continual fresh delight and vigour, is to retract our confessions and to bury and cover them with the mould of new transgressions. Now, take this unto you, you "shall not prosper." What can be said worse? For you are but in a dream of happiness, and you shall one day be shaken out of it, and that fancied pardon shall evanish, and then your sins that you covered in this manner, shall be discovered before the Judge or the world, and you "shall not stand in judgment."

SERMON XVIII.

1 John i. 9.—"If we confess our sins, he is faithful and just to forgive us our sins," &c.

The freedom of God's grace, and the greatness of his wisdom, shine forth most brightly in the dispensation of the gospel, and both of them beautify and illustrate one another. That there is, first, an expiation of sin by the blood of Jesus Christ, that a way is laid down of reconciling the world, and that by the blood of the cross, that peace is purchased and so preached unto sinners, as a thing already procured, and now only to be applied unto the soul by faith,—herein doth the estimable riches of the grace of God expose itself to the view of angels and men. That the great work of redemption is ended, ere it come to us, and there remains nothing, but to publish it to the world, and invite us to come and receive it, and have a part in it,—all is ready, the feast prepared, and set on the table, and there wants nothing but guests to eat of it, and these are daily called by the gospel to come to this table, which the wisdom of the Father hath prepared for us, without either our knowledge or concurrence. Besides, the very terms of proposing the gospel, speak forth absolute freedom. What can be more free and easy than this? Christ is sent to die for sinners, and to redeem them from the curse,—only receive him, come to him, and believe in him. He hath undertaken to save, only do you consent too, and give up your name to him,—ye have nothing to do to satisfy justice, or purchase salvation, only be willing that he do it for you, or rather acquiesce in that he hath done already, and rest on it. But how shall our sins be pardoned, and justice satisfied? Only confess your sins to him, and ye are forgiven, not for your confession, but for Christ, only acknowledge thine iniquity and wrongs, and he hath taken another way to repair his justice than by thy destruction and condemnation. He is so far from extending his justice against thee, that he is rather engaged upon his faithfulness and justice to forgive thee, because of his promise.

Yet, ye would not conceive so of this manner of proposal of forgiveness and salvation, as if the requiring of such a thing as repentance in thee were any derogation from the absoluteness of his grace for it is not required, either to the point of satisfaction to God's justice, and expiation of sin, for that is done already upon the cross. Christ was not offered to save sinners, he was not sent upon the previous condition of their repentance nay, "while we were yet enemies, Christ died for the ungodly." So that to the business of our redemption there was no concurrence upon our part nor influence upon it by our carriage, for he considered us as sinners, and miserable, and so saved us. And now, to the actual application of these preventing mercies,—it is true, it is needful in the wise and reasonable dispensation of God, that sinners be brought to the knowledge and sensible acknowledgment of their sin and misery, and so be upon rational inducements of misery within, and mercy without, of self-indigency, and Christ's sufficiency, be drawn unto Jesus Christ, and so to a partaking of those purchased privileges of forgiveness of sin, peace with God, &c. I say, all this is so far from diminishing a jot of that absolute freedom of grace, that it rather jointly proclaims the riches of grace and wisdom both, that repentance should be given to an impenitent sinner, and faith freely bestowed on an unbelieving sinner, and withal, that remission and salvation, together with faith and repentance, should be brought to us by his death, while we were yet enemies,—this doth declare the most unparalleled bounty and grace that the heart of man can imagine, and withal, that remission of sins is joined to confession, and salvation to faith, herein the wisdom of God triumphs, for what way is it possible to declare that freedom of grace, to the sensible conviction of a sinner, and so to demonstrate it to all men's consciences, except by making them return within, to see their own absolute unworthiness, vileness, and incorrespondency to such mercies, and so drawing an acknowledgment of his grace from the mouths and consciences of all? How shall a soul know that rich superabundant grace, if he know not the abundance of his sins? How shall he profess the one, except he withal confess the other? Let us imagine an impenitent sinner, continuing in rebellion, pardoned and forgiven: and is there any thing more contrary to common sense and reason, to be in God's favour, and yet not accepting that favour, to be a friend, and yet an enemy, to have sins forgiven, and yet not known, not confessed? These, I say, sound some plain dissonancy and discord to our very first apprehensions. Certainly, this is the way to declare the glory of his grace, in the hiding and covering of sin, even to discover sin to the sinner, else if God should hide sin, and it be hid withal from the conscience, both thy sin and God's grace should be hid and covered, neither the one nor the other would appear. Take it thus then,—the confession of sin is not for this end, to have any casual influence upon thy remission, or to procure any more favour and liking with God, but it is simply this, the confession of sin is the most accommodate way of the profession and publication of the grace of God in the forgiving of sins. Faith and repentance are not set down as conditions pre-required on thy part, that may procure salvation or forgiveness, but they are inseparably annexed unto salvation and forgiveness, to the end that they may manifest to our sensible conviction, that grace and freedom of grace which shines in forgiveness and salvation.

"He is just and faithful," &c. Herein is the wonder of the grace of God increased, that when we are under an obligation to infinite punishment for sin, and bound guilty before his justice, that the "most great and potent Lord" who can easily rid himself of all his enemies, and do all his pleasure in heaven and earth, should come under an obligation to man to forgive him his sins. A strange exchange! Man is standing bound by the cords of his own sins over the justice of God,—he is under that insoluble tie of guiltiness. God in the meantime is free, and loosed from the obligation of the first covenant, that is, his promise of giving life to man. We have loosed him from that voluntary engagement, and are bound under a curse. And yet, behold the permutation of grace,—man is loosed from sin, to which he is bound, and God is bound to forgive sin, to which he was not bound. He enters into a new and voluntary engagement by his promise, and gives right to poor creatures to sue and seek forgiveness of him, according to his faithfulness. Yet in this plea, as it becomes us to use confidence, because he gives us ground by his promises, so we should season it with humility, knowing how infinitely free and voluntary his condescension is, being always mindful, that he may in righteousness exact punishment of us for sin, rather than we seek forgiveness from him. And yet seek it we ought, because he hath engaged his faithful promise, which opportunity to neglect, and not to improve, either through fear or security, were as high contempt and disobedience to him, as those sins by which we offend him.

Certainly, the very name of God, revealed to us or known by nature's light, those general characters of his name, mercy and goodness, power and greatness, might suffice to so much, as to make us, in the apprehensions of our own guiltiness and provocations of his holiness, to look no other way than to his own merciful and gracious nature. Suppose we had nothing of a promise from him, by which he is bound, yet, as the very apprehension of the general goodness, and unlimited bounty, and original happiness that is in God, ought naturally to draw the creature towards him in all its wants, to supplicate his fulness, that can supply all necessities, without lessening his own abundance, even so, if we did only apprehend that God is the fountain of mercy, and that he is infinitely above us and our injuries, and that all our being and well being eternally consists in his sole favour, this, I say, alone considered, might draw us to a pouring out our hearts before him, in the acknowledgment of our guiltiness, and casting ourselves upon his mercy, as the term is used in war, when there is no quarter promised, and no capitulation made. It is the last refuge of a desperate sinner, to render unto God upon mercy, to resign himself to his free disposal. Since I cannot but perish, may a soul say, without him, there is no way of escaping from his wrath, I will rather venture, and "go in to the King, and if I perish, I perish." There is more hope in this way to come to him, than to flee from him. Perhaps he may show an act of absolute sovereign goodness, and be as glorious in passing by an offence, as just in punishing it. Do I not see in man, in whom the divine Majesty hath imprinted some characters of conscience and honesty, that it is more generous and noble to forgive than to revenge? And do I not see generally among men, clemency and compassion are commended above severity and rigour, though just, especially towards those who are inferior, weak, unable to resist, and have yielded themselves to mercy. Now, shall I not much more apprehend that of God which I admire in a sinful man? Shall not that be most perfect in him which is but a maimed and broken piece of his image in lost man? Certainly, it is the glory of God to conceal an offence as well as to publish it, and he can show as much greatness and majesty in mercy as in justice, therefore I will wholly commit myself to him. I think a man ought to reason so, from the very natural knowledge he hath of God. But when ye have not only his name and nature published, but his word and promise so often proclaimed, himself come under some tie to receive and accept graciously all sinners that fly in under the shadow of his wings of mercy, then, O with how much persuasion and boldness should we come to him, and lay open our sins before him, who not only may pardon them, and not only is likely to do it, seeing he hath a gracious nature, but certainly will pardon them, cannot but do it, because his faithfulness requireth it! Certainly, he hath superadded his word to his name, his promise to his nature, to confirm our faith, and give us ample ground of strong consolation.

There is another more suitable notion about the justice of God, in forgiving sin. It hath some truth in the thing itself, but whether it be imported here, I dare not certainly affirm. Some take his faithfulness in relation to his word of promise, and his justice in relation to the price and ransom paid by Christ, importing as much as this—whatever sinner comes to God in Christ, confessing his own guiltiness in sincerity, and supplicating for pardon, he cannot in justice refuse to give it out unto them, since he hath taken complete satisfaction of Christ. When a sinner seeks a discharge of all sin, by virtue of that blood, the Lord is bound by his own justice to give it out and to write a free remission to them, since he is fully paid, he cannot but discharge us, and cancel our bonds. So then a poor sinner that desires mercy, and would forsake sin, hath a twofold ground to suit[247] this forgiveness upon—Christ's blood, and God's own word, Christ's purchase and payment, and the Father's promise, he is just and righteous, and therefore he cannot deny the one, nor yet take two satisfactions, two payments for one debt, and he is faithful, so he cannot but stand to the other, that is, his promise, and thus is forgiveness ascertained and assured unto the confessing sinner. If any would take this in relation to confession, as if it reflected upon that which preceded, and the meaning should be, if any man confess his sin, he is just to requite confession with remission,—he cannot in righteousness deny one that deserves it, he is just to return some suitable recompense to such a humble confession, this sense were a perverting of the whole gospel, and would overturn the foundations of grace. For there is no connection between our confession and his remission but that which the absolute good pleasure of his will hath made, besides, that repentance is as free grace given from the exalted Prince, as remission of sins is.

SERMON XIX.

1 John i. 9, 10.—"If we confess our sins, he is faithful and just to forgive us our sins, and to cleanse us from all unrighteousness. If we say we have not sinned, we make him a liar," &c.

And who will not confess their sin, say you? Who doth not confess sins daily, and, therefore, who is not forgiven and pardoned? But stay, and consider the matter again. Take not this upon your first light apprehensions, which in religion are commonly empty, vain, and superficial, but search the scriptures, and your own hearts that ye may know what confession means. It may be said of that external custom of confession that many of you have, that the Lord hath not required it,—"sacrifices and burnt offerings thou wouldest not." Some external submissions and confessions, which you take for compensation for sins and offences against God,—these, I say, are but abomination to the Lord, but "a broken and a contrite heart, O God, thou wilt not despise," Psal. li. 16, 17. And, "Lo, I come to do thy will, I delight in it," Psal. xl. 7, 8. When external profession and confessions are separated from the internal contrition of the heart and godly sorrow for sin, and when both internal contrition and external profession and confession are divided from conformity, or study of conformity to God's will, then they are in no better acceptance with God than those external sacrifices which God rejected, though he had required them, because they were disjoined from the true life of them and spiritual meaning, that is, faith in a mediator, and love to obedience. If confession flow not from some contrition of heart if there be not some inward spring of this kind, the heart, opened and unfolding its very inside before God, breaking in pieces, which makes both pain or sense, and likewise gives the clearer view of the inward parts of the heart, and if it be not joined with affection to God's will and law, earnest love to new obedience, it is but a vain, empty, and counterfeit confession, that denies itself. I suppose, a man that confesses sin which he feels not, or forsakes not, in so doing, he declares that he knows not the nature of sin; he may know that such an action is commonly called sin, and, it may be, is ashamed and censured among men, and therefore he confesseth it; but while he confesseth it without sense or feeling, he declares that he takes it not up as sin, hath not found the vileness and loathsomeness of the nature of it nor beheld it as it is a violation of the most high Lord's laws, and a provocation of his glorious holiness. Did a soul view it thus, as it is represented in God's sight, as it dishonours that glorious Majesty, and hath manifest rebellion in it against him, and as it defiles and pollutes our spirits; he could not, I say, thus look upon it, but he would find some inward soul abhorrence and displeasance at it, and himself too. How monstrous would it make him in his own sight? It could not but affect the heart, and humble it in secret before God; whereas your forced and strained confessions made in public, they are merely taken on then, and proceed from no inward principle. There is no shadow of any soul humiliation, in secret, but as some use to put on sackcloth when they come to make that profession, and put it off when they go out, so you put on a habit of confession in public, and put it off you when you go out of the congregation. To be mourning before the Lord, in your secret retirements,—that you are strangers to. But I wonder how you should thus mock God, that you will not be as serious and real in confessing as in sinning. Will you sin with the whole man, and confess only with the mouth? Will ye not sin with delight, and not confess it with a true sorrow that indeed affects the heart? Now, do you honour God by confessing, when the manner of it declares, that you feel not the bitterness of sin, and conceive not the holiness and righteousness of God, whom you have to do withal? Even so, when you confess sin, which you do not forsake, you in so far declare that you know not sin, what it is you confess, and so, that you have mocked him who will not be mocked; for, what a mockery is it, to confess those faults which we have no solid effectual purpose to reform, to vomit up your sins by confession, that we may with more desire and lust lick up the vomit again, and to pretend to wash, for nothing else, but to return to the puddle, and defile again! My brethren, out of the same fountain comes not bitter water and sweet; James iii. 11. Since that which ordinarily proceeds from you is bitter, unsavoury to God and man, carnal, earthly, and sensual, your ways are a displayed banner against God's will, then lay your account, all your professions and acknowledgments are of the same nature,—they are but a little more sugared over, and their inward nature is not changed, is as unacceptable to God, as your sins are.

I would give you some characters out of the text, to discover unto you the vanity and emptiness of your ordinary confessions. The confession of sin must be particular, universal, perpetual, or constant;—particular, I say, for there are many thousands who confess that they are sinners, and yet do not at all confess their sins; for, to confess sins is to confess their own real actual guiltiness, that which they indeed have committed or are inclined to do. So the true and sincere confession of a repenting people is expressed, 1 Kings viii. 38, "What prayer or supplication soever be made by any man, which shall know the plague of his own heart, and spread forth his hands, then hear thou in heaven, and forgive every man whose heart thou knowest." Now consider whether or not you be thus acquainted with your own hearts and ways, as to know your particular plague and predominant sin. Are you not rather wholly strangers to yourselves, especially the plague of your hearts? There are few that keep so much as a record or register of their actions done against God's law, or their neglect of his will; and therefore, when you are particularly posed about your sins, or the challenge of sin, you can speak nothing to that, but that you never knew one sin by another; that is, indeed, you never observed your sins, you never knew any sin, but contented yourself with the tradition you received that you were sinners. But if any man be used to reflect upon his own ways,—yet generally, the most part of men are altogether strangers to their hearts,—if they know any evil of themselves it is at most but something done or undone, some commission or omission, but nothing of the inward fountain of sin is discovered. I beseech you, then, do not deceive yourselves with this general acknowledgment that you are sinners, while in the meantime your real particular sins are hid from you, and you cannot choose but hide in a generality from God.

Certainly, you are far from forgiveness, and that blessedness of which David speaks, (Psal. xxxii.) for this belongs to the man "that hideth not his sins, in whose heart there is no guile." And this is the plainness and sincerity of the heart, rightly to discern its own plagues, and unfold them to him. David, no doubt, would at any time have confessed that he was a sinner, but mark how heavy the wrath of God was on him for all that, because he came not to a plain, ingenuous, and humble acknowledgment of his particular sins. "I confessed my sin, and mine iniquity I hid not." While you confess only in general terms, you confess other's sins rather than yours, but this is it—to descend into our own hearts, and find out our just and true accusation, our real debt, to charge ourselves as narrowly as we can, that he may discharge us fully, and forgive us freely.

Next, I say, confession must be universal, that is, of all sin, without partiality or respect to any sin. I doubt if a man can truly repent of any sin, except he in a manner repent of all sin; or truly forsake one sin, except there be a divorcement of the heart from and forsaking of all sin; therefore the apostle saith, "If we confess our sins," not sin simply, but sins, taking in all the body and collection of them, for it is opposed to that, "if we say we have no sin," &c. Then there lies a necessity upon us to confess what we have; we have all sin, and so should confess all sins. Now, my meaning is not, that it is absolutely necessary that a soul come to the particular knowledge and acknowledgment of all his sins, whether of ignorance or infirmity, nay, that is not possible, for "who can understand his errors?" saith David, "cleanse thou me from secret sins," Psal. xix. 12. There are many sins of ignorance, that we know not to be sins, and many escapes of infirmity, that we do not advert to, which otherwise we might know. Now, I do not impose that burden on a soul, to confess every individual sin of that kind; but this certainly must be,—there must be such a discovery of the nature of sin, and the loathsomeness of it in God's sight, and the heinous guilt of it, as may abase and humble the soul in his presence, there must be some distincter and clearer view of the dispositions and lusts of the heart, than men attain generally unto, and, withal, a discovery of the holy and spiritual meaning of God's law, which may unfold a multitude of transgressions, that are hid from the world, and make sin to abound in a man's sight and sense—for when the law enters, sin abounds, and to close up this, as there are many sins now discovered unto such a soul, which lay hid before, the light having shined in upon the darkness, and, above all, the desperate wickedness of the heart is presented, so there is no sin known and discerned, but there is an equal impartial sorrow for it, and indignation against it. As a believer hath respect to all God's commands, and loves to obey them, so the penitent soul hath an impartial hatred of all sin, even the dearest and most beloved idol, and desires unfeignedly to be rid of it. Hence your usual public confessions of sin are wiped out of the number of true and sincere confessions, because you pretend to repent of one sin, and in the meantime, neither do ye know a multitude of other sins that prevail over you, nor do you mourn for them, nor forsake them. Nay, you do not examine yourselves that way, to find out the temper of your hearts, or tenor and course of your ways. You pretend to repent for drunkenness, or such like, and yet you are ordinary cursers, swearers, liars, railers, neglecters of prayer, profaners of the Sabbath, and such like, and these you do not withal mourn for. In sum, he that mourns only for the sin that men censure, knoweth and confesseth no sin sincerely. If you would indeed return unto God from some gross evils, you must be divorced in your affections from all sin.

Then this confession should be perpetuated and continued as long as we are in this life, for that is imported by comparing this verse with those it stands between. "If we say we have no sin, if we say at any time, while we are in this life, if we imagine or dream of any such perfection here," we lie. Now, what should we do then, since sin is always lodging in our mortal bodies, during this time of necessary abode beside an ill neighbour? What should be our exercise? Even this,—confess your sins, confess, I say, as long as you have them, draw out this the length of that. Be continually groaning to him under that body of death, and mourning under your daily infirmities and failings. That stream of corruption runs continually—let the stream of your contrition and confession run as incessantly, and there is another stream of Christ's blood, that runs constantly too, to cleanse you. Now, herein is the discovery of the vanity and deceitfulness of many of your confessions, public and private, the current of them soon dries up, there is no perpetuity or constancy in them, no daily humbling or abasing yourselves, but all that is, is by fits and starts upon some transient convictions or outward censures and rebukes, and thus men quickly cover and bury their sins in oblivion and security and forget what manner of persons they were. They are not under a duly impartial examination of their ways, take notice of nothing but some solemn and gross escapes, and these are but a short time under their view.

Now, let me apply a little to the encouragement of poor souls, who being inwardly burdened with the weight of their own guiltiness, exoner themselves by confession in his bosom. As you have two suits, and two desires to him,—one, that your sins may be forgiven, another, that they may be subdued, so he hath two solemn engagements and ties to satisfy you,—one to forgive your sins, and another to cleanse you from all unrighteousness. The soul that is truly penitent, is not only desirous of pardon of sin—that is not the chief or only design of such a soul in application to Christ,—but it is withal to be purified from sin and all unrighteousness, and to have ungodly lusts cleansed away. And herein is the great application of such an one's reality,—it will not suffice or satisfy such an one, to be assured of delivery from wrath and condemnation, but he must likewise be redeemed from sin, that it hath no dominion over him. He desires to be freed from death, that he may have his conscience withal purged "from dead works to serve the living God," Heb. ix. 14. He would have sin blotted out of an accusing conscience, that it may be purged out of the affections of the heart, and he would have his sins washed away, for this end especially, that he may be washed from his sins, Rev. i. 5. Now, as this is the great desire and design of such a heart, in which there is no guile, to have sin purified and purged out of us as well as pardoned, so there is a special tie and obligation upon God our Father, by promise, not only to pardon sin, but to purge from sin, not only to cover it with the garment of Christ's righteousness, and the breadth of his infinite love but also to cleanse it by his Spirit effectually applying that blood to the purifying of the heart. Now, where God hath bound himself voluntarily, and out of love, do not ye lose him by unbelief, for that will bind you into a prison: but labour to receive those gracious promises, and to take him bound as he offers. Believe, I say that he will both forgive you, and in due time will cleanse your heart from the love and delight of sin. Believe his promise, and engagement by promise to both and this will set a seal to his truth and faithfulness. There is nothing in God to affright a sinner, but his justice, holiness, and righteousness, but unto thee who, in the humble confession of thy sins, fliest into Jesus Christ, that very thing which did discourage thee, may now encourage and embolden thee to come, for "he is just and faithful to forgive sins." His justice being now satisfied, is engaged that way to forgive, not to punish.

SERMON XX.

1 John i. 10.—"If we say that we have not sinned, we make him a liar, and his word is not in us."

There is nothing in which religion more consists than in the true and unfeigned knowledge of ourselves. The heathens supposed that sentence, γνωθι σεατον "Know thyself," descended from heaven. It was indeed the motto of the wisest and most religious amongst them. But certain it is, that the true and sincere understanding of ourselves descends from "the Father of lights," and is as great a gift as man is capable of, next to the knowledge of God himself. There is nothing more necessary to man, either as a man or as a Christian, either as endowed with reason or professing religion, than that he should be thoroughly acquainted with himself, his own heart, its dispositions, inclinations, and lusts, his ways and actions, that while he travels abroad to other creatures and countries, he may not commit so shameful an absurdity, as to be a stranger at home, where he ought to be best acquainted. Yet how sad is it, that this which is so absolutely needful and universally profitable, should be lying under the manyest difficulties in the attainment of it? So that there is nothing harder, than to bring a man to a perfect understanding of himself:—what a vile, haughty, and base creature he is—how defiled and desperately wicked his nature—how abominable his actions, in a word, what a compound of darkness and wickedness he is—a heap of defiled dust, and a mass of confusion—a sink of impiety and iniquity, even the best of mankind, those of the rarest and most refined extraction, take them at their best estate. Thus they are as sepulchres painted without, and putrified within—outwardly adorned, and within all full of rottenness and corruption, "the imagination of his heart only evil continually." Now, I say, here is the great business and labour of religion,—to bring a man to the clear discerning of his own nature,—to represent unto him justly his own image, as it is painted in the word of God, and presented in the glass of the law, and so by such a surprising monstrous appearance, to affect his heart to self abhorrency in dust and ashes and to have this representation, however unpleasant, yet most profitable, continually observant to our minds, that we may not forget what manner of persons we are. Truly I may say, if there be a perfection in this estate of imperfection, herein it consists, and if there be any attainment of a Christian, I account this the greatest,—to be truly sensible of himself, and vile in his own eyes.

It was the custom of Philip,[248] king of Macedonia, after he had overcome the famous republic of Greece, to have a young man to salute him first every morning with these words, *Philippe homo es*,—Philip, thou art a man, to the end that he might be daily minded of his mortality, and the unconstancy of human affairs, lest he should be puffed up with his victory, and this was done before any could have access to speak with him, as if it were to season and prepare him for the actions of the day. But O how much more ought a Christian to train up his own heart and accustom it this way, to be his continual remembrancer of himself, to suggest continually to his mind, and whisper this first into his ear in the morning, and mid day, and evening,—*peccator es*, thou art a sinner, to hold our own image continually before us, in prayer and praises, in restraints, in liberties of spirit, in religious actions, and in all our ordinary conversation, that it might salt and season all our thoughts, words and deeds, and keep them from that ordinary putrefaction and corruption of pride and self conceit, which maketh all our ointment stink.

"If we say we have no sin, we make him a liar." Why is this repeated again, but to show unto us, even to you Christians who believe in Christ, and are washed in his blood, how hard it is to know ourselves aright? If we speak of the grosser sort of persons, they scarce know any sin, nor the nature and vileness of any that they know, therefore they live in security and peace, and bless themselves in their own hearts, as if they had no sin. For such, I say, I shall only say unto them, that your self deceiving is not so subtile, but it may soon be discerned; your lie is gross, and quickly seen through. But I would turn myself to you Christians, who are in some measure acquainted with yourselves, yet there is something against you from this word. After ye have once got some peace from the challenge of sin, and hope of pardon, you many times fall out of acquaintance with yourselves. Having attained, by the Lord's grace, to some restraint of the more visible outbreakings of sin, you have not that occasion to know yourselves by, and so you remain strangers to your hearts, and fall into better liking with yourselves, than the first sight of yourselves permitted you. Now, my beloved in the Lord, herein you are to be blamed, that you do not rather go to the fountain, and there behold the streams, than only to behold the fountain in the streams. You ought rather, upon the Lord's testimony of man, to believe what is in you, before you find it, and see it breaking out; and keep this character continually in your sight, which will be more powerful to humble you than many outbreakings. I think we should be so well acquainted with our own natures, as to account nothing strange to them that we see abroad, but rather think all the grossness and wickedness of men suitable and correspondent to our spirits,—to that root of bitterness that is in them. The goodness of God in restraining the appearance of that in us, which is within us in reality, should rather increase the sense of our own wickedness, than diminish it in our view.

Indeed, self love is that which blinds us, and bemists us in the sight of ourselves. We look upon ourselves through this false medium, and it represents all things more beautiful than they are, and therefore the apostle hath reason to say, "We deceive ourselves, and we make God a liar." O how much practical self-conceit is there in the application of truth! There are many errors contrary to the truths themselves, and many deceivers and deceived, who spread them, but I believe there are more errors committed by men in the application of truths to their own hearts, than in the contemplation of them, and more self deceiving than deceiving of others. It is strange to think, how sound, and clear, and distinct a man's judgment will be against those evils in others, which yet he seeth not in himself, how many Christians will be able to decipher the nature of some vices, and unbowel the evils of them, and be quick-sighted to espy the least appearance of them in another, and to condemn it, and yet so partial are they in judging themselves,—self-love so purblinds them in this reflection, that they cannot discern that in themselves, which others cannot but discern! How often do men declaim against pride, and covetousness, and self-seeking, and other evils of that kind? They will pour out a flood of eloquence and zeal against them, and yet it is strange they do not advert, that they are accusing themselves, and impannelling themselves in such discourses, though others, it may be, will easily perceive a predominancy of these evils in them. "Who art thou, O man, who judgeth another, and doest the same thing? Canst thou escape God's judgment?" Rom. ii. 1. Consider this, O Christian, that thou mayest learn to turn the edge of all thy censures and convictions against thyself, that thou mayest prevent all men's judgments of thee, in judging thyself all things that men can judge thee, that is, a chief of sinners, that hath the root of all sin in thee, and so thou mayest anticipate the divine judgment too, "for if we judge ourselves, we shall not be judged." Labour thou to know those evils that are incident to thy nature, before others can know them, that is, in the root and fountain, before they come to the fruit and stream, to know sins in the first conceptions of them, before they come to such productions as are visible, and this shall keep thee humble, and preserve thee from much sin, and thou shalt not deceive thyself, nor dishonour God, in making him a liar, but rather set to thy seal to this truth, and his word shall abide in thee.

There is a common rule that we have in judging ourselves, by comparing ourselves amongst ourselves, which, as Paul saith, "is not wisdom," 2 Cor. x. 12. When we do not measure ourselves by the perfect rule of God's holy word, but parallel ourselves with other persons, who are still defective from the rule, far further from it than anyone is from another, this is the ordinary method of the judging of self love. We compare with the worst persons, and if we be not so bad as they, we think ourselves good. If not so ignorant as some are, we presume that we know, if not so profane as many, we believe ourselves religious. "Lord, I am not as this publican," so say many in their hearts,—there is a curser, a swearer, a drunkard, a blind ignorant soul, that neglects prayer in private and public, and upon these ruins of others' sins, they build some better estimation of themselves. But, I pray you, what will that avail you, to be unlike them, if you be more unlike your pattern than they are unlike you? It must be, others will compare with those that are good, but it is with that which is worst in them, and not that which is best. How often do men reckon this way,—here is a good man, here is an eminent person, yet he is such and such, subject to such infirmities, and here self-love flatters itself, and, by flattering, deceives itself. My beloved, let us learn to establish a more perfect rule, which may show all our imperfections. Let our rule ascend, that our hearts may descend in humility. But when our role and pattern descends to men of like infirmities, then our pride and self conceit ascends, and the higher we be that way in our own account, the lower we are indeed, and in God's account, and the lower we be in ourselves we lose nothing by it; for, as God is higher in our account, so we are higher in God's account, according to that standing rule, Matth. xxiii. 12, "Whosoever shall exalt himself shall be abased, and he that shall humble himself shall be exalted."

SERMON XXI.

1 John ii. 1.—"My little children, these things write I unto you, that ye sin not. And if any man sin, we have an advocate with the Father," &c.

The gospel is an entire uniform piece, all the parts of it are interwoven through other, and interchangeably knit together, so that there can be no dividing of it any more than of Christ's coat that was without seam. If you have it not altogether by the divine lot, you cannot truly have any part of it, for they are so knit together, that if you disjoin them, you destroy them, and if they cease to be together, they cease altogether to be. I speak this, because there may be pretensions to some abstracted parts of Christianity. One man pretends to faith in Jesus Christ, and persuasion of pardon of sin, and in this there may be some secret glorying arising from that confidence, another may pretend to the study of holiness and obedience, and may endeavour something that way to do known duties, and abstain from gross sins. Now, I say, if the first do not conjoin the study of the second, and if the second do not lay down the first as the foundation, both of them embrace a shadow for the thing itself, because they separate those things that God hath joined, and so can have no being but in men's fancy, when they are not conjoined. He that would pretend to a righteousness of Christ, without him, must withal study to have the righteousness of the law fulfilled within him, and he that endeavours to have holiness within must withal go out of himself, to seek a righteousness without him, whereupon to build his peace and acceptance with God, or else, neither of them hath truly any righteousness without them, to cover them, or holiness within, to cleanse them. Now, here the beloved apostle shows us this divine contexture of the gospel. The great and comprehensive end and design of the gospel is, peace in pardon of sin, and purity from sin. "These things I write unto you, that you sin not," &c. The gospel is comprised in commands and promises, both make one web, and link in together. The immediate end of the command is, "that we sin not," nay, but there is another thing always either expressly added, or tacitly understood—"but if any man sin," that desires not to sin, "we have an advocate with the Father." So the promise comes in as a subsidiary help to all the precepts. It is annexed to give security to a poor soul from despair, and therefore the apostle teacheth you a blessed art of constructing all the commands and exhortations of the gospel, those of the highest pitch, by supplying the full sense with this happy and seasonable caution or caveat, "but if any man sin," &c. Doth that command, "Be ye holy as I am holy," perfect as your heavenly Father, which sounds so much unattainable perfection, and seems to hold forth an inimitable pattern, doth it, I say, discourage thee? Then, use the apostle's art, add this caution to the command, subjoin this sweet exceptive,—"but if any man," that desires to be holy, and gives himself to this study, fail often, and fall and defile himself with unholiness, let him not despair, but know, that he hath "an advocate with the Father." If that of Paul's urge thee, "present your bodies a living sacrifice,—and be not conformed to the world," but transformed, and "glorify God in your bodies and spirits," which are his, (Rom. xii. 1, 2, 1 Cor. vi. 20,)—and, cleanse yourselves "from all filthiness of the flesh and spirit," (2 Cor. vii. 1,)—and, "walk in the Spirit," and "walk as children of the light," &c.,—if these do too rigorously exact upon thee, so as to make thee lose thy peace, and weaken thy heart and hands, learn to make out a full sentence, and fill up the full sense and meaning of the gospel, according as you see it done here. But if any man,—whose inward heart-desires, and chief designs are toward these things, who would think himself happy in holiness and conformity to God, and estimates his blessedness or misery, from his union or separation from God,—"sin" then "we have an advocate with the Father, even Jesus Christ the righteous," who hath all that we want, and will not suffer any accusation to fasten upon us, as long as he lives "to make intercession for us."

On the other hand, take a view of the promises of the gospel. Though the immediate and next end of them is to give peace to troubled souls, and settle us in the high point of our acceptance with God, yet certainly they have a further end, even purity from sin, as well as pardon of sin, cleansing from all sin and filthiness as well as covering of filthiness. "These things I write unto you, that ye sin not." What things? Consider what goes before, and what follows after, even the publication of the word of life, and eternal life in him, the declaration of our fellowship with God in Christ the offering of the blood of Christ, able to cleanse all sin, the promise of pardon to the penitent, confession of sin,—all these things I write, "that ye sin not," so that this seems to be the ultimate end and chief design of the gospel, unto which all tends, unto which all work together. The promises are for peace, and peace is for purity, the promises are for faith, and faith is for purifying of the heart, and performing the precepts, so that, all at length returns to this, from whence, while we swerved, all this misery is come upon us. In the beginning it was thus,—man was created to glorify God, by obedience to his blessed will, sin interposeth and marreth the whole frame, and from this hath a flood of misery flowed in upon us. Well, the gospel comes offering a Saviour, and forgiveness in him. Thus peace is purchased, pardon granted, the soul is restored unto its primitive condition and state of subordination to God's will, and so redemption ends where creation began, or rather in a more perfect frame of the same kind. The second Adam builds what the first Adam broke down, and the Son re-creates what the Father in the beginning created, yea, with some addition. In this new edition of mankind, all seems new—"new heavens, and new earth," and that because the creature that was made old, and defiled with sin, is made new by grace. Now, hence you may learn the second part of this lesson that the apostle teaches us; as ye ought to correct, as it were, precepts of the gospel, by subjoining promises in this manner, so ye ought to direct promises towards the performance of his precepts, as their chief end. Whensoever you read it written, "The blood of Christ cleanseth us from all sin,"—"If we confess, he is faithful to forgive our sins,"—"God so loved the world that he gave his Son,"—"He that believeth hath everlasting life," &c.—then make up the entire sense and meaning after this manner, "These things are written that we sin not." Is there a redemption from wrath published? Is there reconciliation with God preached? And are we beseeched to come and have the benefit of them? Then say, and supply within thine own heart, These things are written, published, and preached, that we may not sin. Look to the furthest end of these things, it is, "that we sin not." The end of things, the scope of writings, and the purpose of actions, is the very measure of them, and so that is the best interpreter of them. The scope of scripture is by all accounted the very thread that will lead a man right in and out of the labyrinths that are in it. And so it is used as the rule of the interpretation in the parts of it. Now, my beloved in the Lord, take here the scope of the whole scriptures, the mark that all the gospel shoots at, "These things I write unto you, that ye sin not." You hear, it is true, of pardon of sin, of delivery from wrath, of not coming into condemnation, of covering offences, of blotting them out as a cloud, all these you read and hear of, but what do they all aim at? If you consider not that attentively you shall no more understand the plain gospel, than you can expound a parable without observing the scope of it. Do you think these have no further aim, than to give you peace, and to secure you from fears and terrors, that you may then walk as you list, and follow the guiding of your own hearts? Nay, if you take it so, you totally mistake it. If you do not read on, and had all these things written to this end, "that ye sin not," you err, not understanding, or misunderstanding, the scriptures.

"These things I write unto you, little children." To enforce this the more sweetly, he useth this affectionate compellation, "little children," for in all things affection hath a mighty stroke, almost as much as reason. It is the most suitable way to prevail with the spirit of a man, to deal in love and tenderness with it, it speaks more sweetly, and so can have less resistance, and therefore works more strongly. It is true, another way of terrors threatening, and reproofs, mingled with sharp and heavy words of challenges, may make a great deal of more noise, and yet it hath not such virtue to prevail with a rational soul. The Spirit of the Lord was not in the wind, nor in the earthquake, nor in the fire, but in the still and calm voice which came to Elijah, 1 Kings xix. 11, 12. These suit not the gentle, dove-like disposition of the Spirit; and though they be fit to rend rocks in pieces, yet they cannot truly break hearts, and make them contrite. The sun will make a man sooner part with his cloak than the wind, such is the difference between the warm beams of affection, and the boisterous violence of passions or terror. Now, O that there were such a spirit in them who preach the gospel, such a fatherly affection, that with much pity and compassion they might call sinners from the ways of death! O there is no subject, in which a man may have more room for melting affections, nothing that will admit of such bowels of compassion as this—the multitude of souls posting to destruction, and so blindfolded that they cannot see it! Here the fountain of tears might be opened to run abundantly. The Lord personates a tender hearted father or husband often, "Oh, why will ye die? Ye have broken my heart with your whorish heart. O Jerusalem, how oft would I, but thou wouldst not!" When he, who is not subject to human passions, expresseth himself thus, how much more doth it become us poor creatures to have pity on our fellow-creatures? Should it not press out from us many groans, to see so many perishing, even beside salvation. I wish you would take it so, that the warning you to flee from the wrath to come, is the greatest act of favour and love that can be done to you. It becomes us to be solicitous about you, and declare unto you, that you will meet with destruction in those paths in which you walk; that these ways go down to the chambers of death. O that it might be done with so much feeling compassion of your misery, as the necessity of it requires! But, why do many of you take it so hard to be thus forewarned, and have your danger declared unto you? I guess at the reason of it. You are in a distempter as sick children distempered in a fever, who are not capable of discerning their parents' tender affection, when it crosseth their own inclinations and ways.

SERMON XXII.

1 John ii. 1.—"My little children, these things write I unto you, that ye sin not. And if any man sin, we have an advocate with the Father,", &c.

Christ Jesus came by water and by blood, not by water only, but by blood also, and I add, not by blood only but by water also, chap. v. 6. In sin there is the guilt binding over to punishment, and there is the filth or spot that defileth the soul in God's sight. To take away guilt, nothing so fit as blood for there is no punishment beyond blood, therefore saith the apostle, "without the shedding of blood there is no remission of sin," Heb. ix. 22, and for the stain and spot, nothing is so suitable as water, for that is generally appointed for cleansing. And some shadow of this the heathens had, who had their lustrations in water, and their expiations by blood,[249] but more significantly and plainly, the Jews, who had their purifications by sprinkling of water, (Num. viii. 7.) and expiations by sacrificing of slain beasts. But all these were but evanishing shadows; now the substance is come, Jesus Christ is come in water and blood; in water, to cleanse the spots of the soul, to purify it from all filthiness; and in blood, to satisfy for sin, and remove the punishment. You have both in these words of the apostle, for he labours to set out unto us the true Christ, whole and entire, "these things I write unto you, that ye sin not." Here is the proper end of the water—and "if any man sin, we have Christ a propitiation for our sins." Here is the blood—the end of the blood is to save us, the end of the water is that we sin not, since we are saved. He came in the blood of expiation, because we had sinned. He came in the water of sanctification, that we might not sin. His blood speaks peace to the soul, and the water subjoins, "but let them not return to folly." His blood cries, "behold thou art made whole." And the water echoes unto it, "sin no more, lest a worse thing befall thee," John v. 14. These two streams of water and blood, which are appointed for purity and pardon, run intermingled all along, and so the proper effects of them are interchangeably attributed to either of them; "he hath washed us in his blood," (Rev. i. 5; vii. 14.) "and the blood of Christ cleanseth us from all sin." Then, certainly, this blood cannot be without water, it is never separated from it. The proper effect of blood is to cover sin; but because the water runs in that channel, and is conveyed by the blood thither, therefore it doth cleanse sin, as well as cover it.

"These things I write unto you, that ye sin not." This then is the design of the whole gospel, the great and grand design,—to destroy sin, and save the sinner. There is a treaty of peace made with the sinner, and "Christ is the peace-maker." A tender of life and salvation is made to him, but there is no treaty, no capitulation or composition with sin; out it must go, first out of its dominion, then out of its habitation. It must first lose its power, and then its being in a believer. Yea, this is one of the chief articles of our peace, not only required of us as our duty, that we should destroy that which cannot but destroy us; for, if any man will needs hug and embrace his sins, and cannot part with them, he must needs die in their embracements, because the council of heaven hath irrevocably passed a fatal sentence against sin, as the only thing that in all the creation hath the most perfect opposition to his blessed will, and contrariety to his holy nature,—but also, and especially, as the great stipulation and promise upon his part, "to redeem us from all our iniquities, and purify us to himself, a people zealous of good works;" and not only to redeem us from hell, and deliver us from wrath, Tit. ii. 14. He hath undertaken this great work, to compesce [250] this mutiny and rebellion that was raised up in the creation by sin, else what peace could be between God and us, as long as his enemy and ours dwelt in our bosom, and we at peace with it.

Now, take a short view of these things that are written in the preceding chapter, and you shall see that the harmonious voice of all that is in the gospel, is this, "that we sin not." Let me say further, as "these things are written that we sin not," so all things are done "that we sin not." Take all the whole work of creation, of providence, of redemption,—all of them speak one language, "that we sin not." "Day unto day uttereth speech, and night unto night showeth knowledge: there is no speech or language where their voice is not heard," Psalm xix. 2, 3. And, as in that place, their voice proclaims the glory, majesty, and goodness of God, so they, with the same sound, proclaim and declare, that we should not sin against such a God, so great, and so good. All that we see suggests and insinuates this unto our hearts; all that we hear whispers this unto our ears, "that we sin not, that he made us, and not we ourselves, and that we are the very work of his hands." This speaks our absolute and essential dependence on him, and therefore proclaims with a loud voice, that sin, which would cut off this subordination, and loose from this dependence upon his holy will, is a monstrous, unnatural thing. Take all his mercies towards us, whether general or particular, the transcendent abundance of his infinite goodness in the earth, that river of his riches that runs through it, to water every man, and bring supply to his doors, that infinite variety that is in heaven and earth, and all of them of equal birth-right with man; yet by the law of our Maker, a yoke of subjection and service to man is imposed upon them, so that man is, in a manner, set in the centre of all, to the end, that all the several qualifications and perfections that are in every creature, may concentre and meet together in him, and flow towards him. Look upon all his particular acts of care and favour towards thee, consider his judgments upon the world, upon the nation, or thine own person. Put to thine ear, and hear. This is the joint harmonious melody, this is the proclamation of all, "that we sin not," that we sin not against so good a God, and so great a God. That were wickedness, this were madness. If he wound, it is "that we sin not:" if he heal again, it is "that we sin not." Doth he kill? It is "that we sin not!" Doth he make alive? It is for the same end. Doth he shut up and restrain our liberty, either by bondage, or sickness, or other afflictions? Why, he means "that we sin not." Doth he open again? He means the same thing, "that we sin no more, lest a worse thing befall us." Doth he make many to fall in battle, and turn the fury of that upon us? The voice of it is, that you who are left behind should "sin no more." Is there severity towards others, and towards you clemency? O the loud voice of that is, "sin not!" But alas, the result of all is, that which is written, Psal. lxxviii. 32.—"Nevertheless they sinned still." In the midst of so many concurring testimonies, in the very throng of all the sounds and voices that all the works of God utter, in the very hearing of these, nevertheless to sin still, and not to return and inquire early after God,—this is the plague and judgment of the nation.

But let us return to the words, "these things," &c. "That which is written of the word of life, that which was from the beginning, and was manifested unto us," that is written "that we sin not:" For, saith this same apostle, chap. iii. 5, 8, "And ye know that he was manifested to take away our sins, and in him is no sin;" yea, for this very purpose, saith he, "that he might destroy the works of the devil." Now, this is the great business, that drew the Son out of the Father's bosom,—to destroy the arch-enemy and capital rebel, sin, which, as to man, is a work of Satan's, because it first entered in man by the devil's suggestion and counsel. All that misery and ruin, all those works of darkness and death, that Satan had by his malice and policy wrought upon and in poor mankind, Jesus was manifested in the flesh without sin, to destroy and take away sin out of our flesh, and to abolish and destroy Satan's work, which he had builded upon the ruins of God's work, of the image of God, and to repair and renew that first blessed work of God in man, Eph. iv. 23, 24.

Now, O how cogent and persuading is this; one so high, come down so low, one dwelling in inaccessible glory, manifested in the flesh, in the infirmity and weakness of it, to this very purpose, to repair the creation, to make up the breaches of it, to destroy sin, and save the sinner! What force is in this to persuade a soul that truly believes it, "not to sin!" For, may he think within himself, shall I save that which Christ came to destroy, shall I entertain and maintain that which he came to take away, and do what in me lies to frustrate the great end of his glorious and wonderful descent from heaven? Shall I join hands, and associate with my lusts, and war for them, "which war against my soul," and him that would save my soul? Nay, let us conclude, my beloved, within our own hearts,—Is the Word and Prince of life manifested from heaven, and come to mar and unmake that work of Satan, that he may rescue me from under his tyranny? Then God forbid that I should help Satan to build up that which my Saviour is casting down, and to make a prison for myself, and cords to bind me in it for everlasting. Nay, will a believing soul say, rather let me be a worker together with Christ. Though faintly, yet I resolve to wrestle with him, to pull down all the strongholds that Satan keeps in my nature, and so to congratulate and consent to him, who is the avenger and assertor of my liberty.

Then consider the greatest end and furthest design of the gospel, how it is inseparably chained and linked into this, "that we sin not." We are called to fellowship with the Father and the Son, and herein is his glory and our happiness. Now, this proclaims with a loud voice, "that we sin not," for, what more contrary to that design of union and communion with God, than to sin, which disunites and discommunicates the soul from God. The nature of sin you know, is the transgression of his law, and so it is the very just opposition of the creatures will to the will of him that made it. Now, how do ye imagine that this can consist with true friendship and fellowship, which looseth that conjunction of wills and affections, which is the bond of true friendship, and the ground of fellowship? *Idem velle atque idem nolle, hæc demum vera amicitia est.*[251] The conspiracy of our desires and delights in one point with God's, this sweet coincidency makes our communion, and what communion then can there be with God, when that which his soul abhors is your delight, and his delight is not your desire? "What communion hath light with darkness?" Sin is darkness. All sin but especially sin entertained and maintained, sin that hath the full consent of the heart, and carrieth the whole man after it, that is Egyptian darkness, an universal darkness over the soul. This being interposed between God and the soul, breaks off communion, eclipses that soul totally. Therefore, my beloved, if you do believe that you are called unto this high dignity of fellowship with God, and if your souls be stirred with some holy ambition after it, consider that "these things are written that ye sin not." Consider what baseness is in it, for one that hath such a noble design, as fellowship with the Highest, to debase his soul so far and so low, as to serve sinful and fleshly lusts. There is a vileness and wretchedness in the service of sin, that any soul, truly and nobly principled, cannot but look upon it with indignation, because he can behold nothing but indignity in it. "Shall I who am a ruler," saith Nehemiah, "shall such a man as I flee? and who is there that being as I am, would flee?" Neh. vi. 11. A Christian hath more reason. Shall such a man as I, who am born again to such a hope, and called to such a high dignity, shall I, who aim and aspire so high as fellowship with God, debase and degrade myself with the vilest servitude? Shall I defile in that puddle again, till my own clothes abhor me, who aim at so pure and so holy a society? Shall I yoke in myself with drunkards, liars, swearers, and other slaves of sin? Shall I rank myself thus, and conform myself to the world, seeing there is a noble and glorious society to incorporate with, the King of kings to converse with daily? Alas, what are these worms that sit on thrones to him? But far more, how base are these companions in iniquity, your pot companions? &c. And what a vile society is it like that of the bottomless pit, where devils are linked together in chains?

SERMON XXIII.

1 John ii. 1.—"My little children, these things write I unto you, that ye sin not. And if any man sin, we have an advocate with the Father," &c.

In the gospel we have the most perfect provision against both these extremities, that souls are ready to run upon, the rock of desperate distrust, and the quicksands of presumptuous wantonness. It may be said to be a well-ordered covenant in all things, that hath caveated and cautioned the whole matter of our salvation, in such a way, that there is neither place for discouragement and downcasting, nor yet room for liberty in sin. There is no exemption from the obligation of God's holy law, and yet there is pardon for the breach of it, and exemption from the curse. There is no peace, no capitulation with sin, and yet there is peace concluded with the sinner, who is, by that agreement, bound to fall out with sin. There is no dispensation for sin, and from the perfection of holiness, and yet there is an advocation for the sinner, who aims and studies after it. So that, in sum, the whole gospel is comprised in this,—"he speaks peace to his saint, but let them not return to folly; thou art made whole, sin no more." All that is in the gospel saith this, "that thou shouldst sin no more." But because sin is necessarily incident, therefore all that is in the gospel speaks this further,—though ye be surprised in sin, yet believe, and this is the round in which a believer is to walk,—to turn from pardon to purity, and from pollution again to pardon, for these voices and sounds are interchanged continually. If ye have sinned, believe in Christ the advocate and sacrifice, and, because ye have believed, sin not, but if ye be overtaken in sin, yet believe. And as this is daily renewed, so the soul's study and endeavour in them, should be daily renewed too. If ye have sinned, despair not, if ye be pardoned, yet presume not. After sin there is hope, it is true, because "there is forgiveness with him," but after forgiveness, there must be fear to offend his goodness, for there is forgiveness with him, that he may be feared, Psal. cxxx. 4 And this is the situation I would desire my soul in,—to be placed between hope of his mercy and fear of sin, the faith of his favour and the hatred of sin, which he will not favour, and how happy were a soul to be confined within these, and kept captive to its true liberty.

I spake a little before, how those fundamental truths that are set down before, do all aim at this one mark, "that we sin not," now I proceed. That declaration what God is, verse 5, is expressly directed to this purpose and applied, verse 6—"God is light," and therefore "sin not," for sin is darkness, "he is light," for purity and beauty of holiness, and perfection of knowledge,—that true light in which is no darkness,—that unmixed light, all homogeneous to itself,—therefore "sin not," for that is a work of the night, and of the darkness, that proceeds from the blindness and estrangement of your minds, and ignorance of your hearts, and it cannot but prepare and fit you for those everlasting chains of darkness. Call God what you will, name all his names, styles, and titles, spell all the characters of it, and still you may find it written at every one of them, "sin not." Is he light? Then sin not. Is he life? Then sin not, for sin will separate you from his light and life, sin will darken your souls and kill them. Is he love? Then sin not. "God is love," saith John, O then sin not against love! Hatred of any good thing is deformed; but the hatred of the beautiful image of the original love, that is monstrous. "God is love," and in his love is your life and light, then to sin against him is not simple disobedience, nor is it only grosser rebellion, but it hath that abominable stain of ingratitude in it. Do you read, that it is written, "he is holy?" Then sin not, for this is most repugnant to his holiness,—"his holy eyes cannot see it." Therefore, if thou wouldst have him look upon thee with favour, thou must not look upon sin with favour, or entertain it with delight. Is it written, that he is great and powerful?—Then sin not—that were madness. Is it written, that he is good and gracious? Then it is written, that ye sin not, for that were wickedness, it were an unspeakable folly and madness, to offend so great a God, that can so easily avenge himself; and it were abominable perverseness, and wickedness, to sin against so good and gracious a God, who, though he may avenge himself, yet offers pardon and peace, and beseecheth us to accept it. Is he just? Then sin not, for "he will not acquit the wicked nor hold them guiltless,"—them who do acquit themselves, and yet hold by their sins. And is he merciful? Then, O then, sin not, because he hath acquitted thee, because he is ready to blot out thy guilt! Wilt thou sin against mercy that must save thee? Again, is it written, that the blood of Jesus Christ cleanseth from all sin? That is written, that ye sin not. It is true, it is written, because ye have sinned already, that ye may know how it may be pardoned. But, moreover, it is written, "that ye sin no more," that so more sin may be prevented, at least, deliberate continued walking in sin. So that this blood hath a twofold virtue and use, to be the greatest encouragement to a soul troubled for sin, and the chiefest argument and inducement for a soul not to sin. This medicine, or this plaster, hath two notable virtues, restorative and preservative, to restore the bones that already are broken, through falling in sin and to preserve our feet from further falling in sin. It hath a healing virtue for those bruises that are in the soul, and, besides, it is an anti-hate and sovereign preservative against the poison and infection of sin and the world. What motive is like this? The Son of God shed his blood for our sins, they cost a dear price. O how precious was the ransom! More precious than gold, and silver, and precious stones, because the redemption of the soul is so precious, that it would have ceased forever without it. Now, what soul can deliberately think of this, and receive it with any affection into the heart, but shall find the most vehement persuasion against sin? He cannot but behold the heinousness and infinite evil that is in it, which required such an infinite recompense. And can a soul on that view run to the puddle and defile again, when he sees how dearly the fountain for cleansing was purchased?

Can a believing heart have such treacherous thoughts harboured within it, to crucify afresh the Lord of glory, and, as it were, to trample under feet his blood? No, certainly, he that believes in this blood cannot use it so dishonourably and basely, as it is written, that he sin not, so he reads it, and believes it, that he may not sin, as well as because he hath sinned. Many speak of this blood, and think they apply it to the cleansing of their sin past, but it is rather that they may sin with more liberty, as if the end of vomiting up a surfeit of sin were to surfeit more, and the end of washing, were nothing else but to defile again. Certainly this blood is not for such souls,—not one word of comfort in the word,—not one drop of hope in the blood, to those who pretend to believe in Christ's blood, and continue in sin, as fresh and lively as ever they did, nothing abated of their desires or customs. But if we confess our sins, God will forgive, say you, and this we may do at any time, and this we do daily. Nay, but saith John, this is "written that you sin not," not to encourage you to sin. It is not recorded for this end, that you may live after your own imaginations and former customs, with security and peace, upon this presumption, that pardon is easily procurable, if say, "God have mercy upon me, ere I die." Do not deceive yourselves, for it is written just for the contrary, "that you sin no more, and return no more to folly." If he had said, if we sin, though we confess yet he is just to punish us, you would then be driven to desperation, and from that to a desperate conclusion. Since we must be punished, however, let us not punish ourselves here, in mortifying our flesh,—"let us eat and drink, for to morrow we shall die." Die we must, let us deserve it, for where there is no hope, there is no help for reformation.

But now, when there is such an unexpected proposal of grace, when God, who is free to punish us, becomes indebted by his promise to forgive our debts, we humbly submitting to him, and confessing our guiltiness, this surprisal of clemency and moderation should, yea, certainly will, overcome any heart that truly believes it, and conquer it to his love and obedience. The more easily he forgives sin, the more hardly will a believing heart be drawn to sin. You know any ingenuous spirit will more easily be conquered by kindness and condescendency, than severity and violence. These "cords of love are the bands of a man," suited to the nature of men in whom there is any sparkle of ingenuousness remaining. How often have men been engaged and overcome by clemency and goodness, who could not be conquered by force of arms? Enemies have been made friends by this means, such power is in it to knit hearts together. Augustus, when he was acquainted with the conspiracy of one of his chief minions, Cinna, whom he had made a friend of an enemy, by kindness and courtesy, takes the same way to make of a traitor a constant friend. He doth not punish him as he had done others, but calls for him, and declares unto him his vile ingratitude, that when he had given him life and liberty, he should conspire to take away his prince's life. Well, when he is confounded and astonished, and cannot open his mouth, saith Augustus, I give thee thy life again, first an open enemy, and now a traitor, yet from this day, let an inviolable friendship be bound up between us, and so it proved, for this way of dealing did totally overcome his heart, and blot out all seditious thoughts.[252] But, O how incomparably greater is his condescendency and clemency, whose person is so high and sacred, whose laws are so just and holy, and we so base and wretched,—to pardon such infinite guilt, rebellion, and treachery, against such an infinite majesty, and that, when a soul doth but begin to blush, and be ashamed with itself, and cannot open its mouth! I say, this rare and unparalleled goodness and mercy being considered, cannot but tame and daunt the wildest and most savage natures. Wild beast are not brought into subjection and tamed, but by gentle usage. It is not fierceness and violence can cure their fierceness, but meekness and condescendency to follow their humours and soft dealing with them. As a rod is not bowed by great strength, but broken, even so those things of the promise of pardon for sin, of the grace and readiness of God to pardon upon the easiest terms, are written for this end, that our wild and undaunted natures may be tamed, and may bow and submit willingly to the yoke of his obedience, and may henceforth knit such a sacred bond of friendship and fellowship with God, as may never be broken.

But, say ye, who is he that sins not? Who can say, my heart is pure, and my way is clean? Who can say, I have no sin? And therefore that cannot be expected which you crave. Nay, but saith the apostle, "These things I write unto you, that ye sin not." Because sin is in all, therefore you excuse yourselves in your sins, and take liberty to sin. But the very contrary is the intent of the declaring unto us that we have sin, he shows that none want it, not that ye may be the more indulgent towards it, but the more watchful against it. It is not to make you secure, but rather to give you alarm. Even the best and holiest,—it is an alarm to them, to tell them that sin is *in confinus*, in their very borders, that the enemy is even in their quarters, yea, in their bosom. Certainly, this should so much the more excite us against it, and arm us for it every moment, lest either by fraud or force, by secret undermining or open violence, it draw us away from God. This word, "if we say we have no sin, we lie," is a watchword given to men, a warning to enter in consideration of themselves, for the enemy being within, there is no flying from him. We carry him about with us, and being within, he is less discerned, and therefore we ought to awake, and so walk circumspectly, with eyes in our head, lest we be surprised at unawares, either in that time we know not of, or at that place we least suspect. And to others of you, who have never attained any victory over your sins, and scarce have a discerning of them, I would only say this, that the universality of sin's inhabitation, or being in all men, even the godly, will not excuse sin's domination and reign in you. It is strange, that since the holiest have need of continual watching against this bosom enemy, that ye who have both little knowledge and strength, should think ye may live securely, and not trouble yourselves. If they have need to take heed, how much more have ye, since it is but in them, but it reigns in you?

SERMON XXIV.

1 John ii. 1.—"And if any man sin, we have an advocate with the Father,", &c.

There is here a sad supposition, but too certain, that any man may sin, yea, that all men will sin, even those who have most communion with God, and interest in the blood of Christ. Yet they are not altogether exempted from this fatal lot of mankind. It is incident even to them to sin, and too frequently incident, but yet we have a happy and sweet provision, for indemnity from the hazard of sin,—"we have an advocate with the Father." Grant the probability, yea, the necessity and certainty of that supposal, "if any man do sin," yet there is as much certainty of indemnity from sin, as of necessity of falling into sin. It is not more sure, that we shall carry about with us matter of sorrow and mourning, but that it is as sure, that we have always without us matter of rejoicing.

Let me then speak a word to these particulars. *First*, That sin is incident to the best, even after all persuasions, convictions, resolutions, desires, and designs to avoid sin. *Next*, That it is usual for sins after mercy, convictions, and resolution, to appear so heinous, that they may seem to overtop the mercy of God, and the merits of Christ, a soul is most apt to be troubled with guilt contracted after pardon, and a desire of purity. But withal I would, in the *Last* place represent to you, that there is no ground of despair or discouragement for such an one though there be ground of humiliation and mourning. There is a provision made in the gospel against these continually incident fears, there is a security against the hazard of surprising sins, and, this comfort belongs only to such souls as unfeignedly desire not to sin, and are in some measure persuaded by the grace of God not to sin, not to those who willingly give themselves up to their own lusts. It is as common a doctrine as any, that sin hath some lodging in every man's heart and flesh, and is not totally cast out, but only bound with chains within, that it do not exercise its old dominion over a believer. But I fear, the most common truths, though they be most substantial in themselves, are yet but circumstantial in our apprehensions, and very rarely and extraordinarily have place in the deeper and more serious thoughts of our hearts. They are commonly confessed, it is true, but as seldom considered, I am sure. For who did truly ponder the inclineableness of our nature to sin, the strong propension of the heart to evil, the deceitfulness of sin itself, and the many circumstantial helps and additions it gets to its strength, but would stand in awe, and watch seriously over himself. I dare say, many sin, rather because of a misapprehended immunity from it and a misreckoning of their own measure and strength, than because of the strength of sin itself. I know no one thing makes sin so strong as this,—that we do not apprehend our own weakness, and so give over watchfulness, which is the greatest and best part of our armour of defence, when it is done in faith, and this watch kept on the tower of the Lord's promises. The apprehension of our escaping the pollutions of the world, and of some strength to resist them; this adds no more strength to us, but diminisheth and taketh from our vigilance and so exposeth us, as it were, naked and secure, to the cruelty of our adversary. I would wish every Christian to be thoroughly acquainted, and often conversant in two books of sophistry, I may so term them—the deceitfulness of his own heart, and the deceivableness of sin, Jer. xvii. and Heb. iii. 13. These are the volumes he would daily turn over to learn to discern the sophistications, self flatteries, blindness, darkness, and self love of his own heart, to take off the deceiving mask of pretences and appearances of good, and behold sensibly the true and real inclinations of the heart to wickedness, to passion, pride, uncleanness, malice, envy, and all those affections of the flesh,—to find out the true beating of the pulse of the heart. And indeed this just discerning and discovery of the thief in the soul, is a great part of his arraignment, for if sin be under the view of an eye that hates it, and loves God, much of its power and virtue, which be in darkness, is taken away. I press this the more because I verily apprehend it to be the plague of many Christians, who have some general insight into the matter of good and evil, and espy some more gross corruption in themselves, and have some affection to good. Yet this estrangedness to our own hearts, and the vein or strain of them, the not unbowelling of our hidden affections, and not discerning of the poison of pride, self love, love of the world, and such like lusts, which are intermingled in all that we do, and spread, as it were, universally through the whole man, this, I say, makes most of us to be subject to so many surprisals by sin. We are often routed before we draw up, and often conquered ere we consider. This makes us such unproficients in mortification, so that scarce any sin is killed, while the roots of all sin lie hid under the ground from us. Then withal, I desire you to study how deceivable a thing sin is,—how many deceitful fair pretences it is covered with. It hath the voice of Jacob, but the hands of Esau. Look, what it is that is pleasant or suitable to our natural spirits,—it insinuates itself always under the shadow of that, and if there be not much heedfulness and attention, and much experience of the wiles of that subtile one, it is a great hazard to be catched with it unadvisedly, while we clasp about another thing which is presented as a bait and allurement. Now, is it any wonder that a poor soul be drawn to sin often, when our enemy doth not for the most part profess hostility, but friendship, and under that colour pleads admission within our ports? And, besides, we have a treacherous friend in our bosom, that betrays us into his hands, that is, our own deceitful hearts. These things I mention to put you in remembrance of what condition you are in, in this world, and what posture you should be in. Watch, I say, and when ye have done all, stand with your loins girt, and though you cannot possibly escape all sin, yet certainly it is not in vain thus to set against it, and keep a watch over it, for by this means you shall escape more sin and sin less, as he that aims at the mark, though he do not hit it, yet shall ordinarily come nearer it, than he that shoots only at random, and as the army that is most vigilant and watchful, though they cannot prevent all losses and hazards, yet commonly are not found at such a loss, as those who are proud, confident, and secure.

Now, as it is supposed, that sin is ordinarily incident to the child of God, so it is especially to be caveated, that he despair not in his sins, for it is imported in this provision, that the believer is in great hazard upon new lapses into sin, either of daily incursion, or of a grosser nature, to be discouraged. As there is so much corruption in any man's heart, as will turn the grace of God into wantonness, and incline him upon the proposal of free grace to presume to take liberty to the flesh, so that same corruption, upon another occasion, works another way, upon the supposal of new sins, aggravated with preceding mercy and grace in God, and convictions and resolutions in him, to drive him into despondency and dejection of spirit, as if there were no pardon for such sins. And indeed, it is no wonder if the soul be thus set upon, if we set aside the consideration of the infinite grace of God, that far surpasseth the ill deserts of men. To speak of the very nature of the thing itself, there is no sin in its own nature more unpardonable than sin after pardon; nothing so heinous, aggravated with so many high circumstances, which mingleth it with the worst ingredients, as this sin, after so much grace revealed in the gospel, to the end that we may not sin. Sins washed so freely, in so precious a fountain, and yet to defile again, sins forgiven so readily and easily, the debt whereof, in justice, the whole creation was not able to pay, and yet to offend so gracious a Father, a soul being thoroughly convinced of the vanity, folly, and madness of sin, of the deceitfulness and baseness of its pleasures, and set in a posture against it, as the most deadly enemy; and yet, after all this, to be foiled, deceived, and insnared—here, I say, are very piercing considerations, which cannot but set the challenge very deep into the heart of a Christian and wound him sore. How will he be filled with shame and confusion of face if he look upon God, every look or beam of whose countenance represents unto the soul the vilest and most abominable visage of sin! Or if he look into himself, there is nothing but self condemning there. He finds his own conscience staring him as a thousand witnesses. Thus the soul of a believer being environed, he is ready to apprehend, that though God should have pardoned the sins of his ignorance yet that there is more difficulty in this,—to pardon his returnings to folly, and therefore are some put to harder exercise, and greater terrors, after conversion, than in the time of it. The sins of ignorance being, as it were, removed as a cloud, and scored out in a heap, but the sins of knowledge after mercy, lying more distinctly and clearly in the view of the soul, it is more difficult to blot them out of the conscience, and sprinkle the heart from an evil conscience. These things I speak to you for this reason, that you may be afraid to sin. I suppose that there is no hazard of eternal damnation by sin. Grant that you know beforehand, that if you sin, there is yet forgiveness with him, and there is no hazard of perishing by it, yet, sure I am, it is the most foolish adventure in the world, to take liberty on that account, for though there be indemnity that way, as to thy eternal estate, yet I am persuaded, that there is more damage another way, in thy spiritual estate in this world, than all the gains of sin can countervail. There is a necessary loss of peace and joy, and communion of the Holy Ghost. It is inevitable, in the very ordinary and natural course and connection of things, but that sin, that way indulged, will eclipse thy soul, and bring some darkness of sorrow and horror over it. To speak after the manner of man, and in the way of reason itself, the entertainment of that which God hates will deprive thee of more solid joy and sweetness in him, than all the pleasures of sin could afford. Therefore I dare not say to you, as one too unadvisedly expresseth it, "Fear not, though you do sin, of any hurt that can come by these sins, for if you sin it shall do you no hurt at all."[253] I say, this were indeed but to make you too bold with sin. I had rather represent unto you, that though ye be secured in your eternal estate, and there can come no condemnation that way, yet there is much hurt comes by sin, even in this world, and sure, I think it a very rational and Christian inducement, to prevail with a Christian not to sin, to tell him that he shall make a foolish bargain by it, for he shall lose much more than he can gain. Is there no hurt or loss incident to men, but eternal perdition? Nay, my beloved, there is a loss Christians may sustain by sinning freely, which all the combined advantages of sin cannot compensate. Is not one hour's communion with God, are not the peace of your own consciences, and the joy of the Spirit, such inestimable jewels, that it were more suitable for a man to sell the world, and buy them, than to sell them, and buy a poor momentary trifling contentment, which hath a sting in the tail of it, and leaves nothing but vexation after it? O these bruises in David's bones, these breaches in his spirit, that loss of the joy of his salvation! Let these teach you who are escaped the great hurt of sin, to fear, at least, to be hurt by it this way, more than ever you can expect to be helped by it.

But then, I desire to add this in the third place, that there is provision made against the discouragement of those souls that desire not to sin, and yet sin against their desire. If the challenge I spoke of be written in thy conscience, as it were with the point of a diamond, deeply engraven, yet my beloved, consider, that "if any man sin, we have an advocate," &c. There is an express caution against thy discouragement. Certainly our Saviour hath provided for it. Since the case is so incident, and the supposition so ordinary, it is not conceivable that he hath not caveated and secured thy salvation in such cases, for he knew certainly before he pardoned thee, and visited thee at first, that thou wast to be subject unto this necessary burden of sin, and that it would often times molest and trouble you, and sometimes prevail over you. All this he knew, that when he should order your forces, and draw out against sin, with the greatest desire and resolution, that yet you might be foiled unexpectedly, and this was not unknown to him, when he showed mercy at first. Therefore, since his love is unchangeable, and his wisdom, being infinite, saith it should be so, he would never have cast his love on such persons, if these things, which were then before him, could make him change. Now, I grant there is more wonder in the pardon of following sins, than in the first pardon, and therefore you should still love more, and praise more. But what is this wonder to the wonder of his grace? It is swallowed up in that higher wonder, for his thoughts and ways are not like ours, his voice is, "Return, thou backsliding sinner, to thy first husband, though thou hast played the harlot." Therefore, I desire that whatsoever be presented in that kind, to aggravate your sins, let it humble you more indeed, and make you hate sin, but let it not hinder you to think as highly of his mercy and grace, and to set that in the heavens above it.

SERMON XXV.

1 John ii. 1.—"And if any man sin, we have an advocate with the Father,", &c.

It is the natural office of the conscience to accuse a man in evil doing. As every man by sin is liable to the judgment of the supreme court of heaven, so he is likewise subject to the inferior court of his own conscience, for the most high God hath a deputy within every man's breast, that not only is a witness, but a judge, to fasten an accusation, and pronounce a sentence upon him according to the law of God. And while it is so, that a man is accused in both courts, at the supreme tribunal, and the lower house of a man's own conscience, when man's accuser is within him, and God, his righteous Judge, above him, who can come in to plead such a man's cause? A person self condemned, who shall plead for his absolution? If he cannot but accuse himself, and stop his mouth, being guilty before God of the transgression of all his law, then what place for an advocate to accuse him, or defend his cause? And who is it that can enter in the lists with God, who, because the supreme and highest Judge, must be both Judge and party? Where shall a daysman be found to lay his hands on both, and advocate the desperate-like cause of sinners? Truly, here we had been at an eternal stand, and here had the business stuck for ever, for anything that the creation could imagine, had not the infinite grace and wisdom of God opened themselves to mankind, in opening a door of hope to broken and outlaw sinners. And behold, here is the provision made for the security and salvation of lost souls,—there is one able and mighty to save,—a person found out fit for this advocation, who taketh the broken cause of sinners in hand, and pleads it out, and makes out justice to be for them, and not against them,—"If any man sin, we have an advocate," &c.

There is one thing imported, that sin maketh a man liable to a charge and accusation, and brings him under the hazard of judgment. Indeed it is hard enough to endure an accusing conscience, and a spirit wounded with the apprehension of wrath. When our Saviour would express great affliction, he doth it thus—"A man's enemies shall be those of his own house." If a domestic enemy be so ill, what shall a bosom enemy be, when a man's accuser is not only beside him, but within him,—not only in the house with him, but in the field too,—carried about with him whithersoever he goeth, so that he can have no retiring or withdrawing place from it! Indeed, some poor souls make a mad escape from under the challenge of their consciences, they get away from their keepers to more excess in sin, or make some vain diversion to company, and other things of the world. But the end thereof shall be more bitterness, for that will not still sleep within them, but shall awake upon them with more terror, and one day put them in such a posture, that all the comforts of the world shall be but as a drop of water to a man in a burning fever, or as oil to a flame. But, as I told you, that is not the greatest matter, to be self accused, and self-condemned, if there were not a higher tribunal, which this process originally flows from, one greater than the conscience, who speaks to us in his word, and hath written his charge and sentence against us, and this is it which sets the soul most on edge, and it is but the very apprehension of that higher judgment, which is the gall and wormwood, the poison of those challenges in the conscience. I would desire you to look upon this, and consider that there is a sentence passed in the word of God upon all your actions, that the wrath of God is revealed in the scriptures as due to you, however you may flatter yourselves in your sins, and fancy an immunity from wrath, though you live in sin. I wish ye were once persuaded of this,—that all sinners must once appear before God's tribunal and hear the righteous sentence of the dueness of punishment pronounced; I say, all must once appear, either to hear and believe it, or to see it executed. The wisdom of God requires, that all men's guilt, which is a transgression of the law, should once come to a judicial trial and decision by the law, and either this must be done in your own consciences here, that ye may sist yourselves before him, and take with your sins, and humble yourselves in his sight, and then the matter is put over upon a Mediator, or else you must give him leave, nay he will take leave to cite you to appear, to see the sentence executed which was pronounced, since ye would not apply it to your own hearts. O! happy is that soul that anticipates that great day of final judgment, by a previous self judgment and self trial. Well, then, hath the scriptures included all under sin, that all men might be guilty and every mouth stopped before God, Rom. iii. 19. What shall we do then? Since righteousness and justice is against us, who can plead for us? It would seem that there could be no relaxing, no repealing, no dispensing with this law at least that if there be anything of that kind, that righteousness and judgment can have no hand in it. Yet, behold, what follows, "we have an advocate," &c. And an advocate's office is to sue out the client's right, from principles of justice. Elsewhere Christ hath the office of a Judge, here he is an advocate for the party, and both of these may have a comfortable consideration, John v. 22. "The Father judgeth no man, but hath committed all judgment to the Son." And yet, here we have an advocate with the Father, and that is, with the Father as judge. These do not cross one another, but make out our abundant consolation, that one entire office of our Saviour is represented under all these various notions suited to our capacity. A Judge he is yea, his tribunal is the highest and supreme, from which there is no appeal, the ultimate decision lies here of all capital or soul cases and causes. It is true, the Father doth not wholly divest himself of judgment and authority in the matters of life and death, for the gospel is his contrivance, as it was the Son's, but Christ is, as it were, substituted his vicegerent, in the administration of the second covenant. You read of a preparatory tribunal erected in the word by God the Creator, that is, of the law which condemns us. Now, such is the mercy and grace, and free love of God, that he hath relaxed that sentence as to the persons. He hath not taken that advantage which in justice he had against us, but upon some valuable considerations hath committed to the Son a royal power of prescribing new laws of life and death, and new terms of salvation, and Christ having, at his Fathers will, satisfied the law, in what it did threaten us, he is, as it were, in compensation of such a great service, made Lord and King "both of the dead and living," (Rom. xiv. 9,) and "all things in heaven and earth are given to him," Matt. xxviii. 18, John xiii. 3. And therefore, whatever soul is aggrieved under the accusation and charge of the law, hath liberty, yea, and is called to it, of duty, to appeal unto this new erected tribunal, where Christ sits to dispense life according to the terms of grace and he may be sure the Father will not judge him according to the law, if the Son absolve him in the gospel.

Now, with this it consists, that he who hath all final judgment in his hand, yet is our advocate in another consideration, as we consider God the Father sitting upon the tribunal of justice, and proceeding according to the terms and tenor of his first law, or covenant of life and death. Then Christ comes in with his advocation for poor sinners, and sustains their persons, and maintains their cause, even from the principles of justice. He presents his satisfactory sacrifice and pleads that we are not to be charged with that punishment that he hath suffered, because he hath indeed fulfilled our legal righteousness, and by this means the law's mouth is stopped, which had stopped our mouth, and the sinner is absolved, who was found guilty. Thus you see the salvation and absolution of believers is wonderfully secured, for there is a sentence for it in the court of the gospel, pronounced by the Son. But lest you think he should usurp such an absolute power, then hear, that he is an advocate to plead out the equity and justice of it, before the very tribunal of the law, that the law itself being the rule, the Father himself, who made the law, being the Judge, the poor soul that flies unto him as a refuge, may be saved, since what it craved of us it gets in him, and is as fully satisfied that way, as it could have been by us. Therefore, that same righteousness which bids condemn the sinner, commands to save the believer in Christ, though a sinner. What shall a soul then fear? Who shall condemn? It is Christ that justifieth, for he is judge of life and death and that is much. But it is the Father that justifieth, and that is more whatsoever tribunal you may be cited unto, you may be sure. Is it the gospel? Then the Son is judge. Is it the law? Then the Son is advocate. He will not only give life himself, but see that his Father do it, and warrant you from all back hazards. Nay, before the matter shall misgive, as he comes down from off the throne, to stand at the bar and plead for sinners, who devolve themselves upon him, so he will not spare if need require, to degrade himself further, if I may say so, and of an advocate become a supplicant. And truly he ceased not in the days of his flesh to pray for us, "with strong cries and tears," Heb. v. 7. And now he still lives to make intercession for us. He can turn from the plea of justice, to the intercession and supplication of mercy, and if strict justice will not help him, yet grace and favour he is sure will not disappoint him.

There is a divine contexture of justice and mercy in the business of man's redemption, and there is nothing so much declares infinite wisdom, as the method, order, and frame of it. Mercy might have been showed to sinners, in gracious and free pardon of their sins, and dispensing with the punishment due to their persons, yet the Lord's justice and faithfulness in that first commination might be wronged and disappointed by it, if no satisfaction should be made for such infinite offences, if the law were wholly made void both in the punishment, as also to the person. Therefore in the infinite depths of God's wisdom there was a way found out to declare both mercy and justice, to make both to shine gloriously in this work, and indeed that is the great wonder of men and angels, such a conjunction or constellation of divine attributes in one work. And indeed, it is only the most happy and favourable aspect in which we can behold the divine Majesty. The Psalmist, Psalm lxxxv., expects much good from this conjunction of the celestial attributes, and prognosticates salvation to be near at hand, and all good things, as the immediate effect of it. There is a meeting there, as it were, of some honourable personages, (ver. 10, 11) such as are in heaven. The meeting is strange, if you consider the parties,—Mercy and Truth, Righteousness and Peace. If Mercy and Peace had met thus friendly, it had been less wonder, but it would seem, that Righteousness and Truth should stand off, or meet only to reason and dispute the business with Mercy. But here is the wonder,—Mercy and Truth meet in a friendly manner, and "kiss one another." There is a perfect agreement and harmony amongst them, about this matter of our salvation. There was a kind of parting at man's fall, but they met again at Christ's birth. Here is the uniting principle, "Truth springing out of the earth." Because he who is "the truth and the life, was to spring out of the earth therefore" righteousness will look down from heaven, and countenance the business, and this will make all of them to meet with a loving salutation.

Now, as this was the contexture of the divine attributes in the business of redemption, so our Lord and Saviour taketh upon him divers names, offices, and exercises, different functions for us because he knoweth that his Father may justly exact of man personal satisfaction, and hath him at this disadvantage, and that he might have refused to have accepted any other satisfaction from another person. Therefore he puts on the habit and form of a supplicant and intercessor for us, and so while he was in the flesh, he ceased not to offer up "prayers and supplications with strong cries and tears," and he is said still "to make intercession for us." As he learned obedience, though a Son, so he learned to be a humble supplicant, though equal with God. Because our claim depends wholly on grace, he came off the bench, and stood at the bar, not only pleading but praying for us, entreating favour and mercy to us. And then, he personates an advocate in another consideration, and pleads upon terms of justice, that we be pardoned, because his Father once having accepted him in our stead he gave a satisfaction in value equal to our debt, and performed all that we were personally bound to. So then you may understand how it is partly an act of justice, partly an act of mercy, in God to forgive sin to believers, though indeed mercy and grace is the predominant ingredient, because love and grace was the very first rise and spring of sending a Saviour and Redeemer, and so the original of that very purchase and price. He freely sent his Son, and freely accepted him in our stead, but once standing in our room justice craves that no more be exacted of us, since he hath done the business himself.

A sinner stands accused in his own conscience, and before God, therefore, to the end that we get no wrong, there is a twofold advocate given us, one in the earth, in our consciences, another in the heavens with God. Christ is gone up to the highest tribunal, where the cause receives a definitive sentence, and there he manageth it above, so that though Satan should obtrude upon a poor soul a wrong sentence in its own conscience, and bring down a false and counterfeit act, as it were, extracted out of the register of heaven, whereby to deceive the poor soul, and condemn it in itself, yet there is no hazard above, he dare not appear there, before the highest court, for he hath already succumbed on earth. When Christ was here, the prince of the world was judged and cast out, and so he will never once put in an accusation into heaven, because he knoweth our faithful advocate is there, where nothing can pass without his knowledge and consent. And this is a great comfort, that all inferior sentences in thy perplexed conscience, which Satan, through violence hath imposed upon thee, are rescinded above in the highest court, and shall not stand to thy prejudice, whoever thou be that desirest to forsake sin and come to Jesus Christ.

But how doth Christ plead? Can he plead us not guilty? Can he excuse or defend our sins? No, that is not the way. That accusation of the word and law against us is confessed, is proven, all is undeniably clear, but, he pleads satisfied, though guilty,—he presents his satisfactory sacrifice and the savour of that perfumes heaven, and pacifieth all. He shows God's bond and discharge of the receipt of the sum of our debt, and thus is he cleared, and we absolved. Therefore I desire you, whoever you are that are challenged for sin, and the transgression of the law, if ye would have a solid way of satisfaction and peace to your consciences, take with your guiltiness. Plead not "not guilty." Do not excuse or extenuate, but aggravate your guilt. Nay, in this you may help Satan, accuse yourselves, and say that you know more evil in yourselves than he doth and open that up before God. But in the meantime, consider how it is managed above. Plead thou also "satisfied in Christ though guilty," and so thou mayest say to thy accuser, "If thou hast any thing to object against me, why I may not be saved, though a sinner, thou must go up to the highest tribunal to propone it, thou must come before my judge and advocate above, but forasmuch as thou dost not appear there, it is but a lie, and a murdering be."

Now this is the way that the Spirit advocates for us in our consciences, John xiv. and xv. 26. παρακλετος is rendered here "Advocate," there "Comforter." Both suit well, and may be conjoined in one, and given to both, for both are comfortable advocates,—Christ with the Father, and the Spirit with us. Christ is gone above for it, and he sent the Spirit in his stead. As God hath a deputy judge in man, that is, man's conscience, so the Son, our advocate with God, hath a deputy advocate to plead the cause in our conscience, and this he doth, partly by opening up the Scriptures to us and making us understand the way of salvation in them, partly manifesting his own works and God's gifts in us by a superadded light of testimony, and partly by comforting us against all outward and inward sorrows. Sometimes he pleads with the soul against Satan "not guilty," for Satan is a slanderous and a false accuser, and cares not *calumniari fortiter ul aliquid hæreat*, to calumniate stoutly, and he knoweth something will stick.[254] He will not only object known sins and transgressions of the law, but his manner is to cast a mist upon the eye of the soul, and darken all its graces, and then he brings forth his process, that they have no grace, no faith in Christ, no love to God, no sorrow for sin. In such a case, it is the Spirit's office to plead it out to our consciences, that we are not totally guilty, as we are charged, and this is not so much a clearing of ourselves, as a vindication of the free gifts of God, which lie under his aspersion and reproach. Indeed, if there be a great stress here, and, for wise reasons, the Spirit forbear to plead out this point, but leave a poor soul to puddle it out alone, and scrape its evidences together in the dark,—I say, if thou find this too hard for thee to plead not guilty then my advice is, that ye wave and suspend that question. Yield it not wholly, but rather have it entire, and do as if it were not. Suppose that article and point were gained against thee, what wouldst thou do next? Certainly, thou must say, I would then seek grace and faith from him who giveth liberally. I would then labour to receive Christ in the promises. I say, do that now, and thou takest a short and compendious way to win thy cause, and overcome Satan. Let that be thy study, and he hath done with it.

But in any challenge about the transgression of the law, or desert of eternal wrath, the Spirit must not plead "not guilty," for thou must confess that, but in as far as he driveth at a further conclusion, to drive thee away from hope and confidence to despondency of spirit, in so far the Spirit clears up unto the conscience that this doth nowise follow from that confession of guiltiness, since there is a Saviour that hath satisfied for it, and invites all to come, and accept him for their Lord and Saviour.

SERMON XXVI.

1 John ii. 1.—"We have an advocate with the Father, Jesus Christ the righteous."

There is no settlement to the spirit of a sinner that is once touched with the sense of his sins, and apprehension of the justice and wrath of God, but in some clear and distinct understanding of the grounds of consolation in the gospel, and the method of salvation revealed in it. There is no solid peace giving answer to the challenges of the law and thy own conscience, but in the advocation of Jesus Christ, the Saviour of sinners. And therefore the apostle propones it here for the comfort of believers who are incident to be surprised through the suddenness of sin, and often deceived by the subtlety of Satan, whose souls' desires and sincere endeavours are to be kept from iniquity, and therefore they are made to groan within themselves, and sometimes sadly to conclude against themselves, upon the prevailing of sin. Here is the cordial, I say. He presents to them Jesus Christ standing before the bar of heaven, and pleading his satisfaction in the name of such souls, and so suiting forth an exemption and discharge for them from their sins. So he presents us with the most comfortable aspect, Christ standing between us and justice, the Mediator interposed between us and the Father, so there can come no harm to such poor sinners, except it come through his sides first, and no sentence can pass against them, unless he succumb in his righteous cause in heaven.

The strength of Christ's advocation for believers consists partly in his qualification for the office, partly in the ground and foundation of his cause. His qualification we have in this verse, the ground and foundation of his pleading in the next verse, in that "he is the propitiation for our sins," and upon this very ground his advocation is both just and effectual.

Every word holds out some fitness, and therefore every word drops out consolation to a troubled soul. "With the Father," speaks out the relation he and we stand in to the Judge. He hath not to do with an austere and rigid Judge, that is implacable and unsatisfiable, who will needs adhere peremptorily to the letter of the law, for then we should be all undone. If there were not some paternal affection, and fatherly clemency and moderation in the Judge, if he were not so disposed, as to make some candid interpretation upon it, and in some manner to relax the sentence, as to our personal suffering, we could never stand before him, nor needed any advocate appear for us. But here is the great comfort,—he is Christ's Father and our Father, so himself told us, (John

xx. 17,) "I go to my Father and your Father, and my God and your God." And therefore we may be persuaded that he will not take advantage, even in that which he hath in justice, of us, and though we be apprehensive of his anger, in our failings and offences, and this makes us often to be both afraid and ashamed to come to him, measuring him after the manner of men, who are soon angry, and often implacably angry. We imagine that he cannot but repel and put back our petitions, and therefore we have not the boldness to offer them, yet he ceaseth not to be our Father and Christ's Father. And if ye would have the character of a father, look (Jer. xxxi. 18,) how he stands affected towards ashamed and confounded Ephraim, how his bowels move, and his compassions yearn towards him as his pleasant child. The truth is, in such a case, in which we are captives against our will, and stumble against our purpose, he pities us as a father doth his children, knowing that we are but dust and grass, Psal. ciii. 13-17. See the excellent and sweet application of this relation by the Psalmist—if it stir him, it stirs up rather the affection of pity, than the passion of anger. He pities his poor child, when he cries out of violence and oppression; and therefore, there are great hopes that our advocate Jesus Christ shall prevail in his suits for us, because he, with whom he deals,—the Father,—loves him, and loves us, and will not stand upon strict terms of justice, but rather attemper all with mercy and love. He will certainly hear his well beloved Son, for in him he is well pleased, his soul rests and takes complacency in him, and for his sake he adopts us to be his children, and therefore he will both hear him in our behalf, and our prayers too, for his name's sake.

But this is superadded to qualify our advocate,—he is the Christ of God, anointed for this very purpose, and so hath a fair and lawful calling to this office. He takes not this honour to himself, but was called thereto of his Father, Heb. v. 4. As he did not make himself a priest, so he did not intrude upon the advocateship, "but he that said, Thou art my Son called him to it." If a man had never so great ability to plead in the law, yet, except he be licentiate and graduate, he may not take upon him to plead a cause. But our Lord Jesus hath both skill and authority, he hath both the ability and the office, was not a self intruder or usurper, but the council of heaven did licentiate him, and graduate him for the whole office of mediatorship: in which there is the greatest stay and support for a sinking soul, to know that all this frame and fabric of the gospel was contrived by God the Father, and that he is master builder in it. Since it is so, there can nothing control it or shake it, since it is the very will of God, "with whom we have to do," that a mediator should stand between him and us, and since he hath such a mind to clear poor souls, that he freely chooseth and giveth them an able Advocate, it is a great token that he hath a mind to save as many as come and submit to him and that he is ready to pardon, when he prepares so fit an Advocate for us, and hath not left us alone to plead our own cause.

But the anointing of Christ for it, implies both δυναμιν and εξουσιαν *potentiam et potestatem*, the gifts for it as well as the authority, and the ability as well as the office, for God hath singularly qualified him for it,—given him the Spirit above measure, Isa. lxi. 1. He received gifts not only to distribute to men, but to exercise for men, and their advantage, Psal. lxviii. 18. And therefore the Father seems to interest himself in the cause as it were his own. He furnisheth our Advocate as if it were to plead the cause of his own justice against us, he upholds and strengthens Christ in our cause, as really as if it were his own, Isa. xlii. 1, 6, which expresseth to us the admirable harmony and consent of heaven to the salvation of as many as make Christ their refuge, and desire not to live in sin. Though they be often foiled, yet there is no hazard of the failing of their cause above, because our Advocate hath both excellent skill, and undoubtable authority.

Yea, he is so fully qualified for this that he is called Jesus the Saviour, he is such an Advocate that he saves all he pleads for. The best advocate may lose the cause, either through the weakness of itself, or the iniquity of the judge, but he is the Advocate and the Saviour, that never succumbed in his undertaking for any soul. Be their sins never so heinous—their accusation never so just and true—their accuser never so powerful, yet they who put their cause in his hand, who flee in hither for refuge being wearied of the bondage of sin and Satan, he hath such a prevalency with the Father, that their cause cannot miscarry. Even when justice itself seems to be the opposite party, yet he hath such marvellous success in his office, that justice shall rather meet amicably with mercy and peace, and salute them kindly, (Psal. lxxxv. 10, 11,) as being satisfied by him, that he come short in his undertaking.

But there is another personal qualification needful, or all should be in vain,—"Jesus the righteous." If he were not righteous in himself, he had need of an advocate for himself, and might not plead for sinners, but he is righteous and holy, no guile found in his mouth, without sin, an unblameable and unspotted High Priest, else he could not mediate for others, and such an Advocate too, else he could not plead for others, Heb. vii. 26. As this perfected his sacrifice, that he offered not for his own sins, neither needed he, so this completes his advocateship, and gives it a mighty influence for his poor clients, that he needs not plead for himself. If, then, the law cannot attach our Lord and Saviour, can lay no claim to him, or charge against him, then certainly, all that he did behoved to be for others, and so he stands in a good capacity to plead for us before the Father, and to sue out a pardon to us, though guilty, for if the just was delivered for the unjust, and the righteous suffered for the unrighteous, much more is it consistent with the justice of the Father, to deliver and save the unrighteous and unjust sinner for the righteous Advocate's sake. "If ye seek me, then let these go free," saith he, John xviii. 8. So he in effect pleads with God his Father, O Father, if thou deal with me, the righteous One, as with an unrighteous man, then, in all reason and justice, thou must deal with my poor clients, though unrighteous, as with righteous men. If justice thought she did me no wrong to punish me, the righteous, then let it not be thought a wrong to justice to pardon, absolve, and justify the unrighteous.

Now, if he be so righteous a person, it follows necessarily, that he hath a righteous cause, for an honest man will not advocate an unjust cause. But how can the cause of believers be said to be righteous, when justice itself, and the law, indicts the accusation against them? Can they plead not guilty, or he for them? There is a twofold righteousness, in relation to a twofold rule, a righteousness of strict justice, in relation to the first covenant, and this cannot be pleaded, that our cause is exactly conformable to the covenant of works. We cannot, nor Christ in our name, plead any thing from that, which holds forth nothing but personal obedience, or else personal satisfaction. But yet our cause may be found to be righteous, in relation to the second covenant, and the rule and terms of it, in as far as God hath revealed his acceptance of a surety in our stead and hath dispensed with the rigour of the law, according to that new law of grace and righteousness contempered together. The cause of a desperate lost sinner may be sustained before the righteous Judge, and it is upon this new account that he pleads for us because he hath satisfied in our stead, and now it is as righteous and equitable with God, to show mercy and forgiveness to believing sinners, as it is to reveal wrath and anger against impenitent sinners.

I know there will be some secret whisperings in your hearts upon the hearing of this. Oh! it is true, it is a most comfortable thing for them whose advocate he is. There is no fear of the miscarrying of their cause above, but as for me, I know not if he be an advocate for me, whether I may come into that sentence, "We have an advocate," &c. I confess it is true, he is not an advocate for every one, for while he was here, he prayed not for the world, but them that were given him out of the world, (John xvii.), much more will he not plead for the world, when he is above. He is rather witnessing against the unbelieving world. But yet, I believe his advocation is not restrained only to those who actually believe, as neither his supplication was, John xvii. But as he prayed for those who should hereafter believe, so he still pleads for all the elect not only to procure remission to the penitent, but repentance to the impenitent. There is one notable effect of the advocation and intercession of Christ, which indeed is common to the world, but particularly intended for the elect, that is, the present suspension of the execution of the curse of the law, by virtue whereof there is liberty to offer the gospel, and call sinners to repentance. No question, the sparing of the world, the forbearance and long suffering of God towards sinners, is the result and fruit of our Lord's intercession and advocation in heaven, and so, even the elect have the benefit of it before they believe, but it is so provided, that they shall never sensibly know this, nor have any special comfort from it, till they believe, and so Christ doth not plead for pardon to their sins till they repent. He pleads even before we repent, but we cannot know it; yet he pleads not that pardon be bestowed before they repent, and so the saving efficacy of his advocation is peculiar and proper in the application to believing souls.

Now, consider, I say, whether or not thou be one that finds the power of that persuasion,—"My little children, I write unto you that ye sin not," &c. Canst thou unfeignedly say, that it is the desire and endeavour of thy soul not to sin, and that thou art persuaded to this, not only from the fear and terror of God, but especially from his mercy and goodness in the gospel? This is one part of the character of such as Christ's advocation is actually extended to. Moreover, being surprised with sin, and overcome beside thy purpose, and against thy desire, dost thou apprehend sin as thy greatest misery, and arraign thyself before the tribunal of God, or art thou attached in thy own conscience, and the law pleaded against thee, before the bar of thy own conscience? Then, I say, according to this scripture, thou art the soul unto whom this comfort belongs, thou art called of God to decide the controversy in thy own conscience. By flying up, and appealing to that higher tribunal, where Christ is advocate, thou mayest safely give over, and trust thy cause to him.

But, on the other hand, O how deplorable and remediless is the condition of those souls who have no cause of this kind stated within their own consciences, who are not pursued by Satan and sin, but rather at peace with them, amicably agreeing with them, acting their lusts and will! You who have no bonds upon you, to restrain you from sin, neither the terror of the Lord persuadeth yon, nor the love of Christ constrains you, you can be kept from no beloved sin, nor pressed to any serious and spiritual labour in God's service; and then when you sin, you have no accuser within, or such an one as you suppress, and suffer not to plead it out against you or cite you before God's tribunal. I say unto you, (and, alas! many of you are such) you do not, you cannot know, that you have an interest in this Advocate. You can have no benefit or saving advantage from Christ's pleading, while you remain thus in your sins. Alas! poor souls, what will ye do? Can you manage your own cause alone? Though you defraud and deceive your own consciences now, though ye offer violence to them, do ye think so to carry it above? Nay, persuade yourselves you must one day appear, and none to speak for you, God your Judge, your conscience your accuser, and Satan, your tormentor, standing by, and then woe to him that is alone, when the Advocate becomes Judge. In that day blessed are all those that have trusted in him, and used him formerly as an Advocate against sin and Satan, but woe to those for ever, who would never suffer this cause to be pleaded, while there was an Advocate!

SERMON XXVII.

1 John ii. 2.—"And he is the propitiation," &c.

Here is the strength of Christ's plea, and ground of his advocation, that "he is the propitiation." The advocate is the priest, and the priest is the sacrifice, and such efficacy this sacrifice hath, that the propitiatory sacrifice may be called the very propitiation and pacification for sin. Here is the marrow of the gospel, and these are the breasts of consolation which any poor sinner might draw by faith, and bring out soul refreshment. But truly, it comes not out but by drawing, and there is nothing fit for that but the heart, that alone can suck out of these breasts the milk of consolation. The well of salvation in the word is deep, and many of you have nothing to draw with, you want the bucket that should be let down, that is, the affectionate meditation and consideration of the heart, and therefore you go away empty. You come full of other cares, and desires, and delights, no empty room in your hearts for this, no soul longings and thirstings after the righteousness of God, and therefore you return as you came, empty of all solid and true refreshment. Oh, that we could draw it forth to you, and then drop it into your hearts, and make it descend into your consciences!

In these words, you may consider more distinctly, who this is, and then, for whom he is made a sacrifice, and withal, the efficacy of this sacrifice, and the sufficiency. Who this is, is pointed out as with the finger. "He is," that is, "Jesus Christ, the righteous." The apostle demonstrates him as a remarkable person, as in his evangel the Baptist doth—"Behold the Lamb of God, which taketh away the sins of the world." And the church, (Isa. lxii. 1,) taketh a special notice of this person, "Who is this that cometh from Edom?" And that which maketh him so remarkable, is his strange habit, after the treading the wine-press of wrath alone,—that he was made a bloody sacrifice to pacify God. And to show you how notable a person he is, he is signally and eminently pointed out by the Father, Isa. xlii. 1, "Behold my servant," &c, as if he would have the eyes of all men fixed upon him, with wonder and admiration. And for this end, he singled him out from the multitude, by a voice from heaven, which testified unto him particularly, "This is my well beloved Son, hear him." Therefore the apostle had reason to say, (2 Cor. v. 14.) that he is "one for all," so notable an one, that he may serve for all. He stands in more value in the count of God than all mankind. All creatures are ciphers, which being never so much multiplied, come to nothing, amount not beyond nothing, but set him before them, put Christ on the head of them, and he signifies more than they all do, and gives them all some estimation in the count. And so they stand in Paul's calculation, (Phil. iii.) which he makes with very great assurance and confidence, "Yea, doubtless, I count all dung, but the superexcellent knowledge of Christ,"—Christ is only the figure that hath signification, and gives signification to other things.

But in this business, the consideration of the persons interested, *he* and *us*, maketh us behold a great emphasis in the gospel. *He* a propitiation, and that for *our* sins, is a strange combination of wonders. If it had been some other person less distant from us, that were thus given for us, and standing in our room, then we should have better understood the exchange. Things of like worth, to be thus shuffled together, and stand in one another's place, is not so strange. But between the persons mentioned, *him* and *us*, there is such an infinite distance, that it is wonderful how the one descends to the room of the other, to become a sacrifice for us. O that we could express this to our own hearts, with all the emphasis that it hath! He the Lord, and we the servants; he the King, and we the poor beggars, he the brightness of his Father's glory, and we the shame and ignominy of the whole creation, he counting it no robbery to be equal with God, and being in the form of God, and we not equal to the worst of creatures, because of sin, and being in the form of devils! Had it been a holy and righteous man for sinners, it had been a strange enough exchange, but he is not only holy and harmless, but higher than the heavens. O what a vast descent was this, from heaven to earth, from a Lord to a servant, from an eternal Spirit to mortal flesh, from God to creatures! And to descend thus far for such persons, not only unworthy in themselves, such as could not conciliate any liking, but such as might procure loathing,—as is described, Ezek. xvi., Rom. v. 6, 1 Pet. iii. 18,—"while we were enemies," and might have expected a commissioner from heaven, with vengeance against us. Behold how the mysterious design of love breaks up and opens itself to the world, in sending his own Son for us! And this is exceedingly aggravated from the absolute freedom of it, that there was nothing to pre-engage him to it, but infinite impediments in the way to dissuade him, many impediments to his affection, and many difficulties to his power, and then, no gain nor advantage to be expected from such creatures, notwithstanding of such an undertaking for them.

Now, herein is the strongest support of faith, and the greatest incentive to love, and the mightiest persuasive to obedience that can be. I say, the strongest support of faith, for, a soul apprehending the greatness and heinousness of sin and the inviolableness of God's righteousness, with the purity of his holiness, can hardly be persuaded, that any thing can compense that infinite wrong that is done to his Majesty, though ordinarily the small and superficial apprehension of sin makes a kind of facility in this, or an empty credulity of the gospel. The reason why most men do not question and doubt of the gospel, and of their acceptance before God, is not because they are established in the faith, but rather because they do not so seriously and deeply believe, and ponder their own sins, and God's holiness, which, if many did, they would find it a greater difficulty to attain to a solid and quieting persuasion of the grounds of the gospel: they would find much ado to settle that point of the readiness of God, to pardon and accept sinners. But now, I say, all this difficulty, and these clouds of doubts will evanish at the bright appearance of this Sun of righteousness, that is, at the solid consideration of the glorious excellency of him that was given a ransom for us. Herein the soul may be satisfied, that God is satisfied, when he considers what a person hath undertaken it, even Jesus the righteous, the only Son of God, in whom his soul delighteth, whose glorious divine Majesty puts the stamp of infinite worth upon all his sufferings, and raiseth up the dignity of the sacrifice, beyond the sufferings of all creatures. For there are two things needful for the full satisfaction of a troubled soul, that apprehends the heinousness of sin, and height of wrath, nothing can calm and settle this storm, but the appearance of two things *first* of God's willingness and readiness to pardon sin, and save sinners, *next* of the answerableness of a ransom to his justice, that so there may be no impediment in his way to forgive. Now, let this once be established in thy heart that such an one, so beloved of God and so equal to God, is the propitiation for our sins that, "God hath sent his only begotten Son," for this very business, unrequired and unknown of us then, there is the clearest demonstration of these two things that can be—of the love of God, and of the worth of the ransom. What difficulty can be supposed in it, actually to pardon thy heinous sins, when his love hath overcome infinitely greater difficulties, to send One, his own Son, to procure pardon, John iii. Certainly, it cannot but be the very delight of his heart to forgive sins, since he "spared not his Son" to purchase it, since he hath had such an everlasting design of love, which broke out in Christ's coming. And then, such a person he is, that the merit of his sufferings cannot but be a valuable and sufficient compensation to justice for our personal exemption, because he is one above all, of infinite highness. And therefore his lowness hath an infinite worth in it,—of infinite fulness, and therefore his emptiness is of infinite price of infinite glory, and so his shame is equivalent to the shame and malediction of all mankind. So then, whatsoever thou apprehendest of thy own sins or God's holiness, that seemeth to render thy pardon difficult, lay but in the balance with that first, the free and rich expression of the infinite love of God, in sending such an one for a ransom, and sure, that speaks as much to his readiness and willingness, as if a voice spake it just now from heaven, and then, to take away all scruple, lay the infinite worth of his person, who is the propitiation, with thy sins, and it will certainly outweigh them, so that thou mayest be fully quieted, and satisfied in that point, that it is as easy for him to pardon, as for thee to confess sin and ask pardon, nay that he is more ready to give it thee, than thou to ask it.

But, in the next place I desire you to look upon this as the greatest incentive of affection. O how should it inflame your hearts to consider, that such an one became a sacrifice for our sins, to think that angels hath not such a word to comfort themselves withal! Those innumerable companies of angels, who left their station, and were once in dignity above us have not such glad tidings to report one to another in their societies, as we have. They cannot say, "He is the propitiation for our sins." This is the wonderful mystery, that blessed "angels desire to look into." They gaze upon it, and fix the eyes of their admiration upon "God manifested in the flesh," wondering at the choice of mortal man, before immortal spirits, that he is a ransom for them, and not for their own brethren who left their station. How should this endear him to our souls, and his will to our hearts, who hath so loved us, and given himself for us! Hath he given himself for us, and should we deny ourselves to him, especially when we consider what an infinite disparity is between the worth and difference in the advantage of it. He gave his blessed self a sacrifice, he offered himself to death for us, not to purchase any thing to himself, but life to us. And what is it he requires but your base and unworthy self,—to offer up your lusts and sins in a sacrifice by mortification, and your hearts and affections in a thanksgiving offering, wherein your own greatest gain lies too? For this is truly to find and save yourselves, thus to quit yourselves to him.

The efficacy of this is holden out in the word, "propitiation for our sins." The virtue of Christ's sacrifice is to pacify justice and make God propitious, that is, favourable and merciful to sinners. In which there are three considerable things imported. One is that sin is the cause of enmity between God and man, and sets us at an infinite distance—that sin is a heinous provocation of his wrath. Another is expressed, that Christ is the propitiation,—in opposition to that provocation, he pacifies wrath, and then conciliates favour by the sacrifice of himself. All the expressions of the gospel import the damnable and deplorable estate that sin puts man into, *reconciliation* imports the standing enmity and feud between God and man, *propitiation* imports the provocation of the holy and just indignation of God against man, the fuel whereof is our sins, *justification* implies the lost and condemned estate of a sinner, under the sentence and curse of the law. All that is in the gospel reminds us of our original, of the forlorn estate in which he found us, none pitying us nor able to help us. I would desire that this might first take impression on your hearts,—that sin sets God and man at infinite distance, and not only distance, but disaffection and enmity. It hath sown the seeds of that woful discord, and kindled that contention, which, if it be not quenched by the blood of Christ, will burn to everlasting, so that none can dwell with it, and yet sinners must dwell in it. There is a provoking quality in it, fit to alienate the holy heart of God, and to incense his indignation, which, when once it is kindled who can stand before it? Do but consider what you conceive of wrongs done to you, how they stir your passions and provoke your patience so that there is much ado to get you pacified, and what heinousness must then be in your offences against God, both in regard of number and kind? O that you could but impartially weigh this matter, you would find, that in the view of God all wrongs and injuries between men evanish. "Against thee, thee only, have I sinned."

That relation and respect of sin to God, exhausts all other respects of injuries towards men. It is true, that his Majesty is free from passion, and is not commoved and troubled as your spirits are. Yet such is the provoking nature of sin, that it cries for vengeance, and brings a sinner under the dreadful sentence of divine wrath, which he both pronounceth and can execute without any inward commotion or disturbance of spirit. But, because we conceive of him after our manner, therefore he speaks in such terms to us. But that which he would signify by it is, that the sinner is in as dreadful and damnable a condition by sin, as if the Lord were mightily inflamed with anger and rage. The just punishment is as due and certain as if he were subject to such passions as we are, and so much the more certain, that he is not. Now I desire you to consider, how mightily the heinousness of sin is aggravated, partly by the quality of the persons, and partly by the consideration of his benefits to us. A great man resents a light wrong heavily, because his person makes the wrong heavier. O! what do you think the Most High should do considering his infinite distance from us, his glorious majesty and greatness, his pure holiness, his absolute power and supremacy? What vile and abominable characters of presumption and rebellion do all these imprint upon disobedience! Shall he suffer himself to be despised and neglected of men, when there is no petty creature above another, but will be jealous of his credit, and vindicate himself from contempt? And then, when ingratitude is mingled in with rebellion, it makes sin exceeding sinful, and sinful sin exceeding provoking. To proclaim open war against the holy and righteous will of him to whom we owe ourselves, and all that we are or have, to do evil, because he is good, and be unthankful, because he is kind to take all his own members, faculties, creatures, and employ them as instruments of dishonour against himself, there is here fuel for feeding everlasting indignation, there is no indignity, no vileness, no wickedness to this. All the provocations of men, how just soever, are in the sight of this groundless and vain, like a child's indignation. All are but imaginary injuries, consisting but in opinion, in regard of that which sin hath in the bosom of it against God.

But how shall any satisfaction be made for the injury of sin? What shall pacify his justly deserved anger? Here is the question indeed, that would have driven the whole world to a *nonplus*, if once the majesty and holiness of God had been seen. But the ignorance of God's greatness, and men's sinfulness, made the world to fancy some expiations of sin, and satisfactions to God, partly by sacrifices of beasts, partly by prayer, and repentance for sins.

SERMON XXVIII.

1 John ii. 3.—"And hereby we do know that we know him, if we keep his commandments."

This age pretends to much knowledge beyond former ages, knowledge, I say, not only in other natural arts and sciences, but especially in religion. Whether there be any great advancement in other knowledge, and improvement of that which was, to a further extent and clearness, I cannot judge, but I believe there is not much of it in this nation, nor do we so much pretend to it. But, we talk of the enlargements of divine knowledge, and the breaking up of a clearer light in the point of religion, in respect of which we look on former times, as the times of ignorance and darkness, which God winked at. If it were so indeed, I should think the time happy, and bless the days we live in, for as many sour and sad accidents as they are mixed withal. Indeed, if the variety of books, and multiplicity of discourses upon religion, if the multitude of disputes about points of truth, and frequency of sermons, might be held for a sufficient proof of this pretension, we should not want store enough of knowledge and light. But, I fear that this is not the touchstone of the Holy Ghost, according to which we may try the truth of this assertion, that this is not the rule, by which to measure either the truth, or degrees of our knowledge, but for all that, we may be lying buried in Egyptian darkness, and while such a light seems to shine about us our hearts may be a dungeon of darkness, of ignorance of God and unbelief, and our ways and walk full of stumblings in the darkness. I am led to entertain these sad thoughts of the present times from the words of the apostle, which give us the designation of a true Christian, to be the knowledge of God, and the character of his knowledge, to be obedience to his commands. If, according to this level, we take the estimate of the proportion of our knowledge and light, I am afraid lest there be found as much ignorance of God, and darkness, as we do foolishly fancy that we have of light. However, to find it, will be some breaking up of light in our hearts, and to discover how little we know indeed upon a solid account, will be the first morning star of that Sun of righteousness, which will shine more and more to the perfect day. Therefore we should labour to bring our light to the lamp of this word, and our knowledge to this testimony of unquestionable authority, that having recourse "to the law and to the testimony," we may find if there be light in us or so much light as men think they see. If we could but open our eyes to the shining light of the scripture, I doubt not but we should be able to see that which few do see, that is, that much of the pretended light of this age is darkness and ignorance. I do not speak of errors only that come forth in the garments of new light, but especially of the vulgar knowledge of the truth of religion, which is far adulterated from the true metal and stamp of divine knowledge, by the intermixture of the gross darkness of our affections and conversation, as that other is from the naked truth, and therefore both of them are found light in the balance of the sanctuary, and counterfeit by this touchstone of obedience.

To make out this examination the better I shall endeavour to open these three things unto you, which comprehend the words. 1st, That the knowledge of God in Jesus Christ is the most proper designation of a Christian, "Hereby we know that we know him," which is as much as to say that we are true Christians,—2dly, That the proper character of true knowledge is obedience, or conscionable practising of what we know,—and then, lastly, That the only estimate or trial of our estate before God, is made according to the appearance of his work in us and not by immediate thrusting ourselves into the secrets of God's hidden degrees. "Hereby we know," &c. Here then, in a narrow circle we have all the work and business of a Christian. His direct and principal duty is to know God, and keep his commands, which are not two distinct duties as they come in a religious consideration, but make up one complete work of Christianity, which consists in conformity to God. Then the reflex and secondary duty of a Christian, which makes much for his comfort, is, to know that he knows God. To know God, and keep his commands, is a thing of indispensable necessity to the being of a Christian, to know that we know him is of great concernment to the comfort and well being of a Christian. Without the first, a man is as miserable as he can be, without the sense and feeling of misery, because he wants the spring and fountain of all happiness; without the second, a Christian is unhappy, indeed, for the present, though he may not be called miserable, because he is more happy than he knows of, and only unhappy, because he knows not his happiness.

For the first, then, knowledge is a thing so natural to the spirit of a man, that the desire of it is restless and insatiable. There is some appetite of it in all men, though in the generality of people (because of immersedness in earthly things, and the predominancy of corrupt lusts and affections, which hinder most men's souls to wait upon that more noble inquiry after knowledge, in which only a man really differs from a beast) there be little or no stirring that way, yet some finer spirits there are, that are unquiet this way, and, with Solomon, give themselves, and apply their hearts to search out wisdom. But this is the curse of man's curiosity at first, in seeking after unnecessary knowledge, when he was happy enough already, and knew as much of God and his works as might have been a most satisfying entertainment of his spirit, I say, for that wretched aim, we are to this day deprived of that knowledge which man once had, which was the ornament of his nature and the repast of his soul. As all other things are subdued under a curse for sin, so especially this which man had is lost, in seeking that which he needed not, and the track of it is so obscured and perplexed, the footsteps of it are so indiscernible, and the way of it is like a bird in the air, or a ship in the sea, leaving us few helps to find it out, that most part of men lose themselves in seeking to find it, and therefore, in all the inquiries and searchings of men after the knowledge even of natural things that come under our view, there is at length nothing found out remarkable, but the increase of sorrow, and the discovery of ignorance, as Solomon saith, Eccles. i. 18. This is all the jewel that is brought up from the bottom of this sea, when men dive deepest into it, for the wisest of men could reach no more, though his bucket was as long as any man's, chap. vii. 23. "I said, I will be wise, but it was far from me, that which is far off and exceeding deep, who can find it out?" Knowledge hath taken a far journey from man's nature, and hath not left any prints behind it to find it out again, but, as it were, hath flown away in an instant, and therefore we may ask, with Job, chap. xxviii. ver. 1, 12, "Surely there is a vein for the silver," etc. "But where shall wisdom be found? and where is the place of understanding?" What Utopian isles is she transported unto, that mortal men, the more they seek her, find more ignorance,—the further they pursue, they see themselves at the further distance? Thus it is in those things that are most obvious to our senses, but how much more in spiritual and invisible things is our darkness increased, because of the dulness and earthiness of our spirits that are clogged with a lump of flesh! For God himself, that should be the *primum intelligibile* of the soul, the first and principal object, whose glorious light should first strike into our hearts, Job testifies "how little a portion is known of him." When we cannot so much as understand "the thunder of his power," that makes such a sensible impression on our ears, and makes all the world to stand and hearken to it, then how much less shall we conceive the invisible Majesty of God? In natural things, we have one vail of darkness in our minds to hinder us, but in the apprehension of God, we have a twofold darkness to break through, the darkness of ignorance in us, and "the darkness of too much light" in him—*caliginem nimiæ lucis,* which makes him as inaccessible to us as the other, the over-proportion of that glorious majesty of God to our low spirits, being as the sun in its brightness to a night owl, which is dark midnight to it. Hence it is, that those holy men who know most of God, think they know least, because they see more to be known but infinitely surpassing knowledge. Pride is the daughter of ignorance only, "and he that thinketh he knoweth anything knoweth nothing as he ought to know," saith the apostle, 1 Cor. viii. 2. For he that knoweth not his own ignorance, if he know never so much, is the greatest ignorant, and it is a manifest evidence that a man hath but a superficial touch of things and hath never broken the shell, or drawn by the vail of his own weakness and ignorance, that doth not apprehend deeply the unsearchableness of God, and his mysteries, but thinketh he hath in some measure compassed them, because he maketh a system of divinity, or setteth down so many conclusions of faith, and can debate them against adversaries, or because he hath a form and model of divinity, as of other sciences, in his mind. Nay, my beloved, holy Job attained to the deepest and fullest speculation of God, when he concluded thus, "Because I see thee, I abhor myself," and as Paul speaks, "If any man love God he is known of God, and so knows God," 1 Cor. viii. 3. From which two testimonies I conclude, that the true knowledge of God consists not so much in a comprehension of all points of divinity, as in such a serious apprehension and conception of the divine Majesty as enkindles and inflames these two affections, love and hatred, towards their proper objects, such a knowledge as carries the torch before the affection, such a light as shines into the heart, as Paul's phrase is, 2 Cor. iv. 6, and so transmits heat and warmness into it, till it make the heart burn in the love of God, and loathing of himself. As long as a man doth but hear of God in sermons, or read of him in books, though he could determine all the questions and problems in divinity, he keeps a good conceit of himself, and that "knowledge puffeth up," and swells a man into a vain tumour, the venom of poison blows him up full of wind and self-confidence, and commonly they who doubt least are not the freest of error and misapprehension. And truly, whoever seriously reflects upon the difficulty of knowledge, and darkness of men's minds, and the general curse of vanity and vexation that all things are under, so that what is wanting cannot be numbered, nor that which is crooked made straight,—he cannot but look upon too great confidence and peremptoriness in all points, as upon a race at full speed in the dark night, in a way full of pits and snares. Oftentimes our confidence flows not from evidence of truth, but the ignorance of our minds, and is not so much built upon the strength of reason, as the strength of our passions, and weakness of our judgments.

But when once a man comes to see God, and know him in a lively manner, then he sees his own weakness and vileness in that light, and cries out with Isaiah, "Wo is me, I am a man of polluted lips," and he discerns in that light, the amiableness and loveliness of God that lavisheth his heart after it, and then, as Jeremiah saith, he will not glory in riches, or strength, or beauty, or wisdom, but only in this, that he hath at length gotten some discovery of the only fountain of happiness. Then he will not think so much of tongues and languages, of prophesyings, of all knowledge of controversies, neither gifts of body nor of mind, nor external appendages of providence will much affect him. He would be content to trample on all these, to go over them into a fuller discovery and enjoyment of God himself.

If we search the scriptures, we shall find that they do not entertain us with many and subtile discourses of God's nature, and decrees, and properties, nor do they insist upon the many perplexed questions that are made concerning Christ and his offices, about which so many volumes are spun out, to the infinite distraction of the Christian world. They do not pretend to satisfy your curiosity, but to edify your souls, and therefore they hold out God in Christ, as clothed with all his relations to mankind, in all those plain and easy properties, that concern us everlastingly,—his justice, mercy, grace, patience, love, holiness, and such like. Now, hence I gather, that the true knowledge of God, consists not in the comprehension of all the conclusions that are deduced, and controversies that are discussed anent these things, but rather, in the serious and solid apprehension of God, as he hath relation to us, and consequently in order and reference to the moving of our hearts, to love, and adore, and reverence him, for he is holden out only in those garments that are fit to move and affect our hearts. A man may know all these things, and yet not know God himself, for to know him, cannot he abstracted from loving of him—"They that know thy name will trust in thee, and so love thee, and fear thee." For it is impossible but that this will be the natural result, if he be but known indeed, because there is no object more amiable, more dreadful withal, and more eligible and worthy of choice, and therefore, seeing infinite beauty and goodness, and infinite power and greatness, and infinite sufficiency and fulness, are combined together with infinite truth, the soul that apprehends him indeed, cannot but apprehend him as the most ravishing object, and the most reverend too, and, if he do not find his heart suitably affected, it is an evident demonstration that he doth not indeed apprehend him, but an idol. The infinite light, and the infinite life, are simply one, and he that truly without a dream sees the one, cannot but be warmed and moved by the other.

So then, by this account of the knowledge of God, we have a clear discovery that many are destitute of it, who pretend to it. I shall only apply it to two sorts of persons, one is, of those who have it only in their memories, another, of those who have it only in their minds or heads. Religion was once the legitimate daughter of judgment and affection, but now, for the most part, it is only adopted by men's memories, or fancies. The greatest part of the people cannot go beyond the repetition of the catechism or creed. Not that I would have you to know more: but you do not understand that, only ye repeat words, without the sensible knowledge of the meaning of them; so that if the same matter be disguised with any other form of words, you cannot know it, which showeth, that you have no familiarity with the thing itself, but only with the letters and syllables that are the garments of it. And for others that are of greater capacity, yet, alas! it comes not down to the heart, to the affecting, and moulding, and forming of it. A little light shines into the mind, but your hearts are shut up still, and no window in them. Corrupt affections keep that garrison against the power of the gospel. That light hath no heat of love, or warmness of affection with it, which showeth that it is not a ray or beam of the Sun of righteousness, which is both beautiful for light, and beneficial for influence, on the cold, and dead, frozen hearts of mankind, and by its approaching, makes a spring-time in the heart.

But all men pretend to know God. Such is the self love of men's hearts, that it makes them blind in judging themselves, therefore the Holy Ghost, as he designs a Christian by the knowledge of God, so he characterizeth knowledge by keeping the commandments. "Hereby we know," &c. So that religion is not defined by a number of opinions, or by such a collection of certain articles of faith, but rather by practice and obedience to the known will of God; for, as I told you, knowledge is a relative duty, that is, instrumental to something else, and by anything I can see in scripture, is not principally intended for itself, but rather for obedience. There are some sciences altogether speculative, that rest and are complete in the mere knowledge of such objects, as some natural sciences are. But others are practical, that make a further reference of all things they cognosce upon, to some practice and operation. Now, perhaps some may think that the scripture, or divinity, is much of it merely contemplative, in regard of many mysteries infolded in it, that seem nothing to concern our practice. I confess much of that, that is raised out of the scriptures, is such, and therefore it seems a deviation and departure from the great scope and plain intent of the simplicity and easiness of the scriptures, to draw forth with much industry and subtilty, many things of mere speculation and notion, dry and sapless to the affection, and unedifying to our practice, and to obtrude these upon other men's consciences, as points of religion. I rather think, that all that is in the scriptures, either directly hath the practice of God's will for the object of it, or is finally intended for that end, either it is a thing that prescribeth our obedience, or else it tends principally to engage our affections, and secure our obedience, and so those strains of elevated discourses of God, his nature and properties, of his works, and all the mysteries infolded in them, are directed towards this end, further than mere knowing of them, to engage the heart of a believer to more love, and reverence, and adoration of God, that so he may be brought more easily and steadily to a sweet compliance, and harmonious agreement to the will of God, in all his ways. Nay, to say a little more, there are sundry physical or natural contemplations of the works of God in scripture, but all these are divinely considered, in reference to the ravishment of the heart of man, with the wisdom, and power, and goodness of God. And this shows us the notable art of religion, to extract affection and obedience to God, out of all natural contemplations, and thus true divinity engraven on the soul, is a kind of mistress science, *architectonica scientia*,[255] that serves itself of all other disciplines[256] of all other points of knowledge. Be they never so remote from practice, in their proper sphere, and never so dry and barren, yet a religious and holy heart can apply them to those divine uses of engaging itself further to God and his obedience: as the Lord himself teacheth us—"Who would not fear thee, O King of nations," Jer. x.; and, "fear ye not me who have placed the sand," &c. Jer. v. 22. So praise is extracted, Psal. civ.; and admiration, verses 1, 83. So submission and patience under God's hand is often pressed in Job. Therefore, if we only seek to know these things that we may know them, that we may discourse on them, we disappoint the great end and scope of the whole scriptures; and we debase and degrade spiritual things as far as religion exalts natural things in the spiritual use. We transform it into a carnal, empty, and dead letter, as religion, where it is truly, spiritualizeth earthly and carnal things into a holy use. &c.

HEART-HUMILIATION

Or, Miscellany Sermons, Preached Upon Some Choice Texts, At Several Solemn Occasions.

TO THE READER.

Christian Reader,

This holy preacher of the gospel had so many convictions upon his spirit of the necessity of the duties of humiliation and mourning, and of people's securing the eternal interest of their souls for the life to come, by flying into Jesus Christ for remission of sins in his blood, that he made these the very scope of his sermons in many public humiliations, as if it had been the one thing which he conceived the Lord was calling for in his days; a clear evidence whereof thou shall find manifested in these following sermons upon choice texts, wherein the author endeavoureth, not only to lay before thee the necessity of these duties of soul humiliation, but also showeth thee the gospel manner of performing them, the many soul advantages flowing from the serious exercise of them, and the many soul-destroying prejudices following upon the neglect of them, but above all, thou shalt find him so fully setting forth the sinfulness of sin, and the utter emptiness of self, as may convince the most pharisaically elated spirits, and make them cry out with Ezra, chap. ix. 6, "O my God, I am ashamed, and blush to lift up my face to thee, my God, for our iniquities are increased over our head, and our trespass is grown up unto the heavens." Here thou mayest read such pregnant demonstrations of the righteousness and equity of the Lord's dealing, even in his severest punishments inflicted upon the children of men, as may silence every whisperer against providence, and make them say, as Lam. iii. 22, "It is of the Lord's mercies we are not consumed, even because his compassions fail not." And lastly, thou shalt perceive the inconceivable fitness and fulness of Christ as a Saviour, and his never enough to be admired tenderness and condescending willingness to accept of humble, heart broken, and heart-panting sinners after him, with such plainness of speech demonstrated, as may enable the most bruised reed to quench all the fiery darts of the devil, whereby he laboureth to affright them from making application to Jesus for salvation. Now that the Lord would make those and such-like labours of his faithful servants useful and advantageous to thy soul, Christian reader, is the prayer of thy servant in the gospel of our dearest Lord and Saviour.

SERMON I.

At A Public Fast In July, First Sabbath, 1650.[257]

Deut. xxxii. 4-7.—"He is the Rock, his work is perfect, for all his ways are judgment," &c.

There are two things which may comprehend all religion,—the knowledge of God and of ourselves. These are the principles of religion, and are so nearly conjoined together, that the one cannot be truly without the other, much less savingly. It is no wonder that Moses craved attention, and that, to the end he may attain it from an hard hearted deaf people, he turns to the heavens and to the earth,—as it were to make them the more inexcusable. The matter of his song is both divine and necessary. Throughout it all, he insists upon these two,—to discover what they were in themselves, and what God was to them. He parallels their way with his way, that they, finding the infinite distance, might have other thoughts of themselves and of him both. It is a song, it is true, but a sad song. The people of God's mourning should be of this nature,—mixed, not pure sorrow. It is hard to determine whether there be more matter of consolation or lamentation, when such a comparison is made to the life, when God's goodness and our evils are set before our eyes, which may most work the heart to such affections. Nay, I think it possible they may both contribute to both these. Is there any more abasing and humbling principle than love? How shall the sinner loathe himself in his glorious presence? Will not so much kindness and mercy, so often repeated, as oft as it is mentioned, wound the heart in which there is any tenderness? And, again, when a soul beholds its own ingratitude and evil requital of the Lord's kindness, how vile and how perverse it is, how must it loathe itself in dust and ashes! Yet is not all ground of hope removed. Such a sad sight may make mixed affections. If we be so perverse and evil, then he is infinitely good, and his mercy and goodness are above our evils; if we have dealt so with him, yet is he the Rock that changes not, he is a God of truth, and will not fail in his promise. Nay, though it be sad to be so evil, void of all goodness, yet may the soul bless him for evermore, that he hath chosen this way to glorify his name, to build up his praise upon our ruin. May not a soul thus glory in sad infirmities, because his strength is perfected in them, and made manifest? May not a soul choose emptiness in itself, that it may be beholden to his fulness? How refreshing a view might the saddest look on our misery and emptiness be, if we did behold his purpose of manifesting his glory in it! You see here a comparison instituted between two very unequal parties, God and man; there is no likeness, let be equality in it, yet there is almost an equality in unlikeness. The one is infinitely good and perfect; well, what shall we compare to him? Who is like thee, O God, among the gods? Angels' goodness, their perfection and innocency, hath not such a name and appearance in his sight. So then, there can be no comparison made this way. Let no flesh glory in his sight in anything, but, "let him that glorieth, glory in the

Lord," for in the sight of the glorious Lord, all things do disappear and evanish. But surely nothing, though most perfect, can once come within terms of reckoning beside him for any worth. Moses sees nothing to set beside God, that will appear in its own greatness and native colours, but the creatures' evil and sin; and if this be not infinite absolutely, or equal to his goodness, yet it comes nearest the borders of infiniteness. So then, is God most perfect? Is he infinite in goodness, in truth, in righteousness, &c.—and so infinite, that before him nothing appears good?—"There is none good save one, that is God." Yet we may find another infinite, and it is in evil sinful man; and these two contraries set beside other, do much illustrate each other. It is true that his grace superabounds, and his goodness is more than the creatures' sinfulness; yet, I say, you shall not find anything that cometh nearer the infiniteness and degrees of his goodness, than the sinfulness of men. How much the more glorious he appears, so much the more vile and base doth it appear.

If ye did indeed ponder and weigh these two verses in the balance of the sanctuary, would not your heart secretly ask this question within you, Do I thus requite the Lord? O foolish and unwise! Yea, would you not account yourselves mad, to forsake the fountain of living waters, and dig broken cisterns to yourselves? O of how great moment were this to humble yourselves to-day! This day ye are called to mourning and afflicting your souls. Now, I know not a more suitable exercise for a day of humiliation, or a principle that may more humble and abase your souls, than the serious and deep consideration of these two,—what God is, and hath been to us, and what we are, and have proved to him; what hath made so many formal humiliations that have provoked him to anger? Certainly we do not either seriously think on any of these, or if one of them, yet not on both. The most part of you know no more in such a day, but a name and ceremony of a little abstinence. Is this to sanctify a day to the Lord,—when ye do not so much as the people who bowed down their head for a day, and spread sackcloth under them? I wonder how ye think to pacify his wrath, and are not rather afraid of adding fuel and oil to the flame of his indignation. Ye come here and sit as in former times, and what do ye more either here or at home? There is no soul-affliction, no, not for a day. The most part of you are no more affected with your sins and his judgments, than if none of these things were. Now, I pray you, what shall the Lord say to us, when he speaks to the Jews in such terms, Isa. lviii. 5,—"Is it such a fast that I have chosen, a day for a man to afflict his soul?" And do ye so much as afflict it for a day, or at all? Is this then the fast that he will choose, to abstain from your breakfast in the morning, and at night to compensate the want of it, and no more?[258] Is this an acceptable day to the Lord? The Lord upbraids the Jews, "Wilt thou call this a fast?" And what reason have we to ask you, is it possible ye think ye do indeed fast to the Lord? I cannot think that the most part of you dare say, that ever ye fasted or afflicted your souls.

Always here is the way, if we consider it. To spend a day acceptably to the Lord, enter into a serious consideration of his Majesty, and yourselves. Study on these two till ye find your hearts bear the stamp of them, enlarge your hearts in the thoughts of them. Both are infinite,—his goodness and power and mercy, and your sin and misery,—no end of them. Whatever ye find good in God, write up answerably to it, so much evil and sin in yourselves and the land; and what evil ye find in yourselves and the land, write up so much goodness and mercy in his account. All the names of his praise would be so many grounds of your confusion in yourselves, and would imprint so many notes of reproach and disgrace upon the creature found so contrary to him. This is even the exercise God calls us to this day,—to consider his ways to us, and our ways to him; how he hath walked, and how we have walked. Because ye lose the sight of these two, he sends affliction,—because in our prosperity and peace we forget God, and so ourselves; as ye find this people did, "when they waxed fat they kicked against him, and forgat that he was their Rock." We are so much taken up with our own ease and peace, that we do not observe him in his dealings; therefore doth the Lord trouble our peace, remove those things we are taken up with, make a public proclamation of affliction, and blessed be his name whose end is gracious. He means this,—it is the proclamation of all his judgments,—turn your eyes off your present ease here, consider what I am, and what yourselves are. No nation so soon buries the memory of his mercies, O how soon are they drowned in oblivion! And we forget our own provocations as suddenly. Therefore must he write our iniquities upon a rod, that we may read them in great letters; and he writes his former goodness in the change of his dispensations, when his way to us changes, that we may know what is past. This is the great design that God hath in the world,—to declare himself and his own name, that it may be wondered and admired at by men, and this cannot be but by our ruin, abasing us in the dust. He therefore uses to stain the pride of all glory, that his alone may appear without spot. This is then the great controversy of God with men and nations in all generations. They will not see him alone exalted, and will not bow before him, and see their own vileness. Why doth he overturn kingdoms and thrones? Why doth he shake nations so often? Here it is; God's controversy will never cease, till all men acknowledge him in his highness and holiness, as the sole fountain of all life, and find themselves vile, less than nothing, nay, worse than nothing, and emptiness. If ye would then have God at peace with the land and yourselves, here is the compendious way,—set him up a throne of eminency in your hearts, and put yourselves in the dust, take with your own guiltiness and naughtiness, and impossibility to help yourselves in yourselves. Hold these two still in your eyes, that he may be alone exalted.

Look how unequal a match, ver. 4, 5, "He is the Rock," a rock indeed! If we speak of strength, lo! he is strong; if of stability, he is the Lord, and changes not, "the Ancient of days." Hast not thou heard and considered this, that the Almighty faints not, and wearies not? He holds forth himself in such a name to his people, a ready, all-sufficient, perpetual, and enduring refuge to all that trust in him, and fly unto him as a rock higher than they. And this is the foundation that the church is builded on, against which the gates of hell shall not prevail. God's omnipotency is for defence, his eternity, faithfulness, and unchangeableness to make that sure. His mercy and goodness makes a hole in that rock to enter in, a ready access for poor shipwrecked and broken men, who have no other refuge. This is our rock, on which the church is builded, Jesus Christ, 1 Cor. x. 4.; Matt. xvi. 18. Were God inaccessible in himself, an impregnable rock, how would sinners overcome him, and enter in to him to be saved from wrath? Nay but Jesus Christ hath made a plain way and path, out of the waves of sin and misery, into this rock higher than we; and so the poor soul that is lost in its own eyes, and sees no refuge, is forced to quit the broken ship of created confidence, for fear of perishing. Here doth it find a door in this rock to enter. And there is water to drink of, "a fountain of living waters" comes out of it, and that is Christ.

Now, all these names of his praise rub so many marks of shame on his people. O how sad is the secret reproof and expostulation contained in this commendation of God! He hath been a rock to us, our refuge that we fled unto, and found sure; for as, in our straits, we mounted upon his power and were supported, when "the floods lifted up their waves," yet have we left our rock, gone out from our strength. He offers himself a rock unto us, his fulness and all-sufficiency for us, and yet we leave the fountain of living waters, and dig broken cisterns, had rather choose our own broken ships in which to toss up and down. He abides for ever the same; though we change, he changes not. How may it reprove our backslidings, that we depart from our rock! And where shall we find a refuge in the day of indignation? Is there any created mountain, but some floods of the time will cover? Therefore it is folly and madness to forsake this rock that is still above the floods; "he is mightier than the noise of many waters." It may reprove our unbelief,—we change our faith according to his dispensation, our faith ebbs and flows as the tide of his providence, and thus we are as sticks floating in the water, tossed up and down. But would ye be established as mount Sion? Would ye be unmoveable in the midst of great waters, that they shall not come near unto you? Then, by all means get upon this rock, that abides unmoved in the midst of the waves. Though they should beat upon it, and the wind blow, yet it is proof of all tempests. All things might be driven up and down about you with the Lord's dispensation, but ye should abide the same, and might look round about you on the troubled sea of men's minds, of lands and estates. If you come here, ye may make shipwreck, but ye shall not drown; though ye lose the creature's comfort and defence, yet ye are on your rock, which is established before the rocks and mountains. You may be sure of salvation. He that made the rocks and winds and seas, is your rock.

"His work is perfect." As he doth not trouble himself when all is troubled about him, so he keeps him also in perfect peace, whose mind is stayed on him; so also what he doth among men, though it cannot pass without man's censure, yet it is in itself perfect, complete, without spot or defect. What is the subject of all men's questions, doubts, complaints, censures, expostulations, and such like, of which the world is full? It is some one work of God or other; there is no work of his providence, but some man finds a fault in it, and would be at the mending of it. *Neque Deus cum pluit, omnibus placet*:[259] if he give rain, he displeases many; if he withhold it again, we are as little pleased. The reason of all this misconstruction is, we look on his work by parcels,[260] and take it not whole and entire. [Viewed] so, it is perfect, and cannot be made better. "His works are perfect," in relation to the beginning and original of them, his own everlasting purpose. Men often bring forth works by guess, by their purpose, so no wonder it answer not their desire. But "known to him are all his works from the beginning," and so he doth nothing in time, but what was his everlasting pleasure. Often we purpose well, and resolve perfectly, but our practice is a cripple, execution of it is maimed and imperfect. But all his works are carved out, and done just as he designed them, without the least alteration; and, if it had not been well, would he have thought on it so, and resolved it beforehand? His works are perfect, in relation to the end to which he appointed them. It may be it is not perfect in itself: a blind eye is not so perfect as a seeing eye; nay, but in relation to the glory of his name, who hath a purpose to declare his power by restoring that sight, it is as perfect. And in this sense, all the imperfection of the creatures and creation, all of them are perfect works, for they accomplish the end wherefore they were sent; and so the night declares his name, and utters a speech as well as the day, the winter as the summer, the wilderness as the fruitful field. For what is the perfection of the creature, but in as far as it accomplishes his purpose and end, as the maker of it serves himself with it? And therefore all his work is perfect, for it is all framed in wisdom to his own ends, in number, measure, and weight; it is so exactly agreeing to that, that you could not imagine it better. Again, his work is perfect, if we take it altogether, and do not cut it in parcels, and look on it so. Is there any workmanship beautiful, if ye look upon it in the doing? While the timber lies in one part, and the stones in another, is that a perfect building? When ye see one arm here, another there, and a leg scattered beside them, hath that image any comeliness? Certainly no; but look upon these united, and then they are perfect. Letters and syllables make no sense, till ye conjoin them in words, and words in sentences. Even so is it here; if ye look on the day alone, the light of it being perpetual would weary us, the night alone would be more so; but the interchange of them is pleasant,—day and night together make a distinct language of God's praise. So God hath set prosperity and adversity the one over against the other. One of them, it may be, seems imperfect; nay, but it is a perfect work that is made up of both. Spots in the face commend the beauty of the rest of it.

If ye would then look upon God's work aright, look on it in the sanctuary's light, and ye shall say, "He hath done all well." Join the end with the beginning, and behold they agree very well. Many things among us seem out of order, many things uncomplete, The reformation of England, how great obstruction was in the way of it? Is that now a perfect work? Yes, certainly; for if we knew his end and purpose, it is very well, and could not be bettered by the art of all men; "his thoughts are far above our thoughts." The prosperous and uninterrupted success of that party in England, is it a perfect work? Yes, certainly; for if ye could behold their end, ye would say so; "they are set in slippery places, their foot shall slide in due time."[261]

Entertain this thought in your heart, that he hath done all well. Let not your secret thoughts so much as call them in question. If once ye question, ye will quickly censure them. Hold this persuasion, that nothing can be better than what he doth, nothing can be added, and nothing diminished from them, he doth all in number, weight, and measure. It is so exactly correspondent to his purpose and design, as if it were weighed out, and measured out for that end.

Let this secretly reprove your hearts. The perfection of his works stains our works. O how imperfect are they! And which is worse, how impudent and bold are we to censure his, and absolve our own? If he have a hand in our work, these imperfect works are perfect in regard of him. As we have a hand in his perfect works, his perfect works are imperfect in regard of us.

SERMON II.

> Deut. xxxii. 4, 5.—"He is the Rock, his work is perfect, for all his ways are judgment, a God of truth, and without iniquity, just and right is he. They have corrupted themselves, their spot is not the spot of his children," &c.

There are none can behold their own vileness as it is, but in the sight of God's glorious holiness. Sin is darkness, and neither sees itself, nor any thing else, therefore must his light shine to discover this darkness. If we abide within ourselves, and men like ourselves, we cannot wisely judge ourselves, our dim sparkle will not make all the imperfections and spots appear. But, if men would come forth into the presence of his Majesty, who turns darkness into light, and before whom hell is naked,—O how base and vile would they appear in their own eyes! Is it any wonder that the multitude of you see not yourselves, when holy Isaiah and Job had this lesson to learn? Isaiah gets a discovery of his own uncleanness in the sight of God's glorious holiness, (chap. vi. 5,) which I think made all his former light darkness. He cries out "unclean," as if he had never known it before, and so Job, "Since I saw thee I abhorred myself in dust and ashes." Ye hear much of him, and it doth not abase you, but if ye saw him, ye would not abide yourselves; ye would prefer the dust you tread on to yourselves. Ye who know most, there is a mystery of iniquity in your hearts, that is not yet discerned, ye are but yet on the coast of that bottomless sea of abomination and vileness. Among all the aggravations of sin, nothing doth so demonstrate the folly, yea, the madness of it, as the perfection, goodness, and absolute unspottedness of God. It is this that takes away all pretence of excuse, and leaves the same nothing—no place in which to hide its confusion and nakedness and shame. And therefore it is that Moses, when he would convince this people of their ways, and make them inexcusable, draws the parallel of God's ways and their ways, declares what God is, how absolutely perfect in himself, and in his works, who had given no cause of provocation to them to depart from him, and then, how odious must their departing be! When both are painted on a board before their eyes it makes sin become exceedingly sinful. When the Lord would pierce the hearts of his people, and engrave a challenge with the point of a diamond, he useth this as his pen,—"Have I been a wilderness unto Israel? a land of darkness? Why say my people, We are lords, we will come no more to thee?" Jer. ii. 31. "What iniquity have your fathers found in me, that they are gone far from me, and have walked after vanity?" Jer. ii. 5.

There are two things in sin that exceedingly abuse the creature,—the iniquity of it, and the folly and madness of it. It is contrary to all equity and reason to depart from him that hath made us, and given us a law, to whom we are by so many obligations tied, but what is the folly and madness of it, to depart from the fountain of living waters, and dig broken cisterns that can hold none? verse 13. This is a thing that the heavens may be astonished at, and, if the earth had sense to understand such a thing, the whole fabric of it would tremble for horror at such madness and folly of reasonable souls and this evil hath two evils in it,—we forsake life and love death, go from him and choose vanity. It is great iniquity to depart without an offence on his part. He may appeal to all our consciences, and let them sit down and examine his way most narrowly,—"What iniquity have ye found in me? What cause have ye to leave me!" But when withal he is a living fountain, he is our glory, he is a fruitful land, a land of light, our ornament and attire, in a word, our life and our consolation, our happiness and our beauty; what word shall be found to express the extreme madness of men to depart from such an one, and change their glory into that which doth not profit? If either he were not a fountain of living waters, or if there were any fountain beside, that could yield water to satisfy the insatiable desires of men, it were more excusable, but what shadow shall be found to cover such an iniquity that is both infinite sin, and incompatable loss? It is the scripture's style given to natural men, "fools and simple." All sin hath folly in it, but the people of God's departing from him hath extremity of folly in it, beside iniquity, because they do embrace a dunghill instead of a throne, they make the maddest exchange that can be imagined, glory for shame, life for death,—at least, consolation and peace, for vanity and vexation and anguish of spirit.

If ye would be duly affected with the sight of your own evils, look upon them in this consideration, and, in the view of God, your large portion, ye will be forced to confess yourselves beasts in his sight, Psal. lxxiii. 22. Oh! that men would consider how good and blessed the Lord is, how he is alone, and nothing beside him in heaven and earth,—all broken cisterns, all dung and unprofitable, all vanity and vexation,—he only self-sufficient, all others insufficient, and therefore a proportioned good for our necessity and desires, and I am sure ye would be constrained to cry out with David, "Whom have I in heaven but thee, or in the earth beside thee? It is good for me to draw near to God." Ye would look on drawing near, and walking with him, and before him, not only as the most reasonable thing, but the best thing, most beautiful for you, most profitable for you, and all other ways would be looked on as the ways of death.

"His work is perfect." The Lord looked, and behold all was good that was made. So it was at first. The fabric of this world was an exquisite and perfect work, a suitable demonstration of his infinite wisdom, wonderful in all the parts of it, and in the unity and harmony of the whole. But so also his work of providence is perfect. Divine wisdom hath framed and contrived all, and it cannot be better. If anything seem imperfect in itself, yet it is perfect in relation to his glorious ends he directs it unto. And so would we look on all the works among us. If anything seemed a spot and disgrace of the creation, certainly the sin of men and angels,—nay, but even that is so ordered by his holy sovereignty, that in relation to his majesty, it may be called a perfect work. If ye do but consider what a glorious high throne he hath erected to himself for justice and judgment to be the habitation of it, and mercy and truth to go before it upon the ruins of defaced man, what a theatre of justice he hath erected upon the angels fall, ye would call it as perfect a work as is in the world. His work is one in the world, subordinate to one great design of manifesting his own glorious justice and mercy, omnipotency and wisdom. Now what do ye see of it but parcels? Though ye comprehend all your time in one thought, yet certainly ye cannot judge it aright, for it is but one work that all the several buildings and castings down, all the several dispensations of his providence, from the beginning to the end, make up, and when we think upon these disjoined, limit our consideration within the bounds of our own time, can we rightly apprehend it? Nay, which is worse, we use to have no more within the compass of our thought, but some present thing, and how much more do we err then? What beauty, what perfection can such a small part have? But it is present to him, who beholds with a glance all these parts. Though succeeding in many generations, he sees it altogether, joins the end with the beginning, sees the first mould, the first foundation stone, and the last completing, all flowing from himself, and returning thither, and ending in himself. He hath made an interchange in nature, which might teach us—the night alone hath no beauty. Nay, but it beautifies the day. Your darkest hours and tempests, public and personal, are they perfect works? Yes, certainly, if ye compound them with your sunshines and calms. Several colours make pictures beautiful,—the one is as needful as the other, and if ye did consider your profit more than your honour and pleasure, ye would say so. He doth not model his works according to our fancy to please us, but our good to profit us, and he is wiser than we, and so then it is the most perfect work in itself, that possibly displeaseth us most. Therefore ye would judge of his dealing by another rule than your own satisfaction, for please you and perish you. If he spared the rod, he should hate us indeed, fond love is real hatred. Christians, if ye would judge his works by his word, and not by your sense,—by your well, and not by your will, certainly we would say, as the men did of Christ, "He hath done all well." The world would discover to you a perfection, even in imperfection, a perfection in infirmities, that ye should not only rejoice in them, but glory in them. "Most gladly therefore will I glory," &c. saith Paul. Are infirmities a perfect work? Or is the suffering of Paul, to be buffetted and tempted, a perfect work? What comfort is in it? Yes, much. Infirmities alone are infirmities indeed, nay but infirmities in me, and strength in Jesus, weakness in me, and strength dwelling in me,—these make up one perfect work that could as little want the infirmities as the strength. The glory of God, and our well and consolation, require the one, as well as the other, they could not be complete without any of them. What do ye think of the times now? Are England's apostacy, and Ireland's desolation,[262] perfect works? That great work of reformation, that seemed to be above our shoulders, is now razed to the ground, and the very foundations removed? Is deformation a perfect work? Certainly, if we look on these things in the scripture's light, and consider them in relation to him who is the chief builder, and doth in heaven and earth what he pleaseth, that deformation is a perfect work, though not a perfect reformation. Though we could not inform you of the perfection of it, yet the general might silence us; all this shall be no miss, no mar in the end. His work, at the end of accounts, shall appear so complete, as if it had never had interruption. He is wise, and knows what he doth, if this were not for his glory and his people's good, certainly it should not be. Was not the people wandering in the wilderness forty years a most strange work—a longer interruption of the expected and begun voyage out of Egypt? What human reason would have styled this work with perfection? Did they not often murmur against it? Yet Moses calls this a perfect work also. What if the Lord be digging the ground deeper in England, that the foundation may be the surer? What if he be on a work of judgment, filling the cup of many deluded blasphemers, that he may have another cup of wrath prepared? What if this be his great purpose, to execute vengeance upon a profane generation, that will not abide the very name and form of godliness, by those who pretend to the name of it as their honour? What if the Lord hath defaced all that this kingdom was instrumental in building up in England, that he alone may have the glory in a second temple more glorious?[263] Many things there may be in his mind, and "he is in one mind, and who can turn him? and what his soul desireth, even that he doth, and this may be enough to satisfy us, he sees and knows all his works from the beginning."

And without all controversy he hath provided it so, that the reproach of his name shall be made up with[264] the more shining of his glory, and the afflictions of his people shall be compensed with songs of deliverance. May ye not give him so much credit, as ye would give to a skilful man in his own trade? Ye know it is his name, "excellent in counsel, and wonderful in working." Then take his work, expound it according to his word, and not your apprehension. It may be his work appears not excellent, nay, but if ye knew his counsel, ye would think it so. His wonderful counsel makes all his works excellent, and therefore do not take upon you to judge his works unless ye could wade the depth of his counsels, else ye declare yourselves to be both ignorant and presumptuous. "There is a time to build, and a time to cast down, a time for every thing," saith the wise man. Now, I say, he knows the time and season, he does every thing in his time. If ye come by a workman that is casting down a house that in your appearance seems good, would ye condemn him presently? No, but stay till ye see what he will do next, wait till the due time, and when ye see a better piece of workmanship on that ground, ye shall absolve him. Though God often change his work, do not think he changes his counsel and purposes as men do, no, "he is in one mind, and who can turn him?" Therefore he had that change in his mind when he made the work, when he erected such a throne, he had this in his mind to cast it down within such a space, and so his change—his throwing down—is as perfect in his mind, as his building up. Ye have large and big apprehensions of temporal kingdoms and crowns of government, and such like, as if they were great, yea, only things, but they are not so to him. All this world and its standing, all the kingdoms and their affairs are not his great work and business. He hath a great work, the bringing of many sons to glory, and the completing of Jesus Christ; building of that glorious mystical building, the holy temple made up of living stones, of which Christ is the foundation, and chief corner-stone both, and it is this that he attends to most. Other works among men, though they have more noise, they are less concerned. All these are but in the by, and subservient to his great design, and like the scaffolds of a building, that are, it may be, sometimes very needful. Nay, but when the building is completed, he shall remove all these, he hath no more use of them: kings shall be thy nurse fathers, kings shall bow to thee. He is not much concerned in government nor in governors, but for his little flock's sake, and if these were gathered, all these shall have an end, and the flock alone abide for ever.

"And all his ways are judgment." This is to the same purpose,—his ways and his works are one. And this is the perfection of his work, that it is all right and equal; whether they be in justice or mercy, they are all righteous and holy, no iniquity in them, his ways are straight and equal, exact as if they were measured by an exact even rule, but because we make application of a crooked rule to them, we do imagine that they are crooked, as the blind man judges no light to be, because he sees it not. How may the Lord contend and plead with us, as with that people, Ezek. xviii. 25. Is it possible that any can challenge him and clear themselves, who will be justified of all when he is judged, and before whom no flesh can be justified? And yet, behold the iniquity of men's hearts. There is a secret reflection of our spirits upon his Majesty, as if his ways were not equal, whenever we repine against them, and when we do not take with our iniquity, and stop our mouths with dust. Behold, the Lord will assert his own ways, and plead with all flesh this controversy, that all his proceedings are full of equity. He walks according to a rule, though he be not tied to a rule. He walks according to the rules of wisdom, justice, and mercy, though his illimited sovereignty might be a sufficient ground of clearing of all his proceedings. But we walk not according to a rule, though we be bound to a rule, and a rule full of equity.

Here is the equity and justice of his ways, the gospel holds it forth in a twofold consideration. *First*, If any man turn from his iniquity, and flee unto my Son as the city of refuge, he shall live, he hath eternal life, iniquity shall not be his ruin, although he hath done iniquity. O "who is a God like unto thee, that pardoneth iniquity!" Is not this complete mercy? Whatever iniquity hath been, aggravate it as ye can, though it could have ruined a world yet it could not have ruined thee that turnest in to Jesus Christ from iniquity. What exception can all the world have against this, or his walking according to it? And *on the other hand*, whosoever continueth in sin, though he appear to himself and others never so righteous, if he entertain and love any known sin, and will not part with it for Jesus Christ, shall not he die in his iniquity? Is there any iniquity in this, that he receive the wages of his works—his reward that he eat of the fruit of his own ways, and drink of his own devices? But how many hearts censure this way as a rigid and strict severe dealing! The multitude think it cruelty to condemn any christened soul—to put so many in hell. The civil man will think it is too hard measure that he should be ranked in hell with the profane. But certainly, all mouths shall be stopped one day, and he shall be justified when he judges. Ye that will not justify him in his sayings, and set to your seal to the truth of the word, you shall be constrained to justify him, when he executes that sentence. Ye shall precipitate your own sentence, and rather wonder at his clemency in suffering you so long.

This way of the Lord is equal and right in itself, but it is not so to every one. The just man shall walk in it and not stumble; as in an even way, nothing shall offend him, Hosea xiv. last verse. Yet for as equal and straight as it is, many other transgressors shall fall therein; they stumble even in the noon-day and highway, where no offence is. It is true, often his own people stumble in it, as David, Psal. lxxiii, and xciv. David's foot was slipping, yet a secret hold was by mercy. It often requires a wise and prudent man to understand it, because his footsteps are in the deep waters; Psal. lxxxvii. 19. His way is in the depths of the sea, his paths in great waters, so that men must wait till the Lord expound his own ways, till he come out of the waters, and make them a dry plain. And this is our advantage; the word says, "He is near thee, in thy mouth, and neither above, nor beneath in the depths, that thou needest neither descend nor ascend to know it," Deut. xxx. 11-14. But his way is in the depths, and his footsteps are not known, so that we ought to hold us by the word till he expound his work. His word will teach us our duty, and we may commit unto him his own way; the word is a commentary to expound his ways. David lost the sight of God's footsteps and was like to wander, till he came to the sanctuary, and this shined as a candle in a dark place; he learned there to know the unknown footsteps and to follow them. By all means embrace the word, and be satisfied with it, when ye do not comprehend his work; it teaches as much in general, as may put us to quietness; all his ways are judgment, just and true in all his ways is the King of saints. If I do not comprehend how it is,—no wonder, for he makes darkness his covering, he spreads over his most curious engines and pieces of workmanship a vail of darkness for a season; and "who can behold him when he hides himself?" says Job; and though he withdraw the covering, yet what am I? "Who can by searching find out God?" If I shall examine his way, what rule shall I take to try it by? If I measure by my shallow capacity, or by my crooked way, shall I have any just account of it? Will my arm measure the heavens as his doth? If I examine it, or try it by himself, he is high as heaven and unsearchable. Therefore it becomes us to hearken to his word, and believe its sentence of his work, when reason cannot comprehend it.

One thing, if it were deeply engraven on our hearts, would be a principle, of settling our spirits, in all the mysteries and riddles of providence,—the knowledge and faith of his sovereignty, of his highness, and of his wisdom. Should he give account of his matters to us? He is wise and knows his works; but is he bound to make us know them? His ways are above our thoughts and ways, as heaven is above the earth, Isa. lv. And therefore, O grasshopper in the earth, that dwelleth in tabernacles of clay, do not presume to model his ways according to thy conceptions. One thing is certain,—this is enough for faith, "all his ways are mercy and truth to those that keep his covenant and his testimonies," Psal. xxv. 10. And there is no way or path of God so far above our reach, and unsearchable, as his mercy in pardoning sin; and this is only the satisfying answer to all your objections and scruples. In these ye do but vent your own thoughts: but says the Lord, my thoughts are above your thoughts, as heaven above earth. Ye but speak of your own ways, but my ways are far above yours, they are not measured by your iniquity; and therefore, David subjoins, Psal. xxv. ver. 11, "Pardon my iniquity, for it is great."

SERMON III.

> Deut. xxxii. 4, 5.—"He is the rock, his work is perfect. For all his ways are judgment. A God of truth, and without iniquity, just and right is he. They have corrupted themselves, their spot is not the spot of his children. They are a perverse and crooked generation."

"All his ways are judgment," both the ways of his commandments and the ways of his providence, both his word which he hath given as a lantern to men's paths, and his works among men. And this were the blessedness of men, to be found walking in his ways, and waiting on him in his ways, having respect to all his commandments, and respect to himself in all his works. We all know in general that he doth all well, and that all his commandments are holy and just. Nay, but our practice and affections belie our knowledge; and for the most part, we stand cross in our humours, and affections, and conversation, both to his word and providence, and this is our misery. "Great peace have they that love thy law." What peace then can keep that heart and mind that is daily at variance with his statutes and judgments, when the heart would wish such a command were not, when it is an eyesore to look upon it? "Blessed are the meek." "It is good for a man, both quietly to wait, and hope, and keep silence." How then must that spirit be miserable, that stands cross unto God's dispensations, and would limit the Holy One! Do not our hearts often say, "I do well to be angry, why is it thus with me?" But, "who hath hardened himself against him and prospered?" His counsel must stand; and you may vex yourself, and disquiet your soul in the mean time, by impatience, but you cannot by your thought add one cubit to your stature. You may make your case worse than providence hath made it, but you cannot make it better by so doing, so that at length you must bow to him or be broken. Oh then that this were engraven on our hearts with the point of a diamond! "All his ways are judgment;" that ye might be overcome with the equity of his command and dispensation, and your heart and tongue might not move against them. It was enough of old with the saints, "It is the Lord, let him do what seems good in his eyes." God's sovereignty alone pondered, may stop our mouth; but, if ye withal consider, it is perfect equity that rules all, it is divine wisdom that is the square of his works; then how ought we to stoop cheerfully unto them! One thing, ye would remember, his ways and paths are judgment, and if you judge aright of him, ye must judge his way and not his single footsteps. Ye will not discern equity and judgment in one step or two; but consider his way, join adversity with prosperity, humbling with exalting; take along the thread of his providence, and one part shall help you to understand another. There is reason in all, but the reason is not visible to us in so small parts of his way and work.

"A God of truth." Strange it is that his majesty is pleased to clothe himself with so many titles and names for us. He considers what our necessity is, and accordingly expresses his own name. I think nothing doth more hold forth the unbelief of men, and atheism of our hearts, than the many several titles that God takes in scripture. There is a necessity of a multitude of them, to make us take up God; because we staying upon a general notion of God, rather frame in our imaginations an idol than the true God. As there is nothing doth more lively represent the unbelief of our hearts, than the multitude of promises; men that consider such frequent repetitions of one thing in scripture, so many divers expressions of one God, may retire into their own hearts, and find the cause of it, even the necessity of it. But while we look so slightly on these, we must judge it superfluous and vain. Needed there any more to be said, but, "I am your God, I am God," if our spirits were not so far degenerated unto atheism and unbelief? Certainly that word *Jehovah* holds forth more to angels than all the inculcated names and titles of God to us, because we are dull and slow of heart. Therefore wonder at these two when ye read the scriptures, God's condescendency to us, and our atheism and unbelief of him: they are both mysteries, and exceeding broad. There is not a name of God, but it gives us a name, and that of reproach and dishonour, so that for every one, some evil may be written down. And it is to this purpose Moses draws them out in length, that in the glass of his glorious name, the people might behold their own ugly face. This name is clear, "he is a God of truth," not only a true God, but truth itself: to note his excellency and eminency in it. It is Christ's name, "I am the truth," the substantial truth, in whom all the promises are truth, "are yea and amen." His truth is his faithfulness in performing his promises, and doing what his mouth hath spoken: and this is established "in the very heavens," Psal. lxxxix. 2. His everlasting purpose is in heaven where he dwells; and if any man can ascend up to heaven, if any creature can break through the clouds, then may his truth be shaken. His word comes down among men; nay, but the foundation of it is in heaven, and there is his purpose established; and therefore, there is nothing done in time can impair or hinder it. Ye think this world very sure, the earth hangs unmoveable, though it hang upon nothing. All the tumults, confusions, and reels which have been in the world have never moved it to the one side. Heaven goeth about in one tenour perpetually, keeping still the same distance. Nay, but his truth is more established than so. Heaven and earth depend but upon a word of command, he hath said, "Let it be so," and so it is. Nay, but his word is more established. Of it saith Christ, one jot or tittle of it cannot fail, though heaven and earth should fail. He may change his commands as he pleases, but he may not change his promise, this puts an obligation on him, as he is faithful and true, to perform it, and when an oath is superadded, O how immutable are these two!—when he promises in his truth and swears in his holiness. Is there any power in heaven and earth can break that double cord? Matth. v. 18, Heb. vi. 18. There is no name of God but it is comfortable to some, and as terrible to others. What comfort is it to a godly man that trusts in his word, he is a God of truth! An honest man's word is much, his oath is more. What shall his word be who is a God of truth? Though all men should be liars, yet God is true. Ye who have ventured your souls on his word, ye have an unspeakable advantage, his truth endures for ever, and it is established in the heavens, the ground of it is without beginning, the end of it without end. Ye are more sure than the frame of heaven and earth, for all these shall wax old as a garment. We speak of a naked word of truth, indeed it is no naked word that is God's word. His works of providence, and his dispensation to you, is a naked and bare foundation, nay, a sandy foundation, and ye who lean so much to them, is it any wonder ye so often shake and waver? All other grounds beside the word are uncertain, unstable, this only endures for ever. The creature's goodness and perfection is but as the grass, and the flower of the field. Venture not much on your dispositions and frames, thou knowest not what a day may bring forth, but his truth is to all generations, and it is well tried as gold seven times,—all generations have tried it and found it better than pure gold. His dispensations are arbitrary—no rule to you. He loveth to declare his sovereignty here and to expatiate in the creature's sight beyond its conceiving, but he hath limited himself in his word and come down to us, and laid bonds on himself. Will he then untie them for us? Give him liberty where he loves it, take him bound where be binds himself. How may God expostulate with this generation, as those of little faith? "How long shall I be with you?" saith Christ. How long will Christians tempt the Lord in seeking signs, and will not rest upon his only word and promises? "O adulterous generation, how long shall I be with you and ye will not believe?" Is it not righteousness in him, either to give you no sign at all, or to give you a sign darker than the thing itself, as he did to the Pharisees? Ye will give credit to a man's word, and will ye not believe God's? An honest man will get more trust of us, than the true and living God! Shall he not be offended with this? We declare it unto you, that he is truth itself, and will not fail in his promise, let that be your castle and refuge to enter into. Mercy and truth are two sweet companions to go along with you in your pilgrimage. David prayed for them Psal. lxi. 7. "O prepare thy mercy and truth to preserve me." Who will not be safe within these everlasting arms? What power can break through them? And this he promised to himself, (Psal. lvii. 3.) God shall send them out. Mercy made so many precious promises, and truth keeps them. Mercy is the fountain and source of all our consolation, and truth and faithfulness convey it to us, and keep it for us. It is these two that go before his face when he sits on a throne of majesty, and makes himself accessible to sinners (Psalm lxxxix. 14,) and so they are the pathway he walks in towards those who seek him, Psalm xxv. 10.

But this sweet and precious name, that is as ointment poured forth to those who love him, how doth it smell of death to those who walk contrary to him? "He is a God of truth" to execute his threatenings on those who despise his commands, and though ye flatter yourselves in your own eyes, and cry, "Peace, peace," even though ye walk in the imagination of your own heart, yet certainly "he is a God of truth." I pray you read that sad and weighty word, that will be like a millstone about many men's necks to sink them in hell, Deut. xxix. 20, 21, ye who "add drunkenness to thirst," whose rule of walking is your own lust, and whatsoever pleaseth you, without respect of his commands, and yet flatter yourselves with a dream of peace, know this for a truth, "the Lord will not spare thee, he that made thee will not have mercy on thee. His jealousy will smoke against thee, and all the curses written in this book shall be upon thee, and thy name shall be blotted out from under heaven." It was unbelief of God's threatening that first ruined man, it is this still that keeps so many from the remedy, and makes their misery irrecoverable. The serpent brought them to this question, "Hath God said ye shall die." And then presently the question entertained becometh a conclusion, Ye shall not surely die. Thus ye see how the liar, from the beginning, was contrary to the God of truth, and he murdered us by lying of that God of truth, and it is the same that shuts out all hope of remedy. Ye do not as yet believe and consider that curse that was pronounced against Adam, but is now also inflicted upon us, therefore, there is no solid belief can be of the promises of the gospel, and ye who think ye believe the gospel, do but indeed fancy it, except ye have considered the true curse of God on all flesh. But if any man have set to his seal that God is true in his threatening, and subscribed unto the law, then, I beseech you, add not the unbelief of the gospel unto your former disobedience. He is "a God of truth," in promises and threatenings. It is strange how untoward and froward we are,—a perverse generation. We do not believe his threatenings, but fancy we receive his promises, or else, believing his threatenings we question his promises. But know this for a truth, his last word is more weighty, and the unbelief of it is most dangerous. Ye have not kept his commands, and so the curse is come upon you? Do ye believe that? If ye do, then the gospel speaks unto you, the God of truth hath one word more, "He that believes shall be saved," notwithstanding of all his breaking of the law. If ye do not set your seal to this also, then ye say he is not a God of truth, ye say he is a liar. And as for you who have committed your souls to him, as to a faithful keeper, and acquiesced unto his word of promise for salvation, think how unsuitable it is for you to distrust him in other lesser things. Ye have the promise of this life, whoever hath the promises of the life to come. Therefore do not make him a liar in these. He is "a God of truth," and will let you want no good thing. "Say to the righteous, it shall be well with him, whatever be." Let heaven and earth mix through other, yet ye may be as mount Sion unmoved in the midst of many floods, because of the promises.

"Without iniquity." Who doubts of that, say ye? What needs this be added? Who charges him with iniquity or sin? Nay, but stay and consider, and you shall find great weight in this. It is true, none dare charge him openly, or speak in express terms against his holiness, yet, if we judge of our own and other's practices and dispositions, as the Lord useth to construct of them, if we resolve our murmurings, impatience, self absolutions, and excuses to hold off convictions, into plain language, if we would translate them into a scripture style, certainly it will be found that the most part of men, if not all, use to impute iniquity to God, and accuse him rather than take with accusations laid against themselves. And therefore the Lord useth to go to law with his people. He who is the judge of the world, that cannot do unrighteousness, he who is the potter, and we all the clay, yet he so far condescends to us for convincing us, as sometimes to refer the controversy between him and his people to other creatures, as Micah vi. 2. He calls the mountains and the foundations of the earth to judge between him and his people, and sometimes he appeals unto their own consciences and is content, though judge, to stand and be judged by those who were guilty, as ver. 3 and Jer. ii. ver. 5, and 31. All this supposes, that when the Lord would endeavour to convince them of iniquity, they did rather recriminate, and took not with their own faults. This is a truth generally acknowledged by all, "He who is the judge of the world doth no iniquity," but O! that ye considered it, till the meditation of it were engraven on your spirits, the seal of God's holiness, that ye might fear before him, and never call him to account for his matters. Who can say, I have purged my heart from iniquity? Among men the holiest are defiled with it, and so are all their actions. But here is one that ye may give him an implicit faith so to speak, he is "a God of truth," and can speak no lie, he does no iniquity, and cannot do wrong to any man. Would there be so much impatience amongst you, and fretting against his dispensations, if ye believed this solidly? Would ye repine against his holy and just ways, were it not to charge God with iniquity? Your murmuring and grudging at his dispensations is with child of blasphemies, and he who can search the reins sees it, and constructs so of it. You say by interpretation, that if ye had the government of your own matters, or of kingdoms, ye would order them better than he doth. How difficult a thing is it to persuade men to take with their own iniquity! O how many excuses and pretences, how many extenuations are used that this conviction may not pierce deeply! But all this speaks so much blasphemy,—that iniquity is in God. Ye cannot take with your own iniquities, but ye charge his Majesty with iniquity.

"Just and right is he." Is this any new thing? Was it not said already, that he is "without uniquity, and his ways judgment?" But, alas! how ignorant are we of God, and slow of heart to conceive of him as he is, therefore is there "line upon line, and precept upon precept," and name upon name, if it be possible, that at length we may apprehend God as he is. Alas! our knowledge is but ignorance, our light darkness, while it is shut up in the corner of our mind, and shines not into the heart, and hath no influence on our practice. And the truth is, the belief of divine truths is almost no more but a not contradicting them, we do not seriously think of them as either to consent to them, or deny them. Is there any consideration amongst us now of God's justice and righteousness, though it be frequently spoken of? And what advantage shall we have if ye do not consider them? O how hard is it to persuade men's hearts of this, that God is just, and will by no means acquit the guilty? There are so many delusions drunk in in men's hearts, contrary to his truth. "Let no man deceive you," "be not deceived" with vain words, "know ye not," saith our apostle. These are strange prefaces. Would ye not think the point of truth subtile that there needed so much prefacing unto it? and yet what is it? Even that which all men grant,—God's wrath comes on the children of disobedience, but, alas! few men consider, but deceive themselves with dreams of escaping it. Though men know it, yet they know it not, for they walk as if they knew no such thing.

Always however this is of little moment to affect our spirits now, yet in the day that God shall set your iniquities before your face, and set his justice also before your eyes. O how sad and serious a thing will it be then! If these two verses were engraven on our hearts,—God's justice and holiness, our corruption and vileness,—I think there would be other thoughts among us than there are.

SERMON IV.

Deut. xxxii. 5.—"They have corrupted themselves; their spot is not the spot of his children; they are a perverse and crooked generation."

We doubt this people would take well with such a description of themselves as Moses gives. It might seem strange to us, that God should have chosen such a people out of all the nations of the earth, and they to be so rebellious and perverse, if our own experience did not teach us how free his choice is, and how long-suffering he is, and constant in his choice. His people are called to a conformity with himself, "Be ye holy, for I am holy," (Lev. chap. xix. and xx.) and to a deformity and separation from the rest of the world in their conversation, from whom God had separated them in profession and privileges, Lev. xviii. 24. But behold what unlikeness there is between God and his people. If ye were to paint out to the life a heathen people, you needed no other image or pattern to copy at but this same description of this people. It is this that makes Moses in the preface turn to the heavens and earth, and call them to hear his song, and Isaiah begins his preaching thus, "Hear, O heavens, and give ear, O earth, &c." A strange thing it must be, that senseless creatures are called to wonder at. It must surpass all the wonders and prodigies of nature and art. And what is that? "I have nourished and brought up children, and they have rebelled against me," &c. If we consider what this people seemed once to be, and thought themselves to be, we may easily know how they corrupted themselves. If ye look on them at one time, (Exod. xix. 8, Deut. v. 27,) ye would call them children. There was never a fairer undertaking of obedience than this, "All that the Lord hath spoken we will do," so that the Lord commends them for speaking well, verse 28, "They have well said all that they have spoken," verse 29, "O that there were such an heart in them!" But compare all this people's practice with this profession, and you shall find it exceeding contrary; they indeed corrupted themselves, though they got warning to take heed of it. "Take ye therefore good heed unto yourselves, lest ye corrupt yourselves," Deut. iv. 15, 16. But alas, it was within them that destroyed them; there was not such a heart in them as to hear and obey, but they undertake, being ignorant of their own deceitful hearts, which were desperately wicked. And therefore, behold what corruption ensued and followed upon such a professed resolution. They never sooner promised obedience, but they disobeyed; they did abominable works, and did no good, and this is to corrupt their way, Psalm xiv. 1, &c. We need not instance this longer in this people, we ourselves are a sufficient proof of it. We may make this song our own, "we have corrupted ourselves." Once we had a fair show of zeal for God, of love and desire of reformation of life, many solemn undertakings were that we should amend our ways and doings, but what is the fruit of all? Alas, we have corrupted ourselves more than they. Israel promised, but we vowed and swore to the Most High, reformation and amendment of life in our conversations and callings. Lay this rule to our practices, and are we not a perverse and crooked generation? Oh! that we were more affected with our corruptions, and were more sensible of them, then we could not choose but mourn for our own and the land's departing from God. Did not every man vow and swear to the most high God to endeavour reformation of his life, even a personal reformation?[265] But alas, where is it? "He that is filthy" is "filthy still." Nay, which is worse, the evil man waxeth worse and worse. There is a great noise of a public reformation of ordinances and worship, but alas, the deformation of life and practice outcries all that noise. Nay, certainly all that is done in the public, must come to no account before God since our practices outcry it. Public reformation is abomination, where personal corruptions do not cease. This made the Jews' solemn days hateful, their hands were "full of blood." Isa. i. 15. All that ye have spent on the public will never be reckoned, since ye will not consecrate your lives to God, will not give your lusts up to him. Ye are his enemies in the mean time, though you account yourselves religion's friends. I beseech you consider your ways. Would any of us have thought to have seen such profanity, mocking of godliness, and ignorance in Scotland in so short a time? Nay, it is to be feared that the day is not far off, when ye will corrupt yourselves, and do abominable things, yea, defile yourselves as ill as the nations that know not God.

Every man useth to impute his faults to something beside himself. Ere men take with their own iniquity, they will charge God that gave no more grace, but if men knew themselves, they would deduce their corruption and destruction both from one fountain, that is, from themselves. Ignorance of ourselves maketh us oft undertake fair, and promise so well on our own head. What was the fountain of this people's corruption, and apostatizing from their professions? The Lord hints at it, Deut. v. 29, &c. "Oh that they had such a heart." Alas, poor people, ye know not yourselves, that speak so well. I know thee better than thou dost thyself, I will declare unto thee thy own thought, thou hast not such a heart as to do what thou sayest; there is a desperate wicked heart within thee, that will destroy thee by lying unto thee. If thou knewest this fountain of original corruption, thou wouldest despair of doing, and say, I cannot serve the Lord. Now here is the fountain of the land's corruption this day. Why is our way corrupted? Because our hearts within were not cleansed, and because they were not known. If we had dried up the fountain, the streams had ceased, but we did only dam it up, and cut off some streams for a season; we set up our resolutions and purposes as an hedge to hold it in, but the sea of the heart's iniquity, that is above all things, hath overflowed it, and defiled our way more than in former times. Ye thought upon no other thing, but that presently ye would be all changed people, and would reform without more ado,—and thus it is with you in all your public repentances. But alas! you know not yourselves, it is still within you which will yet corrupt you, and it was within us that hath undone us, we were too confident of ourselves, and it is no wonder that the Lord suffers us to prove ourselves, that we may know what is in our heart. Now, therefore, since ye have so often tried it, I beseech you follow not such a way again. Ye are called to deny yourselves, and to follow Christ and this is a great part of it, that ye may never expect for any good within yourselves, or the helping of any evil. "In me is thy help found." Look to the fountain of life, Jesus Christ, and despair of your own hearts, for they are desperately wicked, so wicked, that if ye knew them, ye would despair of them, and give them over to another hand, who can create a new heart within you. Ye use to impute your backslidings to the times, to temptations, to company, and such like. This is the way that men shift the challenges of sin: the drunkard puts it on his companion, the servant on his master that led him wrong, the people put rulers in the fault, and absolve themselves, and rulers put one another in the wrong, and absolve themselves. But, alas! all of us are ignorant of ourselves; it is not times nor temptations that corrupt us, but ourselves. No man is tempted, saith James, of God, "but every man is tempted when he is drawn away of his own lust and enticed," James i. 14. Temptation were no temptation, if our hearts were not wicked hearts. Nay, many of us are ready to tempt temptations, to provoke the devil to temptations; we cast ourselves open to temptations. Temptations find lust within, and lust within is the mother to conceive sin, if temptation be the father. Times do not bring evils along with them, they do but discover what was hid before. All the evils and corruptions you now see among us, where were they in the day of our first love, when we were as a loving and beloved child? Have all these risen up of late? No certainly, all that you have seen and found were before, though they did not appear; before they were in the root, now you see the fruit. All the apostacy and profanity that hath been vented in these days, was all shut up within the corners of men's hearts at the beginning. Time and temptation hath but uncovered the heart, and made the inside out, hath but opened a sluice to let out this sea of corruption. It is not bred since, but seen since.

Now so it is with us, we have corrupted ourselves, and so we corrupt ourselves still more. Backsliding cometh on as gray hairs, here and there and is not perceived by beholders. *Nemo repente fit turpissimus.*[266] No man becometh worst at first. There are many steps between that and good. Corruption comes on men's ways as in fruits, some one part beginneth to alter, and then it groweth worse, and putrifieth and corrupteth the rest of the parts. An apple rots not all at once, so it is with us. Men begin at leisure, but they run post before all be done. In some one step of our way we take liberty and think to keep the rest clean, but when that part is corrupted, "a little leaven leaveneth the whole lump," and all followeth: and then he that corrupted himself, is ready to corrupt others. "Children that are corrupters," Isa. i. 4. Every one by his example corrupts another, and by corrupting others they again corrupt themselves more. Oh! how infectious an evil is sin, of a pestilentious nature, and truly our hearts are more ready to receive such impressions, than either a world or a devil is to make them.

"Their spot is not." Why doth the Lord take pleasure to reckon their sins, to describe so abominable a people? Is not this Jacob in whom he saw no iniquity?[267] Is not this Israel, whose transgressions are not known?[268] Certainly if this people would have charged themselves so, he would not have done it. He loves to forget, when we remember our sins, but he must remember them when we forget them. What is the Lord's great controversy with men? Here it is,—How can ye say or think that ye are not polluted? Or if ye take with such a general, yet, why is not the conviction of your sin and misery so deeply engraven, as to pursue you out of all hope of remedy in yourselves, (Jer. ii. 22, 23)? "And therefore is thine iniquity marked before me, saith the Lord." God hath determined not to wrong his justice. If men should go away unpunished and unjudged both, where were his righteousness? If there were no record of men's transgressions, were he a righteous judge? Therefore, those who do not judge themselves must leave judgment to him, for once the mouth of all flesh must be stopped, and all become guilty before God. Why pleads the Lord with man? Because man says, "I am innocent, I have not sinned, his anger will turn away," Jer. ii. 35. Will any speak so in terms? No indeed, but the Lord constructs so of the most part, because they do more consider the wrongs done to them, than their own wrongs done to God. All men confess the general, that they are sinners, but who searches and tries his way to find out particulars? And in as far as ye do not charge yourselves with particular guiltiness, until ye be afraid of his anger, as long as the consideration or your sins is so superficial and shallow, that ye apprehend no danger of wrath, or immunity from it, certainly God will plead with you. Justice must so far be glorified, as once to conclude you under the sentence of death; if ye do it not now, then ye leave God to be your judge and party. But if any man shall take with his guiltiness, till his mouth be stopped, and condemn himself in God's sight, I say, mercy and grace in God must not be wronged, he that judges himself shall not be judged of the Lord. What a fair offer is this to you all the Lord offers to you! If ye will in time be your own judges, I will resign my judgment to you. If you will in earnest pass the sentence, I will neither pass it nor execute it. If ye come to the Mediator, Christ Jesus, to escape from the wrath of a judge, you shall meet with a reconciled Father, and with such love in him as shall hide a multitude of offences. O the depth, and height, and breadth of that love! Well then, it shall be a sea to cast your offences into, that shall drown them. Had not his people many spots? Is there any man can say, I have cleansed my heart from iniquity? No, not one. Yet behold, he sees no spots in his people. He doth not make them his people because spotless, but he seeth them spotless, because he makes them his people. There is no covering that can hide men's uncleanness from his piercing eye, but one even Jesus Christ his righteousness, and "Blessed is he whose sins are covered." If this covering were spread over the mouth of all hell, then hell should have a covering from his eyes. If ye therefore strip yourselves naked of your own pretences and leaves, and think not yourselves secure under any created shelter. If ye hide not your iniquity, then it shall be hid indeed, here is a covering that shall hide it from his eyes. There is no spot so heinous, none so ingrained, but the blood of Jesus can wash it as perfectly out, as if it had never been, Isa. i. 16, 17. Though your spots were such as are not incident to his children, yet this blood cleanses from one and all, it is of an infinite nature. But though it be so, that the blood of Christ cleanseth from all sin, that there is a fountain opened in the house of David for sin and for uncleanness, for sin and separation, for such heinous offences as may separate people even from the congregation of the Lord's people, yet there are some sins, some spots, that ordinarily his people are not defiled with, and in this respect they may be called holy and undefiled in the way. There are some marks and characters of unregenerated men so legible and express, that we may even read from men's conversation, that they are not the children of God. Though the blood of Christ wash from all, yet the child of God ordinarily is kept from some kind of spots, so that if a man shall be spotted with them it is no marvel he question if he be a child or not. There are two, which I think so gross and unclean spots that I cannot conceive how a soul washen by Jesus Christ can be defiled with them. One is, a course of profanity. The common walk of the multitude is so gross and profane, so void of God and godliness, that it witnesseth to their face that they are not the sons of God. "He that is born of God sinneth not; he maketh not sin his way and trade to walk into, and please himself into." What are the most part of you, I pray you? Is your spot like the spot of his children? Do not ye declare your sin as Sodom, ye drunkards, who wallow in it daily, and though ye profess repentance, yet never amend? Ye who have a custom of swearing and blaspheming his holy name, do not ye carry in your forehead a spot that is not like his children? The child of God may fall in many particulars, but it is not the spot of a child to continue in them to add drunkenness to thirst, and yet to dream of escaping wrath. I pray you, consider it, for it is of great moment. Do ye carry such a black mark,—the devils mark? O do not think yourselves safe. May not this persuade you? Do but compare yourselves in your converse and walk with an heathen without the church. Set aside your public profession of coming to the church, and hearing the word, and church privileges, and is the difference visible between you and them? Many of you pray no more in secret or in your families than they. Ye curse and swear as they, ye are covetous and worldly as they. If ye can, do but draw a line of difference, and if ye cannot, then I ask, what are ye? Is not this the spot of bastards? Another spot is, hatred of godliness and the godly. This is indeed the most lively image of the devil: who hates his brother is of the devil. He that hates the Son, can he love the Father? he that hates him that is begotten, hates also him that begat him and he that loves him that begat, loves him that is begotten. Now, how can he be begotten of God, who hates that nature he is said to partake of—who hates him that is begotten? I wonder that many of your consciences are not touched with this? How can ye imagine ye are children of God, when there are none of your neighbours that your heart riseth more against, that ye can less abide, than those who seek God most diligently, whose conversation is different from the worlds? Do not flatter yourselves, as if it were hypocrisy ye hated. No, no ye can agree with profanity, and how can ye hate hypocrisy? Ye can agree with a profane hypocrite—with a profane man, that feigns and dissembles repentance but if once he were so thoroughly changed, as to hate his former way, and forsake it, then your antipathy beginneth. What a ridiculous thing is it for profanity to take upon it to censure hypocrisy! Certainly if profanity cast out with hypocrisy, it must be because it hath a form of godliness, which it so much detesteth. It is a strange hatred at godliness that a profane man hath, that he cannot abide the very shadow of it. I beseech you who love not holiness in your own persons, who hate to be reformed yourselves, do not add this height of sin to it, as to hate it in others also. If ye be not godly yourselves, do not add this declared manifest character of a child of the devil to it, to hate godliness in others. There were some hope of you, if ye held it in reverence and estimation where ye saw it. There are many other spots not incident to his children, as this, that men will not take with their sin and the curse. It is a great difficulty to convince the most part of men how miserable they are, how void of God. All the world will not put them out of a good opinion of themselves, and I think this hath been the spot of this people, they would not take with their guiltiness—a stubborn hearted people, wholehearted. There needs no more to declare a number of you not to be God's children, but this,—ye have lived all your time in the opinion and belief that ye were God's children, that ye believed in him, ye never saw yourselves lost and miserable. This was the spot of this people that they esteemed themselves children, though they had many spots that testified to their face that they were no children. They waxed worse and worse, neither mercies nor judgments amended them. "When he slew them," it may be, "they sought him, and flattered him with their mouth, but their hearts were not right with him, neither were they steadfast in his covenant," Psal. lxxviii. 34. Ye would have thought them a godly people, while under the rod for a season, but all that was but extorted and pressed out by violence of affliction, as the groans of a beast under a burden. But a little time declared that it was but flattery, though they thought themselves ingenuous, and therefore they returned to their old provocations, as a sow to the puddle, or a dog to his vomit. And is not this our spot, even the spot of great and small? If any would look upon us in our engagements and vows under trouble, we appear like his people, a praying, repenting, and believing people,[269] but how quickly doth all this prove flattery? Do we not still return to our old ways that we have been exemplarily punished for, and which we so solemnly engaged against? The heat of the furnace dieth out, and they wax colder and harder, a little time wears away all their tenderness. Every man seeks his own things, and no man seeks the things of Jesus Christ. This was this people's sin and spot. "Jeshurun waxed fat and kicked, and lightly esteemed the Rock of his salvation." When their heads were lifted up to government, when they were raised out of the waters of affliction and poverty, then they forgat God, they oppressed the poor and needy, eat up his people as bread, and could not abide to have their faults told them, they said to the seers, "See not, and to the prophets, Prophesy not unto us right things," &c. Isa. xxx. 10. I think likewise, that oppression is not the spot of his children, whoever uses it. And covetousness presses men to it, when power is in their hand to compass it. This is a vile spot, unworthy of any ruler, let be[270] a Christian. It was abhorred among Pagans. O but it cries to heaven, saith the Scripture, it hath a double cry when other sins cry once! The heinousness of it crieth once, and the poor people cry again, and both these come up to the ears of the Lord of hosts, nay, it hath the cry of murder, and another beside. He that is greedy of gain, is said to take away the life of the owners thereof, Prov. i, 19. So he is a murderer before God, and the poor man's blood crieth for vengeance, and then himself seconds it either by prayer, or crying out for misery, Job xxxv. 9. All men's prayers and professions will not outcry these two. The people's many prayers could not be heard, (Isa. i. 15), because their hands were "full of blood," which had a louder cry than their prayers. The poor also oppressing the poor, is like a sweeping rain that leaves nothing behind it.

It is read in the margin, "that they are not his children,—that is their blot." And indeed it is so. It is a great blot and stain in the face of any man whoever he be, that he is not born of God—that he can reckon kindred to none but Adam. But what indignity is it and disgrace, for a people professing his name, yet to have no other generation, to reckon no higher than the earth and the earthly. What is now the great blot of our visible church? Here it is, the most part are not God's children, but called so; and it is the greater blot that they are called so, and are not.[271] O poor saints, esteem your honour and high privilege; ye have received this, to be the sons of God! It is no blot to you that you are poor and despised in the world; but it is and shall be an eternal blot to the great and rich, and wise in the world, that they are not the children of God. Christianity is no blot, though it be in reproach among men, but it is really the glory and excellency of a man; but the want of it, alas! how doth it abase many high and noble, impoverish many rich, and infatuate many wise! Ye think all of you are the children of God, because ye are in the church, and partake of the ordinances and sacraments; and so did this people. But Moses did not flatter these Jews, but told both princes and people in their face, that they were not children of God, because only Israel in the letter, they had not children's manners. O that it might not be said of the most part of you, that ye are not children of God, and that that is your blot and shame! It is the shame of rulers not to be the children of God. They are wise, they are active, they are noble, but one spot disgraceth all, one fly maketh their ointment to stink, they are not gracious, many of them, but sons of men at the farthest reckoning, are not begotten again to a lively hope. "Not many wise, not many noble, not many rich." The scantiness of gracious men is the spot of judicatories,[272] that there are many children of the world, but few children of light in them. O how beautiful and glorious would judicatories be, if all the members were children of light! What glory would there be, if all of them did shine and enlightened one another! But what beauty or comeliness, what majesty can be in rulers or judicatures, when the image of God is not in them! This is also the spot of assemblies, synods, presbyteries, that there are few godly ministers. Alas, that this complaint should be, even among those whose office it is to beget many children to God! How few of them are begotten, or have the image of their Father! And thus church assemblies have no beauty, such as the courts of Jesus Christ should have. O that we were in love with Christianity and grace; that it were our grand question, how shall I be put among the children? The Lord seems to wonder at it, and make a question of it, How can such as we be put among the children? Jer. iii. 19. But he answers it himself, "Thou shalt call me, My Father, and shall not turn away from me." There is no more to do, but to take with[273] your wanderings and wrongs done to God, embrace him in Jesus Christ, and he becomes your Father; and if ye be children, sure ye will resolve to abide in your Father's house, and turn no more to a present world, or your former lusts.

They are a "perverse and crooked generation." What pleasure hath the Lord in speaking thus, when he upbraids none? Certainly, in a manner it is drawn out of him. Would he object our faults, if we did not defend them by obstinacy? Perverseness and crookedness is obstinacy and incorrigibleness against mercies and judgments,—"that that which is crooked cannot be made straight," saith Solomon. Then doth the Lord take notice of sins, when men refuse to return, and so maintain their sins. It is this which heightens provocations, and makes out the controversy,—perverseness in sin. It is not ordinary common infirmities that the Lord punisheth, either in a land or person; but when infirmities are discovered by the light of the word, when the Lord useth means to reclaim men in his providence, and yet no means prevail, then are they reckoned perverse. Now, perverseness is not the spot of his children: the child of God daily bows and folds to him, receives challenges from him, takes with iniquity and yields unto God. O that this title might not be written above the head of this generation deservedly—"This is a perverse and crooked generation!"

SERMON V.

Psal. lxxiii. 28.—"But it is good for me to draw near to God: I have put my trust in the Lord God, that I may declare all thy works."

After man's first transgression, he was shut out from the tree of life, and cast out of the garden, by which was signified his seclusion and sequestration from the presence of God, and communion with him: and this was in a manner the extermination of all mankind in one, when Adam was driven out of paradise. Now, this had been an eternal separation for any thing that we could do, (for we can do nothing but depart by a perpetual backsliding, and make the distance every day wider,) except it had pleased the Lord, of his infinite grace, to condescend to draw near to us in gracious promises and offers of a Redeemer. If he had not made the first journey from heaven to earth, by sending his only Son, we should have given over the hope of returning from earth to heaven. But he hath taken away the greatest part of that distance, in drawing near to our nature; yea, in assuming our flesh into the fellowship of his glorious divinity. He hath stooped so low to meet with us, and offered himself the trysting place[274] between God and us, a fit meeting-place, where there is a conjunction of the interests of both parties, and now, there is no more to do, but to draw near to God in Jesus Christ, since he hath made the great journey to come down to us. We have not that infinite gulf of satisfaction to justice to pass over, we have not the height of divine Majesty, as he is infinitely above us, and offended with us, to climb up unto. Certainly we could not but fall into the lake that is below us, if we were to aim so high. But the Lord hath been pleased to descend to us, in our mean capacity in the flesh, and fill up the immeasurable gulf of justice by the infinite merits and sufferings of his Son in our flesh. And now he invites us, he requests us, to come to him in his Son and have life. We are not come to mount Sinai, that might not be touched, that burnt with fire and tempest, where there were terrible sights and intolerable noises. I say, such a God we might have had to do with a consuming fire, instead of an instructing light,—a devouring fire, instead of a healing Sun of righteousness, considering that there is nothing in us which is not fit and prepared fuel for everlasting burnings. But we are come—and that is the eternal wonder of angels—unto mount Sion to be citizens in the city of God and fellow citizens with blessed angels and glorified spirits, to peace and reconciliation with him who was our judge. And if you ask how this may be? I answer, because we have one Jesus, the Mediator of the new covenant, to come to, whose blood crieth louder for pardon of sinners than all men's transgressions can cry for punishment of sinners, Heb. xii. 18-20, &c.

Let us then consider the first step and degree of union with God,—it consists in faith in Jesus Christ. This is the first motion of the soul in drawing near to God, for, as there is no remission without blood, so no access to God without a mediator. For if you consider what is in Jesus Christ, you will find that which will engage the desire of the heart, as also that which will give boldness and confidence to act that desire. Eternal life is promised and proposed in him,—he offers rest to weary souls, and hath it to give. That which we ignorantly and vainly seek elsewhere, here it is to be found. For personal excellencies, he is the chief infinitely beyond comparison, and for suitableness to us and our necessities, all the gospel is an expression of it, so that he is presented in the most attractive drawing manner that can be imagined. And then, when the desires are inflamed, yet if there be no oil of hope to feed it, it will soon cool again. Therefore, take a view again, and you may have boldness to enter into the holiest by the blood of Jesus. There was some kind of distance kept in the Old Testament,—none but the high priest might enter into the holiest place, but the entry of our High Priest into it, that is, into heaven, hath made it patent to all that come to him and apply his blood. There is a new and living way by the holy flesh of Christ, consecrated and made, of infinite value and use, by the divinity of his person, and, therefore, having such a one of our kindred so great with God, we may draw near with a true heart and full assurance of faith, having our consciences sprinkled, &c, Heb. x. 18-20, &c. Now, since the way is made plain to you, and the entry is opened up in the gospel, do you not find your hearts stir within you to draw near to him? Do you not find a necessity of making peace by such a Mediator? O that ye knew the great distance between God and your natures, and what the hazard is, "Lo! they that are far from thee shall perish," then certainly you would take hold of this invitation, and be easily drawn unto Jesus Christ. But unto you who have adventured to draw near for pardon of sin in Christ, I would recommend unto you that you would draw yet nearer to God. After that the partition wall of wrath and condemnation is removed, yet there is much darkness in your minds and corruption in your natures, that separates from him, I mean, intercepts and disturbs that blessed communion you are called unto. Therefore, I would exhort you, as James, "Draw near to God, and he will draw near to you," chap. iv. 8, and that, wherein this most consists, is in studying that purification of our natures, that cleansing of our hearts from guile, and our hands from offences, by which our souls may draw towards a resemblance of God. This access and drawing near to God in assimilation and conformity of nature is the great design of the gospel. "Be ye holy, for I am holy. Now, ye are agreed, walk with him," (Amos iii. 3), as Enoch "walked with God," Gen. v. 24, that is, labour in all your conversation to set him before your eyes, and to study to be well pleased with him in all things and to please him in all, to conform yourselves to his pleasure in every thing. And this communion in walking especially consists in that communication of the spirit with God in prayer, this is the nearest and sweetest approach when the soul is lifted up to God, and is almost out of itself in him, and this being the ordinary exercise and motion of the soul, it exceedingly advances in the first point of nearness, that is, in conformity with God. Drawing often near in communion with him in prayer, makes the soul draw towards his likeness, even as much converse of men together will make them like one another.

Now, for the commendation of this, "It is good." What greater evil can be imagined than separation from the greatest good? And what greater good, than accession to the greatest good? Every thing is in so far happy and well, as it is joined with, and enjoyeth, that which is convenient for it. Light is the perfection of the earth, remove it, and what a disconsolate and unpleasant thing is it! Now, truly there is nothing suitable to the immortal spirit of man but God, and, therefore, all its happiness or misery must be measured by the access or recess, nearness or distance, of that infinite goodness. Therefore, is it any wonder, that all they that go a whoring from him perish, as every man's heart doth? For we are infinitely bound by creation, by many other bonds stronger than wedlock, to consecrate and devote ourselves wholly to God, but this is treacherously broken. Every man turns aside to vanity and lies, and is guilty of heart whoredom from God, and spiritual idolatry, because the affection that should be preserved chaste for him is prostitute to every base object. So then, this divorcement of the soul from God cannot but follow thereupon, even an eternal eclipse of true and real life and comfort. And whoever draws back from the fountain of life and salvation, cannot but find elsewhere perdition and destruction, Heb. x. ult. My beloved, let us set thus aside all other things which are the pursuits and endeavours of the most part of men. Men's natural desires are carried towards health, food, raiment, life and liberty, peace, and such like, but the more rational sort of men seek after some shadow of wisdom and virtue. Yet the generality of men, both high and low, have extravagant illimited desires towards riches, pleasure, preferment, and all that we have spoken is enclosed within the narrow compass of men's abode here, which is but for a moment. So that, if it were possible that all these forementioned desires and delights of men could attend any man for the space of an hundred years, though he had the concurrence of the streams of the creatures to bring him in satisfaction, though all the world should bow to him and be subject to the beck of his authority without stroke of sword, though all the creatures should spend their strength and wit upon his satisfaction, yet do but consider what that shall be within some few years, when he shall be spoiled of all that attendance, denuded of all external comforts, when the fatal period must close his life, peace, health, and all, and his poor soul also, that was drowned in that gulf of pleasure, shall then find itself robbed of its precious treasure, that is, God's favour, and so remain in everlasting banishment from his presence. Do ye think, I say that man were happy? Nay! O happy Lazarus, who is now blessed in Abraham's bosom, who enjoys an eternity of happiness for a moment's misery! But, my beloved, you know that it is not possible even to attain to that imagined happiness here. All the gain that is found is not able to quit the cost and expense of grief, vexation, care, toiling and sweating that is about them.

But if ye would be persuaded, there is that to be found easily, which you trouble yourselves seeking elsewhere, and believe me, though the general apprehension of men be,—that peace, plenty, preferment, and satisfaction in this life, to compense their pains, are more easily attainable than fellowship and communion with God, yet I am persuaded that there is nothing more practicable than the life of religion. God hath condemned the world under vanity and a curse, and that which is crooked can by no art or strength be made straight, but he hath made this attainable by his gracious promises, even a blessed life, in approaching near to himself, the fountain of all life. And this is a certain good, an universal good, and an eternal good. It will not disappoint you as other things do, of which you have no assurance for all your toilings. This is made more infallible to a soul that truly seeks it in God. It is as certain that they cannot be ashamed through frustration, as that he is faithful. And then it is an universal good, one comprehensive of all, one eminently and virtually all things created, to be joined to the infinite all fulness of God. This advanceth the soul to a participation of all that is in him. This is health, Psalm xlii. 11. Prov. iii. 8. This is light, John viii. 12. It is life, (John xi. 25,) liberty, (John viii. 36,) food and raiment, (Isa. lxi. 10, and John iv. 14,) and what not? It is profit, pleasure, preferment in the superlative degree, and not scattered in so many various streams which divide and distract the heart, but all combined in one. It is the true good of both soul and body, and so the only good of man. And lastly, it is eternal, to be coetaneous with thy soul. Of all other things it may be said, "I have seen an end of them," they were and are not. But this will survive time, and all the changes of it, and then it will begin to be perfect, when all perfection is at an end. Now, from all this, I would exhort you in Jesus Christ to ponder those things in your hearts, and consider them in reference to your own souls, that ye may say with David, "It is good for me to draw near to God."

That which all men seek after, is happiness and well being. Men pursue nothing but under the notion of good, and to complete that which may be called good, there is required some excellency in the thing itself, and then a conveniency and suitableness to us, and these jointly draw the heart of man. But the great misery is, that there is so much ignorance and misapprehension of that which is truly good, and then, when any thing of it is known, there is so little serious consideration and application of it to ourselves, and this makes the most part of men wander up and down in the pursuit of divers things, which are not that true good of the soul, and set their hearts on that which is not, until they find their hearts fall down as wanting a foundation and then they turn about again to some other vanity. And so the wanderings and strayings of men are infinite, because the by ways are innumerable, though the true way be but one. Yea, the turnings and toilings of one man are various and manifold because he quickly loses the scent of happiness in every way he falls into and therefore must turn to another. And thus men are never at any solid setting about this great business, never resolute wherein this happiness consists, nor peremptory to follow it, but they fluctuate upon uncertain apprehensions, and diverse affections, until the time and date of salvation expire, and then they must know certainly and surely the inevitable danger and irrecoverable loss they have brought themselves, to, who would not take notice of the sure way, both of escaping wrath and attaining happiness while it was to be found.

Well, then, this is the great business we have here to do, yea, to make the circle the larger, it is that great business we have to do in this world, to know wherein the true well being and eternal welfare of our souls consist and by any means to apply unto that, as the only thing necessary, in regard of which, all other things are ceremonies, circumstances, and indifferent things. And to guide us in this examination and application, here is one man, who, having almost made shipwreck upon the rocks which men commonly dash upon, and being by the Lord led safely by, and almost arrived at the coast of true felicity, he sets out a beacon, and lights a candle to all who shall follow him, to direct them which way they shall steer their course. Examples teach more effectually than rules. It is easy for every man to speak well upon this point in general, and readily all will acknowledge that here it is, and nowhere else. But yet all this is outcried by the contrary noise of every man's practice. These general grants of truth are recalled in the conversations of men, therefore they cannot have much influence upon any man. But when we hear one speak, and see him walk so too, when we have the example of a most wise man, who wanted not these worldly expectations which other men have, so that he not only propones it to us, but after much serious advisement, after mature consideration of all that can be said of the wicked's best estate, and the godly's worst, setting down resolute conclusions for himself—"It is good for me to draw near to God," yea, so determinate in it, that if none of the world should be of that mind, he would not change it,—though all should walk in other ways, he would choose to be rather alone in this, than in the greatest crowd of company in any other. Now, I say, when we have such a copy cast us, a man of excellent parts in sobriety and sadness, choosing that way, which all in words confess to be the best, should not this awake us out of our dreams and raise us up to some more attention and consideration of what we are doing? The words, you see, are the holy resolution of a holy heart, concerning that which is the chiefest good. You see the way to happiness, and you find the particular application of that to David's soul, or of his soul to it. We shall speak a word of the thing itself, then of the commendation of it, then of the application of it.

For the thing itself,—drawing near to God,—it gives us some ground to take a view of the posture in which men are found by nature, far off from God. Our condition by nature I cannot so fitly express, as in the apostle's words, (Eph. ii. 12,)—"Without Christ, aliens from the commonwealth of Israel, strangers from the covenants of promise, having no hope, and without God in the world." A deplorable estate indeed, hopeless and helpless! No hope in it, that is the extremity of misery, the refuse of all conditions. "Without Christ, and without God." Oh! these are words of infinite weight: without those, without whom it is simply impossible to be happy, and without whom it is not possible but to be miserable,—without the fountain of light, life, and consolation, without which there is nothing but pure darkness, without any beam of light; nothing but death, without the least breathing of life, nothing but vexation, without the least drop of consolation. In a word, without these, and wanting these, whom, if you want, it were good to be spoiled of all being, to be nothing, if that could be, or never to have been any thing. Men will seek death, and cannot find it. O what a loss and deprivement is the loss of God, which makes death more desirable than life, and not to be at all, infinitely preferable to any being! Now, it is true, that the bringing in of multitudes within the pale of the visible church, is some degree of access and nearness to God, for then they become citizens as to external right, in the commonwealth of the church, and have the offers of the promises made to them, in respect of which visible standing, the apostle speaks of the whole church of Ephesus, "but now ye are made near who were far off," (ver. 13,) notwithstanding, that many of them were found afterwards to have left their first love, Rev. ii. But yet, beloved, to speak more inwardly, and as your souls stand in the sight of God, the generality of those who are near hand in outward ordinances are yet far off from God in reality,—"without God and without Christ," as really, as touching any soul-feeling, as those who are altogether without. The bond of union and peace was broken in paradise, sin dissolved it, and broke off that nearness and friendship with God, and from that day to this day, there hath been an infinite distance and separation betwixt man and God. The steps and degrees of it are many. There is darkness and blindness in men's minds. Such ignorance naturally possesseth the multitude, that it wholly alienates them from the life of God, Eph. iv. 18. For what fellowship can light, that pure light, have with such gross darkness as is among us? This certainly is the removal of that Sun of Righteousness from our souls, or the imposition of the clouds of transgression, that makes it so dark a night in the souls of men. And then there is nothing but enmity and desperate wickedness in the heart of man, and this keeps the stronghold of the affections, Rom. viii., Jer. xvii. There cannot be a further elongation or separation of the soul from God, than to turn so opposite, in all inclinations and dispositions, to his holy will, for the distance between God and us is not local in the point of place, for whither shall we go from him who is everywhere? And thus he is near hand every one of us, but it is also real in the deformity and repugnancy of our natures to his holy will. But add unto this, that being thus separated in affection, and disjoined, as it were, in natural dispositions, we cannot draw near to God in any ordinance,—as the word, prayer, &c. Though we may, as that people, draw near with our lips, and ask of him our duty, and seem to delight to know him, yet there is this natural incapacity and crookedness in the heart of man, that it cannot truly approach unto the Father of spirits with any soul-desire and delight. But their hearts are removed far from me, Isa. xxix. 13, Matt. xv. 8. I think men might observe that their souls act not in religious business as they should, but that they remove their souls many miles distant from their bodies,—and they cannot keep any constancy in this approach of prayer to God, cannot walk with him in their conversation, or carry him along in their meditation. But there is one point of estrangement and separation superadded to all, that there is no man can come near to God without an oblation and offering of peace, that there is no approaching to him, but as to a continuing fire, except we can bring a sacrifice to appease, and a present to please Him for our infinite offences. There the difference stands,—we cannot draw near to walk together, till we be agreed. And, truly, this unto man is impossible, for we have nothing so precious as the redemption of our souls,—nothing can compense infinite wrongs, or satisfy infinite justice. Now, this seems to make our nearness again desperate, and to put men furthest off from hope.

Notwithstanding, this is the very purpose of the gospel, preached from the beginning of the world, to remove that distance, and to take impediments of meeting out of the way; for that great obstruction, the want of a sacrifice and ransom, the Lord hath supplied it, he himself hath furnished it; and it was the great design carried on from the beginning of the world. But as the sun, the nearer he is, the more the earth is enlightened: so here, first some dawning of light appears, as a messenger of hope, to tell that the Redeemer shall come,—that the true sacrifice shall be slain; then still the nearer his own appearing, the clearer are the manifestations of him, and the great design is more opened up, till at length he breaks out in glory from under a cloud, and shows himself to the world, to be that Lamb of God that should take away the sins of the world. And now, as the apostle to the Hebrews speaks, chap. vii. 19, "The law hath made nothing perfect, but the bringing in of a better hope did, by the which we draw nigh to God." All the sacrifices and shadows that were under the law did but point at this perfect ransom; and the way of access to God through a Mediator was not so clear; but now the matter is made as hopeful as is possible,—the partition-wall of the law's curses,—the hand-writing against us is removed on the cross,—the enmity slain,—the distance removed by the blood of the cross, being partly filled up by his descent into our nature, partly by his lower descent in our nature to suffer death. And this is the savoury oblation that we have to present to God, and may have boldness to come nigh because of it. And when once our access is made by the blood of Jesus Christ, then we are called and allowed to come still nigher, to cleave and adhere to him as our Father, to pray unto him, to walk with him. Then we should converse as friends and familiars together; then draw nigh to his light for illumination, and to him as the fountain of life for quickening, to place our delight and desire in him,—to forsake all other things, even our wills and pleasures, and to lose them, that they may be found in his; to converse much in his company, and be often in communication with him, and meditation upon him. This is the very design and substance of the gospel. It holds forth the way of making up the breach between man and God, of bringing you nigh who are yet afar off, and nearer who are near hand. O let us hearken to it!

SERMON VI.

Prov. xxvii. 1.—"Boast not thyself of to-morrow, for thou knowest not what a day may bring forth."

There are some peculiar gifts that God hath given to man in his first creation, and endued his nature with, beyond other living creatures, which being rightly ordered and improved towards the right objects, do advance the soul of man to a wonderful height of happiness, that no other sublunary creature is capable of. But by reason of man's fall into sin, these are quite disordered and turned out of the right channel; and, therefore, as the right improvement of them would make man happy, so the wrong employment of them loadens him with more real misery than any other creature. I mean, God hath given to man two notable capacities beyond other things;—one is, to know and reflect upon himself, and to consider what conveniency is in any thing towards himself,—what goodness or advantage redounds to himself from them, and in that reflection and comparison to enjoy what he hath; another is to look forward beyond the present time, and, as it were, to anticipate and prevent the slow motions of time, by a kind of foresight and providence. In a word, he is a creature framed unto more understanding than others, and so capable of more joy in present things, and more foresight of the time to come. He is made mortal, yet with an immortal spirit of an immortal capacity, that hath its eye upon the morrow,—upon eternity. Now, herein consists either man's happiness or misery, how he reflects upon himself, and what he chooseth for the matter of his joy and gloriation, and what providence he hath for the time to come. If those be rightly ordered, all is well; but if not, then woe unto him, there is more hope of a beast than of him.

Man's nature inclines to boasting—to glorying in something, and this ariseth from some apprehended excellency or advantage, and so is originated in the understanding power of man, which is far above beasts. Beasts find the things themselves, but they do not, they cannot reflect upon their own enjoyment of them, and therefore they are not capable of such pleasure; for the more distinct knowledge of things in relation to ourselves, the more delight ensueth upon it. Many creatures have singular qualities and virtues, but they are nothing the happier; for they know them not, and have no use of them, but are wholly destinated to the use of man, who therefore is only said to enjoy them, because he only is capable of joy from them. And this, I suppose, may give us a hint at the absolute incomprehensible blessedness, self-complacency, and delight of God. It cannot but be immeasurably great, seeing the knowledge of himself and all creatures is infinite; he comprehends all his own power, and virtue, and goodness, and therefore his delight and rejoicing is answerable. There is a glorying and boasting then that is good, which man is naturally framed unto; and this is that which David expresses, Psal. xxxiv. 2, "My soul shall make her boast in God;" and Psal. xliv. 8, "In God we boast all the day long, and praise thy name for ever." When the soul apprehends that all-sufficiency, and self-sufficient fulness of God; what infinite treasures of goodness, and wisdom, and power are in him, and so how suitable and convenient he is to the condition of the soul; what a sweet correspondence there is between his fulness and our emptiness—his mercy and our misery—his infiniteness and our unsuitableness; that there is in him to fill and overflow the soul: the apprehension of this cannot but in a manner perfume the soul with the delight. You find how the senses are refreshed, when they meet with their suitable object; how a pleasant smell refresheth the scent; how lively and beautiful colours are delightful to the eye. But much more here, God is the proportioned object of the immortal spirit; he corresponds to all its capacities, and fills it with unconceivable sweetness. But, my beloved, boasting and glorying in him, ariseth not only from the proportionableness and conveniency of him to our spirits; but this must be superadded,—propriety in him. Things are loved, because excellent in themselves, or because they are our own; but we boast in nothing, we glory in nothing, but because it is both excellent in itself, and ours besides. It is the apprehended interest in any thing makes the soul rise and lift up itself after this manner,—to have such a one to be ours,—such a Lord to be our God,—one so high and sublime,—one so universally full, to be made over to thee; here is the immediate rise of the soul's gloriation. And truly, as there is nothing can be so suitable a portion, so there is nothing that can be so truly made ours as God. Of all things a believer hath, there is nothing so much his own as God,—nothing so indissolubly tied unto him,—nothing so inseparably joined. See Paul's triumph upon that account, Rom. viii. Nothing can truly be said to be the soul's own, but that which is not only coetaneous with it, that survives mortality, and the changes of the body, but likewise is inseparable from it. What a poor empty sound is all that can be spoken of him, till your souls be once possessed of him! it cannot make your hearts leap within you, but it cannot but excite and stir up a believer's heart.

Now there may be a lawful kind of gloriation, rejoicing in the works of God, consequent to the first, which is a little stream from that greater river which runs out from it, and flows into it again. A soul that truly apprehends God will take delight to view the works of God, which make such an expression of him, and are a part of the magnificence of our heavenly Father. But this is all in reference to him and not to ourselves; for then it degenerates and loseth its sweetness, when once it turns the channel towards the adorning of the creature. True boasting in God hath necessarily conjoined with it an humble and low esteem of a man's self, Psal. xxxiv. 2, "The humble shall hear thereof, and be glad." As humility and self-emptiness made David go out of himself, to seek satisfaction in God, and having found it, he boasts and triumphs, so there were none capable of understanding his triumph, or partaking with him in his delights, but the humble souls. Now you may perceive how far this boasting here spoken of is degenerated from that, and so how far man's nature is spoiled,—"Boast not thyself," &c. The true boasting we were created unto, hath a sufficient foundation, even such as will bear the weight of triumph, but that which men's spirits are now naturally set upon, cannot carry, cannot sound such gloriation, and therefore this boasting makes men ridiculous. If you saw a man glorying in rags, setting forth himself to be admired in them, or boasting in some vain, despicable, and base thing, you would pity him, or laugh at him as one distempered. The truth is, the natural man is mad, hath lost his judgment, and is under the greatest distraction imaginable since the fall. That fall hath troubled his brains, and they are never settled, till the new creation come to put all right again, and compose the heart of man. I say, all other distractions are but particular, in respect to particular things, but there is a general distraction over all mankind, in reference to things of most general and most eternal concernment. Now, fools and mad persons, they retain the same affections and passions that are in men, as anger, love, hatred, grief, joy, &c., but it is so much the worse, since the judgment, which is the only directive and guide of them, is troubled. Now they are set on wrong objects, they run at random, and are under no kind of rule, and so they hurry the poor man and put him in a pitiful case. Now indeed so it is with us,—since sin entered, the soul is wholly turned off God, the only true object of delight, in which only there can be solid gloriation. The mind of man is blinded, and his passions are strong, and so they are now spent upon empty vanities, and carried headlong without judgment. Oftentimes he glories in that which is his shame, and boasts in that which is his sin, and which will cause nothing but shame, the more weight be laid upon it. There is in man an oblivion and forgetfulness of God, and in this darkness of the ignorance of God, everything is apprehended or misapprehended as present sense suggests, and as it fancies a conveniency or excellency. Thither the soul is carried, as if it were something, and then it is but the east-wind. There is nothing beside God that is a fit matter of boasting, because it lacks one of the essential ingredients—either it is not suitable to the soul, or it is not truly our own. There wants either proportion to the vast capacity and void of our desires, and so cannot fill up that really, but only in a deluding dream or imagination, and therefore will certainly make the issue rather vexation than gloriation, or there wants property and interest in them, for they are changeable and perishing in their own nature, and by divine appointment, that they cannot be conceived to be the proper good of the immortal soul. They cannot be truly our own, because they will shortly cease to be, and before they cease to be, they may in a moment cease to be ours. That tie of interest is a draw knot, whatsoever catcheth hold of the end of it looseth it.

The object of degenerate and vicious boasting is here held out: "Boast not thyself," or "of thyself." Whatsoever be the immediate matter of it, this is always the ultimate and principal object. Since man fell from God, self is the centre of all his affections and motions. This is the great idol, the Diana, that the heart worships, and all the contention, labour, clamour, and care that is among men, is about her silver shrines, so to speak, something relating to the adorning or setting forth this idol. It is true, since the heart is turned from that direct subordination to God, the affections are scattered and parted into infinite channels, and run towards innumerable objects, for the want of that original unity, which comprehends in its bosom universal plenty, must needs breed infinite variety, to supply the insatiable appetite of the soul. And this might be enough to convince you, that your souls are quite out of course, and altogether wandered from the way of happiness because they are poured out on such a multiplicity of insufficient, unsatisfying things, every one of which is narrow, limited and empty, and the combination and concurrence of all being a thing either impossible or improbable to be attained. But we may conceive that men's affections put themselves into three great heads of created things, one of which runs towards the goods or perfections of the mind, another towards the goods or advantages of the body, and a third towards those things that are without us, *bona fortunæ*, riches and honour, &c. Now each of these sends out many streams and rivulets as so many branches from it, but all of them, though they seem to have a direct course towards other things, yet wind about and make a circular progress to the great ocean of self-estimation, whence they issued at first.

You may find all of these, (Jer. ix. 23,) falling under a divine interdiction and curse, as being opposite to glorying in God. While men reflect within themselves, and behold some endowments and abilities in their minds beyond other men, of which wisdom is the principal, and here stands for all inward advantages or qualifications of the soul in that secret reflection and comparison, there is a tacit gloriation, which yet is a loud blasphemy in God's ears. It is impossible almost for a man to recognosce[275] and review his own parts such as ingine,[276] memory, understanding, sharpness of wit, readiness of expression, goodness and gentleness of nature, but that in such a review, the soul must be puffed up, apprehending some excellency beyond other men, and taking complacency in it, which are the two acts of robbery that are in gloriation and boasting. Commonly this arises from unequal comparisons. We please ourselves that we are *deterioribus meliores*, "better than the worst," and build self-estimation upon the ruins of other men's disadvantages, as if it were any point of praise in us that they are worse, like men that stand upon a height, and measure their own altitude, not from their just intrinsic quantity, but taking the advantage of the bottom, whereby we deceive our own selves. I remember a word of Solomon's, that imports how dangerous a thing it is for a man to reflect upon, or search into his own glory, Prov. xxv. 27. "It is not good to eat much honey, so for men to search their own glory is not glory."

To surfeit in the excess of honey or sweet things drives to vomit, and cloys the stomach, ver. 16. Though it be sweet, there is great need, yea, the more need of caution and moderation about it, so for a man either to search into his own breast, and reflect upon his own excellencies, to find matter of gloriation or studiously to affect it among others, and inquire into other men's account and esteem of him, it is no glory—it is a dangerous and shameful folly. Now this is not only incident to natural spirits, upon their consideration of their own advantages, but even to the most gracious, upon the review of spiritual endowments and prerogatives. It is such a subtile and insinuating poison that it spreads universally, and infects the most precious ointments of the soul, and, as it were, poisons the very antidote and counterpoison. So forcible is this that was first dropped into man's nature by Satan's envy, that it diffuses itself even into humility, and humiliation itself, and makes a man proud because of humility. The apostle found need to caveat this, Rom. xi. 18-20, "Boast not," "be not high minded, but fear,"—"thou standest by faith," and chap. xii. 16, "Mind not high things," "be not wise in your own conceits," and 1 Cor. viii. 2, "If any man think that he knoweth anything, he knoweth nothing as he ought to know." All which gives us a plain demonstration of this, that self gloriation and complacency, in reflection upon ourselves, is both the greatest ignorance and the worst sacrilege. It is an argument of greater ignorance for a man to think he knows than not to know indeed. It is the worst and most dangerous ignorance, to have such an opinion of our knowledge, gifts, and graces, for that puffs up, swells with empty wind, and makes a vain tumour and then it is great sacrilege, a robbing of the honour that is due to God. For what hast thou that thou hast not received? That appropriating of these things to ourselves as ours, is an impropriating of them from their right owner, that is, God, 1 Cor. iv. 7. For if thou didst apprehend that thou received it, where then is glorying? I would desire then, that whenever you happen to reflect upon yourselves, and observe any advantage, either natural or spiritual, in yourselves, that you may think this word sounds from heaven, "Let him that glorieth glory in the Lord." Let not the wise man glory in his wisdom, and so not the learned man in his learning, nor the eloquent man in his speaking nor the ingenious man in his quickness nor the good man in his goodness. All these things though sweet, yet will surfeit, gloriation in them is neither glory nor gain, neither honourable nor profitable.

Then the stream of gloriation flows in the channel of bodily gifts as might, strength of body, beauty and comeliness of parts, and other such endowments which, besides that it is as irrational as the former, is a sacrilegious impropriation of the most free and arbitrary gifts of God to ourselves, it is withal absurd, in that it is not so truly of ourselves. These bodily ornaments and endowments do not perfect or better a man as a man, they are but the alterable qualities of the vessel or tabernacle of a man, in which other baser creatures may far excel him. How many comely and beautiful souls are lodged within obscure and ugly cottages or bodies of clay, which will be taken down! And the great advantage is, that the soul of a man, which is a man, cannot be defiled from without, that is, from the body, though never so loathsome or deformed, the vilest body cannot mar the soul's beauty. But then, on the other hand, the most beautiful body is defiled and deformed by the filthiness of sin in the soul, and O how many deformed and ugly souls dwell in beautiful and comely bodies, which truly is no other thing than a devil in an image well carved and painted. Christians, you had need to correct this within you, even a self complacency, joined with despising of others in the consideration of those external gifts God hath given you. What an abominable thing is it to cast up in reproach, or in your hearts to despise any other for natural imperfections, such as blindness, lameness, deformity or such like? Let that word sound always in your ears, Who made thee to differ from another? "Boast not thyself, &c." But there is as strong a stream runs in the third channel as in any, gloriation arising from those outward and extrinsic differences that the providence of God makes among men, such as riches, honour, gain, &c. You find such men, Psalm xlix. 6, Prov. xviii. 11, and x. 15. That which a godly man makes the name of the Lord,—that is, the ground and foundation of his confidence for present and future times,—that the most part of men make their riches, that is, their strong city, and their high wall, their hope and expectation is reposed within it. This is the tower or wall of defence against the injuries and calamities of the times, which most part of men are building, and if it go up quickly, if they can get these several stones or pieces of gain scraped together into a heap they straightway imagine themselves safe, as under a high wall. But there is no truth in it, it is all but in their imagination, and therefore it comes often down about their ears, and offends them, instead of being a defence. Let a man creep, as it were, from off the ground where the poor lie, and get some advantage of ground above them, or be exalted to some dignity or office, and so set by the shoulders higher than the rest of the people, or yet grow in some more abundance of the things at this life, and strange it is, what a vanity or tumour of mind instantly follows! He presently thinks himself somebody, and forgetting either who is above him, to whom all are worms creeping and crawling on the footstool, or what a sandy foundation he stands upon himself, he begins to take some secret complacency in himself, and to look down upon others below him. He applauds, as it were, unto himself, and takes it in evil part to want the approbation and *plaudite* of others. Then he cannot so well endure affronts and injuries as before, he is not so meek and condescending to his equals or interiors. While he was poor he used entreaties, but now he answers roughly, (Prov. xviii. 23,) as Solomon gives the character of him. How many vain and empty gloriations are there about the point of birth and place, and what foolish contentions about these, as if it were children struggling among themselves about their order and rank! There is no worth in these things, but what fancy and custom impose upon them and yet poor creatures boast in these empty things. The gentlemen despise citizens, the citizens contemn the poor countrymen, and yet their bloods in a basin have no different colours, for all this hot contention about blood and birth. "Boast not of thyself." Nay, to speak properly, this is not thyself,—*Qui genus laudat suum, aliena jactat.*[277] Such parents, and such a house are nothing of thy own; these are mere extrinsic things, which are neither an honour to unworthy men, nor a disgrace to one who is worthy.

You see, beloved in the Lord, what is now the natural posture or inclination of our souls in this degenerate and fallen estate. As the rivers of paradise have changed their channels and course since the fall, so hath man's affections, and so hath his gloriation, so that it may be truly said, that our glory is our shame and not our glory. Many glory in iniquity and sin, (Psal. x. 3, and xciv. 4), but that shall undoubtedly be their shame and confusion before men and angels. How many godless persons will glory in swearing heinous and deep oaths, and some have contended about the victory in it! You account it a point of gallantry, but this triumph is like the devils in hell upon the devouring of souls. Some boast of drinking, and being able to drink others under the table, but we should be humbled and mourn for such abominations. Certain I am, that many boast of wicked designs, and malicious projects against their neighbours, if they can accomplish them. They account their glory not to take a wrong without giving a greater, nor to suffer an evil word without twenty worse in recompense. Alas! this boasting will one day be turned into gnashing of teeth, and this gloriation into that gnawing and ever-tormenting worm of conscience. And what will ye do in the day of that visitation? And where shall be your glory? But the most part glory and boast in things that profit not, and will become their shame, because they glory in them, that is, those gifts of God, outward or inward, temporal or spiritual, wherein there is any advancement above others; unto whom I would seriously commend this sentence to be pondered duly, "Boast not" of thyself. Whatsoever thou art, or whatsoever thou hast, boast not of thyself for it, think not much of thyself because of it. Though there be a difference in God's donation, yet let there be none in thy self estimation. Hast thou more wisdom and pregnancy of wit, or more learning than another? Think not more of thyself for that, than thou thinkest of the ignorant and unlearned who want it. Have that same reflection upon thine own unworthiness, that thou would think reasonable another that wants these endowments should have. Is there a greater measure of grace in thee? Boast not, reckon of thyself as abstracted and denuded of that, and let it not add to thy value or account of thyself, put not in that to make it down weight, and to make thee prefer thyself secretly to another. Whether it be some larger fortune in the world, or some higher place and station among men, or some abilities and perfections of body or mind, which may entice thee secretly to kiss thy hand, and bow down to thyself, yet remember that thou boast not, glory not in any thing but in the Lord. Let nothing of that kind conciliate more affection to thyself, or more contempt toward others. Let not any thing of that kind be the rule of thy self judging, but rather entertain the view of the other side of thyself, that is the worst, and keep that most in thy eye, that thou may only glory in God. If thou be a gentleman, labour to be as humble in heart as thou thinkest a countryman or poor tenant should be, if thou be a scholar, be as low in thy own sight as the unlearned should be, if rich, count not thyself any whit better than the poor, yea, the higher God sets thee in place, or parts, the lower thou oughtest to set thyself. "Boast not" of thyself, nor any thing in thyself, or belonging to thyself, for the property of all good is taken from us since the fall, and is fallen into

God's hand since we forfeited it, and there is nothing now properly ours but evil,—that is our self.

SERMON VII.

Prov. xxvii. 1.—"Boast not thyself of to morrow, for thou knowest not what a day may bring forth."

As man is naturally given to boasting and gloriation in something (for the heart cannot want some object to rest upon and take complacency in, it is framed with such a capacity of employing other things), so there is a strong inclination in man towards the time to come, he hath an immortal appetite, and an appetite of immortality; and therefore his desires usually stretch farther than the present hour, and the more knowledge he hath above other creatures, the more providence he hath and foresight of the time to come. And so he often anticipates future things by present joy and rejoicing in them, as he accelerates in a manner by his earnest desires and endeavours after them. Now, if the soul of man were in the primitive integrity, and had as clear and piercing an eye of understanding as once it had, this providence of the soul would reach to the furthest period in time, that is, to eternity, which is the only just measure of the endurance of any immortal spirit. But since the eye of man's understanding is darkness, and his soul disordered, he cannot see afar off, nor so clearly by far. He is now, as you say, sand blind,—can see nothing at such a distance as beyond the bounds of time, can see nothing but at hand.

"To-morrow!" This is the narrow sphere of poor man's comprehension, all he can attain unto is to be provident for the present time. I call it ill present, even that which is to come of our time, because, in regard of eternity, it hath no parts, it hath no flux or succession, it is so soon cut off as a moment, as the twinkling of an eye, and so, though a man could see the end of it, it is but a short and dim sight, it is as if a man could only behold that which is almost contiguous with his eye. These, then, are the two great ruins and decays of the nature of man, he is degenerated from God to created things, and seeks his joy and rest in them, in which there is nothing but the contrary, that is, vexation. And then he is fallen from apprehension of eternity, and the poor soul is confined within the narrow bounds of time, so that now all his providence is to lay up some perishing things for some few revolutions of the sun, for some few morrows, after which, though an endless morrow ensue, yet he perceives it not, and provides not for it, and all his glorying and boasting is only upon some presumptuous confidence and ungrounded assurance of the stability of these things for the time to come, which the wise man finding much folly in, he leaves us this counsel, "Boast not thyself of to-morrow,"—with a most pungent reason, taken partly from the instability and inconstancy of all these outward things in which men fancy an eternity of joy, and partly from the ignorance we have of the future events,—"for thou knowest not what a day may bring forth."

This boasting is an evil so predominant among men, that I know not any more universal in its dominion, or more hurtful to us, or displeasing to God. If it could be so embowelled unto you, as that you might truly discern the many monstrous conceptions of atheism and irreligion that are in it, it were worth the while, but I shall not digress upon the general head, I had rather keep within the limits of the text. Self boasting, you see, is that which is here condemned, and the very name is almost enough to condemn the nature of it. But there is another particular added to restrict that, "of to-morrow." Of all boastings the most irrational and groundless is that which arises from presumption of future things, which are so uncertain both in themselves and to us.

It is worth the observation, that whatever be the immediate and particular matter and occasion of men's gloriation, yet self is the great and ultimate object of it; it is self that men glory in, whatsoever created thing be the reason or occasion of it. "Boast not thyself of to morrow." Here we might stand and take a look of the crookedness and perverseness of man's spirit since his departure from God. Self love and pride were the first poison that the malice of Satan dropped into man's nature, and this is so strong and pestilent, that it has spread through the whole of mankind, and the whole in every man. Every one is infected, and all in every one. What are all the disordered affections in men but so many streams from this fountain? And from these do men's affections flow next, so that there is nothing left uncorrupted, and free of this abominable and vile ingredient, all flowing from self and returning to it again, which is both sacrilegious and unnatural. There is heinous sacrilege in it,—the spoiling of the glorious divine Majesty of his indubitable prerogative and incommunicable right of all the glory, and honour of his creature. There is no usurpation like this for the worm that crawls on the footstool to creep up to the throne, and, as it were, to king it there, to deify and adore itself, and gather in all the tribute of praise and glory and love, that is only due to the Lord God Almighty; and invert and appropriate these to ourselves, which is, as if the axe should boast itself, as if it were no iron, or the staff, as if it were no timber. Hence it is, that of all evils in man's nature, God hath the most perfect antipathy and direct opposition against pride and self love, because it is sacrilege and idolatry in the highest manner. It strikes at the sovereignty and honour of God's name, which is dear to him as himself, it sets up a vile idol in the choicest temple of God, that is, in the heart, and this is the abomination of desolation. Other evils strike against his holy will, but this peculiarly points at the very nature and being of the most high God, and so it is with child of blasphemy,—atheism is the very heart and life of it. And then it is most unnatural, and so monstrous and deformed. For, consider all the creation, though every one of them have particular inclinations towards their own proper ends, and so a happiness suitable to their own nature; yet how diverse, how contrary soever they be, there is no selfishness in them, they all concur and conspire to the good of the whole, and the mutual help of each other. If once that poison should infect the material world, which hath spoiled the spiritual; let once such a selfish disposition or inclination possess any part of the world, and presently the order, harmony, beauty, pleasure, and profit of the whole world should be interrupted, defaced, and destroyed. Let the sun be supposed to boast itself of its light and influence, and so disdain to impart it to the lower world, and all would run into confusion. Again, I desire you but to take a view of this humour in another's person, (for we are more ready to see others evils than our own,) and how deformed is it? So vile is self-seeking and self boasting, that all men loathe it in others, and hide it from others. It disgraces all actions, how beautiful soever, it is the very bane of human society, that which looses all the links of it, and makes them cross and thwart one another.

But, alas! how much more easy is it, to point out such an evil in a deformed visage, than to discern it in ourselves, and how many will hate it in the picture, who love and entertain it in their own persons! Such deceitfulness is intermingled with most desperate wickedness. I verily believe that it is the predominant of every man, good and bad, except in so far as it is mortified by grace. O the turnings and windings of the heart upon itself, in all the most apparently direct motions towards God and the good of men! What serpentine and crooked circumgirations and reflections are there in the soul of man when the outward action and expression seems most regular and directed towards God's glory, and others edification! Whoever of you have any acquaintance with your own spirits cannot but know this, and be ashamed and confounded at the very thought of it. Self boasting, self complacency, self seeking, all those being of kin one to another, are insinuated into your best notions, and infect them with more atheism before God, than the strongest pious affection can instil of goodness into them. How often will men's actions and expressions be outwardly clothed with a habit of condescendency and self-denial! And many may declaim with such zeal and vehemency against this evil, and yet, *latet anquis*, the serpent is in the bosom and his venom may be diffused into the heart, and the poison of self-seeking and self-boasting may run through the veins of humble-like carriage and passionate discourses for self denial. O that we could above all things establish that fundamental principle of Christianity in our hearts, even as we would be his disciples, truly and sincerely, and not in outward resemblance,—to deny ourselves, to renounce ourselves and our lusts, to make a whole resignation of our love, will, glory, and all to him, in whom to be lost it is only truly to find ourselves.

But, though man have this strange self idolizing humour, and a self glorying disposition, yet he is so poor and beggarly a creature, that he hath not sufficient matter within himself to give complacency to his heart, therefore he must borrow from all external things, and when there is any kind of propriety in, or title to them, then he glories in himself for them, as if they were truly in himself. We are creatures by nature most indigent, yet most proud, which is unnatural. No man is satisfied within himself (except the good man, Prov. xiv. 14), but he goes abroad to seek it at the door of every creature, and when there are some plumes or feathers borrowed from other birds, like that foolish bird in the fable, we begin to raise our crests, and boast ourselves, as if we had all these of our own, and were beholden to none, but as things that are truly our own will not be sufficient to feed this flame of gloriation, without the accession of outward things; so present things, and the present time, will not afford aliment enough, or fuel for this humour, without the addition of the morrow.

"Boast not thyself of to-morrow." No man's present possession satisfies him, without the addition of hope and expectation for the future, and herein the poverty of man's spirit appears, and the emptiness of all things we enjoy here, that our present revenue, as it were, will not content the heart. The present possession fills not up the vacuities of the heart, without the supply of our imaginations, by taking so much in upon the head of the morrow, to speak so. As one prodigal and riotous waster, who cannot be served with his yearly income, but takes so much on upon his estate, upon the next year's income, before it come, begins to spend upon it, before it come itself, and then, when it comes, it cannot suffice itself, so the insatiable and indigent heart of man cannot subsist and feed its joy in complacency upon the whole world, if it were presently in its possession, without some accession of hopes and expectations for the time to come. Therefore the soul, as it were, anticipates and forestalls the morrow, and borrows so much present joy and boasting upon the head of it, which when it comes itself, perhaps it will not fill the hand of the reaper, let be[278] pay for that debt of gloriation that was taken on upon its name, or compense the expectation which was in it, see Job xi. 18, 20, viii. 13. Hope is like a man's house to him, but to many it is no better than a spider's web. We have then a clear demonstration of the madness and folly of men, who hang so much upon things without, and suffer themselves to be moulded and modelled in their affections, according to the variety of external accidents. First of all, consider the independence of all things upon us and our choice; there is nothing more unreasonable than to stir our passions upon that which falls not under our deliberation, as the most part of things to come are. What shall be to-morrow, what shall come of my estate, of my places; what event my projects and designs shall have,—this is not in my hand, these depend upon other men's wills, purposes, and actions, which are not in my power, and therefore, either to boast of glory upon that which depends upon the concurrence of so many causes unsubordinate to me, or to be vexed and disquieted upon the fore-apprehension of that which is not in my hand to prevent, is not only irreligious, as contrary to our Saviour's command, Matt. vi. 25, but unreasonable also, as that which even nature condemns. "Take not thought for to-morrow," and so by consequent, "Boast not thyself of to-morrow," and there is one argument from the vanity of such affections. "Thou canst not make one hair black, nor add one cubit to thy stature," &c. To what purpose, then, are either those vexations or gloriations, which cannot prevent evil, nor procure good? Why should our affections depend upon others motions? This makes a man the greatest slave and captive, so that he hath not the dominion and power of himself. But the vanity of such affections is the more increased, if we consider that supreme eternal will, by which all these things are determined, and therefore, it is in vain for creatures to make themselves more miserable, or put themselves in a fool's paradise, which will produce more misery afterwards, and that, for those things which are bound up in that fatal chain of his eternal purpose. Then, in the next place, the folly of men appears from the inconstancy of these things. There is such an infinite variety of the accidents of providence, that it is folly for a man to presume to boast of any thing, or take complacency in it, because many things fall between the cup and the lip,[279] the chalice and the chin, as the proverb is. There is nothing certain, but that all things are uncertain,—that all things are subject to perpetual motion, revolution, and change,—to-day a city, to-morrow a heap. And there is nothing between a great city and a heap but one day, nothing between a man and no man but one hour. Our life is subject to infinite casualties, it may receive the fatal stroke from the meanest thing, and most unexpected, it is a bubble floating upon the water, for this world is a watery element, in continual motion with storm; and in these, so many poor dying creatures rise up, and swim and float awhile, and are tossed up and down by the wind and wave; and the least puff of wind or drop of rain sends it back to its own element. We are a vapour appearing for a very little time—a creature of no solidity—a dream—a shadow and appearance of something; and this dream or apparition is but for a little time, and then it evanisheth, not so much into nothing, for it was little distant from nothing before, but it disappears rather. All human affairs are like the spokes of a wheel, in such a continual circumgiration, as a captive king, who was drawing Sesostris's chariot, said, when he was looking often behind him. The king of Egypt, Sesostris, demanded for what end did he look so often about him? Says he, "I am looking to the wheel, musing upon the vicissitudes and permutations of it, how the highest parts are instantly the lowest." And this word repressed the king's vain glory.[280] Now, in this constant wheeling of outward things, which is the soul that enjoys true quiet and peace? Even that soul that is fixed, as it were, in the centre upon God, that hath its abode in him; though the parts without be in a continual violent motion, yet the centre of the wheel is at much peace, is not violently turned, but gently complies to the changes of the other. And then consider the madness of this,—"Thou knowest not, &c." There are two reasons in the things themselves,—inconstancy, and independency on us; but this is as pressing as any,—our ignorance of them; they are wholly in the dark to us, as it were in the lower parts of the earth. As there is no more in our power but the present hour,—for to yesterday we are dead already, for it is past and cannot return, it is as it were buried in the grave of oblivion, and to-morrow we are not yet born, for it is not come to the light, and we know not if ever it will come,—so there is no more in our knowledge but the present hour. The time past, though we remember it, yet it is without our practical knowledge, it admits of no reformation by it; and the time to come is not born to us, and it is all one as if we were not born to it. And indeed, in the Lord's disposing of all affairs under the sun, after this method, there is infinite wisdom and goodness both, though at the first view men would think it better that all things went on after an uniform manner, and that men knew what were to befall them. Yet, I say, God hath herein provided for his own glory and the good of men,—his own glory, while he hath reserved to himself the absolute dominion and perfect knowledge of his works, and exercises them in so great variety, that they may be seen to proceed from him; and for our good,—for what place were there for the exercise of many Christian virtues and graces, if it were not so? What place for patience, if there were no cross dispensations? What place for moderation, if there were no prosperity? If there were not such variety and vicissitude, how should the evenness and constancy of the spirit be known? Where should contentment and tranquillity of mind have place? For it is a calm in a storm properly, not a calm in a calm,—that is no virtue. If the several accidents of providence were foreseen by us, what a marvellous perturbation and disorder would it make in our duty! Who would do his duty out of conscience to God's command, to commit events to him? Now, there is the trial of obedience, to make us go by a way we know not, and resign ourselves to the all seeing providence, whose eyes run to and fro throughout the earth. Therefore that no grace may want matter and occasion of exercise; that no virtue may die out for want of fuel, or rust for lack of exercise, God hath thus ordered and disposed the world. There is no condition, no posture of affairs, in which he hath not left a fair opportunity for the exercising of some grace. Hath he shut up and precluded the acting of one or many through affliction, then surely he hath opened a wide door, and given large matter for self denial, humility, patience, moderation, and these are as precious as any that look fairest. In a word, I think the very frame and method of the disposing of this material world speaks aloud to this purpose. You see, when you look below, there is nothing seen but the outside of the earth, the very surface of it only appears, and there your sight is terminated, but look above, and there is no termination, no bounding of the sight,—there are infinite spaces, all are transparent and clear without and within. Now, what may this present unto us? One says, it shows us that our affections should be set upon things above and not on things below, seeing below there is nothing but an outward appearance and surface of things,—the glory and beauty of the earth is but skin deep, but heavenly things are alike throughout, all transparent, nothing to set bounds to the affections; they are infinite, and you may enlarge infinitely towards them. I add this other consideration, that God hath made all things in time dark and opaque, like the earth. Look to them, you see only the outside of them, the present hour, and what is beyond it you know no more, than you see the bowels of the earth, but eternity is both transparent and conspicuous throughout, and infinite too. Therefore God hath made us blind to the one, that we should not set our heart, nor terminate our eyes upon any thing here, but he hath opened and spread eternity before us in the scriptures, so that you may read and understand your fortune,—your everlasting estate in it. He hath shut up temporal things and sealed them, and wills us to live implicitly, and give him the trust of them without anxious foresight, but eternity he hath unveiled and opened unto us. Certain it is, that no man, till he be fully possessed of God, who is an all sufficient good (Psal. iv.) can find any satisfaction in any present enjoyment, without the addition of some hope for the future. Great things without it will not content. For what is it all to a man if he have no assurance for the time to come? And mean things with it will content. Great things with little hope and expectation, fill with more vexation instead of joy, and the greater they be, this is the more increased. Again, mean and low things, with great hopes and large expectations, will give more satisfaction, therefore, all mankind have a look towards the morrow, and labour to supply their present defects and wants, with hope or confidence of that. I would exhort you who would indeed have solid matter of gloriation, and would not be befooled into a golden dream of vain expectations of vain things, that ye would labour to fill up the vacuities of present things with that great hope, the hope of salvation, which will be as an helmet to keep your head safe in all difficulties, 1 Pet. i. 3, Heb. vi. 18, 19, Rom. v. 5. It is true, other men's expectations of gain and credit, and such things, do in some measure abate the torment and pain of present wants and indigencies, but certain it is, that such hope is not so sovereign a cordial to the heart, as to expel all grief, but leaves much vexation within. But then also, the frequent disappointment of such projects and designs of gain, honour, and pleasure, and the extreme unanswerableness of these to the desires and hopes of the soul, even when attained, must needs breed infinitely more anxiety and vexation in the spirit, than the hope of them could give of satisfaction, yea the more the expectation was, it cannot choose but the greater shame and confusion must be. Therefore, if you would have your souls truly established, and not hanging upon the morrow uncertainly, as the most part of men are get a look beyond the morrow, unto that everlasting day of eternity, that hath no morrow[281] after it, and see what foundation you can lay up for that time to come, as Paul bids Timothy counsel the rich men in the world, who thought their riches and revenues, their offices and dignities, a foundation and well spring of contentment to them and their children, and are ready to say with that man in the parable, "Soul take thy rest, thou hast enough laid up for many years." "Charge them, says he," &c. 1 Tim. vi. 16-19. O a charge worthy to be engraven on the tables of our hearts, worthy to be written on the ports of all cities, and the gates of all palaces. You would all have a foundation of lasting joy, says he, but why seek you lasting joy in fading things, and certain joy in uncertain riches, and solid contentment in empty things, and not rather in the living God, who is the unexhausted spring of all good things? Therefore, if you would truly boast of to-morrow, or sing a solid *requiem* to your own hearts, there is another treasure to be laid up in store against the time to come,—the time only worthy to be called time, that is eternity, and that is study to do good, and be rich in good works, in works of piety, of mercy, of equity, of sobriety. This is a better foundation for the time to come, or, rather receive and embrace the promise of eternal life made to such,—that free and gracious promise of life in the gospel, and so you may supply all the wants and indigencies of your present enjoyments, with the precious hope of eternal life which cannot make ashamed. But what is the way that the most part of men take to mitigate and sweeten their present hardships? Even like that of the fool in the parable Luke xii. They either have something laid up for many years, or else their projects and designs reach to many years. The truth is, they have more pleasure in the expectation of such things, than in the real possession, but that pleasure is but imaginary also. How many thoughts and designs are continually turning in the heart of man,—how to be rich, how to get greater gain, or more credit? Men build castles in the air, and fancy to themselves, as it were, new worlds of mere possible things, and in such an employment of the heart, there is some poor deceiving of present sorrows, but at length they recur with greater violence. Every man makes romances for himself, pretty fancies of his own fortune, as if he had the disposing of it himself. He sits down, as it were, and writes an almanack and prognostication in his own secret thoughts, and designs his own prosperity, gain, and advantage, and pleasures or joys, and when we have thus ranked our hopes and expectation, then we begin to take complacency in them, and boast ourselves in the confidence of them, as if there were not a supreme Lord who gives a law to our affairs, as immediately as to the winds and rains.

Now, that you may know the folly of this, consider the reason which is subjoined,—"For thou knowest not what a day may bring forth." There is a concurrence of inconstancy in all things, and ignorance in us, which might be sufficient to check our folly of confident and presumptuous expectation from them, and gloriation in them, so that, whether we look about us to the things themselves, or within us to ourselves, all things proclaim the folly and madness of that which the heart of man is set upon. And this double consideration the apostle James opposes to the vain hopes and confident undertakings of men, chap. iv. 13, &c., which place is a perfect commentary upon this text, he brings in an instance of the resolutions and purposes of rich men, for the compassing of gain by merchandise, whereby you may understand all the several designs and plots of men, that are contrived and ordered, and laid down in the hearts of men, either for more gain, or more glory, or more pleasure and ease. Now, the grand evil that is here reproved, is not simply men's care and diligence in using lawful means for their accommodation in this life, or yet their wise and prudent foresight in ordering of their affairs for attaining that end, for both these are frequently recommended and commended by the wise man Prov. vi. 6, and xxiv. 27. But here is the great iniquity,—that men in all these contrivings and actings, carry themselves as if they were absolute independents, without consideration of the sovereign universal dominion of God. No man almost reflects upon that glorious Being, which alone hath the negative and definitive sentence in all the motions and affairs of the sons of men, or considers, that it is not in man that walks to direct his paths; that when all our thoughts and designs are marshalled and ordered, and the completest preparation made for reaching our intended ends, that yet the way of man is not in himself, that all these things are under a higher and more absolute dominion of the most high God. Whose heart doth that often sound unto,—"A man's heart deviseth his way, but the Lord directeth his steps," and so is not bound by any rule to conform his executions to our intentions? For he works all according to the counsel of his own will, and not ours, and therefore, no wonder that the product of our actions does not answer our intentions and devices, because the supreme rule and measure of them is above our power, and without our knowledge. And therefore, though there were never so many devices in the heart of man, never so wisely or lawfully contrived and ordered, though the mine be never so well prepared, and all ready for the firing of it, yet the counsel of the Lord, that shall stand, Prov. xix. 21, and xvi. 9. That higher determination may blow up our best consultations or drown them, for man's goings are of the Lord, how then can a man understand his paths? Prov. xx. 24. And yet the most part of men, in all these things, lose the remembrance of this fatal and invincible subordination to God, and propose their own affairs and actions, as if themselves were to dispose of them, and when their own resolutions and projects seem probable, they begin to please themselves in them, in the forethought of what they will do, or what they may have or enjoy to morrow afterward; there is a present secret complacency and gloriation, without any serious reminding the absolute dependence of all things upon the will of God, and their independence upon our counsels without forecasting and often ruminating upon the perpetual fluctuation and inconstancy of human affairs, but, as if we were the supreme moderators in heaven and earth, so we act and transact our own business in a deep forgetfulness of him who sits in heaven, and laughs at all our projects and practices and therefore, the Holy Ghost would have this secret but serious thought to season all our other purposes and consultations,—"If the Lord will," &c. Whereas though we ought to say and think this, it is scarce minded, and then we know not what shall be to morrow for our life itself is a vapour. Herein is a strong argument,—you lay your designs for to morrow, for a year, for many years, and yet ye know not if ye shall be to morrow. How many men's projects are cast beyond that time that is measured out on God's counsel! And what a ridiculous thing must that be to him, if it be not done with submissive and humble dependence on him! In a word time is with child of innumerable things, conceived by the eternal counsel of God. Infinite and inconceivably various are those conceptions which the womb of time shall at length bring forth to light. Every day, every hour, every minute is travailing in pain, as it were, and is delivered of some one birth or another, and no creature can open its womb sooner, or shut it longer, than the appointed and prefixed season. There is no miscarrying as to him whose decrees do properly conceive them though to us they seem often abortive. Now, join unto this, to make the allusion full, as long as they are carried in the womb of time, they are hid from all the world. The womb is a dark lodging and no understanding nor eye can pierce into it, to tell what is in it, till it break forth, and therefore, children born are said to come to the light, for till then, they are to us in a cloud of darkness, that we cannot tell what they are. So then, every day, every hour, every moment is about to bring forth that which all the world is ignorant of, till they see it, and oh! that then they understood it. We know not whether the morrow's or next hour's birth may be a proportioned child, or a monster, whether it will answer the figure and mould that is in our mind, or be misshapen and deformed to our sense. Men's desires and designs may be said to conceive, for they form an inward image and idea within themselves, to which they labour to make the product and birth of time conformable, and when it answers our preconceived form, then we rejoice as for a man child. But for the most part it is a monster as to our conception, it is an aberration from our rule, it is either mutilated and defective of what we desire, or superfluous or deformed, which turns our expectation into vexation, and our boasting into lamentation. But the truth is, time brings forth no monsters as to the Lord's decrees, which are the only just measures of all things. It may be said of every thing under the sun, as David speaks of himself in the womb, "My substance was not hid from thee, when I was made in secret, and curiously formed in the lowest parts of the earth," &c. Psal. cxxxix. 15. His eyes see all their substance, yet being unperfect, and in his everlasting book all their members are written, the portraiture of every thing is drawn there to the life, and these in continuance are fashioned just as they were written and drawn, and so they exactly correspond to his preconception of them, whatever deformity they may have as to us, yet they are perfect works, and beautiful to him.

SERMON VIII.

Isaiah i. 10, 11, &c.—"Hear the word of the Lord, ye rulers of Sodom, give ear unto the law of our God, ye people of Gomorrah," &c.

It is strange to think what mercy is mixed with the most wrath like strokes and threatenings. There is no prophet whose office and commission is only for judgment, nay, to speak the truth, it is mercy that premises threatenings. The entering of the law, both in the commands and curses, is to make sin abound, that grace may superabound, so that both rods and threatenings are the messengers of Jesus Christ, to bring sinners to him for salvation. Every thing should be measured and named by its end, so, call threatenings promises, call rods and judgments mercies, name all good, and good to you, if so be you understand the purpose of God in these. The shortest preaching in the Bible useth to express itself what it means, though it be never so terrible. This is a sad and lamentable beginning of a prophet's ministry, the first word is, to the heavens and to the earth[282] a weighty and horrible regrate[283] of this people, as if none of them were to hear, as if the earth could be more easily affected than they. The creatures are taken witnesses by God of their ingratitude, and then who shall speak for them? If heaven and earth be against them, who shall speak good of them? Will their own conscience? No certainly, it will, in the day of witnessing and judging, precipitate its sentence, and spare the judge the labour of probation, "a man's enemy shall be within his own house," though now your consciences agree with you. Nay, why doth the Lord speak to them? Because the people consider not, because consciences have given over speaking to them, therefore the Lord directs his word to the dumb earth. Yet how gracious is he, as to direct a second word even to the people, though a sad word? It is a complaint of iniquity and backsliding, and such as cannot be uttered, yet it is mercy to challenge them, yea, to chasten them. If the Lord would threaten a man with pure and unmixed judgments, if he would frame a threatening of a rod of pure justice, I think it should be this, "I will no more reprove thee, nor chasten thee," and he is not far from it, when he says, "Why shall ye be stricken any more?" &c. ver. 5. As if he would say, It is in vain now to send a rod, ye receive no correction. I sent the rod, that it might open your hearts and ears to the word, and seal your instruction,—but to what purpose is it?—Ye grow worse and worse. Well, the prophet compares here sin and judgment, and the one far surmounts the other. Ye would think a desolate country, burnt cities, desolation made by strangers, a sufficient recompense of their corruption and misorders, of their forsaking and backsliding. Ye would think now, if your present condition and the land's pressed you to utter Jeremiah's lamentation, a sadder than which is not almost imaginable, ye would think, I say, that you had received double for all your sins. And yet, alas! how are your iniquities of infinite more desert? All that were mercy, which is behind infinite and eternal punishment. That there is room left for complaint, is mercy, that there is a remnant left, is mercy.

Now, to proclaim unto this people, and convince them that their judgment was not severe, he gives them one word from God. And, indeed, it is strange, that when the rod is sent, because of the despising of the word, that after the despising of both word and rod, another word should come. Always this word is a convincing word, a directing word, and a comforting word. These use to be conjoined, and if they be not always expressed, we may lawfully understand them. We may join a consolation to a conviction, and close a threatening with a promise, if we take with a threatening. Jonah's preaching expressed no more but a threatening and denunciation of judgment, but the people understood it according to God's meaning and made it a rule of direction, and so a ground of consolation. How inexcusable are we, who have all these expressed unto us, and often inculcated, "line upon line, and precept upon precept," and yet so often divide the word of truth, or neglect it altogether. Most part fancy a belief of the promises and neither consider threatenings nor commands. Some believing the threatenings, are not so wise for their own salvation as to consider what God says more, but take it for his last word. Shall not Nineveh rise up in judgment against this generation? They repented at one preaching, and that a short one, and in appearance very defective, and yet we have many preachings of the Son of God and his apostles in this Bible,—both law and gospel holden forth distinctly, and these spoken daily in our audience, and yet we repent not.

This is a strange preface going before this preaching, and more strange in that it is before the first preaching of a young prophet. He speaks both to rulers and people, but he gives them a name such as certainly they would not take to themselves, but seeing he is to speak the word of the Lord, he must not flatter them, as they did themselves. Is not this the Lord's people, his portion and inheritance which he chose out of the nations? Are not these rulers the princes of Judah, and the Lord's anointed? Were they not both in covenant with God, and separated from the nations both in privileges and profession? How then are they "rulers of Sodom" and "people of Gomorrah" likened to the worst of the nations, and not likened to them but spoken of as if they were indeed all one. When ye hear the preface ye would think that the prophet was about to direct his speech to Sodom and Gomorrah, but when you look upon the preaching ye find he means Judah and Jerusalem, and these are the rulers and people he speaks of. Certainly, according as men walk, so shall they be named and ranked. External privileges and profession may give a name before men, and separate men from men before the world, but they give no name, make no difference, before God, if all other things be not suitable to these. "He is not a Jew, saith Paul, who is one outwardly," but he who hath that circumcision in the heart, in the spirit, and not in the letter. Outward profession and signs may have praise of men, but it is this that hath praise of God, Rom. ii. 28, 29. Circumcision and uncircumcision, baptism or unbaptism, availeth nothing, but a new creature. A baptized Christian and an unbaptized Turk are alike before God, if their hearts and ways be one, Gal. vi. 15. All Christians profess faith, and glory in baptism, but it avails nothing except it work by love, Gal. v. 6.

Now, what name shall we give you? How shall our rulers be called? How shall ye, the people, be called? If we shall speak the truth, we fear it will instruct you not, but irritate you, yet the truth we must speak, whether ye choose or whether ye refuse. You would all be called Christians, the people of God, but we may not call you so, except we would flatter you, and deceive you by flattering, and murder you by deceiving. We would gladly name you Christians in the spirit, saints chosen and precious. O that we might speak so to rulers and people! but, alas, we may not call you so except ye were so indeed, we may not call you Christians lest ye believe yourselves to be so. And yet, alas, ye will think yourselves such, speak what we can. Would you know your name then? I perceive you listen to hear what it is. But understand, that it is your name before God, which bears his account of you. What matter of a name among men? It is often a shadow without substance, a name without the thing. If God name you otherwise, you shall have little either honour or comfort in it, when men bless you and praise you, if the Lord reckon you among the beasts that perish, are ye honoured indeed? Well, then, hear your name before God. What account hath he of you? Ye rulers are rulers of Sodom, and ye people are people of Gomorrah. And if ye think this a hard saying, I desire you will notice the way that the prophet Isaiah takes to prove his challenge against them, and the same may be alleged against rulers and people now. We need no proof but one of both, see ver. 23,—"Thy princes are rebellious, because, though they hear much against their sins, yet they never amend them, they pull away their shoulder, if they hear, yet they harden their heart." Is there any of them hath set to pray in their families, though earnestly pressed? Well, what follows? "Every one loves gifts." Covetousness, then, and oppression proves rulers to be rulers of Sodom. Shall then houses stand, "shalt thou reign, because thou closest thyself in cedar?" Jer. xxii. 15. No certainly, men shall one day take up a proverb against them. "Woe to him that increaseth that which is not his, and ladeth himself with thick clay, they shall be for booties to the Lord's spoilers," Hab. ii. 6. Woe to them, for they have consulted shame to their houses, and sinned against their own soul. Their design is to establish their house, and make it eminent, but they take a compendious way to shame and ruin it. Alas, it is too public, that rulers seek their own things, for themselves and their friends, and for Jesus and his interests they are not concerned. But are ye, the people, any whit better? O that it were so! But alas, when ye are involved in the same guiltiness, I fear ye partake of their plagues! What are ye then? "People of Gomorrah." Is not the name of God blasphemed daily because of you? Are not the abominations of the Gentiles the common disease of the multitude, and the very reproach of Christianity? Set apart your public services and professions, and is there any thing behind in your conversation, but drunkenness, lying, swearing, contention, envy, deceit, wrath, covetousness, and such like? Have not the multitude of them been as civil, and carried themselves as blamelessly, and without offence, as the throng of our visible church? What have ye more than they? It is true, ye are called Christians, and ye boast in it. Ye know his will, and can speak of points of religion, can teach and instruct others, and so have, as it were, in your minds a form and method of knowledge,—the best of you are but such. But I ask, as Paul did the Jews in such a case, "Thou that teachest another, teachest thou not thyself? Thou that makest a boast of the law, through breaking of it, dishonourest thou God?" Rom. ii. 17-23. Why then, certainly all thy profession and baptism avail nothing, and will never extract thee from the pagans, with whom thou art one in conversation. Thy profession is so far from helping thee in such a case, that it shall be the most bitter ingredient in thy cup of judgment, for it is the greatest aggravation of thy sin, for through it God's name is blasphemed. If they had not known, they had not had sin. Pagan's sin is no sin in respect of Christians. If ye consider Christ's sermon, Matt. xi., ye will say Isaiah is a meek and moderate man in regard of him. Isaiah calls them people of Gomorrah, but Christ will have them worse, and their judgment more intolerable than theirs. And that not only the profane of them, but the civil and religious like who believe not in him. Well, then, here is the advantage ye get of your name of Christianity, of your privilege of hearing his word daily, ye who never ponder it, to tremble at it, or to rejoice in it, who cannot be moved either to joy or grief for spiritual things, neither law nor gospel moves the most part of you. I say, here is all your gain,—ye shall receive a reward with Gentiles and pagans, yea, ye shall be in a worse case than they in the day of the Lord. The civil Christian shall be worse than the profane Turk, and ye shall not then boast that ye were Christians, but shall desire that ye had dwelt in the place where the gospel had never been preached. It is a character of the nations, that they call not on God, and of heathen families, that they pray not to him, (Jer. x. 25,) and wrath must be poured on them. What, then, are the most part of you? Ye neither bow a knee in secret nor in your families, to God. Your time is otherwise employed, ye have no leisure to pray twice or thrice a day alone, except when ye put on your clothes ye utter some ordinary babblings. Ye cannot be driven to family worship. Shall not God rank you in judgment with those heathen families? Or shall it not be more tolerable for them than for you? And are not the most part of you every one given to covetousness, your heart and eye after it, seeking gain and advantage more than the kingdom of heaven? Doth not every one of you, as you have power in your hand, oppress one another, and wrong one another? Now, our end in speaking thus to you, is not to drive you to desperation. No, indeed, but as there was a word of the Lord sent to such by Isaiah, so we bring a word unto you. That which ruins you, is your carnal confidence. Ye are presumptuous as this people, and cry, "The temple of the Lord, the work of the Lord," &c. as if these would save you. Know, therefore, that all these will never cover you in the day of wrath. Know there is a necessity to make peace with God, and your righteousness must exceed the righteousness of a profession, and external privileges and duties, or else ye shall be as far from the kingdom of heaven as Sodom and Gomorrah. We speak of rulers' sins, that ye may mourn for them, lest ye be judged with them. If ye do not mourn for them in secret, know that they are your sins, ye are companions with them. Many fret, grudge, and cry out against oppression, but who weeps in secret? Who prays and deprecates God's wrath, lest it come upon them? And while it is so, the oppression of rulers becomes the sin of the oppressed themselves.

"Hear the word of the Lord." It were a suitable preparation for any word that is spoken, to make it take impression, if it were looked on "as the word of the Lord," and "law of our God." And truly no man can hear aright unless he hear it so. Why doth not this word of the Lord return with more fruit? Why do not men tremble or rejoice at it? Certainly, because it is not received as God's word. There is a practical heresy in our hearts, which rather may be called atheism—we do not believe the Scriptures. I do not say men call it in question, but I say, ye believe them not. It is one thing to believe with the heart, another thing not to doubt of it. Ye doubt not of it, not because ye do indeed believe it, but because ye do not at all consider it. It is one thing to confess with the mouth, and another thing to believe with the heart, for ye confess the Scriptures to be God's word, not because ye believe them, but because ye have received such a tradition from your fathers, have heard it from the womb unquestioned. O that this were engraven on your heart—that these commands, these curses, these promises are divine truths, the words and the oath of the Holy One! If every word of truth came stamped with his authority, and were received in the name of God himself, what influence would it have on the spirits and the practices of men? This would be a great reformer, would reform more in a month, than church and state hath done these many years. Why are rulers and people not converted and healed for all that is spoken? Here it is, "Who believes our report?" Who believes that our report is thy own testimony, O Lord? When ministers threaten you in God's name,—if his authority were stamped on the threatening, if men did seriously apprehend it were God's own voice, would they not tremble? When the gospel and the joyful sound comes forth, if he apprehended that same authority upon it, which ye who are convinced believe to be in the law, would ye not be comforted? Finally, I may say, it is this point of atheism, of inconsideration and brutishness, that destroys the multitude, makes all means ineffectual to them, and retards the progress of Christians. Men do not consider, that this word is the word of the eternal, and true, and faithful God, and that not one jot of it will fail. Here is a point of reformation I would put you to, if ye mind indeed to reform, let this enter into your hearts and sink down, that the law and gospel is the word of God, and resolve to come and hear preachings so, as the voice "of Jesus Christ, the true and faithful witness." If ye do not take it so now, yet God will judge you so at the end. "He that despiseth you, despiseth me, and he that hears not you, hears not me." If ye thought ye had to do with God every Sabbath, would ye come so carelessly, and be so stupid and inconsiderate before the Judge of all the earth? But ye will find in the end, that it was God whom ye knew not.

SERMON IX.

Isaiah i. 11.—"To what purpose is the multitude of your sacrifices unto me? saith the Lord," &c.

This is the word he calls them to hear and a strange word. Isaiah asks, What mean your sacrifices? God will not have them. I think the people would say in their own hearts, What means the prophet? What would the Lord be at? Do we anything but what he commanded us? Is he angry at us for obeying him? What means this word? Is he not repealing the statute and ordinance he had made in Israel? If he had reproved us for breach of commands, for omission and neglect of sacrifices, we would have taken with it, but what means this reproof for well doing? The Lord is a hard master. If we neglect sacrifices, and offer up the worst of the flock, he is angry, if we have a care of them, and offer them punctually, and keep appointed days precisely, he is angry. What shall we do to please him? I think many of you are put to as great a non plus, when your prayers and repentance and fasting are quarrelled, do ye not say in your hearts, we know not what to do? Ministers are angry at us if we pray not, and our praying they cry out against, they command us to repent and fast, and yet say that God will abhor both these. This is a mystery, and we shall endeavour to unfold it to you from the word. It concerns us to know how God is pleased with our public services and fastings for the most part of people have no more religion. Ye all, I know, desire to know what true religion is. Consult the Scriptures, and search them, for there ye shall find eternal life. We frame to ourselves a wrong pattern and copy of it, and so we judge ourselves wrong. Our narrow spirits do not take in the latitude of the Scripture's religion, but taking in one part we exclude another, and think God rigid if it be not taken off our hand so. But, I pray, consider these three things, which seem to make up the good old way, the religion of the Old and New Testaments—

First, Religion takes in all the commands,—it is universal, hath respect to all the commandments, Psal. cxix. 6. It carries the two tables in both hands, the first table in the right hand, and the second in the left. These are so entirely conjoined, that if you receive not both, you cannot receive any truly.

Secondly, It takes in all the man, his soul and spirit as well as his body, nay, it principally includes that which is principal in the man, his soul and spirit, his mind and affections. If ye divide these, ye have not a man present but a body, and what fellowship can bodies have with him who is a Spirit? If ye divide these among themselves, ye have not a spirit indeed present if the mind be not present, surely the heart cannot, but if the mind be, and the heart away, religion is not religion, but some empty speculation. The mind cannot serve but by the heart, where the heart is, there a man is reckoned to be.

Thirdly, It takes in Jesus Christ as all, and excludes altogether a man's self. He worships God in the spirit, but he rejoices not in himself, and in his spirit, but in Jesus Christ, and hath no confidence in himself, or the flesh, Phil. iii. 3, 8. It includes the soul and spirit, and all the commands, but it denies them all, and embraces Jesus Christ by faith, as the only object of glorying in and trusting in. All a man's self becomes dross in this consideration. Now, the first of these is drawn from the last, therefore it appears first—I say, an endeavour in walking in every thing commanded, of conforming our way to the present rule and pattern, is a stream flowing from the pure heart within. A man's soul and affections must once be purified, before it sends out such streams in conversation. And from whence doth that pure heart come? Is it the fountain and original? No certainly. The heart is desperately wicked above all things, and how will it cleanse itself? But this purity proceeds from another fountain,—from faith in Jesus Christ, and it is this that lies nearest the uncreated fountain Christ himself, it is the most immediate conduit the mouth of the fountain or the bucket to draw out of the deep wells of salvation. All these are conjoined in this order, 1 Tim. i. 5—"The end of the commandment is love." Ye know love is said elsewhere to be the fulfilling of the law, and when we say love, we mean all duties to God and man, which love ought immediately to principle. Now this love proceeds from a pure heart, cleansed and sanctified, which pure heart proceeds from faith unfeigned. So then, we must go up in our searching from external obedience all alongst, till we arrive at the inward fountain of Christ dwelling in us by faith, and then have ye found true religion indeed. Now, ye may think possibly, we have used too much circumlocution: what is all this to the present purpose? Yes, very much. Ye shall find the Lord rejecting this people's public worship and solemn ordinances upon these three grounds,—either they did not join with them the observation of weightier commands, or they did not worship him in them with their spirits, had not souls present, or they knew not the end and use for which God had appointed these sacrifices and ceremonies, they did not see to the end of all, which was Jesus Christ.

First, then, I say the people were much in external sacrifices and ceremonies, commanded of God, but they were ignorant of the end of his commands, and of the use of them. Ye know in themselves they had no goodness, but only in relation to such an end as he pleased they should lead to, but they stayed upon the ceremony and shadow, and were not led to use it as a means for such an end; and so, though they fancied that they obeyed, and pleased God, yet really they wholly perverted his meaning and intention in the command; therefore doth the Lord plead with them in this place for their sacrificing, as if it had been murder. They used to object his commands. What, says the Lord, did I command these things? Who required them? Meaning certainly, who required them for such an end, to take away your sin? Who required them but as a shadow of the substance to come? Who required them but as signs of that Lamb and sacrifice to be offered up in the fulness of time? And forasmuch as ye pass over all these, and think to please me with the external ceremony, was that ever my intent or meaning? Certainly ye have fancied a new law of your own, I never gave such a law; therefore it is said, Psal. l. 13.—God pleads just after this manner, "Will I eat the flesh of bulls, or drink the blood of goats?" &c.; and Micah vi. 7, "Will the Lord be pleased with thousands of rams, or with ten thousands of rivers of oil?" He who hath no pleasure in sinful men, what pleasure can he have in beasts? Therefore, it was to signify to them (who thought God would be pleased with them for their offering) that he could not endure them; it was worse to him to offer him such a recompense, than if they had done none at all. He is only well pleased in his well-beloved Son; and when they separate a lamb or a bullock from the well-beloved, what was it to him more than "a dog's neck" or "swine's flesh?" It was his creature, as these are, and no more, Isa. lxvi. 3. Now that they looked never beyond the ceremonies, is evident, because they boasted in them; they used to find out these as a remedy of their sins, and a mean to pacify God's wrath, Micah vi. 6. Paul bears witness of it, 2 Cor. iii. 13-15. Moses had a vail of ceremonies over his face, and the children of Israel could not steadfastly look to the end of that mystery, Christ Jesus, but their minds were blinded, and are so to this day in the reading of the scriptures; and this vail of hardness of heart shall be done away when Christ returns to them again. Now, I say, it is just so with us. There was never a people liker other than we are like the Jews. We have many external ordinances, preaching, hearing, baptism, communion, reading, singing, praying in public, extraordinary solemnities of fasting and thanksgiving, works of discipline and government, public reproof to sinners, confessions and absolutions. What would ye think if we should change the terms of sacrifices and new moons, and speak all this to you? To what purpose is the multitude of your fasts and feasts, of your preachings and communions, of your praying in secret, and in your families, of conference and prayer with others, of running to and fro to hear preaching, to partake of the Lord's table? I am full of them, I delight not in them. When ye come here on the Sabbath, who required at your hand to tread my courts? Come no more to hear the word, run no more after communions, seek no more baptism to your children, call no more solemn assemblies, it is all iniquity. O, say ye, that is a strange preaching indeed! Must we pray no more, hear no more, sing no more? Did not God command these? Why do ye discharge them? We do not mean so, that these should not be, but they should be in another way: all these want the soul and life of them, which is Jesus Christ in them. Do ye not think yourselves religious, because ye frequent these? The multitude of the people think that these please God, and pacify his wrath: ye have no other thing in your mind but these. If ye can attain any sorrow or grief for sin, or any tears to signify it, presently you absolve yourselves for your repentance. The scandalous who appear in public, think the paying of a penalty to the judge, and bowing the knee before the congregation,[284] satisfies God. Ye miss nothing when ye have these. I speak to the professors of religion also, who pretend to more knowledge than others, when ye have gone about so many duties, ye are well satisfied if ye get liberty in them. If ye can satisfy yourselves, ye doubt not of God's satisfaction; and if ye do not satisfy yourselves in your duties, ye cannot believe his satisfaction. Ye get the ordinance, and miss nothing. Now, I say, in all this ye do not reach to the end of this ministry, Jesus Christ; ye do not steadfastly behold him, to empty yourselves in his bosom, to turn over all the unrighteousness of your holy things upon him who bears it. That which pleaseth you, is not "he in whom the Father is well-pleased," but the measure of your own duty. O, the establishing of our own righteousness is the ruin of the visible Church! This is the grand idol, and all sacrifice to it. Know, therefore, that the most part of your performances are abomination and iniquity, because ye have so much confidence in them, and put them not upon Christ as filthy rags, or do not cover them with his righteousness, as well as your wickedness. I know ye will say, that ye are not satisfied with them, and that is still the matter of your exercise. Well, I affirm, in the Lord's name, from that ground, that ye have confidence in them, for if your diffidence and disquietness arise from it, your confidence and peace must come from it also. Is there any almost that maintain faith, except when their own conditions please them well? And that faith I may call no faith, at least not pure and cleanly entire faith. As for the multitude of you, you must know this, that God is not pleased with your prayers, and fasting, and hearing, &c. because ye have such an esteem of them, because ye can settle yourselves against all threatenings, and never once remember of Jesus Christ, or consider the end of his coming into the world; because ye find no necessity of pardon for your prayers and righteousness, but stretch the garment of these over the uncleanness of your practices. What delight hath the Lord in them, when they are put in his Son's place? Will he not be jealous that his Son's glory be not given to another?

In the *second* place, the Lord rejects their performances, because there was nothing but a mere shadow of service, and no worshipping of God in the Spirit. Ye know what Christ saith, "God is a Spirit, and he that worships him must do it in spirit and in truth," John iv. 24. It is the heart and soul that God delights in, "My son, give me thy heart," for if thou give not thy heart, I care for nothing else. The heart is the whole man. What a man's affection is, that he is. Light is not so,—it brings not the man alongst with it. Christ Jesus hath given himself for us, and he requires that we offer ourselves to him. If we offer a body to frequent his house, our feet to tread in his courts, our ears to hear his word, what cares he for it, as long as the soul doth not offer itself up in prayer or hearing? And this was the sin of this people, Isaiah xxix. 13. "They draw near with the lips, and their heart is far from the Lord." Now are we not their children, and have succeeded to this? Is there any thing almost in our public services, but what is public? Is there any thing but what is seen of men? Ye come to hear, ye sit and hear, and is there any more? The most part have their minds wandering, no thoughts present; for your thoughts are removed about your barns and corns, or some business in your head; and if any have their thoughts present, yet where are affections, which are the soul and spirit of religion, without which it is no true fire but wild fire, if it be not both burning and shining? Are ye serious in these ordinances? Or rather, are ye not more serious in any thing beside? And now, especially, when God's providence calls you to earnest thoughts, when it cries to all men to enter into consideration of their own ways, I pray you, is there any soul-affliction in your fasts even for a day? Is there any real grief or token of it? Not a fast in Scripture without weeping! We have kept many, and have never advanced so far. Shall the Lord then be pacified? Will not his soul abhor them? How shall they appease him for your other provocations, when they are as oil to the flame, to increase his indignation? The most part of Christians are guilty here; we come to the ordinances, as it were, to discharge a custom, and perform a ceremony, that we may have it to say to our conscience that it is done, and there is no more intent and purpose. We do not seek to have soul-communion with God. We come to sermon to hear some new thing, or new truth, or new fashion of it; to learn a notional experience of cases. But alas, this is not the great purpose and use of these things. It is to have some new sense of those things we know. We know already, but we should come to get the truth more received in our love, to serve God in our spirits, and to return to him ourselves in a sacrifice acceptable. This is the greater half, if not the whole of religion,—love to Jesus Christ who loved us, and living to him, because he died for us, and living to him because we love him. Now, all our ordinances and duties should be channels to carry our love to him, and occasions of venting our affections.

Thirdly, The Lord rejected this people's services, because they were exact and punctual in them, and neglected other parts of his commandments; and this is clearly expressed here, "I will not hear" your prayers, though there be many of them. Why? "Your hands are full of blood." Ye come to worship me, and pray to me, and yet there are many abominations in your conversation, which you continue in, and do not challenge in yourselves. Ye have unclean hands; and shall your prayers be accepted, which should come up with pure hands? They took his covenant in their mouth, and offered many sacrifices, but what have ye to do with these things, saith the Lord, since ye hate to be reformed, since ye hate personal reformation of your lives, and in your families? What have ye to do to profess to be my people? Psal. l. 16, 17. The Lord requires an universality, if ye would prove sincerity: if ye have respect to any of his commands, as his commands, then will ye respect all. If ye be partial, and choose one duty that is easy, and refuse another harder,—will come to the church and hear, but will not pray at home,—will fast in public, but not in private,—then, says the Lord, ye do not at all obey me, but your own humour; ye do not at all fast unto me, but unto yourselves. As much as your interest lies in a duty, so much are ye carried to it. And I take this to be the reason why many are so eager in pursuing public ordinances, following communions, and conferences with God's people, ready to pray in public rather than alone. If ye would follow them into their secret chamber, how much indifferency is there! How great infrequency, how little fervency! Well, says the Lord, did ye pray to me when ye prayed among others? No, ye prayed either to yourselves, or the company, or both. Did ye seek me in a communion? No, saith the Lord, ye sought not me, but yourselves: if ye sought me indeed with others, you would be as earnest, if not more, to seek me alone, Zech. vii. 6. And again, the Lord especially requires the weightier matters of the law to be considered. As it was among the Jews, their ceremonies were commanded, and so good; but they were not so much good in themselves as because they were means appointed for another end and use. But the moral law was binding in itself, and good in itself, without relation to another thing; and therefore Christ lays this heavy charge to the Pharisees, "Ye tithe mint and anise," Matt. xxiii. 23. "Woe unto you, for ye neglect the weightier matters of the law, judgment, mercy, and faith: these ye ought to have done, and not left the other undone." Are there not many who would think it a great fault to stay away from the church on the Sabbath or week day, and yet will not stick to swear,—to drink often? "Woe unto you, for ye strain at a gnat, and swallow a camel;" therefore are the prophets full of these expostulations. The people seemed to make conscience of ceremonies and external ordinances, but they did not order their conversation aright; they did not execute judgment, and relieve the oppressed, did not walk soberly, did not mortify sinful lusts, &c. Alas, we deceive ourselves with the noise of a covenant,[285] and a cause of God; we cry it up as an antidote against all evils, use it as a charm, even as the Jews did their temple; and, in the mean time, we do not care how we walk before God, or with our neighbours: well, thus saith the Lord, "Trust ye not in lying words," &c. Jer. vii. 4, 5, 6. If drunkenness reign among you, if filthiness, swearing, oppression, cruelty reign among you, your covenant is but a lie, all your professions are but lying words, and shall never keep you in your inheritances and dwellings. The Lord tells you what he requires of you. Is it not to do justly, and walk humbly with God? Mic. vi. 7. This is that which the grace of God teaches, to deny "ungodliness and worldly lusts," and to "live soberly, righteously, and godly, towards your God, your neighbour, and yourself," Tit. ii. 11, 12; and this he prefers to your public ordinances, your fasting, covenanting, preaching, and such like.[286] "Is not this to know me?" saith the Lord, Jer. xxii. 15, 16. You think you know God when you can discourse well of religion, and entertain conferences of practical cases. You think it is knowledge to understand preachings and scripture; but thus saith the Lord, to do justly to all men, to walk humbly towards God, to walk soberly in yourselves, is more real knowledge of God, than all the volumes of doctors contain, or the heads of professors. Is this knowledge of God to have a long flourishing discourse containing much religion in it? Alas, no! to do justly, to oppress none, to pray more in secret, to walk humbly and soberly, this is to know the Lord. Practice is real knowledge indeed: it argues, that what a man knows, he receives in love, that the truth hath a deep impression on the heart, that the light shines into the heart to inflame it. What is knowledge before God? As much as principles, affection, and action, as much as hath influence on your conversations; if you do not, and love not what you know, is that to know the Lord? Shall not your knowledge be a testimony against your practice, and no more?

SERMON X.

Isaiah i. 16.—"Wash you, make you clean, put away the evil of your doings from before mine eyes; cease to do evil," &c.

If we would have a sum of pure and undefiled religion, here it is set down in opposition to this people's shadow of religion, that consisted in external ordinances and rites. We think that God should be as well-pleased with our service as we ourselves, therefore we choose his commands which our humour hath no particular antipathy against and refuse others. But the Lord will not be so served: as he will not share with the world, and divide the soul and service of man with creatures, so as mammon should get part, and he his part. No, if we choose the one, we must refuse the other; for so will he not suffer his word and commands to be divided: there must be some universality in respect of the gospel and the law, and a conjunction of these two, or we cannot please him.

If religion do not include the gospel, we are yet upon the old covenant of works, according to which none can be justified. If it do not include the law in the hands of a mediator, then we turn the grace of God unto wantonness. If it shut out Jesus Christ and have no use of him, how can either we or our performances stand or be accepted before his holy eyes? If it exclude the law that Christ came to establish, how can he be pleased with our religion? both of these offer an indignity to the Son of God. The sum, then, of Christian religion is believing and sanctification of the Spirit unto obedience. That is the root and fountain, this is the fruit and stream; justification of our persons, and sanctification of our lives and hearts. This is pure religion and undefiled. And therefore Isaiah says, "Wash you, make you clean,"—cleanse in the only true fountain of Christ's blood. It is not your purifications of the law, your many washings with water and hyssop; it is not the blood of bulls and of goats can purge your consciences from dead works: they do but purify your flesh, but cannot wash your souls worse defiled. This blood of Jesus Christ is that clean water that he must sprinkle on you, if you would be clean. If you take any other water, any other righteousness but his, and wash thyself therewith, suppose it be snow water that washeth cleanest—thy most exact conversation, yet, he will plunge thee in the mire, till thine own clothes abhor thee, Job ix. 30, 31. Now, when you have washed your persons (ye need not, save to wash your feet, says Christ,)—your daily conversation, reform it in the virtue of that blood, for we are not called "to uncleanness, but unto holiness," and therefore, "put away the evil of your doings," &c. God hath put away the guilt of your doings by justification, now put ye away the evil of your doings by sanctification, &c. And if ye would know what sanctification is, "cease to do evil," do not return to the old puddle to wallow in it. Ye that are cleansed by this blood, O think how unbeseeming it is to you to defile yourselves again with those things ye are cleansed from! but now, "learn to do well." Ye are given up to Christ, ye must be his disciples, and he will teach you. "Learn of me," saith Christ, (ye need no other law almost but his example, he is a visible and speaking law), yet "seek judgment." As ye ought to look on my example, so especially ponder that word and rule of practice and behaviour that I have left behind me, and given out as the lawgiver of the redeemed. Have I redeemed you, and should not I be the redeemed and ransomed one's king? Is there any society in the world wants a law, order, and government? Neither must ye who are delivered from bondage, enfranchised and made free indeed. Now, ye should of all men most live by a law. And when ye know that rule, then apply it to your several vocations and callings. Let the magistrate act according to it, and every man according to it. Religion consists not in a general notion, but condescends to our particular practice, to reform it. You see then what we would press upon your consciences. It is true religion that we would have you persuaded unto. All men have some kind of religion, even heathens who worship idols, but the true religion respects the true and living God. Now, what is it to worship the true and living God? What is the service of him that may be called religion indeed? Should we be the prescrivers of it?[287] No certainly, he must carve solely in that, or else it cannot please him, therefore "to the law and to the testimony," if ye speak not according to this, and worship not according to this word of God, "it is because there is no light in you." Ye may have a religion before men pure and undefiled, but if it be not so before God and the Father, I pray you to what purpose is it? I am sure it is all lost labour, nay, it is labour with loss, instead of gain. O that ye were persuaded to look and search the scriptures. Think ye to have eternal life out of them?—and think ye to have eternal life by them, who do not labour to know the way of it set down there? Every one of you hath a different model of religion, according to your fancies and breedings, according as your lusts will suffer you. The rule that the most part walk by is the course and example of the world. Is not this darkness, and gross darkness? Others model their duties according to their ability. They will do all they can do with ease, and without troubling themselves, and they think God may be well pleased with that. I pray you consider and hear the word of the

Lord, and law of your God. Hath he set down here the rule and perfect pattern of true religion, and will ye never so much own it, as to examine yours according to it? The scriptures are the touchstone, if you would not have a counterfeit religion deceiving you in the end, when ye have trusted to it, I pray you try it by the word of God. Oh! that this principle were once sunk into your hearts,—I may not walk at random, if I please myself, and satisfy my own will, if that be not also God's will, I shall have neither gain nor comfort of it. His will is manifested in his word,—I will search and find what God hath required of me, for if I be not certain of his will, I may be doing all my days, and sweating out my life, and yet lose my pains and toil. I say, this word of the Lord that Isaiah calls to the people to hear, ver. 10, will at length judge you. Your religion will be tried in the day of accounts according to it, not according to your rules and methods ye have prescribed unto yourselves. Now, if ye in the meantime shall judge yourselves, according to another rule, and absolve yourselves, and in the end God shall judge you according to this word, and condemn you, were ye not fools in neglecting this word?

The whole will of God concerning your duty may be summed up in two, John hath one of them, 1 John iii. 23, "And this is his commandment, that we should believe on the name of his Son Jesus Christ, and love one another, as he gave us commandment," and Paul hath another to the Thessalonians, 1 Thess iv. 3, "This is the will of God, even your sanctification." And these two make up this text, so that it unites both gospel and law. The commandment of the law comes forth, and it is found that we have broken and are guilty, that we cannot answer for one of a thousand. The law entering makes sin abound. Our inability, yea, impossibility of obedience is more discovered. Well, then, the gospel proclaims the Lord Jesus Christ for the Saviour of sinners, and commands us, under pain of damnation, to believe in him,—to cast our souls on him, as one able to save, as one who hath obeyed the law for us, so that this command of believing in Christ is answerable to all the breaches of the law, and tends to make them up in Christ. When he proclaimed the law on mount Sinai, with terror, that which ye hear expressed is not his first commandment, which ye are in the first instance to obey, for all these we have broken, but it hath a gospel command in its bosom, it leads to Jesus Christ, and if ye could read the mind of God in it, ye would resolve all these commands which condemn you and curse you, into one command of believing in the Son, that ye may be saved from that condemnation. And if ye obey this command, which is his last command, and most peremptory, then are the breaches of all the rest made up, the intent of all the rest is fulfilled, though not in your obedience, yet in Christ's, which is better than ours. Believing in Christ presents God with a perfect righteousness, with an obedience even to the death of the cross. When a sinner hears the holy and spiritual sense of the law, and sees it in the light of God's holiness, O how vile must he appear to himself, and how must he abhor himself! What original pollution, what actual pollution, what a fountain within, what uncleanness in streams without, will discover itself! Now, when the most part of men get any sight of this, presently they fall a washing and cleansing themselves, or hiding their filthiness. And what water take they? Their own tears and sorrows, their own resolutions, their own reformations. But alas, we are still more plunged in our own filthiness; that is still marked before him, because all that is as foul as that we would have washen away. What garment do men take to hide themselves ordinarily? Is it not their own righteousness? Is it not a skirt of some duty that is spread over transgressions? Do not men think their sins hid, if they can mourn and pray for a time? Their consciences are eased by reflection upon this. But alas, thine iniquity is still marked! Shall filthiness hide filthiness? Thy righteousness is as a vile garment, as a menstruous cloth, (Isa. lxiv. 6.) as well as thine unrighteousness, how then shall it cover thine nakedness? Seeing it is so then, what is the Lord's mind concerning our cleansing? Seeing stretched out hands and many prayers will not do it, what shall I do? The Lord hath showed thee what thou shalt do, and that is, that thou do nothing in relation to that end, that thou shouldst undertake to wash away the least spot by all thy repentance. Yet must thou wash and make clean, and the water is brought new unto you, even the blood of Jesus Christ that cleanseth from all sin. Wash in this blood, and ye shall be clean. And what is it to wash in this blood? It is to believe in Christ Jesus, to lay hold on the all sufficient virtue of it, to trust our souls to it, as a sufficient ransom for all our sins, to spread the covering of Christ's righteousness over all our righteousness and unrighteousness, as having both alike need to be hid from his holy eyes. Jesus Christ "came by water and by blood," (1 John v. 6), by water to sanctify, and by blood to justify, by the power and cleansing virtue of the Holy Ghost, to take away sin in the being of it, and by the virtue of his blood, to take away sin in the guilt and condemnation of it.

Now, I conceive he presses a twofold exercise upon them in this washing, and both have relation to the blood of Jesus Christ, to wit repentance and faith. If they be not all one, yet they are in this point inseparably conjoined. Repentance waters and saps the roots of believing, which otherwise would dry up; therefore, instead of outward forms and ceremonies of religion, he presseth them to inward sorrow and contrition of heart for sin, that they might present an acceptable sacrifice to God, "a contrite heart." This is more pleasing than many specious duties of men without, Psal. l. 7, &c. But when I press upon you repentance, do not conceive that we would have it preparatory to faith, that ye should sit down and mourn for your sins for a time, till your hearts be so far humbled, and then ye might come as prepared and fitted to Jesus Christ. This is the mistake of many Christians, which keeps them from solid settling. We find it ordinary, souls making scruples and objections against coming to Jesus Christ, because of want of such preparations, of measures of humiliation and contrition, which they prescribe to themselves, or do behold in others. And so they sit down and apply themselves to such a work, apply their consciences to the law and curse; and they find, instead of softening, hardness, instead of contrition of spirit, more dulness and security; at least they cannot get satisfaction to themselves in that they seek, and thus they hang their head over their impenitent hearts, and lament, not so much that repentance is not, as that they cannot find it in themselves. Alas! there are many diseases in this one malady. If it were embowelled unto you, ye would not believe that such a way were so contradictory to the gospel. For, first, ye who are so, have this principle in your hearts, which is the foundation of it: I cannot come to Christ so unclean, I must be a little washen ere I come, the most gross uncleanness and hardness of my heart must be taken away, and so I shall be accepted. Alas, what derogation is this to the blessed Saviour! What absurdity is it! I am too unclean to come to the fountain, I must be a little purged before I come to this fountain that cleanseth from all sin. I pray you, why was the fountain opened? Was it not for sin and uncleanness? And this thou sayest by interpretation, if I were so and so humbled, then I might come, and be worthy to come; when the want of such a measure debars thee as unworthy, doth not the having of it in thy estimation make thee worthy? And so ye come with a present in your hand to Jesus Christ, with a price and reward to him who gives freely. Again, thou deniest Christ to be the only fountain of all grace, and so it is most dishonourable to him. If thou would have repentance before thou come to him, where shalt thou have it? Wilt thou find it in thy heart, which is desperately wicked? Wilt thou seek it of God, and not seek it in the mediator Jesus Christ? God out of a mediator will not hear thee. In a word, there is both extreme sin and extreme folly in this way: great sin, because it contradicts the tenor of the gospel, it dishonours the Lord Jesus, the exalted Prince, as if he were not the fountain of all grace; it is contrary both to the freedom of his grace, and to the fulness of it also. It is great folly, for thou leavest the living fountain, and goest seeking water in a wilderness; thou leavest the garden where all herbs grow, and wanderest abroad to the wild mountains; and because thou canst not find what thou seekest, thou sittest down and weepest beside it. Repentance is in Christ, and no repentance so pleasing to God as the mournings and relentings of a pardoned sinner; but thou seekest it far from him, yea, refusest him for want of that which thou mayest have by choosing him. Therefore we declare this unto you, that whatever ye be, whatever ye want, if ye think ye stand in need of Jesus Christ, embrace him. If ye be exceeding vile in your own eyes, and cannot get repentance as ye would to cleanse yourselves, here is the fountain opened, and ready to wash in. Yet this we must tell you, that no sinner can believe but he that repents,[288] not because repentance is required as a preparation to give a man a warrant and right to believe,—I know no ground of faith but our necessity, and the Lord's promise and command unto us,—but because no soul can truly fly into Jesus Christ to escape sin's guilt, but he that desires to be delivered from sin itself; and therefore the most part of you fancy a faith which you have not, because there is no possibility that men will come out of themselves, till they be pressed out by discovered sin and misery within. Your woulds and wishes after Christ and salvation, that many of you have, are not the real exercises of your soul's flying unto him for salvation. If ye did indeed turn into Jesus Christ, your hearts would turn the back upon sin, and these sins ye seek remission of. Now, all the desire that many men have of Christ, is this,—I would fain have his salvation, if I might keep my sin; I would gladly be delivered from the guilt of sin, if he would let me keep still the sin. But will Christ make any such bargain?

If this blood only wash from sin, O how many lie in their sins, and wallow in their filthiness! "There is a generation pure in their own eyes, and yet are not washed from their filthiness," Prov. xxx. 12. O that ye believed this! If ye be not now washed, eternity shall find you unclean, and woe to the soul that enters eternity with all the pollution of its sins: can such a soul enter into the high and holy place, the clean city? No, certainly; it must be without among the dogs and swine, it must be kept in darkness for ever. It is, then, of great importance that ye be washen from your filthiness. Now, I ask you, is it so or not? Are ye made clean and washen from the guilt of your sins? Every one of you almost will say so and think so; and yet says the scripture, "There is a generation pure in their own eyes, and yet are not washed." Is there a generation such? Is there any such? Oh! then, think it is possible you may be mistaken in the opinion of your own cleanness. Do any conceive themselves pardoned, and yet are not so? Think it is possible you may have deceived yourselves, especially since ye have never examined it. But are there so many so, a whole generation,—the most part of men? Then, as you love your souls, try, for it is certain that the most part of you must be deceived. Is there a generation in the visible church not washen, and yet every one thinks himself clean? Then certainly the most part are in a great delusion. Will ye then once examine whether or not ye be deluded with them? It shall be your peace to know it, while it may be amended. But how comes it to pass, that so many hearing of the gospel, and lying near this fountain, are not cleansed? I think certainly, because they will not have a thorough cleansing, they get none at all. All men would love Christ's blood well to pardon sin, but who will accept of the water to sanctify them from sin? But Christ came with both. Shall this blood be spent upon numbers of you, who have no respect to it, but would still wallow in your filthiness? Would ye have God pardoning these sins ye never throughly resolved to quit? But how is it that so many men are clean in their own eyes, and yet not washed? I think indeed, the reason of it is, they make a kind of washing, which they apprehend sufficient, and yet know not the true fountain. We find men taking much soap and nitre, when convinced of sin, or charged with it, and thereupon soon absolving themselves. If ye ask their grounds, they will tell you, they repent and are sorry for it; they purpose to make amends, and they think amendment a good compensation for the past wrong. They will, it may be, vow to drink no more for a year after they have been drunk; they will confess their sin in public, and all this they do without having any thought of Jesus Christ, or the end of his coming, and can absolve themselves from such grounds, though in the mean time Christ come not so much as in their mind; and therefore are they not really washed. All thy righteousness is unclean before God, and thy repentances defile thee: and yet because of some such duties, though deceivest thyself, and are clean in thine own eyes. These have some beauty in thy eyes, and thou puttest them between thy filthiness and thy eye, and so conceivest that thou art clean. I think a reason also, why many men are clean in their own eyes, and conceive that God hath pardoned their sin, is because they have forgotten it. It is not recent in their memory, and makes no present wound in their conscience: and therefore, they apprehend God such as themselves,—they think he hath forgotten about it also. But oh! how terrible shall it be, when God brings to remembrance, and sets our sins in order before us! Ye think God cares not for your sins, that he forgives them before thee, and thou shalt know they are still marked before him.

Ye who have washen in this blood, ye may rejoice, for it shall make you clean every whit. Your iniquities that so defiled you, shall not be found. O the precious virtue of that blood that can purge away a soul's spots! All the art of men and angels could not reach this. This redemption and cleansing was precious, and would have ceased for ever; but this blood is the ransom, this blood cleanseth, and so perfectly, that it shall not appear, not only to men's eyes, but also God's piercing eye. Sinners, quit your own righteousness,—why defile ye yourselves more? When your eyes are opened, ye will find it so. Here is washing; apply yourselves to this fountain; and if ye do indeed so; if ye expect cleansing from Jesus Christ, I pray you return not to the puddle. Ye are not washen from sin, to sin more, and defile yourselves more; if ye think ye have liberty to do so, ye have no part in this blood.

SERMON XI.

Isaiah i. 16.—"Wash you, make you clean; put away the evil of your doings from before mine eyes; cease to do evil," &c.

There are two evils in sin,—one is the nature of it, another the fruit and sad effect of it. In itself it is filthiness, and contrary to God's holiness; an abasing of the immortal soul; a spot in the face of the Lord of the creatures, that hath far debased him under them all. Though it be so unnatural to us, yet it is now in our fallen estate become, as it were, natural, so that men agree with it, as if it were sunk and drunk into the very soul of man. The other is guilt and desert of punishment and obligation to it. All men hate this, but they cannot hold it off. They eat the tree and fruit of death, they must eat death also: they must have the wages of sin, who have wrought for it. Now, the gospel hath found a remedy for lost man in Jesus Christ; he comes in the gospel with a twofold blessing, a twofold virtue, a pardoning virtue and a sanctifying virtue, "water and blood," 1 John v. 6. He comes to forgive sin, and to subdue sin; to remove the guilt of it, and then the self[289] of it. God's appointment had inseparably joined them; and Christ came not to dissolve the law, but to establish it. If he had taken away the punishment, and left the sin in its being, he had weakened the law and the prophets. That conjunction of sin and wrath, which is both by divine appointment, and suitable also unto their own natures, must stand, that divine justice may be entire; and therefore, he that comes to redeem us from the curse of the law, hath also this commission to redeem from sin and all transgressions of the law, Rom. xi. 26, and Gal. iii. 13. He that turns away the wrath of God from men, turns also ungodliness from them which provoked his wrath; and so he is a complete redeemer, and a complete redeemer he had not been otherwise. If he had removed wrath only, and left us under the bondage of sin, it had not been half redemption; "he that commits sin, is the servant of sin." But this is perfect freedom and liberty, to be made free from sin, for it was sin that subjected us to wrath, and so was the first tyrant and the greatest. The gospel then comes with a joyful sound unto you, but many of you mistake it, and apprehend it to be a doctrine of liberty and peace, and that unto sin; but if it were so, it were no joyful sound. If there were proclaimed a liberty to all men to do as they list, no punishment, no wrath to be feared, I would think that doctrine no glad news, it were but the perpetuating of the bondage of a reasonable soul. But this is glad news,—a delivery and freedom proclaimed in the gospel. From what? Not unto sin, but from sin; and this is to be free indeed. We owe more to Jesus Christ for this, than for redemption from wrath, because sin is a greater evil than wrath; yea, wrath were not so, if sin were not. Therefore he exhorts to wash, and wash so that they may make clean. Take Jesus Christ for justification and sanctification,—employ both the water and the blood that he hath come with. But because all men pretend a willingness to have Christ their Saviour, and their sins pardoned through his blood, who, notwithstanding, hate to be reformed, and would seek no more of Christ: therefore, he branches out that part of the exhortation in several particulars. All men have a general liking of remission of sins, but renouncing of it is to many a hard doctrine. They would be glad that God put their evils out of his sight, by passing them by, and forgetting them; but they will not be at the pains of putting away their evils from his sight; and therefore, the gospel which comprehends these two united, is not really received by many, who pretend to be followers of it. This is his command, that ye believe. Some pretend to obey this, and yet have no regard of that other part of his will, even their sanctification; and therefore their faith is dead, it is a fancy. If ye did indeed believe and receive Christ for pardon of sin, it were not possible but your souls would be engaged and constrained to endeavour to walk in all well-pleasing. But it is an evident token of one that is not washed from his sin, and believes not in Christ, if he conceive within his heart a greater latitude and liberty to walk after the flesh, and be emboldened to continue in sin, because of his grace and mercy; and yet such are the most part of you. Upon what ground do you delay repentance? Upon what presumption do ye continue in your sins, and put over the serious study of holiness, till a more fit time? Is it not from an apprehension of the grace and mercy of God, that ye think ye may return any time and be accepted, and so ye may in the meantime take as much pleasure in sin as you can, seeing ye may get leave also for God's mercy? I pray you consider, that you have never apprehended God's mercy aright, ye are yet in your sins, and certainly as yet are not washed from them.

"Put away the evil," &c. When the Spirit convinces a soul, he convinces a man not only of evil doings but of the evil of his doings; not only of sin, but of the sinfulness of sin; and not only of those actions which are in themselves sinful, but also of the iniquity of holy things. I think no man will come to wash in Christ's blood, till this be discovered. If he see much wickedness, many evil doings, yet he will labour to wash away these by his own tears, and repentance, and well-doing. As long as he hath any good actions, as prayers, fasting, and such like, he will cover his evil doings by them; he will spread the skirts of such righteousness over his uncleanness; and when he hath hid it from his own eyes, he apprehends that he hath hid it from God's also. He will wash his bloody hands with many prayers, and thinks they may be clean enough. We see blasphemers of God's name use to join a prayer for forgiveness with their oath and curse, and they never trouble themselves more. O what mocking of God is this! Now, as long as it is thus, there is no employment for the Son of God's blood; they can do their own turn. Men will not come to Christ, because it is the best way, if they see any else beside. None will come till they see it is the only way; none can wash in Christ, except they wash all. If ye have any thing that needs not washing, his blood is not for you; his righteousness is not known, when ye establish all, or a part of your own. I fear the most part of you have no employment for Christ; ye have extreme need of him, but ye know it not, for there are many things which ye will not number among your sins,—your prayers, your hearing, reading, singing, public and private worship, giving alms, &c. How many of you were never convinced of any sin in these! Do ye not conceive God is well-pleased with you for them? Your conscience hath convinced you, it may he, of gross sins, as drunkenness, filthiness, swearing, &c. But ye are not convinced for your well doing, ye find not a necessity of a Mediator for these. I think many of you never confessed any such thing, except in a general notion. Alas, how ignorant are men of themselves! We are unclean, how can any thing we do cleanse us? Are not we unclean, and do not our hands touch our own works? Shall not then our own uncleanness defile our good actions, more than they can cleanse us? Hag. ii. 13. The ignorance of this makes men go about to build up their old ruined righteousness, and still seek something in themselves, to make up wants in themselves. Always, when the light of God hath discovered you to yourselves, so that ye can turn your eye nowhere, but uncleanness fills it, though your conversation be blameless in the world, so as men can challenge nothing yet ye have found within and without nothing, but matter of mourning, I say, this is an evidence that the Spirit hath sinned and enlightened thy darkness. Now, when thou hast fled unto Jesus Christ for a covering to thy righteousness, as well as unrighteousness, it remains that thou now put away the evil of thy doings,—put not away thy doings, but the evil of them. We challenge your prayers, services, and public duties, even as the prophet did we declare unto you that God is as ill pleased with them, as your drunkenness, whoring, intemperance, &c. The most part of you are no more acceptable when ye come to the church, than when ye go to the tavern,—your praying and cursing is almost all one. What shall we do then, say ye? Shalt we pray no more, and hear no more? No, say I, put not away your prayers and ordinances, but put away the evil of them from before his sight. Rather multiply your doings, but destroy the evil and iniquity of your doings. And there is one evil or two above all, that makes them hateful to him: ye trust too much in them. Here is the iniquity, the idol of jealousy set up: ye make your doings your righteousness, and in that notion they are abomination. There is nothing makes your worship of God so hateful as this, ye think so much of it, and justify yourself by it, and then God knows what it is that ye so magnify, and make the ground of your claim to salvation. It is even an empty ceremony, a shadow without substance, a body without a soul. You speak and look and hear, you exercise some outward senses but no inward affection, and what should that be to him, who is a Spirit?

They did not observe the iniquity of their holy things, and therefore are they marked by him—they are in his sight. They did not see so many faults in their prayers and services, they wondered why God did chide them so much, but God marks what we miss, he remembers when we forget. We cover ourselves with a wall of external duties, and think to hide all the rottenness of our hearts, but it will not be hid from him, before whom hell hath no covering. All hearts are open and naked before him. Your secret sins are in the light of his countenance. Men hear you pray, see you present at worship, they know no more, at least they see no more, nay, but the formality of thy worship, the wanderings of thy mind are in his sight. And, O how excellent a rule of walking were this, to do all in his sight and presence! O that ye were persuaded in your hearts of his all seeing, all searching eye, and all knowing mind! Would ye not be more solicitous and anxious anent the frame of your hearts, than the liberty of your speech or external gesture? O how would men retire within themselves, to fashion their spirits before this all searching and all knowing Spirit! If ye do not observe the evils of your hearts and ways, they are in his sight, and this will spoil all acceptance of the good of them. If ye observe the evils of your well doing, and bring these also to the fountain to wash them, and be about this earnest endeavour of perfecting holiness, of perfecting well doings in the power and fear of God, then certainly he will not set your sins in the light of his countenance, the good of your way shall come before him, and the evil of it Christ shall take away.

"Cease to do evil," &c. These are the two legs a Christian walks on, if he want any of them, he is lame and cannot go equally,—ceasing from evil, and doing good, nay, they are so united, that the one cannot subsist without the other. If a man do not cease from evil and his former lusts, he cannot do well, or perfect holiness. There are many different dispositions and conditions of men, there are generally one of two. Some have a kind of abstinence from many gross sins and are called civil honest men,—they can abide an inquest and censure of all their neighbours, they can say no ill of them. But alas, there is as little good to be said; he drinks not, swears not, whores not, steals not. Nay, but what doth he well? Alas, the world cannot tell what he doth, for he prays not in secret, nor in his family,—he is void of some offences towards men, but there are many duties called to, towards both God and men, he is a stranger to. He oppresses not the poor, nay, but he is not charitable either to give to them, he defrauds no man, but whom helps he by his means? Again, there are others, they will boast of some things done, they pray, they keep the church well, they do many good turns, and yet for all that, they do not cease to do evil. They were drunkards, so they are, they can swear for all their prayers, are given to contention, to lying, to filthiness, &c. Now, I say, neither of these religions is pure and undefiled. Religion is a thorough and entire change, it is like a new creation, that must destroy the first subject, to get place for that which is to come. It is a putting off old garments, to put on new, the putting off an old form and engraven image, to make place for a new engraving. Men do not put a seal above a seal, but deface the old, and so put on the new, men do not put new clothes upon the old, but put the old off, and so they have place for the new. Religion must have a naked man. Godliness is a new suit, that will not go on upon so many lusts, no, no, it is more meet and more conformed unto the inwards of the soul than so. The cold must go out as the heat comes in. Many men do not change their garments, but mend them, put some new pieces unto them. They retain their old lusts, their heart idols, and they will add unto these a patch of some external obedience, but alas, is this godliness? Hypocrisy will be content of a mixture,—sin is the harlot, whose heart could endure to see the child parted. It can give God a part, to get leave to brook the most part; sin will give God liberty to take some of the outward man, if it keep the heart and soul. But God will not reckon on these terms, he will have all the man or nothing, for he is the righteous owner. True godliness cannot mix so, but false and counterfeit may do it well. Other men, again, possibly unclothe themselves of some practices, but they put on new clothing, they reform some passages for fear of censure, or shame, or such like. They are found, it may be, blameless, either because so educated, or their disposition is against particular gross sins, but they are not clothed upon with holiness and well doing, and so they are but naked and bare in God's sight, not beautiful. They have swept their house, and some devil put out or kept out, but because the good Spirit enters not, ordinarily seven worse enter again into such men.

There is a great moment[290] of persuasion in this order of the exhortation, "Wash you," and then, "put away the evil of your doings," and "cease to do evil." Do not continue in your former customs. It is strange, how contrary our hearts are to God, we use to turn grace unto wantonness, we use to take more liberty to sin, when we conceive we are pardoned. But I do not know any more strong and constraining persuasion to forsake sin, than the consideration of the forgiving of it might yield. O what an inducement and grand argument to renouncing of evils, is the consideration of the remission of them! This is even that ye are now called unto, who have fled to Jesus to escape wrath what should ye be taken up with, in all the world but this,—to live to him henceforth, who died for us,—to forsake our own old way, and that from the constraining principle of love to him, 2 Cor. v. 14, 15. O that ye would enforce your own hearts with such a thought, when there are any solicitations to sin, to former lusts! Should I, that am dead to sin, live any longer therein? Rom. vi. 2. Should I who am washed from such pollutions, return again to the pollutions of the world? Should I again defile myself, who am cleansed by so precious blood, and forget him that washed me? Should I return with the dog to the vomit, and with the sow to the puddle? God forbid I pray you consider. If you be Christians indeed, give a proof of it. What hath Jesus Christ done for you? He hath given himself, his own precious blood, a ransom for us, will ye not give up yourselves to him? Will not ye give him your sins and lusts, which are not yourself, but enemies to yourself? Will not ye put away these ills, that he came into this world to destroy? Art thou a Christian, and are there yet so many sins, and works of the devil reigning in thee, and set up in God's sight?

What an inconsistency is this! If thou be his follower, thou must put these away. Give them a bill of divorcement, never to turn again. Many a man parts with his sin, because it leaves him, he puts it not away, temptation goes, and occasion goes away, but the root of it abides within him. Many men have particular jars with their corruptions, but they reconcile again, as differences between married persons. They do not arise[291] to hate their sin in its sinful nature. But if thou hate it, then put it away. And who would not hate that which Christ so hated, that he came to destroy it? 1 John iii. 5. What a great indignity must it be to the gospel, to make that the ground of living in sin, which is pressed, in it, as the grand persuasion to forsake it? Seeing we are washed from the guilt of it, O let us not love to keep the stain and filth of it! Why are we washen? Was it not Christ's great intendment and purpose, to purify to himself a holy people? We are washen from the guilt of our sins, and is it to defile again? Is it not rather to keep ourselves henceforth clean, that we may be presented holy and unblameable in his sight,—that we may seek to be as like heaven as may be. But who ceases to do these evils, that he says are pardoned? Who puts away the evil of these doings, the guilt whereof he thinks God hath put away? Could ye find in your hearts to entertain those evils so familiarly, to pour out your souls unto them, if that peace of God were indeed spoken unto you? Would not the reflex of his love prove more constraining on your hearts? Were it possible, that if ye did indeed consider, that your lusts cost Christ a dear price to shed his blood, that your pleasures made his soul heavy to death, and that he hath laid down his life to ransom you from hell, were it possible, I say, that ye would live still in these lusts, and choose these pleasures of sin, which were so bitter to our Lord Jesus? I beseech you be not deceived,—if ye love the puddle still, that ye cannot live out of it, do not say that ye are washed. Ye may have washen yourselves with soap and nitre, but the blood of Christ hath not cleansed; for, if that blood sprinkled your conscience once, to give you an answer to all challenges, it could not but send forth streams to purify the heart, and so the whole man. The blood and water might be joined, the justifying Saviour, and the sanctifying Spirit, for both these are in this gospel washing, 1 Cor vi. 11, 1 John v. 6. "This is he that came by water and blood, even Jesus Christ, not by water only, but by water and blood." Not by water only, but by blood also, and I say, not by blood only, but by water also. The very purpose of forgiveness is not to lay a foundation for more sin, but that men may sin no more, but break off their sins. It is indeed impossible for a man to amend his ways, till he be pardoned, for his sin stands betwixt him and God. God is a consuming fire—the guilt of it hinders all meeting of the soul with God, at least all influence from him. But when an open door is made in Christ, that men may come and treat with God, notwithstanding of rebellions, and have the curse relaxed, O how may he go about his duty comfortably! Am I escaped from hell, why should I any more walk in the way to it? And now he hath the Spirit given for the asking. There are some cessations from sin, that are not real forsakings of it, and ceasings from it. You know men will abstain from eating for a season, that they may be made ripe for it at another time. Some do not cease from sin, but delay it only, they put it not away, but put it off only for another time, till a fitter occasion and opportunity. And this is so far from ceasing from it, that it is rather a deliberate choice of it, and election of conveniency for it. There may be some pure and simple ceasings from sin, mere abstinence, or rather mere absence of sin for a season, that is not ceasing from doing evil. The Christian's ceasing hath much action in it. It is such a ceasing from doing evil, that it is a putting away of evil, it hath a soul and spirit joined in that cessation. Sin requires violence to put it out where it hath haunted,—it is an intruding guest, and a usurping guest. It comes in first as a supplicant and beggar, prays for a little lodging for a night, and promises to be gone. The temptation speaks but for a little time, even the present time, for a little one,—it seeks but little at first, lest it be denied, but if once it be received into the soul, it presently becomes master, and can command its own time, and its abode. Then ye will not so easily put it out as ye could hold it out, for it is now joined with that wicked, desperate party within you, the heart, and these united forces are too strong for you. According as a lust is one with a man's heart, or hath nearer connection with his heart and soul, it is the worse to put away: for, will ye drive a man from himself? It is the cutting off a right hand, or plucking out of a right eye. To make a man cease from such evils, requires that a stronger power be within him than is in the world. Men may cease for a time, for want of occasions or temptations to sin, when there is no active principle in them, restraining or keeping their souls from such sins as appear after, when no sooner is occasion offered, but they run as the horse to his course, or the stone falleth downward,—they receive fire as easily as dry stubble. That is not Christian ceasing, which is that which the soul argues itself into, from grounds of the gospel. Should I, who am dead to sin, live any longer therein? This is a principle of cessation, and this is true liberty,—when the soul can abstain from present temptations upon such grounds and persuasions of the gospel, then it is really above itself and above the world, then hath it that true victory. Many men cease only from sin, because sin ceases from them, they have not left it, but it hath left them. The old man thinks himself a changed man, because he wallows not in the lusts of the flesh, as in his youth. But, alas! no thanks to him for that, he hath not ceased from his lusts. But temptations to him, or power and ability in him to follow them hath ceased,—there is no change in his spirit within, for he can talk of his former sins with pleasure, he continues in other evils as bad, but more suitable to his age. In a word, he is so inwardly, that if he were in his body, and occasions offering as before, he would be just the same. Some, again, cease from some evils, from some principles, but, alas! they are no Christian principles. What restrains the multitude of civilians from gross scandals? Is it any thing but affectation of a good name and report in the world? Is it not fear of reproach or censure? Is it not because possibly they have no particular inclination to such evils? And yet there are many other evils of the heart as evil though more subtile, that they please themselves in, as pride, covetousness, malice, envy, ambition, &c. What shall all your abstinence be accounted of, when it is not love to Jesus Christ, or hatred of sin, that principles it? It is not the outward abstinence that will commend you such it is, as the principles of it are. And these only are the true Christian principles of mortification,—love of Jesus Christ, which constrains men to live no more to themselves, but to be new creatures, 2 Cor. v. 14, 15; and hatred of sin in its nature as sin a Christian should have a mortal hatred of it, as his mortal enemy. It is not Christianity to abstain from some fleshly lusts, if ye consider them not as your soul's enemies, 1 Peter ii. 11. "Ye that love the Lord hate evil," Psal. xcvii. 10. These are chained together. David's hatred was a soul-hatred, an abhorrency, Psal. cxix. 163, "I hate and abhor lying." It is like the natural antipathies that are among creatures, the soul hates not only the person of it, but the nature of it also. Men often hate sin, only as it is circumstantiate, but Christian hatred is a hatred of the nature, like the deadly feuds, which are enmities against the kind and name. "I will put enmity between thy seed," &c. It is a "perfect hatred," Psal. cxxxix. 22. And so it cannot endure any sin, because all is contrary to God's holiness and offensive to his Spirit. I would think it easier to forsake all evil, and cease from doing any evil, I mean, presumptuously, with a willing mind and endeavour, than indeed to forsake one, for as long as ye entertain so many lusts like it, they shall make way for it. It were easier to keep the whole commandments in an evangelical sense, than indeed to keep any one, for all of them help another, and subsist they cannot one without another, so that ye take a foolish course, who go about particular reformations. Ye scandalous sinners profess that ye will amend the particular fault ye are guilty of, and, in the mean time, you take no heed to your souls and lives, therefore it shall be either in vain, or not acceptable. How pleasant a life would Christians have, if they would indeed be persuaded to be altogether Christians! The halving of it neither pleaseth God nor delights you, it keeps you but in continual torment between God and Baal. Your own lusts usurp over you, and that of Christ in you challenges the supremacy, so ye are as men under two masters, each striving for the place, and were it not better to be under one settled government? If there be any tenderness of God in your hearts, or light in your consciences, they cannot but testify against your lusts, these strange lords. Your lusts, again, they drive you on against your conscience; thus ye are divided and tormented betwixt two,—your own conscience and affections. You have thus the pain of religion, and know not the true pleasure of it. You are marred in the pleasures of sin, conscience and the love of God is a worm to eat that gourd. It is gall and vinegar mixed in with them. Were it not more wisdom to be either one thing or another? If ye will have the pleasures of sin for a season, take them wholly, and renounce God, and see if your heart can endure that. If your heart cannot condescend to that, I pray you renounce them wholly, and ye shall find more exquisite and sure pleasures in godliness, at his right hand. O what a noble entertainment hath the soul in God; the peace and joy of the Holy Ghost is a kingdom indeed!

SERMON XII.

Isaiah xxvi. 3.—"Thou shall keep him in perfect peace, whose mind is stayed on thee, because he trusteth in thee."

All men love to have privileges above others. Every one is upon the design and search after some well-being, since Adam lost that which was true happiness. We all agree upon the general notion of it, but presently men divide in the following of particulars. Here all men are united in seeking after some good; something to satisfy their souls, and satiate their desires. Nay, but they scatter presently in the prosecution of it, because, according to every man's fancy and corrupt humour, they attribute that good unto diverse things; and when they meet with disappointment, they change their opinion of that, but are made no wiser, for they turn from one to another of that same kind, in which their imagination hath supposed blessedness to be; and therefore they will return to that which they first loathed and rejected. Is there, then, no such thing in the world as blessedness? Is it not to be found among men? Are all men's insatiable desires in vain? Is a creature made up and composed of desires, to keep it in continual torment and vexation of spirit? No certainly, it is, and it is found by some. All the world strives about it, but the man only who trusts and believes in God, he it is, who carries it away from them,—who hath this privilege beyond the world. And why do so many miss it? Because they do not see or suspect that it is blessedness indeed which he enjoys; but, on the contrary, their corrupted imaginations represent godliness, and a godly man's self-indigency and dependence on God, as the greatest misery and shame. The godly man hides not his blessedness from the world; no, he proclaims it when he hath found it,—he would that all enjoyed it with him. And if there were no more to declare that it doth not consist in worldly things, this might suffice—they are not communicable to many, without the prejudice and loss of every one. But none will believe his report of his own estate.

If ye would consider, here is that which men toil for,—compass sea and land for; here it is; "near thee in thy mouth." It is not in heaven, that thou shouldst say, How shall I ascend to it? It is not in hell below, that thou shouldst say, Who shall descend? It is not in the ends of the earth. No. It is "near thee, in thy mouth." It is not beyond the sea, but it is "near thee in thy mouth, even the word of faith," which Christ preached, Rom. x. 6-8. And what says that word? Believe with thy heart, and thou shall be saved; trust in God, and depend on him, and ye shall have peace, and that perfect peace; and this peace shall be kept by God himself. "Blessed, then, is the man that trusts in the Lord," Psal. xl. 4. Ye make a long journey in vain; ye spend your labour and money in vain; all the pains might be saved: it is not where ye seek it. Ye travel about many creatures; ye go to many doors, and inquire for happiness and peace, but ye go too far off; ye need not search so many coasts, it is nearer hand, in this word of the gospel—the joyful sound; it is this that proclaims peace. Peace is a comprehensive word, especially in scripture. It was the Jews' salutation, "Peace be to you;" meaning happiness and all good things; it is Christ's salutation, "Grace and peace." Grace is holiness, peace is happiness, and these are either one, or inseparably conjoined as one. This was the angels' song, "Glory to God, peace on earth," Luke ii. 14. Blessedness was restored, or brought near to be restored, to miserable man, by Jesus Christ; and upon the apprehension of this, angels sing. It was this Christ came into the world with; and when he went away, he left this legacy to his children, "My peace I leave you," John xiv. 27. We lost happiness, and all men are on a vain pursuit of it since, but it is found, and found by one of our kin. Our Lord Jesus, our elder brother, he hath found it, or made it, and brought it near us in the gospel for the receiving; and whoso receives him by faith, and trusts in him, receives that privilege, that peace. He endured much trouble to gain our peace; he behoved to undergo misery to purchase our blessedness, and so it is his own, and whoso receives him receives it also.

The news of such a peace might be seasonable in the time of war and trouble, if we apprehended our need of it. It is not a peace from war and trouble, but a peace in war and trouble. "My peace I leave with you," and "in the world ye shall have trouble," John xiv. 27, and xvi. at the end. What a blessed message is it, that there is a peace, and a perfect peace attainable in the midst of wars, confusions, and calamities of the times, public and personal; a perfect peace, a complete peace, even complete without the accession of outward and worldly peace, that needs it not; nay, appears most perfect and entire in itself, when it is stripped naked of them all. Behold what a privilege the gospel offers unto you! ye need not be made miserable, but[292] if you please. This is more than all the world can afford you. There is no man can promise to himself immunity from public or personal dangers, from many griefs and disappointments; but the gospel bids you reckon up all your troubles and miseries that you can meet with in the world; and yet in such a case, if ye hearken to wisdom, there is a peace that will make you forget that trouble. "Her ways are ways of pleasantness, and all her paths are peace," Prov. iii. 17. I will undertake to make thee blessed, says wisdom, the Father's wisdom. When all the world hath given thee over for miserable; when thou hast spent thy substance on the physicians, and in vain, come to me, I can heal that desperate disease by a word. "I create peace," when natural causes have given it over; I create it of nothing; I will keep you "in perfect peace."

You have then here, three things of special concernment in these times; and all times, a blessedness, a perfect peace attainable, the way of it, and the fountain of it. The fountain of it, the preserver of it, is God himself; the way to attain it, is "trusting in God, and staying on him." This sweetness of peace is in God the tree of life. Faith puts to its hand, and plucks the fruit of the tree; hope and dependence on God is a kind of tasting of that fruit and eating of it; and then followeth this perfect peace, as the delightful relish and sweetness that the soul finds in God, upon tasting how gracious he is. God himself is the life of our souls, the fountain of living-waters, the life and light of men. Faith and trusting in God, draws out of this fountain,—out of this deep well of salvation; and staying on God, drinks of it, till the soul be refreshed with peace and tranquillity, such as passeth natural understanding. Christ Jesus is the tree of life, that grows in the garden of God; trusting in him by faith implants a soul in him,—roots a soul in him, by virtue of which union, it springs up and grows into a living branch; by staying and depending upon him, we live by him, and hence springs this blessed and sweet fruit of peace of soul and conscience, which grows upon the confidence of the soul placed in God, as the stalk by which it is united to the tree. Trusting and staying upon God is the soul's casting its anchor upon him in the midst of the waves and storms of sin, wrath, and trouble. The poor beaten sinner casts an anchor within the vail, on that sure ground of immutable promises in Jesus Christ; and then it rests and quiets itself at that anchor, enjoys peace in the midst of the storm,—there is a great calm, it is not moved, or not greatly moved, as if it were a fair day. David flieth unto God as his refuge, anchors upon the name of the Lord, Psal. lxii. 1, 2; and so he enjoys a perfect calm and tranquillity. "I shall not be moved," because he is united to the rock, he is tied to the firm foundation, Jesus Christ, and no storm can dissolve this union, not because of the strength of that rope of faith, it is but a weak cord, if omnipotency did not compass it about also, and so we "are kept by the power of God, through faith unto salvation." The poor wearied traveller, the pilgrim, sits down under the shadow of a rock, and this peace is his rest under it. Faith lays him down, and peace is his rest and sleep. Faith in Jesus Christ is a motion towards him, as the soul's proper place and centre, and therefore it is called a coming to him,—flying to him as the city of refuge. It is the soul's flight out of itself, and misery and sin within, to apprehend mercy and grace, and happiness in Christ. Now, hope is the conjunction or union of the soul with him,—the soul then staying and resting on him, as in its proper place, and so it enjoys perfect peace and rest in its place, so that if ye remove it thence, then ye offer violence to it.

These two things are of greatest importance to you to know, what this perfect peace is, and what is the way to attain it. The one is the privilege and dignity, the other is the duty of a Christian, and these two make him up what he is.

I would think that man perfectly blessed, who is at peace with two things,—God and himself. If a man be at peace with creatures without him, and be at peace with himself, but have war within his own mind, that man's peace is no peace, let be perfect peace. A man's greatest enemy is within his own house. And within indeed, when it is in his bosom and soul, when a man's conscience is against him, it is worse than a world beside. *Conscientia mille testes*,[293] so I say, it is *mille hostes*. It is "a thousand witnesses," and "a thousand enemies." It were better to endure condemnation of any judge, of many judges in the world, than to sustain the conviction of a man's own conscience, when it accuseth, who shall excuse? John viii. 9, Rom. ii. 15. "A merry spirit," saith Solomon, "is a continual feast," Prov. xv. 15. And what must a heart be, which hath such a gnawing worm within it, as an accusing conscience, to eat it out? This is the worm of hell that dies not out, which makes hell hell indeed. This indeed will be a painful consumption, "A broken spirit drieth up the bones," it will eat up the marrow of the spirit and body, Prov. xvii. 22. What infirmity is there which a man cannot bear? Poverty, famine, war, pestilence, sickness, name what you will, but a wounded spirit who can bear? Prov. xviii. 14. And there is reason for it, for there is none to bear it, a sound and whole spirit can sustain infirmities, but when that is wounded, which should bear all the rest, what is behind to bear it? It is a burden to itself. If a man have trouble and war in this world, yet there is often escaping from it, a man may fly from his enemy, but when thy enemy is within thee, whither shalt thou fly? Thou canst not go from thyself, thou carriest about thee thy enemy, thy tormentor.

But suppose a man were at peace within himself, and cried peace, peace, to himself, yet if he be not at peace with God, shall his peace be called peace? Shall it not rather be named supine security? If a man be at variance with himself, and his soul disquieted within, there is more fear than danger if he be at peace with God. It is but a false alarm, that shall end well, but if he have peace in his own bosom, and yet no agreement with God, then destructions are certainly coming, his dream of peace will have a terrible wakening. A man may sleep soundly, and his enemies round about him, because he knoweth not of it, but he is in a worse estate than he that is in great fear, and his enemies either none, or far distant. The one hath present danger, and no fear, the other present fear, and no danger, and which of these think ye best? Sudden destruction awakes the one from sleep, Ezek. vii. 25. Their fear and destruction come both at once, when it is now in vain to fear, because it is past hope, Prov. i. 27. Therefore the Lord swears, that "there is no peace to the wicked," Isa. xlviii. 22. What! Do not they often cry peace to themselves, and put the evil day far off? No men are so without bands in life and death as they, they have made agreement with hell and death, and their own consciences, yet for all that, "thus saith the Lord, there is no peace to the wicked." If God be against us, what is the matter who be with us, for he can make a man's friends his enemies, and he can make a man's enemies to be at peace with him: He makes peace and creates trouble, Isa. xlv. 7. Men can but destroy the body, but he can destroy both body and soul for ever. O what a potent and everlasting enemy is he! There is no escaping from his all-seeing eye and powerful hand, Psal. cxxxix. 7, 8. A man may fly from men, but whither shall he fly from His presence? To heaven?—He is there. To hell?—He is there. The darkness of the night hath been a covering under which many have escaped, and been saved in armies, but darkness is no covering to him, it is all one with light. He is near hand every one of us. The conscience is within us, but he is within the conscience, and how much God is above the creature, so great and dreadful a party is he above any enemy imaginable. Therefore I conclude, that that man only hath perfect peace, who is at peace with God, and with his own conscience. If a man be at peace with God, and not with himself, he wants but a moment's time of perfect peace, for, ere it be long, the God of it will speak peace unto him. But if he be at peace with God and himself, I know not what he wants of the perfect peace, of the "peace, peace," for it is a man's mind that makes peace or war, it is not outward things, but in the midst of peace he may be in trouble, and in the midst of trouble in peace, according as he hath satisfaction and contentment in his own breast, for what is all the grace of a Christian? It is godliness with contentment, it is not godliness and riches, godliness and honour, or pleasure, godliness and outward peace. No, no, contentment compenseth all these, and hath in it eminently all the gain and advantage of these. A man in honour, a rich man, having no contentment in it, is really as poor, as ignominious, as the poor and despised man. If contentment then be without these things, certainly they cannot be missed, for where contentment is not with them, it only is missed, and they not considered. Contentment is all the gain that men seek in riches, and honour, and pleasure, if a godly man have that same without them, he then hath all the gain and advantage, and wants nothing, but some trouble that ordinarily attends them. Outward peace cannot add to inward peace, and so the want of it cannot diminish.

We must begin at the original, if we would know rightly this peace that passeth knowledge. The fountain-head is peace with God, a stream of this is peace of conscience, and peace with the creatures. There is a peace of friendship, when persons were never enemies, and there is a peace of reconciliation, when parties at variance are made one. Innocent Adam had peace once with God as a friend,—angels continue so to this day, but now there is no such peace between men and God, for all are become enemies to God, and aliens from the commonwealth of Israel, that peace was broken by rebellion against God his maker, and all the posterity are born with the same enmity against God. On our part are hearts desperately wicked, whose imagination is only evil continually. On God's part is holy and spotless justice, that is of purer eyes than to behold iniquity, and therefore must destroy it or the sinner. On our part are so many rebellions,—Adam's actual transgression, and all our own sins and breaches of the holy law, as so many breaches of peace. On God's part are so many curses answerable to the breaches of the law: "cursed is every one that abideth not in every thing," &c. This curse is even the proclamation of men to be traitors, and an intimation of the righteous judgment which will come upon them. Adam was in a covenant of peace with God,—"Do, and thou shalt live, if not, thou shalt die." Adam brake this covenant, so the peace is dissolved, and God is no more obliged to give life, but to execute the pain contained in the covenant, and in sign and token of this, look how Adam fled from God's presence, to hide himself when he heard his voice, it was a poor shift, for whither should he go from his presence? But, alas! seeking more wisdom, he lost that he had, seeking divine wisdom, he lost human. Now, there is no more making up this peace on such terms again, we have no capacity to treat with God any more, but blessed be his Majesty, who hath found out the way of agreement and reconciliation. O that ye were once persuaded of your enmity against God! ye are not born friends, though ye be born within the visible church. How dreadful a thing is it, to have the Most High and terrible God against you, to do to you according to your deservings! Ye all know this, we are enemies to God by nature, I pray you, is it but a name? Is it not worthy deep consideration? But who considereth this matter? If ye lose a friend, ye will be troubled, and the more behoveful your friend was, the more troubled you will be. If a great and potent nation proclaimed war against us, we cannot but be sensible of it, but alas! who considereth the great breach that is between God and all men, occasioned by the first man's transgression and rebellion! It is one of the degrees of health, to know the disease, and I may call it a degree of peace, a kind of preparation to peace, to know the enmity, and not generally to know it, but to ponder it till the heart be affected with it, to call a council of all the faculties and affections of the soul to consider the great imminent danger of man's commonwealth. What is it, I pray you, that is the greatest obstruction of men's making peace with God, that makes the breach irreparable, and the wound incurable? It is this, certainly, no man apprehendeth it aright, we entertain good thoughts of our friendship with God, or that it is easy to be reconciled. Who seeth such a wide breach between God and man, that all the merits of angels and men could not make it up? Who seeth the price of redemption so precious, as it must cease for ever, for all that men and angels can do? Is not every man offering God satisfaction, either his tears, or sorrow, or amendment in time coming, or all of them? Do not men undertake to pacify God with external ordinances, and think it may suffice for their sins? Certainly ye are ignorant of the infinite separation between God and man, who imagine a treaty with him yourselves, or that ever ye can come unto speaking terms, and therefore is this war and enmity perpetual; therefore there is no peace, when ye cry, Peace, peace! When ye have peace within you, and say that ye have peace with God, yet certainly, the Lord thy God is against thee, and will not spare thee, Deut. xxix. 19. Many of you bless yourselves in your own hearts, when ye hear the curse and threatening of the law, ye say, God forbid that all that were true. Well, thus saith the Lord, All these curses that are written in this book shall be upon thee, and the Lord shall separate thee unto evil, because ye take not with your enmity, there can be no treaty, a mediator can have no employment from you.

How shall the breach of peace be made up? Since the first covenant cannot be made up again, where shall the remedy be found? God is just and righteous, men are rebellious and sinful, can these meet, and the one not be consumed? Will not God be a consuming fire, and men as stubble before the Lord's presence? Therefore, there must be a Mediator between them, a peace-maker, to make of two one, to take up the difference. And this Mediator must be like both, and yet neither wholly the one nor the other. He must therefore be God and man, that he may be a fit day's man betwixt God and man, and this is our Lord Jesus Christ. In his divinity he comes near to God, in his humanity he comes near to man, in his person he is between both, and he is fit to make peace, and therefore he is "a Prince of peace," Isa. ix. 6. And that he may be a Prince of peace, he must be both, "an everlasting Father" like God, and a young child like unto man. God to prevail with God, and a man to engage for man, and therefore he is called "our Peace," Eph. ii. 14. Our Lord Jesus Christ enters into a covenant with the Father, wherein he undertakes to bear our curse, and the chastisement of our peace. He is content to be dealt with as the rebel, "Upon me, upon me be the iniquity," and so there comes an interruption, as it were, of that blessed peace he had with the Father. He is content that there should be a covering of wrath spread over the Father's love, that he should handle the Son as an enemy, and therefore it is, that sinners are admitted as friends,—his obedience takes away our rebellion. The cloud of the Lord's displeasure pours down upon him, that it might be fair weather to us, the armies of curses that were against us, encounter him, and he, by being overcome, overcometh, by being slain by justice, Satan and sin, overcometh all those, and killeth the enmity on the cross, making peace by his blood, Col. ii. 14, 15, Eph. ii. 15. And it is this sacrifice that hath pacified heaven,—the sweet smell of it hath gone above, and made peace in the high places.

Here, then, is the privilege of a believer,—to be at peace with God, to be one with him, and this indeed is life eternal, to be united unto the fountain of life, in whose favour is life and whose loving kindness is better than life. Is not this a blessed estate? Whatever a man hath done against God is all forgiven and forgotten, it shall never come into remembrance. Are not angels blessed who are friends with God? Such is the soul whose sins are pardoned through Christ,—its sins are as if they never had been. The soul is not only escaped that terrible wrath of God, but being at peace with God, all the goodness that is communicable to creatures, it shall partake of, "that they may be one, as we are one, that they may be perfect in one," John xvii. This Christ prayed for, and this was the end of his death,—to make of two one. So, then, the glory that Christ is partaker of with the Father, we must be partakers of with him, and all this by virtue of that peace with God by him. O if ye knew what enmity with God is! how would it endear and make precious peace with him! The one engageth all that is in God to be against a man; the other engageth all that is in him to be for a man. And is not he then a great one, whether he be a friend or an enemy, is he not the best friend and worst enemy, who hath most power, yea, all power, to employ for whom he will, and against whom he will? What a blessed change is it, to have God, of a consuming fire, made a sun, with healing and consolation! that the righteous, holy, and just God, before whom no flesh can stand, should accept so rebellious sinners, and dwell among them! He had not only power to destroy, but law against us also. What a perfect peace is it, then, that the Judge becometh a merciful Father, and the law of ordinances is cancelled, and that power employed to keep salvation to us, and us to salvation! Ye who have made peace and atonement through Christ's blood, rejoice in the hope of the glory of God, there wants nothing to make you completely blessed, but the clear and perfect sight and knowledge of your estate before God.

Now, when this peace, which is made up in heaven, is intimated unto the conscience, then all the tempests and clouds of it evanish, and this is the peace of believing, which is the soul's resting and quieting itself upon the believing favour of God. There may be a great calm above, good-will in God towards men, and yet great tempests in this lower region, no peace on earth. There is a peace of conscience which is a disease of conscience, a benumbedness of conscience, or a sleep of conscience, when men walk in the imagination of their own hearts, and flatter themselves in their own eyes, will not trouble themselves with the apprehension of the wrath of God. When souls will not suffer their sin, or the curse to enter in, this is that "no peace" which the Lord speaks often of, it is but a dream, and when a man awaketh, alas! what a dreadful sight meets he with first,—"sudden destruction!" Sin enters into the conscience, and the law, the strength of sin, and so that peace endeth in an eternal disquietness. But what is the reason, that notwithstanding of God's justice and men's sins, so many are not afraid of him, so many pass the time without fear of wrath and hell? Is it not because they have taken hold of his strength, and made peace with him? No, indeed, but because they know not the power of his anger, to fear him according to his wrath. Who will spend one hour in the examination of his own ways, in searching out sins, in counting his debt, till he find it past payment? No, men entertain the thoughts of sin, and hell and wrath, as if it were coals in their bosom, they shake them out, they like and love any diversion from them. Oh! ignorance maketh much peace, I would say security, which is so much worse than fear, because it is so far from the remedy, that it knoweth not the evil and danger. It is not the rising of the Sun of righteousness, shining into the soul, that hath cleared them, but their perpetual darkness that blindeth them. I say, then, in the name of Jesus Christ, that ye never knew the peace of God, who knew not war with God, ye know not love, who have not known anger, but this is the soul's true peace and tranquillity, when it is once awakened to see its misery and danger—how many clouds overspread it, what tempests blow; what waves of displeasure go over its head! But when that peace, which is made in the high places, breaketh through the cloud with a voice, "Son, be of good comfort, thy sins be forgiven thee!" when that voice of the Spirit is uttered, presently at its command the wind and waves obey, the soul is calmed, as the sea after a storm, it is not only untroubled, but it is peaceable upon solid grounds, because of the word which speaks peace in Christ. The peace of the most of you is such as ye were born and educated withal. Is it not a created peace, a spoken peace,—the fruit of the lips, and so no true peace? Ye had not your peace from the word, but ye brought it to the word, ye have no peace after trouble, and so it is not the Lord's peace.

The Christian may have peace, in regard of his own salvation and eternal things, and in regard of all things that befalleth in time; the first is, when the conscience is sprinkled with the blood of Jesus Christ, and getteth a good answer to all the challenges and accusations of conscience, and of the law and justice, 1 Pet. iii. 21; when the Spirit of God shines into the soul, with a new light to discover these things that are freely given, 1 Cor. ii. 12. And this is the sealing of the Spirit after believing, Eph. i. 13. When a soul hath put to its seal by believing God's word, and hath acknowledged God's truth and faithfulness in his word, the Spirit sealeth mutually the believer's faith, both by more holiness and the knowledge of it; and how great peace is this, when a soul can look upon all its iniquities when they compass about a man, and outward trouble sharpeneth and setteth on edge inward challenges, and yet the soul will not fear,—it hath answers to them all in Christ's blood, Psalm xlix. 5. This is a greater word than all the world can say. Many men's fearlessness proceedeth from ignorance of sin, their iniquities were never set in order before them; but if once they compassed them about, and wrath, like a fiery wall, compass them about also, so that there were no escaping, O it would be more terrible than all the armies of the world! Ye would account little of a kingdom, ye would exchange it for such a word as David hath upon good grounds.

Now, I say again, the soul that hath thus committed itself to him as a faithful keeper, may have peace in all estates and conditions; and this peace floweth from that other peace. There is a peace which guards the heart and mind, Phil. iv. 6, 7, opposed to carefulness and anxiety; and this Paul is exemplary for, "I have learned in every estate, therewith to be content, to want and abound," &c. ver. 11. The soul of a believer may be in an equal even tenor and disposition in all conditions; it may possess itself in patience. Impatience and anxiety make a man not his own man; he is not himself, he enjoys not himself; he is a burden to himself, and is his own tormentor; but if souls were stayed upon God, certainly they would possess themselves, dwell securely within their own breasts. We may find that the most part of men are exposed to all the floods and waves of the times. They move inwardly, as things are troubled outwardly; every thing addeth moment to their grief or joy; any dispensation casteth the balance, and either weighs them down with discouragement, or lifteth them up with vanity and lightness of mind; but the believer's privilege is to be unmoved in the midst of all the tossings and confusions of the times, Psal. cxxviii. 1, 2. Ye would be as mount Zion if ye trusted in God; no dispensation would enter into the soul to cast the balance upon you; ye might stand upon your rock Jesus Christ, and look about the estates, persons, affairs, and minds of men, as a troubled sea, fleeting, tossed up and down, and ye stand and not be moved, or not greatly moved, Psal. lxii. 2. And this is to be wise indeed. If I would describe a wise man, I would say, he "is one man," beside him no man is one with himself, but various, inconstant, changeable. He is unwise who is unlike himself, who changeth persons according to dispensations: wisdom is the stability of thy times, and faith is wisdom. It establisheth as mount Zion, so as a man cometh out still one,—in prosperity not exalted, in adversity not cast down, in every estate content; and this is the man who is blessed indeed. This were wisdom,—to will the same thing, and nill[294] the same thing. *Semper idem velle, atque idem nolle.*[295] I need not, says Seneca, add that exception, that it be right which you desire, for no one thing can universally and always please, if it be not good and right; so I say, he were both wise and happy, who had but one grief and one joy. Should not a believer's mind be calm and serene, seeing the true light hath shined; it should be as the upper world, where no blasts, no storms or clouds are to eclipse the sun, or cloud it. While our peace and tranquillity is borrowed from outward things, certainly it must change; but a believer's peace and tranquillity of mind, having its rise from above, from the unchangeable word of the Lord, it needeth not to change according to the vicissitudes of providence. He needeth not to care beforehand, because there is one who careth for him; and what needeth both to care? He needeth not be disquieted or troubled after, because it shall turn about to his good; all things shall do so, Rom. viii. 28. He needeth not be anxious about future events, because he hath all his burden cast upon another by prayer and supplication. What needeth he then take a needless burden? Prayer will do that which care pretends and cannot do, and that without trouble. He needeth not be troubled when things are present, for he cannot by his thought either add or diminish, take away or prevent. There is one good and necessary thing that his heart is upon, and that cannot be taken from him; and therefore all things else are indifferent, and of small concernment to him.

Now what wanteth such a man of perfect peace, who is reconciled to God, and at peace within himself? When peace guardeth the heart and mind within, compasseth it as a castle or garrison, to hold out all the vain alarms of external things, may not all the world be troubled about him? What though the floods lift up their voice, if they come not into the soul? If he be one and the same in peace and trouble, prosperity and adversity, do not lament him in the one more than the other. It is the mind that maketh your condition good or bad; but yet, I say, the believer hath likewise peace with all the creatures, which the world hath not, and even in this he is a privileged man. He is in league with the stones of the field, and in peace in his tabernacle, Job v. 23. All things are his, because he is Christ's, and all are Christ's, who is the possessor of heaven and earth, at least the righteous heir of both, 1 Cor iii. 21. The unbeliever hath no right to the creature; though there be a cessation for a time between them and him, yet that is no peace, for they will at length be armed against him. They are witnesses already against him, and groan to God for the corruption that man's sin hath subjected them unto. His table is, it may be, full, yet it is a snare unto him; he getteth ease and quietness outwardly: nay, but it slayeth the fool and destroyeth him. But the godly man is at peace, through Christ's blood, with all crosses and comforts; the sting and enmity of all evils is taken away by Christ. Poverty is made a friend, because Christ was poor; hunger and thirst is become a friend, because

Christ was hungry and thirsty; reproach and contempt is at peace with him, because Christ was despised; afflictions and sorrows are reconciled to him, because Christ was a man of sorrows, and acquainted with griefs; in a word, death itself is become a friend, since Christ subdued it by lasting of it. I may say, the worst things to a natural man are become best friends to the believer; the grave keepeth his body and dust in hope. Death is a better friend than life, for it ministers an entry into glory: it is the door of eternal life: it taketh down the tabernacle of mortality, that we may be clothed upon with immortality. In sum, whatever it be, Christ hath stamped a new quality on it; it cometh through his hand, and so, if it be not good in itself, yet it is good in the use, and in his appointment, Rom. viii. 21. If it be not good, yet it worketh together for our good; it contributeth to our good, because it is in his skilful hand, who can bring good out of evil, peace out of trouble. O that ye were persuaded to be Christians indeed, to love his law, and trust in him. Great peace have all such. This were more to you than peace in the world; your peace should be as a river, for abundance and perpetuity; no drought could dry it up; it should run in time as a large river, and when time is done, it would embosom itself in eternity, in that ocean of eternal peace and joy which the saints are drowned in above; other men's peace is but like a brook that dries up in summer.

SERMON XIII.

Isaiah xxvi. 3.—"Thou shall keep him in perfect peace, whose mind is stayed on thee, because he trusteth in thee."

Christ hath left us his peace, as the great and comprehensive legacy, "My peace I leave you," John xiv. 27. And this was not peace in the world that he enjoyed; you know what his life was, a continual warfare; but a peace above the world, that passeth understanding. "In the world you shall have trouble, but in me you shall have peace," saith Christ,—a peace that shall make trouble no trouble. You must lay your accounts to have such a life as the forerunner had; but withal, as he hath left us his trouble, so hath he left us his peace; the trouble will have an end, but the joy can no man take from you. We have this sure promise to rest upon, in behalf of the church, peace shall be in Israel; a peace that the world knoweth not, and so cannot assault it, or take it away. O that ye would hearken to this word, that ye would trust in the Lord, and stay upon your God, then should your peace be as a river, Isa. xlviii. 18. There is nothing more desired in time of trouble than peace; but all peace is not better than war: some necessary war is better than evil-grounded peace. The kingdoms have been long in pain, labouring to bring forth a safe and well-grounded peace. But, alas! we have been in pain and brought forth wind; when we looked for peace, no good came, and for healing, behold trouble. But how shall we arrive at our desired haven? Certainly, if peace be well-grounded, it must have truth for its foundation, and righteousness for its companion; truth must spring out of the earth, and righteousness look down from heaven. This were the compendious way for public peace, if every man would make his own peace with God. There are controversies with God, between king, nobles, and people; and therefore God fomenteth the wars in the kingdoms. If you would have these ended, make peace with God in Christ, by flying in unto him, and resting on him; more trusting in God would despatch our wars; trusting in the arm of flesh continueth them. Always whatever be, peace or war, here is the business that more concerns you,—your eternal peace and safety; and, if ye were more careful of this, to save your own souls, you would help the public more. If you could be once persuaded to be Christians indeed, we needed not press many duties in reference to the public; and until you be once persuaded to save yourselves, by flying from the wrath to come, it is in vain to speak of public duties to you. We do therefore declare unto you the way of obtaining perfect peace,—peace as a river; if you will quit all self-confidences, flee from yourselves as your greatest enemies, and trust your souls unto the promise in Jesus Christ, and lean all your weight on him, we assure you, your peace shall run abundantly and perpetually. Whoever trusteth in creatures, in uncertain riches, in worldly peace, in whatsoever thing besides the only living and glorious Lord, we persuade him, that his peace shall fail as a brook. All things in this world shall deal deceitfully with you, as a brook which is blackish, by reason of ice; what time it waxeth warm, it shall evanish. You that looked and waited for water in it shall be confounded, because you hoped, and are ashamed because of your expectation. Job vi. 15, &c. The summer shall dry up your peace, and what will ye do? But if you pour out your souls on him, and trust in the fountain of living waters, you shall not be ashamed, for your peace shall be as a river. The elephant is said to trust that he can drink out a river; but he is deceived, for he may drink again,—it runs, and shall run for ever. If any thing would essay to take your peace from you, it is a vain attempt, for it runs like a river; it may be shallower and deeper, but it cannot run dry, because of the living fountain it proceedeth from. There is no other thing can be made sure; all besides this is uncertain, and this only is worthy to be made sure; nothing besides this can give you satisfaction.

Are your hearts asking within you, how shall this peace be attained? If you desire to know it, consider these words, "Whose heart is stayed on thee, because he trusteth in thee." It concerneth you much to know well, what this is that your eternal peace depends on.

Trusting in God, is the leaning of the soul's weight on God. The soul hath a burden above it, heavy and unsupportable, and this the truster casteth upon God; and so he is a loadened and weary man, whom Christ exhorteth to come to him, and he shall find ease for his soul, Matt. xi. 28; Prov. iii. 5. Leaning to ourselves, and trusting in God are opposed. Psal. xxii. 10, trusting is exponed[296] to be "a casting upon God." Psal. xxv. 1, it is called, "a lifting up the soul to him." This one thing is included in the bosom of trusting and believing, that a man hath many burdens too heavy for him, which would sink him down: the believer is such a one as Jehoshaphat, 2 Chron. xx. 12, "O Lord, we have no might against this great company, neither know we what to do." O Lord, I have an army of iniquities against me, a great company compasseth me about; an army of curses as numerous as mine iniquities; both are innumerable as the sand of the sea; I have no might against them, neither know I what to do: nay, the Lord is against me, his wrath is like the roaring of a lion; what can I do against him? The first beginning of trusting in God is distrusting ourselves; and until a man see his duty and burden beyond his strength, his burden greater than he can bear, you will never persuade him to come to Jesus Christ, and lean on him. We will not preach any such doctrine, as to discharge any to come to Christ, till they be wearied and loaden; for, when a man conceiveth that he wanteth that weariedness, whither shall he go to find it? Is there any fountain, but one, Jesus Christ, both of grace and preparations to it, if any such be? But this we preach unto you, that until you be wearied and loaden, you will not cast your burden on Jesus. We need not discharge you to come till you be such, for certainly you will not come. This is the desperate wickedness of our hearts, that we will never forsake ourselves till we can do no better. Until men be as David, "I looked on the right hand, and there was none would know me; refuge failed me," certainly they will not cry to God. Men will look round about them, before they will look up above them; they will cast the burden of their souls upon any thing, upon their own sorrow and contrition, upon their resolution to amend, upon external duties and privileges, upon civil honesty, until all these succumb under the weight of their salvation; and then, it may be, they will ask after him who bare our griefs. I would not willingly speak of preparations to faith, because it putteth men upon searching for something in themselves, upon fashioning their own hearts, and trimming them to come to Christ; whereas there is nothing can be acceptable to him but what cometh from him. But I think all that men intend, who speak of preparations, may be gained this way by holding out unto men the impossibility of coming to Christ, till they be emptied of themselves. Not that the one is a thing going before, to be done by us, but because they are all one; it is one motion of the soul to come out of itself, and into Jesus; it is one thing really to distrust ourselves, and to trust in him; and by this means, when the true nature of faith itself is holden out, men might examine themselves rather by it, whether they have it, than by the preparations of it.

But to come to our purpose, when the soul is pressed under burdens of sin and misery, of duty and insufficiency, and inability to do it, then the gospel discovereth unto the wearied soul a place of reposing and rest. The Lord hath established Christ Jesus, an "ensign to the people;" those who seek unto him shall find his rest glorious, Isa. xi. 10. When there is discovered in us all emptiness and inability, yea impossibility to save ourselves, or perform any duty, then are we led to Jesus Christ, as one who is come with grace and truth, in whom it hath pleased the Father all fulness should dwell; and the turning of the soul over upon him is trusting in him. You would not mistake this; trusting in the Lord in its first and most native acting, is not always persuasion of his good-will and love in particular. No, the soul meets first with a general promise, holding out his good-will in general; and the soul closeth with this, as a thing both good and true,—as faithful in itself, and worthy of all acceptation. This is it that we must first meet with,—an all-sufficient Saviour, able to save to the utmost all that come to him; and the soul's accepting of that blessed Saviour on the terms he is offered, this is believing in him, and trusting to him, as a complete Saviour.

Now when the soul hath disburdened itself upon God, and set its seal to the truth of the promises in the gospel for salvation; if the light of the Spirit shine to discover this unto it, that it hath laid hold on his strength who is able to save to the utmost, then it becometh persuaded of his love in particular; and this is rather the sealing after believing, than believing itself.

When once men have hazarded their souls upon his word, and trusted in him, then they may trust in him for all particulars: he that hath given his Son for us, will he not with him give all things? This, therefore, is the continual recourse of a believer,—from discovered emptiness and insufficiency in himself, to travel unto the fulness and strength of Jesus Christ, that his strength may be perfected in weakness. Yea, when all things seem contrary, and his dispensation writes bitter things against us, yet ought we to trust in him, Job xiii. 15. There is a peace of wilfulness and violence in faith, that will look always towards his word, whatever be threatened to the contrary.

Now, from this faith in God, floweth a constant dependence and stayedness on him, they are stayed on him, because they trusted in him; for faith discovereth in God such grounds, that it may lean its weight upon him without wavering and changing. It considereth his power, his good will, and his faithfulness; he is able to perform, he is willing to do it, and he is faithful, because he hath promised. His greatness and power is a high rock, higher than we, that faith leadeth us unto. His love and good-will in Jesus Christ, maketh an open entry and ready access to that rock; and faithfulness engageth both to give a shelter and refuge to the poor sinner. Would a soul be any more tossed, would there be any place for wavering and doubting, if souls considered his excellent loving-kindness, and great goodness laid up and treasured with him for those that trust in him? Psalm xxxvi. 7. Who would not put their trust under the shadow of his wings, and think themselves safe? Again, if his eternal power were pondered, how he is able to effectuate whatever he pleaseth; what everlasting arms he hath that by a word supports the frame of the world; what he can do, if he stretch out his arm; and then, if these two immutable things, (Heb. vi. 18,) his promise and his oath, were looked upon;—how he hath engaged himself in his truth, and sworn in his holiness; would not a soul lie safely between these three? What strong consolation would such a threefold consideration yield? Would any wind or tempest blow within these walls mounted up to heaven?

Stayedness on God is nothing else but the fixedness of believing and trusting, Ps. cxii. 7, 8, "his heart is fixed, trusting in God; his heart is established." It is even the mature and ripe age of faith. Faith, while it is yet in infancy, in its tender years, neither can endure storms, nor can it confirm us in them; but when it hath sprung up and grown in that root of Jesse, when it is rooted and established in Jesus Christ, then it establisheth the soul. Faith abiding in him and taking root, groweth, confirmed as a tree that cannot easily be moved; and if you establish faith, you shall be established.

There are two particulars which I conceive the trusting soul is stayed on. First, in the meditation of God. Secondly, in expectation from him of all good things. When I say the meditation of God, I take in both contemplation and affection. The most part of men have but few thoughts of God at all; even those who trust in him do not consider sufficiently what a one he is in whom they believe. If faith were vigorous and lively, it would put men to often thinking on him, seeking to know him in his glorious names; the mind would be stayed upon this glorious object, as the most mysterious and wonderful one. How strong are men's minds with their vanities? When they awake, they are not still with God. The meditation of him is a burden to them; any other thing getteth more time and thoughts. But meditation addeth affection to contemplation; men may think long upon the heavens and their course, but their affections are not ravished with them. But thus is the soul stayed on God;—when the soul's desires are towards the remembrance of his name, then affection stayeth the mind upon what it pitcheth on; and certainly the mind giveth but passing looks, constrained thoughts, where the heart is not. Here is David's meditation, Ps. i. "My delight is in the law of the Lord." The soul of a believer should be constant and fixed in the consideration of God, till he be wholly engaged to admiration and wondering. "O Lord, how excellent is thy name," Psal. viii. 1: "and who is like unto thee?" You all say that you believe in God, and know his power,—you know he is good, he is merciful, just, long-suffering, faithful, &c. But what is all this knowledge but ignorance, and your light darkness, when it doth not press you to put your trust in his name? You know; nay, but you consider not what you know. This is trusting, when the mind is stayed on what it knoweth, when all the scattered thoughts and affections are called home, and united in one, to be exercised about this comprehensive object, "the Lord our God." It is not want of knowledge destroyeth you, but want of consideration of what you know, and this is brutishness. Men's hearts do not carry the seal and stamp of their knowledge, because thoughts of God and his word are but as passengers that go through a land, as lightning going through the mind, but warms it not; and so their practice carrieth no impression of it either. How base is it for those who have God for their God, to be so ignorant of him! Would not any man willingly travel about his own possessions? Have you such a large portion, believers, and should ye be taken up with other vanities? Should your hearts and minds be stayed on them, more than the living God? There is a great vanity and levity in men's minds; "The Lord knoweth the thoughts of man that they are vanity." There is an unsettledness of spirit,—we cannot pitch on that upon which we may be stayed; and so all the spirits of men are in a continual motion from one thing to another, for nothing giveth complete satisfaction, and therefore it must go and try one after another, to see if it can find in it what it found not in the former. And such is the inconstancy of the spirit, that it licketh up its vomit; and what thing it refused, it eateth it up as its meat. The time is spent in choosing and refusing, rejecting one thing and taking another, and again returning to what you have rejected. Thus are men tossed up and down, and unstable in all their ways, as a ship without ballasting. Now, faith and trusting in God is the ballast and weight of this inconstant ship: it is the anchor to stay it from being driven to and fro. If once men would pitch upon this one Lord, who hath in himself eminently all the scattered perfections of creatures, and infinitely more,—if you would consider him, and meditate on him, till your souls loved him, would you not be ravished with him? Would you not build your house beside him, and dwell in the meditation of his name? This would fix and establish you in duties—"when I awake, I am still with thee." A little searching and experience discovereth emptiness in all beside; and therefore is it, that the soul removeth sooner from such a particular creature than it expected. But here is One that is "past finding out." The more I search and find, I find him the more above what I can search and find. The creatures are but painted and fair in men's apprehension, and at a distance; but the near enjoyment of them discovereth the delusion, and sendeth a man away ashamed, because he trusted. But the Lord God is, and there is no other. He is not as waters that fail, no liar,—he is an everlasting fountain,—the more you dig and draw, it runs the faster; he will never send any away ashamed that trust in him, because they shall find more than they expected.

Therefore the soul that is stayed on meditation of God, and knoweth him certainly, will be fixed in expectation from him. Our expectation from the creatures changeth, because it is often frustrated. Disappointment meets it. It is above what is in the creature, and so it must meet with disappointment; but as he is above our meditation, so is he far above our expectation; and if a man's experience answer his hope, he hath no reason to change his hope. The Lord hath often done things we looked not for, but we never looked for any thing, according to the grounds of the word, but it was done, or a better than it. He doth not always answer our limitations; but if he give gold, when we sought silver, are we not answered? Are we disappointed? There are three things that use most to disquiet and toss men's spirits,—sin and wrath, future events, and present calamities. Faith establisheth the soul on God in all these, and suffereth it not to be driven to and fro with these winds; it finds a harbour and refuge in God from all these. If he be pursued by the avenger of blood, God's wrath and justice, here is an open city of refuge that he may run to and be safe. If iniquities compass me about, yet I will not fear, but oppose unto that great company the many sufferings and obedience of Jesus Christ. My conscience challengeth and writeth bitter things against me, yet I have an answer in that blood that speaketh better things than Abel's. If sins prevail, he will purge them away. His mercy is above all my sin, and his virtue and power is above my sin. He hath promised, and will he not do it? Oft times men's souls are perplexed and tossed about future events, careful for to morrow. This is a great torment of spirit, it cutteth and divideth it,—putteth a man to his own providence, as if there were no God, but he that trusteth in God is established in this, "His heart is fixed trusting in the Lord." He hath committed his soul to him, and why may he not his body? He hath nothing but his promise for eternal salvation, and may not that same suffice for temporal? He careth for me, saith faith, why then should we both care about one thing? He hath given his Son for me, the most precious gift which the world cannot match, and will he not with him give all these lesser things? And thus the believer encloseth himself within the Father's love and providence, and is fixed, not fearing evil tidings, for what tidings can be evil, seeing our Father hath the sovereign disposing of all affairs, and knoweth what is best for us? Present dispensations often shake men, and drive them to and fro, their feet slip, and are not established, "Thou didst hide thy face, and I was troubled." But if you trusted in God, and considered what is in him to oppose to all difficulties and calamities, you would say, "I shall not be moved, though the floods lift up their voice." If you believed his love, would not this sweeten all his dealing? He maketh all work together for good. Sovereignty, righteousness, and mercy, are sure and firm ground to stand upon in all storms. You may cast anchor at any of those, and lie secure. "It is the Lord, let him do what he pleaseth." This was enough to quiet the saints in old times. Should he give account of his matters to us? Shall the clay say to the potter, why is it thus? His absolute right by creation maketh him, beyond all exception, do what he pleases, but beside this, he is pleased and condescendeth to reason with us, and give account of his matters, to testify to our conscience that he is righteous in all his ways. It was the ground of Jeremiah's settling, Lam iii. "It is of the Lord's mercy that we are not consumed." It should have allayed and stayed Job. Know this, thou art punished less than thy iniquities deserve. Who will set a time to plead with him? Shall any be found righteous before him? And this might stop all men's mouths, and put them in the dust to keep silence, seeing he hath law to do infinitely more than he doth, why should not we rather proclaim his clemency, than argue him so very hard? If to both those you shall add the consideration of his mercy, that all his paths are mercy and truth unto you, even when he correcteth most severely, so that you may bless him as well for rods as for meat and clothing, and count yourself blessed when you are taught by the rod and the word, the one speaking to the other, and the other sealing its instruction,—if you believed that it were a fruit of his love, that "he chasteneth every son whom he loveth," because he will not let you depart from him, will not let you settle upon a present world, and forget your country above, therefore he compasseth you about with hedges of thorns to keep in your way, and therefore he maketh this world bitter and unpleasant, that you may have no continuing city,—if all this were believed would not the soul triumph with Paul, "What can separate me from the love of God?"—not past things, for all my sins are blotted out, and shall be remembered no more, not present things, for they work to good, and are a fruit of his love, not things to come, for that is to come which shall more declare his love than what is past, would not a soul sleep securely within the compass of this power, this love, and faithfulness of God, without fear of dashing or sinking?

Now, judge whether a perfect peace may not flow from all this. May it not be a perfect calm, when the mountains that environ go up to heaven? Not only doth the soul trust in God, but God keepeth the trusting soul in peace. He is the Creator of peace, and the preserver of it,—"I create peace, I keep him in peace." The same power and virtue is required to the preserving of a thing, and the first being of it. Our faith and hope in God is too weak an anchor to abide all storms. Our cords would break, our hands faint and weary, but he is the everlasting God, who faileth not, and wearieth not. He holdeth an invisible gripe of us. We are kept by his power unto salvation, and we are kept by his power in peace. "Thy right hand holdeth me," saith David, and this helpeth me to pursue thee. What maketh believers inexpugnable, impregnable? Is it their strength? No indeed. But "salvation will God appoint for walls and bulwarks." Almighty power is a strong wall, though invisible,—this power worketh in us and about us.

Now, believers, pity the world about you, that knoweth not this peace. When they lie secure, and cry Peace, peace, alas! they are a city open without walls as the plain field,—there is no keeper there, nothing to hold off destruction. Entertain your own peace, do not grieve the Spirit who hath sealed it. If you return to folly after he hath spoken peace to you, I persuade you, you shall not maintain this peace. There may be peace with God, but no peace in thy conscience, as long as the whoredoms of thy heart are to the fore, thou mayest be secure, but security is worse than fear. Know this, that continuing in a course of sin, entertaining any known sin, shall trouble thy peace. If God hath spoken peace to thee, thou shalt not lodge that enemy in peace. "Great peace have they that love thy law." Obedience and delight in it doth not make peace, but it is the way of peace, and much meditation on the blessed word of God is the most excellent mean to preserve this peace, if it be secured with much correspondence with heaven by prayer, Phil. iv. 6, 7. If you would disburden your hearts daily at the throne of grace, peace should guard and keep your heart, and then your peace would be perfect indeed. But because your faith is here imperfect, your requests few and infervent, your follies and iniquities many, therefore is this promised perfection a stranger to the most part of Christians. Always what we want here, we must expect to have made up shortly. Heaven is a land of peace, and all things are there in full age, here all are in minority, it is but yet night, but when the day shall break up, and the shadows fly away, and the Prince of peace shall appear and be revealed, he shall bring peace and grace both with him, and both perfect. To Him be praise and glory.

SERMON XIV.

Isaiah lix. 20.—"And the Redeemer shall come unto Zion, and unto them that turn," &c.

Doctrines, as things, have their seasons and times. Every thing is beautiful in its season. So there is no word of truth, but it hath a season and time in which it is beautiful. And indeed that is a great part of wisdom, to bring forth everything in its season, to discern when and where, and to whom it is pertinent and edifying, to speak such and such truths. But there is one doctrine that is never out of season, and therefore it may be preached in season and out of season, as the apostle commandeth. Indeed to many hearts it is always out of season, and especially in times of trouble and anguish, when it should be most seasonable, when the opportunity may commend the beauty of it, but in itself, and to as many as have ever found the power of it on their hearts, it is always the most seasonable and pertinent doctrine,—I mean the very subject-matter of this text, the news of a Redeemer to captive sinners. It is in itself such glad tidings, and shines with so much beauty and splendour to troubled sinners, that it casteth abroad a lustre and beauty on the feet of the messengers that carry it, Isa. xl. It is a cordial in affliction, whether outward or inward, and it is withal the only true comfort of prosperity. It allayeth the bitterness of things that cross us, and filleth up the emptiness of things that pretend to please us, it giveth sweetness to the one, and true sweetness to the other. Reason then—that should always be welcome to us, which we stand always in need of, that it should always be new and fresh in our affection, which is always recent and new in its operation and efficacy toward us. Other news how great or good soever, suppose they were able to fill the hearts of all in a nation with joy, yet they grow stale, they lose their virtue within few days. What footsteps or remainder is of all the triumphs and trophies of nations, of all their solemnities for their victorious success at home and abroad? These great news, which once were the subject of the discourse of and delight of many thousands,—who report them now with delight? So those things that may cause joy and triumph to some at this time, as they cannot choose but make more hearts sad than glad; so they will quickly lose even that efficacy they have, and become tasteless as the white of an egg, to them that are most ravished with them. But, my beloved, here is glad tidings of a Redeemer come to Zion to save sinners, which have no occasion of sadness in them to any, but to those who are not so happy as to consider them, or believe them, and they are this day, after many hundred, I may say thousand, years since they were first published, as green and recent, as refreshing to wearied souls, as ever they were. Yea, such is the nature of them, and such an everlasting spring of consolation is in them, that the oftener they be told, and the more they be considered, the sweeter they are. They grow green in old age, and bring forth fruit, and are fat and flourishing; and indeed it is the never-dying virtue and everlasting sap of this word of life, that maketh the righteous so, Psal. xcii. 14. This word of a Redeemer at the first publishing, and for a long time, was but like waters issuing out from under the threshold, and then they came to the ankles, when it was published to a whole nation; but still the longer it swells the higher above knees, and loins, till it be a great inexhausted river, and thus it runs at this day through the world, and hath a healing virtue and a quickening virtue, Ezek. xlvii., and a sanctifying virtue, ver. 9-12. Now this is our errand to you, to invite you to come to these waters. If ye thirst, come to be quenched; if ye thirst not, ye have so much the more need to come, because your thirst after things that will not profit you, will destroy you, and your unsensibleness of your need of this is your greatest misery.

That the words may be more lively unto us, we may call to mind, the greatest and deepest design that hath been carried on in the world, by the Maker and Ruler of the world, is the marriage of Christ his Son with the Church. This was primarily intended, when he made the world, as a palace to celebrate it in; this was especially aimed at, when he joined Adam and Eve, in the beginning of time, together in paradise, that the second Adam should be more solemnly joined to the church, at the end of time, in the paradise of heaven; and this the apostle draws out as the sampler and arch-copy of all marriages and conjunctions in the creatures, Eph. v. Now this being the great design of God, of which all other things done in time are but the footsteps and low representations, the great question is, how this shall be brought about, because of the great distance and huge disproportion of the parties, He "being the brightness of the Father's glory," and we being wholly eclipsed and darkened since our fall;—He higher than the heaven of heavens, and we fallen as low as hell into a dungeon of darkness and misery, led away by sin and Satan, lying in that abominable posture represented in Ezek. xvi.; not only unsuitable to engage his love, but fit to procure even the loathing of all that pass by.

Now it being thus, the words do furnish us with the noble resolution of the Son, about the taking away of the distance, and the royal offer of the Father, to make the match hold the better, both flowing from infinite love, in the most free and absolute manner that can be imagined. The Son's resolution, which is withal the Father's promise, is to come into the world first to redeem his spouse, and so to marry her; "and the Redeemer shall come unto Zion," &c. The Father's offer, that he might not be wanting to help it forward, is to dispone,[297] by an irrevocable covenant, having the force of an absolute donation, his word and Spirit to Christ and his seed, to the church, even to the end of the world, (ver. 21). "As for me, this is my covenant." The Son hath done his part, and is to express his infinite love, infinite condescendency, and stooping below his majesty. Now, as for me, I will show my good-will to it in my infinite bounty and riches of grace to the church; he hath given himself for her,—I will give my Spirit; and thus it cannot but hold.

We shall speak a word then of these three: first, what estate and condition Christ findeth his church in, out of which she must be taken to be his spouse; then, what way and course is laid down by the council of heaven, to fill up the infinite distance between Christ and sinners; and, to close all, we shall show you the suitableness of these promises, and the wonderful fitness of this doctrine to the church, at this time Isaiah preached it, and at all times.

The first is supposed in the words. Redemption supposeth captivity or slavery; redemption of persons importeth captivity and slavery of these persons, and redemption of other things that belong to persons, importeth sale or alienation of our right to them. Of both, personal redemption is the greatest and most difficult; yet both we have need of, for our estate and fortune, so to speak, is lost, "for all men have sinned and come short of the glory of God," Rom. iii. 23. That inheritance of eternal life, we have mortgaged it, and given away our right to it. The favour of God and the blessedness of communion with him, was Adam's birthright, and by a free donation was made his proper inheritance and possession, to be transmitted to his posterity. But O! for how small a thing did he give it away,—for a little taste of an apple he sold his estate; and both he and we may lament over it, as the king that was constrained to render himself and all his army for want of water. When he tasted it, "For how small a thing," saith he, "have I lost my kingdom!" Then our persons are in a state of bondage, in captivity and slavery; captives under the wrath of God, and slaves or servants to sin. There needed no greater difference and deformity between Christ and us, than this,—our servitude and bondage to sin, which truly is the basest and most abominable vassalage in the world. The abasement of the highest prince, to the vilest servitude under the basest creatures in his dominion, is but a shadow of that loathsome and ugly posture of our souls. This servitude doth in a manner unman us, and transform us into beasts. Certainly it is that which, in the holy eyes of God, is more loathsome than any thing beside. He seeth not that deformity in poverty, nakedness, sickness, slavery. Let a man be as miserable as Job on his dunghill, it is not so much that, as the unseen and undiscerned posture and habit of their souls, that he abominateth. Now what a match is this, for the highest and holiest prince, the Son of the greatest King, and heir of all things! But if you add to this slavery, that captivity under the curse and wrath of God,—that all men are shut up, and enclosed in the prison of God's faithful and irrevocable sentence of condemnation, and given over by the righteous judgment of God, to be kept by Satan in everlasting chains of darkness,—he keepeth men now, by the invisible cords of their own sins, but these chains of darkness are reserved for both him and men,—now indeed, this superaddeth a great difficulty to the business. The other may be a difficulty to his mind and affection, because there is nothing to procure love, but all that may enforce hatred and loathing. But suppose his infinite love could come over this stay, could leap over this mountain by the freedom of it, yet there is a greater impediment in the way, that may seem difficult to his power, and it is the justice and power of God, enclosing sinners and shutting them up for eternal wrath, till a due satisfaction be had from or for them. You see then, how infinite the distance is betwixt him and us, and how great the difficulty is to bring about this intended union. Angels were sent with flaming swords to encompass the tree of life and keep it from man, but man is environed by the curse of the Almighty God. The justice, the faithfulness, and the power of God do guard or set a watch about him, that there is no access to him to save him, but by undergoing the greatest danger, and undertaking the greatest party that ever was dealt withal, and the strictest and severest too.

This being the case then, the distance being so vast, and the difficulty so great, the distance being twofold, between his nature and ours, and between our quality and his: an infinite distance between his divine nature and our flesh, and besides an extreme contrariety between the holiness of his nature, and the sinfulness of ours,—[there is here] such a repugnancy, as there is no reconciliation of them. You know what Paul speaketh of the marriage of Christians with idolaters: how much more will it hold here? What communion can be between light and darkness, between God and Belial? Is it possible these can be reduced to amity, and brought to so near an union? Yet for all this, it is possible; but love and wisdom must find out the way. Infinite love and infinite wisdom consulting together, what distance can they not swallow up? What difficulty can they not overcome?

And here you have it, the distance undertaken to be removed, both by the Father and the Son,—(for all this while we can do nothing to help it forward; while the blessed plot is going on, we are posting the faster to our own destruction). And this is the way condescended upon; *first*, To fill up that wide gap between his divine spiritual nature, and our mortal fleshly nature, it is agreed upon, that the Son shall come in our flesh, and be made partaker of flesh and blood with the children; and this is meant by this promise, "the Redeemer shall come to Sion;" which is plainly expressed by his own mouth, John xvi. 28, "I came forth from the Father, and am come into the world." There being such a distance between his majesty and our baseness, love maketh him stoop down and humble himself to the very state of a servant, Phil. ii. 7, 8. And thus the humiliation of Christ filleth up the first distance; for "love and majesty cannot long dwell together," *nec in una sede morantur majestas et amor*;[298] but love will draw majesty down below itself, to meet with the object of it. This was the great journey Christ took to meet with us, and it is downward below himself; but his love hath chosen it, to be like us, though he should be unlike himself. How divinely doth the divine apostle speak of it, "And the Word was made flesh, and he dwelt among us," John i. 14. And therefore the children of Adam may in verity say of him, what the holy Trinity, in a holy irony spake of man, "Lo, he is become as one of us." It was a singular and eminent privilege conferred upon man in his first creation, that the Trinity in a manner consulted about him, "Let us make man after our image;" but now when man hath lost that image, to have such a result of the council of the Trinity about it, "let one of us be made man, to make up the distance between man and us,"—O! what soul can rightly conceive it without ravishment and wonder, without an ecstacy of admiration and affection!—that the Lord should become a servant!—the Heir of all things be stripped naked of all!—the brightness of the Father's glory, be thus eclipsed and darkened!—and in a word, that which comprehendeth all wonders in the creation,—who made all things,—be himself made of a woman! and God become a man, and all this out of his infinite love, to give a demonstration of love to the world; so high a person abased, to exalt so base and low as we are! There is a mystery in this, a great mystery, a mystery of wisdom, to swallow up the understanding with wonder; and a mystery of love, to ravish the hearts of men with affection,—depths of both, in the emptiness of the Son of God. The prophet doubted what was commanded, to seek a sign, whether in heaven above, or in the depth beneath; but what he would not ask, God gave in his great mercy, "Behold a virgin shall conceive a Son, and they shall call his name Immanuel;" a sign indeed from heaven, and the height of heaven, because he is God; and a sign from the depth beneath too, because he is man; "God with us," and so composed to unite heaven and earth together; "God with us," that he might at length bring us to be with God. He became *Immanuel*, that he might make us *Immelanu*.[299] If that was given as tidings of great joy, and as the highest and deepest sign of love and favour, at that time to uphold the fainting church; O! how much more may it now comfort us, when it is not a virgin shall conceive, but a virgin hath conceived! May not the joy be increased, that the Redeemer is not to come, but come already, and hath made up that wide separation which was between us and him, by his low condescendency to his union with our nature! This is one step of advancement towards that happy marriage, that the whole creation seems to groan and travail for, Rom. viii. 22. But yet there is a great difficulty in the way. We are in a state of captivity; we are prisoners of justice, have sold ourselves and our happiness; and now our natural inheritance lies in the lake of fire and brimstone,—heirs of wrath, concluded under the curse of God; and indeed, this was insuperable to all flesh; neither men nor angels could ransom us from this. The redemption of the soul of man is so precious, and the redemption of the inheritance of man, that is, heaven, is so precious too, that none in heaven or earth can be found, that can pay the price of them, so that it would have ceased for ever. And here the great design of Christ's union with sinners would have been marred and miscarried, if himself had not undertaken to overcome this too; and indeed, as there could none be found to open the seals of the book of God's decrees concerning his church,—none worthy in heaven or earth but the Lamb, the Lion of the tribe of Judah, he prevailed to open it, and loose the seals thereof, Rev. v. 3-5. So there could none be found in heaven or earth, neither under the earth, worthy to undertake or accomplish this work, or able to open the seals of the book of God's curses, or to blot out the hand-writing of ordinances that was against us, or to open the prison of death in which man was shut up; none, I say, hath been found worthy or prevailed, but the Lamb of God and Lion of the tribe of Judah; and therefore the four and twenty elders that sit round about the throne, and the four beasts, with the innumerable company of angels, and spirits of just men made perfect, fell down before the Lamb, every one of them with harps, and they sung a new song, "Worthy is the Lamb that was slain, to receive power, and riches, and wisdom, and strength, and honour, and glory, and blessing; for thou hast redeemed us to God by thy blood." And every creature says Amen to this, and consents to this, to do him homage; to him who alone was worthy, and as willing to do it as worthy for it. I think the 16th verse of this chapter gives us a sensible representation of this. The preceding discourse from the beginning, holding out the sinful and deplorable condition of that people, and in them, as a type of the desperate wickedness of all mankind, and withal their desperate misery, for Paul, (Rom. iii.) maketh the application for us; and from this, concludeth all under sin, and so all under wrath, all guilty, that every mouth may be stopped; men waiting for light, and behold obscurity; for brightness, but walking in darkness; groping for the wall, like the blind, stumbling at noon-day as in the night, and in desolate places as dead men; all roaring like beasts, and mourning like doves, whenever the apprehension of the terror of God entereth. Now it is subjoined, verse 16, "And he saw that there was no man," &c.; as if he had waited and looked through all the world, if any would appear, either to speak or do for man, if any would offer themselves, and interpose themselves for his salvation. "Therefore his own arm brought salvation, and his righteousness, it sustained him." Therefore the Son of God steps in and offers himself, as if God had first essayed all others, and when heaven is full of wonder and silence, he breaks out in this, "Lo, I come to do thy will," Psal. xl. Since I have gotten a body to be like sinners, I will also come in their place, and I will give my life a ransom for them; and therefore it is subjoined, "the Redeemer shall come to Zion;" he shall come clothed with vengeance and indignation as a garment, against the enemies of his church, sin and Satan, in zeal and burning love to his designed spouse. He shall strengthen himself, and stir up his might and fury against all that detain her captive.

Now, indeed, he is the only fittest person for this business in heaven or earth; for he hath both right to do it, and he only hath might and power to accomplish it. He hath right to the redemption of sinners, because he is our kinsman, nearest of blood to us.

Now, you know the right of redemption belonged to the kinsman, Lev. xxv. 25. And therefore when the nearest kinsman could not redeem Naomi and Ruth's parcel of land, Boaz did it, as being next. And suitable to this, our Lord Jesus, when others as near could not, and were not able, he hath done it, and taken men and angels to witness, that he hath first redeemed us, that he might marry us, as Eph. v.; that he hath purchased us to be his wife. And indeed the very word imports this; *Goel*,[300] a redeemer and kinsman, passing under one word: so Job, "I know that my Redeemer," or my kinsman, "liveth:" and because our kinsman, therefore most interested in our redemption; for, for this end he became partaker of flesh and blood with the children, that he might destroy our greatest enemy, Satan, and redeem us, Heb. ii. 14. And besides, he hath right to redemption, as the Church's husband, because he must mediate between her and all others; none can reach her, except he please, or prosecute a plea against her, as in the case of the wife's making a vow, if her husband consented not, it was void, (Numb. xxx.,) but if he heard of it and held his peace, it was confirmed. Now the Lord Jesus hath known this deplorable estate in which we are captives, and he hath testified his utter dislike of our binding over ourselves to death, and resigning ourselves to Satan; and therefore this bondage in which we are detained, is not confirmed and ratified, but he hath right remaining to redeem us from the hand of all our enemies. But then, he alone hath might and power to do it, for God hath laid help on him, and made him able and mighty to save us to the uttermost. It was not gold or silver, or corruptible things. Suppose the whole earth were turned into gold or precious stones; he must give person for person, and one person equivalent to all—his own life, his own blood for us; and the value of this was infinitely raised by the stamp of his divinity put upon it. The king for the servant,—one that knew no sin for sinners,—yea, God for man. This superadds infinite worth, and makes it an over-ransom, and over purchase, a ransom to buy our persons from hell, a purchase to redeem us to our inheritance, heaven, that we had lost, and these two styles it gets, λυτρον, αντιλυτρον.[301]

Now, you see the great difficulty is overcome and taken out of the way: Christ, being made a curse, hath purchased a redemption from the curse of the law, Gal. iii. 13. But yet, there is another point of vast distance, I may say contrariety and enmity, between us and him. He is holy and undefiled, all fair, and no spot in him; we are wholly defiled and depraved by sin, our souls are become the habitation of devils, and a cage of every unclean and hateful bird; in a word, he hath not only our enemies to overcome, but our own hearts to conquer, and our enmity to take away. This makes the widest separation from him. Now, he filled up much of the distance, with his taking our flesh, and he removed the great difficulty, by dying in our flesh his humiliation to be a man, brought him nearer us, and his further humiliation to be a dying, crucified, and buried man, brought him yet a step nearer us. But nearer he cannot come, for lower he cannot be, except he were a sinner, which would mar the whole design, and take away all the comfort of his likeness to us. Therefore, since he hath come so low down to us, it is suitable we be raised up one step to meet him, and so the exaltation of sinners shall make up all the distance, and bring the two parties to that long since designed, and long desired meeting. Now, for this end and purpose, the Son undertakes the redemption of his church from sin and ungodliness as well as wrath, and therefore you have that which is expressed as the character of the redeemed in this verse. It is exponed as the great point or part of the redemption itself by the apostle, Rom. xi. "The Redeemer shall come to Sion, and shall turn away ungodliness from Jacob." And so his end was not only to be a partaker of our nature, but to make us partakers of the divine nature, and therefore the Father, out of his love to this business, promised to send his Spirit to dwell in our hearts, to make the word sound in our mouths and ears, and the Spirit to work in our hearts, and this exaltation of sinners to the participation of the Holy Spirit, together with Christ's humiliation to partake of our flesh, makes up the full distance, and bringeth Christ and his church to that holy patient impatience, and longing for the day when it shall be solemnized in heaven. The Spirit within us says, Come, and the bride says, Come. Even so come, Lord Jesus. And he waits for nothing, but the completing and adorning of all the rest, that there may be one jubilee for all and for ever. Now I wish we could understand the absolute and free tenor of God's covenant. There is much controversy speculative about the condition of the covenant, about the promises, whether absolute or conditional; and there is too much practical debate in perplexed consciences about this, how to find something in themselves to fit and fashion them for the redemption. But truly, if we would not disjoin and dismember the truth of God, but take it all entirely as one great design of love and mercy revealed to sinners, and so conjoin the promises of the covenant into one bundle, we would certainly find that it hath the voice of Jacob, though it seem to have the hand of Esau; we find an absolute, most free and unconditioned sense, when there is a conditional strain and shadow of words in some places.

The truth is, the turning of souls from ungodliness is not properly a condition exacted from us, as a promise to be performed in us, and the chiefest part of Christ's redemption; and though some abuse the grace of God, and turn it into wantonness and liberty, yet certainly, this doctrine, that makes the greatest part of the glad news of the gospel to be redemption from sin, and the pouring out of the Spirit, is the greatest persuasive to a godly conversation, and the most deadly enemy to all ungodliness.

I thought to have spoken more of that third thing I proponed,[302] but take it in a word. This was always proponed to the church as the strongest cordial, it was given here as the greatest consolation in all their long captivity, that this Redeemer was afterwards to come, whose virtue was then living, and present to the quickening and comforting of souls. It was thought enough to uphold in a most desperate strait, "To us a child is born," Isa. ix. 6. I wish we could take it so. Certainly it was the character of a believer before Christ's coming, that he was one that was looking and waiting for the salvation of Israel, by this Redeemer. But now we are surrounded with consolation before and behind,—Christ already come, so that we may in joy say, Lo! this is our God, we have waited for him! others waited and longed, and we see him,—and Christ shortly to come again without sin, to our salvation. And what could be able to take our joy from us, if we had one eye always back to his first coming, and another always forward to his coming again?

SERMON XV.

Isaiah lxiv 6, 7.—"But we are all as an unclean thing, and all our righteousnesses are as filthy rags," &c.

This people's condition agreeth well with ours, though the Lord's dealing be very different. The confessory part of this prayer belongeth to us now; and strange it is, that there is such odds of the Lord's dispensations, when there is no difference in our conditions; always we know not how soon the complaint may be ours also. This prayer was prayed long before the judgment and captivity came on, so that it had a prophecy in the bosom of it. Nay, it was the most kindly and affectionate way of warning the people could get, for Isaiah to pour forth such a prayer, as if he beheld with his eyes the calamity, as already come. And indeed it becometh us so to look on the word, as if it gave a present being to things as certain and sensible as if they were really. What strange stupidity must be in us, when present things, inflicted judgments, committed sins, do not so much affect us, as the foresight of them did. Love Isaiah! Always,[303] as this was registrate for the people's use, to cause them to still look on judgments threatened, as performed and present, and anticipate the day of affliction by repentance; and also to be a pattern to them, how to deal with God, and plead with him from such grounds of mercy and covenant-interest: so it may be to us a warning, especially when sin is come to the maturity, and our secure backsliding condition is with child of sad judgments, when the harvest seemeth ripe to put the sickle into it.

There is in these two verses, a confession of their own sinfulness, from which grounds they justify God's proceeding with them, they take the cause upon themselves, and justify him in his judging, whether temporal or spiritual plagues were inflicted. In this verse,[304] they take a general survey of their sinful estate, concluding themselves unclean, and all their performances and commanded duties, which they counted once their righteousness: and from this ground, they clear God's dealing with them, and put their mouths in the dust; and so from the Lord's judgment they are forced to enter into a search of the cause of so much sin; and from discovered sin, they pronounce God righteous in his judgment. Perceiving a great difference in the Lord's manner of dealing with them, and their fathers, they do not refound[305] it upon God, who is righteous in all his ways, but retort it upon themselves, and find a vast discrepance between themselves and their fathers, verse 5. And so it was no wonder that God's dispensation changed upon them. God was wont to meet others, to show himself gracious, even to prevent strokes, but now he was wroth with them. Nay, but there is good cause for it. They rejoice and wrought righteousness, but we have sinned. And this may be said in the general,—never one needeth to quarrel God for severe dealing. If he deal worse with one than with another, let every man look into his own bosom, and see reason sufficient; yea, more provocation in themselves than others. Always in this verse, they come to a more distinct view of their loathsome condition. Anybody may wrap up their repentance in a general notion of sin, but they declare themselves to be more touched with it, and condescend on particulars, yet such particulars as comprehend many others. And in this confession, you may look on the Spirit's work, having some characters of the Spirit in it.

I. They take a general view of their uncleanness and loathsome estate by sin; not only do they see sin, but sin in the sinfulness of it and uncleanness of it.

II. They not only conclude so of the natural estate they were born in, and the loathsomeness of their many foul scandals among them; but they go a further length, to pass as severe a sentence on their duties and ordinances as God hath done, Isa. i. and lxvi. The Spirit convinceth according to scripture's light, and not according to the dark spark of nature's light; and so that which nature would have busked[306] itself with as its ornament, that which they had covered themselves with as their garment, the duties they had spread, as robes of righteousness, over their sins to hide them; all this now goeth under the name of filthiness and sin. They see themselves wrapt up in as vile rags as they covered and hid: commanded duties and manifest breaches come in one category. And not only is it some of them which their own conscience could challenge in the time, but all of them and all kinds of them, moral and ceremonial, duties that were most sincere, had most affection in them, all of them are filthy rags now, which but of late were their righteousness.

III. There is an universality, not only of the actions, but of persons; not only all the peoples or multitudes' performances are abomination; but all of them, Isaiah, and one and other, the holiest of them, come in in this category and rank—"we are all unclean," &c. Though the people, it may be, could not join holy Isaiah with themselves, yet humble Isaiah will join himself with the people, and come in, in one prayer. And no doubt, he was as sensible of sin now, as when he began to prophesy; and growing in holiness, he must grow also in sense of sinfulness. Seeing at the first sight of God's holiness and glory, he cried "unclean," &c. Isa. vi. 5, certainly he doth so now, from such a principle of access to God's holiness, which maketh him abhor himself in dust and ashes.

IV. They are not content with such a general, but condescend to two special things, two spiritual sins, viz. omission, or shifting of spiritual duties, which contained the substance of worship. "None calleth on thee," few or none, none to count upon, calleth on thee; that is, careth for immediate access and approaching unto God in prayer and meditation, &c. Albeit external and temple-duties be frequent, yet who prayeth in secret? or if any pray, that cannot come in count, the Lord knoweth them not, because they want the Spirit's stamp on them. This must be some other thing than the general conviction of sin which the world hath, who think they pray all their days; here people, who though they make many prayers, Isa. i., yet they see them no prayers, and no calling on God's name now.

V. To make the challenge the more, and the confession more spiritual and complete, there is discovered to them this ground of their slackness and negligence in all spiritual duties, "None stirreth up himself to take hold on thee." Here is the want of the exercise of faith: faith is the soul's hand and grip, John i. 12; Heb. vi. 18; 1 Tim. vi. 12; Isa. xxvii. 5. Nobody awaketh themselves out of their deadness and security, to lay hold on thee. Lord, thou art going away, and taking good-night of the land, and nobody is like to hold thee by the garment; no Jacobs here, who will not let thee go, till thou bless them; none to prevail with thy Majesty,—every one is like to give Christ a free passport and testimonial to go abroad, and are almost Gadarenes, to pray him to depart out of their coasts. There is a strange looseness and indifferency in men's spirits concerning the one thing necessary. Men lie by and dream over their days, and never put the soul's estate out of question; none will give so much pains, as to clear their interest in thee, to lay hold on thee, so as they may make peace with thee. Now, can there be a more ample and lively description of our estate, both of the land and of particular persons of it? Since this must not be limited to the nation of the Jews, though the prophet spake of the generality of them, yet, no doubt, all mankind is included in the first six verses; and any secure people may be included in the seventh verse, for Paul applieth even such like speeches (Rom. xi. 13.) that were spoken, as you would think, of David's enemies only. Yet the Spirit of God knowing the mind of the Spirit, maketh a more general use of their condition, to hold out the natural estate of all men out of Christ Jesus.

But there are in these two verses other two things beside the acknowledgment of sin:

I. The acknowledgment of God's righteousness in punishing them, for now they need not quarrel God, they find the cause of their fading in their own bosom. They now join sin and punishment together, whereas in the time of their prosperity they separated punishment from sin; and in the time of their security in adversity they separated sin from punishment: at one time making bare confession of sin, without fear of God's justice, at another time fretting and murmuring at his judgments, without the sense of their sin. But now they join both these, and the sight and sense of God's displeasure maketh sin more bitter, and to abound more, and to appear in the loathsome and provoking nature of it, so that their acknowledgment hath an edge upon it. And again, the sight and sense of sin maketh the judgment appear most righteous, and stoppeth their mouth from murmuring. In the time of their impenitency under the rod, their language was very indifferent, Ezek. xviii. 2. "The fathers have eaten sour grapes, and the children's teeth are set on edge;" they have sinned and we suffer; they have done the wrong and we pay for it. But it is not so now, ver. 5. The fathers have done righteousness in respect of us, and thou wast good unto them; but we are all unclean, and have sinned, and so we are punished.

II. They find some cause and ground in God of their general defection; not that he is the cause of their sin, but in a righteous way he punished sin with sin. God hid his face, denied special grace and influence; and so they lie still in their security, and their sin became a spiritual plague. Or this may be so read,—*None calleth on thy name, when thou didst hide thy face from us, and when thou didst consume us because of our iniquities*; and so it serveth to aggravate their deep security, that, though the Lord was departing from them, yet none would keep him and hold him. Though he did strike, yet they prayed not; affliction did not awake them out of security, and so the last words, "Thou hast consumed us," &c., are differently exponed and read. Some make it thus, as it is in the translation, "Thou hast hid thy face," and left us in a spiritual deadness, that so there might be no impediment to bring on deserved judgment. If we had called on thee, and laid hold on thee, it might have been prevented, we might have prevailed with God, but now our defence is removed, and thou hast given us up to a spirit of slumber, and so we have no shield to hold off the stroke,—thou hast now good leave to consume us for our sins. Another sense may be—*Thou hast suffered us to consume in our iniquity, thou hast given us up to the hand of our sins.* And this is also a consequent of his hiding his face. Because thou didst hide thy face, thou lettest us perish in our sins; there needeth no more for our consumption, but only help us not out of them, for we can soon destroy ourselves.

First, Sin is in its own nature loathsome, and maketh one unclean before God. Sin's nature is filthiness, vileness, so doth Isaiah speak of himself, chap. vi. 5, when he saw God's holiness; so doth Job abhor himself, which is the affection which turneth a man's face off a loathsome object, when he saw God, Job xl. 4, and xlii. 6. Look how loathsome our natural condition is holden out by God himself, Ezek. xvi. You cannot imagine any deformity in the creature, any filthiness, but it is there. The filthiness and vileness of sin shall appear, if we consider *first* that sin is a transgression of the holy and spiritual command, and so a vile thing, the commandment is holy and good, Rom. vii. And sin violateth and goeth flat contrary to the command, 1 John iii. 4. When so just and so equitable a law is given, God might have exacted other rigorous duties from us, but when it is so framed that the conscience must cry out, All is equity, all is righteous and more than righteous, thou mightest command more, and reward none. It is justice to command, but it is mercy to promise life to obedience, which I owe,—what then must the offence be, against such a just command, and so holy? If holiness be the beauty of the creation, sin must be the deformity of it, the only spot in its face.

Secondly, Look upon sin in the sight of God's holiness and infinite majesty, and O how heinous will it appear! and therefore no man hath seen sin in the vileness of it, but in the light of God's countenance, as Isa. vi. 5, Job. xl. and xlii. God is of purer eyes than to behold iniquity, he cannot look on it, Hab. i. 13. All other things beside sin, God looketh on them as bearing some mark of his own image, all was very good, and God saw it, Gen. i. and ii. Even the basest creatures God looketh on them, and seeth himself in them, but sin is only God's eyesore, that his holiness cannot away with it, it is most contrary unto him, and as to his sovereignty, it is a high contempt and rebellion done to God's Majesty. It putteth God off the throne, will take no law from him, will not acknowledge his law, but, as it were, spitteth in his face, and establisheth another god. There is no punishment so evil, that God will not own as his work, and declare himself to be the author of it, but only sin, his soul abhorreth it, his holy will is against it, he will have no fellowship with it, it is so contrary to him: contradicteth his will, debaseth his authority, despiseth his sovereignty, upendeth his truth. There is a kind of infiniteness in it, nothing can express it but itself no name worse than itself to set it out, the apostle can get no other epithet to it, Rom. vii. 13, than "sinful" sin, so that it cometh in most direct opposition unto God. All that is in God, is God himself, and there is no name can express him sufficiently. If you say God, you say more than can be expressed by many thousand other words. So it is here—sin is purely sin, God is purely good and holy, without mixture, holiness itself, sin is simply evil, without mixture, unholiness itself. Whatever is in it, is sin, is uncleanness. Sin is an infinite wrong, and an infinite and boundless filthiness, because of the infinite person wronged. It is an offence of infinite Majesty and the person wronged aggravateth the offence, if it be simply contrary to infinite holiness, it must be, in that respect, infinite unholiness and uncleanness.

Thirdly, Look upon the sad effects and consequences of sin,—how miserable, how ruinous it hath made man, and all the creation, and how vile must it be!

I. Look on man's native beauty and excellency, how beautiful a creature! But sin hath cast him down from the top of his excellency, sin made Adam of a friend an enemy, of a courtier with God an open rebel. Was not man's soul of more price than all the world, so that nothing can exchange it? Yet hath sin debased it, and prostituted it to all vile filthy pleasures, hath made the immortal spirit to dwell on the dunghill, feed on ashes, catch vanities, lying vanities, pour out itself to them, serve all the creatures—whereas it should have made them servants, yea, a slave to his own greatest enemy, to the ground he treadeth upon. O what a degenerate plant! It was a noble vine once in paradise, but sin hath made it a wild one, to bring forth sour grapes. What is there in all the world could defile a man? Matt. xv. 20. Nothing that goeth out or cometh in, but sin that proceedeth out of the heart. Man was all light, his judgment sinned into his affections, and through all the man, but sin hath made all darkness, closed up the poor captive understanding, hath built up a thick wall of gross corrupted affections about it, so that light can neither get in nor out. The soul was like a clear running fountain, which yielded fresh clear streams of holy inclinations, desires, affections, actions and emptied itself in the sea of immense Majesty from which these streams first flowed, but now it is a standing putrified puddle, that casteth a vile stink round about, and hath no issue towards God. Man was a glorious creature, fit to be lord over the work of God's own hands, and therefore had God's image in a special manner, holiness and righteousness, God's nature. A piece of divinity was stamped on man, which outshined all created perfections. The sun might blush when it looked on him, for what was material glory to the glory of holiness and beauty of God's image! But sin hath robbed poor man of this glorious image, hath defaced man, marred all his glory, put on an hellish likeness on him. Holiness only putteth the difference between angels in heaven and devils in hell, and sin only hath made the difference between Adam in paradise, and sinners on the cursed ground, Rom. iii. 23.

II. Sin hath so redounded through man unto all the creation, that it hath defiled it, and made it corruptible and subject to vanity, (Rom. viii. 20, &c.,) so that this is a spot in all the creature's face,—that man hath sinned, and used all as weapons of unrighteousness, so that now the creature groaneth to be delivered.

III. It hath brought on all the misery that is come on man, or that is to come, it hath brought on death and damnation as its wages, and the curse of the eternal God, Gal. iii. 13, Rom. vi. 23. How odious then an evil must it be, that hath so much evil in it yea, all evil in the bosom of it! Hell is not evil in respect of sin, for sin deserveth hell, it hath ruined man, and made all the beautiful order of the creation to change.

IV. It separateth man from God, which is worst of all, and this is included in the text, "We are all as an unclean thing," or man is as a leprous man set apart, because of pollution, that may not come to the temple, or worship God, so hath iniquity separated between God and us, Isa. lix. 2. And O how sad a divorcement is this! it maketh men without God in the world, in whom we live, and move, and have our being, in whose favour is life, and at whose right hand are pleasures for evermore. Now poor man is made miserable, deprived of his felicity, which only consisted in enjoyment of God. Sin as a thick partition wall, is come in between, enmity also is come in, and divideth old friends, Eph. ii. 14-17, and now no heavenly or comfortable influence can break through the night of darkness is begun which must prove everlasting. Except the partition-wall be removed, all must wither and decay as without the sun.

V. Look on the price paid for sin, on the cleansing that washeth it away, and you may see unspeakable deformity and vileness in it. The redemption of the soul is precious silver and gold and precious stones will not do it,—that would be utterly contemned. "What!" saith God, "presumptuous sinner, wilt thou give me a farthing in payment of a sum which all the world, sold at the dearest, would not discharge?" Psal. xlix. 7, 8, 1 Pet. i. 18. It is no corruptible thing, but the blood of the Son of

God. O what must the debt be, when the price is so infinite! the Son of God must die, nay, it is not sacrifice or offering—"Lo, I come to do thy will," it is Christ himself that is the ransom, Psal. xl. 6, 7. And it is not much soap or nitre, it is not much repentance and tears that will wash away this filthiness, no, it is of a deeper dye, it is crimson ingrained filthiness, Jer. ii. 22 and Isa. i. 16. Blood of bulls and goats cannot do it, but only the blood of the immaculate Lamb offered up by himself, (Heb. x. 4, 5,) the blood of Him, "who by the eternal Spirit offered up himself without spot unto God," Heb. ix. 14. What must sin be, that must have such a fountain opened for it? It must be strange uncleanness when the blood of Christ only can cleanse it, Zech. xiii. 1.

"We all," &c. Mark, *first*, Sin hath gone over us all, and made all mankind unclean, Rom. iii. 10, 22. Every one of Adam's posterity is born unclean, "For who can bring a clean thing out of an unclean?" Job. xiv. 4. Consider: How sin defaced innocent Adam, how one sin made him so vile, and spoiled him of the divine nature, and so the root was made unclean, and the branches must follow the root, and so are we all born and conceived in sin, Psalm li. 5. We carry in us original corruption, flowing from the first actual sin of Adam, and this maketh poor children, before they do good or evil, to be abominably vile in God's sight, even as the child is set out, Ezek. xvi. Every one cometh of evil parents, all come of Adam the rebel, what a loathsome sight would a child be to us so described, "Cast out in the open field, to the loathing of its person in the day it is born," and what must it all be before God, who is of purer eyes than to behold sin? *Secondly*, Unto all this we have added innumerable actual transgressions as so many filthy streams flowing out at the members, from the inward puddle of original corruption; and so how much more vile are we all nor infants can be, or Adam was in the day he was cast out of paradise! And thus, Rom. iii. from verse 10, are the branches set down in word, thought, and deed; so that all the inclinations and motions and actions of the man are only evil continually. Every man shall find his count past counting; one day's faults would weary you, but what will your whole life do? Known sins are innumerable, what must unknown be? Every man's heart is like the troubled sea, that casteth up mire and dirt daily, and cannot be at rest. The heart is daily flowing and ebbing in this corruption, it cometh out daily to the borders of all the members; and there are some high spring-tides, when sin aboundeth more. When in one member of the tongue a world of evil is, what can be in all the members? And what in the soul, that is more capable than all the world? Well, then, every man hath sinned in Adam, and hath sinned also in his own person, and sealed Adam's first rebellion by so many thousand actions like it. Every man hath approven the sin that first ruined man, and made himself much more loathsome nor Adam was; therefore all mankind may say, "We all are as an unclean thing." Now from all this, we would gladly discover unto you what your condition is by sin; if the Lord would shine, how vile would you be! Always we must declare this unto you in the Lord's name, you are all unclean, not only born in sin and iniquity, not only have you a body of death within you, that hath all the members; but all these members have one time or other acted and brought forth fruit unto death. How vile, then, must you be in God's sight! It is a strange love that you have to yourselves, that you cannot apprehend how God can hate you! But if he find sin in you, wonder rather how he can look upon you; we would then have you to know this, that there can be no fellowship between God and you in your natural estate. As men cannot inhabit a vile person's house, no more can God enter into your souls. There is an absolute necessity of washing, before you can be his house and temple. Hath that one sin of Adam made that glorious person so deformed, that he could not look on himself, but cover himself? And hath it been of so defiling a nature, that it hath redounded in all the posterity; and, as unclean things under the law defiled all they touched, so hath that sin subjected all the creatures to corruption? O then imagine what an unspeakable defilement must be on us all, who are not only guilty of Adam's sin, but of many thousands beside! If one sin have so much loathsomeness in it, what must so many out of number, united in one person, even as in us all? No unclean thing can enter into heaven above: know this for a truth, you cannot see God's face in the case you are born into. You know nothing of sin, who wonder that any should go to hell. No, if you knew anything of sin, you would wonder that ever God should look on such cast out in the open field in their blood.

Next, You must know the insufficiency of all things imaginable, to wash away sin's filthiness, except the blood of Christ. Since you are unclean, do you not ask, how shall we be washed? Indeed many have an easy answer, and pass it lightly. The multitude know no way to cleanse in, but the tears of repentance and mourning; and so, many think themselves clean, when they run and pour out a tear as Esau did for the blessing. But what saith the Lord? "Though thou wash thee with nitre, and take thee much soap, yet thine iniquity is marked." Can such an ingrained uncleanness, can such an infinite spot in the immortal soul, be so lightly dashed out? Many think baptism cleanseth them, but was not this people circumcised, as ye are baptized? And Peter tells us, it is not the washing of water, &c. 1 Pet. iii. 21. Sacrifice and offering will not do it. This people thought, sure they had satisfied God, when they brought a lamb, &c., but all this is abomination. Would not many of you think yourselves cleansed from sin, if you offered all your substance, and the fruit of your body for the sin of your soul? Nay, but you must see an absolute necessity of the opened fountain of Christ's blood, that cleanseth from all sin.

Then we would have you abhor yourselves in dust and ashes, and see nothing in all the creation so vile as you; look on sin in the sight of God's face, and how unholy will it appear! There are many sins, little ones, that in our practice pass for venal and uncontrolled; but look on the filthy loathsome nature of all sin, and hate the least offence, for it hath a kind of infiniteness in it, and blotteth the soul, defileth the person. How great a necessity is there of continual application to the fountain, of dwelling beside it, that you may wash daily! David's so often repeated and inculcated prayer, "Wash me, cleanse me," &c. Psalm li., declareth that he hath apprehended much uncleanness in sin, that it needeth so many applications of the precious blood. And you who have come to Jesus, and are clean, O how much owe you to free grace, that passed by you in your blood, and said, "Live, it is a time of love!" How strange is it, that glorious Majesty cometh to own deformity, and cometh to clothe it with his own garments! Praise the virtue of that blood, that is more precious than the blood of bulls and goats, that can so throughly purge, as you shall have no more conscience of sin.

Unclean sinners, wash you, make you clean,—there is a fountain opened; though sin were as scarlet, it can perfectly change the colour of it. If you wash not while the fountain is open, it will quickly be sealed on you, and then it shall be said, when the angel sweareth by him that liveth forever and ever, that time shall be no more, then shall it be said, "let him that is unclean be unclean still." Now, cleansing is offered in the gospel,—if you will love your loathsomeness so well, as not to dip yourselves in this fountain, then let the unclean be so still. Your repentance will never change your colour, though you should melt in sorrow: and therefore you who have found a way to be saved otherwise nor[307] by Jesus Christ, you shall be deceived. Your tears and mourning that you might have had, though Christ had never come into the world, is all you use to speak of, and build your hope on; and if you speak of Christ, it is in such terms as to buy him by such repentance; so that the truth is, you use but Christ's name as a shadow, you make no use of him; he needed not to have come into the world, for many of you could have done as well without him. But as many of you as cannot find cleansing, who see filth increase by washing, come to Christ Jesus, and say, "If you wilt, thou canst make me clean," Matt viii. 2. Nothing beside Jesus can do it—believe his sufficiency. Nothing beside him will do—believe his willingness; for, for this cause he is an open fountain, that all may come and draw.

SERMON XVI.

Isaiah lxiv. 6, 7.—"All our righteousnesses are as filthy rags, and we all do fade as a leaf, and our iniquities, like the wind, have taken us away."

Not only are the direct breaches of the command uncleanness, and men originally and actually unclean, but even our holy actions, our commanded duties. Take a man's civility, religion, and all his universal inherent righteousness,—all are filthy rags. And here the church confesseth nothing but what God accuseth her of, Isa. lxvi. 8, and chap. i. ver. 11, 12, 13, &c. This people was much in ceremonial and external duties; and therefore they cried, "The temple of the Lord, the temple of Lord!" as if this would have outcried all their other sins; therefore were they proud, and lords in their own estimation, and innocent, Jer. ii. 31, 35. They thought the many good services they did to God might compense all their wrongs, Mic. vi. 6, 7. They gave a price to justice for their sins, even a confession of it, by offering a lamb, &c. and a purpose to amend. But, lo! what sense the prophet hath of all this, "Lord, all our righteousnesses" are filthy likewise. Albeit we have paid the debt of sins with duties, yet now we see all these are sins themselves, and must have another sacrifice; so that all matter of boasting is now removed, and we are stript naked of all righteousness. We covered our filthiness before with duties, now both the one and the other is filthy. We would look upon two sorts of righteousnesses, the natural man's, and the converted man's, upon the one's civility and fair profession, and upon the other's real or true grace in discharge of duties, and we shall find good reason to conclude both the one and the other under filthiness, so that there is no ground of boasting, no inherent righteousness can make us accepted before God.

First, then, Whatever men can do from natural principles, all the flower and perfection of men's actions, both civil and religious, is but abominable before God, as long as their persons are unjustified. Every performance is defiled by the uncleanness of the person; and therefore God heareth not sinners, (John viii.,) that is, unjustified sinners; though they pray much, yet God heareth them not. And this is lively expressed by Hag. ii. 12, 13, 14. As the priest's holy garments and flesh could not make bread or pottage holy, but the unclean body could make these unclean; so this nation's and people's performances and holy duties, could not make them holy, and their persons clean, but their unclean persons and actions made all their performances unclean. The solemn meeting and sacrifice, &c. could not make them accepted, but their unclean persons made their solemn meetings and religious duties vile and abominable in God's sight: and thus to the unclean all things are unclean, even their mind and conscience, Tit. i. 15. The unbelieving man, who is born unclean, and defiled with so much original corruption, and so many actual transgressions, defileth all things he toucheth. As a dead body, or a leprous garment, under the law, made all unclean it touched, and nothing could make it holy by touching of it; so all your civility, all your profession, will never contribute to the cleansing of your person; and your persons shall defile all your most clean actions. God loveth not that stock of Adam, and all that groweth on it must be hateful; he is only well-pleased in Jesus Christ, and with those who are transplanted out of rotten Adam into the true vine Jesus. It is such fruit only that can be acceptable; therefore, until you be sprinkled with clean water, and made clean according to the new covenant-way, you cannot please God. Believe this,—your sins and your duties are one, your oaths and your prayers are in the same account with God. What have you then to build upon, when all this is removed? You must once he stript naked of all coverings; and will not your nakedness then be great? The Pharisee went away unjustified, and the poor repenting sinner justified. What was the reason? There are not many of you have such a fair venture for heaven as he had,—so many prayers, fastings, alms, to ground your hope on. Nay, but all this would never justify his person, because once he was unclean, come of Adam, and had contracted more uncleanness, and all that is like the leprous garment, defiling all that cometh near it; so that whatever hath any dependence on a son of Adam, must contract filthiness. Now, I ask your consciences, have you so many specious coverings to adorn yourself with? Is not your outside spotted, and not so clean as the young civil man and the religious Pharisee? Certainly no; and yet you have no other ground to plead the acceptation of your persons upon, but only this, your prayers and tears, or some such duty performed by you. Well, all is uncleanness, since your persons were once unclean,—no soap nor nitre can wash it, no holy flesh make it holy, no good wishes nor duties can make it acceptable. Did not this people think of their duties as much as you do? and had more reason so to do; for our congregations have not so much form of godliness as they had, and yet God solemnly protested to them that all their works were defiled, even those which they took to wash themselves with. So your repentance and tears must be as filthy as the sin you would wash by it.

Secondly, The uncleanness of men's practice maketh unclean performances. Unclean hands maketh unclean prayers, Isa. i. 15. When men go on in sin, and use their members as instruments of unrighteousness against God, and guiltiness is above their head unrepented of and unpardoned, then whatever the members act for God in religious duties, it must be also abominable; for will God take prayers from such a mouth, that cursing cometh out of? Isa. iii. 10, 11, 12. Shall sweet water come out of one fountain with bitter? Or can a fig-tree bear both thistles and grapes? Certainly, profane conversation must make unclean profession; and therefore your coming to the church and ordinances, your praying in your families, or such like, must of necessity be defiled, since out of the same mouth cometh cursing, railing, lying, filthy speeches. Your tongues are so often employed in God's dishonour, to blaspheme his name, to slander your neighbours, to reproach the saints, that all your prayers must be of the same stamp, and as bitter as the other stream of your actions. When you stretch forth your hands to make many prayers, to take the bread and wine, shall not God hide his face from such hands as are unclean with many abominations, some murdering, some abusing their neighbours, some sabbath breaking, some filthiness? How oft have your hands and feet served you to evil turns? And therefore, your good turns will never come in remembrance. Nay, believe it, you cannot be heard of God, while you cover any offence. And this I may say in general, even to the saints; any known sin given way to, and entertained without controlment, without wrestling against it, hindereth the acceptation of your solemn approaches. If your heart regard iniquity, shall God hear? Psal. lxvi. 18. No, believe it, the least sin that you may judge at first venial, and then give it toleration and indulgence, shall separate between God's face and you. Your prayers are abomination, because of such an idol perked up in the heart beside God, that getteth the honour and worship due to him, and God must answer you according to it, Ezek. xix. 1, 3, 4. God will not be inquired of such as give allowance to sin, Ezek. xiv. 2-4. And, on the other hand, no sin, how great and heinous soever, can hinder God's gracious acceptation, when souls fly unto Jesus and turn their back upon sin, or giveth it no heart allowance. And to the multitude I say, all that you do or touch in a duty must be defiled, because your whole way is unclean, Hag. ii. 12-14. Think you to sin all the week through, and worship God on the Sabbath? Will you lie, swear, commit adultery, rail and curse, and come and stand before me, saith the Lord? No, certainly, you cannot be accepted. And will you hate reformation in your lives, and yet take his covenant in your mouth, and call yourselves by his name, "Christians?" And shall not God challenge you for that, as much as for your swearing, and cursing, and lying, &c.? Indeed the Lord putteth all in one roll, and you need not please yourselves in such things, Psal. i. 16; Jer. vii. 9, 10; for it is all one to you to go to tavern to drink, and come to the sermon,—to blaspheme God's name, and call on it; because the profanity of the one defileth the other, and the holiness of the other cannot make you holy.

Thirdly, The natural man's performances want the uprightness, reality, and sincerity that is required. It is but a painted tomb, full of rottenness within; it is but a shadow without substance, for he wanteth the spiritual part of worship, which God careth for, who will be worshipped "in spirit and in truth," John iv. 24. Now, what is it that the most part of you can speak of, but an outside of some few duties, soon numbered? You hear the preaching, and your hearts wander about your business. You hear, and are not so much affected as you would be to hear some old story or fable told you. A stage play acted before this generation would move them more than the gospel doth; so that Christ may take up this lamentation, "We have piped to you, and you have not danced; lamented to you, and you have not mourned." You use to tell over some words in your prayers, and are not so serious in any approach to God, as in twenty other things of the world. Whatever you plead of your heart's rightness, and have recourse to it, when your conversation cannot defend you, yet your hearts are the worst of all, and have no uprightness towards God; for you know that what duties you go about, it is not from an inward principle, but from education, or custom, or constraint. Are you upright, when you are forced, for fear of censure, to come here, or to pray at home? Is that sincerity and spiritual worship? And for the more polished and refined professors, you have this moth in your performances, and this fly to make your ointment to stink, that you do much to be seen of men. Therefore, what little fervour of spirit is in secret duties, there you may measure your attitude and your life. And O! how wearisome, how lifeless are secret approaches! You would not have many errands to God, if you thought no body looked upon you. And for spirituality, it is a mystery in all men's practice. Who directeth his duty to God's glory? If you get some flash of liberty, you have your desire; but who misseth God's presence in duties, which a world will approve? Who go mourning as without the sun, even when you have the sunshine of ordinances, and walk in the light of them?

And, *Fourthly*, Though your performances had uprightness of heart going along, and much affection in them, yet all are filthy, because of want of faith in Jesus Christ. When you make your duties a covering of your sins, and think to satisfy God's justice for the rest of your faults, by doing some point of your duty, then it cannot choose but be polluted in his sight. And this very thing was the cause of God's rejecting the Jews' righteousness, even because they did not look to the end of the mystery, Christ Jesus: did not pull by the vail of ceremonies, to see the immaculate Lamb of God slain for sin; and therefore doth the Lord so quarrel with them, as if he had never commanded them to do such things, Isa. i. 12, 13, "Who hath required these things at your hands? Bring no more vain oblations;" all is abomination. Even as God should say to you, when you come to the church, Who required you to come? Who commanded you to come to hear the preaching? What have you to do to pray? What warrant have you to communicate? All your praying, hearing, communicating, is abomination; who commanded you to do these things? Would you not think it a foolish question? You would soon answer, that God himself commanded you, and will he not let us do his bidding? Indeed this people, no doubt, have said so in their heart, and wondered what it meant. Nay, but here is the mystery,—you go about these commanded duties not in a commanded way, and so the obedience is but rebellion. You bring offerings and incense, and think that I am pacified when you bring alms,—you judge you have given me a recompence; whereas, all that is mine, and what pleasure have I in these things? I never appointed you sacrifices for this end, but to lead you into the knowledge of my Son, which is to be slain in the fulness of time, and by one offering to perfect all. I commanded you to look on Jesus Christ slain, in the slain Lamb, and so to expect remission and salvation in him; but you never looked to more nor the ceremony, and made that your saviour and mediator; and therefore it is all abomination. When you slay a lamb, and offer incense, it is all one thing as to cut off a dog's neck, or kill a man. So may the Lord say to this generation, I command you to pray, to repent and mourn for sin, to come and hear the word; but withal you must deny all these, and count yourselves unprofitable servants; you must singly cast your soul's burden on Christ Jesus. But now, saith the Lord, who commanded your repentance? For when you sit down to pray, or come in public to confess sin before the congregation, you think you are washen. When you have said, you have sinned, and if you come to the length of tears and sorrow, O then, sure you are pardoned, though in the meantime you have no thought of Jesus Christ, and know no use of him! Therefore, saith the Lord, who commanded you to do these things? You think you have satisfied for your sin, when you pay a penalty; but who requireth this? I will reckon with you for these, as well as the sins you pray and mourn for, because you do not singly look to Christ Jesus. Now, if he had never come to the world, your ground of confidence would not fail you; for you might have prayed as much, mourned and confessed, and promised amendment; and so you pass by the Son of God, in whom only the

Father is well-pleased. Think, then, upon this,—whatever you make your righteousness, there needeth no other thing to make it filthy, but to make it your righteousness. Your confidence in your good heart to God, prayer day and night, and such like, is the most loathsome thing in God's eyes. Except you come to this, to count your prayers, as God doth, among your oaths; to count your solemn duties among profane scandalous actions, as the Lord doth, Isa. i. and lxvi. 3, then certainly, you do adorn yourselves with them, and cover your nakedness of other faults with such leaves as Adam did, but you shall be more discovered. Your garment is as filthy as that it hideth, even because you make that use of it to hide your sin and cover it.

Next, The Lord's children have no ground of boasting either, from their own righteousness; the holiest saint on earth must abhor himself in dust and ashes, and holy Isaiah joineth himself in with a profane people. When he cometh to God to be justified, he cometh among the ungodly,—he bringeth no righteousness with him, he cometh in among them that work not. Now, you shall find good ground why it must be so:

I. There are ordinarily many blemishes in our holiest actions, spots upon our cleanest garments; often formality eateth up the life of duties, and representeth a body without a soul in it. You sit down to pray out of custom, morning and evening; and if there were no more to prove it, this may suffice. When pray you but at such times? You have an ordinary, and go not by it. No advantage is taken of providence, no necessity constraineth when occasion offereth; and so it is like the world's appointed hours. How great deadness and indisposition creepeth in! so that this is the ordinary complaint; yea, all prayers are filled with it,—scarcely any room for other petitions, because of the want of frame for prayer itself. The word is heard as a discourse, and on whom hath it operation to stir up affections, either of joy or of trembling? Christians, you come not to hear God speak, and so you meet with empty ordinances—God is not in them. How often do crooked and sinister ends creep in, and bias the spirit! Men ask, to spend on their lusts, and to satisfy their own ambition. Some would have more grace to be more eminent, or to have a more pleasant life; and this is but the seeking to spend on your lusts. If affection run in the channel of a duty, it is often muddy, and runneth through our corruptions: liberty in duties is principled with carnal affection and self-love. Will not often the wind of applause in company fill the sails, and make your course swifter and freer nor when you are alone? And often much love to a particular[308] maketh more in seeking it. And that which is a moth to eat up and consume all our duties is conceit and self-confidence in going about them, and attributing to ourselves after them. It is but very rare that any man both acted from Jesus Christ as the principle, and also putteth over his work on Christ singly as the end. Alas! too often do men draw out of Christ's fulness, and raise up their own glory upon it, and adorn themselves with the spoils of his honour; for we use to pray from a habit of it, and go to it as men acquainted with it, and when we get any satisfaction to our own minds, O how doth the soul return on itself, and goeth not forward as it goeth! It is so well pleased with itself, when it getteth liberty to approach, that it doth not put all over on Jesus, and take shame to itself. As long as there is a body of death within, holiness cannot be pure and unmixed; our duties run through a dirty channel, and cannot choose but contract filth. While sin lodgeth under one roof so near grace, grace must be in its exercise marred; and therefore the holy apostle must cry, Rom. vii. 19. "The good that I would, I do not: but the evil which I would not, that I do," and verse 24, "O wretched man that I am! who shall deliver me from the body of this death?"

II. Though there were not such blemishes and spots in the face of our righteousness, yet it is here in a state of imperfection, and but in its minority, and so must be filthy in the Lord's sight. It was perfect holiness, according to the perfect rule of God's law, that Adam was to be justified by, according to the covenant of works; exact obedience, not one wanting,—or else all that can be done, came short of righteousness: one breach bringeth the curse on. All obedience, if there be a failing in a little, will not bring the blessing on: he that doth all, liveth; and he that doth not all, is cursed. And therefore, Christians, all you do cannot commend your persons to God, for if he examine you by the rule of the law, O how short will the holiest come! Paul and Isaiah dare not come into such a reckoning; neither is all obeyed, nor any in the measure and manner commanded. And therefore, you might cry down all your performances, when you could challenge them with no particular blot, with this—all is short of the command, and infinitely short. I have been aiming at holiness so long, I have stretched out my strength, and what have I attained? It may be, I have outstripped equals, and there seemeth to be some distance between me and others; nay, but the command is unspeakably more before me nor I am before others. I have reached but a span of that boundless perfection of holiness; it is but a grain weight of the eternal weight of grace, and I must forget it, and stand before God, as if I had lost mind of duties, appear in his presence as if I had attained nothing; for the length that is before my hand drowneth up all attainments.

III. Nay, but put the case were man perfect, yet should he not know his soul, but despise his life: the Lord putteth no trust in his servants, and his angels he chargeth with folly, and the heavens are not clean in his sight; how then must man be abominable, that hath his foundation in the dust, and drinketh in iniquity like water? How should God magnify him? or he be righteous that is born of a woman? Job xxv. 4, 6; xv. 14, 15; and iv. 18, 19. Job was a great length in the sight of his own vileness and God's holiness, when he saw this, "Though I were perfect, yet I would not know it, but despise it; I would not answer him, though I were righteous," chap. ix. 14, 15, 21. So unspeakably pure and clean is his holiness, that all created holiness hath a spot in it before his, and evanisheth, as the stars disappear when the sun riseth, which seem something in the darkness. The angels' holiness, the heaven's glory, is nothing to him, before whom the nations are as nothing; so that it is all the wonder of the world, that ever God stooped so far below himself, even to righteous Adam, as to make such a covenant with him, to account him righteous in obedience. "What is man that thou shouldst magnify him? When I look to the heavens, and the sun, the work of thine hands, Lord, what is man?" What is innocent man in his integrity, that thou shouldst magnify him, to give him a place to stand before thee, magnify him to be a party-contractor with thy glorious Majesty? Psalm viii. 4-6. But now, when this covenant is broken, it is become impossible to a son of Adam ever to stand before God in his perfection, for, how should man be righteous that is born of a woman? Job xv. 14. Since we once sinned, how should our righteousness ever come in remembrance? Therefore hath God chosen another way to cover man's wickedness and righteousness both, with his own righteousness, his Son's divine human righteousness, which is so suited in his infinite wisdom for us. It is a man's righteousness, that it may agree with men, and be a fit garment to cover them; it is God's righteousness, that it may be beautiful in God's eyes, for he seeth his own image in it. And it is not the created inherent righteousness of saints glorified, that shall be their upper garment, that shall be their heaven and glory-suit, so to speak. They will not glory in this, but only in the Lamb's righteousness for evermore. Saint-holiness must have a covering above, for it cannot cover our nakedness; and all the songs of those that follow the Lamb make mention of his righteousness, even of his only. The Lamb is the light and sun of the city, the Lamb is the temple of it; in a word, he is all that is beautiful and glorious. Every saint hath put on the Lord Jesus, and is perfect through his comeliness. At least, if the holiness of spirits of just men made perfect be the glorious habit above; yet all the beauty and glory of it is from Christ Jesus, whose image it is, and the Spirit whose work it is. It shall be still true, all—all our righteousness, as ours, is filthy; and all holiness, as it hath a relation to us, cannot please God. It must be spotted before his pure eyes; but only it is accepted and clean, as it is Christ's and the Spirit's, as it is his own garment put upon us, and his own comeliness making us perfect. It is not so much the inherent cleanness of the Saints' robes that maketh them beautiful in his eyes, as this, that they are washed in the blood of the Lamb, Rev. vii. 14.

Now, from all this we would speak a word to two sorts of you. *First*, There is one great point of religion that is the principal and foundation of all other, even free justification by faith in Jesus, without our own righteousness; and the most part stumble here in the entry. It is the greatest obstruction of souls coming to Christ Jesus, even the ignorant and blind conceit and fancy that almost every man hath of himself and his own performances; the world will not make many believe the half of the evil of themselves that is spoken in the word. If you have a general conviction of sinfulness and misery, yet you think to help it. If you sin, you use to make amends, run to your prayers and repentance to give God a recompence, and satisfy your own consciences. Speak now, is not this the way you think to be saved? I shall do what I can, pray and mourn for sin; and what I am not able to do, God must forgive; you will do all you are able or can, and God's mercy must come in to supply the want of your righteousness. But this is to put a new piece of cloth in an old garment, to make the rent worse. Many of you have no other ground of confidence in the world, nothing to answer the challenge of conscience or satisfy justice, but this,—I repent, I am sorry, I mourn, I shall amend, I resolve never to do the like again. Now, then, from this ground we would declare unto you, in the Lord's name, you are yet unclean, both in persons and actions unjustified, because you have no other covering but your own duties and performances: and let these be examined, and weighed in the balance of the sanctuary, and they will be found light. All your righteousness, saith the Lord, is filthiness; you are unclean, you cannot deny, both by birth and education,—you have often defiled yourselves with sins, you must confess. Now, I ask you, How will you cover that uncleanness and nakedness? How will you hide it from God's eyes and your own consciences? You know no way but this,—I will pray, I will repent and amend. So then you cover yourself with prayer, with sorrow and tears, and a resolution of amending. This, then, is all your covering and ornament,—something done by you, as many will make the wings of two good works stretch themselves out so far as to cover and hide a multitude of offences between them. Therefore I declare, in the Lord Jesus his name, unto you, whose conscience must go along in the acknowledgment and owning of your case, that you have covered yourselves with your own righteousness, that you have taken as filthy rags to cover your nakedness and sin with, as your sins are, and so you have made an addition to your uncleanness, you are more unclean by your prayers and repentance than before; and so God is of more pure eyes than to look graciously on such as you are. You have gone about to establish your own righteousness, and have not known the righteousness of God, and so you have come short of it; you are yet persons in a state of enmity,—God is your judge, you are rebels. It concerns you much to heed this well, to judge of your own actions and persons as God judgeth of them; for if God shall judge one way, and you judge another way, you may be far mistaken in the end. If you have so good an opinion of yourselves and your duties, that you can plead interest in God for them, and absolve yourselves from such grounds; and if God have not the same judgment, but rather think as evil of your prayers as of your cursing, and abhor the thing that satisfieth you, will it not be dreadful in the end? For his judgment shall stand, and you will succumb in judgment, since you crossed God's mind. Therefore we would have you solidly drink in this principle of religion;—that man is so unclean, and God so abhorreth him, that whatever he doth or can do, it cannot make him righteous; that no good action can make him acceptable, and take away the uncleanness of the evil actions; and that any sinful action taketh away all the cleanness of the good actions. Once believe this,—if I should sweat out my life in serving God, and never rise off my knees, if I should give my body to the fire for the truth, if I should melt away in tears for sin, all this is but filthy rags, and I can never be accepted of God for all that, but the matter of my condemnation groweth,—if I justify myself my own mouth proves me perverse: God needeth no more but my good deeds to condemn me for, in all justice: and therefore it is a thing impossible,—I will never put forth a hand, or open a mouth upon that account any more. I will serve God, because it is my duty, but life I will not expect by my service; when I have done all, it is wholly mercy that I am accepted, my good works shall never come in remembrance; I resolve to be found, not having my own righteousness. I will appear among the ungodly sinners, as one that hath no righteousness, that I may be justified only by faith in Jesus Christ. I say, drink in this truth, and let it settle in your hearts, and then we would hear numbers cry, "O what shall I do to be saved?"

Now, *Secondly*, As for you who have fled unto Christ's righteousness only, and have cast away your own as dung and dross, as filthy rags; as you have done right in the point of justification, judge so likewise after it. We would exhort you to judge so of your best actions that are the fruits of the Spirit, judge so of them as you have a hand in them.

"All our righteousness." Mark, Isaiah, a holy prophet, joineth himself in with the multitude. And the truth is, the more holiness, the more humility and self-abasing; for what is holiness, I pray you, but self-denial, the abasing of the creature, and exalting of Christ Jesus? This is the cross that the saints must all bear, "Deny yourself, and follow me." Grace doth not swell men above others; it is gifts, such as knowledge, that puffeth up; charity or love puffeth not up. Men are naturally high-minded, for pride was the first sin of Adam, and grace cometh to level men, to make the high mountains valleys for Christ's chariot; it maketh men stoop low to enter the door of the kingdom. Therefore, if you have attained any measure beyond others, if you would prove it real grace and holiness, do not exalt yourselves above others, be not high-minded, come down and sit among the ungodly, among the unclean, and let not grace given diminish the low estimation of yourself in yourself. There is a growing that is but a fancy, and men's conceit; when men grow above ordinances, above other Christians, and can see none or few Christians but themselves, such a growth is not real. It is but fancy, it is but swelling and wind, and must be pricked to let it out. A holy prophet came in among an unclean people; he did not say, "Stand by, I am holier than thou." Such a man as can find no Christian about him, even though to the judgment of all others, they seek God more than he, such a man hath not real solid grace,—his holiness is profane holiness, and proud holiness; for true holiness is humble holiness, and in honour preferreth others.

There is a great fault among those who have fled to Christ's righteousness in justification, that they use to come full from duties, as a stomach from a honeycomb. Ofttimes we make our liberty and access to God the ground of our acceptation; and according to the ebbings and flowings of our inherent righteousness, so doth the faith and confidence of justification ebb and flow. Christians, this ought not to be; in so doing, you make your own righteousness your righteousness before God; for when the unsatisfaction in the point of duty maketh you question your interest so often, is not the satisfaction of your minds in duties made the ground of your pleading interest? Give you liberty and access, you can believe anything; remove it, and you can believe nothing. Certainly this is a sandy foundation,—you ought to build nothing on performances, you should be as vile in your own eyes, and think your nakedness as open, when you come nearest God, when you have most liveliness, as when he hideth his face, and duty withereth. Will filthy rags be your ornament? No, Christians. Be more acquainted with the unspotted righteousness of the immaculate Lamb of God, and find as great necessity of covering your cleanest duties with it, as your foulest faults, and thus shall you be kept still humble and vile in your own eyes, and have continual employment for Christ Jesus. Your best estate should not puff you up, and your worst estate should not cast you down; therefore be much in the search of the filthiness of your holy actions. This were a spiritual study, a noble discovery to unbowel your duties, to divide them, and to give unto God what is God's, and take unto yourselves what is your own. The discovery of filthiness in them needeth not hinder his praise; and the discovery of grace in them needeth not mar your shame. God hath most glory when we have most shame; these two grow in just proportion,—so much is taken from God as is given to the creature.

Thirdly, We would also press you from this ground to long much to be clothed upon with immortality, to put off the filthy rags of time and earth-righteousness, and to be clothed upon with the white robes of the righteousness of the saints. As you would dwell near the fountain here, and be still washing your garments, and offering all your sacrifices in him who sanctifieth all, so would you pant and thirst for this spotless garment of glory. Glory is nothing but perfect holiness, holiness washen and made clean in the Lamb's blood. Your rags are for the prison and for sojourning; when you come to your Father's house, your raiment shall be changed. Therefore, Christians, every one of you aspire higher. Sit not down in attainments; forget what is behind, and press forward. Let perfect holiness be in your eye and purpose, sit not behind it. All our time-duties have much filthiness,—long for the pure stream that waters the city above. Grace is not in its native place, it is corrupted and mixed here: heaven is the own element of it, and there is grace without mixture. Undervalue all your performances, till you be above, where that which is in part shall be done away, where no unclean thing entereth.

Fourthly, This likewise holdeth out to you a continual necessity of washing. You must take up house beside the fountain opened in the house of David; and never look on any piece of inherent righteousness, but see a necessity of dipping it in the Lamb's blood. And therefore should you pray always in Christ's name, that the prayer which, of itself, would be cast as dung on our face, may have a sweet savour from him. Cover your holiness with Christ's righteousness, and make mention of it only.

SERMON XVII.

Isaiah lxiv. 6.—"And we all do fade as a leaf, and our iniquities, like the wind, have taken us away."

Here they join the punishment with the deserving cause, their uncleanness and their iniquities, and so take it upon them, and subscribe to the righteousness of God's dealing.

We would say this much in general—*First*, Nobody needeth to quarrel God for his dealing. He will always be justified when he is judged. If the Lord deal more sharply with you than with others, you may judge there is a difference between your condition and theirs, as well as in the Lord's dispensation, even as this people do, ver. 5, 6. It is a strange saying, Lam. iii. 33. The Lord "doth not afflict willingly, nor grieve the children of men." That is, as we conceive, the Lord hath not such pleasure in trampling on men, as he might do on the dust of his feet. Though he be absolute sovereign Lord of the creature, and men be but as the dust of his feet, and he may do with his own what he pleaseth, and none ask, what dost thou? yet the Lord useth not to walk according to his own absoluteness,—he hath another ordinary rule whereby he worketh, a rule of justice and equity. Especially in the punishing of men, he useth not to afflict men for his pleasure, as tyrants use to destroy their people. The Lord exerciseth his sovereignty another way, and if he be absolute and unlimited in any thing, it is in showing mercy on men. But in judgment, there may be still some reason gotten for it in the creature beside the will of God; so that, to speak with reverence of his majesty, strokes are often drawn out of his hands. He getteth so much provocation ere he strike, and holdeth off so long,—threateneth, and giveth warning thus before strokes, as if it were against his will to lay on, as if his heart were broken with us.

Secondly, If men knew themselves and their own sinfulness, they would not challenge God with unrighteousness, but put their mouth in the dust, and keep silence. And it is from this ground, that this people do not charge God. Sin is of such infinite desert and demerit, because against infinite majesty, that God cannot go beyond it in punishment; and therefore Jeremiah, when he is wading out of the deep waters of sore temptation and sad discouragement, pitcheth and casteth anchor at this solid ground, "It is of the Lord's mercy that we are not consumed," Lam. iii. 22. What! do I mean thus to charge God, as if he dealt rigorously? No, no: It is his mercy that a remnant is left,—our strokes are not pure justice, our cup is mixed, mercy is the greatest part. Whatever is behind utter destruction, whatever is below the desert of sin, which is hell and damnation, all this must be reckoned up to mercy. That I am yet alive, and so may have hope, this is mercy, "For why should a living man complain?" ver. 39. That a rod is come to awake us out of security, this is mercy, for we might have slept to death. And this wholesome counsel got Job of his friends,—to stay his murmuring and grudging at God's dispensations, Job. xi. 6. Why dost thou complain, Job? Know but thy sins, and there shall be no room for complaint. Look but unto God's secrets of wisdom, and his law, and see it is double to what you have known,—your obligation is infinitely more than you thought upon, and then how great and numberless must iniquities be? "Know, therefore," saith Zophar, "God exacteth of thee less than thine iniquities deserve." God exacteth not according to law, he craveth not according to the obligation, but bids write down fifty in his bill of affliction, when an hundred are written in our bill of deserving. So then, complain not,—it is mercy that life is saved. Are you men, and living men? Wonder at this, and wonder not that you are not wealthy, are not honourable, seeing you are sinners: all that came on Jerusalem maketh not Ezra think God out of bounds, chap. ix. 13. As we are less than the least of God's mercies, and all our goodness deserveth none of them, so is the least sin greater than the greatest of all his judgments, and deserveth still more. Nay, if there were no more but original corruption common to men, and the filthiness that accompanieth men's good actions, yet is God righteous in punishing severely, and this people acknowledge it so. You use to inquire what sin hath such a man done, when so terrible judgments come on? Nay, inquire no more;—he is a sinner, and it is mercy there is not more, and it is strange mercy that it is not so with you also. You use to speak foolishly when God's hand is upon you: I hope I have my punishment here, I hope to suffer here for my sins. Poor souls, if God make you suffer for sins, it will be another matter. Though now your punishment be above your strength and patience, yet it is below your sin. As sin hath all evil in it, so must hell have all punishment in it. The torment of the gravel, racking with the stone, and such like, are but play to hell,—these are but drops of that ocean that you must drink out, and you shall go out of one hell into a worse; eternity is the measure of its continuance, and the degrees of itself are answerable to its duration. There is much impatience even among God's children under the rod, you vex and torment yourselves, and do well to be angry. Any piece of thwarting dispensation, that goes cross to your humour and inclination, imbitters your spirit against God and maketh you go cross to his providence; how often do your hearts say, Why am I thus? What aileth the Lord at me? But, Christians, learn to study your own deservings, and stop your mouth with that, that you may not speak against heaven. If you knew sin well, you would not wonder at judgments, you would rather wonder that you are out of hell. Know what right God hath over you, and how little use he maketh of it against you. When you repine at a little, shall it not be righteousness with God to exact more, and let you know your deserving better? He that thinketh it rigour in God to exact fifty, it is justice that God crave an hundred. If the law require forty stripes, and he give but one, will you not rather commend and proclaim his clemency, than speak of his cruelty? Wonder that God hath spared us so long. Sin is come to great maturity. As pride is said to blossom and bud into a rod, so all sins are blossomed and budded into the very harvest, that the sickle may be put in. If we should have cities desolate, and our land consumed, if we should take up Jeremiah's lamentation, and our case be made parallel to theirs, we have then been punished less than our iniquities deserved.

There are some godless people so black mouthed as to speak against heaven when God correcteth them, they follow the counsel of Job's wife, curse God and die. If God but touch them a little in that which is dearest unto them, they kick against the pricks, and run hard heads with God. As we have known some foolish women, when their only child hath been removed, blaspheme, saying, What can God do more to me?—let him do what he can. O madness and wickedness of men! Cannot God do more when he casteth them into hell? Thou shalt acknowledge that it is more. Some have left off to seek God and turned profane, because of the Lord's correction but you should know that all that is here is but arles.[309] If God had done his worst, you might think yourselves out of his common, nay, but he hath yet more to do, the full sum is to be paid. It were therefore wisdom yet to make supplication to thy judge.

But, *Thirdly*, Sins and iniquities have a great influence in the decay of nations and persons, and change of their outward condition, when it is joined with the wind of God's displeasure. The calamity of this people is set down in excellent terms, alluding to a tree in the fall of the leaf. We, saith he, were once in our land as a green tree busked round about with leaves and fruit; our church and state was in a flourishing condition, at least nothing was wanting to make outward splendour and glory. We were immovable in our own land, as David said in his prosperity, "I shall never be moved," so did we dream of eternity in earthly Canaan. But now Lord, we are like a tree in the fall of the leaf, sin hath obstructed the influence of heaven, hath drawn away the sap of thy presence from among us, so that we did fade as a leaf before its fall, we were prepared so by our sins for judgment,—visible draughts and prognostics of it were to be read upon the condition and frame of all spirits and people, and then did our iniquities raise the storm of thy indignation, and that, like a whirlwind, hath blown the withering leaves off the tree, hath driven us out of our own land, and scattered us among strangers. Sin and uncleanness and the filthiness of our righteousness prepared us for the storm, made us light matter that could resist no judgment, made us matter combustible, and then iniquities, and sin rising up to iniquities, coming to such a degree, hath accomplished the judgment, put fire among us, made us as the birk in Yule even.[310]

First, It is familiar in the Scripture that people in a prosperous condition are compared unto a green tree flourishing, Psal. xxxvii. 35. The wicked's prospering is like a green bay tree spreading himself in power, spreading out his arms, as it were, over more lands to conquer them, over more people, to subject them. And this is often the temptation of the godly, and so doth the Lord himself witness of this people, Jer. xi. 16, "I have called thy name a green olive tree, fair and of goodly fruit." This was once their name, though it be now changed. Now they are called a fading withering tree without both leaves and fruit. Now their place doth not so much as know them, they are removed as in a moment, Psal. xxxvii. 36. And this comparison giveth us to understand something of the nature of human glory and pomp. The fairest and most beautiful excellency in the world, the prosperity of nations and people, is but like the glory of a tree in the spring or summer. Yea, the Scripture useth to undervalue it more than so and the voice commandeth to cry, (Isa. xl. 6, 7, 8,) "All flesh is grass and the goodliness thereof as the flower of the field: the one withereth, and the other fadeth, because the Spirit of the Lord bloweth upon it." A tree hath some stability in it, but the flower of the field is but of a month or a week's standing, nay, of one day's standing, for in the morning the grass is green, and the sun scorcheth it ere night, so that one sun's course shall see it both growing green and fading. So is the goodliness, the very perfection, the quintessence, so to speak, and the abstract of creatures' perfections. Outward accommodation in a world is as fading a thing as the flower is, as smoke is, it is so vanishing that it bides but a puff of his breath to blow it to nothing. Job hath a strange expression, "Thou lookest upon me, and I am not," Job vii. 8. The Lord needeth no more but stare on the most durable creature, and look it not only out of countenance, but also look it into its first nothing—look it out of glory, out of being; and therefore you should not trust in those uncertain things, that can take wings and leave you. When you have accommodation outwardly to your mind do not build your nest in it; these leaves of prosperity will not cover you always, there is a time when they will fall. Nations have their winter and their summer, persons have them likewise, as these must change in nature, so must they do in their lot. Heaven only is one day, one spring perpetually blossoming and bringing forth fruit. There is the tree of life that bringeth forth fruit every month, that hath both spring and harvest all the year over. Christians, sit not down under the green tree of worldly prosperity, if you do, the leaves will come down about you, the gourd you trust in may be eaten up in a night, your winter will come on so as you shall forget the former days as if they had never been. We desire you to be armed for changes; are not matters in the kingdom still going about? All things are subject to revolution and change, and every year hath its own summer and winter, so hath it pleased the Lord to set the one over against the other, that man might find nothing after him, Eccl. vii. 14. Therefore we would have you cast your accounts so as the former days of darkness may return, and the land be covered with mourning clothes.

But would you know what is the original of the creatures' vanity, what is the moth that eats up the glory and goodliness of creatures' enjoyments? Here it is—sin and iniquities. It was sin that first subjected the creation to vanity, Rom. viii. 19, 20. This inferior world was to have been a durable house for an immortal soul, but sin made man mortal, and the world corruptible, and from this proceed all the tempests and disorders that seem to be in the creation. It is this still—it is sin that raiseth the storm of the Lord's wrath, which bloweth away the withered leaves of men's enjoyments. Sin drieth up all the sap and sweetness of the creature comforts,—it maketh the leaves of the tree wither, drives the sap away to the root, hindereth the influence of God's blessing to come through the veins of worldly prosperity. For what is the virtue and sap of creatures? It is even God's blessing, and therefore the bread nourisheth not, but the word and command of God, Matt. iv. 4. That is a right unto the creatures by Jesus Christ, when possession of them is entered into by prayer and thanksgiving, for all right is sanctified by these, and it is the iniquities of men that separate between God and them, Isa. lix. 2. And when God is separated and divided from enjoyments, they must needs be empty shells and husks, no kernel in them, for God "filleth all in all," is all in all, and remove him, and you have nothing—your meat and drink is no blessing, your table is a snare, your pleasures and laughter have sadness in them. At least they are like the vanishing blaze of thorns under a pot, and therefore, when God is angry for sin, men's beauty consumeth as before the moth, Psalm xxxix. 11. When God beginneth to show himself terrible, because of sin, poor man, though of late spreading his boughs out, yet all falleth, and like ice melteth as before the sun, which just now seemed as solid as stone. O but David was sensible of this and could speak from much experience, Psal. xxxii. 3, 4. The anger of the Lord did eat him up, and dried his moisture. It might be read in his countenance,—all the world could not content him, all the showers of creatures' dropping fatness could not keep sap in him. God's displeasure scorcheth so, nay, is within him, that no hiding-place is to be found in the world, no shadow of a rock among all the creatures in such a weary land. Moses and the people knew this well, Psal. xc. 5-9. The Lord's displeasure carried them away, as a flood coming down carrieth all headlong with it, it scorched them and made them wither as grass. When God setteth iniquities before him, and that which is the soul's secret, beginneth to imprint it in visible characters on the rod, and writeth his sin on his punishment, then no wonder that days be spent in vanity and grief, since they are passed over in his wrath, Job xiii. 25. Then doth a soul loathe its dainty meat, and then doth the ox low over his fodder. Meat is laid before him, and he cannot touch it, because of the terrors of the Almighty, and that which before he would not once touch, would not enter into terms of communing with, as the Lord's threatenings, he must now sit down and eat them up as his meat, how sorrowful soever, Job vi. 4-7.

But, *secondly*, when sin hath prepared a man for judgment, then, if iniquity be added to sin, this raiseth the storm, and kindleth the fire to consume the combustible matter. When sin hath given many blows, by preparatory corrections at the root of a man's pleasure and credit, it will at length bring on a fatal stroke that shall drive the tree to the ground. There are some preparatory judgments, and some consummatory, some wither the leaf, and some blow it quite off, some make men like the harvest, ripe to put the sickle of judgment into it. The corruption of a land, the universality of it, and formality in worshipping of God, ripeneth a land for the harvest of judgment,—exposeth it to any storm,—leaveth it open to the Lord's wrath, so that there is nothing to hold his hand and keep off the stroke, but when the wind ariseth, and iniquities have made it tempestuous, then who may stand? It will sweep away nations and people as a flood, and make their place not to know them, so that there shall be neither leaf nor branch left. There is often a great calm with great provocations, and iniquities cry, "Peace, peace!" But when once the cry of it is gone up to heaven, and hath engaged God's anger against a people or person, then it raiseth a whirlwind that taketh all away. Now, all this belongeth to you,—we told you the acknowledgment of sin was yours already, and a wonder it is, that the complaint is not ours also. Always this ought to be an admonition and example to us, on whom the ends of the world are fallen. Therefore we would declare this unto you, that sin and iniquities have judgment in the tail. Now you sit at peace, every one in his own dwelling, and spread forth your branches, but is there not much uncleanness among you? We would have you trouble your carnal peace and security, trouble your ease with thoughts of this. And we have ground to give this warning, because, if there were no more but the iniquity of our holy things—the formality of our service—the commonness of spirit in worship, this might be enough to raise the storm. You know not for what reasons to be afraid of judgment. Look but on original corruption, look on the defilement of your religious actions, and then find ground sufficient of fading away. Though now you sit still, and seem to be so settled, as you would never be moved, you dream of an eternity here—you cleave in your hearts to your houses and lands—you stick as fast to the world, and will not part with it, as a leaf to a tree, yet behold the wind of the Lord may arise, that shall drive you away; take your soul from these things, and then whose shall they be? If you will not fear temporal judgments, yet I pray you fear eternal—fear hell. May not the Lord shake you off this tree of time, and take you out of the land of the living, to receive your portion? There is not only an universal deadness of spirit on the land, but a profane spirit,—iniquities, abominable sins, abound. Every congregation is overgrown with scandals,[311] and for you, none may more justly complain. We are all unclean, sin is not in corners but men declare their sin as Sodom, sin is come to the maturity—defection and apostacy[312] is the temper of all spirits, and, above all, the general contempt and slighting of this glorious gospel, is the iniquity of Scotland,[313] so that we wonder that the withered leaves yet stick to, that the storm is not yet raised, and we blown away. Now, you are like stones—your hearts as adamants, and cannot be moved with his threatening, the voice of the Lord's word doth not once move you. You sin and are not afraid, nay, but when God's anger shall join with iniquity, and the voice of his rod and displeasure roar, this shall make the mountains to tremble, the rocks to move, and how much more shall it drive away a leaf? You seem now mountains, but when God shall plead, you shall be like the chaff driven to and fro. O how easy a matter shall it be to God to blow a man out of his dwelling place! Sin hath prepared you for it, he needeth no more but blow by his Spirit, or look upon you, and you will not be. You who are now lofty and proud, and maintain yourselves against the word, when you come to reckon with God, and he entereth into judgment, you shall not stand—you will consume as before the moth; your hearts will fail you—"who may abide the day of his coming?" It will be so terrible, and so much the more terrible, that you never dreamed of it. If the example of this people will not move you, do but cast your eyes on Ireland,[314] who all do fade as a leaf, and their iniquities have taken them away out of their own land. Shall not the seeing of the eye, nor the hearing of the ear teach you? What security do you promise to yourselves? Have not we sinned as much as they? Were not they his people as well as we? Certainly, since God waiteth longer on you, the stroke must be the greater: provoked patience must turn fury. If you would then prevent this people's complaint, go about such a serious acknowledgment of your sins. "Search your ways, and turn again to the Lord." And let not every man sit down in a general notion of sin, but unbowel it until you see uncleanness, go up to the fountain head, original corruption, go down to all the streams, even the iniquity of holy things. Let every man be particular in the search of his own provocations personal, and every one be public in the general sins of the land, that you may confess out of knowledge and sense, "We are all unclean," &c.

SERMON XVIII.

Isaiah lxiv. 7.—"And there is none that calleth upon thy name, that stirreth up himself to take hold on thee," &c.

They go on in the confession of their sins. Many a man hath soon done with that a general notion of sin is the highest advancement in repentance that many attain to. You may see here sin and judgment mixed in thorough other[315] in their complaint. They do not so fix their eyes upon their desolate estate of captivity, as to forget their provocations. Many a man would spend more affection, and be more pathetic in the expression of his misery, when it is pungent, nor he can do when he speaketh of his sins. We would observe, from the nature of this confession, something to be a pattern of your repentance. And it is this. When the Spirit convinceth, and men are serious in repentance, then the soul is more searching, more universal, more particular in acknowledgment of sins. These are characters of the Spirit's work.

First, The Spirit discovereth unto men, not only sin, but the loathsomeness of sin, its heinous nature, how offensive it is to God's holy eye. Many of you know abundance of evil deeds, and call them sins, but you have never taken up sin's ugly face, never seen it in the glass of the holy law, uncleanness itself, because you do not abhor yourselves. Poor and low thoughts of God make mean and shallow thoughts of sin. You should be as Job, vile, chap. xl. 4, and abhor yourselves in dust and ashes, chap. xlii. 6. As God's holiness grew great in your eyes, sins uncleanness would grow proportionably, Isa. vi. 3, 5. And here your repentance halteth in the very entry.

But, *secondly*, The Spirit discovereth not only the uncleanness of men's natures, and leadeth them up to original corruption, but the Spirit also leadeth men along all the streams, not only those that break out, but those which go under ground, and have a more secret and subtile conveyance. It concludeth not only open breaches of the command under filthiness, but also all a man's own righteousness, though never so refined, it concludeth it also a defiled garment, so that the soul can look no where but see sin and uncleanness in its ornaments and duties. And thus it appeareth before God without such a covering, openeth up its soul, hideth not sin with the covering of duties, but seeth a necessity of another covering for all. Now, therefore, let the most part of you conclude, that you have never yet gotten your eyes open to see sin or confess it, because when you sit down to count your sins, there are many things that you call not sin,—you use not to reckon your praying and repentance among sins. Nay, because you have so much confidence in your repentance and confession, you have never repented. You must see a necessity of a covering of Christ's righteousness above all, faith in Jesus must cover repentance and itself both, with the glorious object of it. But, alas! how soon are many at an end of confession! some particular gross actions may come in remembrance, but no more. Sum up all your confessions, they have never yet pitched on the thousandth part of your guiltiness, no, not in kinds, let be in number.

But, *thirdly*, The spirit convinceth spiritually and particularly both, it convinceth of spiritual sins, as we last said, of the iniquity of holy things, and especially of the most substantial duties, faith and prayer, John xvi. 8, 9. There are not many of you have come this length, to see your want of prayer. No, your own words do witness against you, for you use to say, I pray day and night, I believe in God with all my heart. Now therefore, out of your own mouth shall you be condemned. When the Spirit convinceth you of sin, you will see no faith, no prayer at the first opening of the eyes. But I add, there is no true confession but it is particular: the Spirit useth not to bewilder men's spirits in a general notion only, and a wide field of unknown sins. And such are many of your convictions. You mourn for sin, as you say, and yet you cannot condescend on a particular that burdeneth your conscience; you grant you have many sins, but sit down to count them, and there is a short count of them. Now, do you not reflect back upon former humiliations in public, and former acknowledgments of sins in private? Do you not yet return upon your own hearts to lay home this sad challenge, I have never repented, I do not yet repent? Must not all your solemn approaches be iniquity and abomination, while your souls are not afflicted for sin, while you can see so few sins? The fasting days of Scotland will be numbered in the roll of the greatest provocations, because there is no real and spiritual conviction of sin among us, custom hath now taken away the solemnity, and there remaineth nothing but the very name. Is this the fast that the Lord chooseth? No, believe it, this shall add to your provocation, and rather hasten lingering judgment than keep it off. We would beseech you this day, pray for pardon of former abused fasts. If you had no more to mourn for, this might spend the day and our spirits both, and exhaust all our present supplications—even the wall of partition that stands between God and Scotland, which all our former solemn humiliations hath built up, a great deal higher than other sins could reach.

"There is none that calleth upon thy name." Did not this people make many prayers (Isa. i. 15), before the captivity? And did they not cry, which noteth some fervency in it, and fast, a little before it in Jeremiah's time, (chap. xi. 11, and xiv. 12,) and in the time of it, Ezek. vii. 18, Mic. iii. 4, Zech. vii. 3? How, then, is it that the prophet, now on the watch tower, looking round about him to take up the people's condition, and being led by the Spirit so far as to the case of the captives in Babel, can find no prayer, no calling? And was not Daniel so too? Dan. ix. 13. Lo, then, here is the construction that the Spirit of God putteth on many prayers and fastings in a land, "There is none calleth on thy name," there is none that prayeth faithfully and fervently, few to count upon that prayeth any. It may be there are many public prayers, but who prayeth in secret, and mourneth to God alone? There are many prayers, but the inscription is, "To the unknown God," to a nameless God; your praying is not a calling on his name, as a known God and revealed in the word.

This, then, we would say unto you, that there may be many prayers in your account, and none in God's. There are many prayers of men that God counteth no more of than the howling of a dog.

First, The cry of men's practices is often louder than their prayers, and goeth up to heaven, that the cry of prayer cannot be heard. When men's conversation is flat contrary to their supplications, supplication is no calling on his name, but charming rather. Sodom's abominations had a cry up to God, Gen. xviii. 21. So Abel's blood had a cry for vengeance, which Cain's prayers could not outcry. Thus the Lord would not hear many prayers, Isa. i. 15, because hands and practices were polluted. You that know no worship of God, but in such a solemn duty, your religion is summed up and confined within the limits of temple worship, family exercise, and prayer, certainly the rest of your conversation must speak more. God will not hear but such as worship him and do his will, John iv. 23. Your prayer is a dark parable, if your conversation expone[316] it not. This I speak for this end, to put many of you out of your false ground of confidence. You have nothing but your prayers to trust unto, and for your conversation, you never go about it effectually to reform it, but go on in that which you pray against. We declare unto you the truth, your prayers are abomination, Prov. xxviii. 9. The wicked may have prayers, and therefore think not to please God and flatter him with your mouths, when your conversation is rebellion. Since you hear not him in his commands, God will not hear you in your petitions, Prov. i. 24, 28. You stopped your ear at his reproof, God will stop his ear at your request. If you will go to heaven by your own righteousness, I pray you follow more after it, make the garment more to cover your nakedness: the skirt of a duty is not sufficient.

Secondly, When iniquity is regarded in the heart, and idols set up in God's place, God will not own such a worship, but sendeth a man to the idols he serveth, Psal. lxvi. 18; Ezek. xiv. 9, 4. Do you not often pray to God against a corruption, when your heart cleaveth unto it, and what your mouth saith, your heart contradicteth? Light and conscience often extort a confession of beloved sins, while the temper of the heart hath this language, Lord, grant not my request. And therefore, if there be a prayer for pardon of guilt, yet there is no thorough resolution to quit the sin; and as long as a soul is not resolved to quit the sin, there can be no ingenuous confession of it, and no prayer for removing the guilt can be heard. You cannot employ Christ in his office of mediatorship as a Priest to intercede and offer sacrifice for sin, unless you as sincerely employ him as a Sanctifier and Redeemer; and therefore prayer that separateth Christ's offices, and calleth not on whole Christ, calleth not on his name, for his name is Lord Jesus Christ. How can the Lord be inquired of by such a one who cometh to mock him, putteth up an idol in the heart, and yet prayeth against it, or some other sin, while he is not resolved to quit it? Shall God be resolute to help, when we are not earnest in seeking it? No wonder God answer you according to the idol; no wonder you be given up to serve idols, and your sin grow upon you as a plague for your hypocrisy. When you engage your heart too much to any creature, and come to pray and inquire of the Lord in your necessity, shall it not be righteousness with him, to send you to your god? "When thou criest, let thy companies deliver thee," Isa. lvii. 13. O man, cry unto thy bosom-idol, and let it help thee, since thou trustest to it, and spendest thy heart upon it! Deut. xxxii. 37, 38, "Where is the God that drank the wine of your offerings, and did eat the fat of your sacrifices?" Where is the creature that you have made your heart an altar to, to send up the flames of your choicest thoughts and affections to it? Let this rise up, and help you now, saith the Lord. Therefore we exhort you, if you would have your prayers a delight, be upright in the thing you seek, and see that you entertain no known sin, give it no heart-allowance.

Thirdly, There are many prayers not heard, not known, because the mouth out-crieth the heart. It is the sacrifice of the contrite heart that God despiseth not. The prayers of this people were such, (Isa. xxix. 13,)—they drew near with the mouth, but the heart was far away. It is worship in spirit and truth that God loveth, John iv. 23. Since prayer is a communion of God with the creature, a meeting of one with God, and speaking face to face, God, who is a Spirit and immortal, must have a spirit to meet with, a soul to speak to him. Now, do you not find your hearts gadding abroad even in duty? Is it not most about your corns and lands in the time of solemn worship? Therefore God getteth no more but a carcase to keep communion with: he may have as much fellowship with the stones of the wall, and timber of the house, as he can have with your ears and mouths, while you remove your hearts to attend other things. And I would say more,—if your mind be present, yet your heart is gone; sometimes, yea often, both are gone abroad. Sometimes the mind and thought stayeth, but the affection and heart is not with it, and so the mind's residence is not constant. Your thought may come in as a wayfaring man, but tarrieth not all night, dwelleth not. Now speak to it, even Christians, may not your prayers often have a contrary interpretation to what they pretend? You pray so coldrifely[317] and formally, as God will interpret, you have no mind to it: we ask as we seemed indifferent whether our petition be granted or not. Should the Lord be affected with your petitions, when you yourselves are not affected much? Should his bowels of zeal sound within him, when yours are silent? It is fervent prayer availeth much, James v. 16. A heart sent out with the petition, and gone up to heaven, cannot but bring back an answer. If prayer carry not the seal of the heart and soul in it, God cannot own it, or send it back with his seal of acceptation.

Fourthly, Many prayers are not calling on God's name; and no wonder that when people pray, yet the Spirit says, "None calleth on thy name;" for prayer is made, as to an unknown God, and God is not taken up according to his "name," which are his glorious attributes, whereby he manifesteth himself in his word. To call on God's name, is so to pray to God as to take him up as he hath revealed himself. And what is the Lord's name? Hear himself speak to Moses, Exod. xxxiii. 19, and xxxiv. 6, 7, "The Lord, the Lord God, merciful and gracious, long-suffering, and abundant in goodness and truth. Keeping mercy for thousands: forgiving iniquity, and transgression, and sin, and that will by no means clear the guilty." Now, to call on this name is for the soul, in prayer, to have a suitable stamp on it: every attribute of God taking deep impression in the heart, and so God's name to be written on the very petitions; and shortly, we may say, the spirit should have the impression of God's greatness and majesty, of his goodness and mercy, of his terribleness and justice. This is the order in which God proclaimeth his name. In the entry, the supplicant should behold the glorious sovereignty and infinite distance between God and the creature, that he may have the stamp of reverence and abasement upon his spirit, and may speak out of the dust, as it becometh the dust of the balance and footstool to do to him who sitteth on the circle of the heaven as his throne. And this I must say, there is little religion and godliness among us, because every man is ignorant of God. Even God's children do more study themselves, and their condition, than God's greatness and absoluteness. Who searches God's infiniteness in his word and works till he behold a wonder, and be drowned in a mystery?

O but the saints of old did take up God at a greater distance from the creatures; they waded far into this boundless ocean of God's Majesty, till they were over head and ears, and were forced to cry out, "Who can find out the Almighty to perfection?" All these are but parts of him, his back-parts. There is more real divinity and knowledge of God in one of Job's friends' discourses, one of David's prayers, than now in twenty sermons of gracious men, or many prayers or conferences of saints. But withal you must study his goodness and mercy, and this maketh up the most part of his name. The definition of God hath most of this, so that it may be said truly, that mercy is his delight. Mercy, as it were, swelleth over the rest: God were not accessible, unless mercy did temper it. Behold then greatness to humble, and goodness to make bold, that you may have access. As greatness should leave the stamp of reverence on your petitions, so should mercy and goodness imprint them with faith and confidence; and that the rather, because as Christ is said to be the Father's face, and the image of his person, (2 Cor. iv. 6. and Heb. i. 3,) so may he be called the Father's name, and so doth God himself call him, Exod. xxiii. 20, 21, The angel that went before them in the wilderness, whose voice they ought to obey, his "name is in him;" and this angel is Christ Jesus, Acts vii. 37, 38. So then Christ Jesus is God's name. God, as he revealeth himself in the word, is "God in Christ reconciling the world unto himself," 2 Cor. v. 19. And therefore, Christians, you ought to pray always in Christ's name, and this is to call on his name. Not only encourage yourselves to come to God, because of a mediator, because he is God in Christ, but also offer up all your prayers in the name of Jesus, that his name called on them may sanctify them, otherwise your affectionate prayers cannot be acceptable to God, for he loveth nothing but what cometh through the Son. Prayer must have an evil savour, when it is not put in the golden censer that this angel hath to offer up incense with the prayers of the saints. And likewise you would know God's justice and wrath, that you may serve in fear and trembling: and when trembling is joined with the rejoicing of faith, this is acceptable service. You ought to fear to offend his holiness, while you are before him. Let

God's terribleness have a deep impression on your spirit, both to make sin bitter, and to make mercy more sweet. Thus should prayer ascend with the seal of God's attributes, and then it is a calling on his name. Now, is there any calling on his name among us? Who maketh it his study to take up God in his glorious names? Therefore you call not on a known God, and cannot name him. Now, all of you take this rule to judge your prayers by. Think you not that you make many prayers? You both think it and say it, as you use to say, I pray both day and night. Nay, but count after this rule, and there will be found few prayers in Scotland, albeit you reckon up both private and public. Once scrape out of the count the prayers of the profane and scandalous, whose practice defileth their prayers; and again, blot out the prayers of men's tongues and mouths when hearts are absent, and again, set aside the formal, dwyning,[318] coldrife, indifferent supplications of saints, and the prayers that carry no seal of God's name and attributes on them, prayers made to an unknown God, and will you find many behind? No, certainly,—any of you may take up the complaint in behalf of the land, "There is none that calleth on thy name," or few to count upon. You may say so of yourselves, if you judge thus,—I have almost never prayed, God hath never heard my voice; and you may say so of the land. This would be a well-spent day, if this were but our exercise, to find out the sins of our duties in former humiliations; if the Spirit did so convince you as to blot out of the roll of fasts all the former. If you come this length, as to be convinced solidly that you have never yet prayed and mourned for sin,—I have lived thus long, and been babbling all this while, I have never once spoken to God, but worshipped I know not what, fancied a God like myself, that would be as soon pleased with me as I was with myself,—if the Lord wrought thus on your hearts, to put you off your own righteousness, you should have more advantage in this, than in all your sabbaths and fasts hitherto.

Although the Lord's hand be upon them, and they "fade as a leaf," and are driven into another land, yet none calleth on his name. This maketh the complaint more lamentable, and no doubt is looked upon as a dreadful sign and token of God's displeasure, and of sorer strokes.

Daniel, an eye witness, confirmeth this foretold truth, chap. ix. 13, "All this is come upon us, yet have we not made our prayers to the Lord our God." Well may the Lord make a supposition and doubt of it, Lev. xxvi. 40, 41. After so many plagues are come on, seven added to seven, and again seven times more, and yet they will not be humbled, and when it is even at the door next to utter destruction and consumption, he addeth, "If then their uncircumcised hearts be humbled, and they take with the punishment of sin," &c. We need ask no reason of this, for "bray a fool in a mortar, his folly will not depart from him," Prov. xxvii. 22. Poor foolish man is a foolish man, folly is born with him, folly is his name, and so is he. He hath not so much wisdom as to "hear the voice of the rod, and him that appointeth it." Poor Ephraim is an undaunted heifer. Nature is a "bullock unaccustomed with the yoke," and so it is chastised more and more, Jer. xxxi. 18. Man is like an untamed beast, as the horse, or as the mule. Threatenings will not do it, "God speaketh once, yea twice, and man perceiveth it not," Job xxxiii. 14. God instructeth by the word, and men receive no instruction; all the warnings to flee from the wrath to come are as so many tales to make children afraid. He saith in his heart, "I shall have peace, though I walk in the imagination of my own heart." Since, therefore, he will not incline his ear to the word, God sendeth his rod to seal the word, and yet men are so wild that they fight with God's rods, and will not submit to him; a yoke must be put on Ephraim, a bridle in men's mouth, Psal. xxxii. 9. They will put God to more pains than speaking, and it shall cost them more pain; for he that will not be drawn with the cords of a man, love and entreaties, must be drawn with the cords of a beast, and yoked in a heavy yoke. Yet men are unruly, and the yoke groweth the heavier and sorer that they strive to shake it off. An uncircumcised heart cannot be humbled,—"How can the leopard change his spots? no more can my people return to me," Jer. xiii. 23. It is strange that a people so afflicted will not take with the punishment of their iniquity, but will say in their heart, Wherefore come these things upon me? But here it is, how can an uncircumcised heart be humbled? God may beat on men with rods as on a dog, but he will run away from him still the more, Isa. ix. 13. Nay, it may be there will be more stirring after God, and more awaking by the first stroke of affliction, than when they are continued and multiplied. The uncouthness of rods may affect people something, but when his hand lieth on but a little, custom breedeth hardness, and more and more alienateth spirits from him.

Now we need no more to seal this truth, but our own experience. I think never people might speak more sensibly of it. It hath been the manner of the Lord's dealing with us, to use fair means to gain us, to threaten before he laid on, to give a proclamation before his stroke, and yet it hath been our manner from our youth up to harden ourselves against him, and go on in our own way. Therefore hath the Lord, after long patience, laid on sad strokes, and smitten us, yet have we not turned to him. It may be, when the chastisement was fresh and green, some poured out a prayer, and in trouble visited God, (Isa. xxvi. 16,) but the body of the land hath not known him that smote them, and never ran into their hiding place, but the temptation of the time, like a flood, hath carried them away with it. And for the Lord's children, how soon doth the custom of a rod eat out the sense of it, and prayer doth not grow proportionably to the Lord's rods. The Lord hath expected that some might stand in the gap and intercede, yet few or none called on his name. General corrections of the land hath made general apostacy from God, not a turning in to God; so that we may say, we never entered a furnace, but we have come out with more dross, contracted dross in the fire. Men's zeal and tenderness hath been burnt up, reprobate silver may God call us. We have had so much experience of the unprofitableness of former afflictions, that we know not what the Lord shall do with us. We think it may be the Lord's complaint of Scotland, "Why should you be afflicted any more? you will revolt more and more," Isa. i. 5. What needeth another rod? You are now all secure, it is true, because you are not stricken; nay, but what needeth a rod? For it cannot awake you,—all the fruit of it would be, not to purge away sin, but to increase it. General judgments will prove general temptations, and will alienate you more from me, and make you curse God and the covenant. And indeed, the truth is, we know not what outward dispensation can fall on that can affect this generation, we know not what the Lord can have behind that can work on us. Judgment hath had as much terror, mercies as much sweetness, and as much of God in the one and the other, as readily hath been since the beginning of the world. Only this we know, all things are possible to him which are impossible to us, and if the Spirit work to sanctify the rod, a more gentle rod shall work more effectually; his word shall do as much as his rod.

The case we are now into is just this—"None calleth on thee." It is a terrible one, whether our condition be good or bad outwardly. Our peace hath put us asleep, and the word cannot put men to prayers. Now, the Lord hath begun to threaten, as you have been still in fear of new troubles, and a revolution of affairs again, yet I challenge your own consciences, and appeal to them,—whom hath the word prevailed with to put to prayer? Whom hath the rumour of approaching trouble put to their prayers? Whose spirit hath been affected with God's frowning on the land? And this yet more aggravateth your laziness, in the time that God doth show terrible things to his people in Ireland, giveth them a cup of wormwood, and to drink the wine of astonishment, are not you yet at ease? When your brethren and fellow-saints are scattered amongst you as strangers,[319] yet your hearts bleed not.

Well, behold the end of it,—your case is a sad prognostic of the Lord's hiding his face and consuming us; nay, it is a sure token that his face is hid already. When Job's friends would aggravate his misery, they sum it up in this, "thou restrainest prayer from God." It is more wrath to be kept from much praying, not to be scattered, from your own houses. Therefore, if you would have the cloud of God's anger, that covereth the land with blackness, go over you, and pour out itself on others; if you would prevent the rod, hearken to the word, and stir up yourselves to much prayer, that you may be called his remembrancers. O how long shall prayer be banished this kingdom! The Lord's controversy must be great with us, for since the days of our first love there has been great decay of the spirit of prayer. The children of God should be so much in it, as they might be one with it. David was so much in prayer, as he in a manner defined himself by it, Psal. cix. 4, "I give myself unto prayer." In the original, there is no more but "I prayer." I was all prayer. It was my work, my element, my affection, my action. Nay, to speak the truth, it is the decay of prayer that hath made all this defection in the land. Would you know the original of many a public man's apostacy and backsliding in the cause of God, what maketh them so soon forget their solemn engagements, and grow particular, seeking their own things, untender in seeking the things of God?—would you trace back the desertion up to the fountain-head? Then come and see. Look upon such a man's walking with God in private, such a man's praying, and you shall find matters have been first wrong there. Alienation and estrangement from God himself, in immediate duties and secret approaches, hath made men's affections cool to his interest in public duties. And believe it, the reason why so few great men or none are so cordial, constant, and thorough in God's matters is this,—they pray not in secret; they come to parliament or council where public matters concerning the honour of God are to be debated, as any statesmen of Venice would come to the senate. They have no dependence on God to be guided in these matters; they are much in public duties, but little in secret with God. Believe it, any man's private walking with God shall be read upon his public carriage, whether he be minister or ruler.

There is yet another thing we would have you consider, to endear this duty unto you, and bind upon your consciences an absolute necessity of being much in it, and it is this. Prayer and calling on his name is often put for all immediate worship of God, especially the more substantial and moral part of service. This people was much in ceremonials, and they made these their righteousness; nay, but there was little secret conversing with God, walking humbly with him, loving him, believing in him. Well, then, prayer is, as it were, a compend and sum of all duties; it contains in it, faith, love, repentance; all these should breathe out in prayer. In a word, if we say to you, be much in prayer, we have said all, and it is more than all the rest, because it is a more near and immediate approach to God, having more solid religion in it. If you be lively in this, you are thriving Christians; and if you wither here, all must decay, for prayer sappeth and watereth all other duties with the influence of heaven.

"That stirreth up himself to take hold on thee." This expresseth more of their condition under the rod, and while God was threatening to depart and leave them. None took so much notice of it, as to awake out of his dream, to take a fast hold of God. It was but like the grip a man taketh in his slumbering, that he soon quitteth in his sleep; none awaketh himself, as a bird stirreth up itself with its wings to flight; none do so spread out their sails to meet the wind. This importeth a great security and negligence, a careless stupidity. To take hold, to grip strongly and violently, importeth both faith acted on God, and communion with God; so that the sense is, nobody careth whither thou go,—there is none that stirreth up himself to take violent hold of thee. Men lying loose in their interest, and indifferent in the one thing necessary, do not strongly grip to it. Nobody keepeth thee by prayer and intercession; so that there is no diligence added to diligence, there is no stirring up of ourselves in security.

First, When the Lord seemeth to withdraw, and when he is angry, it is our duty to take hold the more on him; and not only to act faith, and call on him by prayer, but to add to ordinary diligence,—it should be extraordinary.

I. Then, I say, when the Lord is withdrawing and seemeth angry, we ought not to withdraw from him by unbelief, but to draw near, and take hold on him. And the Lord giveth a reason of this himself, Isa. xxvii. 4, 5, "because fury is not in me." It is but a moment's anger, it is not hatred of your persons but sins, it is not fury that hath no discretion in it, no difference between a friend and an enemy; it is but at least a father's anger, that is not for destruction but correction. The Lord is not implacable. Come to him and win him,—"Let him take hold of me, and let him make peace with me, if he will make peace." He is a God whose compassions fail not; and so he is never so angry, but there is room left for manifestation of mercy on those that come to him. God's anger is not an humour and passion as ours is, he can take the poor child in his arms, admit it into his bosom, when outward dispensations frown. Men's anger is like the sons of Belial, briers and thorns, that none may come near to, lest they be hurt; but God angry, is accessible, because his anger is still tempered and mixed with clemency and mercy; and that mixture of mercy is so great and so predominant in all his dispensations here, that they being rightly understood, might rather invite to come, than scare from it. There is more mercy to welcome, than anger to drive away. Look upon the very end and purpose of God's hiding himself, and withdrawing,—it is this; that we may come and seek him early, Hosea v. 15. When God is angry, mercy and compassion principleth it, for anger is sent out to bring in wanderers. His anger is not humour, but resolute and deliberate, walketh upon good grounds, because David in his prosperity missed not God. When all things went according to his mind, then he let God of where he will; therefore, the Lord in mercy must hide his own heart with a frowning countenance, and cover himself with a cloud, that David may be troubled, and so take hold on God, Psalm xxx. 7, 8. Since, then, this is God's purpose, that you may come nearer to him, and since he goeth away that you may pursue; certainly he will never so run away as you may not find him out, nor will he run farther nor he strengtheneth thee to pursue him; thus, Psalm lxiii. 8, God was flying and David pursuing; nay, but the flyer giveth legs to the pursuer, he upholdeth him, as it were against himself: so did the angel strengthen Jacob to overcome himself. Now, shall it not be pleasant to God, that you lay hold on him as your own, even when he seemeth to be clothed with vengeance, seeing he changeth his outward countenance for this very end? He seemeth to go, that you may hold; because when you think he stayeth, you hold not; as the child, while the nurse is near, will look about it, and take hold of any thing; but when she withdraweth, the child cleaveth the faster to her.

But, II. We ought to stir up ourselves more now than any other time: times of God's withdrawing calleth for extraordinary and doubled approaches. So Hos. v. 15, "They will seek me early." And therefore the Lord's children in Scripture have made great advantage of such dispensations. The truth is, as long as we are well dealt with, security creepeth on, and religion is but in a decaying condition. Duties are done through our sleep; we are not as men awaking and knowing what we do, and whither we go. But when the Lord beginneth to trouble us, and hides his face, then it is time to awake out of sleep, before all be gone: and there ought to be, 1. More diligence in duties and approaching to God, because your case furnisheth more matter of supplication; and as matter of supplication groweth, prayer should grow. If necessity grow, and the cry be not according to necessity, it is ominous. And therefore David useth to make his cry go up according to his trouble. In a prosperous condition, though every thing might call a tender-hearted loving Christian to some nearness to God; yet ordinarily, if necessity press not, prayer languisheth and groweth formal. Sense of need putteth an edge on supplication, whereas prosperity blunteth it. The heart missing nothing, cannot go above sublunary things; but let it not have its will here, and the need of heaven will be the greater. Now I say, if you sit so many calls, both from a command, and from your own necessities, you do so much the more sin. Affliction will make even a hypocrite seek him, and pour out a prayer and visit him, Psalm lxxviii. and Isa. xxvi. And if you do not take advantage of all these pressures, you must be so much the more guilty; and therefore God, as it were, wondereth at their obstinacy, "They return not to him that smiteth them!" All this is come upon us, yet have we not prayed. And, 2. It is sent for that end, that you may be more serious; and therefore you ought so much the more to awake, to lay hold on him. This is the way the Lord useth with his secure and wandering children, Psalm cxix. 67. For the Lord findeth us often gripping too strongly to a present world, and taking it in our arms, as if we were never to part with it. Men's souls cleave to outward accommodations; therefore the Lord useth to part us and our idol, that we may take hold of him the faster. It is union with himself that is our felicity, and it is that which God most endeavoureth. When he removeth beloved jewels, it is because they were a stumbling-block, and divorced the soul from God: when he seemeth to withdraw himself his going proclaimeth so much, oh! follow, or perish.

III. It is a very dangerous thing when he withdraweth and you follow not, when he is angry and you care not, do not fly in to make peace with him. Certainly his anger must wax hotter, and desertion will become a spiritual plague; rods must be tempered with much bitterness. What mixture of mercy can be in such a dispensation, where the fruit of it is to harden? But if the Lord's hardest dealing wrought you to more nearness and communion with himself; then certainly you have a fair advantage against the present trouble, and you have your cup mixed. You shall at length bless God for such dispensations; they may be reckoned for good to you.

Next, there ought to be more exercise of faith, and laying hold of the grounds of consolation in God in such a time. 1. For as difficulties grow, faith should fortify itself against them so much the more. The greater the storm be, it should fly the more into the chambers. Faith in the time of a calm day getteth no trial; faith bulketh much[320] because it hath not much to do. But except there be some fresh and new supplies, it cannot hold out in a temptation. But it is a singular proof of a noble and divine faith,—that it can lay hold on him and keep him when he would go,—that can challenge kindness on a miskenning Jesus,[321]—that can stand on the ground of the promises when there is not a foot-breadth of a dispensation to build on. While all things go with you ye have no difficulty to maintain your faith; nay, but when the Lord seemeth to look angry, then awake and gather strength, and take hold on his strength. Look what is in your condition or his dispensation, what is good or ominous, then take hold on the other hand on him, and look what is in him to answer it, and swallow it up. Ye ought to be well acquainted with the grounds of consolation that are in God, in the worst case, and then ye might lay hold on him though he seemed a consuming fire. It is then a time that calleth most for securing your interest in him, a time when there is no external advantage to beguile you, a time when the only happiness is to be one with God. Therefore the man who, in such calamities and judgments, is not awakened to put his eternal estate out of question, he is in a dangerous case. For, do not most part drive over their days, and have no assurance of salvation, they dare not say either *pro* or *contra*. It may be, and it may not be. And this is the length that the most part come,—a negative peace; no positive confidence; no clear concluding, on sure grounds, an interest. Always ye are most called to this, when God afflicteth the land or you: if ye do not then make peace it is most dangerous. 2. The Lord loveth faith in a difficulty best,—it is the singlest and the cleanliest, it is that which most honoureth him, and glorifieth his truth and faithfulness, and sufficiency and mercy; for then it is most purely elevated above creatures, and pitcheth most on God; and therefore bringeth men to this, "No help for my soul, but thou art my portion." And this commendeth God most when he is set alone. Prosperity bringeth him down among creatures, and secure faith maketh little distinction; but awakening faith grippeth strongly and singly, putteth God alone.

Secondly, Oftentimes, when God is departing, none stirreth up himself to lay hold on him. Although there may be praying and doing of many duties, yet there is nothing beyond ordinary. The varieties and accessions of new grounds of supplications doth neither make greater frequency nor more fervency. This our experience may clear unto us both in duties and faith.

I. There is very little diligence in seeking of God in the way and means appointed, even when God seemeth to bid farewell to the land, and go away. Nobody cometh in as an intercessor. Men keep on their old way of praying, and never add to it, come what like. Who is it that riseth above his ordinary, as the tide of God's dispensation is? There ought to be such an impression made by the changes of God's countenance as might be read on the duties of his people. There should be such a distance between your ordinary and such times as between a sleeping man and a waking man, that whatever your attainment of access to God be, ye might stir up and go beyond it according as matters call. Will God count your public fasts a performance of this duty? Alas, we fast sleeping, and none stirreth up himself to these things! Is there any difference betwixt your solemn humiliation and another Sabbath? And is there any difference between a Sabbath and a week-day, save the external duty? Is not this palpably our case? Is there any wakening among us? No, security is both the universal disease and complaint; and it is become an incurable disease since it became a complaint. Doth any of you pray more in private than he used? Or what edge is on your prayers? Alas! the Lord will get good leave to go from us; it feareth me that we would give Christ a testimonial to go over seas. Hold him, hold him! Nay, the multitude would be gladly quit of him,—they cannot abide his yoke, his work is a burden, his word is a torment, his discipline is bands and cords; and what heart can ye then have to keep Christ? What violence can ye offer to him to hold him still? All your entreaties may be fair compliments, but they would never rend his garment.

II. There is no up-stirring to faith among us, and laying hold on Jesus Christ, albeit all his dispensations warn us that it is now high time. There are not many who are about this point, effectually to stir up their faith or to secure their interest. Think ye that conjectures will carry you through difficulties? The multitude think they believe much, but any temptation proveth their mistake. The most part of Scotland would deny God and his Son Jesus Christ, if they were put to it. Always it is a time ye would not lie out from your stronghold,—faith only uniteth you to Christ, and if ye would be kept in any trial, stir up faith.

Thirdly, Prayer and faith, diligence and laying hold on God, must go together and help one another. Not calling on his name, and not laying hold on him go together, and have influence one upon another.

I. Faith hath influence on prayer. Laying hold on God in Christ will make right calling on his name, it learneth men how to call God, to call him Abba, Father. Faith useth to vent itself in prayer. I say, much consideration of God, and claiming into him, and to the grounds of confidence in him, must both make prayer acceptable, and carry the stamp and impression of God's name, or Christ's name, on it, and also make much prayer: for when a soul hath pitched on God as its only felicity, and thus made choice of him, it findeth in him all sufficiency, all things for all things. There is no necessity, but it findeth a supply in his fulness for it; and therefore it applieth a man to the fountain, to draw out of the wells of salvation. There is nothing can be so sweet and refreshing as for such a soul to pour out itself every day in him, to talk with him face to face. Faith engageth the heart to come to God with all things; whereas many difficulties would have been, and the secure or unsettled heart would have gone as many different ways to help them. Faith layeth hold on God, knoweth but one, and bringeth all here; and therefore access to God is a fruit of it, access unto the grace wherein we stand by faith. And again, how can prayer be acceptable as long as faith doth not principle it? It is but like a beast's groaning under a burden. Laying hold on God himself makes a man's duties acceptable, because he speaks and asks; believing that he shall receive, he trusteth God and doth not tempt him. Where lively faith is not entertained there cannot be much affection which is the oil of the wheels. There may be in some bitterness of spirit much vehemency; but that is not a pure flame of divine love that burneth upward to him; and it is soon extinguished, and lasteth no longer nor present sense, and then the soul groweth harder, as iron that had been in the fire.

II. When there is not much prayer and calling, faith cannot lie strong and violent; for prayer is even the exercise of faith, if you wear out of that, faith rusteth. There may be much quietness with little prayer, but there cannot be much, and strong and lively faith, for where it getteth not continual employment it fags. And indeed prayer is a special point of holding God fast, and keeping him, therefore join these, if ye would thrive in anyone of them. Your unbelieving complaints are not prayers and calling on his name, because they are not mixed with faith. As the apostle said of the word, so may it be said of prayer,—your prayers are not profitable, are not heard, because not mixed with faith. Ye use to doubt, that ye may be fervent, to question your interest, that ye may stir up your spirits to prayer. But alas! what a simple gross mistake is that? Poor soul, though thou get more liberty, shall it be counted access to God? Though you have more grief, and your bitterness doth indite more eloquence, shall God be moved with it? Know ye not that you should ask without wavering, and lift up pure hands without wrath and doubting? And yet both are there.

Fourthly, The duty we are called to in such a time when God is angry, is to lay hold on him. We would speak a word more of it. We ought to hold a departing Lord, by wrestling with him in supplication, not to let him depart till he bless, Hos. xii. 3, 4. The application of Jacob's victory over the angel is thus, "Turn ye to the Lord, and wait on him," &c. How had Jacob power over the angel? By supplication and weeping, so that prayer is a victory over God, even the Lord God of hosts. We ought, as it were, to strive against outward dispensation, when it saith, He is gone, when our condition saith, He is gone, or going, we ought to wrestle with it. No submission to such a departing, I mean, no submission that sitteth down with it, and is not careful how it be. Now this time calleth you to such an exercise. The Lord seemeth to be angry with us. There is a strong cloud over the land, and like to pour down upon us—the Lord is drawing a sword again, and beginning now to lay on. Many threatenings would not put us to supplication. Now, what will the laying on of the rod do? If the former days be returning wherein ye saw much sorrow, is it not then high time for the Lord's remembrancers, and for the Lord's children to wrestle with God? As Esau was coming on Jacob, so hath God armed men, and such desperate men, as he hath made a rod to us before. If we be twice beaten with it, it is very just, for before we did not seek in to him who smote us.[322] You would know this, that the Lord is but seeking employment, and if ye would deal with him, ye may make advantage of the present and future calamities. And look to this laying hold on him, this is the chief thing ye should now heed. It is God himself that should be your principal object. Praying should be a laying hold on God, it should meet with himself. For the most part in the time of prosperity, we cannot meet with God singly, we have so much to do with creatures, we keep trysts so punctually with them, so that we cannot keep with God. We have so many things in our affections and thoughts, that God cannot get place, he cannot get us at leisure for the throng of our business, we lose God by catching at shadows. Well then, we are called in such a time of difficulty to come in to God himself, to draw by the vail of ordinances, that we may have communion with God himself. And this is right praying, when the soul getteth such immediate access to God, as it were, to handle him, and see him, and taste him, to exercise its senses on him. Ordinances have been of a long time a covering of his face, and he useth not now to unvail himself in the sanctuary, and let us see his glory God is departed from preaching and praying, and the solemn meeting, so that we meet not with God,—we lay hold on a shadow of an outward ordinance, but not on God himself. Therefore, Christians, make advantage of this time. You may be brought to want ordinances, then lay hold on himself who is the substance and marrow of them. You may be denuded of outward comforts and accommodation here, then lay hold on himself in much prayer. If affliction would blow away the cloud on his face, or would scatter our idols from us, and make us single alone with God, as Jacob was, it were well sent.

II. Your exercise should be to take hold on God by faith. 1. Ye would make peace with God, be much in direct acts of apprehending God himself in Jesus Christ. And this is according as ye take up yourselves with your own misery and necessity. Do but travel continually between your own misery and something answerable in God.

The first thing we would have you do, now when God frowns upon us, is to find out your own lost condition, and how great strangers you have been to him, even when ye have approached in many ordinances, and find a necessity of making peace with God and atonement. Now from this day hold on Christ, as the hope set before you. Look upon that in him which will answer all your necessities, and be suitable to them. It is not matters of outward lot that should go nearest your heart. Let the world go where it will, that which concerneth you most in such a time, is the securing of your soul, for if you lose it, what gain you? what keep you? Your houses, and lands, and lives may be in hazard, nay, but one thing is more worth than all these, and in more hazard. Begin at spiritual things, and ask how matters stand between God and thee.

2. Not only would ye be much in immediate application unto Jesus Christ, but ye would so take hold of him, as ye may be sure ye have him. Make peace, and know that ye have made it, and then shall ye be kept in perfect peace. You would never rest until you can on solid grounds answer the question. And this duty is called for from you at such a time, for "the just shall live by faith," in a troublesome time, Hab. ii. 4. And as ye ought to keep and hold fast confidence and not cast it away in such a time, so should ye all seek after it. Do not only rest in this,—I know not but I may belong to Christ, I dare not say against it. O no, Christians, you should have positive clear grounds of assurance "I am his, and he is mine," "I know that my Redeemer liveth," "God is my portion." And if ye conclude this solidly, I defy all the world to shake and trouble your peace this is perfect peace, "peace, peace," double peace. How can ye choose but be shaken at every blast of temptation, when you are not thus solidly grounded, when you hold not at your anchor?

And, 3. Having thus laid hold on Christ as your own, lay hold on all in him as yours, and for your use. Whatever difficulty the present time or your own condition afford, search but as much in God as may counterbalance it. Answer all objections, from his mercy, goodness, power, wisdom, unchangeableness, and this shall be more nor the trouble. God himself laid hold upon, and made ours, is more nor removing a temporal calamity. It is an eternal weight, to weigh down all crosses and disappointments. For what can present things be? Is there not in the favour of his countenance that which may drown them in oblivion? Are ye like to sink here? Is not God a sure anchor to hold by? And if ye do not this, your trouble is nothing in respect of the danger of your soul. Secure and loose lying out of God, not putting this matter to a full point, is worse nor all your outward fading. Therefore, we exhort you in the Lord's name, to fly into this name of the Lord, as a strong tower to run to and be safe. When the Lord seemeth now to be angry with us, run not away from him, though he should yet clothe himself with vengeance as a garment.

But, *first*, O ye poor people, who have never asked this question, whether have I any interest in Jesus? ask it now, and resolve it in time. If trouble come on, if scattering and desolation come on, and our land fade as a leaf, certainly the Lord's anger will drive you away, What will ye do in the time of his indignation? All of you, put this to the trial,—how matters stand between God and you.

And, *secondly*, If ye find all wrong, do not sink in discouragement, all may be amended, while it is seen wrong in time. Nay, God taketh away outward accommodation, to make you more serious in this. And it is the very voice of rods,—every one fly into your hold, every one make peace with me. You may take hold, and do it feckfully.[323]

Thirdly, You who have fled to Jesus, take more hold of him, you are called also to renew your faith, and begin again. Make peace with God, let your confidence be kept fast, and thus shall ye be immoveable, because he changeth not. God will not go from you if ye believe—hold him by faith. Christ could not do great things in Galilee because of their unbelief, and so he departed from them. As unbelief maketh an evil heart to depart from the God of all life and consolation, so doth it make God depart from us. But faith casteth a knot upon him (to speak with reverence), it fasteneth him by his own word and promise, and he cannot go by it. It is a violent hand laid on God. "I will not let thee go till thou bless me."

Fourthly, Faith and prayer, or holding of God, by believing in him, and much employing him needeth much stirring up unto, and awaking. "That stirreth up himself to take hold on thee." Security is the moth of both these, and eateth out the life of faith and supplication; it maketh prayer so coldrife that it cannot prevail, and faith so weak that it cannot use violence.

I. Security apprehendeth no evil, no need. A secure condition is a dream that one is eating and yet his soul is empty. Look how the people of Laish were quiet and secure, apprehending no evil; destruction cometh then on as an armed man. Always it is much necessity that administers fuel to a man's faith and supplication. David says, (Psal. xxx. 7,) "I said in my prosperity, I shall not be moved." Nay, but many say in adversity, and cry Peace, peace, where no peace is. Security pleadeth innocency, and then believeth immunity. "I am innocent, therefore shall his anger turn away," Jer. ii. 31. Security applieth not sin, and so refuseth the curse of sin and wages of it. And thus is a man in his own eyes a lord, and then he will come no more to God, Jer. ii. 31. It is almost impossible to awake men, by general judgments, to apprehend personal danger, and men never stir out of their nest till it be on fire. We can behold, or hear of our neighbours, spoiling and violence done to them, but till the voice of a cry be heard in our own streets and fields, nobody will take the judgment to themselves. It is well said, that which is spoken to all, is spoken to none, so what is done to all in general, is done to none. The voice of a general rod speaketh not particularly, and maketh not men apprehensive of sad things, and thus men are not pressed unto prayer—are not put out of themselves, it is only necessity that saps the roots of it, and makes it green.

II. Security is lazy and not active, putteth not forth its hand to work, and so dieth a beggar, for only the hand of the diligent maketh rich. Laying hold on God is a duty that requireth much spirit in it; men do not grip things well in their slumbering. There is no duty that needeth so spiritual and lively principles. If a man do not put on such a piece of resolution and edge upon him, he cannot come to the wrestling of prayer and violence of faith. Although the exercise and acting of grace dependeth more upon the Spirit of God's present influence, than upon the soul of man, yet this is the way the Lord communicateth his influence, by stirring up and exciting the creature to its duty, as if it could do it alone. Grace is one thing, and the stirring up of it is another thing. For when we lie by and sleep over our time, and go not about the matter so seriously as it were life and death, it is but a weak hold we can take of God. According to the measure of a man's apprehending necessity, and according to the measure of his seriousness in these things, so will the hand of faith grip, and lay hold with more or less violence. As a man drowning will be put from sleeping, and when one is in extreme hazard all his strength will unite together in one to do that which at any ordinary time it could not do, so ought it to be here. A Christian assaulted with many temptations should unite his strength, and try the yondmost.[324] O but your whole spirits would run together, to the saving of yourselves, if ye were very apprehensive of necessity! The exercise of faith is a dead grip, that cannot part with what it grippeth. Therefore, 1. We must say to you, it is not so easy a thing as you believe, to lay hold on God,—there must be stirring up to it. And when the Lord speaketh of our stirring ourselves, certainly he meaneth this likewise, that he must stir us, ere we stir ourselves. 2. Above all, be afraid of a secure condition: it is the enemy of communion with God and spiritual life. Therefore, look about you, and apprehend more your necessity, and then give no rest and quietness to yourself, till you have employed and engaged him, be as men flying to lay hold on the refuge set before you. 3. It must be a time of little access to God, and little faith, when we are all secure, and nobody goeth about religion as their work and business. We allow ourselves in it, therefore, we do exhort yon, *first*, To purpose this as your end to aim at, and purpose by God's grace to take more hold of God. There is little minding of duty, and that maketh little doing of it. Once engage your hearts to a love and desire of more of this, come to a point of resolution, I must know him more, and trust more in him, be more acquaint with him. And, *secondly*, Put yourselves in the way of duty. It is God that only can stir you up, or apply your hearts to the using of violence to God, but ye would be found in the outward means much, and in these ways God will meet with you, if you wait on him in them.

"For thou hast hid thy face from us." Here is the greatest plague, a spiritual plague. The last verse was but the beginning of sorrows, "We all do fade," &c. But lo, here the accomplishment of misery, God hiding his face, and consuming them in the hand of their sins.

First, The Lord's hiding of his face, and giving up a people to melt away in their sins, punishing with judicial blindness and security, is the worst judgment, it filleth the cup full. This complaint goeth on still worse, and certainly it is worse nor their fading as a leaf and exile out of their land. It is not without reason, that great troubles and afflictions are so expressed, "Thou didst hide thy face," as David said, "Thou didst hide thy face, and I was troubled," importing as much, as it is not trouble that doth trouble, but God's hiding of his face that maketh trouble. It is in so far trouble, as it is a sign of his displeasure, and as the frowns of his countenance are upon it, therefore, the saints, aggravating their affliction, say, "Thou hidest thy face." You know the face is the place wherein either kindness or unkindness appeareth. The Lord's countenance, on face, is a refreshful sweet manifestation of himself to a soul, it is the Lord using familiarity with a spirit, and this made David more glad than corn and wine. Now, the hiding of the face, the withdrawing of his countenance, is, when the Lord in his dispensation and dealing doth withhold the manifestation of himself, either in life or consolation, when he covereth himself with clouds round about, that neither can a soul see into the backside of it—into his own warm heart, nor can the sun beams shine through to quicken and refresh the soul. The Lord draweth over his face a vail of a crossing dispensation, or such like.

There is a desertion of the soul in the point of life and spiritual action, and there is a desertion in regard of consolation. The varieties of the Lord's desertions run upon these two. As a Christian's life is action or consolation, and the Lord's influence is either quickening or comforting, so his withdrawing is either a prejudice to the one or the other. Sometimes he goeth "mourning all the day," nay, but he is "sick of love," sometimes he is a bottle dried in the smoke, and his moisture dried up. The Christian's consolation may be subtracted, and his life abide, but he cannot have spiritual consolation, if he be not lively. This life is more substantial,—comfort is more refreshful,—life is more solid,—comfort sweet, that is true growing solid meat, this but sauce to eat it with.

The hiding here meant is certainly a spiritual punishment. The Lord denying unto this people grace to understand the voice of the rod,—he appearing as a party against them,—leaving them to their own carnal and lazy temper, and thus they lay still under God's displeasure. Now, there is nothing like this.

I. Because it is a spiritual punishment, and estates are not to be valued and laid in the balance with the soul. Albeit men are become so brutish as to abase their souls, and prostitute them to any thing, yet all a man hath is not considerable to it.

II. It is a more excellent thing that is removed by it,—"In his favour is life,"—all felicity and happiness is in God's countenance. If a man have not this, what hath he else? Losses are according as the thing is. Nay, but here is more,—"My Lord is taken from me, my God hath forgotten me." And indeed, if man's true happiness be in communion with God, certainly, any interruption coming in must be sad, and make a man more miserable than the world knoweth. There is a greater emphasis in that word, "Thou hast hid thy face," than if he had said, all the world hideth their face and maketh a scorn of us.

Therefore, *first*, Know what is the worst thing of the times. Many of you think sword and pestilence, and the burdens of the time, the worst things, and if you were now to complain, the saddest complaint would be,—affliction is laid on our loins. But know this, if your cities were desolate, if your land were made a wilderness, and we captives in another land, there is yet a worse thing than all these, and think you not this strange? Nay, I say, there is something worse already in us, that we know not of, and it is this—"Make the hearts of this people hard." A spirit of slumber and deadness from the Lord upon the land, there are multitudes he will never show his face unto, it is still vailed from them, and they know him not. Ye that think all were well if ye had peace and prosperity, and know no hiding of God's countenance—no anger but when he striketh; certainly you know not what his countenance is by all these things men neither know love nor hatred. 2. Whatever calamity come upon you outwardly, deprecate most spiritual plagues and God's deserting. If you have God's countenance, it may make you glad in much sadness. You would be most careful lest any partition-wall came in lest his countenance change on you, if you grieve his Spirit and break his heart. Seek to have his face to shine, and this shall be a sun with healing under his wings. O but Christ's countenance is comely, when it is seen without clouds! but often it is overclouded with much provocation.

Secondly, The Lord's hiding of his face hath influence on the temper of spirits and disposition in duties. The truth is in general, "In him we live, and move, and have our being," and more especially, in many things that are spiritual, we are of our selves able to do nothing. The creature's holiness, and especially our life, is but as the rays that the Sun of righteousness sendeth forth round about him, and if any thing come between it evanisheth. As the marygold that openeth its leaves when the sun riseth, and closeth when it goeth down again, so exactly doth our spiritual constitution follow the motions of his countenance, and depend wholly on them. "Thou hidest thy face, and they are troubled," Psal. xxx 7. The Lord needeth no more but discountenance us, and we are gone.

Always, I. Be more dependent creatures. We use to act as from habits within, without any subordination to the Lord's grace without us, but we find that our sufficiency is not of ourself. How often doth your spiritual condition change on you in an hour? You cannot command one thought of God, or act from any habit of grace, even then when you can bring forth other gifts in exercise. Ye find that grace findeth more difficulties, more interruptions,—therefore learn to attend the changes and motions of his countenance.

II. When you find your heart dead, and you concluded under an impossibility of taking hold of God in a lively manner, then, I pray you, look unto the Lord's suspending of his influence, and let your whole endeavours be at the throne of grace to help it. It will not be your own provoking of yourself to your duty, but you must put yourself upon God, that he may cause his face to shine.

III. Though the Lord's hiding his face be often a cause of our deadness, and his desertion maketh all to wither, yet we have often a culpable hand in it, and he hides his face being provoked so to do. One thing we may mention, grieving of the Holy Ghost whereby we are sealed, quenching the motions of the Spirit, maketh the Spirit cover his face with a vail and hide it. There is here ordinarily a reciprocal or mutual influence. Our grieving him makes him withdraw his countenance, and his withdrawing his countenance maketh us to wither and grow barren.

IV. The most sure and infallible token of the Lord's hiding his face, is security, and a spirit of deadness and laziness, when folk go about duties dreaming, and do all as it were through their sleep. Therefore we may conclude sad things on this land, that the Lord hideth his face from us. And therefore arise, and do not settle and quiet yourself in such a condition. The Lord is angry, needeth any more be said? No more needeth to kind children, but the rod must follow this to make anger sensible.

AN USEFUL CASE OF CONSCIENCE

Learnedly And Accurately Discussed And Resolved, Concerning Associations And Confederacies With Idolaters, Infidels, Heretics, Malignants, Or Any Other Known Enemies Of Truth And Godliness.

SECTION I.

That There Is A Malignant Party Still In The Kingdom.

In the entry to this business, the importunity of not a few makes it needful to speak somewhat to a question which unto this time hath been unquestioned, as beyond all exception, that is, whether there be yet in Scotland a malignant party? Or, whether there be at this time any party who may and ought, in reason and Christian prudence, to be reputed and looked upon as malignants and disaffected to the covenanted cause of God? It seems the more needful to speak somewhat of this, 1. Because some ministers are become slack and silent in this point, as if now there were no need of watchfulness and warning against any such party, 2. Because the expressions of many of the people of the land run that way, that there are now no malignants in Scotland, and that it is but a few factious ministers that will still keep up these names, that they may more easily, with others of their own stamp, weaken and divide the kingdom, for carrying on of their own ends, 3. Because the inclinations and resolutions of the public judicatories, in reference to most of the party who carried that name, do clearly import that they do think they are no more to be looked upon as malignants, as appears from several of their papers, especially the letter written for satisfaction to the presbytery of Stirling. And therefore this must be laid down as the foundation of what follows. That there is still in the land, not only a few persons, but a party considerable for number, power, and policy, who are malignant and disaffected to the covenant and cause of God. We would join heartily in the desire of many, that these and other such like odious names of different parties and factions were taken away, but we cannot join in the reasons of this desire which are ordinarily given. We wish the name malignant were obsolete and antiquate, if so be the thing itself, which is such a root of bitterness, were extirpated out of the church. Yea, though the thing itself remained, if men would hate it for itself, and account it more odious and hateful than the name imports, we would be glad it were no more heard of, because we find this prejudice, by all such appropriated names, that people generally look upon that which goes under that name as the only sin, and as if there were not that root of bitterness, in all which it grows out of, in any, and so conceive themselves good Christians if they fall not under that hateful appellation of malignants. But seeing this bitter fruit of enmity, against godliness and the godly, comes to more ripeness and maturity in many of this generation than in others, who yet are unconverted, and seeing it hath been the custom of the church of God in all generations, to discriminate many more ungodly and known haters of godliness and his people from the common sort of natural people, and to comprehend them under these names of wicked, of malignant, of enemies as may appear in the Old Testament, especially in the Psalms, and that more especially in our days, that name hath been appropriated to such who have declared themselves, in their words or actions, to be haters of godliness and the power thereof, and his people, or have arisen to the height of actual opposition against these, we cannot be blamed for using such a name still, for distinction's sake. We proceed to some reasons.

I. The constant and continued proceedings of the General Assembly and their commissioners for many years past unto this day.

There is not almost any of their warnings, declarations, or remonstrances, which doth not assert this, and warn against it, and that not only before the king's homecoming and taking of the covenant, but also since that time, as is evident by the Declaration emitted by the commission in July last,[325] the Declaration of the Assembly itself, a little after,[326] by the Declaration emitted at Stirling since the defeat at Dunbar,[327] the Causes of the Fast upon that defeat,[328] the Remonstrance to the king at Perth after his escape, together with the Remonstrance given in by them to the parliament,[329] all which do clearly hold forth this truth.

II. Take Christ's rule, "By their fruits ye shall know them." There is a great party in the land that adhere to malignant principles, bring forth malignant fruits, and tread malignant paths, as may appear in these instances. 1. A great many of these who have been formerly engaged in such courses, and under church censures, did lately conjoin together and rise in arms, and drew away the king[330] from the public councils of the kingdom, and refused to lay down arms till they got conditions agreeable to their mind; which course of theirs was justly declared by the commission to carry upon it the stamp of malignancy in an eminent way. 2. The seeking to promote and establish an arbitrary power in the person of the king, as it hath been still the endeavour of the malignant party, so it hath been always taken by the kirk of Scotland as one of their characters; and that there is a party now in Scotland who still hold that principle, and drive this design of arbitrary power, is evident. First, because these same men, who were lately in arms, did not only take up arms upon the king's simple warrant, and without the knowledge, and contrary to the mind of the committee of estates; but also received the act of indemnity,[331] and laid down arms, in obedience to the king's majesty, without so much as mentioning or acknowledging the committee of estates, as is to be seen in a paper subscribed by them,[332] and in the remonstrance of the commission of the General Assembly, dated at Perth, Nov. 29, 1650, the words whereof are these: "Your lordships should likewise consider, whether it doth not encroach upon the present constitution of government of this kingdom, and will not involve your lordships in the guilt of these men's sin, if you shall accept of their laying down of arms, merely upon the profession of obedience to the king's command, without any expression of their respect and obedience to the committee of estates, or any acknowledgment of their sin and offence, which we hope you will look upon as a most unnatural and unseasonable rending of the kingdom, in the time of this heavy oppression by a common enemy, and exposing the kingdom to all misery and ruin."[333] Second, It may be remembered that in the first model of the agreement which was made at Breda,[334] that clause which doth concern the determining of civil matters in the interval of parliament, by such as are authorized by parliament for that effect, and the king's majesty hearkening to their advice, was wholly left out; and any who are acquainted with expressions and inclinations of sundry great ones in the land, are not ignorant of their dislike of a committee of estates, and their desire to have the administration of matters, in the interval of parliament, wholly devolved upon the king's council. And the same spirit that would draw business from the committee to a cabinet council, would at last draw them from the parliament itself, because that is also, if not more, crossing to private interests and designs than a committee of estates. Third instance. There is a party in the land who as in their hearts they do envy, and in their tongues do traduce men that have been steadfast and faithful in the covenant and cause of God, so do they endeavour to the utmost of their power, to bring them into disgrace and contempt, and to get them removed from power and trust, and, upon the other side, study with no less diligence to get places of power and trust, in the army and elsewhere, filled with such as either have been open enemies or secret underminers. Fourth instance. Are there not many who oppose the kingdom of Jesus Christ and work of reformation, not only by holding up that old calumny of malignants, concerning the seditious and factious humour of ministers, and their stretching of themselves beyond their line, and by mocking all faithful and free preaching of the word, and by bearing down the power of godliness, deriding and hating all the lovers and followers thereof, by being impatient of the discipline and censures of the church, but also looking upon the government of the church with an evil eye, and strongly inclining some of them, that church government be put in the hands of a few prelates, most of them that it may be wholly devolved upon the civil government? Fifth instance. There is still a party in the land that endeavour to have the state of the question altered, and to have religion left out of the same, that it being stated upon civil interest, they may take to themselves a greater latitude in their way of carrying on business. This was holden forth to be the design of the malignant party in the year 1648, as appears in the Declaration of the Commission that year in March, and there was a necessary and seasonable warning given against it by the Commission in their Declaration, of the date July 1650.

III. Besides those who are excommunicated, there are yet in the land a considerable number of persons of chief note, who do still lie under censures of the church, some because of their accession to the late unlawful engagement, others because of their accession to the late course of rebellion, about the time of the king's escape from Perth, besides many others of less note.

IV. We suppose that it is most certain and unquestionable, that there was lately a malignant party and faction in the land, very numerous and powerful. How many men of blood, murderers of their brethren, as unnatural and barbarous as the Irish[335] they once joined with, against their country,—how many have watched all opportunities for troubling the peace of the kingdom, and rejoiced in the day of its calamity? How many were the oppressors of those who called on the Lord's name in the time of the Engagement?[336] What multitudes of profane and ungodly mockers of all godliness, and haters and persecutors of the godly, swarming everywhere? If this be truth, as it is indeed, we may say, who hath heard such a thing? Who hath seen such a thing? Shall a nation be born at once? And have they so soon learned to do well, who have been so long accustomed to do evil? When did this catholic conversion fall out, and by what means? Hath the act of indemnity and pardon such influence, to justify these men from all their butcheries and barbarous cruelties? The adding of three thousand to the church in one day, was miraculous in the days of miracles. But behold, a greater miracle than that in the days when miracles are ceased, many thousands added to the church of the friends of the cause of God in one day, and that not by preaching, which is the power of God unto salvation, not by spiritual weapons, which are mighty through God, but by the carnal weapon of an act of indemnity, and the example of one man, the king's conjunction in the cause, which at the best hath not such evidence of reality as to convince any, and change their mind. Sad experience, and the constant testimony of the church of Scotland proves, that malignancy is a weed that hath deeper and stronger roots than to be plucked up so easily; and that, though there be some, yet there be but few in the land who have been once engaged in that way, that have really and indeed abandoned and come off the same.

The point shall more appear by taking off objections that are made to the contrary. It is objected, 1. That these who were formerly esteemed malignants, did oppose the work of God because they could not be persuaded in conscience, that the covenant and cause were contrived and carried on in a warrantable way, those who were most instrumental in it, seeming to them not only to act without authority, but against authority. But so it is, that the king hath now joined in the covenant and added his authority to it, and therefore it needs not be feared that these men will any more oppose it, nay it may be expected, they will no less zealously promote the ends thereof than they did formerly oppose the same.

Answer: This argument supposeth some things that are false, some things at best doubtful, and some things dangerous.

I. It supposeth two falsities: 1. That it was a ground and principle of conscience and respect to the king's authority that made these men to oppose the covenant and work of reformation. If it was the conscience and conviction of the unwarrantableness of it for the want of authority, that stirred them up to oppose the covenant and cause, then why did they subscribe it and join in the defence of the same against the king? 2. It supposeth that the only ground, why they did oppose and undermine the same, was, because the king was of a contrary mind, and refused to join in the covenant, and ratify the same by his authority, which also is false, for there were several other grounds and causes of so doing besides this. We shall name a few, leaving the rest to a further scrutiny (1.) The natural enmity that is in the hearts of all men against the Lord and his anointed, his work and his people, and the power of godliness which doth effectually work in the children of disobedience. (2.) An enmity against the power of parliament and laws. (3.) An enmity against the union of the kingdoms. (4.) An enmity against the power of presbyteries, and the discipline of the church, to which are opposed, a sinful desire of breaking the bonds and casting away the cords of the Lord and his anointed, a desire to establish an arbitrary power and unlimited monarchy, a desire to establish a lordly prelatical power in the persons of a few, or to have the government of the church wholly dependent on the civil power, a desire to dissolve the union of the kingdoms, that they may be thereby weakened and less able to resist malignant designs against religion and liberties, a desire to live loosely without bands in regard of personal reformation.

II. It supposeth something that is at best doubtful, to wit, that the king hath really joined unto the cause of God, there being small evidences of it, and many presumptions to the contrary, especially, 1. His bringing home with him into the kingdom, a number of eminent, wicked and known malignants; his countenancing of, and familiar conversing with such in this nation since his coming,[337] and correspondence with others of them abroad, his deserting of the public councils of the kingdom, to join to a party of bloody and wicked men, raided in arms with his knowledge and by his warrant. 2. His not being convinced of any guilt in his father, because of his opposition to the cause and covenant, notwithstanding of all the blood of the Lord's people shed by him in that opposition. For verifying whereof, we appeal to the knowledge of some noblemen and ministers, who have occasion to know his mind and to be serious with him in this thing.

III. It supposeth something that is of very dangerous consequence. 1. That these men's zeal to the cause or against it, doth ebb and flow according to the king's being against it or for it. Since they follow the cause not for itself but for the king, will they not desert it when the king forsakes it? Can they be accounted real friends of the cause who are known to favour it only, *ad nutum principis*,[338]—as the comedian, *ait, aio, negat, nego*?[339] Is it not all one to follow the cause for the king, and for a man's own interest and advantage? Both are alike extrinsic and adventitious to the cause, both are alike changeable. Eccebulus under Constantius was a precise Christian, under Julian a persecuting apostate; and then again under the next Christian emperor became a Christian. And it is like if he had outlived that emperor till a heathen succeeded, he should have paganized the second time. 2. That very principle that is pretended to unite them to the cause is in itself most dangerous, both to the privileges of parliament and liberties of the people, and to our religion beside. Their principle of opposition was, "They conceived the way followed could not be warrantable without the king's consent and warrant, that people might not vindicate their own just rights and liberties, and their religion, without the king's concurrence, or against him." Now then, the principle of their conjunction to the cause must be this, because it is now clothed with authority which it had not before, and which now makes it warrantable. This principle therefore includes in the bosom of it, the establishing of unlimited and absolute power in kings; the unlawfulness of defensive wars against tyranny and oppression; the king's negative voice, and the dependent power of parliaments upon his pleasure; all which are principles destructive of the cause and our liberties, and the very characters[340] of our enemies from the beginning. Thus they have changed their way, but not their principles, and are now the more dangerous that they may not be looked upon as enemies, but as friends. Seeing it is manifest, that it is not the love of the cause that constrains them, and they know it was not that principle that persuaded the king, but mere necessity, contrary to his own inclination, may we not certainly expect, that according to their principles they will labour to set at freedom the king, whom they conceive imprisoned and captivated by the power of necessity within the limits and bounds of a regulated monarchy, and to loose him from all these chains of involuntary treaties and agreements, and rigid laws and parliaments, that he may then act in freedom and honour according to his own inclination and theirs both? And then farewell religion and liberties.

Objection 2: The most part of these who were formerly malignant, have now repented of that sin, and make profession of their resolution to adhere to the covenant and cause of God, and to bestow their lives and estates in defence thereof. Therefore they are not now to be esteemed malignants.

Answer: We would wish from our hearts that we had no answer to this argument; then should we yield the point in hand, and yield it cheerfully, that there is no malignant party now in Scotland. But, alas! that we have so much evidence convincing our consciences and persuading them to deny what is objected. We acknowledge some have indeed repented, and such we desire to embrace and receive with all tenderness and love, as godly Christians, worthy to be intrusted. But yet the most part of them do still bring forth the same malignant fruits. Their ungodly and wicked practices testify to their face that they have nothing to do to take his covenant in their mouth, seeing they hate to be reformed. The late rising in arms, contrary to their solemn and particular engagements, their bearing down and reproaching the godly, and such as are of known integrity, their studying to fill places of trust with men formerly enemies or underminers, their continuing in their profane and loose walking,—all these are more convincing evidences of their retaining their old principles than any extorted confessions or professions, for sinister respects and ends can be no probable signs of their repentance and change.

We desire these things to be remembered, 1: That the Engagement[341] was carried on, not by open and professed enemies, but such as had made public profession of their repentance, and were thereupon admitted to trust. 2. That upon consideration of the hypocrisy and instability of these men appearing in that and other particulars, the kirk and kingdom of Scotland did take upon themselves strait bonds and engagements to exclude such from trust, until such time as they had given real evidences of the reality of their repentance, and of abandoning their former principles and ways, of which the kirk was to judge impartially as in God's sight. 3. That it hath been confessed and preached by many godly ministers, and was given in by sundry in the time of the search of the Lord's controversy against the land, in November last at Perth, and hath been bemoaned and regretted by many of the people who feared God, that there is a great deal of sin and guilt lying on the kirk of Scotland, for the sudden receiving of scandalous persons, especially malignants, to the public profession of repentance before there was in them any real evidence of their forsaking their former principles and ways.

Objection 3: None are now to be esteemed malignants, in reference to employment and trust, but such as stand judicially declared by kirk and state to be so; for certainly, men are not to lie under the burden of so great a reproach, upon the private whisperings and common reports of others, otherwise, honest men may be wronged, and there shall be no end of confusion, or terminating this controversy, there being no certain rule to walk by in it.

Answer: We acknowledge that surmisings, whisperings, and reports of others are not sufficient, but that a rule is needful. All the question will be, What is that rule? And though the judicial debarring of judicatories be not all, but it must be ruled by another rule, yet are we willing to take it for so much; for even that will prove there is yet a malignant party in Scotland, because many are standing under church censures [albeit we are sorry there is so much precipitancy and haste in taking off the censures].[342] Those involved in the late rebellion are standing under a sentence of the commission,[343] declaring them to be following their old malignant designs; few of them are yet admitted to profession of repentance. We desire it may be considered, that the rule holden forth by the kirk of Scotland 1648, for admitting of persons to trust is of larger extent than judicial sentence or censure; to wit, that they be such against whom there is no just cause of exception or jealousy. 2. Albeit a judicial trial or censure be indeed necessary, for inflicting punishment or censure upon men, yet it is not necessary for avoiding association with them, or debarring them from trust. 3. If none were to be accounted malignants, but they who are judicially declared to be such, what needed the kirk of Scotland have frequently taken so much pains, to give characters to know them by, there being so clear and compendious a way beside? Hath there not been always in the land secret underminers as well as open enemies? And hath not faithful men avoided the one as well as the other? 4. The General Assembly, 1648, declared the taking in of these who followed James Graham[344] to be an association with malignants, though most part of them were then released from church censures.

SECTION II.

That The Present Public Resolutions, Expressed In The Commission's Answer To The Parliament's Query, And The Act Of The Levy, Do Not Exclude That Party.

In the next place, upon supposal and proof, that there is a malignant party and faction still in the land, it is needful to examine, whether the exceptions contained in the answer of the Commission to the Parliament's Query,[345] and inserted into the Act of Levy,[346] be so comprehensive as to include all that party. The exceptions be four: 1. Such as are excommunicated. 2. Such as are forfaulted. 3. Such as are notoriously profane or flagitious. And, 4. Such as have been from the beginning, and continue still, or at this time are, obstinate enemies and opposers of the covenant and cause of God. That these are not comprehensive of the whole malignant party in the land, appears.

First, The rules of the General Assembly framed for the exclusion of all such as ought not to be employed in our armies, are far more comprehensive. The rule is for employing of such only as are of a Christian and blameless conversation, which is turned over by their commissioners into a negative, all that are not notoriously profane or flagitious. Another is, for intrusting only these who have been of known integrity and constant friends to the cause of God from the beginning, which is also turned over into a negative, all that have not been constant enemies. All such, by the Answer, are capable of some trust and employment. The rules agreed upon by the assembly, and ratified by act of parliament, anno 1649, and renewed upon occasion of this invasion, were that no officer nor soldier that followed James Graham should be permitted in the army, nor any officer that was in the Engagement, except such as, upon real evidence of repentance, were particularly recommended by the church, nor any common soldier, but upon sufficient testimony of his repentance. Now, since it is proved that the most part of all such continue still malignants, and retain their old principles, and that the bulk and body of the people are called forth by the public resolution, without such exceptions as were conceived before necessary, for the exclusion of that party, it follows clearly, that the malignant party is not excepted in the present resolutions.

Second. Few of these who were in the late rebellion, and declared, not many days since, to be following a most malignant design and course, are contained under these exceptions, because very few of them are excommunicated or forfaulted, and though more of them be indeed flagitious and profane, yet very few of them will fall under the compass of the exception, notoriously flagitious. Many wicked things will be said to concur to make up a profane man. Some acts will not serve; a habit must be demonstrated, and though that were showed, yet there must be also a notoriety of it, which imports a man to be famous for looseness and profanity, and there are none almost, if any in the land, who have been professed enemies from the beginning, and continue so to this day. James Graham was not such. It is the matter of our sad complaint, that whilst many are enemies, they make profession and semblance of friendship.

Third. These exceptions do not comprehend any who are under censure for malignancy or profanity, except such as are under the sentence of excommunication, and that even such may not be excluded, lest the rule be transgressed, by admitting and employing excommunicated persons, 'tis withal resolved, that these persons shall be relaxed from that sentence, that so they may be immediately in the same capacity of employment with others, whatever formerly hath been their opposition or defection. Some exceptions must be made, for honesty and credit's sake. But the nearest and readiest way is taken to make them ineffectual.

Fourth. These exceptions do not only not reach these who were upon the unlawful engagement and have not as yet given sufficient proof of their abandoning their malignant principles and courses, but come not the length of comprehending these men of blood who followed James Graham and in the most barbarous and cruel way, shed the blood of their own brethren and God's people. Because the most part of these are not excommunicated nor forfaulted, nor notoriously flagitious and profane, nor such as have from the beginning been, and still are enemies. If any will say, that such are comprehended under these exceptions, why did the commission express the exceptions in such terms, as to men's common apprehension do not include many, especially seeing there are known rules, particular and distinct, without ambiguity, and seeing there is such a propension in rulers to employ all without difference, which would undoubtedly take advantage of any thing that seemed to look that way?

It is likewise manifest, that the second part of the answer, relating to the capacity of acting, is loaded with the same inconvenience. 1. There is no positive determination of the qualifications of persons to be intrusted, as in former times it was agreed on by the Assembly and their Commissioners, but that is now referred to the discretion of the parliament, together with such diminutive terms, as give them great latitude to go upon. Before, no trust was given to such persons. Now, it is allowed they shall have some trust, and how much is not determined, nor what degree of it is prejudicial to the cause, which it appears, the parliament's proceedings in nomination of officers unquestioned by the Commission, is a good commentary to expound that they may have any trust, except to be general officers. 2. Our former established rule was, that no persons should be intrusted, but such as are of known integrity, and have been constant friends of the cause. But how far is this diminished? They who are such, only recommended to be especially taken notice of. Less could not be said by any. More ought to have been said by the Commission. And though no such notice be taken of such by the parliament, but on the contrary, those who have been most faithful, and suffered in the late defeat at Hamilton,[347] are used as enemies, worse than malignants in former times, yet there is no testimony given against such things. *Quantum mutatus ab illo cœtu qui quondam fuit!*[348]

Before we enter upon the chief question, we offer these manifest and known truths to consideration:

(1) The occasion of contriving and subscribing first the national covenant, and then the solemn league and covenant, was, the designs and practices of the popish, prelatical and malignant party, against religion and the work of reformation in these kingdoms. (2) Since the contriving and subscribing of the same, it hath been the continual endeavour of that party sometimes by undermining and some times by open opposition to undo the same and to bear down all those that clave honestly thereto and faithfully prosecute all the ends thereof. (3) That there hath been these many years past and still is, such a party, in all the three kingdoms, considerable for number, power, and policy. (4) That that party hath always prosecuted their design under a colour of zeal and respect to the king's authority and interest. (5) That that party hath always been the authors and abettors of much bloodshed, many miseries, and sad calamities to these nations. (6) That the people of God in these kingdoms have taken upon themselves a most solemn and sacred bond of an oath and covenant to discover them and bring them to condign punishment. (7) That it hath been

one of the predominant sins of Scotland under the bond of the covenant to comply with them. (8) That indignation and wrath from the Lord hath been following that party and their designs these years past. (9) That compliances with them hath always been cursed to us of God. (10) That few of that party do really abandon and forsake their corrupt principles and way and join cordially in the cause and covenant. (11) That many of them do, after the profession of their repentance for their opposition to the cause and covenant of God, relapse frequently into the same sin. (12) That sudden receiving of many of them to fellowship and trust, and too great credulity in believing their professions hath often cost this land very dear. (13) That upon consideration of the deep treachery and hypocrisy of these men, and the sad consequences following upon sudden receiving of them without evidence of a change, after long and renewed experience, this land renewed their obligations more strictly in the solemn engagement. (14) That there hath been a design driven these two years past to get that party again in power and trust. (15) That this design hath been testified against by the public resolutions of the judicatories unto this time. (16) That as it hath been driven at very cunningly and actively, by many instruments and arguments of several sorts, so hath it gained ground piece and piece, until at length many of them are brought into the court and to the army and judicatories in the country. And now by the public resolutions they are generally to be employed and intrusted. Thus the design is accomplished. But, (17) These men do not satisfy themselves with some degree of power, but endeavour to engross the whole power of the kingdom into their own hands, and study to bring into contempt, and cull out these who have been and do continue constant in the cause of God. (18) That having power into their hands, they must act according to their own principles and for establishing their own ends. And lastly, That these principles and ends are destructive to the covenant and work of reformation.

SECTION III.

That The Employing Of, And Associating With The Malignant Party, According As Is Contained In The Public Resolutions, Is Sinful And Unlawful.

If there be in the land a malignant party of power and policy, and the exceptions contained in the Act of Levy do comprehend but few of that party, then there need be no more difficulty to prove, that the present public resolutions and proceedings do import an association and conjunction with a malignant party, than to gather a conclusion from clear premises. But that such a conjunction is in itself sinful and unlawful, and besides, a violation of our solemn oaths and engagements, a backsliding from our principles and professions, and a walking contrary to the whole tenor and current of our former resolutions and practices, is now to be made manifest.

First: We reason from that constant, standing and perpetual rule, which the Lord gives concerning the modelling and carriage of the armies of his people in all their wars, Deut. xxiii. 9, "When the host goeth forth against their enemies, then keep thee from every wicked thing." And after, "If there be among you any man that is unclean, by reason of uncleanness that chanceth him by night, then shall he go abroad out of the camp, he shall not come within the camp." (If for ceremonial uncleanness he was to be excluded, much more for moral, as our divines reason from the Old Testament in the point of excommunication, and if for uncleanness not voluntary, much more for voluntary wickedness). The reason of all is given ver. 14: "For the Lord thy God walketh in the midst of the camp, to deliver thee, and to give up thine enemies before thee. Therefore shall thy camp be holy, that he see no unclean thing in thee, and turn away from thee." Even as they would expert a blessing of the Lord, so ought they to keep their camp holy, as he is holy. He gives not such a strict rule for the competency of number, as for the qualifications of the persons, as being the principal thing. Therefore the present conjunction with so many ungodly and wicked men, that have formerly declared themselves enemies to God and his people, and to this day give no evidence to the contrary, is sinful and unlawful.

Second, The Lord hath frequently in scripture declared his dislike and hatred of such associations and conjunctions. The scriptures cited in the General Assembly's declaration in the year 1648, against the Engagement,[349] are sufficient proof of this. We shall take the argument as it is formed by the commissioners of that assembly, in their answer to the observations of the committee of estates upon the assembly's declaration, p. 7. "Every engagement in war, that is pretended to be for religion, and hath in it a confederacy and association with wicked men, enemies of true religion, is sinful and unlawful. But the present engagement in war, as it is held forth in the public resolutions, is pretended to be for religion, and yet hath in it a confederacy and conjunction with wicked men, and enemies of true religion." Ergo, The second proposition is evident from the two first sections.

The first proposition is proved from those scriptures forementioned. God forbade conjunctions and confederacies with the enemies of his cause and people, not only the Canaanites, (Exod. xxxiv. 12, 15, Deut. vii. 2.) and other heathens, such was Asa his covenant with Benhadad, (2 Chron. xvi. to ver. 10,) Ahaz his confederacy with the king of Assyria, (2 Kings xvi. 7, 10, 2 Chron. xxviii. 16,) but also with wicked men of the seed of Abraham, as Jehoshaphat's with Ahab, (2 Chron. xviii. 3: "And Ahab king of Israel said unto Jehoshaphat king of Judah, Wilt thou go with me to Ramoth Gilead? And he answered him, I am as thou art, and my people as thy people, and we will be with thee in the war," compared with chap. xix. 2. "And Jehu the son of Hanam the seer, went out to meet him, and said to king Jehoshaphat, Shouldst thou help the ungodly, and love them that hate the Lord? therefore is wrath upon thee from before the Lord,") and with Ahaziah, (2 Chron. xx. 35: "And after this did Jehoshaphat king of Judah join himself with Ahaziah king of Israel, who did very wickedly,") which being reproved for, he would not again join with Ahaziah, 1 Kings xxii. 49: "Then said Ahaziah the son of Ahab unto Jehoshaphat: Let my servants go with thy servants in the ships." But Jehoshaphat would not. And then Amaziah's association with 100,000 of Israel, 2 Chron. xxv. 7, 8, 9, 10: "But there came a man of God to him, saying, O king, let not the army of Israel go with thee for the Lord is not with Israel to wit, with all the children of Ephraim. But if thou wilt go, do it, be strong for the battle. God shall make thee fall before the enemy, for God hath power to help and to cast down. And Amaziah said to the man of God, But what shall we do for the hundred talents which I have given to the army of Israel? And the man of God answered, The Lord is able to give thee much more than this. Then Amaziah separated them, to wit, the army that was to come to him out of Ephraim, to go home again wherefore their anger was greatly kindled against Judah, and they returned home in great anger." The sin and danger of such associations may further appear from Isa. viii. 12, 13: "Say ye not, A confederacy, to all them to whom this people shall say, A confederacy, neither fear ye their fear, nor be afraid. Sanctify the Lord of hosts himself, and let him be your fear, and let him be your dread," Jer. ii. 18 "And now,—what hast thou to do in the way of Assyria, to drink the waters of the river?" Psal. cvi. 35. "But were mingled among the heathen, and learned their works," Hosea v. 13. "When Ephraim saw his sickness, and Judah saw his wound, then went Ephraim to the Assyrian, and sent to king Jareb, yet could he not heal you, nor cure you of your wound," and chap. vii. 8, 11. "Ephraim, he hath mixed himself among the people, Ephraim is a cake not turned, Ephraim also is like a silly dove without heart, they call to Egypt, they go to Assyria," 2 Cor. vi. 14, 15. "Be ye not unequally yoked together with unbelievers, for what fellowship hath righteousness with unrighteousness? and what communion hath light with darkness? And what concord hath Christ with Belial? or what part hath he that believeth with an infidel?" And if we should esteem God's enemies our enemies, and hate them with perfect hatred, how can we then join with them as friends? Psal. cxxxix. 21.

The committee of estates at that time endeavoured to elude the strength of these scriptures, and vindicate their engagement from the falling within the compass of them. But the commission of the Assembly that year took the mask off their evasions. Would to God we had no other party to deal with now! It was the evil and complaint of that time, that church and state were divided. But what an evil time are we now fallen into, that the union of those in this point, is the complaint of many of the godly? The commission, in their letter to Stirling presbytery,[350] sets up the committee's answer in a new dress, and holds it out for satisfaction to our consciences. All that is answered may be reduced to three or four heads.

I. There is made a great difference between an invasive and defensive war as if in the one, choice of instruments ought to be sought, but in the case of just and necessary defence, all subjects may be employed.[351]

To which we answer, 1. That the scriptures cited conclude most expressly against conjunctions of that kind in defensive wars. Such was Asa's covenant, such was Ahaz his confederacy. Were not the reproofs of the prophets directed particularly against the people's seeking of help from Egypt and Assyria, in the case of their own just and necessary defence? Jer. ii. 18, Hosea v. 13, and vii. 8, 11, Isa. viii. 12, 13, 2 Chron. xvi. to ver. 10. 2. The law and rule given, Deut. xxiii. is general, regulating all their wars whether defensive or offensive, and it is strange that any should imagine such a difference where the law makes none, nay, when the ground of the law is moral and general, equally respecting all wars. Is there any ground of conscience, why wicked persons may not be kept in the camp when we invade others, and yet these may be employed and intrusted when we defend ourselves? If there be any reason to prefer the one to the other in this point, we conceive defensive war should have the preference, because when the Lord brings upon us an unjust invasion, he is ordinarily pursuing a controversy against us. And therefore we ought to be most tender and circumspect, that there be no unclean thing in the camp, and put away every wicked thing from us, even the appearance of evil, lest we add oil to the flame of his indignation, and he seeing such an unclean thing in us, turn yet further from us, except we say, that we need not take care to have God in the camp with us, when we are upon just and necessary defence, seeing our cause is so good. 3. There is more hazard and danger to our religion and liberties in having a wicked malignant army at home among us, than abroad in another nation. While they are here, they have the power of the sword, and can command all, but there might be some hope and endeavour for vindicating our own liberties and religion while they are abroad, as it fell out in the time of the Engagement.

II. It is answered, that there is a difference between this case and the Engagement, because there was then no necessity of choosing such instruments, a competency of power might be had, but now it is not so, and therefore the scriptures mentioned do not militate against the present case. *Answer 1.* The scriptures cited will obviate this. What made Israel and Judah run to Egypt and Assyria for help, but their weakness and necessity? Their wound was incurable, and their bruise grievous, as Jeremiah often laments, and particularly chap. viii. 20-22, and x. 19, &c., and yet this did not excuse them for going to Egypt or Assyria to heal their wound, Hosea v. 13, and vii. 8, 11. The scripture holds out infidelity and distrust in God as the ground of such association, (2 Chron. xvi. 7-9, Isa. viii. 12, 13,) which proceeds from the incompetency of means as the occasion of it. 2. Suppose there was a necessity for the calling forth the body of the common people, yet certainly there is no necessity of employing any such persons of whom the question is, and putting them in places of trust. There is none can deny but there are, besides all secluded persons, many that might fill the places of trust and power. Therefore the plea of necessity is but a pretence to cover some design, that under its specious and plausible covering, the power of the land may be engrossed into the hands of malignants, and so by this means all power and trust may return, as the rivers to the sea or fountain, as they judge the king, that so in his person there may be established an unlimited and arbitrary power. 3. Necessity is a very plausible argument and strong plea to carnal reason for any thing, but it cannot be a good ground, in point of conscience, for that which is sinful in itself. Now that this is sinful in itself appears, from the word of God simply condemning such associations, upon moral, and so general and perpetual grounds. Now, in such a case of necessity, we are called either to trust in God, in the use of competent means, seeing in such cases we have so many promises, or if all help be gone which God allows us to make use of, we must wait on him till he brings salvation with his own arm.

But because the plea of necessity is the strongest that is made use of for the present public resolutions, we must consider it a little more. It is alleged, that the best part of the land is under the feet of the enemy, and so no help can be had from it, and for other parts of the land which are yet free, there is not much choice of persons, and the testimony of faithful men in the state declares, that when all that are called forth of these places are gathered, it cannot amount to a power competent enough, and therefore in such a question of the existence of second means, the knowledge whereof immediately depends on sense and experience, these who are not acquainted should give credit to the testimony of faithful witnesses, and that a competency of power must be had, according to the ordinary way of Providence, in relation to which we must act, except we would tempt God by requiring of him wonders.[352]

Answer. Suppose the enemy's army to consist of 20,000 or above, are there not more fencible persons in the shires on the north side of Forth? Believe it who please we cannot stop our own consciences, and put out our own eyes. Let the rolls of several shires be looked to, and it shall confute that testimony. Nay, are there not more persons not formerly secluded, in all those shires? What meant the levy appointed immediately after Dunbar? Was not 10,000 foot, and 1,400 horse put upon these shires which are not under the power of the enemy, and yet the rules of exclusion were not abandoned? Now all these, or most part of them, are yet in the country not levied. Money was taken instead of men, the levies obstructed so that there was little addition to the strength of the forces that remained, the forces diverted by the insurrection of the malignants in the north, at the King's command or warrant,—all which hath such pregnant presumption of a design carried on to necessitate the kingdom to employ that party, by the cunning politicians of the time, by obstructing the levies, raising the malignants, and then pacifying them by an act of indemnity, and at last openly and avowedly associating with them. Thus the design is accomplished which was long since on foot.

2. If satisfying courses had been studied by the public judicatories to carry on all the godly in the land with their resolutions, there had accrued strength from the parts of the land be south Forth, which would have compensated all that competency of power that the conjunction of the malignants makes up and, it may be, would have been more blessed of God. 3. If there be no help required nor expected from those parts of the kingdom be south Forth, wherefore did the commission write to the presbyteries in those bounds that they might concur actively in their stations for the furtherance of the levies, and choose ministers to go out with them?

III. It is answered. That the confederacies reproved were unlawful, because they were either with heathens, or with idolaters, strangers, and foreigners. This is answered to the case of Amaziah, &c., and so it seems not to make against the present case, the employing all subjects in the just and necessary defence of the kingdom.[353]

Answer 1. This answer at one blow cuts off all the strength of the General Assembly's reason against the association with malignants in that year. There might be some few persons idolaters, but there was no party and faction such, and yet they can deny association with the English malignants from those scriptures, yea not only with them but with our own countrymen that were in rebellion with James Graham, who were neither idolaters nor foreigners. We need no other answer than the Commission at that time give to the committee of estates using that same evasion, pg. 10, 11. 2. The ground and reason whereupon such associations are condemned, is more general and comprehensive. Jehoshaphat was reproved for joining with Ahab, because he was "ungodly, and hated the Lord," which is properly in our terms, because he was a malignant and profane man. It was a strange mocking of scripture to restrict ungodliness, in that place, to the sin of idolatry. Confederacy with the Canaanites and other nations was forbidden on this ground, "that the people be not insnared, and learn not their works." Now, is not the company of, and communion with ungodly men, of the same general profession, but mockers and haters of the power thereof, as infectious and insnaring? Nay, it is more apt to insnare because of the profession. Paul would have as much distance kept with a brother walking unorderly as a pagan. For such a one as walks contrary to his profession of the true religion, does evidence more ungodliness and wickedness, than an ignorant and superstitious papist that walks precisely according to his profession. There is some principle of conscience stirring in the one, but it is seared in the other with a hot iron. God ranks such, who are uncircumcised in heart, with the uncircumcised in flesh. Ought not his people to do so too? 3. The rule of modelling armies and purging the camp is most comprehensive, Deut. xxiii. Not only idolaters and foreigners, but every wicked thing and unclean thing, was to be removed out of the camp. Now, seeing those examples are transgressions of this law, what reason is there to make the only ground of reproving and condemning of them to be, because idolaters were associated with, as if any other might be joined with, that is not an idolater? 4. That reason against Amaziah's conjunction with Israel is wrested, by some expounding it thus God is not with them, is not understood, in regard of a state of grace, as appears, nor in regard of God's prospering providence, because he was often with them in that regard but it must be understood in regard of an idolatrous profession. But we reply, that it is true it is not understood in regard of a state of grace, nor simply in regard of his prospering providence, but *ut plurimum*,[354] the Lord for the most part crossing them till they were cut off from being a nation. But especially it is to be meant in regard of a course opposite to God, according as the Lord speaks, 2 Chron. xv. 2. "The Lord is with you while ye be with him, but if ye forsake him he will forsake you." If any will restrict this to idolatry, he hath no ground from scripture for such a limitation, but being engaged in the business, he wrests the scriptures to his own destruction. Sure we are, there are many palpable forsakings of God, and God's forsaking of men, beside idolatry and false worship. 5. That which is said "That God did not command Amaziah to dismiss any of his own subjects." Either it makes not much to the present business, or else it strikes against the law of God itself, that commanded such strict purging of the camp. From whom I pray you? Certainly from wicked Israelites, from wicked countrymen. Therefore, if there was any such among the men of Judah, he ought to have put them out of the army as well as the Israelites. Nay, the command of dismissing the Israelites, was, really and upon the matter, a command to purge his camp of all that was of the stamp of the Israelites. It is strange that the civil difference of strangers and citizens should make such difference in the point of conscience. Ought we not to hate the Lord's enemies with a perfect hatred, not as Englishmen, not as strangers, but as enemies? Levi knew not his brother. This was his honour. But many now for respect to their brethren, know not God. It is the moral quality that the law of God respects, without respect of persons and countries. To be a citizen, if not qualified, doth no more plead for employment, *in foro conscientiæ*[355] and before God, than to be a stranger and qualified doth impede trust and employment *in foro conscientiæ* and before God.

IV. It may be answered (and it is by some), That those scriptures plead, that there should be no conjunction with wicked men in a quarrel of religion, but seeing our present business is the defence of the kingdom, all subjects, as subjects, stand in capacity of employment for that end, though in reference to the defence of religion there must be a choice.

Answer 1. The Commission have vindicated themselves in a letter to Stirling presbytery from that imputation, that it is said, they state the quarrel and cause merely upon civil things in the answer to the parliament's query.[356] But certainly there is just ground given to these that are watching for any such thing to state the cause so, because they do, contrary to all former custom and practice, mention the defence of the kingdom only, as it had been of purpose to make the employing of all members of the body or subjects of the kingdom for its defence more plausible.

But we answer to the point. The associations and conjunctions that are condemned in the cited scriptures are some of them for civil quarrels so far as we know, some of them in the point of just and necessary defence of the kingdom, and yet that doth not justify them. 2. The rule given them, Deut. xxiii., was regulating all their wars and clearly holds forth, that all subjects as subjects and members of the politic body, though as such there is an obligation lying on them to defend the whole, yet are not in actual and nearest capacity to the performance of that duty, if they be wicked and unclean. And the reason is, because the Lord would have the wars of his people his own wars, and all that they do, to his glory, Num. xxi. 14. 2 Chron. xx. 15, Col. iii. 17. More especially in such solemn undertakings, there ought to be a difference between his people, acting for self defence, and other nations. 3. Although the defence of the kingdom and defence of the cause, be different in themselves, yet are they inseparable. Whoever is intrusted with the defence of the kingdom really and *de facto*,[357] he is *eo ipso*[358] intrusted with the defence of the cause. Therefore the people of God, who ought always to have religion first in their eye, ought, especially in raising forces for self preservation, to level at religion, and direct the choice of instruments in relation to that mark, that they destroy not Christians, while they save subjects and preserve our bodies to destroy our souls.

Third Reason. That which is dissonant from and contrary unto all our former resolutions and proceedings, oaths and engagements, confessions and humiliations, must needs be most unlawful, or they themselves, as to that point, were unlawful. But the present resolutions and proceedings are dissonant from, and contrary to all these. Ergo, either our present or our former resolutions and practices were unlawful, either we were wrong before, or we are not right now. The second proposition maybe made manifest from, 1. The present resolutions are contrary to the solemn league and covenant in the fourth article and the sixth,—to the fourth, because we put power in the hands of a malignant party, power of the sword, which is inconsistent in the own nature of it with either actual punishing of them, or endeavouring to bring them to punishment, unless it be intended to bring them all forth, and expose them to the slaughter for a sacrifice for the land, which may be the Lord's mind indeed, howbeit they know not his thoughts,—and to the sixth article, because it is a declining to the contrary party, even that party against whom the covenant was at the making expressly contrived. And as the declaration of the General Assembly 1648, hath it, it is a joining with one enemy to beat another, with a black devil to beat a white.[359]

It is most ingeniously answered, that the present resolutions are not contrary to the covenant, because such as are described in the covenant are not allowed to be employed, meaning that these men are not now malignants. What needs men make such a compass to justify the public resolutions, seeing there is so easy and ready a way straight at hand? This one answer might take off all the arguments made against them, that there is no malignant party now, which is the foundation that being removed all the building must fall to the ground. But we have in the first article evinced that, which had been scandalous to have proved, if it had not been questioned. If it were indeed true, that no malignants are allowed to be employed, what need the Commission in their letter to Stirling presbytery take so much pains from scripture and reason to justify the present resolutions, when the clearing of that one point had cleared all? As for the declaration of the Assembly, anno 1648, it is answered, *that none are to be employed, that continue notourly*[360] *in the courses of malignancy*, which was done that year. Whereas the malignant party that was then associated with, would have engaged to be faithful to all the ends of the covenant, many of them were such as had been in covenant, and made show of their repentance for their defection from it; and so there is no difference in this particular.

2. The Solemn Acknowledgment of public sins is so clear and peremptory in this that it makes us tremble to think on it. *Page 6*, "Should we again break his commandments and covenant, by joining any more in affinity with the people of these abominations, and take in our bosom these serpents, which have formerly stung us almost to death? This, as it would argue much folly and madness, so, no doubt, it would provoke

the Lord to consume us till there be no remnant, nor escaping." Let the 6th article also be considered.[361] Join to this the Declaration of the commission, upon report of this enemy's invading, *p. 6* where it is declared, that malignants shall not be associated with, nay, not countenanced and permitted to be in our armies. The General Assembly after this, upon the enemy's entry into Scotland, gives serious warning to the rulers, to take heed of snares from that party and that the rather, because men ordinarily are so taken with the sense of danger, as not to look back to that which is behind them, &c. How often have we sentenced ourselves unto wrath and consumption if we shall fall into this sin again? All these and the like, are endeavoured to be taken off, by saying that our engagements in this point were conceived in a way of prosecution of the cause, but to be no impediment of the just and necessary defence, which we are bound to by nature's law, which no human law can infringe.

But we reply, (1) It is strange, our prosecution of the cause these years past should be contradistinguished from the defence of it and the kingdom. It was conceived that our war in England was defensive, not invasive, that it was necessitated for the defence even of our kingdom, but it seems it is now questioned. But passing what was acted abroad, certainly all our wars at home were merely defensive, both against unjust invasion and seditious insurrections. Now our solemn engagements were conceived, in relation to our actings at home especially, and modelling our armies for the defence of our liberties and religion. We know well enough that a just invasive war is a rare accident in the world, and that the flock of Jesus Christ is for the most part, obnoxious to the violence of others, as sheep among wolves, but are not often called to prey upon others. (2) To call our solemn engagements and declarations grounded upon our oaths and the word of God, human laws and constitutions that must cede to nature's law, is indeed ingenious dealing, because to justify the present proceedings, there can be no more expedite way than to condemn bypast resolutions for the peremptoriness of them, and to make them grounded on politic considerations, which are alterable, but it imports a great change of principles. We conceive that all human laws that are not for the matter grounded on the word of God, that oblige not conscience, but in the case of scandal and in regard of the general end, are alterable and changeable, whenever they come in opposition to the law of nature, self defence, and the law of God written in his word. And therefore that act of parliament, mentioned by the Commission, discharging all subjects from rising without the king's command, which was made use of against our first taking arms, was no ways binding on the subjects not to rise in defence of their religion and liberties when in hazard.[362] And we wonder that that law should be compared to our solemn engagements, which are grounded upon oaths and God's word, as touching the very matter and substance of them, as if our engagements did no more bind us now, in case of defence, than that law did bind us then. Royalists might be excused for preferring the king's will to God's, but we cannot be pardoned for equalizing them; and especially while we consider that that forementioned act undoubtedly hath been intended for the establishing of an arbitrary and absolute power in the king's hand, that the subjects may not have liberty to save themselves, except the king will. Where God hath given us liberty by the law of nature, or his word, no king can justly tie us, and when God binds and obliges us by any of these, no king or parliament can loose or untie us. (3) The Declaration of the Commission and Assembly upon this invasion, renews the same bond of our former engagements, yea, and speaks expressly in the case of fewness and scarceness of instruments, against the unbelief of people that are ready in danger to choose any help.[363] Therefore that which is said in answer, that at that time there was a choice of instruments which now is not, may indeed condemn and falsify the declarations at that time, in the supposition of the paucity of instruments, and in the application of that doctrine and divine truth to that time, but it doth not speak any thing against the application of that truth therein contained to our time, it being more manifest, that we have greater necessity and less choice of instruments, and so in greater hazard of unbelief, and overlooking what is behind us.

3. It is of all considerations the most confounding, to reflect upon our former humiliations and fasts. How often hath it been confessed to God, as the predominant public sin of Scotland, countenancing and employing the malignant party? But when we call particularly to mind the first solemn fast after the defeat at Dunbar, astonishment takes hold on us, to think, that is now defended as a duty, which, but some months ago, was solemnly confessed as a sin. The not purging of the army, the obstructing of that work, and great inclinations to keep in and fetch in such persons, and the repining at, and crying out against all that was done in the contrary, were then reckoned as the great causes of God's wrath, and his sad stroke upon us. What distraction may this breed in the hearts of the people of the land to hear that same thing complained of as a great sin to day, and commended as a necessary duty to morrow? Is not all the land presently called to mourn for the king's sins, of which this is one, the designing a conjunction with the malignant party, and giving them warrant to rise in arms for the defence of the kingdom? Now, how shall they be able to reconcile these in their own minds,—at the same time to mourn for that as a sin in the king, which they hear commended as the duty of the parliament—to fast to day for that as the king's sin, which they must go about to morrow as their own duty? "Tell it not in Gath, publish it not in Askelon, lest the daughters of the Philistines rejoice." Heathens may rise in judgment against this generation *Semper idem velle atque idem nolle hæc demum sapientia est.*[364] If any wise man be *ubique et semper sibi par et idem*,[365] what ought a godly man to be?

Fourth Reason. That which is an uncertain mean of preservation of the kingdom, and a more certain mean of destruction of religion, is utterly unlawful. But the employing and intrusting of all men promiscuously, according as is holden out in the public resolutions, is at best an uncertain mean of the preservation of the kingdom, and is a more certain mean of the destruction of religion. *Ergo*, It is utterly unlawful. The first proposition cannot be denied. When any less good comes in opposition with a greater good, the lesser good in that respect becomes evil. We may not endanger certainly a greater good for the probable and uncertain attainment of the lesser. The second proposition I know will be denied, as it was denied in the time of the engagement by the committee of estates. They said, the danger of religion was not infallible, that it might eventually fall out so, but not by any casualty. And thus it is pleaded now, that the danger of religion is not inevitable, but that the danger of the kingdom is certain and so these being laid in the balance together, we ought, to eschew a certain danger of the kingdom's destruction, rather hazard a probable danger of religion.

But we shall clear this and confirm the reason. 1. The danger of the kingdom is indeed great, but it is not so certain and inevitable in case of not employing the malignant party, because there may be some competency of power beside. Now the delivery and preservation of the kingdom from this danger, by conjunction with that party, is rather improbable, because we have sentenced ourselves to destruction if ever we should do such a thing again. We are standing under a curse, whereto we have bound over ourselves, and beside, God is in a special manner pursuing that generation, and hath raised up this enemy for their destruction so that we may with greater probability expect to partake of their plagues, and to fall under our own curse, than to be delivered, or be instruments of deliverance to the kingdom. Or, at the best, it is uncertain. For what is more uncertain than the event of war? The battle in this sense may be said peculiarly to belong to the Lord. Now, on the other hand, the danger of religion is certain and inevitable, though not simply in itself and absolutely, (because the Lord doth in heaven and earth what he pleases,) yet with a moral certainty and infallibility, which is often as great as physical certainty. Suppose these men having the power of the sword, prevail, will they not employ it according to their principles, and for attaining their own ends, which both are destructive to religion? What is more certain than that men act and speak from the abundance of the heart, when there is no outward restraint? It should be a great wonder if they who are so accustomed to do evil, should cease to do evil, when they have power and convenience to do it. Power and greatness hath corrupted many good men. Shall it convert them? Can men expect other fruits from a tree than the nature of it yields? Will one seek figs on thorns, or grapes on thistles? 2. We do not see what defence it can be, for the present, to the kingdom, at least the godly and well affected in the kingdom, who will be as much troubled in their persons and estates by that party, as by the common enemy. It is known what threatenings the country is filled with, which vent that inveterate malice and hatred to all the well affected in the kingdom, which they have kept within their breast of a long time and now they find opportunity of outing it. It is as clear as daylight, that the most part of all the secluded persons look upon these that opposed them in the Engagement, and shut them out of places of trust, and capacity of employment, as enemies, and as great enemies as the secretaries. And that we may know what to expect when they have full power in their hands they have already so lifted up their head, that no godly man can promise himself security in many places, and especially the faithful gentlemen and people of the West,[366] who have given more proof of their faithfulness to the cause and kingdom against the common enemy, than any others in the land, yet are they daily suffering violence from these preservators of the kingdom, while they are sufferers under the feet of the enemy. When they have no common enemy, whom, I beseech you, will they prey upon, seeing they do it already while they have an enemy?

But it is replied, That none of the least suspicion are allowed to be in such trust and power, as may be prejudicial to religion, and that an oath is to be taken of all, which is to be conceived as particular, binding, and strict as possible.

Answer 1. What a manifest receding is it from former principles, that it is now conceived, that all places of trust, excepting some few of eminent note, may be filled with secluded and debarred persons, without the prejudice of religion! It is certain that most part of the officers, nominated by the parliament and shires, are not only such, of whom there is just ground of suspicion, but such as have been enemies by actual opposition to the cause of God, or known underminers thereof. Can it be said in good earnest, that none, of whom is any suspicion, shall have such trust as may be prejudicial? Sure we are, there are many just grounds of suspicion and jealousy of general persons,[367] who have chief trust in our armies and this the public judicatories are not ignorant of. 2. Oaths and covenants are but like green cords about Samson to bind these men. Would we have them yet once again perjured? Then may we tender an oath to them. Put power in their hand, and then make them swear to employ it well. 'Tis as ridiculous as to give a madman a sword, and then persuade him to hurt none with it. There is no more capitulation with such persons, retaining their old principles, than with the floods or winds. These whom that sacred bond of covenant hath not tied, what oath can bind? Except you can change their nature, do not swear them to good behaviour. Can a leopard change his spots?

Fifth Reason. That which gives great offence and scandal, and lays a stumbling-block in the way, both of the people of the land and our enemies, especially in the way of the godly, that is unlawful. But the present association and conjunction with all persons in the kingdom (excepting a few, if any) is scandalous and offensive to the whole land, to the godly especially, and also to the enemy. Therefore it is unlawful. The *major*[368] is beyond all exception, if we consider how peremptory Christ and his apostles are in the point of offence, which yet few Christians do consider. We ought not only to beware of the offence of the godly, but even of wicked men, even of our blaspheming enemies. "Give no offence neither to the Jew nor Gentile, nor to the church of God." Christ would not offend and scandalize his malicious enemies. The *minor*[369] is proved. 1. There is great offence given to the godly in the kingdom by the public resolutions, concerning that conjunction with the malignant party, under the name and notion of subjects. (1) Because it is known that the most part of them are tender in that point, what fellowship they act with, and this hath been remonstrate unto the commission and committee of estates, from several synods. Now the present resolution layeth that stumbling block in their way, that they cannot act in the defence of the kingdom, because there is no way left them for the performing of that duty, but that which they in their consciences are not satisfied with. It is a sad necessity and snare that is put upon them, that they cannot perform their bound duty, which they are most desirous of, without sin, because of the way that is taken. (2) Is it not matter of offence and stumbling to them, to be necessitated by law to that which was their affliction? The mixture that was in our armies was their grief, and their comfort was that the judicatories were minting at[370] their duty to purge them. But now there is no hope of attaining that, all doors are shut up by the public resolutions. (3) It undoubtedly will weaken their hands, and make their hearts faint, so that they cannot pray with affection and in faith, for a blessing upon such an army,[371] the predominant and leading part whereof have been esteemed, and are really enemies to God and his people. (4) Is it not a great offence that any thing should proceed from the public judicatories that shall lay a necessity upon many godly in the land, to suffer, because they cannot in conscience go along with it? *Next*, It scandalizeth the whole land. What may they think within themselves, to see such dissonancy and disagreement between present and former resolutions and practices? What may they judge of this inconstancy and levity of the commission, and thus be induced to give no respect and reverence to them in their resolutions? Is it not, at least, a very great appearance of evil to join with that party, that we did declare and repute, but some few weeks since, to be wicked enemies of religion and the kingdom, and look henceforth on them as friends without so much as any acknowledgment of their sin had from them? Shall not they be induced to put no difference between the precious and the vile, not to discern between him that fears God and him that fears him not, when the public resolutions put no difference? Then, how will it confirm all the malignant party in their wickedness? May they not think our solemn vows and engagements, our rigid resolutions and proceedings, were but all contrived and acted out of policy, and that interest and advantage, and not conscience, principled them? Have they not an occasion given them to persecute all the godly, and vent their long harboured malice against these who have been most zealous for reformation and purging of the land? Nay, they are put in the capacity that they have desired, for acting all their resolutions and accomplishing their designs. And last of all, the present proceedings will not only encourage and animate the common enemy, but confirm them in all the imputations and calumnies they have loaded our church with. May they not have ground to think, that we are but driving on a politic design, and do not singly aim at God's glory,—that it is not grounds of conscience that act us, but some worldly interest, when they look upon the inconstancy and changeableness of our way and course, which is so accommodated to occasions and times? Can they think us men of conscience, that will join with all these men of blood, before we will so much as speak with them? It is replied, that the scandal is taken, and not given, which must not be stood upon in the case of a necessary duty. But, 1. We cleared, that there is no necessity of that conjunction, therefore the scandal is given, seeing it is known beforehand that it will be taken. 2. There are many grounds of offence given by the present resolutions, as appears by what is said. If it were no more, it is a great appearance of evil, it is very inductive of many evils, a most fit occasion of all that is spoken, and besides, it is in itself sinful, contrary to God's word, and our oaths.

Sixth Reason. That which makes glad all the wicked and enemies of God in the land, and sad many, if not most part, of the godly, hath much appearance and evidence, if not certainty, of evil. But the public resolutions and proceedings are such. *Ergo*,—Or thus—That which makes glad all the wicked, and heightens the hopes and expectations of the malignant party, and makes sad none almost but the godly, and discourages their spirits, that, proceeding from the public judicatories, cannot be right and lawful. But so it is, that that which proceeds from the public judicatories makes glad all the hearts of the wicked, and makes sad none almost but the godly, heightens the hopes of the malignants, and makes them say, their day is coming, "lo we have seen it," and discourages the godly, and makes them almost say, "Our hope is cut off, our glory is departed." *Ergo*, It cannot be right, at least it hath a great and convincing appearance of evil.

This argument may be thought more popular than either philosophical or scriptural. But such an argument the General Assembly, 1648, made use of against the Engagement. It is no ways imaginable, how the wicked and ungodly in the land would so insult and rejoice in this day, if they saw not some legible characters upon it, which were agreeable to their own principles and ends. The children of God are, for the most part, led by the Spirit of God, and taught the way they should choose, John xvi. 13, Psal. xxv. 12. So that readily they do not skunner[372] at courses approven of God. But the children of the world being, at best, led by their own carnal minds and senses and, for the most part, acted by a spirit of disobedience and enmity against God, they use not to rejoice at things that do not suit with their carnal hearts, and are not engraven with the character of that which is imprinted in their spirits. We see now that the wicked walk on every side, when the vilest men are exalted. And when the wicked rise, the righteous is hidden, and when they bear rule, the people mourneth, but when righteous men are in authority, the people do rejoice, and when the righteous rejoiceth, there is great glory, Ps. xii. 8, Prov. xxviii. 12, and xxix. 2.

Seventh Reason. That which is the accomplishment and perfecting of the malignant design that hath been driven on these years past, especially since the Unlawful Engagement, cannot be a course approven of God. But the present course is the accomplishment of that design. *Ergo*, That there hath been a design, for a long time driven and endeavoured, both at home and abroad, with much policy and industry, by many turnings and windings, and by arguments of several kinds, as the exigence of the times did furnish,—and that the design was, to have all such persons in trust and power again, who had been secluded, that so they might compass their own ends—hath not been denied hitherto and we are persuaded no man that fears God and observes the times, is ignorant of it. Let the public papers of the treaty at Breda,[373] and the public papers of this kingdom and church at home, be consulted. They bear witness for us. Was not the foundation of it laid in Holland, and many of them in both nations, brought home with the king contrary to public resolutions, and by the prevailing influence of some in the state, kept in the kingdom, contrary to public resolutions? Was not the work of purging judicatories and armies obstructed, the godly discountenanced and discouraged, great endeavours used to raise the malignants in the South and in England, and, since the defeat, to raise all without exception in the North, but when that could not be obtained, by the withstanding of honest men in the state? The levies appointed, which would have been a considerable force for the defence of the kingdom, were rendered wholly ineffectual, partly by taking money for men, partly by raising the malignant party, and then pretending to go against them, they were pacified by an act of indemnity the fruit and result of all which is, this present conjunction with them, and putting the power of judicatories and armies in their hand. Thus the design is completed.

Eighth Reason. That which will increase the Lord's indignation and controversy against the land yet seven times more, that is very unlawful and unseasonable. But so it is that confederacy and association with the people of these abominations, will increase the Lord's indignation and controversy seven times more. *Ergo*, The assumption was as manifest and uncontroverted as the proposition, a few months ago, but it is begun now to be questioned by some, *qui quod sciunt nesciunt, quia sapiunt*[374] But we shall evince it. 1. We are standing under such a sentence, which we deliberately and sincerely passed upon ourselves, in the days of our vows to God, that if we did ever any more join with the people of these abominations, the Lord would consume us till there was no remnant. And this was not done in rashness but in sobriety, and with a scripture precedent, Ezra ix. 12, 13. 2. Our experience hath made this clear to us, we never did mingle ourselves among them, but the Lord did pursue us with indignation, and stamped that sin, as in vive[375] characters, upon our judgment. God hath set upon that rock, that we have so oft split upon, a remarkable beacon. Therefore we do not only in our solemn engagements, bind ourselves over to a curse, in case of relapsing, but pass the sentence of great madness and folly on ourselves. *Piscator ictu sapit.*[376] Experience makes fools wise, but it cannot cure madness. Did not that mixture provoke God at Dunbar?[377] And is this the way to appease him, to revolt more and more? 3. Conjunction and confederacy with that party, doth necessarily infer a communion in blessings and plagues, we must cast in our lot with them, and have all one purse. Now it hath been confessed and declared by this church, that God hath a notable controversy with that party, that this enemy is in an eminent way to bear them down and crush them. Therefore if we join with them, we must resolve to partake of their plagues, and have that controversy pleaded against us also.

It is answered, That indignation need not be feared simply on this account, because the means are lawful and necessary, else, if this have any force, it will conclude, that we should lie down and do nothing, because God's indignation is upon the whole land.

But we reply, 1. Though it be true, that this enemy is the rod of God's indignation against the whole land, yet it is certain to us, and hath been formerly unquestioned, that they are raised up in a special way, to execute God's wrath on malignants, and God doth arm them with power in a signal manner for that end. Besides, the Lord's anger and indignation against his enemies is such, as will burn and none can quench it. It is of another nature than his wrath against his own people, which is a hiding of his face for a moment. He corrects us in measure and judgment, but leaves us not altogether unpunished. But he makes an end of other nations especially these that rise up to actual enmity and hatred of his people, and shedding of their blood. And therefore, if any man would not meet with wrath and sore displeasure, he would stand at a distance with such as God hath appointed for destruction, we mean, as long as they carry in their foreheads the mark of the beast. When God hath such a remarkable controversy against a people, then "he that helpeth and he that is helped shall both fall together," Isa. xxxi. 3. All that is in league with them, shall fall with them by the sword, Ezek. xxx. 5 and xxxii. 21. 2. Since it is known that the malignant party have not changed their principles, and so they cannot but in prosecuting this war establish their old quarrel and follow it viz. the king's arbitrary power, the interest of man above God's, or the kingdom's interest, we leave it to be judged impartially, whether or not these that associate with them, do espouse that quarrel and interest, at least expose themselves to all that wrath and indignation, which hath hitherto followed that quarrel, seeing they must have common blessings and curses. Will not that quarrel holden up by most part of the army, be a wicked thing, an Achan in the camp, that will make God turn away from it, and put Israel to shame?

Having thus established the truth, in the next place, we come to take off what objections are made to the contrary.

First: It is argued from human authority. The uncontroverted and universal practice of all nations in all generations, is, to employ all subjects in the case of necessary just defence. It was the practice of our reformers, who took into the congregation, and received all that, upon acknowledgment of their error, were willing to join, though they had been on the contrary faction. Such an universal practice of Christian nations, though it be not the ground of our faith, yet it is apparent that it cannot want reason for it.[378]

Answer 1: This will plead as much against the exceptions added in the answer to the query and act of levy, for seeing other nations except none, in the case of necessary defence, why should we except any? And if once we except any upon good and convincing grounds, upon the same ground we ought to except far more. 2: Mr. Gillespie, in his Treatise of Miscellany Questions,[379] makes mention that the city of Strasburg, 1529, made a defensive league with Zurich, Berne, and Basil; because they were not only neighbours, but men of the same religion. And the Elector of Saxony refused to take into confederacy those who differed from him in the point of the Lord's supper, lest such sad things should befall him, as befell these in Scripture, who used any means of their own defence. This rule was good *in thesi*,[380] though in that case misapplied. Now then, if they made conscience of choosing as the means of their own defence, a confederacy with foreigners, may not the same ground lead us to a distance from our own countrymen, as unqualified, who have nothing to commend them but that they are of the same nation, which is nothing in point of conscience? 3: The practice of other nations that are not tender in many greater points, cannot be very convincing, especially, when we consider that the Lord hath made light to arise, in this particular, more bright than in former times. God hath taken occasion of illustrating and commending many truths unto us in this generation, from the darkness of error, and of making straight many rules, from the crookedness of men's practice and walking. Is not the Lord now performing the promise of purging out the rebels from among us and them that transgress? God hath winked at former times of ignorance. But now, the Lord having cleared his mind so to us, how great madness were it to forsake our own mercy, and despise the counsel of God against our own souls? (1) As for that instance of our reformers there could not have been any thing brought more prejudicial to that cause, and more advantageous for us. After they were twice beaten by the French in Leith, and their forces scattered, and the leaders and chief men of the congregation forced to retire to Stirling, John Knox, preaching upon the eightieth Psalm, and searching the causes of God's wrath against them, condescends upon this as the chief cause, that they had received into their councils and forces such men as had formerly opposed the congregation, and says, God never blest them since the Duke had come among them. See Knox's Chron.[381] (2) It cannot be showed that ever they took in a party and faction of such men, but only some few persons, which, though it was not altogether justifiable, was yet more excusable. But now the public resolutions hold forth a conjunction with all the bloody murderers in the kingdom (excepting very few), and these without profession of repentance in many, and without evidence of the reality of it almost in any. (3) These persons were not such as had once joined with the congregation, and relapsed and became enemies to it, but they turned to the protestant religion from popery. But ours is a different case.

Second. It is argued from scripture. Three scripture instances are brought to justify the present proceedings. The first instance is from the practice of God's people in the book of Judges, who, when for defection from religion they were brought under oppression, yet when any governor was raised by God for their defence, they gathered and came all out promiscuously, notwithstanding a great part of them had been in the defection. Yet it is not found that their governors are reproved for this, but rather sad curses on them that came not out to the work, Judges v. 15, 16, 17, 23. The second instance is from the story of the kings, very like the first. When, after defection, gracious reforming kings arose, and had to do against foreign invasion, we find them not debarring any subjects, but calling them out promiscuously. Neither is this laid to their charge, that they called out such and such subjects, though we may perceive by the story of the prophets, that the greater part of the body of the people were wicked, &c.

We answer to these two instances jointly. 1. We may by the like reason prove, that which is as yet uncontroverted (we know not how long), that we ought at no time to make choice of instruments, neither in case of prosecution of the cause and the invasion of others, nor yet in the time when choice is to be had, and so, that all our former engagements, resolutions, and proceedings, in the point of purging judicatories and armies, was superfluous and supererogatory, because we read not that the reforming kings and judges, whenever they had an invasive war, and in the times that they had greatest plenty and multitudes of people, did ever debar any of their subjects from that service, but called them out promiscuously. Neither is this laid to their charge, though we may perceive that the greater part of the people were wicked under the best kings. Therefore we may lawfully employ any subjects of the kingdom in any of our wars. And we may look upon all indifferently, without any discerning of persons that fear God and them that fear him not, as in good capacity to be intrusted, even when otherwise we have choice of good instruments. Certainly it follows, by parity of reason. For if you conclude that, from the calling forth all promiscuously, and no reproof given for it, in the case of necessary defence, then we may conclude, from the calling forth of all promiscuously, and in the case of an invasive war, and no reproof recorded, that neither, in such a case, is it sinful to make no difference, and that with strong reason, because it being more easy in such a case to choose instruments, and no necessity pleading for it, if it had been sinful, the prophets would have rather reproved it, then rebuked them for using such means in a case of necessity. 2. We may argue after that manner, that in the case of necessary just defence, there should be no exceptions made at all of any persons, because we read not that the judges or kings debarred any subjects, neither that they were rebuked for so doing. Therefore the instances militate as much against the exceptions added in the answer to the query, as against us, unless it be said that there were no such persons among that people, which were as groundless rashness as to say that they gave all evidence of repentance. 3. Seeing the judges and the reforming kings of Judah were so accurate and exact in cleaving to the law of God, and walking according to it in all other things, it were more charitable and Christian judgment to say, that since they are not reproved for any fault in this particular, that they were also exact to walk according to the rule, (Deut. xxiii.) in so great a point as this. 4. Men's practice is often lame and crooked, and therefore must be examined according to the rule, but it were not fair dealing to accommodate the rule to men's practice. Seeing then we have so clear and perfect a rule (Deut. xxiii.), which must judge both their practice and ours, we see not how their practice can be obtruded as a rule upon us, which itself must be examined according to a common and general rule. If it be not according to that law, we hold it to be sinful in itself, and so no precedent for us; albeit the prophets did not reprove it in express and particular terms (as they did not reprove man stealing, &c.), yet they rebuked it by consequence, in as far as they rebuked the kings for association with wicked Israelites, which is condemned upon grounds common to this very case in hand. 5. We see not any ground for such promiscuous calling forth of the people by the judges. Barak's business, as that of Jephthah and Gideon, was done by no great multitudes of people, but a few choice men. 6. As the oppression was heavy and continued long, so the repentance of the people was solemn, and their deliverance a fruit of this. 7. Their case and ours is very different. None of Israel or Judah did fight against the profession of the true religion, and shed the blood of their fellow subjects who were for the defence of the same. Israel in the days of the judges, and Judah in the time of the reforming kings, was not divided the one half against the other, upon opposition and defence of the true religion, and the better part, after many experiences of the treachery and enmity of the most of the worst part, solemnly engaged to God not to admit them to employment and trust, but upon real evidence of repentance of which they should judge as in the sight of God. And last of all, did ever Israel or Judah, in the days of their judges and reforming kings, admit into their armies a party and faction of such as had given no real evidence of their abandoning their former course, and such a party, as had been long studying to get the power of armies and judicatories in their own hands for attaining their own ends? But all those are in our case.

The third instance from scripture, is from 1 Sam. xi., which is alleged to be a clear practice, and stamped with divine approbation. In the case of Jabesh-Gilead besieged by a foreign enemy, Saul commands all to come forth for defence of their brethren, under pain of a severe civil censure. Now, what Saul did in this business, the Spirit of God is said to act him to it, and what the people did, was from the fear of God, making them obey the king. And then Samuel in this acting concurs jointly, and makes no opposition. And last of all, the people came forth as one man, and yet (chap. x. 27) many men of Belial were among them, who malignantly opposed Saul's government, contrary to God's revealed will.

To which we answer, 1. The stamp of divine approbation is not apparent to us, success doth not prove it. Neither the Spirit coming on Saul, nor the fear of God falling on the people, will import a divine approbation of all that was done in the managing that war. That motion of the Spirit is no sanctifying motion, but a common, though extraordinary, impulse of Saul's spirit to the present work, which, doubtless, was in the king of Babylon, whom God raised up, fitted and sent for the destruction of many nations albeit that work in his hand was iniquity. That fear of God that fell upon the people, was but a fear of the king imprinted by God, and it is more peculiarly attributed to God, because the people did despise and contemn him, which makes their reverence and fear to be a more extraordinary thing upon a sudden. Then Samuel, not opposing the course in hand, doth no more import his approbation of all that was done in it, than his not reproving the men of Belial doth prove that he approved of their opposition. 2. It doth not appear that the men of Belial were a great faction and party, there is something in ver. 12 speaks against it. It is not like the people would put a faction and party to death. 3. Neither doth it appear that they were in the army. For that which is said, that all the people came out as one man, doth only import, that the body and generality of them came forth, and that it was a wonder so many came forth so suddenly at the command of the king, who was but mean and abject in their eyes. It is certain that all fencible persons were not present, because the whole army being numbered, ver. 8, was but 330,000. And who will say there was no more men in Israel, when they had 600,000 such, and above, before their coming into the land? Seeing then, many have staid at home, it is most probable that these men of Belial would not come, seeing they despised Saul's mean and low condition in their heart and thought him unfit to lead their armies, till he should prove what was in him. That which is said, ver. 12, doth not prove they were in the camp. It might be conveniently spoken of absent persons. 4. It is not certain that these men were wicked and scandalous in their conversation, haters of godliness and of their brethren, but that they stood at distance only with Saul, in the point of his election, which indeed was blame worthy, seeing God had revealed his mind in it. And therefore they are called men of Belial, as Peter was called Satan, for opposing Christ's suffering.

Some other scriptures are alleged by some, as David's employing of such men, &c., all which are cleared in Mr. Gillespie's Treatise of Miscellany Questions, quest. 14.

Third. It is argued from reason. And, 1. That which any is obliged to do for another's preservation by the law of God and nature, and which he cannot omit without the guilt of the other's destruction, that may the other lawfully require of him to do when he needs it, and when it may be done without the undoing of a greater good. But so it is, that every subject is obliged by the law of nature, oath and covenants, and the law of God, to endeavour to their power, the preservation of the kingdom against unjust violence. And the safety of the kingdom stands in need of many subjects' assistance who were secluded. And it may be done without undoing a greater good than is the preservation of religion. *Ergo.*

This argument hath an answer to it in the bosom of it. (1) We shortly deny the assumption, in relation to the two last branches, both that the kingdom's preservation stands in necessity of these men's help, and that their help tends not to the undoing of a greater good, seeing there is no reason given to confirm these two points, wherein the nerve of the business lies. We refer to a reason of our denial of them given p. 22.[382] (2) It is true that the obligation to such a duty lies upon all, but that obligation is to be brought into act and exercise in an orderly and qualified way, else what need any exceptions be in the act of levy? Excommunicated persons are under the same obligation, yet the magistrate is not actually obliged to call such, but rather to seclude them. Are not all bound to come to the sacrament who are church members? Yet many are not in a capacity to come, and so ought neither to presume to come nor be admitted. Are not all subjects obliged to defend the cause of God, and to prosecute it? And yet many, because of their enmity to the cause of God, are actually incapable of employment in the defence or prosecution thereof. (3) The law of nature is above all human laws and constitutions, they must cede whenever they come in opposition to it. *Salus populi* is *suprema lex*[383] in relation to these. But, in relation to the law of God, it is not so. Sometimes the law of nature must yield to positive commands of God. Abraham must sacrifice his son at God's command. The law of nature obliges us to the preservation of ourselves, but it does not oblige to every mean that may be found expedient to that end, unless it be supposed lawful and approven of God. Therefore the Lord in his written word doth determine what means we may use for that end, and what not. But, (4) We conceive that the law forbidding association and confederacy with known wicked and ungodly persons, is included in the law of nature, as well as the law that obliges us to self preservation. That is grounded on perpetual reason, as well as this. Nature bids me preserve myself, and nature binds me to have one friend and foe with God. The heathens had a notion of it. They observed, that Amphiaraus, a wise and virtuous man, was therefore swallowed up in the earth with seven men and seven horses, because he had joined himself and associated with Tydeus, Capaneus, and other wicked commanders marching to the siege of Thebe. Mr Gill. Miscell. Quest. chap. 14 p. 171.[384]

2. The second reason is framed thus *in hypothesi.*[385] Such as are excluded are a great part, if not the greater part of the remnant of the land, if rules of exclusion be extended impartially. Now, they having their lives and liberties allowed them, must either in these things be insured by the interposing of a competent power for their defence, or else they must have liberty to act for themselves. But so it is, that we cannot interpose a competent power for their protection. *Ergo*, They must have liberty to act for themselves. *Nam qui dat vitam dat necessaria ad vitam.*[386]

We answer, (1) It is not certain that such as are excluded are the greater part of the land. However, it is certain, that though the rule had been kept, and endeavours had been used to walk according to it, yet many whom it excludes would have been taken in. There is a great difference between endeavour of duty, and attaining its perfection. If the rule had not been quite destroyed, so great offence could not have been taken, though it had not been strictly urged in all particulars. (2) We still affirm, upon evident grounds to us, that there is a power competent in the land, beside the malignant party, which may protect the land and insure their lives and liberties. (3)[387] We are persuaded many of that party, who have been so deeply involved in blood guiltiness and barbarous cruelties should neither have lives nor liberties secured to them, because they ought not to be permitted to live. But the not taking away so much guilty blood from the land by acts of justice, is the cause that so much innocent and precious blood is now shed. Our rulers have pardoned that blood which God would not pardon, and therefore would not pardon it to the land because they pardoned it to the murderers.

SECTION IV.

That It Is Not Lawful For The Well Affected Subjects To Concur In Such An Engagement In War, And Associate With The Malignant Party.

Some convinced of the unlawfulness of the public resolutions and proceedings, in reference to the employing of the malignant party, yet do not find such clearness and satisfaction in their own consciences as to forbid the subjects to concur in this war, and associate with the army so constituted. Therefore it is needful to speak something to this point, That it is as unlawful for the subjects to associate and join in arms with that party as it is for the parliament to employ them. For these reasons:

1. The scriptures before cited against associations and confederacies with wicked and ungodly men do prove this. The command prohibiting conjunction with them and conversing, &c. is common both to magistrates and people, for the ground of it is common to both—The people's insnaring, helping of the ungodly, &c. It were strange doctrine to say, that it is not lawful for the parliament to associate in war with the malignants, lest the people be insnared and yet it is lawful for the people to associate with them upon the command of the parliament, seeing the insnaring of the people hath a more immediate connexion with the people's conjunction with them nor[388] with the parliament's resolution about it. Had it not been a transgression in all the people to have joined with these men before the parliament's resolution about it? How then can their resolution intervening loose the people from their obligation to God's command? Shall it be no sin to me, because they sin before me? Can their going before me in the transgression, exempt me from the transgression of that same law which obliges both them and me? 2. The people were reproved for such associations as well as rulers, though they originated from the rulers. The prophets speak to the whole body. "What hast thou to do in the way of Egypt?" &c. Jer. ii. 18. And Isa. xxxi. "Wo

to them that go down to Egypt." Psal. cvi. "They mingled themselves," &c. The Lord instructed Isaiah, and in him all his own people, all the children whom God had given him, saying, "Say ye not, A confederacy, to all them to whom this people shall say, A confederacy," Isa. viii. 12. When all the people were going on in such a mean of self defence, the Lord instructed him and the disciples among whom the testimony was sealed, that they should not walk in the way of this people. When Jehoshaphat was reproved for helping the ungodly, were not all his people reproved that went with him? They were the helpers of the ungodly as well as he. If Amaziah had refused to dismiss the army of Israel whom God was not with, doubtless it had been the subject's duty to testify against it, and refuse to concur and act in such a fellowship.

3. If the association and conjunction with malignants be only the sin of the parliament, and not the sin of the people, who do upon their command associate with them, then we cannot see how people can be guilty of association with malignants at any time, and in any case. To join with them in an ill cause is not lawful indeed. But neither may we join with good men in an evil cause. Suppose then the cause be good and necessary (as no war is just if it be not necessary), in what case or circumstances shall association with them be unlawful for the people? If it be said, in case the magistrate command it not, we think that strange divinity, that the sole command of the magistrate should make that our duty, which in absence of his command is our sin, and that not because of the absence of his command but from other perpetual grounds. Certainly, whenever association with them is a sin, it is not that which makes it a sin, because the magistrate commands it not, but because God forbids it. And it is as strange, that the unlawful and sinful resolution of parliament should make that lawful to me which otherwise had been unlawful. It is known that human laws oblige not, but as they have connexion with God's word. Now if that law, enjoining a confluence of all subjects for the defence of the kingdom, be contrary to the word, in as far as it holds out a conjunction with malignant and bloody men, how can it be lawful to me, in obedience to that ordinance, to associate with these men? If it be said

to be lawful in the case of necessity, that same necessity is as strong a plea for the magistrate's employing them, as for the people's joining with them, and if it do not justify that, it cannot excuse this. If the lawfulness of the mean must be measured by the justice and necessity of the end, then certainly any mean shall be lawful in the case of just and necessary defence, then we may employ Irish cut throats, then we may go to the devil for help, if expediency to compass such a necessary and just end be the rule of the lawfulness of the mean.

4. The whole land is bound by the covenant and solemn engagement not to associate with the malignant party. *Ergo*, It is as sinful for the people to join with them as for the magistrate to employ them. Are we not all bound by covenant, to endeavour to bring malignants to condign punishment, and to look on them as enemies? And is not conjunction and confederacy with them, on the people's part, as inconsistent in its own nature with that duty, as the magistrate's employing them is inconsistent with his covenanted duty? When all the people did solemnly engage themselves not to join any more with the people of these abominations, was the meaning of it, we shall not join until our rulers join first, or, we shall not join with them in an ill cause? No indeed, but, we shall not employ them in a good cause, or join with any party of them in it. If that engagement be upon every one in their station, let us consider what every man's station in the work is. The ruler's station and calling is to choose instruments, and levy forces for the defence thereof. The subjects station and calling is, to concur in that work, by rising in defence of the cause and kingdom. Now, what did the subject then engage unto? Certainly, unless we mock God, we must say, that as the magistrate engaged not to employ that ungodly generation in a good cause, so the subject engaged not to join with any such party even in a good cause. If this be not the meaning of our engagements and vows, we see not how the subjects are in capacity to break them, as to that precise point of association.

In sum, All the reasons that are brought to prove the unlawfulness of the public resolutions, may with a little variation be proportionably applied to this present question. Therefore we add no more but a word to an objection or two.

Objection 1. A necessary duty, such as self preservation is, cannot be my sin. But it is the subject's necessary duty to rise in defence of the kingdom. *Ergo,*

Answer. A necessary duty cannot be a sin in itself, but it may be a sin in regard of some circumstances, in which it ceases to be a necessary duty. It is a necessary duty to defend the kingdom. But it is neither a duty nor necessary to do it in such a conjunction and fellowship, but rather a sin. If I cannot preserve myself, but by an unlawful mean, then self preservation in such circumstances is not my duty.

Objection 2. Jonathan did assist Saul in a war against the Philistines invading the land, and no doubt many godly joined and died in battle. Now this is commended in scripture, as may be seen in David's funeral[389] upon them, although it was known that Saul was an hater of God's people and a persecutor, and that God had a controversy with him, and that these 3,000 that assisted him against David were also ungodly and wicked men.

Answer 1. These scriptures speak nothing to commend that particular act of Jonathan's conjunction in war with his father. David in his epitaph speaks much to the commendation of both Saul and Jonathan, as of excellent warriors, and of Jonathan as a kind and constant friend to him, but there is nothing touched of that point. If that place be pressed, it will follow with much more evidence, that Saul was as good a man as Jonathan, and that the people of God had great loss in his death. But none of these must be pressed rigorously from a speech wherein he vents his affection and grief. 2. Suppose the natural bond of Jonathan to Saul his father, and the civil bonds of the people to Saul their king, did oblige them to join with him against the common enemy, yet we think they ought not to have associated with these persecuting servants, and the 3,000 that pursued David, but they ought to have pleaded for a purging of the army. 3. It is not probable that there were many godly persons employed in that army. David complains of that time, (Psal. xii.) that the godly man ceased, and the faithful from among the children of men and that the wicked walked round about when the vilest men were exalted. 4. Many of the laws of God have not been much taken notice of, even by godly men, until the Lord hath taken occasion to reprove them particularly, and so to mind[390] them of their duty. It is likely the rule, (Deut. xxiii.) had not been considered till the time of Jehoshaphat and Amaziah.[391] However it be, they had not so many solemn and particular ties of oaths, and covenants, and vows, and confessions, as we have lying on us. 5. Let no man wonder that such particular escapes are not always reproved in scripture, who considers that the fathers' polygamy, though so frequent among them, was not laid to their charge.

Objection 3. Separation from the army, because of the sin of magistrates, in employing such unqualified persons, is paralleled to separation from church worship, because of the sin of the false worshippers, and because the guides of the church do not exclude them. *Answer 1.* We have particular commands about this, and many examples of it, which we have not about separation from a true church, and lawful worship. Union and conjunction with an enemy renders conjunction, and their fellowship, more dangerous and infectious than conjunction in a church state. Judah might not separate from these Israelites in lawful ordinances, or from the ordinance [because] of their presence. And yet they might not help them nor take help from them. Paul did not exhort any to separate from the worship at Corinth, because of the presence of scandalous persons at it and yet he charges them not to converse with such brethren as walk disorderly. Notwithstanding of union in church and state, we may look on many as such as should not be joined with in some other bonds. It is not lawful for a godly man to marry a profane woman, though a visible professor, he may not join in such a tie, although he ought not to separate from church worship for her presence. *Besides*, there is a conjunction in arms for one cause, as necessarily makes men partakers of the same blessings and cursings, and therefore we should give the more diligent heed, when we partake with them in lawful things. 3. Are we all tied, by such particular oaths and solemn vows, not to join with the scandalous persons of a congregation in lawful worship, as we are, not to associate with the malignant party in the defence of the cause of God, and kingdom? It cannot be said. Therefore the cases are not paralleled.

We shall close all with a testimony of one of the Lord's most faithful witnesses, Mr. Gillespie, whose light in this case was once very seasonably held forth, and effectual to the preventing of the declining of this land and we hope it will not be wholly forgotten by them, with whom it had weight then. In his letter to the General Assembly, 1648, he sayeth, "I am not able to express all the evils of compliance, they are so many. Sure I am, it were a hardening of the malignant party, a wounding of the hearts of the godly, a great scandal to our brethren of England, an infinite wronging of those who, from their affection to the covenant and cause of God, have taken their life in their hand, who, as they have been strengthened and encouraged, by the hearing of the zeal and integrity of the well affected in this kingdom, and how they oppose the late Engagement, so they would be as much scandalized to hear of a compliance with malignants now. Yea, all that hear of it may justly stand amazed at us, and look on us as a people infatuated, that can take in our bosom the fiery serpents, that have stung us so sore. But above all, that which would heighten these sins to the heavens is this, that it were not only a horrible backsliding, but a backsliding into that very sin, which was especially pointed at, and punished by the prevalency of the malignant party, God justly making them thorns and scourges, who were taken in as friends, without any real evidence, or fruits of repentance. Alas! shall we split twice upon this same rock, yea, run upon it, when God has set a beacon on it? Shall we be so demented as to fall back to the same sin, which was engraven in great letters in our late judgment? Yea, I may say, shall we thus out face and out dare the Almighty, by protecting his and our enemies, when he is persecuting them, by making peace and friendship with them, when the anger of the Lord is burning against them, by setting them on their feet, when God hath cast them down? O! shall neither judgments nor deliverances make us wise? I must here apply to our condition the words of Ezra, 'And after all this is come upon us for our evil deeds, and for our great trespasses, seeing that thou our God hast punished us less than our iniquities deserve, and hath given such deliverance us this, should we again break thy commandments, and join in affinity with the people of these abominations, wouldest thou not be angry with us till thou hast consumed us, so that there should be no remnant nor escaping?' O happy Scotland! if thou canst now improve aright, and not abuse this golden opportunity, but if thou wilt help the ungodly, or love them that hate the Lord, wrath upon wrath, and woe upon woe, shall be upon thee from the Lord.

"This testimony of a dying man (who expects to stand shortly before the tribunal of Christ) I leave with you my reverend brethren," &c. And again in his Testimony against association and compliance with malignants, written two days before his death, he says, "Seeing now, in all appearance, the time of my dissolution is very near, although I have, in my latter will, declared my mind of public affairs, yet I have thought good to add this further testimony, that I esteem the malignant party in these kingdoms the seed of the serpent, enemies to piety, and Presbyterian government, (pretend what they will to the contrary,) a generation that have not set God before them. With the malignants are to be joined the profane and scandalous, from all which, as also from heresies, and errors, the Lord I trust is about to purge his churches. I have often comforted myself, and still do, with the hopes of the Lord's purging of this polluted land, surely the Lord has begun, and will carry on that great work of mercy, and will purge out the rebels. I know there will be always a mixture of hypocrites, but that cannot excuse the conniving at gross and scandalous sinners. This purging work, which the Lord is about, very many have directly opposed, and said, by their deeds, we will not be purged nor refined, but we will be joining, and mixing ourselves with those whom the ministers preach against, as malignant enemies to God and his cause. But let him that is filthy, be filthy still, and let wisdom be justified of her children. I recommend to them that fear God, sadly and seriously to consider, that the Holy Scripture doth plainly hold forth, 1. That the helping of the enemies of God, or joining and mingling with wicked men, is a sin highly displeasing. 2. That this sin hath ordinarily insnared God's people into divers other sins. 3. That it hath been punished of God with grievous judgments. 4. That utter destruction is to be feared, when a people, after great mercies and judgments, relapse into this sin, Ezra ix. 13, 14. Upon the said and the like grounds, for my own exoneration, that so necessary a truth want not the testimony of a dying witness of Christ, also the unworthiest of many thousands, and that light may be held forth, and warning given, I cannot be silent at this time, but speak by my pen, when I cannot by my tongue; yea, now also by the pen of another, when I cannot by my own; seriously and in the name of Jesus Christ, exhorting all that fear God, and make conscience of their ways, to be very tender and circumspect, to watch and pray that they be not insnared in that great dangerous sin of conjunction, or compliance with malignant or profane enemies of the truth, under whatsomever prudential considerations it may be varnished over, which if men will do, and trust God in his own way, they shall not only not repent it, but to their greater joy and peace of God's people, they shall see his work go on, and prosper gloriously. In witness to the premises, I have subscribed the same with my hand at Kirkaldy,[392] December 15th, 1648. Mr. Frederick Carmichael,[393] at Markinch, and Mr. Alex Moncreiff,[394] minister at Scoonie,

Sic Sub.
GEORGE GILLESPIE.
F. C. *Witness*
A. M. *Witness*

SECTION V.

Scriptures Showing The Sin And Danger Of Joining With Wicked And Ungodly Men.

When the Lord is punishing such a people against whom he hath a controversy, and a notable controversy, every one that is found shall be thrust through: and every one joined with them shall fall, Isa. xiii. 15. They partake in their judgment, not only because in a common calamity all shares, (as in Ezek. xxi. 3.) but chiefly because joined with and partakers with these whom God is pursuing; even as the strangers that join to the house of Jacob partake of her blessings, chap. xiv. 1. To this purpose is Isa. xxxi. 2, 3, and Ezek. xxx. 5, 6, 8. The mingled people and those that are in league with Egypt partake in her plagues, and those that uphold that throne that God so visibly controverts with, their power shall come down, and all its helpers shall be destroyed, as it is Jer. xxi. 12, 20, 24. And this is the great reason of these many warnings to go out of Babylon, Jer. l. 8. and li. 6. Remember that passage, 2 Kings i. 9, 10, 11, 12. The captain and messenger of the king speaks but a word in obedience to his wicked master's command, and the fifty are but with him, and speak not: but their master's judgment comes on them all.

Consider how many testimonies the wise king, in his Proverbs, gives against it. Chap. i. from ver. 10, to 19. "My son, if sinners entice thee, consent thou not. If they say, Come with us, let us lay wait for blood, let us lurk privily for the innocent without cause. Let us swallow them up alive as the grave, and whole as those that go down into the pit. We shall find all precious substance, we shall fill our houses with spoil. Cast in thy lot among us, let us all have one purse. My son, walk not thou in the way with them; refrain thy foot from their path. For their feet run to evil, and make haste to shed blood," &c. Here are the practices and designs of wicked men expressed in their own nature. But certainly they would colour them over with fair pretences. Their purpose is to undo men, especially godly men that classed and purged them. Yea, it is the profession of many, and they scarce lie privily, or have so much wisdom as to conceal their designs till their fit opportunity, but before the power be confirmed in their hand, they breathe out cruelty against all the innocent in the land, and promise themselves great gain by it, and are already dividing their estates among them, saying we "shall find all precious substance," ver. 13. But, my son, if thou fear God, though they entice thee with specious arguments of nature, and necessity, and country privileges, yet consent not. Venture not thy stock in one vessel with them. Cast not in thy lot among them. "Walk not in the way with them: refrain thy foot from their path:" for they are not come to the height of iniquity, they are running on to it. And if thou join, thou wilt cast thyself in a miserable snare; for either thou must go on with them to their designed and professed evils, or be exposed to their cruelty.

Chap. ii. from ver. 10. to the end. "When wisdom entereth into thine heart, and knowledge is pleasant to thy soul; discretion shall preserve thee, understanding shall keep thee to deliver thee from the way of the evil man, from the man that speaketh froward things, who leave the paths of uprightness, to walk in the ways of darkness," &c. If thou take the word of God for a lamp to thy feet, and it enter into thy soul, and be received in love and affection, it will certainly keep thee from the evil men's way, who have already left the righteous paths to walk in the ways of darkness, who rejoice in nothing so much as in the sorrows and miseries of the godly, and delight in one another's wickedness. And it will keep thee chaste to thy husband Christ Jesus, and preserve thee from committing fornications with Egypt as Aholah and Aholibah, and joining so nearly with the degenerated seed of Abraham, who are but as strangers. For come near their house and paths, and they will lead thee to destruction with them or make thee a more miserable life. But these that go to them return not again quickly. They are like fallen stars. Shall they ever be set in the firmament again? It is safest to walk with good and righteous men, for God's blessing and promise is on them. His curse and threatening is on the wicked. Therefore thou may fear wrath on that account, if thou join with them.

Chap. iv. ver. 14-20 "Enter not into the path of the wicked, and go not in the way of evil men. Avoid it, pass not by it, turn from it, and pass away. For they sleep not except they have done mischief, and their sleep is taken away except they cause some to fall. For they eat the bread of wickedness, and drink the wine of violence. But the path of the just is as the shining light, that shineth more and more unto the perfect day. The way of the wicked is as darkness, and they know not at what they stumble." It was said, chap. iii. 23, that the man who keeps wisdom and the fear of God in his heart, should walk in the way and not stumble. That safety hath ease in it here. Their steps are not straitened, as when a man walks in steep and hazardous places, who cannot choose but it will be. If a man enter into the path of wicked men, he must either go along in their way with them, and then it is broad indeed, or, if he think to keep a good conscience in it, he will be pinched and straitened. Therefore it is most free for the mind and conscience to avoid and pass by that way "for they sleep not," &c. They will never be satisfied till they have done a mischief, they will live upon the ruins of the poor country. And how wilt thou join in that? Or how can thou eschew it, if thou walk with them? If it were no more, it is a suspected by path, that thou never travelled into. O pass by it, or, if thou be entered, turn out of it. If thou wilt enter upon the apprehension of some light and duty in it, know that it is but evening, the sun is setting, and thou wilt be benighted ere it be long, and thou shalt stumble then, and not know whereupon, even on that, thou seest not now and thinkest to eschew and pass by. Then from ver. 23, to the end, "Keep thy heart with all diligence, for out of it are the issues of life, &c." Except thou keep thy heart and whole man, thou cannot escape falling into some temptation. O keep thy heart diligently on the knowledge and lore of the truth. Take heed to thy words. Look not a squint but directly to that which is good. Give not a squint look to any unlawful course, for the necessity or utility, it may be that seems to attend it. But look straight on, and ponder well the way thou walkest in, that thou run to no extremity either to one parte or other, that thou walk in the middle way between profanity and error. Thou heldest these ways hitherto for extremes. Ponder, I beseech thee, then, before thou walkest in any of them. See whether they be really come to thee, or thou to them. Mark who is changed.

Chap. v. 8 to the 15. "Remove thy way far from her, and come not near the door of her house, lest thou give thine honour unto others, and thy years unto the cruel. Lest strangers be filled with thy wealth, and thy labours be in the house of a stranger. And thou mourn at last when thy flesh and thy body are consumed, and say, How have I hated instruction, and my heart despised reproof, and have not obeyed the voice of my teachers, nor inclined mine ear to them that instructed me! &c." If thou would be safe from snares, remove from the way and house of the strange woman. Thou must fall in Aholah and Aholibah's whoredoms (Ezek. xxiii.) except thou come not near them. If thou keep not from that assembly and congregation, thou shall be "almost in all evil." If thou join with them, thou cannot but partake of their sins and plagues; and so thou shalt say after, when thou cannot well mend it, "I was near gone, my steps almost gone," and all the assembly of his people shall witness to it.

Chap. vi. 16, 17, 18, 24, 25. "These six things doth the Lord hate, yea seven are an abomination unto him. A proud look, a lying tongue, and hands that shed innocent blood, an heart that deviseth wicked imaginations, feet that be swift in running to mischief. To keep thee from the strange woman, from the flattery of the tongue of a strange woman. Lust not after her beauty in thine heart, neither let her take thee with her eye lids." This describes both our enemies, the malignant party and the sectarian. Pride, violence, cruelty, lying, is the very character of the one. Flattery, beauty of pretended religion, false witnessing and charging of the Lord's people, and seeking to sow discord among these that were one in heart and work, is the character of the other. Now, keep thee from both these abominations, and do not think it is in thy power not to be infected with the contagion of their fellowship. "Can a man take fire in his bosom and his clothes not be burnt? Can one go on hot coals and not burn his feet?" So whoever associates and goes in friendly to either of them "shall not be innocent," ver. 27, 28, 29.

Chap. vii. 14, &c. "I have peace offerings with me, this day have I paid my vows." They pretend religion on both sides. And our church says, the malignants have satisfied them, and repented, even like the peace offerings and vows of the whore. She began with her devotion, that she might with more liberty sin more, and have that pretence to cover it, and by means of her offerings, she got a feast of the flesh, even as they by profession of repentance are admitted to trust, and by offering for the like sin, a new sin is covered, and vows undertaken never to be kept. Therefore take heed of these snares. "For she hath cast down many strong," ver. 26. Many a tall cedar hath fallen by that fellowship. It is the way to hell, ver. 27. See chap. viii. 13.

Chap. x. shows us the very different estate of the godly and wicked, both in regard of light and knowledge concerning duty, and of blessings promised. Ver. 6, 9, 11, 20, 23. "Blessings are upon the head of the just, but violence covereth the mouth of the wicked. He that walketh uprightly, walketh surely, but he that perverteth his ways, shall be known. The mouth of a righteous man is a well of life, but violence covereth the mouth of the wicked. The tongue of the just is as choice silver, the heart of the wicked is little worth. It is as a sport to a fool to do mischief but a man of understanding hath wisdom," &c. Ver. 24, 25, 28, 31, 32, which show us, that if the Lord's mind be revealed to any concerning the present courses, it must be to his poor people that wait on him, and not to all the wicked and ungodly in the land, who almost only are satisfied and clear in the course, who yet before were never satisfied. And beside, though the Lord be chastising his people, yet one may join with them without fear of wrath and indignation on that account, and with hope of partaking of their blessings, when he cannot and dare not join with a wicked party pursued with wrath and indignation in the same dispensation, which may be more clear from chap. xi. 3, 5, 8. "The integrity of the upright shall guide them, but the perverseness of transgressors shall destroy them. The righteousness of the perfect shall direct his way, but the wicked shall fall by his own wickedness. The righteous is delivered out of trouble, and the wicked cometh in his stead." And verses 10, 11, show the different condition of people under wicked rulers and godly. All the wicked now rejoice. None shouts but they. They think their day is come. The godly generally hang their head and are discountenanced, even as Psal. xii. The 21 and 31 verses show, that when godly men are chastised and punished in the earth for their sins, "much more the wicked," especially when the godly were chastised for partaking with them, according to 1 Pet. iv 17, 18, Isa. x 12, and xlix. 26.

Chap. xii. 13. "They are snared by the transgression of their lips." Their ordinary common speeches they drop out with, declare them, and make their cause, more hateful than other pretences, it is covered with, would permit. Yea, they speak like the piercings of a sword, against the godly, ver. 18. If our state and church had a lip of truth, they would speak always the same thing. They would not carry in their talk and writings, as now every common understanding perceives. We may find their writings made up of contradictions. For "a lying tongue is but for a moment," ver. 19. It is but for a moment indeed before the judicatory; and then out of doors it contradicts itself, as in the mock repentances. But sorrow and anguish will come to these, who before they would speak of terms of peace with one enemy, would associate in war with another. "But to the counsellors of peace is joy," ver. 20. The present course contradicts this. Ver. 26. "The righteous is more excellent than his neighbour: but the way of the wicked seduceth them." They think these malignants better than the west country forces. They would condescend to any terms to get their help, though it were to reverse the Act of Classes,[395] to give them indemnity, yea, not so much as to condemn their way: but they will not so much as clear the state of the quarrel, or choose a better general[396] for all their help. Their way seems good in their own eyes, ver. 15. But it were wisdom to hearken to the counsel of the godly.

Chap. xiii. 10. "Only by pride cometh contention, but with the well-advised is wisdom." There is nothing keepeth up our contention and wars but pride: no party will condescend to another. We will not say we have done wrong in bringing in the king. They will not say they have done wrong in invading. But it were wisdom to fall lower and quit those interests. Ver. 16. "Every prudent man dealeth with knowledge: but a fool layeth open his folly." A wise man would count before the war, if he can accomplish it: and if he cannot, then he would send messengers of peace, and cede in all things he may without sin. If it be but more honour and wealth to our king,[397] should we destroy the kingdom to purchase that? Our rash and abrupt proceedings show our folly. Ver. 20. "He that walketh with wise men shall be wise: but a companion of fools shall be destroyed." A man will be, must be, assimilated to his company, and then partake of their judgment or blessings.

Chap. xiv. He that is accustomed to speak truth in private, will in his common speech be a faithful witness in public: but a man accustomed to lying, dissembling, swearing in private, will not stick to forswear himself, to make professions and vows contrary to his mind in public, ver. 5. (and also chap. xii. 17. and vi. 19.) Such men seek wisdom and make a show of religion, but find it not; whereas it is easy to godly men to find it, to find repentance and salvation, ver. 6. Go away from foolish men, and break off society with ungodly men. Be not privy to their counsels. Use them not as special friends, when thou perceivest that all means are used in vain to reclaim them from their damnable way and principles, ver. 7. The knowledge a godly man hath serves to direct his way, and is given of God for it. But all the wit and skill of such wicked men is deceit. They themselves are beguiled by it in opinion, and practice, and hope. And they also beguile others, ver. 8. Sin makes fools agree: but among the righteous, that which is good makes agreement (in the old translation[398]), ver. 9. It is only evil will unite all the wicked in the land as one man. For it is a sport to them to do mischief, chap. x. 23. Albeit our way seem right in our eyes, yet because it is a backsliding way, and departing from unquestionably right rules, the end will be death, and we will be filled with our own devices. O! it shall be bitter in the belly of all godly men when they have eaten it, ver. 12, 14. and chap. i. 31. "The simple believeth every word;" giveth credit to every vain word that is spoken. But a prudent man looketh well to men's goings, ponders and examines whether their professions and practices agree, what weight is in their words, by the inspection of their deeds, and of their ordinary speaking, and does not account a coined word before a judicatory sufficient to testify repentance. And as he gives not present credit to their professions, who have so often proven treacherous, so he himself scares at every appearance of evil, and keeps himself from it; whereas foolish souls rage and are confident, think any thing lawful if they can have any pretence for it, or use of it, ver. 15, 16. Then, what a great difference is between wicked men and godly men, both in their lot, when God is correcting both, and in their disposition! Wisdom that rests in the one's heart, is manifested; wickedness in the other's heart appears also. In the midst of such men there is no other thing, ver. 32, 33.

Chap. xv. 8, ("The sacrifice of the wicked is an abomination to the Lord; but the prayer of the upright is his delight,") expresses how provoking a thing the outward professions and sacrifices of wicked men, continuing in their wickedness; what an abomination that commonly called public repentance, or ecclesiastical holiness is, when men are visibly unholy and ungodly in their conversation. And therefore he pleaded always with that people, that his soul abhorred their external ceremonies, because of the uncleanness of their hands. He pleaded that he never commanded them, though indeed he did command them. Yet those were aberrations and departings from the express rule and command,—to accept or be pleased with these sacrifices and ceremonies,—when there was no evidence of real repentance. To this purpose are chap. xxi. 4, 27; Isa. i. 11; and lxvi. 3; Jer. vi. 20; and vii. 22; Amos v. 22,—all which show that it is but a mocking of the Lord, and perverting of his law, and profaning of his ordinances, to accept the profession of repentance in those who walk contrary thereto, and to count them ecclesiastically holy enough, who say, they repent, though a thousand actions witness the contrary. Of such the Lord says, "What hast thou to do to take my covenant in thy mouth, seeing thou hatest to be reformed?" Psal. l. 16, 17. They have no right to it. They should not be admitted to it for it is a taking the Lord's name in vain. The 16th verse tells us, that it had been better to possess our own land in quietness than to venture what we have for the uncertain conquest of England, and restitution of the king parallel with Eccl. iv. 8.

Chap. xvi. 7. "When a man's ways please the Lord he maketh even his enemies to be at peace with him." Can our States[399] way then please the Lord, seeing they cannot find the way of peace,—they will not walk in it, and seeing they make the godly in the land to fall out with them, and none to be at peace but the wicked, who may thereby get opportunity to crush the godly? Ver. 17 "The highway of the upright is to depart from evil." This is the highway only, to depart from evil, not carnal policies, nor advantages. He thinks the stepping aside to any of these is not the highway. Can then men change their way, and go cross to it and keep the right way in both? No, the godly have this high way and keep it. Chap. xvii. 11. "An evil man seeketh only rebellion, therefore a cruel messenger shall be sent against him." Evil men seek only rebellion, and delight in no other thing. But the King of kings shall send a cruel messenger, he arms men with wrath and power against them. Ver. 13, speaketh sadly to the English, and to our State, that rewarded the west country evil for good. Ver. 14, 19, tell us how we should advise before we begin a war, and leave no mean of composing difference and state unessayed. We did more in it than the English, but not all we might have done. Ver. 15, with chap. xviii. 5, is a dreadful sentence against the public judicatories, that all their resolutions, papers, and practices, justify the wicked and ungodly as honest faithful men, and condemn all approven faithful men, that cannot go along in such courses, or were earnest to have them repent, as both malignants and sectaries. Do they not pronounce all malignants friends, and absolve them from the sentences and classes they stand under? And do they not put the godly in their place? They relax the punishment of the one, and impute transgression to the other, and so bring them under a law. See Exod. xxiii. 7, Prov. xxiv. 24, Isa. v. 23, and the 29th verse of this chapter. It is not good to punish godly men, who have given constant proof of their integrity, for abstaining from such a course, at least having so much appearance of evil, that many distinctions will never make the multitude to believe that we are walking according to former principles, because their sense observes the quite contrary practices, &c.

Chap. xviii. 2, ("A fool hath no delight in understanding, but that his heart may discover itself") shows that if the present cause and course were of God, and tended so much to his glory, fools or wicked men would have no such delight in it. For they delight in nothing but what is agreeable to their humour, to discover themselves, &c. Ver. 3 gives the true reason, why our public judicatories and armies are so base and contemptible, why contempt and shame is poured on them, because, "when the wicked comes, then also comes contempt, and with the vile man reproach." Ver. 13 "He that answereth a cause before he hears it, it is folly and shame unto him." Many pass peremptory sentence upon the honest party in the west before they hear all parties, and be thoroughly informed, and this is a folly and shame to them. They hear the state and church, and what they can say for their way, and indeed they seem just, because they are first in with their cause, and they will not hear another. But he that comes after will make inquiry, and discover those fallacies. Ver. 24 "There is a friend that sticketh closer than a brother." A godly neighbour, not so near in natural bonds to us, that is a surer friend than many brethren in the flesh. These bonds of country and kindred, should all cede to God's interest. See chap. xvii. 17.

Chap. xix. 22. "A man's desire is his kindness and a poor man is better than a liar." The godly that cannot concur in the public cause, being disabled, through an invincible impediment of sin lying in the way and means made use of, are better friends, and have more real good will to the establishment and peace of the land, than any ungodly man, let him be never so forward in the present course. Ver. 10. Pleasure and its attendants are not comely for a wicked man, (i.e. a foolish man) much less for a servant, (i.e. men enthralled in their lusts,) to rule over princes (i.e. godly men, highly privileged by God). All things that are good do ill become them, but worst of all to have power and superiority over good men, ver. 25, joined with chap. xxi. 11. Ringleaders of wickedness, refractory and incorrigible persons, should have been made examples to others, and this would have prevented much mischief. The scripture gives ground for putting difference between the scorner and simple, seducers and seduced.

Chap. xx. 6, xxi. 2, and xvi. 2. "Most men will proclaim every one his own goodness, but a faithful man who can find?" It is no great wonder that malignants say they repent, and the state and church say they keep the same principles. For who will say any evil of himself? Ver. 8. Magistrates should scatter away evil men with their countenance, by denying it to them, and looking down on them. How, then, do our rulers gather them? Ver. 3, shows that war and strife should not be kept up but in extreme necessity. Fools "will be meddling." Ver. 11, shows that the best way of judging of men is by their doings and fruits, not strained words and confessions. But those who, upon a bare profession, pronounce a notour[400] malignant a friend, having no proof of his integrity, and will not have any judged such, but such as judicially are debarred, yet contrary to all the testimony of works and fruits, judge and condemn honest men as traitors, though not judicially convicted. Certainly divers measures are an abomination to the Lord, as in ver. 10. Then in ver. 25 sacrilege is described, and covered perjury, which is a snare to the soul that commits it. He "devoureth that which is holy," i.e. applieth to a common use these things God hath set apart, and commanded to be kept holy, as our profaning of repentance and absolution, by casting such pearls to swine, and for our own advantage, making a cloak of them to bring in wicked men, contrary to the very nature and institution of the ordinance, also our prostituting of our covenant and cause, most holy things to maintain unholy or common interests,—our committing his holy things to them that will devour them. "And after vows to make inquiry," to dispute now, that we did not bind ourselves in the case of necessity, not to employ wicked men, whereas the ground is perpetual and holds in all cases, shows either temerity, in swearing,—or impiety, in inquiring afterward and changing. See Deut. xxiii. 21. Then ver. 26. "A wise king scattereth the wicked, and bringeth the wheel over them." O that our magistrates were so wise! Is the act of levy a scattering of the wicked? Is the act of indemnity a bringing the wheel over them? Psal. ci. 8. "I will early destroy," &c.

In Chap. xxi. 10. "The soul of the wicked desireth evil, his neighbour findeth no favour in his eyes." The wicked's principles can carry nowhere but to evil, and to do evil to good men. Ver. 8. His way and life is full of horrible and tragical chances. But a good man's work is easy and pleasant, directs to a good and peaceable end, Isa. xxvi. 7. Ver. 12. A righteous man should have his wit about him, to consider ungodly houses and families, and persons that God hath visible controversies with, that he may not communicate with them in their judgments. Ver. 16. It is a sad wandering out of the way, when a man leaves the congregation of the living to abide among the dead,—dead in sins and appointed to death. It is a great judgment as well as sin. Ver. 27, with the 4, and places before cited, show how abominable the external professions and pretences of wicked men are, when contradicted by their practice, especially if they do it but out of a wicked mind, when they intend to effect some mischief, under the colour of repentance and being reconciled to the church, as Absalom's vow at Hebron, as Balaam and Balak and the Pharisees, who under pretence of long prayers devoured widows' houses, as Jezebel's fast, and as the people, (Isa. lviii. 4.) who fasted for strife and debate, and to strike with the fist of wickedness. All men know that the church is the ladder to step up upon to go to preferment, and repentance the door to enter to places of trust.

Chap. xxii. 3. "A prudent man foreseeth the evil and hideth himself, but the simple pass on and are punished." He is a wise man that knows the judgment of the Lord, as the stork and swallow the time of their coming, that in the consideration of sins and threatenings, and comparing things spiritual with spiritual, apprehendeth judgment coming on such a course and such a party, and hides himself, goes aside, retires to a covert, by avoiding these evils, and the least fellowship with them that bring it on, and eschewing such a society as hath the cloud hanging directly above their head. But simple idiots and blind worldlings go on headlong, and dread nothing, and are punished, ver. 5. Most grievous plagues and punishments and all manner of unhappiness encumbereth their wicked life. Therefore he that would keep himself pure and clean (1 John v. 18.), and save his own soul, shall be far from them, shall keep himself far from such people. He prays with Job, "Let their counsel be far from me." Job xxi. 16, 17. Because their good is not in their hand, their candle is oft put out, &c. And he resolves with Jacob, My soul shall not enter into their secret, to have such intimacy with them as join counsels with them, Gen. xlix. 6. And ver. 10, 11, Cast out of thy company, family, jurisdiction, the scorner that contemns the godly men, and mocks instruction for such men are infectious, and able to corrupt all they converse with. But cast him out, and contention shall go out with him. It is such only that mars the union of the godly, that stirs up strife, and foments divisions. Thou shalt have more peace, and be more free from sin and shame. But sound hearted upright men, who deal faithfully, not to please but to profit,—you should choose these to intrust and rely upon, those should be friends of kings. Ver. 14. As a harlot's allurements are like pits to catch men, so the allurements of wicked ungodly men, their power, policy, &c., and their fair speeches and flatteries, are a deep ditch to catch men in to this spiritual whoredom and fornication spoken of. Ezek. xxiii. And he whom God is provoked with, by former wickedness, falls into it, Eccl. vii. 26, Ver. 24, 25. "Make not friendship with an angry man and with a furious man thou shalt not go," &c. And is not association in arms with such, as friends against an enemy, a making friendship with them we are sworn to hold as enemies? If we may not converse with a furious passionate man, how then with men of blood, enraged, whose inveterate malice hath now occasion to vent against all the godly? For thou wilt learn his ways, as we have always seen it by experience, and thou wilt get a snare to thy soul. If thou go not in his ways you cannot agree, you will fall out and quarrel, and that is a snare to thee. Ver. 28. "Remove not the ancient land-mark which thy fathers have set." If it be so dreadful and accursed to remove our neighbour's marks and bounds, O! how much more to change and alter God's land-mark, his privileges, oaths and covenants, &c. And chap. xxiii. 10, 11, Deut. xix. 14 and xxvii. 17.

Chap. xxiii. 1, 7. "When thou sittest to eat with a ruler, consider diligently what is before thee. For as he thinketh in his heart so is he," &c. Consider diligently what men are, not what they pretend and seem to be. For as they think, so are they, not as they pretend with their tongue and countenance, but as they think in their heart, which is better evidenced by their common and habitual speaking and walking, than any deliberate and resolved profession contrived of purpose. But if thou consider not this, the morsel thou hast eaten thou shalt vomit up. Thou shalt dearly pay for thy credulity, and lose all thy sweet words. Ver. 23. "Buy the truth and sell it not," &c. Do not we sell the truth, and cause, and all, into the hands of the enemies of all? whereas we ought to ransom the kingdom's liberty and religious interest, with the loss of all extrinsic interest that does but concern the accession of one's honour. Yet we sell, endanger, and venture all for that.

Chap. xxiv. 1. "Be not thou envious against evil men, neither desire thou to be with them." Godly men's hearts are often tickled to be acquainted with, in league and friendship with wicked men, when they have power, that they may not be hurt by them. But seeing there is no society between light and darkness, let not the godly desire to be with them, (as in chap. xxiii. 17,) but rather to be in God's fear always. That is good company. The reason is (verse 2,) their heart studies the destruction of the godly, (why then would thou walk with thine enemy?) and you shall hear nothing but mischief on their lips. Ver. 12. It is not according to men's words but works they should be judged. And why do not we follow that rule in our judging? Do we mock God as one mocks another? Job xxxiv. 11, Psal. lxii. 12, Jer. xxxii. 19, Rom. ii. 6, Ver. 21, &c. Men given to change, false deceitful men, meddle not with such, if thou either fear God or respect man. For such will be sure to no interest but their own. Then calamity shall come suddenly. Therefore have nothing to do with them. For "who knoweth the ruin of them both," of them and all other wicked men, or of both them and the king, if wicked? Also to the wise and godly this belongs, "It is not good to have respect of persons in judgment," whether he be king or nobleman. A righteous state respects not the person of the prince and mighty, saith Job. But he that says to the righteous, you are wicked sectaries, and also malignants, because ye will not approve all their resolutions, and to the wicked, "thou art righteous," to the malignants, you are the honest men, the blessed of the Lord,—who did ever to this day fall under Meroz' curse, should the people approve him? No certainly, "Him shall the people curse, and the nations shall abhor him," or them. But a blessing on them that would reprove our sins and search them out, ver. 25. The malignant party are even speaking so as the classers and purgers did to us, even so will we do to them. But God will render to them according to their work, ver. 29.

Chap. xxv. 2. "It is the honour of kings to search out a matter." It is a king and judge's glory to search out a matter, to try dissemblers before they trust them. God's glory is to pardon. Man's glory is to administer justice impartially. Ver. 4, 5, show what need there is of purging places of trust, especially about the king. Dross cannot be melted. Take what pains you will, it will not convert into a vessel and become useful. This mixed in, obstructs all equity, justice, and piety, where it is. The ruler should be the refiner to purge away this dross, and the army, or judicatory, or kingdom, is a vessel. You shall never get a fined vessel for use and service till you purge away the dross, Psal. ci. 4. Then, (ver. 8) we should follow peace with all men as much as is possible, never to begin strife or draw the sluice of contention. But if we be wronged, we should not for all that go out hastily to strife, till, 1. The justice and equity of the cause appear, 2. That the matter whereabout we contend be of great moment, a ground to found a war upon, 3. That we first use all means of peace and agreement possible, 4. That we overmatch not ourselves with those who are too strong for us, (see chap. xvii. 14) "lest" thou be brought to that extremity that "thou know not what to do." Thus Christ adviseth, Luke xiv. 31. I am persuaded this would plead much in reason to yield security to England, so be it our wrong were repaired, and no more done. Ver. 19 shows what the employment of unfaithful men, who mean nothing less than they pretend, is. They fail when most is expected, and hurt beside, as Job's friends, chap. vi. 15. And ver. 26. A righteous and upright man, consenting with a wicked man in sin, or, through fear of him, not daring to do his duty, turning to him and his way, or dallying and flattering him in his iniquity, is like "a troubled fountain," is not good and profitable for edification nor correction, having troubled the purity of his soul through the mud of carnal respects and interests. Corruption within is the mire, the wicked's seducements are like the beast's trampling it with his foot. And he is like a corrupt, infected, and poisoned fountain, more ready to infect and draw others by his example. Ver. 27. A man should not seek honour and preferment that is base and shameful. None of the trees longed for sovereignty but the bramble.

Chap. xxvi. 1. "As snow in summer and as rain in harvest, so honour is not seemly for a fool." It is as unseemly, prodigious, and destructive a thing, to give honours, promotions, and trust to a wicked man, as snow and much rain in harvest, a reproach and punishment more becomes him than honour, the reward of goodness (as ver. 3), a whip, rod, and bridle are more for him, to restrain him from wrong and provoke him to goodness. Ver. 6. He that commits an errand or business to a wicked man and intrusts him with it, is as unwise in so doing, as if he did cut off the messenger's feet he sent. He deprives himself of the means to compass it. He sends a lame man to run an errand. He is punished by himself as if he had cut off his own feet, and procureth sorrow and discontent to himself, as if he were compelled to drink nothing but what is contrary to his stomach. Ver. 7. All good speeches halt and limp in evil men's mouths, for there is no constancy in their mouths. Within they are very rottenness. "Out of the same mouth come blessing and cursing," James iii. 10. Their very words agree not, the public and extraordinary crosses the private and ordinary. And their actions have less harmony with their words. Professing they know God, in works they deny him &c. Ver. 8. To give a madman a weapon, what else is it but to murder? To bring shot to an ordinance which may do much mischief to himself and others, is to be accessory to that mischief. So to give "honour to a fool." He hath given power to them and put them in a capacity to do evil, and set them on work again to perfect their designs against good men. Ver. 9. As a drunken man, with a thorn in his hand, can make no use of it, but to hurt himself and others, so wicked men's good speeches and fair professions commonly tend to some mischief. These but cover their evil designs and yet the covering is shorter than that it can hide them. Ver. 10. Wicked rulers (look the margin[401]) grieve and molest the subjects: and the means to effect this is, to employ the fool and transgressor, to give offices and countenance to evil men, which may be instruments of their lust, so Abimelech, Judges ix. 4, so Jezebel, 1 Kings xxi. 10, so in Neh. vi. 12. Ver. 11. The dog, feeling his stomach surcharged, goes to the grass,—as our malignants to profess repentance,—and casts up that which troubles him, by a feigned confession. But because there is no change in his nature, he is inwardly stirred by his old principles to lick up that vomit, to commit and practise what he professed repentance for, yea, and to profess the same he pretended sorrow for. When power is confirmed in their hand they will return to their folly. Ver. 17. What else is our interposing ourselves in the king's quarrel concerning England, though we have interest in it to endeavour it in a peaceable way, if he were fit for it, yet in comparison of our kingdom and religion's safety, which may be ruined by war, it is no such matter as belongeth to us. And so it falls out, we are like a man taking a dog by the ears to hold him, we have raised up many enemies, and provoked them to bite us. We cannot hold them long from destroying him, and we provoke them more by holding them, in espousing his quarrel, as Jehoshaphat joining with Ahab. We had done well to interpose ourselves between the king and them to make peace, but to side with one party was not well done. Verses 18, 19. Furious and bloody men take all opportunities to hurt others, especially good men, and so deceive those employed. But they do it under a pretence. As a scorner reproacheth under a pretence of sport, so they, under other pretences, of wrongs done, of the country's defence, &c. Verses 20, 24, show the way to prevent trouble and keep peace. As a contentious turbulent person would inflame a whole country and put them by the ears, so a person, though not contentious in his own nature, yet having many contentious interests following him, which he will not quit, or commit to God's providence, as our king was. O it is the destruction of a nation to have such a person among them. He hath broken the peace of two kingdoms. Verses 23, 24, 25, 26. Burning lips, hot and great words of love and friendship, and a wicked heart revenging its enmity, and minding nothing less than what is spoken, is like a potsherd, a drossy piece covered over with the fairding[402] of hypocrisy, or, like a sepulchre garnished and painted, he dissembles and speaks vanity, and flatters. Psal. xii. 3. But he lays up his wicked purposes close within him till a time of venting them. Therefore when he speaks so fair and courteously, be not confident of him, trust him not too far till thou have proof of his reality.

Put not thyself and thy dearest interests into his mercy. This is wisdom, and not want of charity, Jer. xii. 6; Micah vii. 5. Cain, Joab, and Judas, are proofs of this. It may be covered a time, but not long. *Naturam expellas furca licet, usque recurret.*[403] All the world shall be witness of it, Psal. cxxv. So then, (ver 21.) the calumniator and false accuser, who openly professes his hatred and malice, and the flatterer that seems to be moved with love, both of them produce one effect, viz., ruin and calamity.

Chap. xxvii. 3, 4. "A stone is heavy, and the sand weighty, but a fool's wrath is heavier than them both," &c. We see what we may expect of the enraged, exasperated malignant party. Their wrath against all the godly, for their faithful secluding and purging them out of places of trust, is weighty and insupportable like the sand of the sea. It will crush them under it if God support not. It is like a swelling river, or a high spring tide, it goes over all banks, since the state and church have drawn the sluice and let it out. But when it is joined with envy and malice, against godliness and piety itself, who can stand before that? No means can quench that heat. Ver. 6: Faithful men's reproofs, remonstrances, and warnings, applied in love and compassion, are better than an enemy's kisses and flatteries, than his oils and ointments are. Therefore we would pray against the one, and for the other, that God would smite us with the mouth of the righteous, but keep us from the dainties of the wicked Joabs, Judases, and Ahithophels. Verse 8 speaks sadly against ministers that withdraw from their charges so unnecessarily, as a bird that wandereth too long from her nest: the young starve for cold or famine, or are made a prey. So these who, having no necessary call to be elsewhere, especially not being members of the Commission, yet stay not with their flocks, are guilty of their soul's ruin. Ver. 10: O how doth this speak against the present course of judicatories! They have forsaken their old faithful friends, when they proved ever constant, and have gone in to their wicked countrymen's house in the day of their calamity. But a neighbour in affection and piety, is nearer than a brother in flesh and near in habitation.

Chap. xxviii. 1: "The wicked fleeth when no man pursueth; but the righteous is bold as a lion." Wicked men are now chosen for stoutness and courage, but they have no sure foundation for it. It is but like the rage and temerity of a madman or drunkard. But godly men, once satisfied in grounds of conscience about their duty, would have been bold as lions. A good conscience would have made them bold, Psal. cxii. 7, 8, Lev. xxvi. 36. Now, ver. 2, behold the punishment of our sins, our governors are changed, there is almost a total alteration, and we are faces about, which cannot but bring ruin to the land, especially when men of understanding and piety are shut out. Ver. 4, with chap. xxix. 27: It is a great point and argument of declining and forsaking the law of God, when men praise the wicked, change their names though they themselves be not changed, and leave off contending with, or declaring against them, and do rather plead for them. But godly men, that keep the law, contend with, discountenance, and oppose them, as David, "I hate them that hate thee," and earnestly contend with them. Thus they are kept from partaking with other men's sins. Ver. 5: It is not very likely that all the ungodly should now understand the duty of the times and discern the right way, and that so many that fear God understand it not, seeing the Lord's secret is revealed to them, Psal. xxv. 14. Verses 6, 7: A poor man, and weak means, if they be of upright men, are better and stronger than many rich and strong perverters. A companion of evil men and a keeper of the law agree not in one person; the one is an honour, the other a shame to all that have interest in them. Ver. 9: Their prayers and professions are abomination, no acceptation of those that turn away their ears from obedience to the law, who walk contrary to it. Ver. 10: These cunning and crafty men that have enticed some godly men, and led them on in the present course, shall themselves smart for it, when the godly seduced shall see good things after all this. Ver. 12: When wicked men have power and trust, good men hide and retire themselves from such a congregation or assembly of the wicked. See chap. x. 10, 11. Should we thus choose our own plague, tyranny, oppression, calamity, and misery, and cast away our own glory? Then, (ver. 13) repentance requires time and ingenuous confession, and real forsaking. If both these join not, it is but a covering and hiding of sin. If a man confess, and yet walk and continue in them, he is but using his confession as a covering to retain his sins, and such shall not find mercy of God, or prosper before men. Ver. 14: It is not so despisable a thing to fear alway, and to be very jealous of sin as it is now made. It is counted a reproach to have any scruples at the present course. But happy is he that abstaineth from all appearance of evil, but he that emboldeneth himself, and will not question any thing that makes for advantage, falls into mischief. Ver. 15, 17 show the lamentable condition of a people under wicked rulers. They are beasts and not men towards the people, especially towards the best, Dan. vii. 4, 5, Zeph. iii. 3. Ver. 17: How doth that agree with our sparing of bloody men, of our soliciting for their impunity, of our pardoning them? Are they not, by the appointment of God's law, ordained for destruction, and haste to it? Should any then stay them? Should they not then far less employ them? And, (ver. 24) if it be so heinous to take our father's goods upon this pretence, because they are our own, how much more sacrilege is it to rob God of his interests, and give over his money to bankrupts, and say it is no transgression to rob the land of its defence, and make them naked, as Ahaz his confederacy did? Certainly it is murder. Ver. 28 and chap. xxix. 2 and xi. 12 and xxviii. 28 are to one purpose. We have forsaken our own mercy and wronged our own souls; and destroyed ourselves in choosing our own judgment, and making our own rod to beat us withal. Chap. xxix. 1: We being so often reproved by his word and providence for the sin of association with the wicked, and being so lately punished for it, and having so lately reproved ourselves for it in our declarations and fasts, yet to harden our necks, what can we expect but utter destruction, and that without remedy, as we sentenced ourselves? Ezra ix. 13 and xiv. 13, Isa. xxx. 13, 14. Shall not this iniquity be to us a breach ready to fall, even this iniquity of going down to Egypt for help, &c. Then, (ver. 6) there is a snare to entrap thy feet in the sins of the wicked; if thou be joined with them, thou cannot well escape. Ver. 8: Wicked profane contemners of God and his people bring ruin on a city or commonalty, they set it on fire and blow it up. But godly men pacify wrath, turn away judgments, and purge all from provocations, which is the only means to turn it away.

Ver. 16 shows, when wicked men gather together, and grow in state and power, they grow worse, and sin with greater boldness, and transgression then overflows the land, *tanquam ruptis repagulis*.[404] There is no obstacle. See Psal. xii. And ver. 24 shows, he that is partner and fellow receiver with a thief, or conceals such offenders, endangers his own destruction; and he that stays with, and associates with wicked men, must hear cursing and cannot bewray it. He will see many abominations, that though he would, he cannot remedy. Ver. 25: Fear of man and of the land's danger, hath brought many into a snare, to run from the Lord to an arm of flesh, but he that trusts in the Lord shall be safe. Ver. 27: Here is the deadly enmity between the two seeds, they cannot reconcile well. See ver. 10 and chap. xxi. 3. It is no wonder the godly abominate such men who are God's enemies and the land's plague.

Chap. xxx. 11, 14 describes the malignant party, who make nothing of the godly magistrates or their mother church and land, but curse, malign, oppose as much as they could, and are oppressors, monstrous tyrants, mankind beasts, or beastly men. The subject of their cruelty is the godly afflicted man. They eat up all and will not leave the bones, as the prophet complains, "I lie among men whose teeth are as spears and arrows, and their tongue a sharp sword." And then, ver. 12, 13, 20 describe our enemies, the invaders. They think themselves godly and righteous, yet are not purged from their filthiness. They are given up to strong delusions to believe lies, and there is no lie greater than this, that they are a godly party in a godly cause and way. They wipe their mouth after all their bloodshed, and say, I have done no evil. They wash their hands, as Pilate, as if they were free of the blood of these just men, whose souls cry under the altar. Ver. 21-23: It is a burden to the world and a plague to mankind, when servants, unworthy men, and persons unfit for high places are set in authority, and when wicked men have their desire of plenty and honour, (chap. xix. 10.) and when an odious woman, or men of hateful vicious dispositions, come to preferment and are espoused by a state,—nought they were while alone, but worse now when they have crept into the bed and bosom of the state; her roots were nought before, but now she is planted in rank mould, and will shoot forth her unsavoury branches and blossoms,—and when handmaids, kept in a servile estate because of their disposition and quality, get their masters ushered out, and they become heirs, at least possessors of the inheritance or trust. Ver. 33 shows how necessarily war and contention follow upon unnecessary provocations by word or deed, such as we have given many to England, though indeed they have given moe.[405] And lastly, chap. xxxi. 20, 26, 31 shows how word and work should go together, and men should be esteemed and praised according to their works and fruit of their hands.

A TREATISE OF CHRISTIAN LOVE.

John xiii. 35. "By This Shall All Men Know That Ye Are My Disciples, If Ye Have Love One To Another." First Printed At Edinburgh In 1743.

TO THE READER.

This treatise concerning Christian Love, was composed by the pious and learned Mr. Hugh Binning who was minister of the gospel at Govan, near to Glasgow. He was much celebrated and esteemed in this church, for several practical treatises, frequently printed for the benefit of the public, but this is not inferior to any of them.

Though there have been many excellent discourses in late years on this divine subject, yet, considering that there never was a time wherein a treatise of this kind was more seasonable and necessary than the present, when the love of many, of too, too many, is waxed cold, and this holy fire is almost extinguished, this cannot be thought to be superfluous.

The author was a minister of a most pacific temper, and this amiable grace and virtue did illustriously shine forth in him; and in this discourse, he breathes with a spirit of love in the most affecting and gaining manner, so that, I dare say, that, though it be above ninety years since he composed it, it does not fall short of any performance of this kind that has since appeared in public.

This treatise, with a great number of excellent sermons, preached by this able minister of the gospel, many of which have never been printed, in a manuscript in folio, was found in the late Rev. Mr. Robert Wodrow, minister at Eastwood, his library, and all care has been taken to publish it faithfully, without any alteration either by adding or diminishing any thing from it.

This divine subject of Christian love he lays a great stress upon; he shows that there is a greater moment and weight in Christian charity, than in the most part of those things for which some Christians bite and devour one another. It is the fundamental law of the gospel, to which all positive precepts and ordinances should stoop. Unity in judgement is very necessary for the well being of Christians, and Christ's last words persuade this, that unity in affection is most essential and fundamental. This is the badge that he left to his disciples; if we cast away this upon every different apprehension of mind, we disown our Master, and disclaim his token and badge.

Mr. Binning treats of this subject in a most sublime and pathetic strain; he explains the nature of this grace, discourses of the excellent properties and blessed effect and fruits of it, in a ravishing and captivating manner. There is such a variety of beauties in this treatise, that they deserve to be noticed in this preface, and particularly, his admirable commentary on the 13th chapter of the First Epistle to the Corinthians, wherein he outstrips all that went before him and, in fine, he enforces the exercise of this grace with the most convincing argument and the most powerful motives. And now, not to detain the reader from the perusal, it is earnestly wished that the end of the publication may, by the blessing of God, be obtained, which is, that Christians in our days may be as the primitive ones,—of one mind and of one heart, and that they may love one another with a pure heart fervently.

CHAPTER I.

The beauty and excellency of this world consists, not only in the perfection and comeliness of each part in it, but especially in the wise and wonderful proportion and union of these several parts. It is not the lineaments and colours that make the image or complete beauty, but the proportion and harmony of these, though different severally. And truly that is the wonder, that such repugnant natures, such different parts, and dissentient qualities, do conspire together in such an exact perfect unity and agreement, in which the wisdom of God doth most appear, by making all things in number, weight and measure. His power appears in the making all the materials of nothing, but his wisdom is manifested in the ordering and disposing so dissonant natures into one well agreeing and comely frame; so that this orderly disposition of all things into one fabric, is that harmonious melody of the creation, made up as it were of dissonant sounds, and that comely beauty of the world, resulting from such a proportion and wise combination of divers lines and colours. To go no further than the body of a man, what various elements are combined into a well ordered being, the extreme qualities being so refracted and abated as they may join in friendship and society, and make up one sweet temperament!

Now, it is most reasonable to suppose, that, by the law of creation, there was no less order and unity to be among men, the chiefest of the works of God. And so it was indeed. As God had moulded the rest of the world into a beautiful frame, by the first stamp of his finger, so he did engrave upon the hearts of men such a principle, as might be a perpetual bond and tie to unite the sons of men together. This was nothing else but the law of love, the principal fundamental law of our creation, love to God, founded on that essential dependence and subordination to God, and love to man, grounded upon that communion and interest in one image of God. All the commandments of the first and second table are but so many branches of these trees, or streams of these fountains. Therefore our Saviour gives a complete abridgment of the law of nature and the moral law, "Thou shalt love the Lord thy God with all thy heart, and with all thy soul, and with all thy mind, this is the first and great commandment. The second is like unto it, Thou shalt love thy neighbour as thyself," Matth. xxii. 37, 38, 39. And therefore, as Paul says, "Love is the fulfilling of the law," Rom. xiii. 10. The universal debt we owe to God is love in the superlative degree, and the universal debt we owe one another is love in an inferior degree, yet of no lower kind than that of our selves. "Owe no man any thing, but to love one another" (Rom. xiii. 8), and that collateral with himself, as Christ speaks. Unto these laws all other are subordinate, and one of them is subordinate to the other, but to nothing else. And so, as long as the love of God may go before, the love of man should follow, and whatever doth not untie the bond of divine affection, ought not to loose the knot of that love which is linked with it. When the uniting of souls together divides both from God, then indeed, and only then, must this knot be untied that the other may be kept fast.

But this beautiful and comely frame of man is marred. Sin hath cut in pieces that divine love that knit man to God; and the dissolving of this hath loosed that link of human society, love to our neighbour. And now all is rents, rags, and distractions, because self love hath usurped the throne. The unity of the world of mankind is dissolved, one is distracted from another, following his own private inclinations and inordinate affection, which is the poison of enmity, and seed of all discord. If the love of God and of one another had kept the throne, there had been a coordination and co-working of all men in all their actions, for God's glory and the common good of man. But now self love having enthroned itself, every man is for himself, and strives, by all means, to make a concurrence of all things to his own interest and designs. The first principles of love would have made all men's actions and courses flow into one ocean of divine glory and mutual edification, so that there could not have been any disturbance or jarring amongst them, all flowing into one common end. But self-love hath turned all the channels backward towards itself, and this is its wretched aim and endeavour, in which it wearies itself, and discomposes the world, to wind and turn in every thing, and to make, in the end, a general affluence of the streams into its own bosom. This is the seed of all division and confusion which is among men, while every man makes himself the centre, it cannot choose but all the lines and draughts of men's courses must thwart and cross each other.

Now, the Lord Jesus having redeemed lost man, and repaired his ruins, he makes up this breach, especially restores this fundamental ordinance of our creation, and unites men again to God and to one another. Therefore he is our peace, he hath removed the seeds of discord between God and man, and between man and man. And this is the subject of that divine epistle which the beloved apostle, full of that divine love, did pen, "God is love, and in this was the love of God manifested, that God sent his only begotten Son into the world. And he that loveth is born of God, and knoweth God, but we love God, because he loved us first, and if God so loved us, we ought also to love one another." 1 John iv. This is the very substance of the gospel, a doctrine of God's love to man, and of man's love due to God, and to them who are begotten of God, the one declared, the other commanded. So that much of the gospel is but a new edition or publication of that old ancient fundamental law of creation. This is that paradox which John delivers, "I write no new commandment unto you, but an old commandment, which you had from the beginning; again, a new commandment I write unto you, which thing is true in him and you, because the darkness is past, and the true light now shineth," 1 John ii. 7, 8. It is no new commandment, but that primitive command of love to God and men, which is the fulfilling of the law; and yet new it is, because there is a new obligation superadded. The bond of creation was great, but the tie of redemption is greater. God gave a being to man, that is enough. But God to become a miserable man for man, that is infinitely more. Fellow creatures, that is sufficient for a bond of amity. But to be once fellow captives, companions in misery, and then companions in mercy and blessedness, that is a new and stronger bond. Mutual love was the badge of reasonable creatures in innocency. But now Jesus Christ hath put a new stamp and signification on it; and made it the very differential character and token of his disciples, "By this shall all men know that ye are my disciples, if ye love one another." And therefore, when he is making his latter will, he gives this testamentary commandment to his children and heirs, "A new commandment give I unto you, that ye love one another, as I have loved you, that ye also love one another." New indeed!

For though it be the same command, yet there was never such a motive, inducement, and persuasive to it as this: "God so loved that he gave me, and I so loved that I gave myself, that is an addition more than all that was before," John xiii. 34, 35.

There is a special stamp of excellency put on this affection of love, that God delights to exhibit himself to us in such a notion. "God is love," and so holds out himself as the pattern of this. "Be ye followers of God as dear children, and walk in love," Eph. v. 1, 2. This is the great virtue and property which we should imitate our Father in. As God hath a general love to all the creatures, from whence the river of his goodness flows out through the earth, and in that, is like the sun conveying his light and benign influence, without partiality or restraint, to the whole world, but his special favour runs in a more narrow channel towards these whom he hath chosen in Christ; so in this a Christian should be like his Father, and there is nothing in which he resembles him more than in this, to walk in love towards all men, even our enemies. For in this he gives us a pattern, Matt. v. 44, 45: "But I say unto you, Love your enemies, bless them that curse you, do good to them that hate you, and pray for them which despitefully use you, and persecute you, that ye may be the children of your Father which is in heaven; for he maketh his sun to rise on the evil and on the good, and sendeth rain on the just and on the unjust." To do good to all, and to be ready to forgive all, is the glory of God, and certainly it is the glory of a child of God to be merciful as his Father is merciful, and good to all, and kind to the unthankful. And this is to be perfect as he is perfect. This perfection is charity and love to all. But the particular and special current of affection will run toward the household of faith, those who are of the same descent, and family, and love. This drawn into such a compass, is the badge and livery of his disciples. These two in a Christian are nothing but the reflex of the love of God, and streams issuing out from it. A Christian walking in love to all, blessing his enemies, praying for them, not reviling or cursing again, but blessing for cursing, and praying for reviling, forgiving all, and ready to give to the necessities of all, and more especially, uniting the force of his love and delight, to bestow it upon these who are the excellent ones, and delight of God, such a one is his Father's picture, so to speak. He is partaker of that divine nature, and royal spirit of love. Gal. vi. 10: "As we have therefore opportunity, let us do good unto all men, especially unto them who are of the household of faith." 1 Thess. iii. 12, 13: "And the Lord make you to increase and abound in love one towards another, and towards all men, even as we do towards you, to the end he may establish your hearts unblameable in holiness before God, even our Father, at the coming of our Lord Jesus Christ, with all his saints."

It is foretold by our Lord Jesus Christ, that in the last days the "love of many shall wax cold," Matt. xxiv. 12. And truly this is the symptom of a decaying and fading Christian and church. Love is the vital spirits of a Christian, which are the principles of all motion and lively operation. When there is a deliquium[406] in these, the soul is in a decay; it is so comprehensive an evil, as alone is sufficient to make an evil time. And besides, it is the argument and evidence, as well as the root and fountain, of abounding iniquity, because this is the epidemical disease of the present time, love cooled, and passion heated, whence proceed all the feverish distempers, contentions, wars and divisions, which have brought the church of God near to expiring. Therefore being mindful of that of the apostle, Heb. x. 24, I would think it pertinent to consider one another, and provoke again unto love and to good works. It was the great charge that Christ had against Ephesus, "Thou hast left thy first love." I shall therefore show the excellency and necessity of this grace, that so we may remember from whence we have fallen and repent, that we may do the first works, lest he come quickly and remove our candlestick, Rev. ii. 4, 5.

CHAPTER II.

I. Then, it might endear this Christian virtue unto us, that God propones himself as the pattern of it, that Christ holds out himself as the rare example of it for our imitation. It is what doth most endear God to creatures, and certainly it must likewise appreciate them one to another. 1 John iv. 7, 8: "Beloved, let us love one another; for love is of God, and every one that loveth, is born of God, and knoweth God. He that loveth not knoweth not God; for God is love." Matt. v. 44, 45, "But I say unto you, Love your enemies, bless them that curse you, do good to them that hate you, and pray for them which despitefully use you, and persecute you, that you may be the children of your Father which is in heaven; for he maketh his sun to rise on the evil and on the good, and sendeth rain on the just and on the unjust." Eph. v. 1, 2: "Be ye therefore followers of God, as dear children, and walk in love, as Christ also hath loved us, and hath given himself for us, an offering and a sacrifice to God, for a sweet smelling savour." John xiii. 35: "By this shall all men know that ye are my disciples, if ye love one another." Now the following of so rare an example, and imitating of so noble and high a pattern, doth exalt the soul into a royalty and dignity, that it dwells in God and God in it. 1 John iv. 16. This is the highest point of conformity with God, and the nearest resemblance of our Father. To be like him in wisdom, that wretched aim, did cast men as low as hell, but to aspire unto a likeness in love, lifts up the soul as high as heaven, even to a mutual inhabitation.

II. It should add an exceeding weight unto it, that we have not only so high a pattern, but so excellent a motive, "God so loved," and "herein is love, not that we loved God, but that he loved us, and sent his Son to be the propitiation for our sins," therefore, "If God so loved us, we ought also to love one another," 1 John iv. 9, 10, 11. "Walk in love, as Christ also hath loved us, and hath given himself for us," Eph. v. 2. Here are the topics of the most vehement persuasion. There is no invention can afford so constraining a motive, God so loving us, sinful and miserable us, that he gave his only begotten Son, that we might live through him, and Christ so loving us, that he gave himself a sacrifice for sin. O then! who should live to himself, when Christ died for others? And who should not love, when "God spared not his own Son, but delivered him up for us all?" "God commendeth his love to us, in that while we were yet sinners, Christ died for us," Rom. viii. 32, and v. 8 and xiv. 7, 8.

III. Join to this so earnest and pressing a command, even the latter will of him to whom we owe that we are, and are redeemed. That is the burden he lays on us. This is all the recompence he seeks for his unparalleled love, "This is my command, that as I have loved you, ye love one another," John xiii. 34. Your goodness cannot extend to me, therefore I assign all the beneficence and bounty ye owe to me, I give it over to these whom I have loved, and have not loved my life for them. Now, says he, whatsoever ye would count yourself obliged to do to me, if I were on the earth among you, do it to these poor ones whom I have left behind me, and this is all the testimony of gratitude I crave. Matth. xxv. 34 to 40: "Then shall the King say unto them on his right hand, Come ye blessed of my Father, inherit the kingdom prepared for you from the foundation of the world. For I was an hungered, and ye gave me meat; I was thirsty and ye gave me drink; I was a stranger, and ye took me in; naked, and ye clothed me; I was sick, and ye visited me; I was in prison, and ye came unto me. Then shall the righteous answer him, saying, Lord, when saw we thee an hungered, and fed thee? or thirsty, and gave thee drink? When saw we thee a stranger, and took thee in? or naked, and clothed thee? Or when saw we thee sick, or in prison, and came unto thee? And the King shall answer, and say unto them, Verily I say unto you, Inasmuch as ye have done it unto one of the least of these my brethren, ye have done it unto me." "These ye have always with you, but me ye have not always." It is strange how earnestly, how solicitously, how pungently he presses this exhortation, John xiii. 34, 35, "A new commandment I give unto you, that ye love one another as I have loved you, that ye love one another. By this shall all men know that ye are my disciples, if ye have love one to another," and xv. 12 and 17, "This is my commandment, that ye love one another as I have loved you. These things I command you, that ye love one another," and his apostles after him, 1 Thess. iv. 9, "But as touching brotherly love, ye need not that I write unto you, for ye yourselves are taught of God to love one another." Coloss. iii. 14, "And above all these things, put on charity, which is the bond of perfectness." 1 Pet. iv. 8, "And above all things have fervent charity among yourselves, for charity shall cover the multitude of sins." But above all, that beloved disciple, who being so intimate with Jesus Christ,—we may lawfully conceive he was mured to that affectionate frame by his converse with Christ,—has been most mindful of Christ's testamentary injunctions. He cannot speak three sentences but this is one of them. All which may convince us of this one thing, that there is a greater moment and weight of Christianity in charity than in the most part of these things for which Christians bite and devour one another. It is the fundamental law of the gospel, to which all positive precepts and ordinances should stoop. Unity in judgment is very needful for the well being of Christians. But Christ's last words persuade this, that unity in affection is more essential and fundamental. This is the badge he left to his disciples. If we cast away this upon every different apprehension of mind, we disown our Master, and disclaim his token and badge.

IV. The apostle Paul puts a high note of commendation upon charity, when he styles it the bond of perfection. "Above all things," says he, "put on charity, which is the bond of perfectness," Col. iii 14. I am sure it hath not such a high place in the minds and practice of Christians now, as it hath in the roll of the parts and members of the new man here set down. Here it is above all. With us it is below all, even below every apprehension of doubtful truths. An agreement in the conception of any poor petty controversial matter of the times, is made the badge of Christianity, and set in an eminent place above all which the apostle mentions, in the 12th verse, "bowels of mercies, kindness, gentleness, humbleness of mind, meekness, long suffering." Nay, charity itself is but a waiting handmaid to this mistress.

But let us consider the apostle's significant character he puts on it. It is a bond of perfection, as it were, a bundle of graces, and chain of virtues, even the very cream and flower of many graces combined. It is the sweet result of the united force of all graces. It is the very head and heart of the new man, which we are invited to put on, "Above all put on charity." All these fore-mentioned perfections are bound and tied together, by the girdle of charity and love, to the new man. When charity is born and brought forth, it may be styled *Gad*,[407] for a *troop* cometh, *chorus virtutum*,[408] "a troop or company of virtues" which it leads and commands. Charity hath a tender heart, for it hath "bowels of mercies,"—such a compassionate and melting temper of spirit, that the misery or calamity, whether bodily or spiritual, of other men, makes an impression upon it. And therefore it is the Christian sympathy which affects itself with others' afflictions. If others be moved, it moves itself through comfort and sympathy. This is not only extended to bodily and outward infirmities, but, most of all, to infirmities of mind and heart, error, ignorance, darkness, falling and failing in temptation. We are made priests to God our Father, to have compassion on them who are ignorant and out of the way, for that we ourselves are also compassed with infirmity, Rev. i. 6 and Heb. v. 2. Then, love hath a humble mind, "humbleness of mind," else it could not stoop and condescend to others of low degree, and therefore Christ exhorts above all to lowliness. "Learn of me, for I am meek and lowly in heart." If a man be not lowly, to sit down below offences and infirmities, his love cannot rise above them. Self-love is the greatest enemy to true Christian love, and pride is the fountain of self-love, because it is impossible that, in this life, there should be an exact correspondence between the thoughts and ways of Christians. Therefore it is not possible to keep this bond of perfection unbroken, except there be a mutual condescendence. Self-love would have all conformed to it, and if that be not, there is the rent presently. But humbleness of mind can conform itself to all things, and this keeps the bond fast. Then charity, by the link of humility, hath meekness chained unto it, and kindness. Love is of a sweet complexion, meek and kind. Pride is the mother of passion, humbleness the mother of meekness. The inward affection is composed by meekness, and the outward actions adorned by gentleness and kindness. O that sweet composure of spirit! The heart of the wicked is as the troubled sea, no rest, no quiet in it, continual tempests raising continual waves of disquiet. An unmeek spirit is like a boiling pot, it troubles itself and annoys others. Then, at length, charity, by lowliness and meekness, is the most durable, enduring, long-suffering thing in the world, "with long suffering, forbearing one another in love." These are the only principles of patience and longanimity. Anger and passion is expressed in scripture under the name of haste, and it is a sudden, furious, hasty thing, a rash, inconsiderate, impatient thing, more hasty than speedy. Now the special exercises and operations of these graces are in the 13th verse, "forbearing one another, and forgiving one another," according to Christ's example. And indeed these are so high and sublime works, as charity must yoke all the fore-mentioned graces, unite them all in one troop, for the accomplishing of them. And the great and sweet fruit of all this is comprehended in the 15th verse, "The peace of God rule in your hearts, to the which ye are called in one body." Peace with God is not here meant, but the peace which God hath made up between men. All were shattered and rent asunder. The Lord hath by his Son Jesus Christ gathered so many into one body, the church, and by one Spirit quickens all. Now where love is predominant, there is a sweet peace and harmony between all the members of this one body. And this peace and tranquillity of affections rules and predominates over all these lusts, which are the mineries[409] of contentions, and strifes, and wars.

V. Add unto this another special mark of excellency that this apostle puts on charity, or Christian love. "The end of the commandment is charity, out of a pure heart, of a good conscience, and of faith unfeigned," 1 Tim. i. 5. If this were duly pondered, I do believe it would fill all hearts with astonishment, and faces with confusion, that they neglected the weightier matters of the law, and over stretched some other particular duties, to fill up the place of this, which is the end, the fulfilling of the law. It appears by this that charity is a cream of graces. It is the spirit and quintessence extracted out of these cardinal graces, unfeigned faith, a good conscience, a pure heart. It is true, the immediate end of the law, as it is now expounded unto us, is to drive us to believe in Jesus Christ, as it is expressed, Rom. x. 4. "Christ is the end of the law for righteousness to every one that believeth." But this believing in Christ is not the last end of it. Faith unfeigned in a Mediator is intentionally for this, to give the answer of a good conscience in the blood of Christ, and to purify the heart by the water of the Spirit, and so to bring about at length, by such a sweet compass, the righteousness of the law to be fulfilled by love in us, which by divine imputation is fulfilled to us. Now consider the context, and it shall yield much edification. Some teachers (1 Tim. i. 4.) exercised themselves and others in endless genealogies, which, though they contained some truth in them, yet they were perplexing, and brought no edification to souls. Curiosity might go round in such debates, and bewilder itself as in a labyrinth, but they did rather multiply disputes than bring true edification in the faith and love of God and men. Now, says he, they do wholly mistake the end of the law, of the doctrine of the scripture. The end and great purpose of it is love, which proceeds from faith in Christ, purifying the heart. This is the sum of all, to worship God in faith and purity, and to love one another. And whatsoever debates and questions do tend to the breach of this bond, and have no eminent and remarkable advantage in them, suppose they be conceived to be about matters of conscience, yet the entertaining and prosecuting them to the prejudice of this, is a manifest violence offered to the law of God, which is the rule of conscience. It is a perverting of scripture and conscience to a wrong end. I say then, that charity and Christian love should be the moderatrix of all our actions towards men. From thence they should proceed, and according to this rule be formed. I am persuaded if this rule were followed, the present differences in judgment of godly men, about such matters as minister mere questions, would soon be buried in the gulf of Christian affection.

VI. Now to complete the account of the eminence of this grace, take that remarkable chapter of Paul's, 1 Cor. xiii., where he institutes the comparison between it and other graces, and in the end pronounces on its behalf, "the greatest of these is charity." I wonder how we do please ourselves, as that we had attained already, when we do not so much as labour to be acquainted with this, in which the life of Christianity consists, without which faith is dead, our profession vain, our other duties and endeavours for the truth unacceptable to God and men. "Yet I show you a more excellent way," says he in the end of the former chapter. And this is the more excellent way, charity and love, more excellent than gifts, speaking with tongues, prophesying, &c. And is it not more excellent than the knowledge and acknowledgment of some present questionable matters, about governments, treaties, and such like, and far more than every punctilio of them? But he goes higher. Suppose a man could spend all his substance upon the maintenance of such an opinion, and give his life for the defence of it, though in itself it be commendable, yet if he want charity and love to his brethren, if he overstretch that point of conscience to the breach of Christian affection, and duties flowing from it, it profits him nothing. Then certainly charity must rule out external actions, and have the predominant hand in the use of all gifts, in the venting of all opinions. Whatsoever knowledge and ability a man hath, charity must employ it, and use it. Without this, duties and graces make a noise, but they are shallow and empty within. Now he shows the sweet properties of it, and good effects of it, how universal an influence it hath on all things, but especially how necessary it is to keep the unity of the church.

Charity "is kind" and "suffereth long," (μακϱοθυμηω), it is longanimous or magnanimous and there is indeed no great, truly great, mind but is patient and long suffering. It is a great weakness and pusillanimity to be soon angry. Such a spirit hath not the rule of itself, but is in bondage to its own lust, but "he that ruleth his spirit is greater than he that taketh a city." Now, it is much of this affection of love that overrules passion. There is a greatness and height in it, to love them that deserve not well of us, to be kind to the unfaithful, not to be easily provoked, and not soon disobliged. A fool's wrath is presently known. It is a folly and weakness of spirit, which love, much love cures and amends. It suffers much unkindness, and long suffers it, and yet can be kind.

"Charity envieth not." Envy is the seed of all contention, and self-love brings it forth. When every man desires to be esteemed chief, and would have pre-eminence among others, their ways and courses must interfere one with another. It is this that makes discord. Every man would abate from another's estimation, that he may add to his own. None lives content with his own lot or station, and it is the aspiring beyond that, which puts all the wheels out of course. I believe this is the root of many contentions among Christians,—the apprehension of slighting, the conceit of disrespect, and such like, kindles the flame of difference, and heightens the least offence to an unpardonable injury. But charity envieth not where it may lie quietly low. Though it be under the feet of others, and beneath its own due place, yet it envieth not, it can lie contentedly so. Suppose it be slighted and despised, yet it takes it not highly, because it is lowly in mind.

"Charity is not puffed up, and vaunteth not itself." If charity have gifts and graces beyond others, it restrains itself, with the bridle of modesty and humility, from vaunting or boasting, or any thing in its carriage that may savour of conceit. Pride is a self admirer, and despises others, and to please itself it cares not to displease others. There is nothing so incomportable[410] in human or Christian society, so apt to alienate others' affections, for the more we take of our own affection to ourselves, we shall have the less from others. O these golden rules of Christian walking! Rom. xii. 10, 16, "Be kindly affectioned one to another with brotherly love, in honour preferring one another. Mind not high things, but condescend to men of low estate. Be not wise in your own conceits." O but that were a comely strife among Christians, each to prefer another in unfeigned love, and in lowliness of mind, each to esteem another better than himself! Philip. ii. 3. "Knowledge puffeth up," says this apostle (1 Cor. viii. 1) "but charity edifieth." It is but a swelling and tumour of the mind, but love is solid piety and real religion.

Then charity doth nothing unseemly, "behaveth not itself unseemly," 1 Cor. xiii. 5. Vanity and swelling of mind will certainly break forth into some unseemly carriage, as vain estimation, and such like, but charity keeps a sweet decorum in all its carriage, so as not to provoke and irritate others, nor yet to expose itself to contempt or mockery. Or the word may be taken thus, it is not fastidious. It accounts not itself disgraced and abused, to condescend to men of low estate. It can with its Master bow down to wash a disciple's feet, and not think it unseemly. Whatsoever it submits to in doing or suffering, it is not ashamed of it, as that it were not suitable and comely.

"Charity seeketh not her own things." Self denial and true love are inseparable. Self love makes a monopoly of all things to its own interest, and this is most opposite to Christian affection and communion, which puts all in one bank. If every one of the members should seek its own things, and not the good of the whole body, what a miserable distemper would it cause in the body? We are called into one body in Christ, and therefore we should look not on our own things only, but every man also on the things of others, Philip. ii. 4. There is a public interest of saints, mutual edification in faith and love, which charity will prefer to its own private interest. Addictedness to our own apprehension, and too much self overweening and self pleasing is the grand enemy of that place to which we are called into one body. Since one Spirit informs and enlivens all the members, what a monstrosity is it for one member to seek its own things, and attend to its own private interest only, as if it were a distinct body!

Charity "is not easily provoked." This is the straight and solid firmness of it, that it is not soon moved with external impressions. It is long suffering, it suffers long and much. It will not be shaken by violent and weighty pressures of injuries, where there is much provocation given, yet it is not provoked. Now to complete it, it is not easily provoked at light offences. It is strange how little a spark of injuries puts all in a flame because our spirits are as gunpowder,—so capable of combustion through corruption. How ridiculous, for the most part, are the causes of our wrath! For light things we are heavily moved, and for ridiculous things sadly, even as children who fall out among themselves for toys and trifles, or as beasts that are provoked upon the very show of a colour, as red or such like. We would save ourselves much labour, if we could judge before we suffer ourselves to be provoked. But now we follow the first appearance of wrong, and being once moved from without, we continue our commotion within, lest we should seem to be angry without a cause. But charity hath a more solid foundation. It dwells in God, for God is love, and so is truly great, truly high, and looks down with a steadfast countenance upon these lower things. The upper world is continually calm and serene. No clouds, no tempests there, no winds, nothing to disturb the harmonious and uniform motion, but it is this lower world that is troubled and tossed with tempests, and obscured with clouds. So a soul dwelling in God by love, is exalted above the cloudy region. He is calm, quiet, serene, and is not disturbed or interrupted in his motion of love to God or men.

Charity "thinketh no evil." Charity is apt to take all things in the best sense. If a thing may be subject to diverse acceptations, it can put the best construction on it. It is so benign and good in its own nature that it is not inclinable to suspect others. It desires to condemn no man, but would gladly, as far as reason and conscience will permit, absolve every man. It is so far from desire of revenge, that it is not provoked or troubled with an injury. For that were nothing else but to wrong itself because others have wronged it already, and it is so far from wronging others, that it will not willingly so much as think evil of them. Yet if need require, charity can execute justice, and inflict chastisement, not out of desire of another's misery, but out of love and compassion to mankind. *Charitas non punit quia peccatum est, sed ne peccaretur*,[411] it looks more to prevention of future sin, than to revenge of a bypast fault, and can do all without any discomposure of spirit, as a physician cuts a vein without anger. *Quis enim cut medetur irascitur?* "Who is angry at his own patient?"

Charity "rejoiceth not in iniquity." Charity is not defiled in itself, though it condescend to all. Though it can love and wish well to evil men, yet it rejoiceth not in iniquity. It is like the sun's light that shines on a dunghill, and is not defiled, receives no tincture from it. Some base and wicked spirits make a sport to do mischief themselves, and take pleasure in others that do it. But charity rejoices in no iniquity or injustice, though it were done to its own enemy. It cannot take pleasure in the unjust sufferings of any who hate it, because it hath no enemy but sin and iniquity and hates nothing else with a perfect hatred. Therefore whatever advantage should redound to itself by other men's iniquities, it cannot rejoice, that iniquity, its capital enemy, should reign and prevail. But it "rejoiceth in the truth." The advancement and progress of others in the way of truth and holiness is its pleasure. Though that should eclipse its own glory, yet it looks not on it with an evil eye. If it can find out any good in them that are enemies to it, it is not grieved to find it and know it, but can rejoice at any thing which may give ground of good construction of them. There is nothing more beautiful in its eyes than to see every one get their own due, though it alone should come behind.

Charity "beareth all things." By nature we are undaunted heifers, cannot bear any thing patiently. But charity is accustomed to the yoke,—to the yoke of reproaches and injuries from others, to a burden of other men's infirmities and failings. We would all be borne upon others' shoulders, but we cannot put our own shoulders under other men's burden, according to that royal law of Christ, Rom. xv. 1. "We that are strong ought to bear the infirmities of the weak, and not to please ourselves" and Gal. vi. 2. "Bear ye one another's burdens, and so fulfil the law of Christ," that is the law of love, no question.

Charity "believeth all things." Our nature is malignant and wicked, and therefore most suspicious and jealous, and apt to take all in the worst part. But charity hath much candour and humanity in it, and can believe well of every man, and believe all things as far as truth will permit. It knows that grace can be beside a man's sins. It knows that itself is subject to such like infirmities. Therefore it is not a rigid and censorious judger; it allows as much latitude to others as it would desire of others. It is true it is not blind and ignorant. It is judicious, and hath eyes that can discern between colours. *Credit omnia credenda, sperat omnia speranda.* "It believes all things that are believable, and hopes all things that are hopeful." If love have not sufficient evidences, yet she believes if there be some probabilities to the contrary, as well as for it. The weight of charity inclines to the better part, and so casts the balance of hope and persuasion; yet being sometimes deceived, she hath reason to be watchful and wise, for "the simple believeth every word." If charity cannot have ground of believing any good, yet it hopes still. *Qui non est hodie, cras magis aptus erit,*[412] says charity, and therefore it is patient and gentle, waiting on all, if peradventure God may "give them repentance to the acknowledging of the truth," 2 Tim. ii. 25. Charity would account it both atheism and blasphemy, to say such a man cannot, will not find mercy. But to pronounce of such as have been often approven in the conscience of all, and sealed into many hearts, that they will never find mercy, that they have no grace, because of some failings in practice and differences from us, it were not in sobriety but madness. It is certainly love and indulgence to ourselves, that make us aggravate other men's faults to such a height. Self love looks on other men's failings through a multiplying or magnifying glass, but she puts her own faults behind her back. *Non videt quod in mantica quæ a tergo est.*[413] Therefore she can suffer much in herself but nothing in others, and certainly much self forbearance and indulgence can spare little for others. But charity is just contrary. She is most rigid on her own behalf, will not pardon herself easily, knows no revenge but what is spoken of 2 Cor. vii. 11, self revenge, and hath no indignation but against herself. Thus she can spare much candour and forbearance for others, and hath little or nothing of indignation left behind to consume on others.

"Charity never faileth." This is the last note of commendation. Things have their excellency from their use and from their continuance; both are here. Nothing so useful, no such friend of human or Christian society as charity, the advantage of it reacheth all things. And then, it is most permanent and durable. When all shall go, it shall remain. When ordinances, and knowledge attained by means and ordinances, shall evanish, charity shall abide, and then receive its consummation. Faith of things inevident and obscure shall be drowned in the vision of seeing God's face clearly. Hope of things to come shall be exhausted in the possession and fruition of them. But love only remains in its own nature and notion, only it is perfected by the addition of so many degrees as may suit that blessed estate. Therefore methinks it should be the study of all saints who believe immortality, and hope for eternal life, to put on that garment of charity, which is the livery of all the inhabitants above. We might have heaven upon earth as far as is possible if we dwelt in love, and love dwelt in and possessed our hearts. What an unsuitable thing might a believer think it, to hate him in this world whom he must love eternally, and to contend and strive with these, even for matters of small moment, with bitterness and rigidity, with whom he shall have an eternal, uninterrupted unity and fellowship? Should we not be assaying here how that glorious garment suits us? And truly there is nothing makes a man so heaven-like or God like as this, much love and charity.

Now there is one consideration might persuade us the more unto it, that here we know but darkly and in part, and therefore our knowledge, at best, is but obscure and inevident, ofttimes subject to many mistakes and misapprehensions of truth, according as *mediums* represent them. And therefore there must be some latitude of love allowed one to another in this state of imperfection, else it is impossible to keep unity, and we must conflict often with our own shadows, and bite and devour one another for some deceiving appearances. The imperfection and obscurity of knowledge should make all men jealous of themselves, especially in matters of a doubtful nature, and not so clearly determined by scripture. Because our knowledge is weak, shall our love be so? Nay, rather let charity grow stronger, and aspire unto perfection, because knowledge is imperfect. What is wanting in knowledge let us make up in affection, and let the gap of difference in judgment be swallowed up with the bowels of mercies and love, and humbleness of mind. And then we shall have hid our infirmity of understanding as much as may be. Thus we may go hand in hand together to our Father's house, where, at length, we must be together.

CHAPTER III.

I may briefly reduce the chief persuading motive to this so needful and so much desiderated grace into some three or four heads. All things within and without persuade to it, but especially the right consideration of the love of God in Christ, the wise and the impartial reflection on ourselves, the consideration of our brethren whom we are commanded to love, and the thorough inspection into the nature and use of the grace itself.

In consideration of the *First*, a soul might argue itself into a complacency with it and thus persuade itself, "He that loveth not, knoweth not God, for God is love," 1 John iv. 8. And since he that hath known and believed the love that God hath to us, must certainly dwell in love, since these two have such a strait indissoluble connexion, then, as I would not declare to all my atheism and my ignorance of God, I will study to love my brethren. And that I may love them, I will give myself to the search of God's love, which is the place, *locus inventionis*,[414] whence I may find out the strongest and most effectual *medium* to persuade my mind, and to constrain my heart to Christian affection.

First then, when I consider that so glorious and great a Majesty, so high and holy an One, self sufficient and all sufficient, who needs not go abroad to seek delight, because all happiness and delight is enclosed within his own bosom, can yet love a creature, yea and be reconciled to so sinful a creature, which he might crush as easily as speak a word, that he can place his delight on so unworthy and base an object, O! how much more should I, a poor wretched creature, love my fellow creature, ofttimes better than myself, and, for the most part, not much worse? There is an infinite distance and disproportion betwixt God and man, yet he came over all that to love man. What difficulty should I have then to place my affection on my equal at worst, and often better? There cannot be any proportionable distance betwixt the highest and lowest, between the richest and poorest, between the most wise and the most ignorant, between the most gracious and the most ungodly, as there is between the infinite God and a finite angel. Should then the mutual infirmities and failings of Christians, be an insuperable and impassable gulf, as between heaven and hell, that none can pass over by a bridge of love to either? "If God so loved us," should not we love one another? 1 John iv. 11. And besides, when I consider that God hath not only loved me, but my brethren who were worthy of hatred, with an everlasting love, and passed over all that was in them, and hath spread his skirt over their nakedness, and made it a time of love, which was a time of loathing, how can I withhold my affection where God hath bestowed his? Are they not infinitely more unworthy of his than mine? Since infinite wrongs hath not changed his, shall poor, petty, and light offences hinder mine? That my love concenter with God's on the same persons, is it not enough?

Next, That Jesus Christ, the only begotten of the Father, full of grace and truth, who was the Father's delight from eternity, and in whom he delighted, yet, not withstanding, could rejoice in the habitable places of the earth, and so love poor wretched men, yet enemies, that he gave himself for them, that God so loved that he gave his Son, and Christ so loved that he gave himself a sacrifice for sin, both for me and others, O! who should not or will not be constrained, in beholding this mirror of incomparable and spotless love to love others? (1 John iv. 9, 10, 11.) "In this was manifested the love of God towards us, because that God sent his only begotten Son into the world, that we might live through him. Herein is love, not that we loved God, but that he loved us, and sent his Son to be the propitiation for our sins. Beloved, if God so loved us, we ought also to love one another." Eph. v. 2. "And walk in love, as Christ also hath loved us, and hath given himself for us, an offering and a sacrifice to God for a sweet smelling savour," especially when he seems to require no other thing, and imposes no more grievous command upon us for recompence of all his labour of love. John xiii. 34, 35. "A new commandment I give unto you, That ye love one another, as I have loved you, that ye also love one another. By this shall all men know that ye are my disciples, if ye have love one to another." If all that was in me did not alienate his love from me, how should any thing in others estrange our love to them? If God be so kind to his enemies, and Christ so loving that he gives his life for his enemies to make them friends, what should we do to our enemies, what to our friends? This one example may make all created love to blush and be ashamed. How narrow, how limited, how selfish is it!

Thirdly, If God hath forgiven me so many grievous offences, if he hath pardoned so heinous and innumerable injuries, that amount to a kind of infiniteness in number and quality, O how much more am I bound to forgive my brethren a few light and trivial offences? Col. iii. 13. "Forbearing one another, and forgiving one another, if any man have a quarrel against any, even as Christ forgave you, so also do ye." Eph. iv. 32. "And be ye kind one to another, tender hearted, forgiving one another, even as God for Christ's sake hath forgiven you." With what face can I pray, "Lord, forgive me my sins," when I may meet with such a retortion, thou canst not forgive thy brethren's sins, infinitely less both in number and degree? Matth. vi. 15. "But if ye forgive not men their trespasses, neither will your heavenly Father forgive your trespasses." What unparalleled ingratitude were it, what monstrous wickedness, that after he hath forgiven all our debt, because we desired him yet we should not have compassion on our fellow servants even as he had pity on us! O! what a dreadful sound will that be in the ears of many Christians, "O thou wicked servant, I forgave thee all thy debt, because thou desiredst me! Shouldest not thou also have had compassion on thy fellow servants, even as I had pity on thee? And his lord was wroth, and delivered him to the tormentors, till he should pay all that was due unto him. So likewise shall my heavenly Father do also unto you, if ye from your hearts forgive not every one his brother their trespasses," Matth. xviii. 32, 33, 34, 35. When we cannot dispense with one penny, how should he dispense with his talents? And when we cannot pardon ten, how should he forgive ten thousand? When he hath forgiven my brother all his iniquity, may not I pardon one? Shall I impute that which God will not impute, or discover that which God hath covered? How should I expect he should be merciful to me, when I cannot shew mercy to my brother? Psal. xviii. 25. "With the merciful thou wilt show thyself merciful." Shall I, for one or few offences, hate, bite, and devour him for whom Christ died, and loved not his life to save him? Rom. xiv. 15 and 1 Cor. viii. 11.

In the next place. If a Christian do but take an impartial view of himself, he cannot but thus reason himself to a meek, composed, and affectionate temper towards other brethren. What is it in another that offends me, when if I do search within, I will not either find the same, or worse, or as evil in myself? Is there a mote in my brothers eye? Perhaps there may be a beam in my own; and why then should I look to the mote that is in my brother's eye? Matth. vii. 3. When I look inwardly, I find a desperately wicked heart, which lodges all that iniquity I beheld in others. And if I be not so sensible of it, it is because it is also deceitful above all things, and would flatter me in mine own eyes, Jer. xvii. 9. If my brother offend me in some things, how do these evanish out of sight in the view of my own guiltiness before God, and of the abominations of my own heart, known to his holiness and to my conscience? Sure I cannot see so much evil in my brother as I find in myself. I see but his outside. But I know my own heart; and whenever I retire within this, I find the sea of corruption so great, that I wonder not at the streams which break forth in others. But all my wonder is that God hath set bounds to it in me or in any. Whenever I find my spirit rising against the infirmities of others, and my mind swelling over them, I repress myself with this thought, "I myself also am a man," as Peter said to Cornelius when he would have worshipped him. As he restrained another's idolizing of him, I may cure my own self idolizing heart. Is it any thing strange that weak men fail, and sinful men fall? Is not all flesh grass, and all the perfection and goodliness of it as the flower of the field? Isa. xl. 6. Is not every man at his best estate altogether vanity? Psal. xxxix. 5. Is not man's breath in his nostrils? Isa. ii. 22. And am not I myself a man? Therefore I will not be high minded but fear, Rom. xi. 20. I will not be moved to indignation, but provoked to compassion, knowing that I myself am compassed with infirmities, Heb. v. 2.

Secondly, As a man may persuade himself to charity by the examination of his own heart and ways, so he may enforce upon his spirit a meek and compassionate stamp, by the consideration of his own frailty, what he may fall into. This is the Apostle's rule, Gal. vi. 1. "Brethren, if a man be overtaken in a fault, ye that are spiritual," and pretend to it, "restore such an one in the spirit of meekness." Do not please yourselves with a false notion of zeal, thinking to cover your impertinent rigidity by it. Do as you would do if your own arm were disjointed. Set it in, restore it tenderly and meekly, considering yourselves that ye also may be tempted. Some are more given to reproaching and insulting than mindful of restoring. Therefore their reproofs are not tempered with oil that they may not break the head, but mixed with gall and vinegar to set on edge the teeth. But whenever thou lookest upon the infirmities of others, then consider thyself first, before you pronounce sentence on them, and thou shalt be constrained to bestow that charity to others which thou hast need of thyself. *Veniam petimusque damusque vicissim.*[415] If a man have need of charity from his brother, let him not be hard in giving it. If he know his own weakness and frailty, sure he may suppose such a thing may likely fall out that he may be tempted and succumb in it. For there needs nothing for the bringing forth of sin in any but occasion and temptation, as the bringing of fire near gunpowder. And truly he who had no allowance of love to give to an infirm and weak brother, he will be in *mala fide*, in an evil capacity, to seek what he would not give. Now the fountain of uncharitable and harsh dealing is imported in the 3d verse, "If any man thinks himself to be something when he is nothing, he deceives himself." Since all mortal men are nothing, vanity, altogether vanity, and less than vanity, he that would seem something, and seems so to himself, deludes himself. Hence is our insulting fierceness, hence our supercilious rigour. Every man apprehends some excellency in himself beyond another. Take away pride, and charity shall enter, and modesty shall be its companion. But now we mock ourselves, and deceive ourselves, by building the weight of our pretended zeal upon such a vain and rotten foundation, as a gross practical fundamental lie of self conceit of nothing. Now the Apostle furnishes us with an excellent remedy against this in the 4th verse, "Let a man prove himself and his own work, and then he shall have rejoicing in himself alone, and not in another."—a word worthy to be fastened by the Master of assemblies in the heart of all Christians! And indeed this nail driven in would drive out all conceit. Hence is our ruin, that we compare ourselves among ourselves, and in so doing we are not wise,

2 Cor. x. 12. For we know not our own true value. Only we raise the price according to the market, so to speak. We measure ourselves by another man's measure, and build up our estimation upon the disesteem of others, and how much others displease, so much we please ourselves. But, says the Apostle, let every man prove his own work, search his own conscience, compare himself to the perfect rule; and then, if he find all well, he may indeed glory of himself. But that which thou hast by comparison with others is not thine own. Thou must come down from all such advantages of ground, if thou would have thy just measure. And indeed, if thou prove thyself and thy work after this manner, thou wilt be the first to reprove thyself, thou shalt have that glory due unto thee, that is none at all. For every man shall bear his own burden, when he appears before the judgment seat of God. There is no place for such imaginations and comparisons in the Lord's judgment.

Thirdly, When a Christian looks within his own heart, he finds an inclination and desire to have the love of others, even though his conscience witness that he deserves it not. He finds an approbation of that good and righteous command of God, that others should love him. Now hence he may persuade himself—Is it so sweet and pleasant to me to be loved of others, even though I am conscious that I have wronged them? Hath it such a beauty in my eye, while I am the object of it? Why then should it be a hard and grievous burden to me to love others, though they have wronged me, and deserve it no more than I did? Why hath it not the same amiable aspect, when my brother is the object of it? Certainly no reason for it, but because I am yet carnal, and have not that fundamental law of nature yet distinctly written again upon my heart, "What ye would that others should do to you, do it to them," Matth. vii. 12. If I be convinced that there is any equity and beauty in that command, which charges others to love me, forgive me, and forbear me, and restore me in meekness, why should it be a grievous command that I should pay that debt of love and tenderness to others? 1 John v. 3. "For this is the love of God, that we keep his commandments, and his commandments are not grievous."

In the third place. Consider to whom this affection should be extended. More generally to all men, as fellow creatures, but particularly and especially to all who are begotten of God, as fellow Christians. "And this commandment have we from him, that he who loveth God love his brother also. Whosoever believeth that Jesus is the Christ is born of God, and every one that loveth him that begat, loveth him also that is begotten of him," 1 John iv. 21, and chap v. 1. "As we have therefore opportunity, let us do good unto all men, especially unto them who are of the household of faith," Gal. vi. 10. "O my soul, thou hast said unto the Lord, Thou art my Lord, my goodness extendeth not to thee: but unto the saints that are in the earth, and to the excellent in whom is all my delight," Psal. xvi. 2, 3. And this consideration the Holy Ghost suggests to make us maintain love and unity. Love towards these runs in a purer channel—"Ye have purified your souls in obeying the truth through the Spirit unto the unfeigned love of the brethren, see that ye love one another with a pure heart fervently, being born again, not of corruptible seed, but of incorruptible, by the word of God, which liveth and abideth for ever," 1 Pet. i. 22, 23. We are begotten of one Father, and that by a divine birth, we have such a high descent and royal generation! There are so many other bonds of unity between us, it is absurd that this one more should not join all. "One Lord, one faith, one baptism, one body, one spirit, called to one hope, one God and Father of all," Eph. iv. 2-6. All these being one, it is strange if we be not one in love. If so many relations beget not a strong and warm affection, we are worse than infidels, as the apostle speaks, 1 Tim. v. 8. "If a man care not for his own house, his worldly interests, he is worse than an infidel," for he has a natural affection. Sure then this more excellent nature, a divine nature we are partakers of, cannot want affection suitable to its nature. Christianity is a fraternity, a brotherhood, that should overpower all relations, bring down him of high degree, and exalt him of low degree; it should level all ranks, in this one respect, unto the rule of charity and love. In Christ there is neither Jew nor Gentile. There all differences of tongues and nations are drowned in this interest of Christ, Col. iii. 11. "Thou hast hid those things from the wise and prudent, and revealed them unto babes," Luke x. 21. And "God hath chosen the weak and foolish to confound the mighty and wise," 1 Cor. i. 27. Behold all these outward privileges buried in the depths and riches of God's grace and mercy. Are we not all called to one high calling? Our common station is to war under Christ's banner against sin and Satan. Why then do we leave our station, forget our callings, and neglect that employment which concerns us all, and fall at odds with our fellow-soldiers, and bite and devour one another? Doth not this give advantage to our common enemies? While we consume the edge of our zeal and strength of our spirits one upon another, they must needs be blunted and weakened towards our deadly enemies. If our brother be represented unto us under the covering of many faults, failings, and obstinacy in his errors, or such like, if we can behold nothing but spots on his outside, while we judge after some outward appearance, then, I say, we ought to consider him again under another notion and relation, as he stands in Christ's account, as he is radically and virtually of that seed, which hath more real worth in it than all worldly privileges and dignities. Consider him as he once shall be, when mortality shall be put off. Learn to strip him naked of all infirmities in thy consideration, and imagine him to be clothed with immortality, and glory, and think how thou wouldest then love him. If either thou unclothe him of his infirmities, and consider him as vested now with the robe of Christ's righteousness, and all glorious within, or adorned with immortality and incorruption a little hence; or else, if thou clothe thyself with such infirmities as thou seest in him, and consider that thou art not less subject to failing, and compassed with infirmities, then thou shalt put on, and keep on, that bond of perfection, charity.

Lastly. Let us consider the excellent nature of charity, and how it is interested in, and interwoven with all the royal and divine gifts and privileges of a Christian. All of them are not ashamed of kindred and cognation with charity. Is not the calling and profession of a Christian honourable? Sure to any behoving soul it is above a monarchy; for it includes an anointing both to a royal and priestly office, and carries a title to a kingdom incorruptible and undefiled. Well then, charity is the symbol and badge of this profession, John xiii. 35. "By this shall all men know that ye are my disciples, if ye have love one to another." Then, what is comparable to communion with God, and dwelling in him? Shall God indeed dwell with men, said Solomon? That exalts the soul to a royalty, and elevates it above mortality. *Quam contempta res est homo si supra humana se non exerat!* "How base and contemptible a thing is man, except he lift up his head above human things to heavenly and divine!" And then is the soul truly magnified while it is ascending to its own element, a divine nature. What more gracious than this, for a soul to dwell in God? And what more glorious than this, God to dwell in the soul? *Charitas te domum Domini facit, et Dominum domum tibi. Felix artifex charitas quæ conditori suo domum fabricare potest!* "Love makes the soul a house for the Lord, and makes the Lord a house to the soul. Happy artificer that can build a house for its master!" Love bringeth him, who is the chief among ten thousand, into the chambers of the heart. It lays him all night between its breasts; and is still emptying itself of all superfluity of naughtiness, and purging out all vanity and filthiness, that there may be more room for his Majesty. And then love dwells in God, in his love and grace, in his goodness and greatness. The secret of his presence it delights in. Now this mutual inhabitation, in which it is hard to say whether the Majesty of God does most descend, or the soul most ascend, whether he be more humbled or it exalted, this brotherly love, I say, is the evidence and assurance of it. "If we love one another, God dwells in us, and his love is perfected in us. God is love, and he that dwelleth in love dwelleth in God, and God in him," 1 John iv. 12, 16. For the love of the image of God in his children, is indeed the love of God whose image it is, and then is the love of God perfected, when it reacheth and extends from God to all that is God's, to all that hath interest in God—his commandments, (1 John v. 3. "This is the love of God, that we keep his commandments, and his commandments are not grievous," 1 John iv. 21, "And this commandment have we from him, that he who loveth God love his brother also,") his children, (1 John v.

1, "Whosoever believeth that Jesus is the Christ is born of God, and every one that loveth him that begat, loveth him that is begotten of him,") his creatures, (Mal. ii. 10, "Hath not one God created us, why do we deal treacherously every man against his brother?") The love of God being the formal, the special motive of love to our brethren, it elevates the nature of it, and makes it divine love. He that hath true Christian love, doth not only love and compassionate his brother, either because of its own inclination towards him, or his misery and necessity, or his goodness and excellency. These motives and grounds do not transcend mere morality, and so cannot beget a love which is the symptom of Christianity. If there be no other motives than these, we do not love so much for God as for ourselves; for compassion interesting itself with another man's misery, finds a kind of relief in relieving it. Therefore the will and good pleasure of God must be the rule of this motion, and the love of God must begin in it and continue it. And truly charity is nothing else but divine love in a state of condescent,[416] so to speak, or the love of a soul to God manifested in the flesh. It is that love moving in a circle from God towards his creatures, and unto God again, as his love to the creatures begins in himself and ends in himself, 1 John iii. 17. Is it not a high thing to know God aright? "This is life eternal to know thee, the only true God, and Jesus Christ whom thou hast sent," John xvii. 3. That is a high note of excellency put on it, this makes the face of the soul to shine, now brotherly love evinceth this, that we know God, "Beloved, let us love one another, for love is of God, and every one that loveth is born of God, and knoweth God. He that loveth not, knoweth not God, for God is love," 1 John iv. 7, 8. Love is real light, light and life, light and heat both. "When your fathers did execute judgment, and relieve the oppressed, &c. was not this to know me? saith the Lord," Jer. xxii. 15, 16. The practice of the most common things, out of the love of God, and respect to his commands, is more real and true religion than the most profound and abstracted speculations of knowledge. Then only is God known, when knowledge stamps the heart with fear and reverence of his Majesty and love to his name, because then he is only known as he is a true and living God.

Love is real light and life. Is it not "a pleasant thing for the eye to behold the sun?" Light is sweet, and life is precious. These are two of the rarest jewels given to men. "He that saith he is in the light, and hateth his brother, is in darkness even until now, and knoweth not whither he goeth; because darkness hath blinded his eyes, but he that loveth his brother abideth in the light, and there is none occasion of stumbling in him," 1 John ii. 9-11. "We know that we have passed from death unto life, because we love the brethren; he that loveth not his brother, abideth in death," 1 John iii. 14. The light of Jesus Christ cannot shine into the heart, but it begets[417] love, even as intense light begets heat, and where this impression is not made on the heart, it is an evidence that the beams of that Sun of righteousness have not pierced it. O how suitable is it for a child of light to walk in love! And wherefore is it made day light to the soul, but that it may rise up and go forth to labour, and exercise itself in the works of the day, duties of love to God and men? Now in such a soul there is no cause of stumbling, no scandal, no offence in its way to fall over. When the light and knowledge of Christ possesses the heart in love, there is no stumbling block of transgression in its way. It doth not fall and stumble at the commandments of righteousness and mercy as grievous, "therefore love is the fulfilling of the law," Rom. xiii. 10. And so the way of charity is the most easy, plain, expedient, and safe way. In this way there is light shining all alongst it, and there is no stumbling block in it. For the love of God and of our brethren hath polished and made it all plain, hath "taken away the asperities and tumours of our affections and lusts." *Complanavit affectus.* "Great peace have all they that love thy law, and nothing shall offend them." Love makes an equable and constant motion, it moves swiftly and sweetly. It can loose many knots without difficulty, which other more violent principles cannot cut, it can melt away mountains before it, which cannot be hauled away. Albeit there be many stumbling blocks without in the world, yet there is none in charity, or in a charitable soul. None can enter into that soul to hinder it to possess itself in meekness and patience. Nothing can discompose it within, or hinder it to live peaceably with others. Though all men's hands be against it, yet charity is against none. It defends itself with innocence and patience. On the other hand, "He that hateth his brother is in darkness even till now." For if Christ's light had entered, then the love of Christ had come with it, and that is the law of love and charity. If Jesus Christ had come into the soul, he had restored the ancient commandment of love, and made it new again. As much of the want of love and charity, so much of the old ignorance and darkness remains. Whatsoever a man may fancy of himself that he is in the light, that he is so much advanced in the light, yet certainly this is a stronger evidence of remaining darkness, for it is a work of the darkest darkness, and murdering affection, suitable only for the night of darkness. And such a man knows not whither he goes, and must needs incur and fall upon many stumbling blocks within and without. It is want of love and charity that blinds the mind and darkens the heart, that it cannot see how to eschew and pass by scandals in others, but it must needs dash and break its neck upon them. Love is a light which may lead us by offences inoffensively, and without stumbling. In darkness men mistake the way, know not the end of it, take pits for plain ways, and stumble in them. Uncharitableness casts a mist over the actions and courses of others, and our own too, that we cannot carry on either without transgression. And this is the misery of it, that it cannot discern any fault in itself. It knows not whither it goeth, calls light darkness and darkness light. It is partial in judgment, pronounces always on its own behalf, cares not whom it condemn, that it may absolve itself.

Is there any privilege so precious as this, to be "the sons of God?" 1 John iii. 2. What are all relations, or states, or conditions, to this one, to be the children of the Highest? It was David's question, "Should I be the king's son in law?" Alas! what a petty and poor dignity in regard of this, to be "the sons of God," partakers of a divine nature? All the difference of birth, all the distinction of degrees and qualities amongst persons, besides this one, are but such as have no being, no worth but in the fancy and construction of them. They really are nothing, and can do nothing. This only is a substantial and fundamental difference. A divine birth carries along with it a divine nature, a change of principles, from the worst to the best, from darkness to light, from death to life. Now, imagine then, what excellency is in this grace, which is made the character of a son of God, of one begotten of the Father, and passed from death to life? 1 John iii. 10, 14. "In this the children of God are manifest, and the children of the devil. Whosoever doth not righteousness is not of God, neither he that loveth not his brother. We know that we have passed from death unto life, because we love the brethren, he that loveth not his brother, abideth in death." 1 John iv. 7. "Beloved, let us love one another, for love is of God, and every one that loveth is born of God, and knoweth God." And truly it is most natural, if it be so, that the children of our Father love each other dearly. It is monstrous and unnatural to see it otherwise. But besides, there is in this a great deal of resemblance of their Father, whose eminent and signal property it is, to be good to all and kind even to the unthankful, and whose incomparable glory it is to pardon iniquity, and suffer long patiently. A Christian cannot resemble his Father more nearly than in this. Why do we account that baseness in us which is glory to God? Are we ashamed of our birth, or dare we not own our Father? Shall we be ashamed to love them as brethren whom he hath not been ashamed to adopt as sons, and whom Christ is not ashamed to call brethren?

CHAPTER IV.

We shall not be curious in the ranking of the duties in which Christian love should exercise itself. All the commandments of the second table are but branches of it: they might be reduced all to the works of righteousness and of mercy. But truly these are interwoven through other. Though mercy uses to be restricted to the showing of compassion upon men in misery, yet there is a righteousness in that mercy, and there is mercy in the most part of the acts of righteousness, as in not judging rashly, in forgiving, &c. Therefore we shall consider the most eminent and difficult duties of love, which the word of God solemnly and frequently charges upon us in relation to others, especially these of the household of faith.

I conceive we would labour to enforce upon our hearts, and persuade our souls to a love of all men, by often ruminating upon the words of the Apostle, which enjoin us to "abound in love towards all men," 1 Thess. iii. 12. And this is so concerning, that he prays earnestly that the Lord would make them increase in it, and this we should pray for too. An affectionate disposition towards our common nature is not a common thing. Christianity enjoins it, and it is only true humanity, Luke vi. 36, 37. "Be ye therefore merciful, as your Father also is merciful. Judge not, and ye shall not be judged, condemn not, and ye shall not be condemned, forgive, and ye shall be forgiven." Now in relation to all men, charity hath an engagement upon it to pray for all sorts of men, from that Apostolic command, 1 Tim ii. 1: "I exhort therefore, that first of all, supplications, prayers, intercessions, and giving of thanks be made for all men." Prayers and supplications, earnest prayers out of affection, should be poured out even for them that cannot, or do not pray for themselves. Wherefore are we taught to pray, but that we may be the mouth of others? And since an intercessor is given to us above, how are we bound to be intercessors for others below, and so to be affected with the common mercies of the multitude, as to give thanks too! If man, by the law of creation, is the mouth of the stones, trees, birds, beasts, of heaven and earth, sun and moon and stars, how much more ought a Christian, a redeemed man, be the mouth of mankind to praise God for the abounding of his goodness, even towards these who are left yet in that misery and bondage that he is delivered from?

Next, Charity by all means will avoid scandal, and live honestly in the sight of all men. The apostle says, "Give none offence, neither to the Jews nor to the Gentiles, nor to the church of God," 1 Cor. x. 32. And he adds his own example, "Even as I please all men in all things, not seeking my own profit, but the profit of many, that they may be saved," ver. 33. Charity is not self addicted. It hath no humour to please. It can displease itself to profit others. I do verily think there is no point of Christianity less regarded. Others we acknowledge, but we fail in practice. This scarce hath the approbation of the mind. Few do conceive an obligation lying on them to it. But O how is Christianity, the most of it, humanity? Christ makes us men as well as Christians. He makes us reasonable men when believers. Sin transformed our nature into a wild, beastly, viperous, selfish thing. Grace restores reason and natural affection in the purest and highest strain. And this is reason and humanity, elevated and purified,—to condescend to all men in all things for their profit and edification, to deny itself to save others. Whatsoever is not necessary in itself, we ought not to impose a necessity upon it by our imagination and fancy, to the prejudice of a greater necessity, another's edification. Indeed charity will not, dare not sin to please men. That were to hate God, to hate ourselves, and to hate our brethren, under a base pretended notion of love. But I believe, addictedness to our own humours in things not necessary, which have no worth but from our disposition, doth oftener transport us beyond the bounds of charity than the apprehension of duty and conscience of sin. Some will grant they should be tender of offending the saints. But they do not conceive it is much matter what they do in relation to others, as if it were lawful to murder a Gentile more than a Christian. That is a bloody imagination, opposite to that innocent Christian, Paul, who says (Philip. ii. 15.), we should be "blameless and harmless, the sons of God, without rebuke, in the midst of a crooked and perverse generation," among whom we should shine "as lights." And truly it is humanity elevated by Christianity, or reason purified by religion, that is the light that shines most brightly in this dark world. And he says (in Col. iv. 5.), "Walk in wisdom toward them that are without," and (1 Thess. iv. 12.) "walk honestly toward them that are without,"—avoiding all things, in our profession and carriage, which may alienate them from the love of the truth and godliness walking so, as we may insinuate into their hearts some apprehension of the beauty of religion. Many conceive, if they do good, all is well—if it be a duty, it matters nothing. But remember that caution, "Let not then your good be evil spoken of," Rom. xiv. 16. We would have our eyes upon that too, so to circumstantiate all our duties, as they may have least offence in them, and be exposed to least obloquy of men, 1 Pet. ii. 12. "Having your conversation honest among the Gentiles, that whereas they speak against you as evil doers, they may by your good works which they shall behold, glorify God in the day of visitation."

Then, *Thirdly*, Charity follows peace with all men, as much as is possible, Heb. xii. 14. "If it be possible as much as lieth in you, live peaceably with all men," Rom. xii. 18. Many spirits are framed for contention. If peace follow them, they will flee from it. But a Christian having made peace with God, the sweet fruit of that upon his spirit is to dispose him to a peaceable and quiet condescendency to others, and if peace flee from him, to follow after it, not only to entertain it when it is offered, but to seek it when it is away, and to pursue it when it runs away. (Psal. xxxiv. 14, which Peter urges upon Christians, 1 Pet. iii. 8, 9, 10, 11.) "Finally, be ye all of one mind, having compassion one of another, love as brethren, be pitiful, be courteous. Not rendering evil for evil, or railing for railing, but contrariwise, blessing, knowing that ye are thereunto called that ye should inherit a blessing. For he that will love life, and see good days, let him refrain his tongue from evil, and his lips that they speak no guile. Let him eschew evil, and do good; let him seek peace, and ensue it." I think, since we obtained the mercy to get a Peace maker between us and God, we should henceforth count ourselves bound to be peace makers among men. And truly such have a blessing pronounced upon them, Matt. v. 9. "Blessed are the peace makers." The Prince of peace pronounced it, and this is the blessedness, "they shall be called the children of God," because he is "the God of peace," and to resemble him in these, first in purity, then in peace, is a character of his image. It is true, peace will sometimes flee so fast, and so far away, as a Christian cannot follow it without sin, and that is breach of a higher peace. But charity, when it cannot live in peace without, doth then live in peace within, because it hath that sweet testimony of conscience, that, as far as did lie in it, peace was followed without. Divine wisdom (James iii. 17.), "is first pure, then peaceable, gentle, and easy to be entreated, full of mercy and good fruits, without wrangling and without hypocrisy." If wisdom be peaceable and not pure, it is but a carnal conspiracy in iniquity, earthly and sensual. But if it be pure it must be peaceable. For the wisdom descending from above hath a purity of truth, and a purity of love, and a purity of the mind and of the affection too. Where there is a purity of truth, but accompanied with envying, bitter strife, rigid judging, wrangling, and such like, then it is defiled and corrupted by the intermixture of vile and base affections, ascending out of the dunghill of the flesh. The vapours of our lusts arising up to the mind, do stain pure truth. They put an earthly, sensual, and devilish visage on it.

Charity, its conversation and discourse, is without judging, without censuring, Matth. vii. 1. Of which chapter, because it contains much edification, I shall speak more hereafter. James iii. 17. "Without partiality, without hypocrisy." The words in the original are, αδιακριτος και ανυποκριτος, (without judging and wrangling, and without hypocrisy), importing, that great censurers are often the greatest hypocrites, and sincerity has always much charity. Truly, there is much idle time spent this way in discourses of one another, and venting our judgments of others, as if it were enough of commendation for us to condemn others, and much piety to charge another with impiety. We should even be sparing in judging them that are without, 1 Cor. v. 12, 13. Reflecting upon them or their ways, hath more provocation than edification in it. A censorious humour is certainly most partial to itself, and self indulgent. It can sooner endure a great beam in its own eye, than a little mote in its neighbour's, and this shows evidently that it is not the hatred of sin, or the love of virtue, which is the single and simple principle of it, but self love, shrouded under the vail of displeasure at sin, and delight in virtue. I would think one great help to amend this, were to abate much from the superfluity and multitude of discourses upon others. "In the multitude of words there wants not sin," and in the multitude of discourses upon other men, there cannot miss the sin of rash judging. I find the saints and fearers of God commended for speaking often one to another, but not at all for speaking one of another. The subject of their discourse (Mal. iii. 16.) certainly was of another strain,—how good it was to serve the Lord, &c.—opposite to the evil communication of others there registered.

Charity is no tale bearer. It goeth not about as a slander to reveal a secret, though true, Prov. xx. 19. It is of a faithful spirit to conceal the matter, Prov. xi. 13. Another man's good name is as a pledge laid down in our hand, which every man should faithfully restore, and take heed how he lose it, or alienate it by back-biting. Some would have nothing to say, if they had not other's faults and frailties to declaim upon, but it were better that such kept always silent, that either they had no ears to hear of them or know them, or had no tongues to vent them. If they do not lie grossly in it, they think they do no wrong. But let them judge it in reference to themselves. "A good name is better than precious ointment," (Eccles. vii. 1.) "and rather to be chosen than great riches," Prov. xxii. 1. And is that no wrong, to defile that precious ointment, and to rob or steal away that jewel more precious than great riches? There is a strange connection between these. "Thou shalt not go up and down as a tale-bearer, nor stand against the blood of thy neighbour," Lev. xix. 16. It is a kind of murder, because it kills that which is as precious as life to an ingenuous heart. "The words of a tale bearer are as wounds, and they go down to the innermost parts of the belly," Prov. xviii. 8 and xxvi. 22. They strike a wound to any man's heart, that can hardly be cured, and there is nothing that is such a seminary of contention and strife among brethren as this. It is the oil to feed the flame of alienation. Take away a tale-bearer, and strife ceaseth, Prov. xxvi. 20. Let there be but any (as there want not such who have no other trade or occupation), to whisper into the ears of brethren, and suggest evil apprehensions of them, they will separate chief friends, as we see it in daily experience, Prov. xvi. 28. "Revilers" are amongst these who are excluded out of the kingdom of God, 1 Cor. vi. 10. And therefore, as the Holy Ghost gives general precepts for the profitable and edifying improvement of the tongue, that so it may indeed be the glory of a man, (which truly is no small point of religion, as James expresses, Chap. iii. 2. "If any man offend not in word, the same is a perfect man,") so that same spirit gives us particular directions about this, "Speak not evil one of another, brethren. He that speaketh evil of his brother, and judgeth his brother, speaketh evil of the law, and judgeth the law," (James iv. 11.) because he puts himself in the place of the Lawgiver, and his own judgment and fancy in the room of the law, and so judges the law. And therefore the Apostle Peter makes a wise and significant connection, 1 Pet. ii. 1. "Laying aside all malice, and all guile, and hypocrisies, and envies, and all evil-speakings." Truly, evil speaking of our brethren, though it may be true, yet it proceeds out of the abundance of these, in the heart, of guile, hypocrisy, and envy. While we catch at a name of piety from censuring others, and build our own estimation upon the ruins of another's good name, hypocrisy and envy are too predominant. If we would indeed grow in grace by the word, and taste more how gracious the Lord is, we must lay these aside, and become as little children, without guile, and without gall. Many account it excuse enough, that they did not invent evil tales, or were not the first broachers of them; but the Scripture joins both together. The man that "shall abide in his tabernacle" must neither vent nor invent them, neither cast them down nor take them up, "He backbiteth not with his tongue, nor taketh up a reproach against his neighbour;" (Psal. xv. 3.) or *receiveth not* or *endureth not*, as in the margin. He neither gives it nor receives he it, hath not a tongue to speak of others' faults, nor ear to hear them. Indeed he hath a tongue to confess his own, and an ear open to hear another confess his faults, according to that precept, "Confess your faults one to another." We are forbidden to have much society or fellowship with tale-bearers; and it is added, Prov. xx. 19, "And meddle not with such as flatter with their mouth," as indeed commonly they who reproach the absent, flatter the present; a backbiter is a face-flatterer. And therefore we should not only not meddle with them, but drive them away as enemies to human society. Charity would in such a case protect itself, if I may so say, by "an angry countenance," an appearance of anger and real dislike.

“As the north wind drives away rain,” so that entertainment would drive away a “backbiting tongue,” Prov. xxv. 23. If we do discountenance it, backbiters will be discouraged to open their pack of news and reports: and indeed the receiving readily of evil reports of brethren, is a partaking with the unfruitful works of darkness, which we should rather reprove, Eph. v. 11. To join with the teller is to complete the evil report; for if there were no receiver there would be no teller, no tale-bearer. “Charity covers a multitude of sins,” 1 Pet. iv. 8; and therefore “above all things have fervent charity among yourselves,” says he. What is above prayer and watching unto the end, above sobriety? Indeed, in reference to fellowship with God, these are above all; but in relation to comfortable fellowship one with another in this world, this is above all, and the crown or cream of other graces. He whose sins are covered by God’s free love, cannot think it hard to spread the garment of his love over his brother’s sins. Hatred stirreth up strife, all uncharitable affections, as envy, wrath. It stirreth up contentions, and blazeth abroad men’s infirmities. But “love covereth all sins,” concealeth them from all to whom the knowledge of them doth not belong, Prov. x. 12. Love in a manner suffers not itself to know what it knoweth, or at least to remember it much. It will sometimes hoodwink itself to a favourable construction. It will pass by an infirmity and misken[418] it, but many stand still and commune with it. But he that covereth a transgression seeks love to bury offences in. Silence is a notable mean to preserve concord, and beget true amity and friendship. The keeping of faults long above ground unburied, doth make them cast forth an evil savour that will ever part friends. Therefore, says the wise man, “He that covereth a transgression seeketh love: but he that repeateth a matter separateth very friends,” Prov. xvii. 9. Covering faults christianly, will make a stranger a friend; but repeating and blazing of them will make a friend not only a stranger, but an enemy. Yet this is nothing to the prejudice of that Christian duty of reproving and admonishing one another, Eph. v. 11. “Have no fellowship with the unfruitful works of darkness, but rather reprove them.” Love commands to reprove in the “spirit of meekness,” (Gal. vi. 1.) as a man would restore an arm out of joint. And therefore thou "shall not hate him in thy heart, but shall in any ways reprove him, and not suffer sin upon him," Lev. xix. 17. And he that reproves his brother after this manner from love, and in meekness and wisdom, "shall afterward find more favour of him than he that flatters with his tongue," Prov. xxviii. 23. To cover grudges and jealousies in our hearts, were to nourish a flame in our bosom, which doth but wait for a vent, and will at one occasion or other burst out. But to look too narrowly to every step, and to write up a register of men's mere frailties, especially so as to publish them to the world; that is inconsistent with the rule of love. And truly, it is a token of one "destitute of wisdom to despise his neighbour; but a man of understanding will hold his peace." He that has most defects himself, will find maniest[419] in others, and strive to vilify them one way or other; but a wise man can pass by frailties, yea, offences done to him, and be silent, Prov. xi. 12.

CHAPTER V.

Humility is the root of charity, and meekness the fruit of both. There is no solid and pure ground of love to others, except the rubbish of self-love be first cast out of the soul; and when that superfluity of naughtiness is cast out, then charity hath a solid and deep foundation: "The end of the command is charity out of a pure heart," 1 Tim. i. 5. It is only such a purified heart, cleansed from that poison and contagion of pride and self-estimation, that can send out such a sweet and wholesome stream, to the refreshing of the spirits and bowels of the church of God. If self-glory and pride have deep roots fastened into the soul, they draw all the sap and virtue downward, and send little or nothing up to the tree of charity, which makes it barren and unfruitful in the works of righteousness, and fruits of mercy and meekness. There are obstructions in the way of that communication, which only can be removed by the plucking up of these roots of pride and self-estimation, which prey upon all, and incorporate all in themselves, and yet, like the lean kine that had devoured the fat, are never the fatter or more well-favoured.

It is no wonder, then, that these are the first principles that we must learn in Christ's school, the very A B C of Christianity: "Learn of me, for I am meek and lowly in heart, and ye shall find rest unto your souls," Matth. xi. 29. This is the great Prophet sent of the Father into the world to teach us, whom he hath, with a voice from heaven, commanded us to hear: "This is my well-beloved Son, hear him." Should not the fame and report of such a Teacher move us? He was testified of very honourably, long before he came, that he had the Spirit above measure, that he had "the tongue of the learned;" (Isa. l. 4.) that he was a greater prophet than Moses, (Deut. xviii. 15, 18.) that is, the wonderful Counsellor of heaven and earth, (Isa. ix. 6.) the "Witness to the people," a Teacher and "Leader to the people." And then, when he came, he had the most glorious testimony from the most glorious persons,—the Father and the Holy Ghost,—in the most solemn manner that ever the world heard of, Matth. xvii. 5. "Behold, a voice out of the cloud, which said, This is my beloved Son, in whom I am well pleased; hear ye him." Now, this is our Master, our Rabbi, Matth. xxiii. 8. This is the Apostle and High Priest of our profession (Heb. iii. 1.); "the light of the world and life of men," John viii. 12. and vi. 33, 51. Having, then, such a Teacher and Master, sent us from heaven, may we not glory in our Master? But some may suppose, that he who came down from heaven, filled with all the riches and treasures of heavenly wisdom, should reveal in his school unto his disciples, all the mysteries and profound secrets of nature and art, about which the world hath ploded since the first taste of the tree of knowledge, and beaten out their brains to the vexation of all their spirits, without any fruit, but the discovery of the impossibility of knowing, and the increase of sorrow by searching. Who would not expect, when the Wisdom of God descends among men, but that he should show unto the world that wisdom, in the understanding of all the works of God, which all men have been pursuing in vain; that he by whom all things were created, and so could unbowel and manifest all their hidden causes and virtues, all their admirable and wonderful qualities and operations, as easily by a word, as he made them by a word; who would not expect, I say, but that he should have made this world, and the mysteries of it, the subject of all his lessons, the more to illustrate his own glorious power and wisdom? And yet behold, they who had come into his school and heard this Master and Doctor teach his scholars, they who had been invited to come, through the fame and report of his name, would have stood astonished and surprised to hear the subject of his doctrine; one come from on high to teach so low things as these, "Learn of me, I am meek and lowly." Other men that are masters of professions, and authors of sects or orders, do aspire unto some singularity in doctrine to make them famous. But behold our Lord and Master, this is the doctrine he vents! It hath nothing in it that sounds high, and looks big in the estimation of the world. In regard of the wisdom of the world, it is foolishness, a doctrine of humility from the most High! A lesson of lowliness and meekness from the Lord and Maker of all! There seems, at first, nothing in it to allure any to follow it. Who would travel so far as the college of Christianity to learn no more but this, when every man pretends to be a teacher of it?

But truly there is a majesty in this lowliness and there is a singularity in this commonness. If ye would stay and hear a little longer, and enter into a deep search of this doctrine, we would be surcharged and overcome with wonders. It seems shallow till ye enter but it has no bottom. Christianity makes no great noise, but it runs the deeper. It is a light and overly knowledge of it, a small smattering of the doctrine of it, that makes men despise it and prefer other things, but the deep and solid apprehension of it will make us adore and admire, and drive us to an *O altitudo!* "O the depth both of the wisdom and knowledge of God!" Rom. xi. 33. As the superficial knowledge of nature makes men atheists, but the profound understanding of it makes men pious so all other things, *vilescit scientia*, "grow more contemptible by the knowledge of them." It is ignorance of them which is the mother of that devout admiration we bear to them. But Christianity only, *vilescit ignorantia, clarescit scientia*, is common and base, because not known. And that is no disparagement at all unto it, that there is none despises it, but he that knoweth it not, and none can do any thing, but despise all besides it that once knows it. That is the proper excellency and glory of it.

All arts and sciences have their principles, and common axioms of unquestionable authority. All kind of professions have some fundamental doctrines and points which are the character of them. Christianity hath its principles too. And principles must be plain and uncontroverted; they must be evident by their own light, and apt to give light to other things. All the rest of the conclusions of the art are but derivations and deductions from them. Our Master and Doctor follows the same method. He lays down some common principles some fundamental points of this profession, upon which all the building of Christianity hangs. "Learn of me, for I am meek and lowly." This was the high lesson that his life preached so exemplarily, and his doctrine pressed so earnestly, and in this he is very unlike other teachers who impose burdens on others, and themselves do not so much as touch them. But he first practises his doctrine and then preaches it. He first casts a pattern in himself, and then presses to follow it. Examples teach better than rules, but both together are most effectual and sure. The rarest example and noblest rule that ever was given to men are here met together.

The rule is about a thing that has a low name, but a high nature. Lowliness and meekness in reputation and outward form, are like servants, yet they account it no robbery to be equal with the highest and most princely graces. The vein of gold and silver lies very low in the bowels of the earth, but it is not therefore base, but the more precious. Other virtues may come with more observation, but these, like the Master that teaches them, come with more reality. If they have less pomp, they have more power and virtue. Humility, how suitable is it to humanity! They are as near of kin one to another, as *homo* and *humus*,[420] and therefore, except a man cast off humanity, and forget his original, the ground, the dust from whence he was taken, I do not see how he can shake off humility. Self knowledge is the mother of it, the knowledge of that *humus* would make us *humiles*.[421] Look to the hole of the pit from whence thou art hewn. A man could not look high that looked so low as the pit from whence we were taken by nature, even the dust, and the pit from whence we are hewn by grace, even man's lost and ruined state. Such a low look would make a lowly mind. Therefore pride must be nothing else but an empty and vain tumour, a puffing up. "Knowledge puffeth up," not self knowledge. That casts down, and brings down all superstructures, razes out all vain confidence to the very foundation, and then begins to build on a solid ground. But knowledge of other things without, joined with ignorance of ourselves within, is but a swelling, not a growing, it is a bladder or skin full of wind, a blast or breath of an airy applause or commendation, will extend it and fill it full. And what is this else but a monster in humanity, the skin of a man stuffed or blown up with wind and vanity, to the shadow and resemblance of a man; but no bones or sinews, nor real substance within? Pride is an excrescence. It is nature swelled beyond the intrinsic terms or limits of magnitude, the spirit of a mouse in a mountain. And now, if any thing be gone without the just bounds of the magnitude set to it, it is imperfect, disabled in its operations, vain and unprofitable, yea, prodigious like. If there be not so much real excellency as may fill up the circle of our self estimation, then surely it must be full of emptiness and vanity, fancy and imagination must supply the vacant room, where solid worth cannot extend so far. Now, I believe, if any man could but impartially and seriously reflect upon himself, he would see nothing of that kind, no true solid and real dignity to provoke love, but real baseness and misery to procure loathing. There is a lie in every sin, but the greatest and grossest lie is committed in pride, and attribution of that excellency to ourselves which is not. And upon what erroneous fancy, which is a sandy and vain foundation, is built the tower of self estimation, vain gloriation, and such like? Pride, which is the mother of these, says most presumptuously, "By the strength of my hand I have done it, and by my wisdom, for I am prudent," (Isa. x. 13.) "I am and none else besides me," Isa. xlvii. 10. It is such a false imagination, as "I am of perfect beauty," "I am and none else," "I am a god," (Ezek. xxvii. 3. and xxviii. 2.) which swells and lifts up the heart. Now what a vain thing is it, an inordinate elevation of the heart upon a false misapprehension of the mind? The "soul which is lifted up, is not upright in him," Hab. ii. 4. It must be a tottering building that is founded on such a gross mistake.

Some cover their pride with the pretence of high spiritedness, and please themselves in apprehensions of some magnanimity and generosity. But the truth is, it is not true magnitude, but a swelling out of the superabundance of pestilent humours. True greatness of spirit is inwardly and throughout solid, firm from the bottom, and the foundation of it is truth. Which of the two do ye think hath the better spirit, he that calls dust, dust, and accounts of dung as dung, or he that, upon a false imagination, thinks dust and dung is gold and silver, esteems himself a rich man, and raises up himself above others? Humility is only true magnanimity, for it digs down low, that it may set and establish the foundation of true worth. It is true, it is lowly, and bows down low. But as the water that comes from a height, the lower it comes down the higher it ascends up again, so the humble spirit, the lower it fall in its own estimation, the higher it is raised in real worth and in God's estimation. "He that humbles himself shall be exalted, and he that exalts himself shall be abased," Matt. xxiii. 12. He is like a growing tree, the deeper the roots go down in the earth, the higher the tree grows above ground, as Jacob's ladder, the foot of it is fastened in the earth, but the top of it reaches the heaven. And this is the sure way to ascend to heaven. Pride would fly up upon its own wings. But the humble man will enter at the lowest step, and so goes up by degrees, and in the end is made manifest. Pride catches a fall,[422] and humility is raised on high; it descended that it might ascend. "A man's pride shall bring him low, but honour shall uphold the humble in spirit," Prov. xxix. 23. "Pride goeth before destruction, and an haughty spirit before a fall." But "before honour is humility," Prov. xvi. 18. and xviii. 12. The first week of creation, as it were, afforded two signal examples of this wise permutation of divine justice, angels cast out of heaven, and man out of paradise, a high and wretched aim at wisdom brought both as low as hell. The pride of angels and men was but the rising up to a height, or climbing up a steep to the pinnacle of glory, that they might catch the lower fall. But the last week of the creation, to speak so, shall afford us rare and eminent demonstrations of the other, poor, wretched, and miserable sinners lifted up to heaven by humility, when angels were thrown down from heaven for pride. What a strange sight, an angel, once so glorious, so low, and a sinner, once so wretched and miserable, so high! Truly may any man conclude within himself, "Better it is to be of an humble spirit with the lowly, than to divide the spoil with the proud," Prov. xvi. 19. Happy lowliness, that is the foundation of true highness! "But miserable highness that is the beginning of eternal baseness." "Blessed are the poor in spirit, for theirs is the kingdom of heaven," Matt. v. 3. Blessedness begins low, in poverty of spirit. And Christ's sermon upon blessedness begins at it, but it arises in the end to the riches of a kingdom, a heavenly kingdom. Grace is the seed of glory, and poverty of spirit is the seed, first dead before it be quickened to grow up in fruits. And indeed the grain "is not quickened except it die," (1 Cor. xv. 36) and then it gets a body, and "bringeth forth much fruit," John xii. 24. Even so, grace is sown into the heart, but it is not quickened except it die in humility, and then God gives it a body, when it springs up in other beautiful graces, of meekness, patience, love, &c. But these are never ripe till the day that the soul get the warm beams of heaven, being separated from the body, and then is the harvest a rich crop of blessedness. Holiness is the ladder to go up to happiness by, or rather our Lord Jesus Christ as adorned with all these graces. Now these are the steps of it, mentioned Matt. v., and the lowest step that a soul first ascends to him by, is poverty of spirit, or humility. And truly the spirit cannot meet with Jesus Christ till he first bring it down low, because he hath come so low himself, as that no soul can ascend up to heaven by him, except they bow down to his lowliness, and rise upon that step.

Now a man being thus humbled in spirit before God, and under his mighty hand, he is only fit to obey the apostolic precept "Be ye all of you subject one to another," 1 Pet. v. 5. Humility towards men depends upon that poverty and self emptying under God's mighty hand, ver. 6. It is only a lowly heart that can make the back to bow, and submit to others of whatsoever quality, and condescend to them of low degree, Rom. xii. 16, Eph. v. 21. But the fear of the Lord humbling the spirit will easily set it as low as any other can put it. This is the only basis and foundation of Christian submission and moderation. It is not a complemental condescendence. It consists not in an external show of gesture and voice. That is but an apish imitation. And indeed pride often will palliate itself under voluntary shows of humility, and can demean itself to undecent and unseemly submissions to persons far inferior, but it is the more deformed and hateful, that it lurks under some shadows of humility. As an ape is the more ugly and ill favoured that it is liker a man, because it is not a man, so vices have more deformity in them when they put on the garb and vizard of virtue. Only it may appear how beautiful a garment true humility is, when pride desires often to be covered with the appearance of it, to hide its nakedness. O how rich a clothing is the mean-like garment of humility and poverty of spirit! "Be ye clothed with humility," 1 Pet. v. 5. It is the ornament of all graces. It covers a man's nakedness by uncovering of it. If a man had all other endowments, this one dead fly, would make all the ointment unsavoury, pride. But humility is *condimentum virtutum,* as well as vestimentum.[423] It seasons all graces, and covers all infirmities. Garments are for ornament and necessity both. Truly this clothing is alike fit for both, to adorn and beautify whatsoever is excellent, and to hide or supply whatsoever is deficient: *ornamentum et operimentum.*[424]

The apostle Paul gives a solemn charge to the Romans (Rom. xii. 3), that no man should think high of himself; but soberly, according to the measure of faith given. That extreme undervaluing and denial of all worth in ourselves, though it be suitable before God (Luke xvii. 6, 7, 10, Prov. xxx. 2, 3, Job xlii. 6, 1 Cor. iii. 7), yet is uncomely and incongruous before men. Humility doth not exclude all knowledge of any excellency in itself, or defect in another, it can discern, but this is the worth of it: that it thinks soberly of the one, and despises not the other. The humble man knows any advantage he has beyond another, but he is not wise in his own conceit. He looks not so much upon that side of things, his own perfections and others' imperfections. That is very dangerous. But he casts his eye most on the other side, his own infirmities and others' virtues, his worst part and their best part, and this makes up an equality or proportion. Where there is inequality, there is a different measure of gifts and graces, there are diverse failings and infirmity, and degrees of them. Now, how shall so unequal members make up one body, and join unto one harmonious being, except this proportion be kept, that the defects of one be made up by the humility of another? The difference and inequality is taken away this way, by fixing my eye most upon my own disadvantages and my brother's advantages. If I be higher in any respect, yet certainly I am lower in some, and therefore the unity of the body may be preserved by humility. I will consider in what I come short, and in what another excels, and so I can condescend to them of low degree. This is the substance of that which is subjoined. (Rom. xii. 16) "Mind not high things, but condescend to men of low estate. Be not wise in your own conceits." And this makes us meet in honour to prefer one another, taking ourselves up in the notion of what evil is in us, and another up in the notion of what good is in him. Rom. xii. 10, "Be kindly affectioned one to another, with brotherly love, in honour preferring one another." Thus there may be an equality of mutual respect and love, where there is an in equality of gifts and graces, there may be one measure of charity, where there are different measures of faith, because both neglect that difference, and pitch upon their own evils and another's good.

It is our custom to compare ourselves among ourselves, and the result of that secret comparison is estimation of ourselves, and despising others. We take our measure, not by our own real and intrinsic qualifications, but by the stature of other men's, and if we find any disadvantage in others, or any pre-eminence in ourselves, in such a partial application and collation of ourselves with others (as readily self love, if it find it not, will fancy it), then we have a tacit gloriation within ourselves, and a secret complacency in ourselves. But the humble Christian dares not make himself of that number, nor boast of things without his measure. He dare not think himself good, because, *deterioribus melior*, "better than others who are worse." But he judges himself by that intrinsic measure which God hath distributed unto him, and so finds reason of sobriety and humility, and therefore he dare not stretch himself beyond his measure, or go without his station and degree, 2 Cor. x. 12-14. Humility makes a man compare himself with the best, that he may find how bad he himself is. But pride measures by the worst, that it may hide from a man his own imperfections. The one takes a perfect rule, and finds itself nothing. The other takes a crooked rule, and imagines itself something. But this is the way that unity may be kept in the body, if all the members keep this method and order, the lowest to measure by him that is higher, and the higher to judge himself by him that is yet above him, and he that is above all the rest, to compare with the rule of perfection, and find himself further short of the rule than the lowest is below him. If our comparisons did thus ascend, we would descend in humility, and all the different degrees of persons would meet in one centre of lowliness of mind. But while our rule descends, our pride ascends. The scripture holds out pride and self estimation as the root of many evils, and humility as the root of many good fruits among men. "Only through pride comes contention," Prov. xiii. 10. There is pride at least in one of the parties, and often in both. It makes one man careless of another, and out of contempt not to study equity and righteousness towards him, and it makes another man impatient of receiving and bearing an injury or disrespect. While every man seeks to please himself, the contention arises. Pride in both parties makes both stiff and inflexible to peace and equity, and in this there is a great deal of folly. For, by this means, both procure more real displeasure and dissatisfaction to their own spirits. "But with the well advised is wisdom." They who have discretion and judgment will not be so wedded to their own conceits, but that in humility they can forbear and forgive for peace' sake. And though this seem harsh and bitter at first, to a passionate and distempered mind, yet O how sweet is it after! There is a greater sweetness and refreshment in the peaceable condescendence of a man's spirit, and in the quiet passing by any injury, than the highest satisfaction that ever revenge or contention gave to any man. "When pride comes, then comes shame, but with the lowly is wisdom," Prov. xi. 2. Pride groweth to maturity and ripeness. Shame is near hand it, almost as near as the harvest. If pride come up, shame is in the next rank behind it. But there is a great wisdom in lowliness. That is, the honourable society that it walks in. There may be a secret connection between this and the former verse, "divers and false balances are abomination to the Lord, but a just balance is his delight." Now, if it be so in such low things as merchandise, how much more abominable is a false spiritual balance in the weighing of ourselves! Pride hath a false balance in its hand, the weight of self love carries down the one scale by far.

Lowliness of mind is the strongest bond of peace and charity. It banishes away strife and vain glory, and makes each man to esteem another better than himself, (Philip. ii. 3) because the humble man knows his own inside, and only another's outside. Now certainly the outside is always better and more specious than the inside, and therefore a humble man seeing nothing but his neighbour's outside, and being acquainted throughly with his own inside, he esteems another better than himself. Humility, as it makes a man to think well of another, so it hinders him to speak evil of his brother. James iv. He lays down the ground work in the 10th verse, "Humble yourselves in the sight of the Lord, and he shall lift you up." He raises his superstructure, verses 11, 12: "Speak not evil one of another, brethren. He that speaketh evil of his brother, and judgeth his brother, speaketh evil of the law, and judgeth the law, but if thou judge the law, thou art not a doer of the law, but a judge. There is one lawgiver, who is able to save, and to destroy. who art thou that judgest another?" For truly the very ground of evil speaking of that nature, is some advantage, we conceive, that may redound to our own reputation, by the diminution of another's fame. Or, because we are so short sighted in ourselves, therefore we are sharp sighted towards others, and because we think little of our own faults, we are ready to aggravate other men's to an extremity. But in so doing we take the place of the judge and law upon us, which judges others, and is judged by none. So we judge others, and not ourselves. Neither will we suffer ourselves to be judged by others. This is to make ourselves the infallible rule, to judge the law.

Humility levels men to a holy subjection and submission to another, without the confusion of their different degrees and stations. It teaches men to give that respect and regard to even one that is due to his place or worth, and to signify it in such a way as may testify the simplicity of their estimation, and sincerity of their respect. Eph. v. 21, "Submit yourselves one to another in the fear of God." 1 Pet. v. 5, "All of you be subject one to another, and be clothed with humility." Now, if humility can put a man below others, certainly it will make him endure patiently and willingly to be placed in that same rank by others. When others give him that place to sit into, that he had chosen for himself, will he conceive himself wronged and affronted, though others about him think so? Nay, it is hard to persuade him of an injury of that kind, because the apprehension of such an affront hath for its foundation the imagination of some excellency beyond others, which lowliness hath razed out. He hath placed himself so low for every man's edification and instruction, that others can put him no lower, and there he sits quietly and peaceably. *Bene qui latuit bene vixit.*[425] Affronts and injuries fly over him, and light upon the taller cedars, while the shrubs are safe.

Qui cadit in plano, (vix hoc tamen evenit ipsum,)
Sic cadit, ut tacta surgere possit humo.[426]

He sits so low, that he cannot fall lower, so a humble man's fall upon the ground is no fall indeed, but in the apprehension of others, but it is a heavy and bruising fall from off the tower of self conceit.

Now the example that is given us, "Learn of me," is certainly of greater force to persuade a man to this humble, composed, and quiet temper of spirit, than all the rules in the world. That the Son of God should come down and act it before our eyes, and cast us a pattern of humility and meekness, if this do not prevail to humble the heart, I know not what can. Indeed this root of bitterness, which is in all men's hearts by nature, is very hard to pluck up, yea, when other weeds of corruption are extirpated this poisonable one, pride groweth the faster, and roots the deeper. Suppose a man should be stript naked of all the garments of the old man, this would be certainly nearest his skin and last to put off. It is so pestilent an evil, that it grows in the glass window as well as on the dunghill and, which is strange, it can spring out of the heart, and take moisture and aliment from humility, as well as from other graces. A man is in hazard to wax proud that he is not proud, and to be high minded because he is lowly. Therefore, it is not good to reflect much upon our own graces, no more than for a man to eat much honey.

I know not any antidote so sovereign as the example of Jesus Christ, to cure this evil, and he himself often proposes this receipt to his disciples, (John xiii. 13-17) "Ye call me Master and Lord, and ye say well, for so I am. If I then, your Lord and Master, have washed your feet ye also ought to wash one another's feet. For I have given you an example, that ye should do as I have done to you. Verily, verily, I say unto you, the servant is not greater than his lord, neither he that is sent greater than he that sent him. If ye know these things, happy are ye if ye do them." Matt xi. 29, 30, "Take my yoke upon you, and learn of me, for I am meek and lowly in heart and ye shall find rest unto your souls. For my yoke is easy, and my burden is light." Matt. xx. 27, 28, "And whosoever will be chief among you, let him be your servant. Even as the Son of man came not to be ministered unto, but to minister, and to give his life a ransom for many." Might not that sound always in our ears, the servant is not above his lord, the "Son of man came not to be ministered unto, but to minister?" O whose spirit would not that compose? What apprehension of wrong would it not compensate? What flame of contention about worth and respect would it not quench? What noise of tumultuous passions would it not silence? Therefore, the apostle of the Gentiles prescribes this medicine, (Phil. ii. 5-8) "Let this mind be in you, which was also in Christ Jesus who, being in the form of God, thought it not robbery to be equal with God, but made himself of no reputation, and took upon him the form of a servant, and was made in the likeness of men, and being found in fashion as a man, he humbled himself, and became obedient unto death, even the death of the cross." If he did humble himself out of charity, who was so high, how should we humble ourselves, both out of charity and necessity, who are so low! If we knew ourselves, it were no strange thing that we were humble, the evidence of truth would extort it from us. But here is the wonder, that he who knew himself to be equal to God, should notwithstanding become lower than men, that the Lord of all should become the servant of all, and the King of glory make himself of no reputation! That he pleased to come down lowest, who knew himself to be the highest of all, no necessity could persuade it, but charity and love hath done it. Now, then, how monstrous and ugly a thing must pride be after this! That the dust should raise itself, and a worm swell, that wretched, miserable man should be proud, when it please the glorious God to be humble, that absolute necessity shall not constrain to this, that simple love persuaded him to! How doth this heighten and elevate humility, that such an one gives out himself, not only as the teacher, but as the pattern of it. "Learn of me, for I am meek and lowly in heart, and ye shall find rest unto your souls."

SEVERAL SERMONS UPON THE MOST IMPORTANT SUBJECTS OF PRACTICAL RELIGION.

THE PUBLISHER TO THE READER.

There are no sermons I know of any divine or pastor in this kingdom, that have been more frequently printed, or more universally read and esteemed, than the elegant and judicious discourses of Mr. Binning, which were published after his death, at different times, in four small volumes. As there was a great demand for these valuable writings, about twenty six years ago; so these printed copies of them were compared with his own manuscript copy now in my hand, carefully revised, and then printed, in a large 4to of 641 pages, by Robert Fleming, Printer at Edinburgh, in the year 1735, to which was prefixed a short account of his Life, chiefly taken from the large memoirs of his Life, that the Reverend Mr. Robert M'Ward, some time minister of the gospel at Glasgow, wrote, in a long letter to the Reverend Mr. James Coleman, Minister of the gospel at Sluys in Flanders, who translated Mr. Binning's Sermons into High Dutch, and printed them for the benefit of the Christian congregations in Holland and Flanders. Some of the most memorable particulars of this great man's life have been also published, anno 1753, by the reverend, learned, and industrious Mr. John Wesley, late Fellow of Lincoln college, Oxford, in his Christian Library, which contains about fifty volumes in 8vo of Extracts from, and Abridgments of, the choicest pieces of practical Divinity, we have printed in our language. It is prefixed to Mr. Binning's Sermons upon the first and part of the second chapters of the first Epistle of John, in the 29th volume of that useful work.[427]

Mr. Binning's elegant and judicious Treatise of Christian Love was first printed from a manuscript in my hand, at Edinburgh, 1743, in an octavo pamphlet of forty-seven pages, in short print, by Robert Fleming, to which he hath prefixed a short preface. And the publisher tells us, "That he had revised about twenty four sermons, upon very edifying and profitable subjects, to print in a separate volume, from which they [his readers] should receive as great improvement and satisfaction, as from any of his printed treatises, which every person may easily discover from the style and language to be Mr. Binning's genuine compositions, as his manner of writing can scarcely be imitated by any other person." These sermons were carefully transcribed some little time ago, and revised by the assistance of a friend, and are now printed in this small volume . . . And not to detain the reader further from the serious and candid perusal of this book, I shall only add, that I have faithfully transcribed these sermons from the manuscript copy without the smallest alteration of his sentiments. I have endeavoured to rectify a few grammatical errors of the transcribers and the old form of spelling, and altered a few words not now used in our modern sermons, for words of the same meaning. As I have added several sermons of this author upon the kingdom of God, which I transcribed since the proposals of this book were printed, so I could not insert the sermons upon Acts xxvi. 18; Acts xiv. 11, 12, without almost doubling the price, which I feared would not be agreeable to some of the encouragers of this work. I intend to put the other sermons I have transcribed, or may yet copy, into the hands of some friends to revise before they be printed; as also Mr. M'Ward's Life of this worthy gentleman, taken from his own papers . . .

It is my sincere wish, that all the readers of this book may be builded up in spiritual wisdom and goodness unto eternal life.

Brousterland, September 12th, 1760

SERMON I.

1 John iii. 23.—"And this is his commandment, That we should believe on the name of his Son Jesus Christ, and love one another."

It is a common doctrine often declared unto you, that the most part of those who hear the gospel do run, in their pretended course to heaven, either upon a rock of dashing discouragement, or the sands of sinking presumption. These are in all men's mouths; and no question they are very dangerous, so hazardous, as many fools make shipwreck either of the faith, or a good conscience,—of the faith, by running upon and dashing upon the rock,—of a good conscience, by sitting down upon the quicksand. But I fear that which is commonly confessed by all is cordially believed by few, and so, little regarded in our course and conversation. All Christians pretend to be making a voyage heaven-ward, and that is only home-ward. Now the gospel is given us to direct our course, and teach us how to steer between these two hazards, both safely and surely. This is the shore that shall guide us, and conduct to our intended haven, that is heaven, if we set our compass by it, and steer our course accordingly. Yet strange it is to behold the infinite wanderings and errors of men, on the one hand or the other:—some presuming upon the news of mercy, and the sound of God's grace, to walk after the imagination of their own hearts, and to live and continue in sin, for which Christ died, that he might redeem us from it, fancying a possibility of living in sin, and escaping wrath, and so abusing the tender of grace to promote licentiousness;—others, again, apprehending the wrath of God, and their just deservings, abusing the notion of God's justice, and the perfection of his holiness, to the prejudice of the glory of his grace and mercy, and their own salvation. This is certainly the cunning sleight of Satan, with the deceitfulness and ignorance of our own hearts, that leads men, and sometimes one and the same man, at diverse times, to contrary misapprehensions of divine truths. The wind of temptation gets fires to one corner of the house and then to another, and sometimes over-persuades the notion of mercy, and another time overstretches the apprehension of his justice; and yet in effect there is no true persuasion of any of them, but a cloud or shadow is apprehended instead of them.

Now I say, there is one cure for both these,—the right apprehension of the gospel in its entire and whole sum, the right uptaking of the light which shines in a dark place, and is given to lead us to our place of rest—to have a complete model, and a short summary of the gospel, always in our heart and eye. For truly it is the apprehending of parcels of divine truth, which leads men into such opposite mistakes and courses. To remedy this, we have some brief comprehensive models of the gospel set down by the Holy Ghost, and none in better terms than this here: "This is his commandment, that ye believe," &c. You have it in two words, faith and love. This is the form of sound words which we should hold fast, 2 Tim. i. 13. This is the mould of doctrine delivered by Christ and his Apostles. It is the separation of these two in some men's fancy, that leads too many in such paths of destruction. Truly they can as little be divided as the sun's light and heat, but the motions and shadows of them may, and it is the following the shadows of some of them which shipwrecks souls. Now not only the common multitude of the hearers of the gospel are in hazard of this, but even God's own children, who have believed in him.

The taking up of these things apart, creates the heart much trouble and perplexity, and occasioneth much sin and stumbling. I do think it is the ignorance and advertency of this conjunction, that makes our case both more sad and sinful than otherwise it would be. And these two indeed have a mutual influence upon one another, loosing reins to sin more freely, for it unquestionably disturbs the soul's peace, and procures it much bitterness. And again, the quitting hold of the promise of grace in Christ Jesus, and the indulging our own sad and sullen apprehensions, cannot but in the issue disable the soul from the duties of love, and expose it unto the violence of every temptation. As these two do mutually strengthen one another, the faith of Jesus Christ, and the lively apprehension of his grace and goodness, so they are the most noble and effectual persuasives to live unto him, and to walk in love. Besides, faith is the mean and way which God hath appointed to convoy his influence unto the soul; and then again, love carrying itself actively in duties to God and men, bestirring itself for God and those who are beloved of God, it brings in a supply to faith, and returns by a straight compass to the spring from whence it first issued, and increases it still more. Believing on the name of the Son sends forth the stream of holy affection to him, and all begotten of the Father, and this returns again by the circuit of obedience to his commands and submission to his easy yoke, to unbosom itself in the fountain from whence it first issued; and whereas faith was at first one simple soul adherence to a Saviour, and a hearty embracing of him, this accession of the fruits of it exalts it unto that height of assurance, and gives that evidence which it wanted; and faith being thus strengthened, and rooted, and built up to the top of assurance of God's grace, love, and salvation, it becomes more able to bear the yoke of his commands, which are not grievous. The spring of believing, thus swelled by the concurrence of so many streams, it breaks forth the more, and sends out more love and delight in God, and more charity, compassion, and meekness towards men. And this is the circle and round Christianity runs, until that day come that the head-spring of faith shall be obscured and shrivelled up in the great sea of the love of God, which shall overflow all the saints' graces in due time, when we shall see God face to face.

This is a true Christian, which this apostle so beloved of God describes. Here is one under a commandment, and not above it, as some fondly conceive. He is a keeper of his commands, and a doer of these things which are pleasant in God's sight. This is no legal notion, if it be right taken.

It is not the bondage of the creature to be under the command of God, truly it is the beauty and liberty of a reasonable soul. Some speak of all subjection unto a law as slavery, but is it not an infinitely greater slavery to be at liberty to sin, and serve our own lusts? O wretched and base liberty! the Son indeed makes us truly free, and that from sin; and he is truly a Redeemer who redeems us from all iniquity, John viii. 32; Psal. cxxx. ult.; Tit. ii. 14.

But this commandment here spoken of, would not indeed be gospel, unless there was a prior command, a brighter precept, given by the Father to the Son. I find two commands given by the Father, and received by the Son, which two you may conjoin and make one of, as here faith and love are made one commandment. The first is, John x. 18, "I lay down my life of myself, no man taketh it from me. This commandment have I received from my Father, and no other." John xii. 49, 50, "The Father gave me a commandment, what I should say and speak, and I know that his commandment is life everlasting." This is more expressly and clearly set down, John vi. 39, 40, "This is the Father's will that sent me, that of all that he gave me I should lose none, but raise them up at the last day. This is the will of him that sent me, that every one which seeth the Son, and believeth on him, should have everlasting life." Here, then, beloved in the Lord, is the foundation of our hope, and that which makes all commandments given by God to us to come under a gospel notion, that which makes Christ's yoke easy, and his burden light, and his commands not grievous. The great commandment was imposed upon our Saviour. The great weight of that wrath due to our sins was put upon his shoulders. This was the Father's will, that he should lay down his life for his sheep; this command he received willingly, and obeyed faithfully and fully. And by his obedience to this, that great obligation to satisfy God's justice, and pay a ransom for our souls is taken off us; inasmuch as he died, justice cannot come and demand it at our hand. Now, therefore, there is another commandment given to Christ, which directly concerns us, and it is this in substance: "I will and command that thou who hast come in the place of sinners, and resolvest to die for them, that thou give eternal life to whom thou wilt, even to as many as believe in thy name; I give to thee the absolute disposal of life and death; I command thee to preach life everlasting to all pious souls, that shall flee unto thee upon the apprehension of the danger of death, and that thou bestow that life upon them, and raise them up at the last day to be partakers of it." This is the commission the Father gave to the Son, a sweet commission for poor sinners, and the charter of our salvation. And for this errand he was anointed with the Holy Spirit, and sent into the world; nay, the commission extends further than grace, even to eternal glory also. Christ has received commandment of the Father, to give repentance and remission of sin, both to give faith, and love, and all other graces, else it were defective. Thus Christ comes instructed to the world. He lays open his commission in preaching the gospel. He obeys the first commandment in his own person, by offering up himself upon the cross a sacrifice for sins, and he is about the fulfilling the next commandment, that is, the giving life to them that believe: and that he may accomplish it, having ascended himself unto heaven to intercede for us, he also sent his ambassadors into the world, to whom he hath committed the word of reconciliation, and he gives them commission to publish and proclaim this commandment in his own name. This is his command, that ye "believe on the name of his Son Jesus Christ." And this we do proclaim in his name, since he has gotten a commandment to give life everlasting to believers. This, then, is his charge to you, to come and receive it from him. Come and embrace him, and ye shall have life and all in him. This is the hardest and heaviest burden he imposes upon you, the weight of your life and salvation he hath taken upon himself. But O! now come and lay hold on him, who is thus offered unto you. Know that you are lost and undone in yourselves, consider the impossibilities you lie under to escape his wrath. Behold the anger of God hanging over your head, ready to be revealed in flaming fire, and a tempestuous cloud of eternal misery. Will ye consider that ye are born heirs of wrath? Your natural inheritance is in the lake of fire; and whatsoever your endowments by nature, or your privileges by birth be, nothing shall exeem you from this. Shall not then this Saviour be welcome to you? For truly faith is but a cordial salutation and embracement of our blessed Redeemer. The soul brings him into the house, and makes him welcome, and he is standing ready to come in to your heart, and to bring in salvation with him.

Now whatever soul hath obeyed this commandment by belief of the truth, and receiving of Christ into the heart, there is but one commandment behind, and it is not grievous, viz., love me, and love one another; love me, and live unto me. This is an easy yoke; and there is good reason for it, though it had never been required to love him, and live to him, who loved not his life unto the death for us. There is mention made only of brotherly love here, but certainly the other love to God flowing from the sense of his love, is the right wing of the soul, and brotherly love the left; and by these the pious soul mounts up to heaven with the wings of an eagle. The love of our brother is but the fruit and consequent of this love, but it is set down as a probation, and clear evidence of the love of God in our souls.

Love is commanded as the very sum and substance of the whole law, as the fountain of all other duties. Things are compacted in their causes, and lie hid within the virtue of them. Truly this is the way to persuade and constrain you to all the duties of godliness and righteousness, of piety towards God, and charity towards men,—if once we could fasten this chain of affection upon your hearts, and engage your souls by love to God and man. We cannot but beat the air, while we seek to persuade you to the serious practice of religious duties, of prayer in secret and in your families, of reading and meditation upon the word, of sanctifying the Sabbath, of dealing justly and moderately with all men, of sobriety and temperance in your conversation, of denying ungodliness and worldly lusts, of walking humbly with God and towards men, of restraining and subduing your inordinate lusts and passions; I say, it is almost in vain to press these things upon you, or expect them from you, till once the Spirit of power and love enter into your hearts; and indeed the spirit of love is a powerful spirit, the love of God possessing the heart within, cannot but conform all within and without to his love and good pleasure. Love only can do these things which are pleasant in his sight, for it doth them pleasantly, heartily, and cheerfully; and God loves a cheerful giver, a cheerful worshipper. Brotherly love is rather expressed, because little or not at all studied by the most part. Other duties to God, if men come not up in practice to them, yet they approve them in their soul and mind. But there is scarce a notion of the obligation of charity and love towards our brethren, yea, not so much as in the minds of Christians, let be in their practice. It is the special command which Christ left to his disciples when he was going away, John xiii. 35. But, alas! we have forgotten it, it is so long since.

SERMON II.

1 John iii. 23.—"This is his commandment, that," &c.

We commonly make many rules in religion, and turn it into a laborious art, full of intricate questions, precepts, and contentions. As there hath been a great deal of vanity in the conception of speculative divinity, by a multitude of vain and unedifying questions which have no profit in them, or are beneficial to them that are occupied therein, but only have stirred up strife and envy, and raised the flame of contention in the Christian world; so I fear that practical divinity is no less vitiated and spoiled in this age amongst true Christians (by many perplexed cases relating to every condition), than the other among the schoolmen. Hereby it seems to me, that Christ and his apostles did not suppose it to be so perplexed a business as we now do make it; neither did the hearers weary themselves or others with so many various objections against the practice of the fundamental commandment of the gospel, believing in Jesus Christ. The plain nature of the gospel being holden forth and received, I am persuaded, was and is able (like the sun arising in brightness) to dispel and scatter all these mists and clouds which do arise both in the one and other, from ignorance at first, and which are elevated to a greater height by the custom of the times. The matter, my brethren, is not so dark as you make it. Here it is plainly and simply expressed: "This is his commandment, that ye believe in the name of his Son;" and then, "love one another." Ye all know that we had commandments given us by God, which were by nature impressed on the heart of man; but by his fall into sin, the tables of the law (which I may say were in Adam's mind and heart, understanding and affection), those two tables were broken in the fall, and since there could be no obedience, because of ignorance and perversion, the tables breaking in pieces, their ruptures have produced these two opposite principles. The fall of man hath broken his mind, and so darkened his understanding, and broken his will, and put it in a wrong set. This appointed it, set it in a posture of enmity against God. However, we are by this fall utterly disabled to stand up before God in acceptable obedience. There is no man breathing, how blameless soever he be before the world, but must fall down as guilty before God in many things, yea, in all things. But the law being thus obliterated out of men's consciences, as he lost ability to obey, so he lost almost all conscience of sin and disobedience. He not knowing his charge and obligation, could not accuse himself for falling in rebellion. Therefore it pleased the Lord to cause the law to be written in tables of stone in mount Sinai. He transcribes the commandments over again, that all the world may see their obligation, and how infinitely short they have come in their subjection, and how just their condemnation may be. For this purpose, the Lord causes proclaim the old bond in the ears of men with great majesty and authority, as it became the Lawgiver, that all may become guilty, and stop their mouth before God, Rom. iii. 19. He would once have all men knowing that they are under infinite breaches of his commandments, that they may see themselves also subject to his judgment. Now, what do you think of a soul that stands at the foot of this mountain, and hears a dreadful accusation read against it, to all which the conscience within must subscribe unto, and both together pronounce the person guilty and liable to eternal punishment? I say, what can such a soul do, who has with trembling heard his voice? Satisfaction there cannot be given for an infinite offence against an infinite nature. The curse and sentence which was the sanction and confirmation of this commandment is just, and there appears no way how, without violation of God's justice, it can be repealed. Obedience to these commandments is now both impossible and unprofitable;—impossible, I say, because of the weakness and wickedness of the flesh, that has no ability nor willingness but to offend and disobey; and unprofitable, because it cannot at all relax the former sentence of condemnation. Now obedience, being a present duty, cannot pay old debts, or satisfy for our former rebellions, and so it must leave a man to seen condemnation. I fear this is a puzzle that all consciences must come unto here, or elsewhere. Here is a strait indeed.

But yet there is an enlargement, there is a way found out of bringing the soul out of the miry clay, and deep pit of misery; and it is this, God hath found out a ransom for himself, without our procurement, or consent, or knowledge. He hath provided a satisfaction to his justice in his Son Jesus Christ. Having laid upon him our iniquities, he exacts of him our deserved punishment, and makes him a curse who knew no sin. Now this being done, the Lord sends forth to all poor sinners who are trembling at mount Sinai this proclamation,—this is my last and most peremptory command, that ye believe in the name of my Son Jesus Christ. This is my well-beloved Son, in whom I am well-pleased, hear ye him. Have ye heard me the lawgiver condemning you? Now go and hear him, the Mediator and Saviour, absolving you, for I have committed all judgment unto him. Though I pronounce the sentence in this world against you, yet I have committed all the execution of it to him, and if you come to him, you may prevent it. You have broken all my former commandments, and I have pronounced a sentence against you for that. But now I give a new commandment instead of all the former, which if you obey, then the sentence of death is relaxed. You who cannot obey the law and give satisfaction in your own persons, I charge you to flee unto my Son Christ, who hath given me full satisfaction both to the curse, by suffering, and to the command, by obedience, and lay hold on his righteousness as your own, and in him ye are justified, and delivered from all these sentences and hard writings against you. I give a new commandment as the cure and remedy of all broken commandments. Believe on this name, in which is salvation. Take his obedience and suffering for your cure, and present me with that, I shall be as well satisfied as with your own personal satisfaction.

This now is very plain business. All commands are broken. There is yet one published in the gospel to help all, and it is in substance to embrace and welcome Jesus Christ for all, to seek our life and salvation in him, to take him as a priest to offer sacrifice for us, and expiate our sins, and to come to him as a prophet to seek wisdom and illumination, and all grace from him; to choose him as our King, henceforth to submit to his easy yoke of government. Now I say there will be no more debates about this. Will ye yet dispute whether ye may believe or not? Will ye inquire after this whether you have a warrant or not? Truly such a question would occasion much jealousy and provocation among men. If a man had signified as much willingness by command, by invitation, by request, by frequent repetition of these, yet to call in question or dispute whether or not I may go to such a person, will he make me welcome, were it not the greatest affront I could put upon him? Would it not alienate his affection more than any thing, to be jealous of his real kindness to me.

I would desire to hold out unto you the sin, the danger, and the vanity of such a way. I say the sin is great, it is no less than the highest and most heinous disobedience to the gospel, which of all others is of the deepest dye. You have disobeyed the law, and broken all the ten commandments. And will ye therefore disobey the gospel, too, and break this fundamental commandment? Is it not enough that ye have broken the rest, and will ye break this also, which was given for the cure of all?

Consider, I say, this is his commandment. Now commands should be obeyed, and not disputed, coming from an infallible and uncontrollable authority. Would ye not silence all the rebellions of your hearts against the commands of praying, hearing, reading, dealing justly, and walking soberly, with this one word, it is his command, it is his sovereign will? And why do ye not see the stamp of that same authority upon this? Now if you consider it aright, it hath more authority upon it than upon others, because it is his last command, and so would be taken as most pungent and weighty. When your hearts rise up to question and dispute this matter, I pray you cut all these knotty objections with the sword of his commandment. You use to go about to loose them by particular answers and untie them at leisure with art and skill, but truly it would be a readier and wiser course to cut them in pieces at one stroke, by this piercing and pungent precept. If your reasons and scruples be weighty, and you cannot get answers to overbalance them, I pray you put this weighty seal of divine authority into the balance, and sure I am it will weigh down all. Consider then the danger of it. It is the last and most peremptory command, after which you may expect no other, but the execution of justice. How sad and severe is the certification, "He that believeth not is condemned already," and "the wrath of God abideth on him." There needs no new sentence to be pronounced against you. Why? Because, if you believe not, that prior sentence of the law is yet standing above your heads to condemn you, that wrath abides on you. This is the only way to remove it, to come to him, who hath taken it on himself, after the breach of all commands. Ye have this retreat, this refuge to flee unto, a new command to come unto the Son, and have life; but after this disobedience of the Son, you have none. There is nothing after unbelief, but ye are turned over, or rather left over, in the hand of the law and divine justice. Therefore it is the most dangerous and damnable thing to disobey this. It is to refuse the very remedy of sin. Consider also what vanity and uselessness is in these debates. What an unreasonable and senseless thing is it to dispute against our own soul, and against our own happiness! All is wrapt up here, and we do no less than the highest act of self-murder that can be. He that hateth me, wrongs his own soul. What an unreasonable thing then is it, because ye are miserable, to refuse mercy; because ye are unclean, therefore to maintain that ye are not to come to the blessed fountain of cleansing; because ye have broken the rest of the commands, therefore ye may not obey this? Is there any sense or reason in such things; because I am a sinner, therefore I will not come to a Saviour? Alas! to what purpose was the Son sent and given, and for what end came he? Was it not to seek and to save such as are lost and undone, and to deliver them from misery? What do you gain by such questions? For at length you must turn and enter in at the door of a naked command and promise, when you have wearied yourselves to find that in your hearts which is not in them, to seek waters in the wilderness, and springs in the desert, qualifications and graces in your own hearts to warrant your boldness in coming to the promise. I say, when you have sought and all in vain, you must at length come to this fountain in which is all grace and happiness. If you had what you seek, yet if ye would indeed believe in Christ, you must deny them and look upon yourselves as ungodly, to be justified by faith. Why then do you grasp after that which can do you no good, (though you had it), I mean, in point of your acceptation? Consider it, my beloved, that the honour of God and your own happiness lies most in this, nay not only that, but your holiness too, which you pretend to seek after, lies in it. Till you come to Christ, it is in vain to seek it elsewhere.

SERMON III.

1 John iii. 23.—"And this is his commandment," &c.

There are different tempers of mind among men, some more smooth and pliable, others more refractory and froward. Some may be persuaded by love, who cannot be constrained by fear. With some a request will more prevail than a command. Others again are of a harsher disposition. Love and condescension doth rather embolden them, and therefore they must be restrained with the bridle of authority. It would seem that the Lord hath some regard to this in the administration of the gospel. He accommodates himself to the diverse dispositions of men, and (if we may say with respect to him which yet can be no disrespect, seeing he hath humbled himself lower) he doth become all things to all men, that he may gain some. You see the gospel sometimes running in the channel of love and kindness, sometimes in the channel of authority and majesty. God sometimes stoopeth down to invite, and affectionately to beseech sinners to come unto his Son for life. He hath prepared a marriage and banquet for us in Christ. He hath made all things ready for the receiving, for the eating, and he sends forth his servants to entreat and invite all such, who have no bread and clothing, who are poor and lame, to this wedding. He gives an hearty invitation to all that stand at an infinite distance from God, and so are feeding upon empty vanities without him, to come and enjoy the riches of his grace, which runs as a river in Christ between these two golden banks, the pardon of sin, and the purification of our soul from its pollution. You have a hearty invitation, Isa. lv. 1, 2, 3, "Ho, every one that thirsteth, come to the waters." But he comes yet lower to request and obtest poor sinners, as if he could have advantage by it; he will not stand[428] to be a supplicant at any man's door, to beseech him to be reconciled to God, 2 Cor. v. 14, 19, 20. As if we could do him a favour and benefit, he requests us most earnestly. Truly it is strange that this doth not melt the heart, and make it fall down into the belief and obedience of the truth. Affection is the most insinuating and prevailing thing with an ingenuous spirit, most of all when it is accompanied with majesty in the person that hath it, and humility in the carriage and disposition. For a great personage to descend out of love, to affectionate and humble requests and solicitations, this cannot but have a mighty influence on any spirit that is not wild and savage. But because the heart of man is desperately wicked, and hath lost that true ingenuity and nobleness of spirit, and is now become stubborn and froward, as a wild ass, or as a swift dromedary traversing her ways, therefore the Lord takes another way of dealing with men suitable to their froward natures; he gives out his royal statute backed with majesty and authority; "This is his command," &c.—that when fair means could not prevail, other means more terrible might reduce lost rebellious men. He hedges in our way with threatenings and promises annexed to the commandment, "He that believeth has everlasting life, but he that believeth not is condemned already, and shall not see life, but the wrath of God abideth on him." He declares all men traitors if they come not in to his Son, to be reconciled to God, before the decree of wrath pass forth.

Truly it is a wonder that there should be any need either of an invitation, or a request, or a command, or a threatening; that we should need to be invited, or requested, or commanded, or threatened to our own happiness. Might not a bare and simple offer, or proposal of Jesus Christ, his nature, and offices, of the redemption and salvation purchased by him, suffice? What needed more, but to declare unto us that we are lost and utterly undone by nature, and that there is a refuge and remedy provided in Christ? Surely in any other thing of little importance, we needed no entreaty. Were it not a good enough invitation to a man that is like to starve for hunger, to cast meat freely before him; or to a man that is in hazard of drowning, to cast a cord to him? We would seek no other persuasion to go and dig for a treasure of gold, than to show us where it is hid. But strange is the rebellious and perverse disposition of man's heart. What an enmity is in it to the ways of God! What strange inclination to self-murder, ever since man destroyed himself! We cannot express it unto you; but you may perceive it well enough, both by the Lord's frequent obtesting, and protesting to us in his word, and the experience of the great barrenness of all such means. Whence is it, I pray you, that there should need so many means to persuade you to that which is your own advantage, and to call you to shun the ways of destruction? And whence is it that notwithstanding of all those invitations, entreaties, commandments, promises and threatenings often sounding in your ears, yet the most part are not reduced to obedience, nor reclaimed from the ways of death, and do not take hold of the path of life. Truly it may plainly point out to you the desperate wickedness of the heart, the stubbornness and rebelliousness of our disposition, and if once we could persuade you of this we had gained a great point which few do seriously consider, and so do not abhor themselves.

The commandments mentioned in the text are these two, to believe in Christ, and to love our brother. It is no wonder they are recommended with so much seriousness and earnestness; for they are both the most comprehensive, and the most pleasing commandments. They are most comprehensive; for it appears that all the commands spoken of in the preceding verse, are summed up in this one precept, "And this is his commandment," &c. And that they are most pleasant in God's sight is evident, for the true Christian being described from this, that he does these things that are pleasing in God's sight,—that he is one that studies to conform himself to his good pleasure, this is subjoined, as the two most pleasing exercises of Christianity, "This is his commandment," that is, his pleasing commandment, that ye should believe in Christ, and love one another.

This command of believing in Jesus is comprehensive, because it takes in all precepts, and that under a threefold consideration. It takes them all in as broken and transgressed by men, as fulfilled by Christ, and also takes them all in as a rule of righteousness, according to which the believer ought henceforth to walk.

The command of believing in Christ doth first of all import this—that a sinner should examine himself according to the law of God,—that he should lay his whole life and course his heart and ways, down before the perfect and holy commandments,—that he may stop his own mouth with shame and silence, and find himself guilty before God. Many use to speak of humiliation preparatory to believing, and the work of the law preparatory to the gospel. But truly I conceive it would be more fitly expressed, if it were holden out thus, that it is one of the essential ingredients in the bosom of believing, and one of the first articles of the gospel law, to charge all sinners to acknowledge their sin and misery, to discern their own abounding iniquity, and danger of perishing by it, how guilty they are before God, and how subject to his judgment, that so finding themselves undone, they may have recourse to a Saviour.

Truly the Spirit's work is to convince of sin, and then of righteousness, and when we are commanded to believe, the first part of our believing is crediting and subscribing to the law, to the justice and righteousness of God against us, and then the believing and acknowledging the gospel is the end and purpose to that. "Ye believe in God, believe also in me." This takes in completely the two books of saving faith towards God as a Lawgiver and Judge, and faith towards our Lord Jesus Christ as a Saviour and Redeemer; and it doth but beget misapprehensions in many, when the one is looked upon as a condition without which we shall not be welcome to the other. Truly, I think, both are proposed as essentials of saving faith; none of them in such a way as to procure right and warrant to the other, but only in such an order as is suitable to any reasonable nature to be wrought upon, and that is all. It is only required of you, upon that account, because fleeing unto a Saviour for refuge is a rational and deliberate action, which necessarily includes the sense of misery without him. But the sense of sin and misery is not urged as one thing which ye should go about to prepare, and fit yourselves for more welcome at Christ's hand as commonly it is taken. Here it is easy to understand how the command of believing belongs unto all who hear it, even to the vilest and grossest sinners, who are yet stout, hard hearted, and far from righteousness, (Isa. xlvi. 12.) those who are spending their money for that which is not bread, and their labour for that which satisfies not, and those whose hearts are uncircumcised, and their lives profane. And yet the commandment of coming to the Son and believing on him for life, is extended unto them all. All are invited, requested, commanded, and threatened to this duty. There is no bar of exclusion set down in the gospel to hold out one, and let in another; as many suppose these promises, that sound condition wise, to be limitations and restrictions of the right and warrant to persons to believing. Indeed it is true all are not exhorted at the first hand to assurance of God's love, and an interest in Christ. There is no question that none have right to this seal, but them who have believed and set to their own seal to the character or truth of the word. But all are charged to believe in Christ that is, out of a sense of their own lost estate, to embrace a Saviour for righteousness and strength. Neither is there any fear that men can come too soon to Christ. We need not set down exclusions or extractions, for if they be not sensible of sin and misery, they will certainly not come to him at all. And therefore the command that enjoins them to believe on the Son, charges them also to believe that they are lost without him. And if the most presumptuous sinners would once give obedience to this commandment, really there would be no fear of presumption in coming too soon unto Jesus. A sense of sin is not set as a porter, to keep out any who are willing to come in, but rather to open the door, and constrain them that were unwilling to enter in, so that if the least measure of that can do this, we are not to stand till we have more, but to come to the Prince exalted to get remission of sins, and more true gospel sorrow which worketh repentance unto salvation from dead works. You should not therefore understand any promises in the scriptures so, as if there were any conditions set down to seclude any from coming, who are willing to come. For they do but declare the nature and manner of what they are invited to, that no man may mistake believing, and take his own empty presumptions or fancies, which embolden him to sin more, for that true faith which is full of good fruits.

Now, in the text, the pious soul, having once subscribed to the guilt and curse of all the commandments by believing the law, he looks also upon the Son, Jesus Christ, and finds the law fulfilled, the curse removed, all satisfied in him. He finds all the commandments obeyed in his person, all the wrath due for the breach of them pacified and quenched by his sufferings. And he gives a cheerful and cordial approbation of all this. He receives Christ as the end of the law for righteousness, which Christ made up by obedience and suffering to supply our disobedience. We should stay or rest upon this, as that which pacifies the Father's wrath to the full. This is what gives the answer of a good conscience, and pacifies every penitent soul, and secures his title to heaven. Now this presents God with a full atonement and obedience to all the law, which he accepts from a believer as if it were his own. This is the large comprehension of believing, it takes in its arms, as it were, in one bundle,[429] all the precepts and curses, and devolves them over on Christ, puts them in an able hand, and then takes them all, as satisfied and fulfilled by him, and holds them up in one bundle to the Father. And hence it proceeds, in the third place, that believing on the Son takes in all again to be the rule of walking and the mark to aim at. Finding such a perfect exoneration of bygones[430] in Christ and standing in such favour with God, the soul is sweetly constrained to love and delight in the divine laws. And truly this is the natural result of faith. I wish you may rightly observe this conjunction, that this is inseparably knit with it, love to God and men, delight to do his will, to love him, and live unto him. Do not deceive yourselves with vain words. If you find not the smartness of the gospel, and the doctrine of grace laying this restraint upon the heart, ye are yet in your sins. This is the reasoning of a believing soul. Shall I, who am dead unto sin, live any longer therein? Shall I not delight in those commandments, when Christ hath delivered me from the curse of the law? Though such a one fall, and come short, yet the pressure of the heart is that way. But then attend unto the order, ye must first believe on the Son, and then love him, and live unto him. Ye must first flee unto his righteousness, and then the righteousness of the law shall be wrought in you. Therefore do not weary yourselves to no purpose. Do not wrong your own souls by seeking to prevent this order, which was established for your joy and salvation. Know that you must first meet with satisfaction in all the commands of Christ, before obedience to any of them be accepted, and having met with that, know that the sincere endeavour of thy soul, and the affectionate bensal[431] of thy heart to thy duty, is accepted. And if ye find yourselves thereafter surcharged with guilt and unanswerable walking, yet ye know the way is to begin at this again, to believe in the Son. This is the round you must walk, as long as ye are in the body. When you are defiled, run into the fountain, and when you are washed, study to keep your garments clean, but if defiled again, get your hearts washed from wickedness. "These things," says John, "I write to you that ye sin not," who believe but if any sin, who desire not to transgress, you have a propitiation for the sins of the whole world.

Now love is a very comprehensive command. It is the fulfilling of the whole law, Rom xiii. 10, Matth. xxii. 37, 38. It is indeed the true principle and pure fountain of our obedience unto God and men. All fruits of the Spirit are moral virtues that grow out of the believer. Whether pleasant unto God, or refreshing unto men, they are all virtually in this root of love, all the streams are compacted in this fountain. Therefore he names one for all, viz. brotherly love, which is the bond of perfection, Col. iii. 14. It is a bundle of many divine graces, a company or society of many Christian virtues combined together. They are named bowels of mercies, long suffering, kindness, humbleness of mind, meekness, forbearance, and forgiveness, all which are tied to the believer's girdle by charity, so that where love is, every good comes. After it a troop of so many sweet endowments and ornaments also come, and where this is wanting, (as truly it is the epidemical disease of the time), there are many sins abounding, for when iniquity abounds "the love of many shall wax cold," Matt. xxiv. 12. Oh! that is our temper or rather our distempered nature,—love cold, and passion hot! When charity goes away, these wild and savage beasts of darkness come forth, viz. bitter envying and strife, rigid censuring and judging, unmercifulness and implacableness of spirit upon others' failings and offences. Self love, that keeps the throne, and all the rest are her attendants. For where self love and pride is, there is contention, strife, envy, and every evil work, and all manner of confusion. Thus they lead one another as in a chain of darkness, Prov. xiii. 10, James iii. 16. Think not that love is a complimental word, and an idle motion of loving, it is a more real thing, a more vital thing. It hath bowels of mercy, they move themselves when others are moved, and they bring their neighbours misery into the inmost seat of the heart, and make the spirit a solemn companion in misery. And it is also exercised in forbearing and forgiving. Charity is not easily provoked, therefore it can forbear, is easily appeased, therefore it can forgive, it is not soon displeased, or hard to be pleased, "forbearing and forgiving one another in love." Study then this grace more. See it to be the fulfilling of the law, for "the end of the commandment is charity, out of a pure heart, a good conscience, and faith unfeigned." The end of the law is not strife and debate, nor such intricate and perplexed matters as minister endless questions and no edification. Though men pretend conscience and scripture, yet the great end of both is violated, that is charity, which mainly studies edification in truth and love. And therefore it is a violent perversion of the commandment, or word, to overstretch every point of conscience, or difference, so far as to the renting of Christian peace and unity. What hath kindled all these names of bloody war, what hath increased all these fiery contentions among us, but the want of this? As James says of the tongue, so I may speak of uncharitableness and self love, they set on fire the course of nature, and they are set on fire of hell. The true zeal and love of God, is like that elementary fire of which they speak, that in its own place hath a temperate heat, and doth not burn or consume what is about it. But our zeal is like the fire that is mixed with some gross matter, a preying, devouring, and consuming thing, zeal down in the lower region of man's heart, it is mixed with many gross corruptions, which are as oil and fuel to it, and gives it an extreme intemperate destroying nature.

But then consider, that this commandment of love is our Lord and Saviour's last testamentary injunction to his disciples, John xiii. 34, 35. "A new commandment I give unto you, that ye love one another, as I have loved you, that ye also love one another. By this shall all men know that ye are my disciples, if ye have love one to another." It is Christ's latter will, and given us as a token and badge of discipleship. Every profession hath its own signs and rules, every order their own symbol, every rank their own character. Here is the differential or peculiar character and livery of a Christian, brotherly love,—"By this shall all men know that ye are my disciples, if ye have love one to another," &c. I remember a story of a dying father who called his sons to him on his death bed, and having sent for a bundle of arrows, he tried them one by one if they could break them, and when they had all tried this in vain, he caused loose the bundle, and take the arrows one by one, and so they were easily broken, by which he gave them to understand, that their stability and strength would consist in unity and concord, but, if love and charity were broken, they were exposed to great hazard.[432] I think our Lord and Saviour gives such a precept unto his disciples at his departure out of this world,—"A new command I give unto you," &c. (John xiii. 34)—to show them that the perfection of the body, into which they were all called as members, consisted in that bond of charity. And indeed love is not only a bond or bundle of perfection in respect of graces, but in regard of the church too. It is that bond or tie which knits all the members into one perfect body, Col. iii. 14, 15, 16. Without this bond, all must needs be rents, rags, and distractions.

Now I shall add but one word of the other, that these commands are pleasing in God's sight. And truly believing in the Son must be grateful to him, not only from the general nature of obedience to his will, but also because this doth most honour both to the Father and to the Son. The Father counts himself much honoured, when we honour the Son, and there is no honour the creature can be in a capacity to give unto him like this, to cast all our hope, and hang all our happiness upon him, (John v. 23, 24), to set to our seal that he is true and faithful, (John iii. 33), which is done by believing. But most of all, this is pleasing in his sight because the Father's good pleasure concentres in the same point with the soul's good pleasure, that is, on the well beloved Son, Christ. Therefore faith must needs be well pleasing to the Father, for what is faith else but the soul's complacency and satisfaction in the Son. As the Father is already well pleased with his death and sufferings, so he propones and holds him out in the gospel, that you may be as well pleased with him as he is. This is believing indeed, to be pleased with him as the Father is pleased, and this pleases the Father too. Oh that you could understand this! The gospel is not brought unto you, that you may reconcile God, and procure a change in his affection, but for this end, to beseech you to be reconciled unto God, to take away all hostile affections out of your heart. And this is the business we have to do, to persuade you that the Father holds him abundantly contented with his Son. "This is my beloved Son, in whom I am well pleased." And to move you to be as well contented with him as he is, he says, "Hear him. I hear him for you, hear ye him for me. I hear him interceding for you, hear ye him beseeching you." Now this may take down all ground of jealousy concerning our welcome and acceptance, it cannot but be an acceptable and pleasing thing to God, that the affection and desire of the soul fall in and embosom itself with his good pleasure upon Christ his Son.

And then, in the next place, it is well pleasing to God that ye love one another, not only because he shall see his own image and likeness in your love, (for there is nothing in which a Christian more eminently resembles his Father, or more evidently appears to be a child of the Highest, than in free loving all, especially the household of faith, and forbearing and forgiving one another, and so he cannot choose but like it well), but especially, because your love concentres too, and meets upon the same objects with his love, these whom the Father so loved, that he gave his only begotten Son for them, and the Son so loved them, that he gave himself for them. If these be thy delight, and thou forbear them as the Father and the Son hath done, that conspiracy of affections into one point cannot but be pleasing unto him. Now, if these please him so well, whom should they not please?

SERMON IV.

James iii. 14.—"But if ye have bitter envying and strife in your hearts, glory not," &c.

It is a common evil of those who hear the gospel, that they are not delivered up to the mould and frame of religion that is holden out in it, but rather bring religion into a mould of their own invention. It was the special commendation of the Romans, that they obeyed from the heart that form of doctrine into which they were delivered, (Rom. vi. 17) that they who were once servants, or slaves of sin, had now become voluntary captives of truth, and had given themselves up to the gospel, to be modelled and fashioned by it; and if so, then certainly the most substantial points of religion would be most deeply engraven upon them. Every thing would have its own due place with us, if we were cast in the primitive mould of godliness, but when we cast godliness in a mould of our own apprehension, they cannot choose but a miserable confusion and disorder will follow in the duties of religion. For according as our fancy and inclination impose a necessity upon things, so we do pursue them, and not according to the real weight that is in them. I find the scripture laying most weight upon the most common things, placing most religion in the most obvious and known things, and for other things more remote from common capacity, I find them set far below, in the point of worth and moment, even these things that seem least. But I find that order quite perverted in the course of Christians. Some particular points that are not so obvious to every understanding, are put in the first place, and made the distinguished character of a Christian, and others again, in which true and undefiled religion doth more consist, are despised and set in a low place, because of their ceremonies. I think this apostle hath observed this confusion, and hath applied himself to remove it, by correcting the misapprehensions of Christians, and reducing their thoughts and ways to the frame of true Christianity. Even as Christ dealt with the Pharisees, who brought in such a confusion in religion, by imposing a necessity upon ceremonies, and an indifferency upon the very substance itself, truly, I think, it may be said unto us, you tithe mint, anise, and cummin, and pass over judgment and the love of God, these things ye ought to have done, and not to leave the other undone. Ye neglect the weightier matters of the law, judgment, mercy, faith and truth, and in the room of these ye have misplaced things, that are higher in God's esteem from an apprehension of their necessity. Thus by your traditions and opinions of things so remote from the kingdom of God, ye have made the unquestionable commandments of God of none effect, Matth. xv. 6. You think possibly, if this apostle was coming out to preach unto you this day, that he would certainly resolve you in many controverted points, and would bring some further light to the debates of the time. But truly I think if he knew the temper of our spirits, he would preach over this sermon to us again, "My brethren, be not many masters," &c. I suppose he would bring that old primitive light of pure and undefiled religion, the splendour of which our present ways and courses could not endure, but would be constrained to hide themselves in darkness. What would you think of such a sermon as this, "If any man among you seem to be religious, and bridleth not his tongue, this man's religion is vain?" Jam. i. 26. "If any man offend not in word, the same is a perfect man," Jam. iii.

2. This is accounted a common and trivial purpose. But believe it, sirs, the Christian practice of the most common things, hath more religion in it than the knowledge of the profoundest things, and till you learn to do what you know, it is a mockery to study to know further what to do. There is a strange stirring of mind after more light and knowledge in some particulars of the time. But I would fain know, if there be as much ardour and endeavour to practise that which we have already. To him that hath shall be given, to him that makes use of his knowledge for the honour of God, and the good of mankind, and their edification, more shall be given, but from him that hath not, shall be taken away even that which he hath, and yet really and cordially hath not, because he hath no use of it. Therefore he may by inquiry find more darkness, because his old light shall rather be put out. Do you not all know that ye should bridle your tongues, that it is a great point of that Christian victory over the world to tame and danton[433] that undantoned wild beast, to quench that fire brand of hell? Do ye not all know that we should be swift to hear, slow to speak, and slow to wrath? And as the apostle Paul speaks on another subject, "Doth not even nature itself teach you when you have but one tongue, and two ears, that ye should hear much, and speak little?" Are not our ears open, and our tongue enclosed and shut up, to teach us to be more ready to hear than to speak? Now I say, till Christians learn to practise these things that are without all controversy, you may make it your account never to want controversy, and never to get clearness. For to what purpose should more light be revealed, when that which is revealed is to no purpose?

But it is in vain to think to reform the tongue, till you have the heart first reformed. They say the belly hath no ears. Truly the tongue is all tongue, and has no ears to take an admonition or instruction. We must, then, with the apostle, retire into the heart, and abate from the abundance of the superfluity and naughtiness that is within; and therefore our apostle descends to the cure of pride, envy and strife in the heart, that are fountains of all that pestiferous flood which flows out of every man's mouth. "Is there any wise man among you?" &c. And indeed this is the orderly proceeding both of nature and grace. Nature begins within to probe among the superfluous and noisome humours which abound in the body, and desolate the members, and doth not think it sufficient to apply external plasters. Grace must begin within too, to purge the heart, for out of the abundance of the heart the mouth speaks, the eye looks, and the feet walk. If there be no destroyer in the members or outward man, it is not the preserving of rules and cautions that will suffice to restrain, to abate, or to cure, but the disease must be ripped up to the bottom, the cause found within, as our apostle doth here. Hence, says he, proceed all these feverish distempers among you, your hot and passionate words, your evil speakings and reproachings, your contentions and wars about matters either civil or religious. Whence are all these? From a vain persuasion of wisdom, from a foolish imagination of some excellency in yourselves, and some inward affection to be accounted something of among men. "Who is a wise man," &c. You would be accounted wise, and so you do account yourselves, and this begets strife and envy in the heart, and predisposeth the mind to strife and contention with others. And therefore he takes the mask off, by deciphering the very nature of such a wisdom; he embowels that pretended wisdom in religion and gives it its own name, and because things are best known, and most livelily comprehended in their opposition and comparison with one another, he shows wherein true wisdom and religion consist, and sets the one against the other, that the deformity of the one and the beauty of the other may appear. We shall then speak a word of this that is supposed, and then of that which is expressed, the descriptions of true wisdom, and pretended wisdom. I conceive this interrogation, "Is there a wise man among you?" imports chiefly these two one is,—that it is the natural disease of all men to esteem themselves something, and desire to be esteemed such by others; another is,—that the misapprehension of that wherein true wisdom and excellency doth especially consist, is the ground of many miscarriages in the seeking or venting of that.

It was an ancient remark, that "vain man would be wise, though he be born like a wild ass's colt." Empty man is wise in his own eyes, and would be so in other men's too. He hath no reality nor solidity, but is like these light things which the wind carries away, or the waters bear above, and tosses hither and thither, yet he apprehends some solid and real worth in himself, and would impose that apprehension upon others. And truly this is a drunkenness of mind, which makes a man light and vain, to stagger to and fro. It is a giddiness of spirit, that makes him inconstant and reeling, but insensible of it. Though he be born as stupid and void of any real wisdom and excellency, as a wild ass's colt, yet he hath this madness and folly superadded to all that natural stupidity, that he seems to be wise and understanding, and truly it was a more ancient disease than Job's days. We may trace the steps of its antiquity to be from the very beginning, and there we shall find the true original of it. What was it, I pray you, did cast the angels out of heaven, down to the lowest hell, to be reserved in chains for everlasting darkness? I do not conceive what their natures so abstracted from all sensual lusts could be capable of, but this spiritual darkness and madness of self conceit, and an ambitious aspiring after more wisdom, whence did flow that malcontent and envious humour, in maligning the happiness of man. And this was the poison that Satan, the chief of these angels, did drop into man's nature, by temptations and suggestions of an imaginary wisdom and happiness, "You shall be as gods knowing good and evil." And truly this poison is so strong and pestilent, that having once entered into the body, it spreads through all the members, it infects all the posterity that were in Adam's loins. Being once distilled into the lump, it diffuses itself through the whole, such a strange contagion is it. That wretched aim at a higher wisdom, hath thrown us all down into this brutish and stupid condition, to be like wild asses colts. Yet this false and fond imagination of wisdom and excellence remains within us, which is so much the nearer madness, that now there is no apparent ground left for such a fairly.[434] And if one of a cubit's height should imagine himself as tall as a mountain, and accordingly labour to stretch out himself, we would seek no other sign of madness. Truly this malignant and poisonable humour is so subtile that it hath insinuated itself into all the parts and powers of the soul, and steals in without observation into all our thoughts, purposes, affections, ways, and courses. It is of so infectious and pestiferous a nature, that it defiles all that is in the man, and all that comes out of the man.

The apostle speaks of covetousness, that it "is the root of all evil." Truly I think that comprehends many inordinate affections in it. Now, both self love and earth love arise from some false imagination of that which is not. Whether it be an imagination of some excellency in ourselves, or some worth in these worldly and earthly things, man first makes a god of it, and then worships it. Therefore covetousness is called idolatry, self idolatry and earth idolatry. We first attribute some divinity to ourselves like these people (Isa. xliv. 17) to their idols. We then fall down and worship ourselves, but we do not consider in our heart, that we are but dust. And then we ascribe some divinity to the perishing things of the world, and then worship them, but do not consider that they are earthly and perishing vanities. Thus we feed upon ashes, a deceived heart hath turned us aside, and we cannot deliver our own souls, by discovering the lie that is in our right hand. We feed partly on the element of the air, by seeking that of others that we have of ourselves, and partly upon the element of the earth, by the love of this world. And these two degenerated evils, are the root of all evils, self estimation, and creature affection.

I think this apostle in this one word "Is there any wise man among you, or any endowed with knowledge" and that word, "glory not," strikes at the root of all the forementioned and aftermentioned evils. From whence I say doth that promptitude and bensal[435] to speak, that slowness and difficulty to hear, that readiness and inclination to pride, (reproved, James i. 19, 20) proceed? Is it not from an overweening conceit of our own wisdom, that we are so swift to speak, and so slow to hear, and that we would teach others and yet be taught of none? We are so much in love with our own apprehensions, that we imagine they shall find as much esteem and affection among men, and so being like barrels full of liquor, in our own conceit, we are like to burst if we vent not, and are as incapable of taking from others as of retaining what is within. The word of God was a fire in Jeremiah's heart that would have consumed him, if he had not given it vent. Truly self love is a fire that must vent one way or other, or it would burn up all within by displeasure, and then it is the over apprehension of some excellency in ourselves, which so disposes us to anger, that makes us combustible matter, like the spirit of gunpowder, for the least spark of injury or offence, will set all in a flame. It is certainly the fond imagination of some great worth in ourselves, that is the very immediate predisposition to the apprehension of an injury. Humility cannot be affronted, it is hard to persuade of an injury. Why? Because there is no excellency to be hurt or wronged. Therefore Christ conjoins these, "meek and lowly in heart," (Matth. xi. 29,) lays poverty of spirit down as the foundation of meekness, Matth. v. 3-5. Whence is it that we accept of men's persons by judging according to the outward appearance, and are so ready to displease our brethren, especially these who are inferior to us in body, or mind, or estate? Is it not from this root, self admiration? This makes us elevate ourselves above others, and to intrude ourselves among these who are chiefest in account. Whence doth our unmercifulness and rigidity towards other men proceed, but from this fountain, that we allow so much licence and indulgence to ourselves, that we can have none to spare for others, and that we do not consider that we ourselves stand in need of more mercy from God, and cannot endure a mixture of judgment in it? Therefore we have judgment to others without mercy, James ii. 13. And is not this self pleasing humour the fountain of that contentious plea after the pre-eminence, and censorious liberty of judging others, and usurping authority over them? James iii. 1, "My brethren, be not ye many masters." Truly this is the root of all contentions and strifes. It is this which rents all human and Christian society. This looses all the pins of concord and unity. This sets all by the ears, and makes all the wheels reel through other. The conceit of some worth beyond others, and the imagination of some pre-eminence over them, even in the best creatures—he best, and he best, that is the plea, he greatest, and he greatest, that is the controversy. As bladders puffed up with wind, they cannot be kept in little room, but every one presses another, but if the wind were out, they would compact in less room, and comply better together. The apostle implies this, when he puts every man in mind of his own failing, "in many things we offend all," and if this were considered, it would abate our security, and cool our heat and fervour, and moderate our rigour towards others. There would not be such strife about places of power and trust, if we were not swelled in our own apprehensions to some eminency. And is not this the very fountain which sends out all these bitter streams of the tongue, these evil speakings one of another, these sharp and immoderate censures of our neighbours? Truly this is it, every man accounts himself to be wiser and more religious than his brother, to have more knowledge, and so he cannot endure any difference in opinion, to have more holiness, and so he cannot bear any infirmity in practice. But the way to help this, would be to humble ourselves before God, James iv. 10. Lowliness and meekness are the ground stones of these Christian virtues which preserve Christian society, Eph. iv. 2, 3. And is not this, I pray you, the foundation of wars, strifes, contentions, and jealousies? "From whence come wars and fightings among you?" Is it not from these imperious lusts which war in our members? Only from pride cometh contention, Prov. xiii. 10. The head spring of all envy, also issues out from pride, and this divides, in many streams and waters, all our courses and ways, with putrified and pestilent corruptions. While every man hath this opinion of himself, all is done in strife, no condescendence, no submission one to another, Phil. ii. 3. While all make themselves the centre, it cannot otherwise happen, but designs, courses, thoughts, and ways, must interfere and jar among themselves. Self-seeking puts all by the ears, as you see children among themselves, if an apple be cast to them. Any bait or advantage of the times yokes them in that childish contention, who shall have it? All come, strive, and fight about it, and it is but a few can have it, and these that get it cannot keep it long. Others will catch it from them. Now what vain things are these, which can neither be gotten, nor kept, but by strife? Oh that we could seek better things, which may be both sought and kept, without emulation or strife!

Now the other thing is, that the misapprehension of that wherein true excellence consists is the ground of many evils. "Who is a wise man?" &c. You all affect the title, and ye seek the thing, as ye suppose. But alas! ye mistake that wherein it consists. Truly there is in all men (ever since we tasted of the tree of knowledge of good and evil) a strange innate desire of knowledge, and affectation of wisdom, and desire of excellence. But since the first endeavour in paradise succeeded ill, there hath nothing gone well since. We weary ourselves to catch vanities, shadows, and lies. "How long, O ye sons of men, will ye love vanity, and follow after lies?" That divinely taught prophet could not but pity the children of men. And as Paul speaks to the Athenians of another purpose, "Him whom ye ignorantly worship, we show unto you," so he declares unto men that which they ignorantly and vainly seek elsewhere. This I assure you consists in this, that ye show out of a good conversation your works with meekness and wisdom.

All our mischief proceeds from this, that we misapprehend and mistake that which we would gladly have. And so once being in the wrong way, that cannot lead to our purposed end, the faster we run, the farther we go from it. The more we move in affection and diligence, the less we indeed promove in reality to the attaining what we seek. How greatly have we fallen! I might instance this in many things, but I shall be content with these two. There is a desire in all men after happiness, but there is a fundamental error in the imagination supposing it to consist in the enjoyment of temporal pleasure, honour, advantage, or the satisfaction of our own natural inclinations. Now this leads all mankind to a pursuit after these things. But how base a scent is it? And how vain a pursuit is it? For the faster they move in that way, the further they are from all solid and true contentment. Again, in all godly men, there is something of this rectified, and they suppose religion to be the only true wisdom, and this wisdom the only true happiness. But oftentimes there are even mistakes in that too. As many of the world call sweet bitter, and bitter sweet, because of the vitiated and corrupted palate; so the godly, being in some measure distempered, call that which is not so sweet sweetest, and that which is not so bitter, bitterest. They change the value of things, and misplace them out of that order in which God hath set them. One great mistake is this. We impose a great deal of weight and moment upon these things in religion, which are but the hay and stubble, or pins in the building, and we esteem less that wherein the foundation and substance of true religion consists. We have an over-apprehension of a profession, and an undervaluing thought of practice. We overstretch some points of knowledge, and truth of the least value;[436] and have less value for the fundamental statutes of the gospel, faith and love, mercy and judgment. This our Saviour reproved in the Pharisees. "I will have mercy (says God) and not sacrifice." A ceremony of opinion in some particulars of the time hath more necessity with us than the practice of true godliness: and this is the root of the most part of these vain janglings, strifes of words, and perverse disputings of men, whereof cometh envy, strife, malice, evil surmisings, and no edification in faith and love, which were so frequent in the primitive times, and so often hammered down by Paul. This is it, a misapprehension of the value of them. Fancy imposes a worth and necessity upon them. But Paul doth always oppose unto them true godliness (1 Tim. vi. 3, chap. iv. 7), and prescribes that as the cure, that true godliness in practice of what we know, and charity towards our brethren, may be bigger in our apprehension, and higher in our affection. Would ye then know, my brethren, wherein true religion consists, and wherein genuine Christianity stands? It is in showing out of a good conversation, our works with meekness and wisdom. I reduce it to these two words, in joining practice to knowledge, and meekness to both; and this makes our religion to shine before men, and glorify our heavenly Father.

Wherein then do ye think this mystery of wisdom which the gospel reveals consists? Not in the profound and abstracted speculations of God, or the secrets of nature,—a work about which learned men have racked their inventions, and beaten their brains to no other purpose, than the discovery of the greatness of man's ignorance. It doth not consist in the sounding of the depths of divinity, and loosing all these perplexing knots of questions, and doubts, which are moved upon the scripture, in all which men really bewray their own ignorance and misery. "The world by wisdom knew not God." Living right is the first point of true wisdom. It costs many men great expenses to learn to know their own folly, to become fools, that they may become wise, 1 Cor. iii. 18. Man became a fool by seeking to become wiser than God made him; and that is all the result of our endeavours after wisdom since, Rom. i. 22. But here is the great instruction of Christianity, to bring man down low from the height of presumption and self-estimation, and make him see himself just as he is by nature, a fool, and a wild ass's colt. Nebuchadnezzar had much ado to learn this lesson. It cost him some years brutality to learn to know his brutishness, and when that was known his understanding returned to him.

Now this is the first and hardest point of wisdom. When it is once learned and imprinted on the heart, O what a docility is in the mind to more! What readiness to receive what follows! It makes a man a weaned child, a little simple child, tractable and flexible as Christ would have all his disciples. A man thus emptied and vacuated of self-conceit, these lines of natural pride being blotted out, the soul is as a *tabula rasa*, "an unwritten table," to receive any impression of the law of God that he pleases to put on it; and then his words are all "plain to him that understandeth, and right to them that find knowledge," Prov. viii. 9. Then I say it is not difficult to understand and to prove what is the good and acceptable will of God, Rom. xii. 2; Eph. v. 10-17. It is not up unto heaven, that thou shouldest say, who shall ascend to bring it down? Neither is it far down in the depth, that thou shouldest say, who shall descend and bring it up from hence? But it is near thee, "in thy mouth, and in thy heart," &c. Rom. x. 6, 7, 8. "He hath showed thee, O man, what is good, and what is required of thee, but to do justly, to love mercy, and to walk humbly with thy God," Micah vi. 8. There is the plain sign of Christian wisdom, the abridgment of all that is taught in the school of Christ. Here is the course of moral philosophy, "The grace of God hath appeared, to teach us to deny ungodliness, and worldly lusts, and to live soberly, righteously, and godly in this world." And when the scholar is brought along by these degrees, he is at length laureated[437] in that great day of our Saviour's appearance. Then he hath the degree of glory and immortality conferred upon him. He is a candidate of immortality and felicity, Tit. ii. 12, 13.

We are in the Christian school like many scholars who labour to know so many things, that indeed they know nothing well; as the stomach that devours much meat, but digests little, and turns it not into food and aliment, incorporates it not into the body. We catch at many great points of truth, and we really drink in none of them; we let none sink into the heart, and turn into affection and practice. This is the grand disease of the time, a study to know many things, and no study to love what we know, or practise any thing. The Christian world is all in a flame, and the church is rent asunder by the eager pursuit and prosecution of some points of truth, and this is the clamour of all men, who will show us our light? Who will discover some new thing unto us? But in the mean time we do not prove the unquestionable acceptable will of our God; like a fastidious squeamish stomach, that loathes what it receives, and always longs for something else. Thus the evil is vented here. Who is a wise man, do ye think? Not he who knows many things, who hath still a will to controversy, who hath attained some further light than others of them; not he, brethren, but he that shows out of a good conversation, his works with meekness of wisdom, he that proves and practiseth as well as knows, the good will of God. "For hereby do we know that we know him, if we keep his commandments. He that saith, I know him, and keeps not his commands, is a liar, and the truth is not in him," 1 John ii. 3, 4. This proves that knowledge is not in the head, but in the heart, and that it is not captivated and shut up in the mind, but that a man is delivered up as a captive to the truth, Rom. vi. 16.

All men complain of the want of light and knowledge, though perhaps none think they have much. But is the will of God so dark and intricate? Is it so hard to understand? Truly it is plain, "He hath showed thee what is good," he hath showed thee what to do; but that thou neglectest to do, and therefore men know not what to do further. Do ye not all know that ye should walk soberly, righteously, and piously, and humble yourselves to walk with God, and in lowliness of mind each should esteem another better than himself? Ye should forbear and forgive one another, as God for Christ's sake hath forgiven you. Ye should not seek great things for yourselves, especially when God is plucking up what he hath planted, and casting down what was built. Ye should mind your country above more, and live as sojourners here. Are not these words of wisdom all plain and obvious to the meanest capacity? Now, my beloved, with what face can ye seek more knowledge of God, or inquire for more light into his mind, when you do not prove that known and perfect will of his? When you do not occupy your present talent, why do ye seek more? "To him that hath shall be given." Truly it is the man that fears and obeys as far as is revealed, to whom God shows his secret, and teaches the way he should choose, Psal. xxv. 12. I know not a readier way to be resolved in doubtful things, than to study obedience in these things that are beyond all doubt. To walk in the light received, is the highway to more light. But what hope is there of any more light from the Lord, when our ways and courses, and dispositions and practices, even in our endeavours after more knowledge, cannot endure the light of that shining will of God, that is already revealed? In ordering our conversation, we catch at the shadow of our points of truth, and lose the substance that was in our hands, lowliness, meekness, charity, long suffering, sobriety of mind and actions, and heavenly mindedness. All these substantial we let go, that we may get hold of some empty unedifying notions. We put out our candle that is already enlightened, that is, the knowledge of good conversation that we may seek more light, and that is the way to find darkness and delusion. Because they received not the truth in love, that they might be saved, God gave them up to strong delusions and the belief of lies, 2 Thess. ii. 10, 11. There is the ground of delusions, truth received, but not loved or obeyed, many things known, but the stamp and seal not impressed on the heart we express in the conversation. Therefore God is provoked to put out that useless light of truth and deliver that man captive to delusions, who would not deliver his soul a captive to truth. And is not this righteousness, that he who detained the known truth in unrighteousness of affection and conversation, be himself detained and incarcerated by strong delusions of mind and imagination?

As a good conversation and good works should be joined to knowledge, and meekness must be the ornament of both, this meekness of wisdom is the great lesson that the wisdom of the Father came down to teach man. "Learn of me, for I am meek." And truly the meekness of that substantial wisdom of God Jesus Christ, is the exact pattern and copy, and the most powerful motive and constraint to this kindness of Christian wisdom. Our Saviour did not cry nor lift up his voice in the streets. He made little noise, nor cried with pomp, he was not rigorous, nor rigid upon sinners. Though he was oppressed and afflicted yet he opened not his mouth, being reviled he reviled not again, being cursed, he blessed. Though he could have legions of angels at his command, yet he would show rather an example of patience and meekness to his followers, than overcome his enemies. If many of us, who pretend to be his disciples, had the winds, rains, heavens, and elements at our commandment, I fear we would have burned up the world. We would presently have called for fire from heaven, to devour all whom we conceived enemies to him, or ourselves, and that under the notion of zeal. Zeal it is indeed, but such as is spoken of in the next verse. "If ye have bitter envying (the word is bitter zeal) in your hearts, glory not, nor lie against the truth." Christ's zeal was sweet zeal. It might well consume or eat him up within, but it did not devour others without. "The zeal of thy house (says he) hath eaten me up." But our zeal is like the Babylonian furnace, that burnt and consumed these that went to throw the pious children into it. At the first approaching it gets without the chimney, and devours all around it. If the meekness or gentleness of a person who received the greatest injuries that ever any received, and to whom the greatest indignities were done, and who endured the greatest contradiction of sinners, if his calm composed temper do not soften our spirits, mitigate our sharpness, and allay our bitterness, I know not what can do it. I do not think but if any man considered how much long suffering God exercises towards him, how gentle and patient he is, after so many provocations, how Jesus

Christ doth still forgive infinite numbers of infinite wrongs done to his grace, how slow he is to wrath, and easy to be entreated, surely such a man would abate much of his severity towards others, he would pursue peace with all men, and esteem little of wrongs done unto him, and not think them worthy of remembrance, he would not be easily provoked, but he would be easily pacified. In a word, he could not but exercise something of that gentleness and meekness in forbearing and forgiving, as Christ also forgave him and truly there is no ornament of a man like that of a meek and quiet spirit, 1 Pet. iii. 4. It is both comely and precious, it is of great price in God's sight. It is a spirit all composed and settled, all peace and harmony within. It is like the heavens in a clear day, all serene and beautiful, whereas an unmeek spirit is for the most part like the troubled sea, tossed with tempests, winds, and dashed with rains, even at the best, it is but troubled with itself. When there is no external provocation, it hath an inward unrest in its bosom, and casts out mire and dirt. Meekness is so beseeming every man, that it is even humanity itself. It is the very nature of a man restored, and these brutish, wild and savage dispositions put off. Meekness is a man in the true likeness of God. But passion, and the evils which accompany it, is a man metamorphosed and transformed into the nature of a beast, and that of a wild beast too. It hath been always reckoned that anger is nothing different from madness, but in the continuance of it. It is a short madness. But what is wanting in the continuance is made up in the frequency. When spirits are inclined to it, there is a habitual fury and madness in such spirits. It is no wonder then, these are conjoined, meekness and wisdom, for truly they are inseparable. Meekness dwells in the bosom of wisdom. It is nothing else but wisdom, reason, and religion ruling all within, and composing all the distempered lusts and affections, but anger rests in the bosoms of fools, it cannot get rest but in a fool's bosom, for where it enters, wisdom and reason must go out, Eccles. vii. 9. "A fool's wrath is presently known," Prov. xii. 16. For if there were so much true and solid wisdom as to examine the matter first, and to consider before we suffer ourselves to be provoked, we would certainly quench anger in the very first smoking of an apprehension of a wrong. We would immediately cast it out, for there is nothing so much blinds and dimmeth the eye of our understanding, and when this gross vapour rises out of the dunghill of our lusts, nothing so much uncovers our shame and nakedness. "A prudent man covereth shame," but hastiness and bitterness takes the garment off our infirmity, and exposes us to mockery and contempt, Prov. xii. 16. There is not a greater evidence of a strong solid spirit, than this, to be able to govern this unruly passion, whereas it is taken far otherwise. Meekness is construed by some to be simplicity and weakness, and many imagine some greatness and height of spirit in the hotter natures, but truly it is far otherwise. "For he that is slow to anger, is better than the mighty, and he that ruleth his own spirit, than he that takes a city." Wrath is an impotency and weakness. It hath no strength in it, but such as ye would find in madmen. But this is true magnanimity, to overcome thyself, and "overcome evil with good."

As there is nothing which is a greater evidence of wisdom, so there is nothing a better help to true wisdom than this. For a meek spirit is like a clear running fountain, that ye see the bottom of, but a passionate spirit is like a troubled fountain, the shadow of truth cannot be seen in it. A glass that is pure and cleanly, renders the image lively, but if it be besmeared with dust, you can see nothing, so is a composed mild spirit apt to discern the truth without prejudice. And indeed it is the meek whom God engages to teach his ways, Psal. xxv. 8, 9. He that receives with meekness the ingrafted word, is in the readiest capacity to receive more. When the superfluity of naughtiness is cast out, and all the faculties of the soul composed to quietness and calmness, then his voice will best be heard, and himself readiest to receive it. Our affection keeps a continual hurry within the tumultuous noise of our disordered lusts, that are always raging and controlling the voice of God, so that we cannot hear his teaching. A passionate temper of spirit is very indocile. There are so many loud sounds of prejudices within, that the truth cannot be heard. But a meek spirit hath all quietness and silence, as Cornelius and his house had waiting for the mind of the Lord. And such he delights to converse with most, and reveal most unto, for it gets readiest entertainment. Let me tell you, beloved in the Lord, you disoblige the Lord (if I may speak so) and hinder him to reveal any more of his mind to you, ye disengage him to teach you his way in those dark and untrodden paths, because ye do not study this meekness in the wisdom and knowledge ye have already, nor his meekness and moderation in seeking further knowledge. And it is no wonder he be provoked by it, to choose your delusions, because it is certainly these graces of meekness, charity, patience, gentleness, long suffering, humbleness of mind, and such like, which go always in a chain together. These are an ornament of grace upon the head, and a crown of glory, and that chain about the neck, Solomon mentions, Prov. iv. 9. Now when you cast off your crown of glory, your noblest ornament, your chain of dignity, should he give such precious pearls to swine? When you trample under foot the greater commandments of mercy, judgment, sobriety, humility, meekness, and charity, should he reveal lesser commandments, or discover his will in lesser matters? Consider the manner of expression here, "Let him show forth out of a good conversation," &c. Truly it is good works with meekness of wisdom, it is a good conversation, with a true profession, that shows forth a Christian, and shows him most before men. "Let your light (says Christ) so shine before men." What is the shining beauty of Christian light? It is the works of piety, charity, equity, and sobriety. These glorify the Father, and beautify all his children. You may easily conceive what that is, that chiefly commends religion to the ignorant world. Is it not the meekness of Christian wisdom? Is it not this harmless simplicity, that divine-like candour, that shines in every true Christian? Will rigidity, severity, passion, blood, violence, persecution, and such like, ever conciliate the hearts of men? Have such persons any beauty, any light in them, except a scorching consuming light? The light of a good Christian is like the light of the sun, of a sweet, gentle, and refreshing nature, conveying influence to all, doing good to the household of faith. Peter will tell you what that is, that will most engage the hearts of the world, to a reverend esteem of true religion, 1 Pet. ii. 12. It is a conversation honest, and void of offence, giving to every one their own due, honouring all men, loving the brotherhood, not using our liberty for a cloak of maliciousness, and not overstretching it, to the loosing of other natural or civil bands. When men see Christianity making us do that really and cheerfully, which even nature itself teacheth all to do that makes the light of it shining and beautiful. Are not these higher mysteries of faith, than some conceive? It is not other points of truth and profession, that are either above natural reason, or seem something opposite to it, that can engage natural beholders, and far less the prosecution of a temporal worldly interest of the people of God, to the destruction of all opposite to it, at least to the diminishing of all other men's gain and advantage, the engrossing of all earthly privileges into the hands of saints. That is such a thing that never entered into the heart of the shining lights of the primitive times. O how doth the stream of their exhortations run cross to this notion! I am sure there is nothing in its own nature, such a stumbling block to the world or represents religion so odious and abominable to other men, as when it stands in the way, and intercepts all these natural immunities or privileges of life, or estate. This makes natural men to hate it, even at a distance, and become irreconcilable enemies unto it. Since it will not let them live by it, they are engaged not to let it live by them. I wish indeed all the places of power and trust in every nation, were in the hands of godly men, not so much for the interest of the godly as for the public interest, because men fearing God, and hating covetousness, can only rule justly and comfortably. But to monopolize all power and trust to such a particular judgment and way (as it is now given out) is truly, I think, inhuman and unchristian. These deserve not power and trust who would seek it, and engross it wholly to themselves.[438] But there is another thing which savours greatly of the flesh, at least of that spirit which Christ reproved in his disciples, to take away men's lives, liberty, and livelihood given by their Creator, upon every foot of opposition and enmity to our way and interest. Is this to love our enemies, blessing them that curse us, or praying for them that despitefully use us, or persecute us? Let us remember we are Christians, and this is the rule of Christianity, that stops even the mouth of adversaries. But some still find an evasion for this. They will say they are God's enemies, and not my particular enemies only. But I pray you were not the enemies of Christians in these days more properly enemies to Christ than now? For they had nothing then to persecute them for, but the very profession of that name. And truly I confess in our days we make more particular enemies, by particular injuries and disobligements, than either our profession or practice of religion make. But to put it out of all doubt, we learn that they are persecutors, and do all manner of evil against us, for Christ's name sake. I have said this because I know nothing that more darkeneth and obscures religion nor such worldly and temporal interests, so eagerly pursued, and nothing makes it more to shine among men, than a good conversation with meekness of wisdom.

SERMON V.

James iii. 14.—"But if ye have bitter envying," &c.

The cunning of Satan, and the deceitfulness of our own hearts, are such that when a grosser temptation will not prevail with conscience in some measure enlightened, then they transform themselves into angels of light, and deal more subtilely with us. And there is no greater subtilty of Satan, nor no stronger self deceit, than this, to palliate and cover vices with the shadow of virtue, and to present corruptions under the similitude of graces. It is common unto all temptations to sin, to have a hook under their bait, to be masked over with some pleasure or advantage or credit. But when such earthly and carnal pretences do not insinuate strongly unto a believing heart that has discovered the vanity of all that which is in the world, so dare not venture upon sin for all the pleasures which attend it, then he winds about and tarries and changes his likeness unto light, conscience, and duty, presents many works of darkness and corruption under the notion of duty and honesty, according as he finds the temper of a man's spirit to be. I can give no instance more pregnant, and even common, than this which is given here, viz., contentions and strivings among brethren, bitter envying, maligning and censuring one another, which are very manifest works of the flesh, and works of darkness, fitter for the night than the day, and for the time of ignorance, nor the time after the clear light hath shined. Now if Satan were about to persuade a church or a Christian of this, how do ye think he would go about it? Would he present some carnal advantage to be gained by it, some more profit or preferment from it? May be that might be very taking with some more unconscientious self seeking spirits, and I fear it be too much taken with many. But sure it will not relish with every man. It will not entice him that hath the fear of God, and the love of Jesus stirring within him. Therefore he must seek about, and find some false prophet, that may come out in the name of the Lord, and disguise himself, and by such means he will do it. Let a point of truth or conscience come in debate, let a notion of religion, and one far off from an interest in Christ be in the business, and then he can take advantage to make a man overreach himself in it. He will present the truth as a thing of so great weight and consequence, that he must contend for it, and empty all his wit and power and parts for it. This good intention being established, he raises up men's passions under a notion of zeal, and these be promoved under that pretence for such an end. Whatsoever mean may be sought, profitable for that end, all is chosen and followed without discretion or knowledge of what is good or evil. It is apprehended that the good principle of conscience, of duty, and the good intention, may justify all. And by that means he hath persuaded the churches of Christ, and the Christian world, unto more rigidity, severity, cruelty, strife, contention, blood, violence, and such works of darkness, than readily have been found in the times of ignorance. Is Christendom a field of blood, rather than any other part of the world? Truly this is the reproach of Christianity. By this, God's name is daily blasphemed. Here our apostle sets himself to unmask this angel of light, and to decipher him in his own proper nature and notion. He takes off the vizard of religion and wisdom, and lets you see the very image of hell under it. "But if ye have bitter envying and strife, glory not." Ye glory as if ye had the truth, you glory in your zeal for it, you boast that ye are the wise men, the religious men, and so you take liberty upon the account of envy, to malign, despise, and contend with others. Glory not, if you cherish such strifes and contentions, to the breach of Christian peace and concord. You are liars against the truth, which you profess. Do not think these proceed from true zeal, nay, nay, it is but bitter envy, and bitter zeal. Do not flatter yourselves with an apprehension of wisdom, or knowledge, or religion. That is wisdom indeed, but mark of what nature. It is earthy, sensual, and devilish. And indeed, that is a foolish wisdom, to say no worse of it.

You see, then, what need we have of the exhortation of the apostle (Eph. vi. 11), "Put on the whole armour of God, that ye may be able to stand against the wiles of the devil." Truly we may stand against his darts, and violent open thrusts at our conscience; when we,[439] being ignorant of his devices, and not acquainted with his depths (2 Cor. ii. 11, Rev. ii. 24) will not be able to stand against his ways. For we have a great and subtile party to wrestle with, principalities and powers, and spiritual wickedness in high places, or heavenly things (as some render the word). He exercises much wickedness, spiritual invisible wickedness in heavenly and religious things, in which it is hard to wrestle, unless we be endowed with faith, knowledge, and righteousness, and shod with the gospel of peace, the peaceable gospel reducing our spirits to a peaceable temper. I conceive there is nothing the world hath been more abused with, than the notion of zeal, justice, and such like, and there is nothing wherein a Christian is more ready to deceive himself than this. Therefore I conceive the Holy Ghost has undeceived us in this, and hath of purpose used the word zeal as often in a bad sense as in a good one, and usually chooses to express envy and malice by it, though another word might suit as well, and be more proper. So here bitter zeal, ζηλος φρενος, is reckoned among the works of the flesh, Gal. v. 20. And we are exhorted to walk honestly as in the day, not in strife and envy, or zeal. And therefore the apostle rebukes sharply the Corinthians: "Are ye not carnal, and walk as men, whereas there is among you envying, or zeal, and strife," 1 Cor. iii. 3. Zeal is a vehemency of affection in any earnest pursuit, or opposition of a thing, and to make it good, it must not only be fixed upon a commendable and good object, but must run in the right channel, between the banks of moderation, charity, and sobriety. If it overflows these, certainly that excess proceeds not simply and purely from the love of God, or the truth, but from some latent corruption or lust in our members, which takes occasion to swell up with it. I find in scripture the true zeal of God hath much self denial in it. It is not exercised so much concerning a man's own matters, as concerning the matters that are purely and merely concerning God's glory. It is the most flexible, condescending, and forbearing thing in those things that relate to ourselves and our own interests. Thus Moses is commended as the meekest man, when Aaron and Miriam raise sedition against him, Num. xii. 3. He had not affections to be commoved upon that account. But how much is he stirred and provoked upon the apprehension of the manifest dishonour of God, by the people's idolatry? How many are lions in their own cause, and in God's as simple and blunt as lambs? And how much will our spirits be commoved when our own interest lies in the business, and hath some conjunction with God's interest, but if these are parted, our fervour abates, and our heat cools? I lay down this, then, as the fundamental principle of true zeal, it is like charity that seeketh not its own things.

But to make the nature of it clear, I give you three characters of it, verity, charity and impartiality. I say it hath truth in it, a good thing for the object, and knowledge of that good thing in the subject, for the principle of it: "It is good to be zealously affected always in a good thing," Gal. iv. 18. Zeal is an evil thing, hath something of the impatient and restless nature of the devil in it. There is nothing we should be more deliberate and circumspect in, than what to employ or bestow our affections upon. We should have a certain persuasion of the unquestionable goodness of that which we are ardent and vehement to obtain, else the more ardour and vehemency, the more wickedness is in it. The Jews had a zeal for God, but not according to knowledge, and that is a blind impetuous self will. For if a man take a race at his full speed in the dark, he cannot but catch a fall.[440] The eager and hot pursuits of men are founded upon some gross misapprehensions.

Secondly, There must not only be a goodness supposed in the object, but some correspondence between the worth and weight of that goodness and the measure of our desires and affections, else there wants that conformity between the soul and truth which makes a true zeal of God. I mean this, the soul's most vehement desires should be employed about the chiefest good, and our zeal move in relation to things unquestionably good, and not about things of small moment, or of little edification. This is the apostolic rule, that not only we consider that there be some truth in the thing, but that we especially take notice, if there be so much truth and goodness as requires such a measure of vehemency and affection. Therefore in lesser things we should have lesser commotion, and in greater things greater, suitable to them. Otherwise the Pharisees who exercised their zeal about trifles, and neglected the weightier matters of the law, (Matt. xxiii. 23.) would not have been reproved by Christ. And indeed this is the zeal to which we are redeemed by Christ. Tit. ii. 14. Be ye zealous of good works, of works that are unquestionably good, such as piety, equity, and sobriety. There is nothing more incongruous than to strain at a gnat and swallow a camel, to spend the vital spirits upon things of small concernment to our own or others' edification, and to have nothing to spare for the weightier matters of true godliness. It is as if a man should strike a feather or the air with all his might: He must needs wrest his arms. Even so, to strike with the spiritual sword of our affections, with such vehemency, at the lighter and emptier matters of religion, cannot choose but to disjoint the spirit, and put it out of course, as there is a falsehood in that zeal that is so vehement about a light matter, though it have some good in it. For there is no suitable proportion between the worth of the thing and the vehemency of the spirit. Imagination acts in both. In the one it supposes a goodness, and it follows it, and in the other, it imposes a necessity and a worth far beyond that which really is, and so raises up the spirit to that height of necessity and worth that hath no being but in a man's imagination. I think there is no particular that the apostle doth so much caveat. For I find in 1 Tim. i. 4 he takes off such endless matters that minister questioning rather than godly edifying, and gives us a better subject to employ our zeal upon, ver 5, the great end and sum of all religion, love to God and man, proceeding from a pure heart, a good conscience, and faith unfeigned, from which we must needs swerve, when we turn aside to such empty and vain janglings, ver 6. For truly we have but narrow and limited spirits, and it must needs follow, when we give them very much to one thing, that they cannot attend another thing seriously, as Christ declares, (Matt. vi. 24.) "no man can serve two masters," &c. And therefore there is much need of Christian wisdom to single out and choose the most proper and necessary object. For as much as we give other things that have not so much connexion with that, we take from it as much; and the apostle counsels us, (1 Tim. iv. 7.) rather to exercise ourselves unto true godliness, and to the most substantial things in it, rather than vain things, and opposition of science, chap vi. 3-5, 20. There he opposes the wholesome words of Christ, and the doctrine that is according to godliness, unto questions, and strifes of words, whereof comes envy, railings, evil-surmisings, and perverse disputings of men of corrupt minds. And it is very observable that he is pressing the duties of believing servants towards their masters, whether believers or infidels, that the name of God be not blasphemed, nor the gospel evil spoken of. For there is nothing so much exposes it to misconstruction, as when it is stretched and abused unto the prejudice of natural and civil duties, and doubtless there would be many doubts and questions about it in these days, some contending for worldly pre-eminence over the Pagans, and some for the levelling of all Christians. But, says he, "If any man teach otherwise," or contend about this, "he is proud, knowing nothing," &c. He hath forsaken the substance of true godliness, which consists in good works shining before men, and disabuses the notion of Christian liberty to the dishonour of Christ, and hath supposed gain, a worldly carnal interest of the godly, to be piety, and so pursues that fancy of his own. He renews this in the Second Epistle, (chap. ii. 14-16.) showing that these strifes about words, albeit they seem to be upon grounds of conscience at the beginning, yet they increase unto more ungodliness, ver. 23. And unto Titus he gives the same charge very solemnly, (Tit. iii. 8, 9.) "I will that thou affirm constantly, that they who believe in God should be careful to maintain good works. But avoid foolish and unlearned questions," &c. For "this is a faithful saying." But again,

Thirdly, Zeal must have charity with it, and this all the scriptures cited prove. It must be so tempered with love, that it vents not to the breach of Christian peace and concord. Charity envieth not, or is not zealous. When zeal wants charity, it is not zeal but envy. And hence it is that there are so frequent and fervent exhortations to avoid such questions as may gender strifes, and contentions, and malice. Now certainly there was some truth in them, and something of conscience also in them. Yet he dissuades entirely the prosecution of them to the rigour, as men are apt to do, but wills us rather to have faith in ourselves. And truly I think the questions that did then engender strifes, and rent the church, were as much if not more momentous nor the most part of these about which we bite and devour one another,—the questions of the law, the circumcision, and eating of things sacrificed to idols, of things indifferent, lawful, or not lawful. Yet all these he would have subordinated unto the higher end of the commandment, charity, 1 Tim. i. 4, 5. And when he exhorts the Corinthians to be zealous for spiritual gifts, he would yet have them excel in these things which edify the church, 1 Cor. xiv. 1-12. "Covet earnestly the best gifts," says he, and yet he shows them a more excellent way, and that is charity, (1 Cor. xiii. 1.) to do all these things for the good and edification of the church, rather than of our own opinion, 1 Cor. xii. 3; chap. xiv. 12. I find where the word zeal is taken in a bad sense it hath these works of darkness attending it, wrath, strife, malice, &c. Gal. v. 20; 1 Cor. iii. 3; Rom. xiii. 13. It is accompanied with such a hellish crowd of noisome lusts. Let me add a differential character of it. It is uncharitable, contentious, and malicious. It can do nothing, condescend to nothing, and is conversant about nothing, but what pleases our own humour, for the peace and unity of the church. It is a self-willed impetuous thing, like a torrent that carries all down before it. But truly right zeal runs calmly and constantly within the banks; it will rather consume its own bowels within with grief, than devour others without.

SERMON VI.

Matth. xi. 28.—"Come unto me, all ye that labour, and are wearied," &c.

It is the great misery of Christians in this life, that they have such poor, narrow, and limited spirits, that are not fit to receive the truth of the gospel in its full comprehension; from whence manifold misapprehensions in judgment, and stumbling in practice proceed. The beauty and life of things consist in their entire union with one another, and in the conjunction of all their parts. Therefore it would not be a fit way to judge of a picture by a lineament, or of an harmony by a discrepant, nor of the world by some small parcel of it; but take all the parts together, all the notes and draughts, as conjoined by art in such an order, and there appears nothing but beauty and consent. Even so it falls out in our conceptions of the gospel. The straitness and narrowness of our spirits takes in truth by parcels, disjointed from the whole, looks upon one side of it, and sees not the other. As for example, sometimes there appears unto us our duty and strait obligation to holy walking and this being seen and considered alone, ordinarily fills the soul with some fear, jealousies, and confusion. Another time, there rises out from under the cloud, the mercy and peace of Christ in inviting, accepting, and pardoning sinners, by his blood, that cleanses from all sin; and in that view (such is our weakness and shortness of sight) there is nothing else presented but pardoning grace; and hence there is occasion given to the corruption of our hearts, to insinuate secretly and subtilely unto us some inclinations to more liberty, and indulgence to the flesh. Thus you see what stumbling in practice, and disorder in walking, this partial way of receiving the truth occasioneth. But it hath no less influence upon the many controversies and differences in doctrine and opinion, about grace and works. For from whence arise these mistakes on both hands, but from the straitness of our apprehensions, that we do not take the truth of God in its full latitude, but being eager upon one part and zealous of it, we almost lose the remembrance, and sometimes fall, in wrangling with the other? Many that proclaim the free grace of the gospel, their fault is, not that they make it freer than it is, for truly it is as free of any Antinomian can apprehend it, but rather because they take it not in its entire and full complexion, which best declares the freedom of it, as comprehending both the pardon of sin and purity from sin, grace towards us and grace within us; and so, while they only plead for the one, they seem at least to oppugn the other. And, in like manner, others apprehending the necessity, beauty, and comeliness of holiness and new obedience, are much in pressing and declaring this in opposition to the other way; in which there may be some mistake, not in making it more meritorious than it is, but at leastwise[441] in such a manner it may be holden out, as may somewhat obscure the freedom of God's grace. The occasion of both these misapprehensions may be from the scattering of these diverse parcels of truth, as so many pearls in the field of the scripture; one is found here, and one takes it up, as if there were no more; here is repentance, and away he goes with that, without conjoining these scattered pieces into one body. But yet our Saviour sometimes gives us complete sums and models of the gospel, in which he presents all at one view at once, and especially in these words now read. The sum of all the gospel is contained in two words, "Come unto me," and "take my yoke upon you." All the duty of a Christian, and all his encouragement is here. His duty is to believe in Christ, and to give himself up to his obedience, and become his disciple, and to follow his example; and his encouragement is the rest promised, rest to his soul,—which is the only proper seat, of rest or disquiet. It is most capable and sensible of both,—and this rest includes in its bosom, not only peace and tranquillity of mind here, which all the creatures combined cannot give, but all felicity besides; that eternal rest from all the labours of this life, and complacency in the fruition of God for ever. You see, then, what is the full invitation of the gospel. It is nothing else but come, and have rest. "Take on an easy yoke, and ye shall find rest. Come and be happy. Come and receive life. That which you seek elsewhere, both ignorantly and vainly, here it is only to be found. Come (says Christ), and I promise to give it unto you. Wait upon me by obedience, and you shall at length find by experience, that rest which I am willing to give you."

I desire you may consider both the order and the connexion of these integral parts of the gospel. The order of the gospel is a great part of the gospel. In some things method is arbitrary, and it matters not which go before, or which follow after, but here they become essential, and so a great part of the matter itself. There must be first coming to Christ, and then taking on his yoke; first believing, then obeying his commandments. This is as essential an order, as is between the fruit and the root, the stream and the fountain, the sun-beam and the sun. Will any man expect fruit till he plant? There must then first be the implanting of the soul into Christ by faith, and then in due season follow the fruits of obedience by abiding in him. The perverting of this order makes much disorder in the spirits and lives of Christians. But how can it choose but all must wither and decay, if the soul be not planted by this river, whose streams gladden the city of our God, if the roots of it be not watered with the frequent apprehension and consideration of the grace of Christ, or the riches of God's mercy? The way and method of many Christians is just opposite to this. For you labour and weary yourselves, how to attain some measure and satisfaction in the latter, before you adventure the first, to have the heart humbled by godly sorrow, and the soul inflamed by love to God, and the yoke of his obedience submitted unto; while in the mean time you deliberately suspend the exercise of faith, and apprehension of the pardoning grace of Christ. Now, how this can consist either with sound reason or religion, I do not see. For were it not a point of madness to seek fruits from a tree that is lying above ground, and to refuse to plant it till it give some experience of its fruitfulness in the air? And what can be more absurd, than to imagine to have the Spirit of Christ working in the heart godly sorrow, or Christian love, and so renewing it again to his image, and yet withal Christ not received into the heart by faith? Do you not know that this is his first entrance into the soul? He enters there by the door of faith, and a soul enters into him at the door of the promise by faith. How then do ye imagine he shall work in you, before you will admit him to come in to you? Besides, either you apprehend that you may attain to such gracious qualifications by your own industry without Christ, which is blasphemous to his name and office; for if you may, what need have you of him? Or, if you believe that he is the only treasure of all grace and wisdom, and that all things are delivered to him of the Father, then how do you seek these things without him? It must be wretched folly to seek them elsewhere, and not come to him. And indeed it is observable, that this exhortation to come unto Christ is subjoined unto ver. 27, "All things are delivered unto me by the Father." And therefore, seeing all grace, and life, and happiness is enclosed in me, seeing without me there is nothing but a barren wilderness, in which you may toil and labour, and weary yourselves in fruitless pursuits, come hither where it is originally and plentifully seated, and you cannot miss your end, nor lose your labour. And for the farther illustration of this subject, I shall only add that,

Secondly, There is another woful mistake possesses your minds who take up this way, for certainly you must think that there is some worth or dignity in it, whereby you intend to recommend yourselves unto Christ. For to what purpose is that anxious and scrupulous exaction of such previous qualifications, if it be not to give some more boldness and confidence to thy mind, to adventure to believe the promises and come to Christ, because thou thinkest thou canst not come when thou art so unclean and so unworthy? And therefore thou apprehendest that thou canst so purge thyself from sin and adorn thyself with graces, as may procure some liking, and procure some favour at Christ's hand, which is indeed very opposite to the tenor of the proposal of free grace in the gospel in which there is nothing upon the creature's part required as a condition or qualification to make them the more welcome in coming to Christ.

Let this word then abide with you: "Come unto me, and take my yoke upon you, and learn of me," which in substance is this, Come and cast your burdens on me first, and then take my burden upon you. O it is a blessed exchange! Cast your heavy burden upon my back, and take my light burden on yours. For what is it to invite them that labour and are ladened to come, but to come and repose themselves for rest upon him? And that is directly to lay over that which burdens and ladeneth them upon him. There is an unsupportable burden of sin, the guilt of sin, and there is an intolerable weight of wrath. "Mine iniquities are gone over mine head (Ps. xxxviii. 4.) and as an heavy burden they are too heavy for me." And when the wrath of God is joined to this burden, the name of the Lord burning with anger, how may you conceive a soul will be pressed under that burden, which is so heavy, that it will press the mountains into valleys, make the sea flee out of its place, and the earth tremble? Now here is the invitation. Is there any penitent soul that feels the burden of the weight of sin and wrath? Let them come and disburden their souls of care, fear, and anxiety, in this blessed port of rest and refuge for poor sinners. Is there a yoke of transgressions wreathed about thy neck, and bound by the hand of God, (Lam. i. 14) a yoke that neither men nor angels are able to bear? Then, I beseech you, come hither, and put over your yoke upon Jesus Christ. Tie it about him for God hath laid upon him the iniquities of us all, and he bore our sins. He did bear the yoke of divine displeasure, and it was bound about his neck with God's own hand, with his own consent. Now, here is the actual liberty and the releasement of a soul from under the yoke, here is its actual rest and quiet from under the pain of this burden, when a soul is made to consent unto, and willingly to put over that burden upon Christ. And this freedom and vacancy from the unsupportable yoke of guilt, will certainly dispose the soul, and make it more capable of receiving the easy and portable yoke of his commandments. I or you may easily perceive how easy love maketh all things, even difficulties themselves. Let once a soul be engaged that way to Christ, (and there is no possibility of engaging it in affection without some taste and feeling, or believing apprehension of his love and sufficiency for us,) and you will see that the rough way will be made plain and the crooked way straight, heavy things light, and hard things easy. For what command can be grievous to that soul who apprehends that Christ hath taken the great weight of wrath off it, and carried away the intolerable pain of its guiltiness, which would have pressed and depressed it eternally, without any hope of relaxation or ease? Hath he borne a yoke bound on by the majesty of God, and fastened with the cords of his displeasure? And can it be so heavy to a believing soul to take up that obedience which is fastened with the cords of love? And besides, how much will faith facilitate this, and make this yoke to be cheerfully and willingly submitted to, because it delivers the soul from those unsufferable cares and fears, which did quite enervate its strength, and take away its courage? For, I pray you, what is there in a soul under the fear of wrath, that is not totally disabled by that heavy pressure for any willing or cheerful obedience? The mystery[442] of the spirit is spent that way, the courage of the soul is defeated, the heart is weakened, and nothing is suitable to the yoke of Christian love and obedience. But when once a soul apprehends Christ, this is a reposition of all his cares and burdens, and comes to exoner[443] his soul in him, and cast his burthen upon him. Then the soul is lightened as it were for this journey, then he may walk in the ways of obedience, without the pressing fear and pushing anguish of the dread of condemnation of the law. To conclude this head, nothing will make you take up this yoke willingly, or bear it constantly, except you be delivered from the other yoke that was so heavy even to Christ, and that made him cry, "My soul is exceeding heavy and troubled, and what shall I say? Father, save me from this hour."

Now, these who are here in the text invited to come unto Christ,—you see them described to be labouring and heavy laden persons. "Come unto me, all ye that labour," &c. At least it seems to hold forth a previous qualification and condition of believing, without which we may not venture to come unto Christ. Indeed it is commonly so taken, and mistaken. Many conceive that the clause is restrictive and exclusive, that is to say, that this description of burdened and wearied sinners is a limitation of the command of believing, and that it circumscribes the warrant of coming to Christ, as if none might lawfully come unto him but these that are thus burdened, and thus it is supposed to be a bar, set upon the door of believing at which sinners must enter in to Christ, to hold out, and shut out all those who are not thus qualified for access, which I truly conceive is contrary to the whole strain and current of the dispensation of the gospel. Therefore I take it to be rather declarative, or ampliative, or both. I say, it is partly for declaration, not of the warrant to come, but of the persons who ordinarily do come to Christ. It declares not simply and universally who should come, but those who actually do come unto Christ. Take it thus then. All persons who hear the gospel are invited to come unto our Saviour without exception, the blind, the lame, those on the highways, not only the thirsty and the hungry, (Isa. lv. 1.) but those who have no thirst or hunger for righteousness, but only for things that do not profit (ver. 2), not only the broken hearted, that desire to come near to righteousness, but even the stout hearted that are far from righteousness. Such are commanded to hearken, and incline their ear, Isa. xlvi. 12, lv. 2, 3. Now, this command that reaches all, gives an immediate actual warrant and right to all to come, if they will. For what is required previous to give warrant to obedience, but the command of obedience? And therefore the Jews were challenged, because they would not come to Christ that they might have life. Now then there is no bar of seclusion set upon the door of the gospel, to keep out any soul from entering in. There is no qualification or condition prescribed by the gospel, and without which if he come, he is actually welcomed and received by Christ, whatsoever you suppose he wants. It is true, men's own security and unbelief will exclude them from Christ, but that is no retraction on the gospel's part. It is a bar set on a man's own heart, that shuts him up from coming to the patent entry of the gospel.

Therefore I take it thus, that though all ought to come to Christ, and none that are indeed willing are debarred for the want of any supposed condition, yet none will actually and really come, till they be in some measure sensible of the weight of their sins, and the wrath of God, till they are labouring under the feeling of their own misery and desperate condition. And whatsoever be the measure of this, if it give so much uneasiness to a man that he can be content with rest and ease in Christ, he may, and certainly ought, to come unto Jesus, and cast all his burdens upon him. I think then, that way that is in so frequent use among Christians, to sit down, and essay to bring our hearts to some deep humiliation, and so to prescribe and order it, as we will deliberately delay, and suspend the thoughts of believing, till we have attained something of this,—I say, this way crosses the very intention of Christ in uttering these words, and such like. For certainly he meant to take away impediments, and not to cast delays in our way. And therefore I said the word was rather for ampliation, that is, rather to encourage these who accounted themselves excluded, than to exclude any who desire to come. "Come unto me, every one, but especially you that labour, ye should make the greatest haste. Come unto me even though ye apprehend the wrath of God to be intolerable, and have foolishly wearied yourselves in seeking rest by other ways. Ye that are most apprehensive of your sins, and so are apt to doubt of any acceptation,—you that think yourselves worse than any, and so to have least warrant to come to me,—yet come, and I will by no means cast you out, but give rest to your souls." So that it is not intended to exclude those who are most ready to think themselves excluded, because they see so much sin in themselves.

Therefore, my beloved, without further disputing about it, let me exhort you in the name of Jesus Christ, who here invites and commands you, that you would at once put a period to this, and bring it to some conclusion. Since you are diseased and disquieted in yourselves, and cannot find rest in your own bosoms, I beseech you come here, where it is most likely to be found, and it is most certain, if you come you shall find it. Do not continue wrangling and contesting about the matter; for what is that but to increase your labour, and vexation, and add to your heavy burden? It will be so far from giving you any ease in the result of it, that it will rather make your wounds more incurable, and your burdens more intolerable, which is both opposite to the intention of the gospel and the nature of believing. Here then is your rest, here is your refreshing rest. Here it is in quiet yielding to his gracious offers, and silent submitting to the gospel, not in bawling or contending with it, which is truly a contending against ourselves. Isa. xxviii. 12. This is the rest, wherewith you may cause the weary to rest. It is nowhere else, not in heaven or earth, for there is no back that will take on this burden or can carry it away from us. There is no disburdening of a sinner of guilt and wrath, in any other port or haven, but in Christ, who is the city of refuge. Wheresoever you think to exoner yourselves besides this, you will find no refreshing, but a multiplication of burdens and cares. Your burden shall be rolled over upon you again with double weight. Therefore, my beloved, if you will not hear this, consider what follows, viz. you shall refuse this rest and refreshing and restlessly seek another rest. You may go and be doing, but you shall fall backward, and be broken and snared. Your burden shall fall back upon you, and you shall fall and be broken under it. That which the Lord said to Israel when they would flee to Egypt, is most true in this case. "In returning, and in rest ye shall be saved, in quietness and confidence shall be your strength;" but alas! they would not, that is a sad close.

SERMON VII.

Matt. xi. 20.—"Take my yoke upon you, and learn of me," &c.

Self love is generally esteemed infamous and contemptible among men. It is of a bad report every where, and indeed as it is taken commonly, there is good reason for it, that it should be hissed out of all societies, if reproaching and speaking evil of it would do it. But to speak the truth, the name is not so fit to express the thing, for that which men call self love, may rather be called self hatred. Nothing is more pernicious to a man's self, or pestilent to the societies of men than this, for if it may be called love, certainly it is not self love, but the love of some baser and lower thing than self, to our eternal prejudice. For what is ourselves, but our souls? Matt. xvi. 26, Luke ix. 25. For our Lord there shows that to lose our souls, and to lose ourselves, is one and the same thing. But what is it to love our souls? Certainly it is not to be enamoured with their deformed shape, as if it were perfect beauty? Neither can it be interpreted, any true love to our souls, to seek satisfaction and rest unto them, where it is not at all to be found, for this is to put them in perpetual pain and disquiet. But here it is that true self-love, and soul love centereth, in that which our Saviour propounds, namely, to desire and seek the everlasting welfare of our souls, and that perpetual rest unto them, after which there is no labour nor motion any more. Therefore, to draw unto himself the souls of men the more sweetly, and the more strongly too, he fasteneth about them a cord of their own interest, and that the greatest, real rest; and by this he is likely to prevail with men in a way suited to their reasonable natures. "Come unto me, all ye that labour and are wearied, and I will give you rest." Self interest is ordinarily exploded, at least disowned and disclaimed in men's discourses, as a base, wretched, sordid thing, which, though all men act by it, yet they are all ashamed to profess. But yet, if the interest be so high as indeed to concern self, and that which is truly our self, then both nations and persons count it the most justifiable ground of many of their actions, self preservation. But yet there is a higher interest than that, that relates to the eternal interest of our souls. And truly to own and profess, and prosecute that interest of soul preservation, of eternal rest to our souls, is neither ignoble, nor unbeseeming a Christian; neither is it any way inconsistent with the pursuance of that more public and catholic interest of God's glory, in respect of which all interests, even the most general and public, are particular and private. For this is the goodness of our God, that he hath bound up his own honour and our happiness in one bundle together; that he hath knit the rest of our precious souls, and the glory of his own name inseparably together, not only to condescend to our weakness, but to deal with us suitably to our natures. He proposes our own interests chiefly, to draw us to himself, and allows this happy self seeking in which a man loses himself, that he may be found again in Christ. Seeing then it is thus, that elsewhere, wheresoever you turn yourselves, within or without, there is no rest, but endless labour, and fruitless toil, (you find this already by experience, you who apprehend the weight of your sins, and the greatness of divine wrath,) that there is an intolerable pressure upon your souls already, and that this is nothing diminished, but rather augmented, by your vain labours and inquiries after some ease and peace,—your endeavours to satisfy your own consciences, and pacify God's wrath some other way, having filled you with more restless anxiety, and seeing there is a certain assurance of true rest and tranquillity here, upon the easiest terms imaginable, that is, "come to Jesus Christ, all ye who are disquieted and restless, and he will give you rest,"—O should not this be an invincible and irresistible attractive to your hearts, to draw them to our Redeemer over all impediments? The rest is perfect happiness; and yet the terms are easy. Only come and embrace it, and seek it nowhere else. There is a kind of quietness and tranquillity in the seeking and attaining this rest. All other rests are come to by much labour and business. Here Christ would have you,—who have laboured in vain for rest, and lost your toil and your pains,—to come at it, by ceasing from labour, as it were, that which you could not attain by labour, to come by it, *cunctando* (by keeping quiet), which you could not gain *pugnando* (by fighting). There is a quiet and silent way of believing promises, and rolling yourselves upon Christ offered in them, which is the nearest and most compendious way to this blessed rest and quietness, which, if you think to attain by much clamour and contention of debate or dispute, or by the painful labour and vexation of your spirits, which you call exercise of mind,—you take the way about, and put yourselves further off from it. Faith has a kind of present vacancy and quietness in it, in the very acting of it. It is not a tumultuous thing, but composes the soul to quietness and silence, to a cessation from all other things but the looking upon Christ holden out in the gospel, and this in due time will give greater rest and tranquillity. Consider what the Lord speaks to the people that would take a journey upon them to Egypt, (Isa. xxx. 15). "In returning and rest shall ye be saved, in quietness and confidence shall be your strength." Their peace was near hand, but they would travel abroad to seek it, and they find trouble. Their strength was to sit still and be quiet, and trust in the Lord. Nay, but they would not sit still, but flee and wander abroad to their old house of bondage, and therefore, says the Lord, you shall flee. Now, may not this represent the folly and madness of souls that are under the fear of wrath and sense of sin, and be as it were a type of it? Our rest is in resting on a Saviour, our peace is in quiet confidence in him, it is not far off, it is in our mouth. "The word is near" (says Paul), it is neither in heaven above, nor in the depth below. We need not go abroad and search for that happiness we want. It is nigh at hand in the gospel, but while we refuse this, and give ourselves to restless agitation and perplexity about it, sometimes we apprehend that we are eased in our travels and endeavours, but it shall prove to us no better than Egypt a house of bondage. Wheresoever we seek shelter out of Christ, we will find it a broken reed, that not only will fail under us, but in the rent will split our hand, and pierce us through with many sorrows. To conclude then this head, coming to Christ with our burdens is a motion towards rest. For he adds, "I will give you rest." But moreover, there is a kind of rest in this motion. It is an easier, plainer, and pleasanter motion, than these troubled and laborious windings and wanderings of our hearts after vanity. He persuades you to walk in this path of pleasantness and peace, and you shall find a great rest at the end of it, "receiving (says Peter) the end of your faith the eternal salvation of your souls."

Now the next thing in the text is, having come to Jesus, and found rest and happiness in him, we must take his yoke upon us. And this is the other integral part of the gospel, of which I desire you to consider these few particulars, that occur in the words,—The order in which it is to be taken on,—The nature of this yoke,—And the most ready and expeditious way of bearing it.

The method and order in which Christ's yoke is to be taken upon us, is first, To come unto our Saviour, and give over the yoke of our transgressions to him, and then to take up the yoke of his commandments from him, to believe in his promises, and rest our souls on them, and to take up the yoke of his precepts, and proceed to motion, and walking in that rest. Now this method hath a double advantage in it, for the real receiving and carrying of Christ's yoke. It gives vacancy and room for it, and it gives strength and furniture[444] for it. It expels that which would totally disable you to bear it, and brings in that comfortable supply, which will strengthen and enable you to bear it. Consider what posture a soul is put into, that lives under the terror of God, and is filled with the apprehension of the guilt of sin and the greatness of God's wrath. I say, such a soul, till he have some rest from that grievous labour, is fit for no other more pleasant labour, until he be something disburthened of that which is like to press him down to hell. He is not very capable of any new burden, until the yoke of his transgressions that is wreathed about his neck be taken off. Do ye think he can find any vacant room for the yoke of Christ's obedience? When a soul is under the dominion of fear and terror, under the power of grief and anguish, do ye think he is fit for any thing, or can do any thing, but groan in that prison of darkness, under these chains? Such a soul is in bondage, under servitude, and can neither take up this yoke of liberty nor walk in it. The strength and moisture of the spirit is drunk up by the poison of these arrows, and there remains neither attention, affection, nor spirit for any thing else. Therefore here is the incomparable advantage that redounds from this way of coming first to Christ, and exonering our cares and fears in his bosom, and in disburthening our sins upon him, who hath taken them on, and carried them away, as that scape goat sent unto the wilderness on which they laid the sins of the people. By this means, I say, you shall have a vacancy for the yoke of Christ and liberty to all your faculties, your understanding, will, and affections, (which are no better than slaves and captives, *non sui juris*, while they are under these tyrannous passions of fear and horror,) to attend the obedience of Christ and the drawing of his yoke. This will relieve your souls out of prison, and then you will be fit for employment. Besides this, there is furniture and help brought into the soul, which enables it to this; and without which, though it were not pressed under a burden of sin and wrath, yet it would neither be able nor willing. There is that supply and strength that faith brings from Christ, which arises from our mystical implantation in him, from hence flows that communication of his grace to a believer. The law came by Moses, but grace and truth by Jesus Christ, John i. 16, 17. Now this efficacy and virtue that is in Christ the head, is transmitted unto the members of his body by believing in him. Indeed the very apprehension of such a Saviour may have some quickening virtue in it, but certainly the great influence of life is annexed to it by his gracious promises, "Because I live, ye shall live also," John xiv. 19. "As the living Father who sent me, lives in himself, and I have life by the Father, so he that believes on me, shall live by me," John vi. 57. "Abide in me, and I in you, and ye shall bring forth much fruit." He hath graciously appointed the derivation of that life to us, to be conjoined with our right apprehensions, and believing meditations of him, making, as it were, faith the opening of his house, to let in his fulness to us. Now, besides this more mysterious and supernatural furniture and supply, there is even something that is naturally consequent to it, some enabling of the soul for holy obedience, flows naturally from the love of Christ. And when ever a believer apprehends what he has done for him, finds some rest and relaxation in him, it cannot but beget some inward warmth of love to him who so loved us. "Faith worketh by love," says Paul. The way it goes to action is by affection. It at once inflames that, and then there is nothing more active and irresistible. It hath a kind of indefatigable firmness in it, it hath an unwearied strength to move in the yoke all the day long. In a word, nothing almost is impossible or too hard for it, for it is of the nature of fire to break through all, and over all impediments. Nothing is so easy but it becomes uneasy to a soul under fear, and nothing so difficult but it becomes easy to a soul wherein perfect love has cast out fear. For love makes a soul to move supernaturally in divine things, as a natural or co-natural agent, freely, willingly, and constantly. If they be not suitable to our natures as corrupted, and so, grievous to love, then, as much as it possesses the heart, it makes the heart co-natural to them, and supplies the place of that natural instinct that carries other creatures to their own works and ends, strongly and sweetly. 1 John v. 3, Psal. cxix. 165, Neh. vii. 10, Col. iii. 15. Now you may judge whether or not you can possibly expect so much advantage in any other method or way you take. This I leave to your own consideration and experience.

And so I come to the next thing proposed, *secondly*, To consider what this yoke is, and what is the nature of it. And may I not upon this head justly enough distinguish a twofold yoke, of doctrine and discipline, that is, the yoke of Christ's commandments and laws, which both, in his love and wisdom, he hath imposed upon us, for the regulation of our lives? And this we are to take on by an obedience cheerful, willing, and constant. But there is another yoke mentioned in scripture, namely, the yoke of his chastisements and correcting, such a one as Ephraim (Jer. xxxi. 18) was tried with, and was long or he could learn to bear it. It is good for a man to bear this yoke in his youth, Lam. iii. 27. Now whether or not this be meant here, I do not contend. The first is the chief intent, and it is not needful to exclude this altogether, since it is not the smallest point of Christianity to take up the one yoke by submission, as well as to take up the other by obedience. How ever it be, obedience must be taken so largely, as it cannot but comprehend the sweet compliance, and submission of the will to God's will in all cross-dispensations, which is no little probation of the loyal and obedient temper of the heart. Both yokes must be taken up, for so Christ speaks of his cross, "If any man will be my disciple, he must take up his cross and follow me," Matt. xvi. 24, 25. It must be lifted up upon our shoulders, as it were, willingly, and cheerfully, we actually concurring, as it were, to the bearing of it, and the receiving it. But there is this difference between the one yoke and the other, the one cannot be imposed upon us, neither can we bear it, except we actively and with our own consent and delight take it up. Though God may impose laws upon us, and give us righteous and faithful commandments, which indeed lay a strait obligation and tie upon us under pain of disloyalty, and rebellion, to walk in them, yet it never becomes our yoke, and is never carried by us, until there be a subsequent consent of the soul, and a full condescension of the heart, to embrace that yoke with delight. Till we yoke ourselves unto his commandments, by loving and willing obedience, we have not his yoke upon us. "Thy people shall be made willing in the day of thy power." It is not terrors and constraints, but the bands of love will bind us to this yoke. It must be bound upon us by the cords of love, not of fear. He is a true king, not a tyrant, he loves *imperare volentibus*, "to rule every man with his own consent," but a tyrant "rules every man against his will," *nolentibus imperat.* But as to the other yoke of his discipline, his cross, whether it be for his sake, or whether it be the general cross of our pilgrimage here, and the vicissitudes and changes of this life, it is not in our arbitrament to bear a cross, or have a cross or not. Have it we must, bear it we must, whether we choose or refuse it. There is no man can be exempted from some yoke of this kind. No man can promise himself immunity from some cross or other, if not in poverty, yet in abundance, if not in contempt and reproach yet in honour and greatness. There is nothing of that kind that will not become weighty with itself alone, though nothing be superadded to it. So then, since every man must have a yoke, he hath only the advantage who takes it up, and bears it patiently. For if he thus sweetly comply and yield to God's will, he will not so much bear his cross, as his cross will bear him. If thou take it up, it will take thee up and carry thee. If thou submit and stoop willingly to God's good pleasure, thou wilt make it a more easy yoke, and light burden. *Ducunt volentem fata, nolentem trahunt.*[445] If thou be patient, his dispensation will gently and sweetly lead thee to rest, but an impatient soul is dragged and drawn after it against the hair, and yet he must follow it. There is this mighty disadvantage in our impatient unsubjection to God's will, that it makes that a yoke which is no yoke, no cross a cross, an easy yoke hard, and a light burden heavy, and yet notwithstanding we must bear it. A yoke, a cross, we cannot escape, whithersoever we go, whithersoever we turn ourselves, because we carry ourselves about with us, and our own crooked perverse apprehensions of things which trouble us more than the things themselves. Now consider the reasonableness of taking on the yoke of Christ's obedience. Should we not with David, offer ourselves willingly, and present ourselves even before we are called? "Lo I come, to do thy will, O God. I delight in thy law, it is in my inward part," Psal. xl. 8. There is no yoke so reasonable, if you consider it as imposed by Christ our King and Lawgiver. Hath he not redeemed us from the house of bondage, from the vilest and basest slavery, under the most cruel tyrants, Satan, and death, and hell? Heb. ii. 15. Hath he not asserted and restored us into the true liberty of men, and of the sons of God? The Son hath made us free, (John viii. 32) when we were under the most grievous yoke of sin and wrath, and the eternal curse of God. He hath put his own neck under it and become a curse for us, that he might redeem us from the curse of the law, and so he hath carried away these iron chariots, these yokes of brass and iron, whereby Satan kept us in subjection, and now been established our careful King, not only by the title of the justest and most beneficial conquest that ever was made, but by God's solemn appointment upon the hill of Zion, Psal. ii. 6. And being exalted a Prince to give us salvation, were it not most strange if his kingdom should want laws, which are the life and soul of republics and monarchies? Ought not we to submit to them gladly, and obey them cheerfully? Should not we absolutely resign ourselves to his will, and esteem his commandments concerning all things to be right? What command should be grievous to that soul, which is delivered from the curse of all the commandments, and is assured never to enter into condemnation? If there were no more to say, were it not monstrous ingratitude to withdraw ourselves from subjection to him, or yield obedience to any other strange lords, as our lusts are? Would it not be an unexemplified unthankfulness to requite rebellion to him, for so much unparalleled affection? Since we are not our own, but bought with a price, we are not *sui juris*,[446] to dispose of ourselves. All reason should say, that he who payed so dear for us should have the use of us. And that is nothing but glory he seeks from us, that we offer and consecrate soul and body to him, to come under his yoke. As for the gain, it redounds all to ourselves, and that as the greater gain too.

Now a word to the last thing proposed, for I can only hint at it. The most excellent and ready way of bearing this yoke, is to learn of him, to present him as our pattern, and to yield ourselves to him, as his disciples and scholars, not only to learn his doctrine, but to imitate his example and practice, "to walk even as he walked." And herein is great moment[447] of persuasion, Christ puts nothing upon you, but what he did take upon himself. There is so much more reason for you to take it up, that it is his own personal yoke, which he himself carried, for he delighted to do the Father's will. It was his meat and drink to work in that yoke. Now there are two things especially wherein he propones himself the exemplar or pattern of our imitation, viz., his humility and meekness of spirit. He was "meek and lowly in heart." And these graces have the greatest suitableness to capacitate and dispose every man for taking, and keeping the yoke of Christ. Humility and lowliness bows his back to take on the least of his commands. This makes him stoop low, and makes his shoulders fit for it, and then meekness arms him against all difficulties and impediments that may occur in it.

SERMON VIII.

Matt. xi. 29.—"Take my yoke upon you," &c.

Christianity consists in a blessed exchange of yokes between Christ and a pious soul. He takes our uneasy yoke, and gives his easy yoke. The soul puts upon him that unsupportable yoke of transgressions, and takes from him the portable yoke of his commandments. Our burden was heavy, too heavy for angels, and much more for men. It would crush under it all the strength of the creatures, for who could endure the wrath of the Almighty? Or, "what could a man give in exchange for his soul"? Nay, that debt would drown the whole creation, if they were surety for it. Notwithstanding, Christ hath taken that burden upon him, being able to bear it, having almighty shoulders, and everlasting arms for it. And yet you find how heavy it was for him, when it pressed out that groan from him, "Now is my soul sore amazed, very heavy, and exceeding sorrowful even unto death, and what shall I say?" That which carried it away from us, hath buried it in his grave, whither it pressed him down. It gets him very low under it, but he hath got above it and is risen again, and whereas in vain there was a stone put above him, and sealed, he hath rolled a stone above that yoke and burden, that it cannot be able to weigh down any believing soul to hell; for that weight which depressed his spotless soul, would have depressed the sons of men to eternal darkness. Now for his burden, we observe that it is of another nature, to speak properly, than other burdens. It is not a heavy yoke or burden, but a state of liberty, an ornament, a privilege. It is a chain of gold about a saint's neck, to bind Christ's laws about them, every link of that chain is more precious than rubies or diamonds. If there be any burden in it, it is the burden of honour, the burden of privilege, and incomparable dignity, *honos* not *onus* or *onus honoris*.[448] This is that which he puts upon us, or rather that which a believer receives from him. Now I will not have you so to take it, as if Christ did not propose the terms thus, "If you will be willing to take on the yoke of my laws, I will take on the yoke of your sins and curses." Nay, it is not such an exchange as is thus mutually dependent; for it hath pleased the Father without consulting us, and the Son without our knowledge or consent, to conclude what to do with the heavy and unsupportable burden of sinners. The Father "laid upon him the iniquities of us all, and he" of his own accord "hath borne our griefs, and carried our sorrows," (Isa. lii. 4-6) and that burden did bruise him; yea, "it pleased the Lord to bruise him," and it pleased himself to be bruised. O strange and unparalleled love, that could digest so hard things, and make so grievous things pleasant! Now I say, he having thus taken on our burden already, calls upon us afterward, and sends forth proclamations, and affectionate invitations, "Come unto me, all ye poor sinners, that are burdened with sin, and wearied with that burden; you who have tired yourselves in these byways, and laboured elsewhere in vain, to seek rest and peace: you have toiled all night and caught nothing, come hither, cast your net upon this side of the ship, and you shall find what you seek. I have undertaken your yoke and burden, why then do you laden yourselves any more with the apprehension of it? The real and true burden of wrath I have already carried away, why then do ye weary yourselves with the imagination of it? Only come to me, and see what I have done, and you shall find rest and peace."

Now this being proponed absolutely unto sinners, and they being invited to consent to that which Christ has done in their name, in the next place he comes to impose his easy yoke upon us, not at all for any recompence of what he hath done, but rather for some testimony of gratitude and thankfulness on our part, and for the manifestation of grace and love on his part. I do indeed conceive, that the imposition of the yoke of Christ's laws upon believers, is as much for the declaration of his own love and goodness, as the testification of our thankfulness. If you consider the liberty, the beauty, and the equity of this yoke, it will rather be construed to proceed from the greatest love and favour, than to tend any way to recompence his love. Herein is perfect liberty, Psal. cxix. 32, 45. It is an enlargement of heart, from the base restraint and abominable servitude of the vilest lusts, that tyrannize over us, and keep our affections in bondage. O how narrow bounds is the liberty of the spirits of men confined unto, that they serve their own lusts! Sin itself and the lusts of the flesh, are a grievous yoke, which the putting on of this yoke looses them from: and when the heart is thus enlarged with love and delight in Christ, then the feet unfettered, may walk at liberty, and run in the way of God's commandments. "I will walk at liberty," when I have a respect to thy ways, Psal. cxix. 45. O how spacious and broad is that way in reality, which to our first apprehension and the common construction is strait and narrow! The truth is, there is no straitness, no bondage, no scantiness, but in sin. That is the most abominable vassalage, and the greatest thraldom of the immortal spirit; to be so basely dragged by the flesh downward, to the vilest drudgery, and to be so pinched and hampered[449] within the narrowness of created and perishing things. To speak properly, there is no slavery but this of the spirit; for it is not so contrary to the nature and state of the body, (which by its first institution was made a servant,) to be under the dominion of men, and further we cannot reach. Yea, it is possible for a man, while his body is imprisoned, to be yet at greater freedom than those who imprisoned him. As his mind is, so he is. But to be a servant of sin and unrighteousness, must totally degrade the soul of man. It quite defaces that primitive glory, and destroys that native liberty, in which he was created. Therefore to have this sin taken off us, and the yoke of Christ's obedience put on us, to be made free from sin, and become the servants of righteousness, that is the soul's true liberty, which sets it forth at large to expatiate in the exceeding broad commandments, and in the infinite goodness of God, where there is infinite room for the soul.

When, then, I consider how beautiful this is for a reasonable spirit, to be under the law of him that hath made it and redeemed it, I cannot but think that Christ doth rather beautify and bless, than burden. The beauty of the world consists in that sweet order, and harmonious subordination of all things, to that law God hath imposed upon them, or engraves upon their natures. If we should suppose but one of the parts of the world to swerve from the primitive institution, what a miserable distraction would ensue? How deformed would this beautiful and adorned fabric become? How much more is it the beauty, grace, and comeliness of an intelligent being, to be under the law of him that gave him a being, and to have that written in his heart,—to be in a manner transformed by the shining glory of these laws, to be a living law? What is it, I pray you, deforms these fallen angels, and makes them devils? Why do we paint a good angel in a beautiful and comely image, while the devils are commonly represented in the most horrid, ugly, and monstrous shape and visage? Is it not this that makes the difference, that the one is fallen from a blessed subordination to the will of God, and the other keeps that station? But both are equal in nature, and were alike in the beginning.

Add unto this, the equity of Christ's yoke. There is nothing either so reasonable in itself, or yet so suitable to ourselves. For what is it that he puts upon us? Truly no new commandment; it is but the old command renewed. It is no new law, though he hath conquered us, and hath the right of absolute dominion over us; yet he hath not changed our fundamental laws. He changes only the present tyrannical yoke of sin: but he restores us, as it were, to our fundamental liberty we formerly enjoyed, and that sin forced us from, when it conquered us. Christ's yoke is not a new imposition. It is but the ancient yoke that was bound upon man's nature by God the Creator. The Redeemer doth not invent or contrive one of his own; he only looses off the yoke of iniquity, and binds on that sweet yoke of obedience and love to God. He publishes the same laws, many of which are already written in some obscure characters upon our own minds; and he again writes them down all over in our hearts. There is nothing superadded by Jesus Christ, but a chain of love to bind this yoke about our necks, and a chain of grace and truth to keep his laws. And truly these make the yoke easy, and take away the nature of a burden from it. O what mighty and strong persuasions! O what constraining motives of love and grace doth the gospel furnish, and the rarest cords to bind on Christ's yoke upon a reasonable soul,—cords of the most unparalleled love!

I shall only add unto all this, that as herein Christ hath expressed or completes the expression of his love upon his part; so upon our part it becomes us to take on his yoke, in testimony of our thankfulness. We owe our very selves unto him. What can be more said? We owe ourselves once and again; for we are twice his workmanship, first created by him, and then renewed or created again unto good works. We are bought with a price, we are not our own. Can there be any obligation imagined beyond this? Let us therefore consecrate ourselves to his glory. Let all who believe the gospel dedicate themselves to its obedience, not so much for salvation to themselves, as their obligation to their Saviour. We are not called so much to holiness and virtue that we may be saved, as, because we are saved, to be blameless before God in love. O how gracious and honourable a disposition of this kind would it be, to serve him more out of gratitude for what he hath done, than merely for the reward that he will give!

SERMON IX.

Rom. xv. 13.—"Now the God of hope fill you with all joy and peace in believing," &c.

It is usual for the Lord in his word to turn his precepts unto promises, which shows us, that the commandments of God do not so much import an ability in us, or suppose strength to fulfil them, as declare that obligation which lies upon us, and his purpose and intention to accomplish in some, what he requires of all: and therefore we should accordingly convert all his precepts unto prayers, seeing he hath made them promises. This gives us ground, as it were, to retort his commands by way of requests and supplications. The scripture here gives us a precedent, and often elsewhere hath made his command a promise. It is then in the next disposition, and nearest capacity, to be turned into the form of a supplication. The joy promised in the preceding verse is elsewhere commanded; and this immediately disposes the sinner to receive a new form of prayer, from a believing heart, and that not only for himself, but for others. You see how frequently such holy and hearty wishes are interjected in his writings. And indeed such ejaculations of the soul's desires, whether kept within, or vented, will often interrupt the thoughts and discourses of believers, but yet they break no sentence, they mar no sense, no more than the interposition of a parenthesis. Such desires will follow by a kind of natural resultance upon the lively apprehension of any divine excellent thing, and secret complacency in it, and a stirring of the heart to be possessed with it, will almost prevent deliberation. Such an attractive power the excellency of any object hath in the heart, that it draws it and engages it almost before any consultation be called about it. Now there is something of this in these objects which we are naturally delighted with. All at least that they want the apprehension supplies, and this draws the heart forcibly after them, as it were, with out previous advisement. Yet because of the limitation, emptiness, and scarcity of these things, commonly the desires of men are contracted much within themselves, and run towards a monopoly of those things. They are so poor and narrow, that they cannot be enjoyed of more, without division, and the dividing them cannot be without diminution of each man's contentment, and therefore men's wishes ordinarily are stinted within their own satisfaction and possession, and cannot without some restraint of reason extend further to other men. But this is the vast difference between spiritual things and bodily, eternal things and temporal, that there is no man possessed of spiritual good, but he desires a community. It is as natural upon the apprehension of them to enlarge the soul's wishes to other men, because there is such excellency, abundance, and solidity discovered in them, as that all may be full, and none envy or prejudge another. They are like the light that can communicate itself to all, and that without diminution of its splendour. All may see it without prejudice one to another. They are such an ocean that every one may fill their vessel, and yet nothing less for them that come after. And therefore the soul that wishes largely for itself, will not find that inward discontent at the great abundance of another, which is the inseparable shadow of earthly and temporal advantages. It is cross to men's interest, that love gain or preferment, or any such thing, that others grow rich, or are advanced high in the world, for it intercepts what they desire. But it is not at all the interest of a godly soul that others be worse than himself, but rather the salvation and happiness of all men is that interest which alone he espouses.

Now for this, my beloved, before we proceed further, you may find how the pulse of your souls beats, and what your temper is, by considering what is the ordinary unrestrained and habitual wishes of your hearts. Certainly as men are inclined so they affect, and so they desire, and these unpremeditated desires that are commonly stirred up in the hearts of men, argue much the inward temper and inclination of the heart, and give the best account of it. I think if men would reflect upon themselves, they will find that earthly things are vain, while they put on another beauty, and have a more magnificent representation in their minds, and so draw after them the choicest of their affections, that they cannot spare much real affection for spiritual things, which are apprehended more slightly and darkly, and make the lighter and more superficial impression. But certainly this will be the most natural beating of a holy heart and the ordinary breathing of it, to desire much of this spiritual treasure for themselves and others. You know what the thoughts and discourses of merchants turn most upon. It is to have good winds, fair weather, good markets, and all things that may facilitate gain, and husbandmen wish for good seasons, timely showers, and dry harvests, that there may be plenty. And generally what men's hearts are set upon, that they go abroad fervently and incessantly in longing desires after. Now truly this is the Christian's inward motion, and this is his salutation, wherewith he congratulateth others. "The God of hope fill you with all peace and joy in believing." His gain lies in another airth.[450] His plenty is expected from another field, and that is from above, from the God of hope, the sweetest name (if all the rest be answerable) to be dealt withal, either for gain or plenty, for it is hope that makes labour sweet, and if it answer expectation then all is well. Therefore, in the sowing the seed of prayers and supplications, with tears, for this harvest of joy, and in trafficking for this treasure of peace, it is good that we have to do with the God of hope, who cannot make us ashamed; for he that soweth must sow in hope, 1 Cor. ix. 10. And therefore, though we sow in tears, yet let us mingle hope therewith, and the harvest shall be joy, and the plenty, affluence of peace in the Holy Ghost. Now if we believed this, would not our sorrows be deep, and our labours sweet?

In the words you have read, there is the highest wish of a holy heart for himself and them he loves best; that one desire, if he had no occasion ever to present himself to God, but once, that he would certainly fall upon, or some such like, to be filled after this manner with all peace and joy in believing. These are the fruits of the Spirit he desires to be filled with, and feed upon,—peace as an ordinary meal, and joy as an extraordinary desert, or as a powerful cordial; and to supply what here is wanting at present, the hope of what is to come, and that in abundance. This is even an entertainment that a believer would desire for himself, and these who have his best wishes, while he is in this world. He would despise the delicacies of kings, and refuse their dainties, if he might sit at this table that is spread on the mountain of God's church, a full feast which fills the soul with peace, joy, and hope, as much as now it is capable of. Now these precious fruits you see in the words show the root that brings them forth, and the branch that immediately bears them. The root is the God of hope, and the power of the Holy Ghost. And a soul being ingrafted as a living branch by faith into Christ, receives virtue to bring forth such pleasant fruits, so that they grow immediately upon the branch of believing, but the sap and virtue of both come from the Holy Ghost, and the God of hope. Or to take it up in another like notion. This is the river which gladdeneth the city of God with its streams, that waters the garden of the Lord with its threefold stream. For you see it is parted in three heads, and every one of them is derived from another. The first in the order of nature is peace,—a sweet, calm, and refreshing river, which sometimes overflows like the river Nilus, and then it runs in a stream of joy, which is the high spring tide but ordinarily it sends forth the comfortable stream of hope, and that in abundance. Now this threefold river hath its original high, as high as the God of hope, and the power of the Holy Ghost, but the channel of it is situated low, and it is believing in Christ.

To begin then with the first of these. Truly there is nothing can be spoken that sounds more sweetly in the ears of men than peace and joy. They need nothing to commend them, for they have a sufficient testimonial, and letters of recommendation written upon the affections of all men. For what is it that all men labour and seek after but this? It is not any outward earthly thing that is desired for itself, but rather for the peace and contentment the mind expects in it. And therefore, this must be of itself the proper object or good of the soul, which, if it can be had immediately, without that long and endless compass about the creatures, certainly a man cannot but think himself happy, and will have no missing of other things, as if a man could live healthfully and joyfully without meat, and without all appetite for it, no doubt but he would think himself the happiest man in the world, and would think it no pain to him to want the dainties of princes, but rather that he were delivered from the wearisome necessity others laboured under. Just so is it here, there is nothing would persuade a man to travel, and toil all his lifetime, about the creatures, and not to suffer his soul to take rest, if he did believe to find that immediately without travel, which he endures so much travel for. And therefore the believing Christian is only a wise man, who is instructed where the things themselves, true peace and joy, do lie, and so seeks to be filled with the things themselves, for which only men seek other things, and not as other men who catch at the shadows, that they may at length find the substance itself, for this were far about, and labour in vain.

Peace is so sweet and comprehensive a word, that the Jews made their usual compellation, "Peace be unto you,"[451] importing all felicity, and the affluence of all good. And indeed our Saviour found no fitter word to express his matchless good-will to the well-being of his disciples nor this (Luke xxiv. 36.), when he saluted them after his resurrection, "Peace be unto you," which is as much as if he had wished absolute satisfaction, all contentment and happiness that themselves would desire. Now this peace hath a relation to God, to ourselves, and our brethren. I will exclude none of them from the present wish; for even brotherly concord and peace suits well with the main subject of this chapter, which is the bearing of our neighbours' infirmities, and not pleasing ourselves, and such like mutual duties of charity. But certainly the other two relations are most intrinsic to happiness, because there is nothing nearer to us than the blessed God; and next to him, there is nothing comes so near us as ourselves. The foundation of all our misery, is that enmity between man and God, which is as if heaven and earth should fall out into an irreconcilable discord, and upon that should follow the suspension of the light of the stars, and the withdrawing of the influences of heaven, and the withholding the refreshment of the early and latter rain. If such dissension fell between them, that the heavens should be as brass to the earth, and would refuse the clouds when they cry for rain, or the herbs and minerals when they crave the influences from above, what a desolate and irksome dwelling-place would the earth be? What a dreary habitation would we find it? Even so it is between God and men. All our being, all our well-being, hangs upon the good aspect of his countenance. In his favour is all our life and happiness; yet since the first rebellion, every man is set contrary to God, and in his affections and actions denounces war against heaven, whence hath flowed the sad and woful suspension of all these blessings, and comfortable influences, which only beautify and bless the soul of man. And now there is nothing to be seen but the terrible countenance of an angry God, the revengeful sword of justice shaken in the word; all above us as if the sun were turned into blackness, and the moon into blood, and behold trouble and darkness, and dimness of anguish.

Now whenever a soul begins to apprehend his enmity and division in sad earnest, there follows an intestine war in the conscience. The terrors of God raise up a terrible party within a man's self, and that is the bitter remembrance of his sins. These are mustered and set in order in battle-array against a man, and every one of these, as they are thought upon, strike a dart into his heart. They shoot an arrow dipped in the wrath of God, the poison whereof drinketh up his spirit, Job vi. 4. Though the most part of souls have now a dead calm, and are asleep like Saul in the field in the midst of his enemies, or as Jonas in the ship in the midst of the tempest, yet when they awake out of that deep stupidity, God will write bitter things against them, and make them to possess their iniquities; and they shall find that he hath numbered their steps, and watched over their sin, and sealed it as in a bag, to be kept in record. Then he will renew his witnesses against them, and put their feet in the stocks, and they shall then apprehend that changes and war are against them, and that they are set as a mark against God, and so they will be a burden to themselves, Job vii. 20. What a storm will it raise in the soul! Now to lay this tempest, and calm this wind, is the business of the gospel, because it reveals these glad tidings of peace and reconciliation with God, which can only be the ground of a perfect calm in the conscience. Herein is the atonement and propitiation set forth, that which by its fragrant and sweet smell hath pacified heaven, and appeased justice; and this only is able to pacify the troubled soul, and lay the tumultuous waves of the conscience, Eph. ii. 13-20; Col. i. 19-22. This gives the answer of a good conscience, which is like the sweet and gentle breathing of a calm day after a tempest, 1 Pet. iii. 21. Now it is not so much God reconcileable to sinners, as God in Christ reconciling sinners to himself, 2 Cor. v. 19. Though some men be always suspicious of God, yet they have more reason to suspect their own willingness. For what is all the gospel but a declaration of his love, and laying down the enmity, or rather, that he had never hostile affections to his elect, and so was all this while providing a ransom for himself, and bringing about the way to kill the enmity? And having done that by the blood of Christ, he will follow us with entreaties of reconcilement, and requests to lay down our hostile affections, and the weapons of our warfare; and for him we have no more ado but to believe his love, while we were yet enemies. This, I say, carried into the heart with power, gives that sweet calm and pleasant rest to the soul, after all its tossings. This commands the winds and waves of the conscience, and they obey it. It is true that many find no trouble within, and some, upon terrible apprehensions of sin and wrath, find ease for the time in some other thing, as a diversion to some other object, and turning aside with Cain to build cities, to worldly pleasures, or employments, or company, that the noise of them may put the clamours of their conscience to silence. Some parleys and cessations men have, some treaties of this kind for peace with God; but alas! the most part make no entire and full peace. They are always upon making the bargain, and cannot close it, because of their engagements to sin, and their own corrupt lusts. And therefore many do nothing else than what men do in war, to seek some advantage, or to gain time by their delays: but O the latter end will be sad, when he shall arm you against yourselves! Were it not better, now while it is to-day, not to harden your hearts? Now, joy is the effect of peace, and it is the very overflowing of it in the soul, upon the lively apprehension of the love of God, and the inestimable benefit of the forgiveness of sins. It is peace in a large measure, pressed down, and running over, breaking without the ordinary channel, and dilating itself to the affecting and refreshing of all that is in man: "My heart and my flesh shall rejoice." This is the very exuberance and high sailing-tide of the sea of peace that is in a believer's heart. It swells sometimes upon the full aspect of God's countenance beyond the ordinary bounds, and cannot be kept within in gloriation and boasting in God. When a soul is so illustrated with the Holy Ghost, as to make a kind of presence and possession of what is hoped for, that makes the soul to enlarge itself in joy. This makes the inward jubilation, the heart as it were to leap for joy. Now, truly this is not the ordinary entertainment of a Christian. It is neither so universal nor constant as peace. These fruits so matured and ripe, like the grapes of Canaan, are not set down always upon the table of every Christian, nor yet at all to some. It is enough that he keep the soul in that healthful temper, that it is neither quite cast down or discouraged through difficulties and infirmities. It is sufficient if God speak peace to the soul, though it be not acquainted with these raptures of Christianity. This hath so much sense in it, that it is not meet to be made ordinary food, lest we should mistake our pilgrimage for heaven, and fall upon the building of tabernacles in this mount. For certainly the soul would conclude it good to be here, and could not so earnestly long for the city and country of heaven, if they had any more but some tastes of that joy to sharpen their desires after the full measure of it. It is a fixed and unchangeable statute of heaven, that we should here live by faith, and not by sense. And indeed, the following of God fully, in the ways of obedience, upon the dim apprehensions of faith, is more praiseworthy, and hath more of the true nature of obedience in it, than when present sweetness hath such a predominant influence. Besides, our vessel here is weak and crazy, and most unfit for such strong liquor as the joys of the Holy Ghost. Some liquors have such a strong spirit in them that they will burst an ordinary bottle; and as our Saviour says, "No man puts new wine in old bottles, for they will burst," Matt. ix. 17. Truly the joy of heaven is too strong for our old ruinous and earthly vessels to bear, till the body "put on incorruption," and be fashioned like unto Christ's own glorious body; for it cannot be capable of all the fulness of this joy. And yet there is a kind of all fulness of peace and joy in this life, "fill you with all joy and peace." Indeed the fulness of this life is emptiness to the next. But yet there is a fulness in regard of the abundance of the world. Their joys and pleasures, their peace and contentation in the things of this life, are but like "the crackling of thorns under a pot," that makes a great noise, but vanishes quickly in a filthy security, Eccles. vii. 6. It is such, that like the loudest laughter of fools, there is sorrow at the heart, and in the end of it is heaviness, Prov. xiv. 13. It is but at the best a superfice, an external garb drawn over the countenance, no cordial nor solid thing. It is not heart joy, but a picture and shadow of the gladness of the heart in the outward countenance; and whatever it be, sorrow, grief, and heaviness follow at its heels, by a fatal inevitable necessity. So that there is this difference between the joys and pleasures of the world, and dreams in the night; for the present there is more solidity, but the end is hugely different. When men awake out of a dream, they are not troubled with it, that their imaginary pleasure was not true. But the undivided companion of all earthly joys and contentment is grief and vexation. I wonder if any man would love that pleasure or contentment if he were assured to have an equal measure of torment after it, suppose the pain of the stone, or such like. But when this misery is eternal, O what madness and folly is it to plunge into it! "I said of laughter, It is madness, and of mirth, What doth it?" But the Christian's peace and joy is of another nature. Yet as no man knoweth the "hidden manna," the "new name," and the "white stone," but he that hath it, (Rev. ii. 17) so no man can apprehend what these are, till he taste them and find them. What apprehension, think ye, can a beast form of his own nature? Or what can a man conceive of the angelical nature? Truly this is without our sphere and that without theirs. Now certainly the wisest and most learned men cannot form any lively notion of the life of a Christian, till he find it. It is without his sphere and comprehension, therefore it is called "the peace of God which passes all understanding," (Phil. iv. 7), a "joy unspeakable and full of glory," 1 Pet. i. 8. Suppose men had never seen any other light but the stars of the firmament, or the light of a candle, they could not conceive any thing more glorious than the firmament in a clear night. Yet we that have seen the sun and moon, know that these lights are but darkness unto them. Or, to use that comparison that the Lord made once effectual to convert a nobleman, if a man did see some men and women dancing afar off, and heard not their music, he would judge them mad, or at least foolish, but coming near hand, and hearing their instruments, and perceiving their order, he changes his mind. Even so, whatever is spoken of the joy of the Spirit, or the peace of conscience, and whatsoever is seen by the world of abstaining from the pleasures of the world, the natural mind cannot but judge it foolishness, or melancholy, because they do not hear that pleasant and sweet harmony, and concert of the word and Spirit, in the souls of God's children. Else if they heard the sweet Psalmist of Israel piping, they could not but find an inward stirring and impulse m themselves to dance too.

Now the third stream is hope, "that ye may abound in hope," because this is not the time nor place of possession. Our peace and joy here is often interrupted, and very frequently weakened. It is not so full a table as the Christian's desire requires. Our present enjoyments are not able to mitigate the very pain of a Christian's appetite, or to supply his emptiness. Therefore there must be an accession of hope to complete the feast and to pacify the eagerness of the soul's desire, till the fulness of joy and peace come; and if he have spare diet otherwise, yet he hath allowance of abundance of hope, to take as much of that as he can hold, and that is both refreshing and strengthening. Truly there is nothing men have, or enjoy, that can please, without the addition of hope unto it. All men's eyes are forward to futurity, and often men prejudice themselves of their present enjoyments, by the gaping expectation of, and looking after things to come. But the Christian's hope being a very sure anchor cast within the vail, upon the sure ground of heaven, it keeps the soul firm and steadfast, though he be not unmoved, yet from tossing or floating; though it may fluctuate a little, yet his hope regulates and restrains it. And it being an helmet, it is a strong preservative against the power and force of temptations. It is that which guards the main part of a Christian, and keeps resolutions after God untouched and unmaimed.

Now, my beloved, would you know the fountain and original of these sweet and pleasant streams? It is the God of hope, and the power of the Holy Ghost. There is no doubt of power in God, to make us happy and give us peace. But power seems most opposite to peace, especially with enemies and it seems whatsoever he can do, yet that his justice will restrain his power from helping us. But there is no doubt but the God of power, as well as hope, both can and will do it. He hath this style from his promises and gracious workings, because he hath given us ground of hope in himself. He is the chief object of hope, and the chief cause of hope in us too. Therefore we would look up to this fountain, for here all is to be found.

But I haste to speak a word of the third thing proposed, viz.: The channel that these streams run into. It is believing, not doing. Indeed this stream once ran in this channel. But since paradise was defaced, and the rivers that watered it turned another way, this hath done so too. It is true, that righteousness and holy walking is a notable mean to preserve this pure, and unmixed, and constant. For indeed the peace of our God will never lodge well with sin, the enemy of God, nor can that joy, which is so pure a fountain, run in abundance in an impure heart. It will not mix with carnal pleasures and toys. But yet the only ground of true peace and joy is found out by believing in another. Whatsoever ye do else to find them, dispute and debate never so long about them, toil all night and all day in your examinations of yourselves, yet you shall not catch this peace,—this solid peace, and this surpassing joy, but by quite overlooking yourselves and fixing your hearts upon another object, that is, Jesus Christ. "Peace and joy in believing," and what is that believing? Mistake it not. It is not particular application at first. I delight rather to take it in another notion, for the cordial absent and consent of the soul to the promises of the gospel. I say but one word more, viz.: meditation and deep consideration of these truths is certainly believing, and believing brings peace, and peace brings joy.

SERMON X.

Matth. xi. 16.—"But whereunto shall I liken this generation?"

When our Lord Jesus, who had the tongue of the learned, and spoke as never man spake, did now and then find a difficulty to express the matter herein contained. "What shall we do?" The matter indeed is of great importance, a soul matter, and therefore of great moment, a mystery, and therefore not easily expressed. No doubt he knows how to paint out this to the life, that we might rather behold it with our eyes, than hear it with our ears, yet he uses this manner of expression, to stamp our hearts with a deep apprehension of the weight of the matter, and the depth of it. It concerns us all, as much as we can, to consider and attend unto it.

Two things are contained here. The entertainment Christ gets in the world, of the most part, and, the entertainment he gets from a few children, of whom he is justified. I say, it concerns you greatly to observe this,—for Christ observed it very narrowly,—what success both his forerunner and himself had. Christ begins here to expostulate with the multitudes, and with the scribes and Pharisees about it. But ere all be done he will complain to the Father. He now complains unto you, that he gets not ready acceptance amongst you, if it be possible that you may repent of the great injury done to the Son of God, no not so much to Christ, as your own souls, for "all who hate me love death, and he that sinneth against me wrongeth his own soul," Prov. viii. 36. Wo unto your souls, for you have not hurt Christ, by so much despising him. Ye have not prejudiced the gospel, but ye have rewarded evil to yourselves, Isa. iii. 9. I say, Christ now complains of you to yourselves, if so be you will bethink yourselves in earnest, and return to yourselves, but if ye will not, he will at length complain to the Father. When he renders up the kingdom, and gives an account of his administration unto God, he will report what entertainment ye gave his word. For he will say, "I have laboured in vain, and spent my strength for nought with such a man. All threatenings, all entreaties would not prevail with him to forsake his drunkenness, his swearing, his covetousness, his oppressions," &c. You know Christ's last long prayer, John xvii. He gives an account in it what acceptance he had among men, when he is finishing his ministry. These are the men he now speaks unto in the text, "Whereunto shall I liken this generation?" Thus he speaks of them to his Father. "O righteous Father, the world hath not known thee, but I have known thee." Well then, this is not so light a matter as ye apprehend. Ye come to hear daily, but know ye not that ye shall give an account of your hearing? Know ye not that there is one who observes and marks all the impressions which the word makes on your consciences? He knows all the blows of the sword of the word, that returns making no impression on your consciences. Christ says to the multitudes here, "And what went ye out for to see?" I pray you what went ye out to see, seeing ye have not believed his report? Why went ye out unto the wilderness? Know ye who spake, or in whose authority? May we not speak in these terms unto you, when we consider the little fruit of the gospel? What do you come to see, and what do ye come to hear every Sabbath, and other solemn days? I pray you ask at your own hearts, what your purpose is. Wherefore do ye come together so often? Men are rational in their business. They do nothing but for some purpose. They labour, and plough, and sow, in order to reap. They buy and sell to get gain. They have many projects and designs they still seek to accomplish. And shall we be only in matters of salvation and damnation so irrational? Shall we in the greatest thing of the greatest moment, because of eternal concernment be as perishing brutish beasts, that know not what we aim at? Christ will in the end ask you, what went ye out of your own houses so often to hear? What went you out to see? I pray you what will ye answer? If ye say, we went to hear the word of the Lord, then he shall answer you, and why did not ye obey it? Then why did ye not hear it as my word, and regard it more? If ye shall say, we went to hear a man speak some good words unto us for an hour or two, then is Christ also engaged against you, because he sent him, and ye despise him, for he says, "He that despises me, despises him that sent me," so ye shall be catched both the ways. If ye think this to be God's word, I wonder why ye do not receive it, with the stamp of his authority in your hearts. Why do ye not bow your hearts to it, for it shall endure for ever, and judge you? Why do you sit[452] so many fair offers, so many sad warnings? Are not the drunkards warned every day by this word, that the curse of the Lord shall come upon them? Is not every one of you, according to your several stations and circumstances, warned to forsake your wicked ways, and your evil thoughts, to flee from the wrath to come, before the decree of the Lord pass forth, and before his fury burn as an oven? And if ye think these to be the true words of the eternal God, and the sayings of the Amen, the faithful and true witness, and the truth itself, if ye believe it as ye profess to do, why do ye not get out of the way of that wrath, which continues upon these sinners daily? Shall ye escape the judgment of God? Shall not his word overtake you though ministers that speak unto you will not live for ever? But these words they speak will surely take hold of you, as they did your fathers, so that ye shall say, "Like as the Lord of hosts hath said he will do unto us, so hath he done," Zech. i. 6. If ye do not think this is God's word, I beseech you, why do you come hither so oft? What do ye come to hear? Why take ye so much needless pains? Your coming here seems to speak that ye think it to be God's word and yet your conversation declares more plainly that ye believe it not. Yet Christ takes notice of you and O that ye, beloved, would search yourselves that so ye might hear the word as in the sight of the all seeing God, and in his sight, who will judge you according to it; a sermon thus heard, would be more profitable than all that ever ye heard. Now to what purpose speak we of these things unto you, and why do we choose this discourse, when ye expect to hear public things? I will tell you the reason of it. Because I conceive this is the great sin of the times, and the most reprehensive and fountain sin, the root of all our profanity and malignity, even this which Christ points out in this similitude. The great blessing and privilege of Scotland is the gospel. Ye all must grant this. Now, then, the great misery and sin of this nation is, the abuse and contempt of the glorious gospel, and if once we could make you sensible of this, ye would mourn for all other particular sins.

The words are very comprehensive. Ye shall find in them the different manifestations of God in his word, reduced to two heads. The Lord either mourns to us to make us mourn, or joys to us to make us dance. A similitude and likeness is the end of all the manifestations of himself, that we be one with him. Therefore when he would move our affections in us, he puts on the like, and clothes himself, in his word and dispensation, with such a habit as is suitable. So ye have both law and gospel. He laments in the one, he pipes in the other. Both sad and glad dispensations of his providence may be subordinate to these; the one, I mean his judgments, representing that to our eyes which his law did to our ears, making that visible of his justice, which we heard; the other, I mean mercies, represents that to our eyes, which the gospel did to our ears, making his good will, his forbearance, and long suffering, and compassion visible, that men might say, "As we have heard so have we seen in the city of our God." Now these should stir up suitable affections in men. This is their intendment and purpose, to stir up joy and grief, sorrow for sin, on the one hand, and joy in the Lord's salvation on the other hand; hatred of sin by the one, and the love of Christ by the other.

But what is the entertainment[453] these get in the world? Ye shall see it different. In some it meets with different affections, or it makes them, and moves them, and these do justify wisdom. The accomplishment and performance of God's purposes, in the salvation of souls, justifies his word. They justify Christ by believing in him; Christ justifies us, by making us to believe in him, and applying his own righteousness to us. He that believes justifies the word, and Christ in the word, because he sets to his seal that God is true; and Christ likewise justifies the believer, by applying his righteousness unto him. The believer justifies wisdom, by acknowledging it as the Father's wisdom; Christ justifies the believer by making him and pronouncing him righteous, and a son of God. But in others, and in these a great many, it generally meets with hard hearts, stupid and insensible, incapable of these impressions. You know music is very apt to work upon men's spirits, and doth stir up several passions in them, as joy or grief. Now Christ and his ministers are the musicians that do apply their songs to catch men's ears and hearts, if so be they may stop their course and not perish. These are blessed Sirens[454] that do so, and pipe, day and night, in season and out of season, some sad and woful ditties of men's sin and God's wrath, of the day of judgment, of eternal punishment, that if it be possible, men may fore-apprehend these ills, before they fall into them without recovery. These are the boys in the market places that strive to sadden your hearts, and make you lament in time, before the day of howling, and weeping, and gnashing of teeth. These also have as many joyful and glad ditties, sweetening the sad. It may be, diverse men have diverse parts of this harmony. John had the woful and sad part, Christ took the joyful and glad part; so the one answered the other, and both made a complete harmony. It may be, one man in one spring mixes these two, and makes good music alone. The one part is intended to move men to grief, and mourn once, that they may not mourn for ever; the other to comfort in the meantime these that mourn, to mix their mourning with their hope of that blessed delivery in Jesus Christ. Now what is the entertainment these get from the most part? They can neither move men to one affection nor another; they will neither mourn nor dance. As the children complain of some rude and rustic spirits, that are uncapable of music, and cannot discern one spring[455] from another, so does Christ complain of a generation of men, they can neither repent nor believe, they care for none of these things. His threatenings and denunciations of wrath are a small thing to them, and his consolations appear also to be inconsiderable. Then souls are otherwise taken up, that they have no sense to discern the transcendent excellency of eternal things. We would then press upon your consciences these three things. First, That the word of God comprehending the law and gospel, contains both the saddest ditties and the most joyful and sweet songs in the world. Next, We would discover unto you the great sin, and extreme stupidity of this generation, of which ye are a part, that ye may know the controversy God hath with the land. And then at length, we would labour to persuade you to the right use of this gospel, and justifying of wisdom, if ye would be his children.

The law is indeed a sad song and lamentation, it surpasses all the complaints and lamentations among men. Ye know the voice in which it was given at Sinai. It was delivered with great thunders, great terrors accompanied it. The law is a voice of words and thunder, which made these that heard it entreat that it should not be spoken to them any more; for they could not endure the word that was commanded, Heb. xii. 18, 19. Ye would think if they were holy men, they would not be afraid of it, but so terrible was that sight, and that voice, that it even made holy Moses himself exceedingly fear and quake. It made a great host, more numerous than all the inhabitants of Scotland, to tremble exceedingly. And why was it so sad and terrible? Even because it was a law that publishes transgression, for "by the law is the knowledge of sin." If there were no fear of judgment and wrath, yet I am sure there is none that can reasonably consider that excellent estate in which he was once, that throne of eminency above the creatures, that height of dignity in conformity and likeness to God, that incomparable happiness of communion with the supreme Fountain of life; none I say, none can duly ponder these things, but they will think sin to be the greatest misery of mankind. They must be affected with the sense of that inestimable treasure they lost. And how sad a consideration is it to view that cloud of beastly lusts, of flesh and earth, that was interposed between the Sun of righteousness, and our souls, which hath made this perpetual eclipse, this eternal night and darkness! How sad is it to look upon our ruin, and compare it with that stately edifice of innocent Adam! How are we fallen from the height of our excellency, and made lower than the beasts, when we were once but a little lower than the angels! But then if ye shall consider all that followed upon this the innumerable abominations of men, so contrary to that holy law and God's holiness, that hath flowed from this corrupt fountain, and hath defiled so many generations of men, that they are all bruises and putrified sores, and in nothing sound from the head to the foot,—the soul within becomes the sink of all pollution, the members without the conduits it runs through, and weapons of unrighteousness against our Maker. And what a consideration is this alone, how vile and ugly doth that holy and spiritual law make the most refined and polished civilian? He that hath poorest naturals,[456] most extracted from the dregs of the multitude, oh how abominable will he appear in this glass, in this perfect law of liberty! So that men would despise themselves, and repent in dust and ashes, if once they did see their own likeness. Ye would run from yourselves as children that have been taken up with their own beauty, but are spoiled with the small pox. Let them look unto a glass, and it will almost make them mad. But if we shall stay, and hear out the trumpet which sounds louder and louder, there will be yet more reason of trembling. For it becomes a voice publishing judgment and wrath, for therein is the wrath of God "revealed from heaven, against all ungodliness and unrighteousness of men," Rom. i. 18. It speaks much of all men's sins "that every mouth may be stopped," but the voice waxed louder and louder, the spring grows still sadder, that "all the world may become guilty before God," Rom. iii. 19. It publishes first the command, and then follows the sad and weighty curse of God. "Cursed is every one that abides not in all things which are written in the law," (Gal. iii. 10) as many curses as breaches of the law. And what a dreadful song is this! Ye shall be punished with everlasting destruction, from the presence of the Lord, and the glory of his power? If he had said, ye shall be eternally banished from God, what an incomparable loss had this been? Men would lead an unpleasant life, who had fallen from the expectation of an earthly kingdom, but what shall it be to fall from the expectation of a heavenly kingdom? But when withal there is an eternal pain with that eternal loss, and an incomparable pain with incomparable loss, everlasting destruction from God's presence, joined with this, always to be destroyed, and never to be made an end of! It is the comfort of bodily torments, and even of death itself, that it shall be quickly gone, and the destruction ends in the destruction of the body, and so there is no more pain. But here is an eternal destruction,—not a dying, and then a death, but an eternal dying without tasting death. Now consider (if ye can indeed think) what it is to have a law of enmity, and a hand writing of ordinances against us, as many curses written up in God's register against us, as there were transgressions of the law multiplied and God himself engaged to be against us, to have no mercy on us, and not to spare us! Could any heart endure, or any hands be strong, if they would duly apprehend this? Would the denunciation of war, the publishing of affliction, the sentence of earthly judges, would they once be remembered beside this? If ye would imagine all the torments and rackings that have been found out by the most cruel tyrants against men, all to be centred in one, and all the grief and pain of these who have died terrible deaths, to be joined in one, what would it be to this! It would be but as a drop of that wrath and vexation that wicked souls find in hell, and are drowned into, and that everlastingly without end.

But we must not dwell always at mount Sinai. We are called to mount Zion, the city of the living God, to hear a sweet and calm voice of peace, to hear the sweet and pleasant songs of the sweet Psalmist of Israel, and of our glorious Peacemaker, Christ Jesus, the desire of all nations, and the blessing of all the families of the earth. His song is a joyful sound, and blessed are they that hear it. I am come, says Christ, "to seek and to save that which was lost." I am come to save sinners, and the chief of sinners. Let all these who find their spirits saddened by the terrible law, or who find themselves accursed from the Lord, and cannot be justified by the law of Moses, come unto me. Cast your souls upon me, and ye shall find ease to them. Are ye pressed under the heavy burden of sin and wrath? Come unto me, and I will give you ease. Put it over upon me. Do ye think yourselves not wearied nor burdened enough, and yet ye would be quit of sin and misery? Do your souls desire to embrace this salvation? Come unto me, and I will not cast you out. Whoever comes, on whatsoever terms, in whatsoever condition, I will in no case cast you out. Do not suppose cases to exclude yourselves. I know no case. Ye who cannot be justified by the law of Moses, come unto me, and ye shall be justified "from all things from which ye could not be justified by the law of Moses." Ye who have no righteousness of your own, and see the righteousness of God revealed with wrath against you, now come to me, I have a righteousness of God, beside the law, and will reveal it to you. Ye have a band of enmity, and handwriting of ordinances against you, but come unto me, for I have cancelled it in the cross, and slain the enmity, so it shall never do you any harm. In a word, this is the messenger whose feet are beautiful, that publishes glad tidings of peace. This is the Mediator, who reconciles us unto God. The whole gospel and covenant of grace is a bundle of precious promises. It is a set of pleasant melodious songs, that may accompany us through our wearisome pilgrimage, and refresh us till we come unto the city, where we shall all sing the song of the Lamb. What a song is liberty to captives and prisoners, light to them that sit in darkness, opening of the eyes to the blind, gladness of spirit to those who are heavy in spirit! Ye would all think salvation and remission of sins a sweet song. But if ye would discern it, ye would find nothing sweeter in the gospel than this redemption from all iniquity, from sin itself, and from all kind of misery. How lovely and pleasant a thing is that! When Christ hath piped unto you the remission of all sins in his own blood, then he plays the most sweet spring, the renunciation of sin, and dying to this world, by his death and resurrection. Many listen to the song of justification, but they will not abide to hear out all the song. He is our sanctification and redemption, as well as our righteousness. Always to whomsoever he is pleasant, when he puts his yoke upon them, he will be more pleasant in bearing it. Whosoever gladly hears Jesus singing of righteousness and holiness, they shall also hear him sing of glory and happiness. Those who dance at the springs of righteousness and sanctification, what an eternal triumph and exultation waits on them, when he is singing the song of complete redemption!

Are these things so? Is this the law, and this the gospel? Do they daily sound in our ears, and what entertainment, I pray you, do they get from this generation? Indeed, Christ's complaint hath place here, whereunto shall our generation be likened? For he hath lamented to us and we have not mourned; he hath piped to us, and we have not danced. We will neither be made glad nor sad by these things. How long hath the word of the Lord been preached unto you, and whose heart trembled at it? Shall the lion roar, and the beasts of the field not be afraid? The lion hath roared often to us. God hath spoken often, who will not fear? And yet who doth fear? Shall a trumpet be blown in the city, in congregations every day, that terrible trumpet of Mount Sinai that proclaims war between God and men, and yet will not the people be afraid? Amos iii. 6, 8. Have not every one of you heard your transgressions told you? Are ye not guilty of all the breaches of God's holy law? Hath not the curse been pronounced against you for these, and yet who believes the report? Ye will not do so much as to sit down and examine your own guiltiness, till your mouth be stopped and till ye put it in the dust before God's justice. And when we speak of hell unto you, and of the curses of God passed upon all men, you bless yourselves in your own eyes, saying, peace, peace, even though ye walk in the imagination of your own hearts, add sin to sin, and "drunkenness to thirst," Deut. xxix. 20. Now, when all this is told you, that many shall be condemned and few saved, and that God is righteous to execute judgment and render vengeance on you, ye say within yourselves, For God's sake, is all this true? But where is the mourning at his lamentations, when there is no feeling or believing them to be true? Your minds are not convinced of the law of God, and how shall your hearts be moved? Christ Jesus laments unto you, as he wept over Jerusalem, "How often would I have gathered thee, and thou wouldst not!" What means he? Certainly, he would have you to sympathize with your own condition. When he that is in himself blessed, and needs not us, is so affected with our misery, how should we sympathize with our own misery! God seems to be affected with it, though there be no shadow of turning in him. Yet he clothes his words with such affections, "Why will ye die?" "O that my people had hearkened unto me!" He sounds the proclamation before the stroke, if it be possible to move you to some sense of your condition, that concerns you most nearly. Yet who judges himself that he may not be judged? The ministers of the Lord, or Christians, may put to their ear, and hearken to men in their retiring places, but who repents in dust and ashes, and says, "What have I done?" Jer. viii. 6. But every man goes on in his course without stop. The word ye hear on the Sabbath day against your drunkenness, your oppressions, your covetousness, your formality,

&c., it doth not lay any bands on you to keep you from these things. Long may we hearken to you in secret, ere we hear many of you mourn for these things, or turn from them. Where is he that is afraid of the wrath of God, though it be often denounced against him? Do not men sleep over their time, and dream of escaping from it? Every man hath a refuge of lies he trusts in, and will not forsake his sins.

Again, on the other hand, whose heart rejoices within them to hear the joyful sound? Because men do not receive the law, and mourn when he laments, they cannot receive the gospel. It cannot be glad news to any but the soul that receives sad tidings, the sentence of death in its bosom. Therefore Christ Jesus is daily offered and as often despised, as a thing of nought, and of no value. Ye hear every day of deliverance from eternal wrath, and a kingdom purchased unto you, and ye are no more affected, than if we came and told you stories of some Spanish conquest, that belonged not unto you. Would not the ears and hearts of some men be more tickled with idle and unprofitable tales, that are for no purpose but driving away the present time, than they are with this everlasting salvation? Some men have more pleasure to read an idle book, than to search the holy scriptures, though in them this inestimable jewel of eternal life be hid. The vain things of this present world have a voice unto you of pleasure, and profit, and credit. They will pipe unto you, and ye will listen unto their sound, but ye know not that the dead are there, and that it is the way to the chambers of hell. These indeed are Sirens[457] that entice passengers by the way with their sweet songs, and having allured them to follow, lead them to perishing. Here is the voice that is come down from heaven, the "Word that was with God," and he is "the way, the truth, and the life." He is gone before you, and undertakes to guide you. He comes and calls upon simple men. The Father's Wisdom calls the simple ones to understand wisdom, to find life and peace. Will ye then so far wrong your own souls as to refuse it? And yet the most part are so busied with this world and their own lusts, that the sweetest and pleasantest offers in the gospel sound not so sweet unto them as the clink of their money, or the sound of oil and wine in a cup. Any musician would affect them more than the sweet singer of Israel, the anointed of the God of Jacob. Always[458] these souls that have mourned and danced according to Christ's motions, and whose hearts have exulted within them at the message and word of reconciliation,—blessed are ye. Ye are of another generation, children of wisdom, ye who desire to hear his voice. "Let me hear thy voice." O thou that dwellest in the gardens, the companions hear thy voice, "for thy voice is sweet, and thy countenance is comely." If this be the voice of thy heart, blessed art thou. Thou mayest indeed dance, who hath rejoiced in his salvation, or who hath mourned at his lamentation, thy dancing is but yet coming, for his piping is but yet coming. When all the companies of wisdom's children shall be gathered together in that general assembly of the first born, Christ Jesus, the head of all principalities, and in special the head of the body the church, shall lead the ring, and there shall be eternal praises and songs of those that follow the Lamb. They shall echo into him, who shall begin that song of the hallelujah, Salvation, blessing, honour, glory, and power to the Lamb, &c.

Now, whereunto shall this generation be likened, that are not affected with these things? What strange stupidity and senselessness is it, that men are not affected with things of so great and so near concernment? It would require the art of men to express the obstinacy of some Christian professors, or rather a pen steeped in hell. He would be thought unnatural that would not grieve at his friend's death or loss. And what shall they be called that will not sympathize with themselves, that is, their souls? If we speak to you of corporal calamities, and ye could not be moved, it were great stupidity. But what stupidity is it, that men will not consider their own souls? What shall ye profit, if ye lose your precious souls, and be cast away? It is the greatest loss that is told you, and the greatest gain. Your affections are moved with perishing things, every thing puts them up or down, and casts the balance with you. What deep ignorance and inconsideration is it, that ye who can mourn for loss of goods, of children, of health, of friends, that ye cannot be moved to sorrow for the sin of your soul, for the eternal loss of your soul! Other sorrows cannot profit you, but this is the only profitable mourning. If ye were told your sin and misery, to make you despair and mourn eternally, ye had some excuse to delay, and forget it as long as ye can. But when all this is told you, that you may escape from it, will ye not consider it? When ye are desired to mourn, that ye may be comforted for ever, will ye not mourn? We would have you to anticipate the day of judgment, that ye may judge yourselves, and then ye shall not be judged. What folly and madness is this to delay it till endless, irremediless mourning come, a day that hath no light mixed with darkness! Those that now mourn at that law, and for their sin, and dance at the promises of the gospel, may well be called children of wisdom, and O how may this generation be said to be begotten of foolishness, as their father, and wildness, as their mother! For is there any such folly as this, to lose a man's self absolutely and irrecoverably, for that which they cannot have always? Is there any such folly as to refuse this healing medicine, for the little bitterness which is in it, and then to incur eternal death?

Now what should we do then? What doth the word of God call you to do? This is it, to mourn and rejoice, and this is to justify wisdom. These two are the pulse of a Christian. According as he finds his grief and joy, so is he. All of you have these affections, but they are not right placed. They are not pitched upon suitable objects. The worldling hath no other joy but carnal mirth, no other grief but that which is carnal, these are limited within the bounds of time. Some loss, or some gain, some pleasure or pain, some honour or dishonour, these are the poles all his affections turn about on. Now then we exhort and beseech you, as ye would flee from the wrath to come, consider it now and fear it. As ye would not partake with this untoward generation in their plagues, so be not like them in their stupidity.

Ye are called to consider your sins and God's wrath, that ye may turn unto the Lord, and then you will hear the voice of peace crying unto thee, "Be of good comfort, thy sins are forgiven thee." If ye submit unto the justice of God, or unto the holiness and righteousness of his law in condemning you, you justify wisdom in part, but ye who have justified wisdom thus far, do not condemn wisdom after it. Justify the gospel, in believing upon Jesus Christ. Receive it as a true and faithful saying with your hearts, and this shall justify you. And if ye justify the wisdom of God in prescribing the righteousness of Christ unto you, ye will also justify wisdom in prescribing a rule of holiness and obedience unto you, and count all his paths pleasantness and peace. Ye must dance at the commandments, as well as the promises, because all God's precepts are really promises. Ye have nothing to do but to believe them as the way, and then to dance until ye all sing the song of the Lamb with the saints above.

Now if ye believe his law and gospel, and be suitably affected with these, ye are led also to sympathize with all the dispensations of his providence. Doth God lament to you in his works as well as his word? O then, Christians, we exhort you to mourn. Yet mourning because of his lamentable providence, should be joined with rejoicing in his word. "God hath spoken in his holiness, I will rejoice." We are a stupid generation, that can neither see, nor hear, neither can we be affected with what we see, nor hear. Do not his judgments go forth as a lamp that burneth, yet who considers? Doth not the lion roar, but who is afraid? Is there not a voice publishing affliction? Hath not God's rod a loud voice, and yet who hears it? Who fears? We do not receive agreeable impressions of the Lord's dealing with us, but every man puts the day of evil far from him. He will not apprehend public rods, till they become personal, and therefore they must become personal. If ye were mourning in a penitent manner, as a repenting soul laments, would not our fast days have more soul affliction attending them? If ye did dance as God pipes in his providence, would not our solemn feasts have more soul rejoicing, and heavenly mirth? Alas for that deep sleep that has fallen upon so many Christians! How few stir up themselves to take hold upon God, though he hides his face, and threateneth to depart from us? For the Lord is with you while ye are with him; if ye seek him, and feareth for him with all your heart, you will find him, but if ye forsake him he will forsake you.

SERMON XI.

[It is extremely probable that this was one of the probationary discourses which the author delivered before the Presbytery of Glasgow, previous to his ordination. The following is an extract from the Record of that Presbytery: "Dec. 5, 1649. The qlk daye Mr. Hew Binnen made his popular sermon 1 Tim. i. ver. 5 'The end of ye commandment is charity.'—Ordaines Mr. Hew Binnen to handle his controversie this day fifteen dayes, De satisfactione Christi."—*Ed.*]

1 Tim. ii. 5.—"Now the end of the commandment is charity out of a pure heart, and a good conscience, and faith unfeigned."

In this chapter the apostle, after the inscription of this epistle, repeats a former commandment that he had given to Timothy, how he should both teach himself, and by authority, committed unto him by an extraordinary commission, see that other ministers teach so also. Paul almost in all his epistles, sets himself against legal preachers, and false teachers. It was a common error in the primitive times, to confound the law and grace, in the point of righteousness, or to make free justification inconsistent with the moral law. Therefore our apostle makes it his chief study to vindicate the doctrine of the gospel. He preaches the gospel, and yet is not Antinomian. He preaches the law, and yet is no legal preacher. He exalts Christ more than the Antinomian can do, and yet he presses holiness more than the mere legalist can do. He excludes the law in the point of justification and pardon, and then brings it in again to the justified man's hand. If these words were rightly understood, and made use of, it would put an end to the many useless controversies of the present time, and reform many of our practices.

There are as many practical abuses among Christians concerning the law and the gospel, as there are speculative errors among other sects. In the former verse, he more particularly directs him what to take a care of, that men may neither spend their own, or their neighbour's time, in foolish, unnecessary, or impertinent questions, that tend nothing to the edification of the body of Christ, or in building them up in our most holy faith, the doctrine of Christ Jesus, and faith in it. And in this verse, he shows the true meaning and purpose of the law, and commandment, when he meets these doctors, and draws an argument against them from their own doctrine. They boasted of the law, and were counted very zealous of it, but as it is said of the Jews, they had a zeal of God, but not according to knowledge, because they did not submit unto the righteousness of God. They were also zealous for the commandment, but neither God nor the commandment would give them thanks. Why? Because they wholly mistake and pervert the meaning and purpose of the law. As long as they make the law inconsistent with the gospel, or would mix it with it, in the point of justification, they do it not unto edification in faith (as it is read), and as they ought to do, verses 4, 5, 6. We think this evangelic sentence, but rawly,[459] yea, legally exponed by many, when they look upon the words as they lie here, "the end of the commandment is love," for love worketh no evil, and is the fulfilling of the whole law, and this love is described to be pure and sincere, by the following properties. But we conceive the main business is not to describe love, or to oppose this unto their contentions about trifling questions. We choose rather to understand the text another way, according to the order of nature, which also the words themselves give ground for, "The end of the commandment is love out of a pure heart," out "of faith unfeigned." So then, according to the phraseology and meaning of the words, love is not first, but faith must be first, and primarily intended, so that the sense of the words is this, The end of the commandment is unfeigned faith, from whence flows a good conscience, a pure heart, and love, or the end of the commandment is faith, which is proved unfeigned by these effects, that it gives the answer of a good conscience, it purifies the heart, worketh by love, the effect of faith which is love, being to our knowledge more sensible than faith itself. We think it then more native[460] to make a pure heart, and love, marks of unfeigned faith, than faith and a good conscience the marks of love. This exposition is yet more confirmed by parallel places, Rom. x. 4, "The end of the law is Christ for righteousness, unto them that believe." This is most principally intended, and even before love. Now it is all one to speak of faith as to speak of Christ. For faith and Christ are inseparably joined, and faith comes not as a consideration in the gospel, abstracted from Christ the object of it, as some enemies of Christ affirm. It justifies us not as an act or work, but as an instrument, whereby we apprehend Christ and his righteousness. For faith abstracted from Christ is but an empty notion, and among the dung and loss that Paul would quit to be found in Christ, Phil. iii. 7-9. Now this sense only fits the scope and purpose, and leads on strongly against the false teachers. When Paul brings his argument from the law, which they defended against the gospel, they made the commandment to contradict the gospel. Paul makes the commandment to contradict them, and agree with the gospel, and to be so far from disagreeing with it, that it hath a great affinity with it as the mean to the end as that which is unperfect, without its own complement and perfection. Faith in Jesus Christ alone for salvation, quieting a man's conscience, is the very intent of the law, and the command was never given since Adam, to justify men by obedience to it, but to pursue men after Christ. And to satisfy you more fully, and clear it up he says, though the end of the command be not to justify, but to pursue a man from it to Christ, yet the command suffers no prejudice by this means, but rather is established by faith, the end of it, because this faith persuades the heart, and makes a man obey out of love to God, whereas before it should never have gotten any obedience, while men sought salvation by it.

You see then, there is an admirable harmony and consent between these things that are set at variance, both in the opinion and practice of the times. For what seems more contrary than the cursing commanding law, and the absolving promising gospel? Yet here they are agreed. Doth not justice go cross to mercy in the ordinary notion? Yet here there is a friendly subordination of justice to mercy, of the law to the gospel. Behold how faith is environed with the law, commanding and cursing on the one hand, and obedience to the command on the other hand, how faith is the middle party. A good conscience could never meet with the command since Adam's fall. A pure heart, and the obedience of love, had casten out[461] with the command, but here is the union, the meeting of old friends. Faith is the mediator, as it were, and the gospel comes between them, and so they dare meet again. Christ Jesus, who is our peace to make two one, comes in the middle, and takes away the difference. The law never meets with an obedient servant, or friend, till it meet first with Christ. It can find none righteous in all the world, none upright. Here you have the law's command and curse reconciled with the gospel's promise, and absolution reconciled with new obedience unto the command, the command leading to Christ, and Christ leading the man just back again to the command, the command serving Christ's design, and Christ serving the command. And this is the round that the believer shall go about in, until sin shall be no more. He shall be put over from one hand to another, till Christ shall be all in all. The command shall put him to Jesus, and Christ shall lead him back again, under a new notion, to his old master.

We may consider in the text a twofold relation that faith stands in, the relation of an end, and of a cause. Faith hath the relation of an end unto the commandment, of a cause unto a good conscience and a pure heart, and love, for these are said to be out of faith, which notes this dependence of a cause and fountain. The command is for faith, and a pure heart and love are from faith. We shall use no other division but consider the method of these effects that flow from faith. There is an order of emanation and dependence. There is a chain here. The first link nearest faith is a good conscience. The second link is a pure heart. The third is love, the hand follows the heart, and the heart follows the conscience.

We need not be subtile in seeking our purpose on these words, we think there is more in the plain words than we can speak of. We shall only resolve the verse in these propositions, without more observations. *First*, Faith in Jesus Christ is the end of the commandment, or law. *Secondly*, There is a faith feigned, and a faith unfeigned, a true and a false faith.

Thirdly, Unfeigned faith gives the answer of a good conscience. *Fourthly*, Faith purging the conscience, purifies the heart. *Fifthly*, Faith purifying the heart, works by love. Here then is the substance of all the gospel, and all this makes up an entire complete end. Faith purifying the heart, purging the conscience, and working by love, is the end of the commandment.

First, The end of the commandment or law (for a part is put for the whole) is faith in Christ or Jesus Christ apprehended by faith, which is all one. For ye cannot abstract faith from Christ, for the whole gospel is a shadow without him. Grace and glory is but a beam of the Sun of righteousness, that if ye come between it and Christ, it evanishes presently, Rom. x. 4, "Christ is the end of the law for righteousness to every one that believes." And if Christ be the end of the law, then faith is the end of it, because faith is the profession of Christ, and union with him. But consider, I. That the end is not taken here for the consumption or destruction of a thing. Christ is not the end of the law in that sense, though indeed, if the Antinomian speak ingenuously, his sense would be this, Christ makes an end of the law, contrary to Christ's own express meaning, "I came not to destroy the law but to fulfil it," Matt. v. 17. II. The end is either the intention or scope of a thing, the original word imports both. III. There is an end principally and directly intended in the thing, or work itself, and an end adventitious, and of the work. We may speak either of the end the law, of its own nature, is ordained unto, or the end of the Lawgiver in promulgating the law. These may be different. Next, concerning the law, consider, I. That the law may be taken strictly in a limited sense, as it comprehends only the command, and the promise of life, and the curse on the breach of it, and in this sense, it is frequently taken in Paul's epistles to the Romans, and Galatians, and opposed to faith and the gospel, as the gospel contains promises of salvation to penitent sinners. Or, II. It may, or useth to be so extended, as to comprehend all the administrations made under Moses, or all God's mind revealed under the Old Testament; now, in this sense, it comprehends the gospel, and covenant of grace in it, as we shall hear. Faith in Christ is the intention and scope of the law. Indeed, faith in Jesus is not the intention of the law itself, as it is only made up of commandments, promises, and curses. For the law as it commands, hath nothing to do, but to be a rule and obligation to men, and as it curses, it condemns men, and speaks nothing of Jesus Christ, or a way to make up the breach of the law. The gospel is not contained in the law, but rather accidental to it. For Jesus Christ comes with the gospel, as if some unexpected cautioner would come in, when the Judge is, as the angel that held Abraham's hand,—when he was to slay his son, and offer him up a burnt offering,—giving sentence to deliver him. It is an exception from the curse.

But Christ is directly intended and pointed out by the law. If ye consider the whole administration of Moses, that is, the law and covenant of works, though it was preached after the fall, yet it was never preached alone without the gospel, and so if ye consider the whole administration of God's mind and ordinances, Christ is principally aimed at. For, 1. The doctrine Moses delivered in mount Sinai contained a covenant of grace. If you look to the preface of the ten commandments, it is even the chief gospel promise, and article of the covenant. For how could God come to terms with men after sin, but in terms of grace? and on no other terms can man stand before God, nor God be his God. And likewise, seeing the gospel was preached in paradise, and afterwards to Abraham, God could not be false in his promise made to Abraham, neither could the promulgation of the law that followed make that null which went before, Gal. iii. 17. What meant all the ceremonial law? It shadowed out Jesus Christ, the only sacrifice and propitiation. And this is the sum of the gospel salvation to penitents believing in Christ, and looking through the sacrifices unto him, and thus David's righteousness was the imputation of righteousness, and not inherent holiness, Psal. xxxii. 1, 2; Rom. iv. 5. But 2. It used to be a question, whether the law delivered upon mount Sinai was a covenant of works or not. Some say, that the law which was delivered upon mount Sinai was indeed a covenant of works, though they confess it was preached with the covenant of grace, and not delivered to them to stand by it or of intention to get righteousness by it, but to be subservient to the covenant of grace. Others speak absolutely that the law upon mount Sinai was a covenant of grace. We conceive this is but a contention about words. The matter is clear in itself, (1) That neither is now the gospel preached without the law, as ye may see in Christ's sermon upon the mount, and his sermon to the young man, (Matt. chapters v., vi., vii., Mark x. 17,) nor yet was then the law preached without the gospel, as ye may see in Exod. chap. xx. The preface to the commandments, and the second command contains much of the gospel in them. Deut. xxx. 6, 7, &c., compared with Rom. x. 6, &c., where Paul notes both the righteousness of faith and of the works of the law. (2) Those who say the law on mount Sinai was a covenant of works, do not assert that God gave it to be a covenant of works, out of intention that men should seek salvation thereby, but they make it only a schoolmaster to lead us unto Christ, and to discover our sinful condition; and those who say it was a covenant of grace, consider it in relation to God's end of sending it, and as it takes in all the administration and doctrine of Moses. So there needs be no difficulty here. The matter seems clear, that the covenant of works was preached by Moses, and so it was by Paul, (Rom. x., Gal. iii.) and that neither Paul nor Moses preached the covenant of works, but as a broken covenant; not as such that men could stand unto, or be saved by. No man can preach the gospel, unless he preach the covenant of works; not because both concur to the justification of a sinner, but because the knowledge of a man's own lost condition under the one, presses him to flee to the other.

Now I say, Christ Jesus, or faith in him, is the scope and intention of the law. It is the scope and intention of the lawgiver, in giving out the law. God hath never given a command or curse since Adam's fall, but for this end, to bring sinners unto Christ. This is the end revealed, and appointed by him in his word. This we shall clear from some texts of scripture, because it is very material, Rom. v. 20, 21. It might be questioned from the former words, since death hath reigned before Moses, for sins against nature's light, what means the new entry of the written law? What was the end of the promulgation of it on mount Sinai? He answers, "the law entered that sin might abound;" that is, the world knew not sin, the letters of nature's light were worn out and rusty; men thought not of their miserable condition by nature, and did not charge themselves before God; therefore a new edition and publication of the law must be given, that all men may know how much they owe, and how they were guilty in a thousand things they never dreamed of. But wherefore serves this? That grace might superabound where sin had abounded. The Lord would have sin abounding in men's knowledge, and their charge to be great and weighty, that God's pardoning grace might be more conspicuous, and the discharge more sweet. We also learn, (Gal. iii. 19.) that the same question was moved, "Wherefore then serves the law? Seeing the covenant of grace was preached to Abraham, what meant the publishing of a covenant of works upon mount Sinai?" He answers, "It was added because of transgression, till the seed should come, to whom the promise was made;" and as it is said, Rom. v. 13, "For until the law sin was in the world." It abounded in all places of the world before the law came; but men did not impute it unto themselves, nor condemn themselves as guilty. Therefore the law was added to discover many hidden transgressions, and to show them the curse they deserved. Now this law is not against the promise or covenant of grace, (ver. 21.) which it behoved to be if it were not given of intention to drive men to Christ. But the 22d verse speaks out clearly the end of it, "the scripture hath concluded all men under sin," and under the curse both. To what end? That the promise by faith in Christ might come, or be given to believers. And ver. 24, "The law" was a "schoolmaster" and teacher, to lead us unto Christ. The very doctrine of a command impossible for man to keep, was, as it were, a proclamation of Christ Jesus to him, a complete teaching of the necessity of some other way of salvation. The law exacted obedience rigorously, even such as we could not perform, and cursed every degree of disobedience. This, if there were no more, speaks that a man cannot stand to such terms, and therefore he must flee to Jesus Christ, who mends the broken covenant.

Again, the apostle, 2 Cor. iii. 13, 14, while he speaks of the excellency of the ministry of the gospel beyond the ministry of Moses, notwithstanding all the material glory that accompanied that ministration, as the shining of Moses' face, &c., now opens up a great mystery here,—Moses' face shining while he was with God upon the mount. This holds forth the glory of the law as in respect of God. By counsels and inventions they saw no more but temporal mercies in it, and were not able to fix their eyes on that glory; the carnal Israelites did not break through the ministry of the law and death, to see Jesus there, because a vail was upon their hearts. They thought God had been dealing with them in the terms of a covenant of works, and they would stand to all God had said, and undertook indeed very fairly, "All which God hath commanded, we will do, and be obedient." But though[462] they perverted God's meaning of the law, and did not see Jesus intended; for they did not look steadfastly to the end of that mystery. Now what was it the vail hid them from? For the same vail is yet on them to this day, while they read Moses and the prophets, and when they shall be converted it shall be done away in Christ, they shall then see him in Moses' law. So then, the end of this ministry of the law was Jesus Christ, and this they could not behold.

Now from all this it is very clear, that Jesus Christ, or faith in him, was the great purpose and end of the law, and covenant of works. The world was lying in sin, and none sought God, no not one; neither knew they well what sin was. Therefore God sends his gospel from mount Sinai, and publishes his law in a terrible manner, that they might know the way and manner of the God they served, and see that their obligation was infinitely beyond their ability or performance. But, poor souls! they clearly mistake the matter, and stand to the terms of the covenant of works, as if they were able to perform them. But God did not leave them so. For he adds a ceremonial law, and sacrifices, to shadow out Christ Jesus. Now, says God, though ye have undertaken so well, yet I know you better than ye do yourselves. Ye will never keep one word of what you say. Therefore, when ye sin bring a sacrifice, and look to my Son, the Lamb that is to be slain and offered up, and ye shall have pardon in him.

II. Christ Jesus apprehended by faith, is the accomplishment and perfection of the law. 1. Because Christ Jesus, or faith laying hold upon him, accomplishes the same end that the law was ordained for of itself. The law was appointed to justify men, that it might be a rule of righteousness according to which men might stand before God and live. Now when the law was weak through the flesh, and could not give life, (Rom. viii. 3; Gal. iv. 21.) and the law ordained to life, wrought more death, and made sin exceeding sinful, (Rom. vii. 10-13.) therefore Jesus Christ came in the flesh, to do what the law was unable to do, and to bring many sons unto glory, that the just might live by faith, Gal. iii. 11. The law should never have gotten its end, no man should have stood before God, but the curse only would have taken place, and the promise would have been of no effect. Therefore, Jesus comes, and gives obedience to the law, and delivers men from the curse of it, and by faith puts men in as good, and even in a better condition, than they would have been by the promise; so that the justified sinner may come before God, as well as innocent Adam, and have as great confidence and assurance, and peace by faith, as he could have had by inherent holiness. Imputed righteousness comes in as a covering over the man's nakedness, and doth the turn[463] of perfect inherent holiness.

2. Christ, or faith laying hold on him, is the end or accomplishment of the law, because faith in Christ fulfils the righteousness of the law, in respect of a believer's personal obedience. Although the believer gave not perfect obedience, and so cannot stand in terms of justice, yet he gives sincere and upright obedience, which the law should never have got. The command wrought sin and death, by occasion of corruption, and never would any point of it be fulfilled by men. For as long as the curse was standing, no obedience could be acceptable till justice was satisfied, and though that might have been dispensed with, yet there is none that are righteous, none seek after God. No good principles of obedience were in us, but all are corrupt, and have done abominable works, and all our righteousness is as a menstruous cloth; and though upright obedience could have been yielded, yet the law exacted perfect obedience. But now faith in our Redeemer absolves a man from the curse of the law, so that now he is not looked upon as an enemy, but a friend; and then it puts a

man upon obedience to the command from new motives and principles: and thus the righteousness of the law is fulfilled in us, who walk after the Spirit, Rom. viii. 4. And that imperfect obedience is accepted of God, and received off his hand, by virtue of the sacrifice and atonement of Christ. The law would accept of no less, no not of nine commandments, if the tenth was broken. But now God in Christ accepts of endeavours and minting,[464] and so is the law in some way or other accomplished. And faith leads a man on till he be perfected. He walks by faith from strength to strength, till he appear before God, and be made holy as he is holy. Faith in Christ is the end of the law.

3. Because whatever faith wants of perfect and personal obedience, it makes up in Christ's obedience, and thus is the law thoroughly accomplished, for what it wants in the believer it gets in Christ. Paul would have the Romans take this way, Rom. vi. 11: "Likewise reckon ye yourselves dead indeed unto sin, but alive unto God through Jesus Christ." Ye may gather by good consequence, that since Christ hath died to sin as a public person so ye should die with him unto sin, and mortify sin with him. And thus may ye have consolation against your imperfect personal mortification. Ye were thoroughly mortified in Christ. So the believer may look unto Jesus, as one who hath given obedience even unto the death, and that, not in his own name but for us, that the imperfect holiness and obedience of every sound believer, may have his complete righteousness to cover it, and come next the Father's eye. And thus is the law fulfilled, and this way doth faith not make void, but establish the law, Rom. iii. 31. And as the law got better satisfaction in the sufferings of Christ, who became a curse for us, than in all the punishment we could endure, so it gets more satisfaction to the command by his obedience than if our personal had been perfect. Christ was "made under the law, that we might receive the adoption of sons," (Gal. iv. 4) and the Son's being made under the law is of more worth than all our being under it. Now faith puts that obedience of God Man in the law's hand. When we do God's will, he brings out Christ Jesus, "Lo, (says he) I come, I delight to do thy will," Psal. xl. 7-9. In a word, faith in Jesus accomplishes the law,

in the commands, in the promise, in the curse, as might be easily shown, if your time would allow.

(1) In the curse, because it lays hold upon Christ, who was "made a curse for us," (Gal. iii. 13) and so gives complete satisfaction to the Lord's justice in that point. It holds up the sacrifice and propitiation of our Saviour, and justice says, I am satisfied. It holds up the ransom, (Job xxxiii. 24) and therefore Christ says, "Deliver them from going down to the pit, for I have found a ransom." Again we also observe, (2) That faith in Christ also fulfils the commandments of the law, because it is the fountain of new obedience unto the law. It hath a respect unto all God's righteous judgments. It purifies the heart into the obedience of them, and it works by love, and so it is the end of the law for righteousness. It not only gives the answer of a good conscience unto all challenges and curses from Christ's blood, but daily derives virtue out of Jesus Christ, to bring forth fruit unto God. What it cannot reach by doing, it supplies by believing, and laying hold upon Christ's obedience. And this is the righteousness of the law fulfilled in us. Let us also,

(3) Look upon the promise of life, and it is accomplished also by faith in Christ. For the law could not have given life, and so the promise would now be in vain; but Christ by faith justifies the sinner, and he lives, yea, hath eternal life in him, and so all the three are strengthened and established. Faith is the most comprehensive commandment, 1 John iii. 22, 23. It is put for all the commandments, (1) By acknowledgment of the breach of all, and so it magnifies the law, and makes it honourable, and subscribes to the sentence of justice and the authority of the command; (2) By satisfaction, because it gives a price for the breach of it, and puts the Cautioner[465] in the craver's hand; (3) By obedience, because after this, it hath a respect to all God's laws, and endeavours after new obedience to every one of them.

The improvement of all this is extremely plain. It may serve to discover unto us how we disappoint God of his end in giving unto us the command. And the law was given for the best purposes. But, the most part of men have no end, no use of the law. God hath given it for some end, but they know it not. They live without God, and without rule in the world. Men walk as if there was no law, nor command, nor curse. There are but two ends the command was ordained for, the first instituted end which it naturally tends unto is life, (Rom. vii. 10) and the second end for which God hath appointed it since the first is missed, is to pursue men to Jesus Christ, and convince them of sin, to make them once die that they may live, Rom. vii. 9. But the most part know neither of these ends. A carnal profane generation will not seek life by the righteousness of the law; their iniquities testify against them even to their face, and their sin is found hateful. There is not so much as an endeavour among too many Christian professors, either to approve themselves unto men, or their own consciences in their outward walking. They walk without any regard of a command, or rule, as it were by guess. Their own rule is what pleases them best. What suits their humours, and crosses God's word, that they will do, as if they knew not the curse, or were afraid of the sentence of condemnation. They walk in peace, and have no changes, they walk in the imagination of their vain hearts. They cannot say, and none will say for them, they seek life by the law, their contempt of it is so palpable, and yet no other end of it they know so it is to them as if God had never appointed it. Again,

2. There are many wrong and false ends, or uses of the law, when we make it the immediate mean to life and righteousness, and seek justification by it. And this was the end that these false teachers would have made of it. This is the end that the Israelites looked to. "All that the Lord hath commanded, will we do." O that was a great undertaking! Poor men, they knew not what they said. They thought upon no other thing but obedience to the command, and so made it a covenant of works. Thus did the people that followed Christ, John vi. 28. And the young man that came to Christ said, "What good thing shall I do, to inherit eternal life?" Here doing was preferred to living by faith, Rom. x. 1-23. The Jews did so, and missed the right way. And few of you will take[466] with this, that ye seek to be justified by your own works; and yet, it is natural to men, they will not submit to God's righteousness. There is need of submission to

take Christ. O would not any think all the world would be glad of him, and come out and meet him bringing salvation? Would not dyvours[467] and prisoners be content of a deliverance? Were it any point of self denial for a lost man, to grip a cord cast unto him? Yet here must there be submission to quit your own righteousness. It were of great moment to convince you of this, that ye are all naturally standing to the terms of a covenant of works, ye who are yet alive, and the commandment hath not slain you, with Paul, Rom. vii. 9, 11. Ye are yet seeking life by the law, if ye have not applied the curse unto yourselves. After application of yourselves to the command, ye are yet seeking life by it. Ye adorn yourselves with some external privileges, in some external duties of religion, some branches of the second table duties, and come to God with these. Some think to satisfy God for their faults, with an amendment in time to come. Some think God cannot punish some faults in them, because they have some good things in them. Ask many men the ground of their confidence, and in all the world they know not how to be saved, unless their prayers do it, or their keeping the kirk.[468] But this is not the end that God hath sent out the law for. Ye cannot now stand to such a bargain. The law is now weak through the flesh, and it is now impossible for it to give life. Though you would pray never so much, all is but abomination. And would not many of you think ye were in a fair venture for heaven, if no man living could lay any thing to your charge, but were you unblameable in all the duties of the first and second table? [Could you say,] though you know nothing as by yourselves, that you were frequent and fervent in prayer, reading, and meditation; and as far advanced as Paul, or David, or Moses, or Job, sure ye would think yourselves out of doubt of heaven? Nay, but in this, ye may see ye are seeking righteousness by the law. Though ye were so far advanced, yet God, who is of purer eyes than to behold iniquity, would look to your sins, and pass by your righteousness, and all that would be as menstruous rags before him; and therefore Paul was much wiser, who said, "though I know nothing by himself, yet am I not hereby justified." 3. Many make the law an end, when God hath only made it a mean. God hath appointed the law for some other use, namely, to be subservient to Christ and the gospel. But oftentimes we make the law the end of all God's speaking to us, and so conclude desperate resolutions from it, (Rom vii. 9). "When the law came, sin revived, and I died." Here the man is slain by the commandment, and not yet come to the healing Physician at Gilead. We use to gather desperation of the command, when it presses so perfect and exact obedience, such as we cannot yield. When it craves the whole sum, without the abatement of a farthing, we sit down under the sense of an impossibility to obey, and will not so much as mint[469] at obedience. Because we cannot do as we ought, we will not do as we can. Because we cannot do in ourselves we conclude nothing can be done at all. This is to make the command the last word, and the end of God's speaking. Doth not the child of God frequently sit down and droop over his duty, while he looks upon the Egyptian taskmaster, the command, charging the whole work and portion of brick, and giving no straw to work upon? So are many in duties. While the aim and eye is upon some measure according to the perfect rule, the hands fall down feeble, and none is wrought at all, and they do not look if there be another word from God posterior to the command, a word of promise. We use also to gather desperate conclusions of the curse, and make the law according to which we examine ourselves, the end of God's manifesting his mind unto us, and do not look upon it as a way leading to some other thing. When ye have tried yourselves, and applied your own ways and state unto the perfect rule, God's verdict of all men's condition is true in you, "all have sinned, and come short of the glory of God," "there is none righteous, no, not one," and so if necessitated to apply the dreadful sentence of the judgment to yourselves, ye stay there, and sit down to lodge with the sentence of condemnation, as if that were God's last word to sinners. Is not this to make the law the end, which is but appointed for another end? The curse is not irrepealable. Why then do ye pass peremptory conclusions, as if there was no more hope, but it were perished from the Lord?

II. To discover unto us the right end and use of the law, the great design and purpose of God in making such a glorious promulgation of the law on mount Sinai, and delivering it by the ministry of angels, in the hands of a mediator. The end which God hath been driving at these six thousand years, is this only, that men may come to Jesus Christ and believe in him. The end wherefore the covenant of works hath been preached since Adam's fall, is only this, to make way for a better covenant of grace, that men may hearken to the offer of it. Now faith in Jesus Christ hath two special actings, either upon Christ for justification of the person, and eternal life and salvation, or for sanctification of the person and actions, in the fruits of new obedience. And in the text, unfeigned faith is described from both these, and gives the answer of a good conscience, that is, of absolution from the curse, by the blood of Jesus, and makes him as quiet as he had never sinned. And then it purifies the heart, and worketh by love.

Now the law is a mean appointed of God, and instituted to lead to both these, and Christ in these. The law is appointed to lead a man to faith in Christ, for salvation and righteousness, and the suitableness of it to that end, we comprehend thus: 1. It convinces of sin; "The law entered that the offence might abound," and "was added because of transgressions," Rom. v. 20, Gal. iii. 19. This is the end of God's sounding the trumpet, and declaring our duty, "that every mouth may be stopped" before God, and that none may plead innocence before his tribunal. While men are without the law, they are alive, and think well of themselves, but the entering of the commandment in a man's conscience, in the length, breadth, and spirituality of it, makes sin to appear exceeding sinful. Sin was in the house before, but was not seen before, and now when the bright beam of a clear, spiritual, holy law, carrying God's authority upon it, is darted into the dark soul, O what ugly sights appear! The house is full of motes. Ye cannot turn the command where it will not discover innumerable iniquities, an universal leprosy. For all the actions that were called honest, civil and religious before, get a new name, and they being seen in God's light, are called rottenness, and living without the law, Rom. vii. 9 &c. Think ye, but the woman of Samaria knew her adultery, before Christ spake to her? Nay, but Christ speaks according to the law and makes it a mean of faith. He tells her all that ever she did. He tells her indeed what she knew before, but in another manner. Men know their actions, but the Lord discovers the sinfulness of them, as offensive to God's holy majesty, and pure eyes. It will force a man to give his sin the right name, it will take away all excuses and shifts, and aggravate sin, that it may become exceeding sinful. But further, 2. This is not the last end of it. Not only is it ordained to stop all mouths, but to make all flesh guilty before God, "For by the deeds of the law shall no flesh be justified," Rom. iii. 18, 19. It convinces of an impossibility to stand before God, and so it kills a man. And now the man asks, "What shall I do to be saved?" He cannot stand before God in terms of justice, where none can stand, and so either must some other delivery come, or he is gone. Now here he is put from making satisfaction, "Who can abide with everlasting burnings?" He sees himself standing under the stroke of justice; and where can he go from God's presence? If he go to heaven, he is there, if to hell, he will find him out, the light and darkness are alike to him, Psal. cxxxix. 7-11. Not only the cries of sinful man, but of wretched and miserable man, are heard from him! Now these are the steps the law proceeds by. But it must not stay there, or else it is not come to the end of it. It must put a man within the doors of the covenant of grace. The law is a messenger sent to pursue a man out of his own house of self confidence and security, he was like to perish in, and not to know it. Now by discovering his sinful and cursed condition, it brings him out of himself, and out of all created things. But the end is not yet attained, till it put him in Christ's hand, and enter him in the border of the city of refuge and this is the end of the abounding of sin by the law, that grace may superabound, Rom. v. 20. And this is the end of the concluding him under sin, and making him guilty before God, that the promise of faith may be given him, and another righteousness revealed by faith, Rom. iii. 20, 21, Gal. iii. 23. And now he is at peace, being justified by faith, and rests as a stone in its own place (Rom. v. 1, 2), and the law hath nothing to do with him; he is out of its jurisdiction. 3. Now when it hath pursued him unto Christ for salvation, yet the command is still useful, and appointed yet for faith in Jesus, in performing new obedience. The Christian's daily walking is but the turning of the old round, as the sun doth this day go about the compass it did the first day, so his life is but a new conversion still. When he is now settled on Jesus for salvation, he must yet be put by[470] the command. It discovers his dally sins, and so he is put to Jesus, the open Fountain for all sin and uncleanness. And the command comes out in perfection, and discovers his shortcoming and inability, and therefore he is put to Jesus for strength. And this is the end of the perfect rule upon believers, that they, comparing duty with their ability, may be forced to make up their inability for duty by faith in Christ.

III. We may know from this what great encouragement we have to believe, and how great warrant, since not only God commands faith itself (1 John iii. 23.), but he hath appointed faith to be the end of all other commands, and hath given the whole law for this end. For "without faith it is impossible to see God." Faith is that which God loves best in all obedience. What is it that makes faith so precious? Certainly not the act itself, but the precious object of it, Jesus Christ, in whom the Father is well pleased. Faith glorifies God in his justice and mercy most, and abases the creature. Now what an obligation lies on us to believe? It is usual to question a right and warrant of faith, when we have no doubt of other commands. But, in all reason, any command might be questioned before faith. There is no duty admits of less disputing. Hath not God put it out of all controversy? What warrant have ye to pray, or to sanctify the Sabbath? Is it not because God commands these duties? And do ye not go about them in obedience to God, notwithstanding of the sense of your own inability? How comes it then that ye make any more scruple of this? Hath not the same authority that gave the ten commands, given also this new command? And shall not disobedience be rebellion, and worse than witchcraft?[471] But when besides all this, it is the appointed end of all the commands, so that ye may say, it is commanded in all the commands and the whole law,—command and curse is a virtual kind of commanding faith,—then what shall disobedience be? When ye break one command, ye are guilty of all. Much more here, not only because of God's authority stamped upon all, but because it is the common end of all. If ye could once come to believe that ye had as good warrant to believe in Christ as to abstain from cursing God's name, and as great obligation, what could ye answer for disobedience?

IV: This is a point of great consolation also. What more terrible than the law? Nothing in all the world. Nothing in all the word so dreadful as the trumpet on Sinai, sounding louder and louder. The judge and law gives voice. Yet if ye could look to the end of it and if the vail that was on the Jews' heart be not upon yours, O how comfortable shall it be! Doth not a command and curse form a dead sound in an awakened man's ears, and strike unto his heart like a knife? But if he knew this, it would be a healing medicine. Would not many sinners wish there would be no such thing in the Bible as a condemning law, when they cannot get it escaped? But look to the end of it, and see gospel saving doctrine in the very promulgation of it. When it was published, it made the Jews all to tremble and cry out, and even holy Moses himself was afraid. But there is more consolation than terror here. This condemning law is delivered in a Mediator's hand, even Jesus Christ, Gal. iii. 19, 20. Who was he that spake out of the cloud, and fire, and came and set down his throne on Sinai, accompanied with innumerable angels? Deut. xxxiii. 2, Acts vii. 53. It was Jesus Christ that spoke to Moses in the mount, and in the bush also, Acts vii. 35, 38. Is it then the Mediator's law, whose office it is to preach glad tidings, and the day of salvation? Sure then it needs be dreadful to no man. For if he wound, he shall heal, and he comes to bind up the broken hearted. Ye may look on the command and curse as messengers sent by mercy, to prepare you, and make his way straight before his face. The end of the law is not to condemn you, to stop your mouth, and make you guilty. That is not the last work it is appointed for, but the Mediator hath another end, to bring you to the righteousness of faith, to save you without yourselves. Therefore ye may more willingly accept the challenge, since it comes in so peaceable terms. What should be terrible to you in all God's word and dispensation, since the ministry of condemnation and death is become the port[472] of heaven and life? What must all his other dealings be? Surely there is nothing in the world, but it must lead to this end also. Prosperity and adversity, the end of them is faith, conviction and challenges. Be not then as men without hope, when you are challenged, for the challenge comes from a Mediator who would have you saved.

V: You may see hence how injurious they are to grace who cry down the law. The Antinomian cannot be a right defender and pleader for faith (the end of the command), when he opposes the command that leads to that end. He can not exalt Christ aright, or lead men to him, when he will not come under the pedagogue's hand to be led to Christ. The law, even as a covenant of works, is of perpetual use to a believer, because it lays a blessed necessity upon him to abide with Christ. It is a guard put before the door, to keep him, as it was a schoolmaster to bring him to Christ, and makes a man subordinate to the gospel as a mean to the end, and so it ought to be used. So then it is against the truth [to say] that the Israelites were under the law, and not Christians. The law came not to be a mean of life and righteousness unto them, but that the offence might abound, that so grace might superabound. The law was not intended, but Christ was intended, and this end they could not fix their eyes upon, by reason of the hardness of their hearts. It is also false, that Christian believers are wholly exeemed[473] from the command and law. No, he hath use of all that leads to Jesus Christ, and the law itself becomes gospel under that notion. The command stands in its integrity, that he may be convinced of shortcoming and inability, and so may believe in Christ. The curse also stands, and condemns him for new sins, that he may believe in Christ, who justifies the ungodly. Again, it is not truth, that the law is no mean of conversion, though not in its own virtue and power, but as it is delivered in a Mediator's hand, and applied by the Spirit of grace and the gospel.

Use VI: We exhort you not to disappoint God of his end, and if he hath given the law for this end, never rest till ye be at the end. Let the law enter into you once, or enter ye into it. Ye cannot come to Jesus unless it lead you. Let it enter into your consciences, with God's power and authority as his law, and examine yourselves by it, else ye shall never believe in Christ. 2. Accept all the challenges of the law, let it enter till your mouth be stopped. Read your obligation well, that ye may see how much ye owe. 3. Let faith be the issue and result of all the applications of the law to yourselves. Ye go in the law's hand to Christ, but sit not down with it, or else you will not go free till ye have paid the last farthing. Make faith in Christ the end of the curse condemning you, that he may absolve you, the end of the command, commanding, that he may give strength and fulfil in you the righteousness of the law. God never sent a condition to you, but that you may believe, and be established. 4. Let it be your exercise to travel between an impossible command, and Christ Jesus by faith, through whom all things are possible. Write always down how much ye owe, that ye may see grace superabounding. Sit not down to examine the duty, or go not about it in your own strength. Be not discouraged though ye find no strength. Ye are called in such a case to believe. Nay, in a word, what is all the Christian's employment? Faith exhausts it all. Look on the command, and it calls for believing. Look upon the curse and it calls also for believing.

SERMON XII.

1 Tim. i. 5.—"Now the end of the commandment," &c.

We come now, as was proposed, to observe, *Thirdly*,[474] That faith unfeigned is the only thing which gives the answer of a good conscience towards God. Conscience, in general, is nothing else but a practical knowledge of the rule a man should walk by, and of himself in reference to that rule. It is the laying down a man's state, and condition, and actions beside the rule of God's word, or the principles of nature's light. It is the chief piece of a man. The man is as his conscience is. It is a man's lord. As a wing to a bird, or as a rudder to a ship, so is conscience to a man in all his ways. The office of conscience is ordinarily comprehended in three styles it gets. It is a law or rule, a witness, and a judge, or a light, a register, and a recorder, and an executioner. For the conscience its first act is some principle of nature's light, obliging it as a rule to walk by, or some revealed truth of God, whereof the conscience is informed. Now the conscience, in the second place, comes to examine itself according to the rule, and there it bears witness of a man's actions or state, and faithfully records and depones.[475] And at length the conscience pronounces the sentence upon the man, according as it has found him, either accusing or excusing, condemning or absolving. Now a good conscience is diversely taken in scripture, I. A good conscience is an honest clean conscience, bearing testimony of integrity and uprightness in walking, such as Paul had, 2 Cor. i. 12, "Our rejoicing is this, the testimony of our conscience, that in simplicity, and godly sincerity, we have had our conversation in the world." Heb. xiii. 18, "We trust we have a good conscience, in all things willing to live honestly." Acts xxiv. 16, "Herein do I exercise myself in having a conscience void of offence, towards God and man." 1 Pet. iii. 16, "Having a good conscience, that whereas they speak evil of you, as of evil doers, they may be ashamed that falsely accuse your good conversation in Christ." II. A good conscience is a conscience calmed and quieted, that hath gotten an answer to all challenges, the blood and resurrection of Jesus, 1 Pet. iii. 21. And this we take to be meant here. The good conscience is the conscience that is sprinkled with Christ's blood, from dead works, to serve the living God, Heb. ix. 14. For the guilty man that comes to Christ, and washes in the fountain opened for sin, hath no more conscience of sins, Heb. x. 2. And therefore it is called a pure and clean conscience, 2 Tim. i. 3, "I thank God, whom I serve from my forefathers, with a pure conscience," &c.; the stain of guilt is taken away. Now I say, faith only gives the answer of a good conscience. The man that comes to Christ hath an ill conscience, when he hath examined himself according to the law, and given out faithful witness of his own state and condition, and accordingly pronounced sentence,—a sentence condemnatory. He finds himself lying under God's curse, and so the conscience from a judge turns a tormentor, and begins to anticipate hell, and prevent[476] the execution of wrath. All the world cannot answer this challenge, or absolve from this sentence, until faith come and give a solid answer, that may be a ground of peace. And its answer is good and sure, because it dips the conscience in the blood of the Son of God. For the blood of bulls and of goats could not do it, the redemption of the soul was precious. Faith puts the soul over head and ears in the fountain opened, and it comes out like snow, or wool, though it were like scarlet or crimson. The law condemned, and the conscience subscribed itself sinful, and concluded itself lost in sin; but faith in Christ pleads before mercy's throne, where judgment and justice also sit. It pleads its cause over again, and gets the former sentence repealed. The conscience gave in the charge against the man, but faith sits down and writes the discharge; and so he is as free as if all his debt was paid, or never contracted. Faith puts the Cautioner in the creditor's hand, and goes free. As the law writes down a charge of sin and curses, faith sets against it as many sufferings in Christ, as many blessings in the Blessing of all nations. And when the conscience that condemned itself by faith again absolves itself, O what a calm, what a perfect peace is it then kept in! What a continual feast doth it enjoy! Prov. xv. 15. Make him never such a great man in the world, he would utterly despise it, and count himself more blessed in the pardon of sin, and the friendship of God, than all the enjoyments of this world. He is better in some respect than if he had never sinned, for his sin is, as it were, not before God. And withal he hath got not only acquittance from guilt, but acquaintance with Jesus Christ, the Blessing of the nations, and the Desire of all the families of the earth. Now may he triumph and boast in Christ Jesus. Who shall condemn? It is God that justifies, it is Christ that died, and is risen again. He may say with David, "I will not fear, though my iniquities compass me about;" and with Job, "If he cause quietness, who can give trouble?" We observe then that,

I. Before a man come to Christ, he has an ill conscience; for either he is at peace with himself, and absolves himself, saying, I shall have peace, though I walk in the abominations of my heart, Deut. xxix. 19; or he also says, "Because I am innocent," therefore God will turn away his wrath,

Jer. ii. 35. He cries peace, peace, when there is no peace, (Ezek. xiii. 10.) and that is but a desperate condition, and a bad conscience, if any can be so called. This is the secure and seared conscience, that either doth not judge itself, because a man hath beaten it flint hard, or is constantly absolving itself upon false grounds. That is the conscience that in all the creation is nearest the desperate conscience, that shall never have a good answer. His sin is but lying at the door like Cain's, and shall enter in when judgment comes. He is but flattering himself in his own eyes, till his iniquity be found hateful, and till sudden destruction comes as an armed man. Look upon Deut. xxix. 20, and see such a man's case. There is no peace for him, the Lord will not pity nor spare him, but pour upon him all the curses of the law, even when he blesses himself in his own eyes. In short, he is such as is awakened to see where he is, and condemns himself according to the word; and that is a better and a more hopeful conscience than the former, yet it is but an ill conscience. Conscience doth act its part aright, and in so far it is good, but the man is but in a miserable condition. Withal it gives such a wound to the soul, as none can bear it. All the sad affections which take up men's spirits come in, and this is the worm which never dies in hell, and the fire which shall never be quenched. Anger, grief, hatred, despair, always dwell with an ill conscience. This is both the resemblance of hell, and the sparks which come from that devouring fire. But, II. When the troubled conscience, tossed up and down, and looking upon all hands for help, and all refuge failing them, and no person caring for their soul, when it gets once a look of Jesus, and roweth unto his shore, O what a change! He commands the winds to calm, and the waves to cease, and says unto him, Son, be of good comfort, thy sins are forgiven. Faith finds in Jesus ample grounds of answering all challenges, of silencing all temptations, of overcoming all enemies, and commands the soul to go into its place of refuge. "Return unto thy rest, O my soul, for the Lord hath dealt bountifully with thee," &c. Psal. cxvi. 7-9.

We shall now shut up all with the application in some uses. Use I. We may learn hence how few have a good conscience. Faith is a rare thing, but a good conscience is much rarer. And here we may notice, 1. That the conscience which is dead and sleeping, is not a good conscience: every quiet and calm conscience is not a good one. Ye may dream over your days with the foolish virgins, and take rest in a pleasing delusion, and cry peace, peace, and yet the end of it will be worse than the beginning. A conscience that acts not at all, nor judges itself, is, as it were, no conscience; either ignorance hath blinded it, and keeps it in the dark, or wickedness hath stopped its mouth. You think your conscience good because it tells you few of your faults, it troubles you not; but that conscience must once speak, and do its office, it may be in a worse time for you. 2. It is not a good conscience that always speaks good, and absolves the man. God may condemn when it absolves. When ye walk according to false principles and grounds, and either take a wrong rule, or know not how to apply the rule to yourselves, shall God approve of false judgment? Your conscience is erring and deludes you. But, 1. The good conscience is not only a quiet conscience, but a quieted conscience. It not only hath peace, but peace after trouble. Ye then that have no peace, but what ye had all your days, it is but a mere fancy. The answer of a good conscience quiets the distempered mind, it comes by the sprinkling and washing of Christ's blood. He that hath peace on solid grounds with God, hath once taken up his enmity against him. 2. The good conscience hath been once an evil conscience, when it met with the command. The man has once been under the law, before he came to faith, and examined himself, and his conscience condemned him as not righteous, and out of Christ. Ye then that never examined your state, according to the perfect and holy law, and never judged yourselves, ye cannot believe in Jesus, and so can have no good conscience. 3. The good conscience flows nearest from faith answering the challenges of the law. Some have had sore distempers of conscience, and puddling exercises of terror. But how they were eased or quieted they cannot tell, but their spring-tide ebbed, and they bubbled no more. It went away at will, and did wear out with time. This is not a good conscience, that knows not distinctly the grounds of faith to oppose to the law's condemnation. Some turn to build cities with Cain, and pass the time pleasantly, or in some business, that they may beguile their challenges. But this is not the conscience that faith makes good. Now, set apart all these who do not examine themselves at all, nor judge themselves, but live in a golden dream, who have never been arraigned before God's tribunal, or summoned by his deputy to appear before his judgment-seat; and join unto these all persons who, judging themselves, take other rules of absolution than the word gives, who after trial absolve themselves, and withal those, who, condemning themselves, yet flee not unto this city of refuge, this blood of sprinkling, to get a solid answer in the word to all their challenges, and O how few are behind! It is but as the gleaning after the vintage. Nay, many believers have not a good conscience, though they have a right to it, because they settle not themselves on the grounds of faith, and go not on from faith to faith. There must be some sense of faith, before faith answer rightly, and give peace to the mind.

Use II. Ye see the way to get a good conscience. Believe much, and maintain your faith. It is as simple and poor a mistake as can befall a soul. Ye think because ye have not peace after your believing, therefore it was not unfeigned and true faith: and therefore ye will not believe, because ye cannot get peace. But believe that ye may have a good conscience. Would ye know your sins are pardoned before ye believe? How precious should faith be unto you, when by faith ye may not only overcome the world, but, as it were, overcome God in judging, that the soul may be justified when it is judged? Ye will not get challenges[477] answered by your own integrity and uprightness, or by your performing of duties. No, no, these cannot be sufficient grounds of your peace. Lay down the solid and satisfying grounds of faith, of imputed righteousness, and of salvation by Jesus Christ, and this shall be a foundation of lasting peace. Sense makes not a good conscience, there is much lightness and vanity in it, and the rule it proceeds by is changeable, but faith establishes the soul, and makes it not ashamed.

SERMON XIII.

1 Tim. i. 5.—"Now the end of the commandment," &c.

Fourthly, Faith purging the conscience purifies the heart (Acts xv. 9.), and hope also purifies the heart (1 John iii. 3.), which is nothing else but faith in the perfection and vigour of it. This includes, I. That the heart was unclean before faith. II. That faith cleanses it, and makes it pure. But "who can say, I have made my heart pure (Prov. xx. 9.), I am clean from my sin?" Is there any man's heart on this side of time, which lodges not many strange guests? In answer to this we may observe, that there is a legal purity, and a gospel purity. A legal purity is a sincere and full conformity to God's holy will and command, in thought, affections, inclinations, and actions, and, in this sense, who can say, I have made my hands clean? The old corruption sticks to the heart and cannot be thoroughly scraped out, there are many lurking holes for uncleanness to be hid in. Corruption is engrained in him, and it will not be the work of one day to change it. The whole head is sick, and the whole body full of sores. All the corners of the heart are full of filthiness and idols, and though the house be now sweeped and garnished, and all things look better in it, yet there are many hidden places of rottenness undiscovered, and it is the soul's continual exercise to purify itself as he is pure. But evangelical purity and cleanness is that which God reconciled in Christ takes to be so, and that which in Christ is accepted, and is a fount of his clean Spirit dwelling in the heart. The heart formerly was a troubled fountain, that sent out filthy streams, as a puddle. Corruption was the mud among the affections and thoughts, but now a pure heart is like a clear running water, clean and bright like crystal. Now this purity consists in the washing of regeneration, and sanctification by the Spirit of holiness. Jesus Christ came both by water and blood, 1 John v. 6. He came by blood, to sprinkle and purge the conscience, that it might have no more conscience of sins, Heb. x. 2, ix. 14. And he also came by water, that is, the washing and cleansing virtue of the Spirit of grace, to purge and cleanse us from all filthiness of the flesh and spirit. There are two things in sin that Jesus came to destroy, the guilt and offence of sin, whereby the sinner is bound over to condemnation, and lies under the Judge's curse, and the spot of sin, which also Christ came to destroy. He did both in his own person, and he is to perfect this in us personally, who were judicially reckoned one with him, Rom. vi. 3-12, 1 John iii. 5. Now Jesus Christ hath come with blood to sprinkle the conscience from dead works, and give it a good answer to the challenges of the law, and an ill conscience. And he hath come likewise with water, to wash and cleanse us from the spots, and filth, and power of sin. The first removes the guilt, the latter removes the filth of sin, and both are done by faith, which is our victory over the world, and this is the way how faith overcomes the world by the water and blood. 1 John v. 4-6. The blood of Jesus Christ is holden by faith with a twofold virtue of cleansing, from the guilt, and from the filth of sin, and thus cleanses us from all unrighteousness, 1 John i. 7. According to the promise of the covenant (Ezek. xxxvi. 25, 26.), the application of the blood of sprinkling hath two effects. One is for justification, "ye shall be clean," another is, "from all your filthiness and idols will I cleanse you," that is sanctification. I. Now this purity consists in this, that the pure heart regards not iniquity in the inward man, nor delights in sin, Psal. lxvi. 18. He sets not up his idols in God's place, Ezek. xxxvi. 25. The cleansing of the heart is from idols. Although he cannot get himself purified as Christ is pure, and though iniquity be in his heart, yet he regards it not. He looks not upon it as a guest approven and accepted. Sin may be an intruding guest, but sin is not welcomed with all his heart. He dare not take that pleasure in sin that another man would do. He hath a worm that eats up his pleasure when he departs from God, or his thoughts go a-whoring from him. The unbelieving man's heart is a house full of idols, but the entry of faith by God's Spirit makes their Dagon to fall. But, II. The pure heart hath much of the filthiness taken away that filled it before, and so it is denominated from the best part. It is washed and cleansed from a sea of corruption, and the body of sin that did reign within the heart was formerly like an impure fountain, that sent out nothing but rotten stinking waters. Unto him were all things unclean, for his heart and conscience was defiled, Tit. i. 15. Nothing was pure to him, it ran continually in a stream of unclean thoughts and affections. But now he is purified, and to the believer "all things are pure:" the ordinary strain and current of his thoughts and affections run more clearly free of the earthly quality they had, more sublimated, more spiritualized, and he is named by that. Though, it may be, temptation may trouble the fountain, and make it run unclean and earthly, yet it will settle again, and come into its own posture, and the dreg fall to the bottom, and the clean water of the Spirit be the predominant. But a standing puddle will run foul as long as it runs, corruption goes through all. It is not a corner of the heart, but the whole heart.

III. A pure heart is like a running fountain, if it be defiled, it is always casting out the filth, and is about returning to a right state. But an impure heart is like a standing puddle that keeps all it gets. If by temptation the pure heart and affections be stirred, and the filth that is in the bottom come up to the brim, it hath no rest nor peace in that condition, but works it out again, and it hath this advantage, that it is purer and clearer after troubling nor[478] it was before. For much of the filth would run out that had been lying quiet before. But an impure heart keeps all, and vents none. If ye trouble it, ye will raise an ill smell, and when it settles, it falls but to the bottom again, and there is as much to work upon the next time. In a word, the believer when he sins, and his heart goes wrong, he weeps over his heart, and has no peace till it be cleansed. He washes in the fountain of Christ's blood. When a natural transgression gets up, he sets himself against it and the root of it both, and bears down the original corruption, which is the fountain of all sin (Psal. li. 5), and at every descent he brings away something of that puddle. He is upon the growing hand by the exercise of faith and repentance. Look upon him after he has seen and been sensible of his sins, and ye would say it is not the man ye saw. He hates sin more than he did formerly. We also notice,

IV. That purity is sincerity and uprightness (James iv. 8), "Purify your hearts, ye double minded." Hypocrisy is filthiness and abominable to God.

He then is a sincere man, that hath any honesty of heart toward God. When his actions are not right, his heart doth not approve them, Rom. vii. When he cannot come up to his duty, his desire comes before performance. A sincere man hath a respect to all God's commandments.

V. The pure man is still purifying himself "even as God is pure." As he who hath called him is holy, so he is holy in all manner of conversation. He never thinks he is clean enough, and so he aspires after greater purity, and is named a saint, rather from his aim and endeavour, than from his attainment. He cries, unclean, unclean, am I, and holy, holy, Lord God, art thou. He hath taken up his lodging near the opened fountain, and dwells there, never to remove thence, till he have his robes clean and white in the blood of the Lamb. No unclean thing can enter into heaven, and he is trimming himself against that day, and setting apart all superfluity of naughtiness, and filthiness, and still all his righteousness is as menstruous rags. He is cleansing his house, every day casting out something, searching out all the corners of it, lest the unclean thing, and the Babylonish garment be hid. His pattern is to walk even as Christ walked, 1 John ii. 6.

Now faith and a good conscience have influence on this purifying the heart. I. Because faith lays hold upon the cleansing virtue of Christ's blood. It applies Jesus Christ who came by water and blood, and his blood purges the conscience from dead works, to serve the living God. The blood that was offered up by the eternal Spirit, of how great virtue must it be when applied to the heart and conscience, Heb. ix. 14. No wonder it makes that like wool which was formerly like scarlet. Now faith in Jesus Christ applies that blood. It is the very hand that sprinkles it. Faith takes up house beside the opened fountain, and dwells there. Faith takes Jesus for sanctification as well as justification, 1 Cor. i. 30. Faith looks upon a judicial union with Christ crucified, and sees his perfect offering once offered to sanctify all, and therefore makes continual applications with David, "Purge me with hyssop, and I shall be clean, wash me, and I shall be whiter than the snow." II. Faith purifies the heart, because it lays hold on the promises, and makes use of the word, 2 Cor. vii. 1. Faith having such promises, cleanses the man from all filthiness of the flesh and spirit.

The proper order of faith is the word, and the word is the truth by which we are sanctified and made clean, John xvii. 17. There are many precious promises of sanctification and holiness, and faith draws the virtue of purifying the heart out of the promises, and applies the promise to his impure heart, and it is purged. III. Faith purifies the heart also by provocation and upstirring, in as far as it gives the answer of a good conscience. For the man who hath gotten a solid answer to all his objections in Christ's blood, and hath the continual feast of joy and peace in believing, O how will he abhor himself, and repent in dust and in ashes! Faith takes up God's holiness and purity, and loathes itself with Job, and cries, unclean. The believer will thus reason and conclude,—shall I any more delight and live in sin, since I am dead unto it by Jesus Christ? Rom. vi. 1, 2. He falls in with the beauties of holiness, and so cannot abide his own. Faith begets hope, and hope purifies the heart. Shall then the man who expects to see God, and be a citizen of the new Jerusalem, where no unclean thing can enter, shall he walk in his former lusts, like the wicked world, and not make himself ready for the continuing city he goes to, and adorn himself for the company of the blessed God and angels?

Let us now conclude, by applying all which hath been said in some uses. Use I. We may see from what hath been hinted, how little faith is among you. Faith purifies the heart, but if ye examine yourselves, your hearts will be found unclean, and such as the Holy Ghost cannot dwell in. The temple in which God's Holy Spirit resides must touch no unclean thing, 2 Cor. vi. 16, 17. Are not many men's corruptions rank and lively? Unclean hands are an infallible demonstration of an unclean heart, James iv. 8. These things which proceed out of the heart may teach you what is within the heart. The streams may let you know what is in the fountain Mark vii. 15-22, James iii. 11, 12. What need ye any more proof of yourselves? Sinners, look to your hands, and your outward man, and learn from them to know your hearts. These things proceed out of the heart and defile the whole man. The profanity of the most part of men's practices, cursing and swearing &c., is a bitter stream that cannot proceed from a good fountain. It is a wonder how the world satisfy themselves with a dream of faith. What influence hath your faith had upon your heart and conversation? Are ye not as earthly and worldly as ever, as unclean as ever? Ye think your hearts good, but if your conversation be not good, your hearts are not good. Will any person think his sins are pardoned, when he wallows in them? Do they believe they shall obtain the remission of these sins they are not purging themselves from? No, no, the blood and water must go together and the Spirit's sanctifying with Christ's justifying.

Use II. The children of God may hence gather the ground and reason of their little progress in sanctification. Why are your hearts so unclean, and why is there so much corruption yet living in your thoughts and affections, that it cannot keep within the heart, but, as a full fountain, must run out in streams of external actions? It is even this, ye do not believe much, and though this be told you, yet ye will not believe it; ye take ways of your own to purge out your corruptions, and it will not do. All your resolutions, prayers, sad experiences, &c., are of no more virtue than the blood of bulls and goats. Ye must then apply the blood of the Son of God, which was offered up by the eternal Spirit. It is but a poor fancy to suspend believing till ye see a pure heart. How shall ye get a pure heart? Is it not folly to forbear planting till ye see fruits, or to pluck up your tree because it bears not the first day? Abide in Christ, and ye shall bring forth much fruit. Believe, and believe, and believe again, till faith be answered by a good conscience, till that sweet echo be given unto the Lord's comforting voice, "Thy sins, which are many, are forgiven thee." Be much in laying hold upon the precious promises, and then your heart shall fall out of love with this present evil world, and shall relish spiritual things. But who will believe this report? Ye go away convinced that this is the only way to purify yourselves, and yet ye continue puddling in your old way. May God persuade your hearts to do better.

SERMON XIV.

1 Tim. i. 5.—"Now the end of the commandment," &c.

Fifthly, Faith purging the conscience, and purifying the heart, works by love. Love is the fruit of faith. Love is the stream that flows out of a pure heart and a good conscience. By love, we mean principally love to God, or Jesus Christ, and then love to the saints next to our Saviour. This is often mentioned in scripture, "Hope maketh not ashamed, (Rom. v. 5) because the love of God is shed abroad in your hearts by the Holy Ghost." This love is the consequence of the peace which a justified man obtains by faith, Rom. v. 1, 2; 2 Cor. v. 14. The constraining love of Christ flows from this ground, that a man judges Christ to have died for him, from faith's taking up of Christ in that noble expression of his love, (John v. 40, 42.) "And ye will not come unto me that ye may have life. I know you, that ye have not the love of God in you." Faith works by love. Love is faith's hand put out in action for Christ, and as the mind commands the outward man, whether it will or not, so doth faith command love, Eph. iii. 17. The rooting and building up in love is a fruit of Christ's dwelling in the heart by faith. Love is the branch that grows in faith's root. These are often joined together, and comprehend the substance of the law and gospel, 1 Tim. i. 14, 2 Tim. i. 13. Faith fulfils the obedience to the gospel, and love is the fulfilling of the whole law, (Rom. xiii. 10) so that faith leads a man back again to the command, that he fled to faith from. Faith hath reconciled them and taken up the difference. We shall then show how faith and a good conscience and a pure heart contribute to love.

First, Faith is the eye and sense of the soul to take up Jesus Christ. Nothing is loved but as it is known and apprehended to be good. The affections of themselves are blind, and cannot go forth but as led by the direction of faith. Faith is the mind to present love's object. The world sees no beauty nor form in the commands, that they should desire them. Even Jesus Christ himself is but foolishness to a natural mind, he neither knows his need of him, nor Christ's suitableness to his need. But faith is the first opening of the eyes, when we are turned from darkness to light, and from the power of sin and Satan unto God, Acts xxvi. 18. Christ becomes the believer's wisdom, righteousness, sanctification, and redemption, 1 Cor. i. 30. The day spring from on high visits them who sit in darkness, to guide their feet in the way of peace, Luke i. 78, 79. The light of the knowledge of the glory of God shining in the face of the Sun of righteousness, doth arise and shine into their hearts. The man sees himself in a dangerous condition, and says, Oh I where am I? And faith discovers, on the other hand, all things in Christ Jesus suitable to such a case. He sees nothing but vanity, emptiness, and misery, sin, and condemnation in the creature, he sees grace, mercy, holiness, righteousness and free salvation in Christ. Set these beside one another, and judge ye if the soul cannot choose to run out in affection and longing desire. Oh! says he, to be one with him. Faith presents all the motives and attractives of the heart, and then there needs no more to make it love. Faith discovers a man's self unto himself, and lets him see all misery within, complete woe within doors, and it holds forth bread without the ports[479] for the saint, and salvation for the lost. It brings in an amiable person, who is fairer than the children of men, who is all love, and hath no spot in him. Is it not a sweet word, a Redeemer to captives, a Saviour to sinners? And will not the soul rise up, and go forth out of itself? And will it not choose to flit[480] unto him who is the desire of all nations? Will it not go unto him for food and clothing? Love then is the soul's journey and motion towards Jesus, whom faith hath brought in such a good report of. But,

Secondly. When faith hath given the answer of a good conscience, and brought Jesus nearer hand to the soul, or the soul nearer unto him, then love is stronger, and grows like a fire that many waters cannot quench. It is like jealousy, that is cruel as the grave, many floods cannot drown it. Union is the ground of love, union in nature, or sympathy, or likeness, is the ground of affection. According as faith brings Christ nearer to the heart, the flame increases. All things are desired and loved as good, but more desired, as not only good in themselves, but good unto us. Gold in the Indies will not much move the heart, but bring it hither, and ye shall see who loves it. The first act of faith puts a man in great need of a Saviour, and discovers a possibility of redemption through Jesus, and in so far he is loved. But when once faith has gone that length as to make a good conscience, and to calm and silence the woes of a troubled mind, by the actual application of that desired possible redemption, and when it can particularly apply the common salvation, O then what burning affection! "Who is a God like unto thee, who pardoneth iniquity, and passest by the transgression of his heritage, because he delights in mercy?" "Whom have I in heaven but thee? and there is none upon earth that I desire besides thee." "I will love the Lord, because he hath heard my voice, I will call upon him so long as I live," as if it had never loved before. They will love much to whom much is forgiven. Love, without such a faith, is full of jealousies and suspicions, but when faith hath brought in Christ to dwell in the heart, then it is rooted and built up in love, (Eph. iii. 17) and then perfect love casts out fear, 1 John iv. 18. Love before such an assurance, is but a tormenting love, and hath much fear in it, saying, "Oh I may want him, and then I will be more miserable than if I had not known him." But faith, giving the answer of a good conscience, casts out horror and fear, and then perfects love, and the soul then closes with Christ as a Mediator and friend, and closes with God as a merciful Father, now reconciled unto him through Christ, and not any more as a stern or severe Judge. But,

Thirdly. When faith hath purified the heart, and cleansed the affections, then the soul burns with a purer flame of affection and zeal to God, and is, as it were, delivered from the earthly weight put upon it. When the heart is purified, love is like the flame, whereas, if he be not so purged, there may be some heat and fire latent in the ashes, covered with corruption. But a pure heart is a spiritual heart, and minds spiritual things, (Col. iii. 1) and it is a heart going back unto its own place, Christ hath touched it with his own heart, and with his salvation, and it looks aye[481] sure to him in the heavens. The love of the world is inconsistent with the love of the Father, 1 John ii. 15. The love of the world plucks the heart downward, and the lusts of the flesh are so many weights upon the believer, that he can not mount up in a spiritual cloud of divine affection to Jesus Christ. But the pure and spiritual heart is now more refined, and delivered from these impediments, and it is like a pure lamp of oil burning upward. When a man's heart is engaged to any thing of this world, love cannot be perfect. For love is a man's master, and no man can serve two masters.

SERMON XV.

Matt. vi. 33.—"But seek ye first the kingdom of God and his righteousness," &c.

This is a part of Christ's long sermon. He is dissuading his disciples and the people from carnal carefulness and worldly mindedness. The sermon holds out the Christian's diverse aspects towards spiritual and external things. What is the Christian's disposition in regard to the world, how should he look upon food, raiment, and all things necessary in this life? "Be careful for nothing." "Take no thought for your life, what ye shall eat, or drink," &c. "Seek them not as your chief good." But what is his disposition towards spiritual and eternal things, and how ought ye to look upon them? "Seek them, set your heart upon them, look upon them as your treasure, and where your treasure is, let your heart be there also." So then you see here two callings and employments of a man in the world,—two universal callings that comprehend all men, one natural to us, and unlawful, the other divine, and lawful, the one paganish, the other Christian. What is the employment of all men out of Christ? There are many different callings and employments among men. One spends his time and thoughts one way, and another another way, but all of them agree in one general, whatever they are: Their heart is here. The thoughts they have are bounded and circumscribed in this present world. They are careful for nothing else but what concerns their back and belly,[482] or their name and credit. Take the best of them, whose employment seems most abstracted from the common affairs and distractions among men, yet their affections run no higher than this present world. On the other hand, what should be the exercise and employment of a Christian? It is even this, whatever he be, or whatever his occupation be among men, he drives a higher trade with heaven, that should take him up. The world gets but his spare hours. He is upon a more noble and high project. He aspires after a kingdom. His heart is above where Christ is, and where his treasure is. And these things exhaust his affections and pains. Christ Jesus once takes the man's heart off these baser things, that are not worthy of an immortal spirit, let be[483] a spirit who is a partaker of a divine nature. But because the creature cannot be satisfied within itself, its happiness depends upon something without itself, (and this speaks out the vanity of the creature, and something of God, that is peculiar to him, to be self sufficient,) therefore Christ changes the object of the heart, and fixes the spirit upon a nobler and divine exercise. Since the spirit of a man cannot abide within doors without starving, it must run out upon something, therefore Jesus Christ hath described its bounds and way, its end and period. Before, a man sought many things, because not one was satisfying, that the want of one might be supplied by another; and therefore he was never near the borders of contentment and happiness, because still a thousand things are wanting. But now, Christ puts the soul upon a satisfying and self sufficient object. And here the streams of affection may run in one current, and need not divide or go contrary ways.

First: We have here then the Christian's calling and employment in this world, opposed to the carefulness and worldly mindedness of the men of this world, "Seek ye the kingdom of God." *Secondly*: His encouragement and success in two things, one is expressed, the other implied. That which is expressed, is seeking the kingdom of God, of grace and glory. If ye seek this kingdom, all temporal things shall be laid to your hand, all these things that ye need "shall be added unto you." The other imported is, ye shall get the kingdom who seek it. For the words, "added unto you," suppose the first and principal intent to be gotten. Then the Christian's success and encouragement is this, ye shall have the thing ye seek and more also. It was said to Solomon, "Because thou hast sought wisdom, therefore thou shalt get all other things." Because, O Christian, thou sought the kingdom of God, and not this present world which Satan is prince of, therefore thou shalt get according to thy word, and thou shalt also get what thou asked not, 1 Kings iii. 11-13. He hath success in the main business, and there is a superplus besides, some accession to his portion, that comes of will, so to speak. The kingdom of God in the New Testament is sometimes restricted to the elect, the word of the gospel, and the administration of it, by the Spirit of grace in the hearts of his people. This is frequently called "the kingdom of heaven," and "of God," Matth. xiii. 33. Sometimes the kingdom of God is taken for the state of grace, a new principle of spiritual life, that grows up to the perfect day, and this kingdom is within us, Luke xvii. 21. It is taken also for heaven, the kingdom of glory, Luke xxii. 16. Both these must be sought after, (Luke xii. 31.) and received, (Luke xviii. 17.) and must suffer violence, Matth. xi. 12. The righteousness thereof may be taken for the righteousness of God by faith, Rom. x. 3, chap. iii. 21, 22, 2 Cor. v. 21, Rom. iv. 11, 13, Rom. ix. 30, chap. x. 6, Heb. xi. 7, Phil. iii. 9.

We would observe here: I. That the Christian his name and occupation is to be a wanter and a seeker. II. The great exercise and employment he should have in this world, that which should swallow up his affections, thoughts, and endeavours, should be the kingdom of God and his righteousness, which is clearly expressed in three things: 1. His first and chief care should be to be at peace with God, and to be adorned with Christ's righteousness; 2. To have the kingdom of God within him, a throne of judgment erected for Christ to rule the whole man, by his Spirit according to the word; 3. To be made an heir here, and a possessor hereafter, of the everlasting kingdom of glory; 4. No man can either be a subject of God's gracious kingdom here, or his glorious kingdom hereafter, without the imputed righteousness of the Son of God, and whoever seeks righteousness must also seek the kingdom of God. These are joined together, and there is a great opposition between seeking of the world, and seeking grace and glory. Whoever is careful in these things cannot be diligent here. But rather seek the kingdom of God (Luke xii. 31) also implies, 5. That whatever a man be, or his profession be, except he seek this way of righteousness, and yield himself unto God's kingdom of grace, and unless Christ rule in him, he is but a pagan, or infidel Gentile, in God's account. We return to the first of these, namely:

1st. That the Christian is a seeker. This is the ordinary description of a child of God, Psal. xxiv. 6, Psal. xxvii. 8. Many, at this time, call themselves Seekers.[484] They profess they seek a true church, and seek ordinances purely dispensed, but find none. But the child of God, the good Christian that seeks according to Christ's appointment, seeks not these things as if they were not, but he seeks God in ordinances, he seeks Christ in the church, he seeks grace and glory, honour and immortality, and eternal life. He is in the church, he hath the ordinances rightly administered, yet he wants the most part, till he find Jesus Christ in all these. Many seek corn, wine, or any worldly good thing, saying, "Who will show us any good?" Fie upon such a lax and indifferent spirit, that hath no discretion or sense of things that are good, that sees not one thing needful, and no more good than is necessary. But the child of God is a seeker different from these also, he seeks the favour and countenance of God, Psal. iv. 6, 7. He seeks wisdom above all things, Prov. ii. 4. He seeks but one good thing, because there is but one good thing necessary. The seeking Christian is a wanter, one that hath nothing, and finds it so. He wants, and knows he wants, else he would never seek. What wants he? Nay, rather ask, what hath he? It may soon be told what he hath, but it is hard to tell what he wants. Look what he hath, and ye find little or nothing, and therefore ye may conclude he wants all things. The text tells what he wants: (1) He wants righteousness; (2) He wants grace; (3) He wants glory, and hath no right to it. Men seek not what they carry from the womb. Therefore all men have come into the world with three great wants. (1.) Ye want righteousness. Ye cannot stand before God in the terms of strict justice. There is nothing ye have, or can do, but it is a menstruous cloth, Isa. lxiv. 6. All your religion and prayers will never commend you to God's holy justice. The scripture hath passed this sentence upon you all, "There is none righteous, no not one," Rom. iii. 10. The righteousness that the law of God requires is perfect, and complete, and exact. Either lay down the whole sum, or if it want a farthing it is no payment. Keep all the nine commands, but if ye break the tenth the nine will not suffice. Now all of you have sinned and corrupted your ways, and it is impossible to make up the want. As the redemption of the soul is precious and ceases for ever, so the broken and dyvour[485] man having become a bankrupt, shall never make up or pay his debt to all eternity. He hath once broken the command, and all your keeping afterwards will not stand for the obedience ye should always have given to it. Therefore sinners of the posterity of Adam, and wretched men by nature, see this great want and impossibility to recover it in yourselves. (2.) Ye likewise want all grace by nature. There is no delusion more ordinary than this, that the world thinks grace is very common. But believe it, Sirs, that all men came from the womb without grace, get it as ye will. Look what the scripture speaks of the whole race of Adam, "There is no fear of God before their eyes," Rom. iii. 18. They are without Christ, without hope, and without God in the world, aliens from the covenants of promise, Eph. ii. 1-3, 12. Let grace be as common as can be, yet all of you once wanted it. Ye have it not by birth, nor by education, nor by baptism. Ye think perhaps a baptized soul cannot be graceless, but know it for a truth that ye have neither legal righteousness nor evangelical holiness. All of you have wofully fallen from righteousness, and therefore ye lie, with Adam's posterity, without hope in the world Grace and truth must come from above by Jesus Christ Grace and glory are the gifts of God. (3.) The sinner also comes short of the glory of God, Rom. iii. 23. All sinners are born heirs of hell and wrath, without the hope of happiness. There is none born with a title to the kingdom of heaven, or any right to it. Man in his fall lost his right to eternal life and immortality, and hath purchased a doleful right to the Lord's wrath and to hell fire. Ye think it strange that any christened or baptized person should be damned, but the scripture knows no difference. "Neither circumcision nor uncircumcision availeth any thing, but a new creature, and faith which worketh by love." Neither to be a member of the visible church nor a pagan avails any thing, "for all have sinned and come short of the glory of God." Now what have ye since ye want righteousness? Ye want grace and ye want glory, and in the place of these ye have unrighteousness, all sin, all God's curses and wrath, and this makes up complete misery. In a word, ye want God and Christ, and this is all, and enough for all, Eph. ii. 12. Ye have, by nature, more sibness[486] with Satan, and nearer relation to him, than to God, and if ye want God, what can ye have beside? Your abundance is want. As all things are theirs who are Christ's, so nothing is theirs who are not God's. In short, there is not in all the creation such a miserable creature as man, whom God hath magnified and exalted above the angels, and the rest of the works of his hands. Now all men want these, but no man knows this but the Christian, whose eyes Christ hath opened, and to whom he hath given eye salve. Laodicea was blind and saw not, but she thought she was rich enough, when she had nothing, Rev. iii. 17, 18. The man, who will discourse well on all the miseries of this life, and human infirmities, may be ignorant of these things. There is no man but knows some want. But what is it he misses? Nothing but what concerns his present being and well being in this world, and so the world may supply it. But the Christian wants something this vain world will not make up. "Whom have I in heaven but thee? And there is none upon the earth I desire beside thee," says the soul that hath found God. And whom want I in heaven but thee? (Psal. lxxiii. 25, 26) says the soul that seeks God. He wants God's favour, and the light of his reconciled countenance, Psal. iv. 6. If ye ask him, what seek ye, what want ye in all the world? He answers, "And now. Lord, what wait I for?" My heart and "my hope is in thee," Psal. xxxix. 7. None needed ask at Mary, "Whom seekest thou?" Any body that knows her, knows her want. It is he, the Christ Jesus, and she thinks all the world should want him, and seek him with her, and thinks no body should be ignorant of him; for she speaks to the gardener, as if there had been no other in the world, John xx. 15. But,

2dly. His wants put him to seeking, to diligence. He misses something, and O it is a great something, infinitely more than he is worth in the world! He wants being and well being. He thinks himself as good as lost, and he comes at length to some point of resolution, with the lepers of Samaria, (2 Kings vii. 3, 4.) "Why sit we here till we die? If we enter into the city there is famine, if we sit still we perish, if we go out we may find bread." And so the poor soul, with Mordecai and Esther, comes to this conclusion, "If I perish, I perish;" nothing but perishing as I am, I will go and seek salvation in Jesus Christ, and it may be I will find it. Who knows but he may turn again? Resolution is born a man at first, a giant. It goes out to the utmost border of want the first day. Wanting makes desire, and desire, attended with some hope, makes up resolution and purpose, and when the soul is thus principled, then in the third room,[487] it comes forth to action. Desire and hope give legs to the soul for the journey, and now the wanting Christian ye shall find with his hand in every good turn, his feet in every ordinance. Ye shall find him praying, reading, and hearing. It is true, resolution is born a man, and practice is born but a child, and scarcely will come up in many years to the stature of resolution. Always[488] diligence and violence is the qualification of his practice, (Heb. xi. 6, Matth. xi. 12) and this is written upon his using of means, "How love I the Lord! I am sick of love." The Christian's diligence in the use of means proclaims his earnest desire to obtain, whereas many a man's practice speaks but a coldrife and indifferent spirit. That is a neutral who cares not whether he obtain or miss. Some Christians have some missings of God, and spiritual things, but alas! their want, and sight of want, makes them twice miserable, because it puts not their hand to action. The slothful and sluggard's desire slays him, because his hands refuse to labour, Prov. xxi. 25. O! but he finds many difficulties in the way. Though he have half a wish, or a raw[489] desire after Christ, yet it never comes farther than a conditional wish. A beggar may wish to be a king. He comes to no purpose in it and therefore his way is called a hedge of thorns. Whereas a seeking Christian finds a plain path where he goes, Prov. xv. 19. The sluggard says, "There is a lion in the way, and a lion in the streets." He concludes upon the means and duties of religion before ever he try them, Prov. xxii. 13, Prov. xix. 24. How lazy is he! He will not bring his hand out of his bosom, when he hath put it in. Thus the lazy and secure Christian is a brother to a great waster, his desire consumes him. He hath no more religion than a spunk[490] of desire; and he sits down with this spark of his own kindling, and the life of religion thrives not upon his hand, Prov. xviii. 9, 12. His seeking must have violence with it, Matth. xi. 12. But we may also observe concerning the Christian, that he is,

3dly. Defined on this side of time as a seeker. In heaven he is an enjoyer, and he seeks no more; for how can the ox low over his fodder? He sits down to eat the fruit and sweat of his labour, and well may he triumphantly say, as the ancient philosopher said, "I have found, I have found."[491] But here he is a seeker still. Whatever he miss, he is still a seeker, and whatever he find, he is yet a seeker. He is named not from his finding, but his seeking, not from his enjoyment or attainment, but from his endeavour and aim. Though he find righteousness in Jesus, and remission of sins, yet he is a seeker of grace; though he be justified, yet he seeks holiness. There are many who would seek no more of God than pardon of sin. Let him deliver them from hell, and they will trouble God with no more requests. Doth not some of your own consciences speak, that ye would seek no more from Christ than to be saved from an ill hour, and to be found in him; whereas Paul was not content with this, but made an holy gradation, as we read, Philip iii. 8, &c. He desired to know the power of Christ's resurrection, and to be made conformable to him by any means; and now, when he is found in Christ, and justified, he counts not himself well, or perfect and complete, or to have attained that which he struggled earnestly for. Would not many be content with a Saviour, but they love not to hear of a king to rule over them, nor of his laws to regulate their lives by? They love an imputed holiness, as well as righteousness. But the true seeker seeks grace within him. Though he be justified, or freed from guilt and condemnation, and have the righteousness of Christ to cover him, and though he should never come into condemnation for sin, yet he seeks the death and destruction of it in his soul, and the life of holiness implanted and perfected in his inward man. Though he is sure of heaven, yet he would have God's image upon his spirit, and whole man.

4thly. Whatever degree of grace he have or attain, yet he is still a wanter, and still a seeker. He counts not himself to have attained, or to be already perfect, but presses forward to gain the mark and prize of God's high calling, Phil. iii. 13, 14. He stands at no pitch, but forgets what is behind, and overlooks it, he thinks it not worthy to come in reckoning. There is still so much before his hand, that he apprehends it to be lost time to reckon what is passed. His aim is to perfect holiness in the fear of God. He endeavours to be holy as God is holy, who is the completest pattern of unspotted purity and uprightness, and to be holy in all manner of conversation. He goes from strength to strength, till he appear blameless before God; he seeks grace for grace, Psal. lxxxiv. 5-8. And truly the man who seeks the exact copy or pattern, Jesus Christ, who is gone before his people into heaven, and he who knows the spiritual command in all its dimensions, he will not say "I have found," but will still want more than he hath, and seek what he wants. There are some professors who have attained some pitch and degree, as it were, the first day, and never advance further. They have gotten a gift of prayer, some way of discharging duties, some degree in profession, and they want no more. Look on them some years after, and ye would say, they have sought no more. And truly he who seeks no more shall never be able to keep what he hath already, as a fire must soon die away if ye add not new fuel to it. Christians are not green in old age, because they have come to a pitch in their religion, and stand there. No, religion should not come to its stature hereaway.[492] This is but the time of its minority. Grace should be still on the growing hand. The grace of God is but a child here. Heaven and eternity make up the man. Glory is the man, who was once the child grace.

5thly. The good Christian is still a seeker till Christ be all in all, till he apprehend that for which he is apprehended. As long as he is in this world he is a seeker. Whereof, ye will say? Not only of more grace here, but of glory hereafter. Here he hath no continuing city, but he seeks one to come, Heb. xiii. 14. He is a pilgrim on earth, embracing the promises afar off, and seeking his country, even heaven itself, Heb. xi. 13, &c. All your present enjoyments in this world, your own houses and lands, would not make you think yourselves at home, if ye were Christians at the heart. Ye would miss consolation, ye would want happiness in the affluence of all created things. And therefore, Christians, do ye want nothing when all things go according to your mind? Is there no hole in your heart that a world cannot fill up? This is not well. Ye ought to seek a city, while ye are in your own country, and ye should never think yourselves at home till ye be in heaven. The Christian gets some taste of the fruits of the land, some clusters in the wilderness and house of his pilgrimage, and this makes him long to be there. This inflames the soul's desire, and turns it all in motion to seek that which was so sweet. If hope be so sweet, what shall the thing possessed be? If a grape brought a savour and taste so refreshful, what must the grapes plucked from the tree of life be, and the rivers of pleasures, which are at God's right hand, for evermore be? Sit not down then, Christians, upon your enjoyments, whether they be worldly or spiritual, but aspire to high things.

SERMON XVI.

Matth. vi. 33.—"But seek ye first the kingdom of God," &c.

II. The Christian's chief employment should be to seek the kingdom of God, and the righteousness thereof. "Seek first," &c. Upon this he should first and chiefly spend his thoughts, and affections, and pains. We comprehend it in three things. *First*, He should seek to be clothed upon with Christ's righteousness, and this ought to take up all his spirit. This is the first care and the chief concern. Did not this righteousness weigh much with Paul, when he counted all things but loss and dung, that he might be found in Christ, not having his own righteousness, but the righteousness which is by faith in Jesus Christ? Phil. iii. 8, 9. Now this righteousness is of more concernment than all the world beside. For it is God's righteousness, (Rom. x. 3, 4; 2 Cor. v. 21.) and this holds out a threefold excellence in it. (1.) It is God's righteousness, because he alone devised it, and found it out. All the world could not have imagined a way possible to save lost mankind, or ever one sinner of that wretched number. Satisfaction to justice was needful, and there was none righteous among Adam's posterity. But here God himself in his everlasting counsel hath found it out, and all hath flowed from his love. The mission of Jesus Christ to be the propitiation for our sins, comes from this blessed fountain, 1 John iv. 9, 10; Rom. iii. 24, 25. God hath been framing this righteousness from all eternity, and even this world seems to be made for this end. All God's dispensation with Adam, his making a covenant of works with him, his mutability and liableness to fall, and so governing all things in his holy providence that he should fall from his own righteousness, and involve all his posterity in the same condemnation with himself,—all this seems to be in respect of God's intention and purpose, even ordained for this end, that the righteousness of Jesus Christ might be commended to you, far more than all the dispensation of the law upon Sinai, more than the curse and the command, the thunder and the lightning. The very condemnation of the scripture was all in God's own mind and revealed will also, as the means appointed to lead sinners to this righteousness, Rom. x. 4. Therefore, how precious should that be to us, that God keeps and preserves the world for?

(2.) By this righteousness alone, we can stand before God, and therefore it is termed God's righteousness; and is not this enough to make it lovely in the eyes of all men? This is the righteousness without the law, though it was witnessed both by the law and the prophets. This is the only righteousness that justifies, when all men are found guilty before God, Rom. iii. 19, &c. Now, what is it in this world can profit you, if ye want this? Condescend[493] upon all your pleasures and heart-wishes, let you have them all, and now, poor soul, pray what hast thou? Though thou hast gained the world, thou losest thy soul, that thou should use the world with? Let you then get what you so eagerly pursue in the world, what will ye do when your soul is required by the hand of justice? "Then whose shall these things be?" Luke xii. 20, 21. By all these things, a man neither knows love nor hatred, as Solomon speaks of external enjoyments, Eccles. ix. 1. But hear the way, O men! how ye may stand before God; here it is only. Will it profit you to enjoy the world, and bless God? And when all these things leave you, and ye leave them, what will ye do,—for riches will not go to the grave with you? All that is here cannot help you in that day, when ye must stand before the Judge of all flesh. If a man be not found in Christ he is gone, and if he be found in him, then the destroying angel passes by, death hath a commission to do him good, God is become his friend in Jesus. If ye could walk never so blamelessly in this world, all this will not come as righteousness in God's sight, nor stand before him. It is only the righteousness of Christ that can be a covering to sinners. But,

(3.) This is God's righteousness, because it is the righteousness of Christ who is truly God, and so it is divine. This is the most excellent piece in all the creation, that comes from Jesus Christ his life, death, and resurrection. And let all men's inherent holiness blush here and be ashamed. Let all your prayers, good wishes, your religious obedience be ashamed, let them evanish as the stars before the sun. The righteousness of Christ is the bright sun that makes all the dim sparkles of nature, civil honesty, and even religious education, disappear. Let even angels blush before him, for they are not clean in his sight, but may be charged with folly. Innocent Adam was also a glorious creature, but the second Adam, the life-giving Spirit and the Lord from heaven, hath an infinitely transcendent and supereminent excellency and prerogative beyond him, and all the creation of God. Look then upon this Jesus how he is described, as the "brightness of the Father's glory and the express image of his person," (Heb. i. 1-3; Col. i. 15, &c.) and wonder that such a glorious one should become our righteousness, that he should take our sins upon him, (2 Cor. v. 21; 1 Pet. ii. 24) and make over his righteousness to us. This is the righteousness of the saints in heaven, Rev. xix. 8. This is the glory of the spirits of just men made perfect. Think ye, my friends, that the glorious saints shall wear their own holiness upon their outside in heaven? No, no, the righteousness of Christ shall cover them, and that shall be the upper-garment that all the host of heaven must glory in. Now this is the thing that the child newborn, if he had the use of reason, should first cry for, before he ever get the breast, to be reconciled to God in Christ. Would ye then spend your time and thoughts upon other things, if ye knew what need ye have of his righteousness, and how suitable it were to your need? Should not the beggar seek food and clothing? Should not the sick man seek health, and the poor man riches? Here they are all in Christ's righteousness. Ye are under the curse of God. This righteousness redeems from the curse. Ye are sinners, and none of you righteous, no not one. But Christ was made sin for us, that we might be made the righteousness of God in him. O sinners, wonder at the change! Hath Christ taken on your sins, that his righteousness might become yours, and will ye not do so much as seek it? But many a man beguiles his own soul, and thinks he seeks this righteousness in the gospel. Therefore ye would know what it is to seek his righteousness. If ye seek it, ye want your own righteousness. And who of you have come this length, to judge yourselves that ye be not judged? It is a great difficulty to convince the multitude of sin. That general notion, that we are all sinners, is but the delusion that many souls perish in. Never any will deny themselves to seek another righteousness, till they be beaten and driven out of their own. There is need of submission to take and receive this righteousness, let be to seek it, And now tell me, can ye say that ye have seen all in yourselves as dung and dross, that ye count all things but loss for the excellency of the knowledge of Christ Jesus, (Phil. iii. 8, 9.) that ye have seen all your own privileges and duties loss, and are ye even sensible that prayer will no more help you than the cutting off a dog's neck? Ye that lay so much weight upon your being baptized, and upon outward privileges, are ye void of righteousness? No, ye seek to establish your own, and do not submit to the righteousness of God. In a word, all who are ignorant of this righteousness of God in Christ, ye all seek to establish your own. There needs more. But not one of twenty of you can tell what this is, it is a mystery. Ask at any of you, how ye shall be saved, ye will say, by prayer to God, and the mercy of God. Ye cannot tell the necessity of Christ's coming into the world.

Secondly, Ye must see an impossibility to attain a righteousness, or to stand before God another way. When ye miss this righteousness and are convinced of sin, it is not the running to prayer will help or mend it. When ye see the broken covenant, ye fall upon doing something, to mend your faults, with some good turns, and some will make a few good works answer all the challenges of sin. Alas! this is a seeking of your own righteousness. Many a poor broken man seeks to make up his fortune. Poor wretched sinners are building up the breach of the old covenant, putting up props under an old ruinous house, seeking to establish it, and rear it up again. But ye will never seek Christ till ye cannot do better, till ye be desperate of helping yourselves without him. Now I appeal to your consciences. Who among you was ever serious in this matter, to examine your own condition, whether you were enemies or friends? Ye took it for granted all your days. But never a man will betake himself to an imputed righteousness, but only he that flies, taking with[494] his enmity, and is pursued by the avenger of blood, and flies in to this righteousness as a city of refuge.

Thirdly, Ye must seek this righteousness, and what is it to seek it? It is even to take it and to receive it. It is brought to your door. It is offered. And the convinced sinner hath no more to do but hearken, and this righteousness is brought near unto him. Prayer to God, and much dealing with him, is one of the ways of obtaining this righteousness. But coming to Jesus Christ is the comprehensive short gate,[495] and therefore it is called "the righteousness of faith," and "the righteousness of God by faith." Now shall ye be called seekers of Christ's righteousness, who will not receive it when it is offered? Ye who have so many objections and scruples against the gospel and the application of it, ye in so far are not seekers, but refusers of the gospel, and disobedient. Christ's righteousness should meet with a seeker not a disputer. Any thing God allows you to seek, certainly he allows you to take and receive it, when it is brought unto you. And therefore, whoever have need of Jesus Christ, not only refuse him not, but stay not till they find him come to them. This is a noble resolution, I will give myself no rest till I be at a point in this. Seek him as a hid treasure, as that which your happiness depends upon.

(1) The kingdom of grace is worthy of all your affections and pains. That despised thing in the world called grace is the rarest piece of the creation, and if we could look on it aright, we would seek grace, and follow after it. Grace extracts a man out of the multitude of men that are all of one mass. Grace separates him from the rest of the world, and to this purpose are these usual phrases in scripture, "Such were some of you," "Once ye were darkness, but now are ye light in the Lord," "Among whom ye had your conversation in times past, fulfilling the desires of the flesh." All men are alike by nature and birth, there is no difference. Grace brought to light by the gospel makes the difference, and separates the few chosen vessels of glory and mercy from the world, and now "they are not of the world, as I am not of the world." All the rest of men's aims and endeavours cannot do this. Learning makes not a man a Christian. Honour makes not a man differ from a Gentile or Pagan. Riches make you no better than infidels. Speak of what ye will, you shall never draw a man entirely out of the cursed race of Adam, never distinguish him from Gentiles before God, till the Spirit of regeneration blow where he listeth. And this is grace's prerogative, beyond all other things. All other excellent gifts, even the gift of preaching, praying, all these are common, so to speak, and in a manner befall to all alike. Your external calling is but common, but he gives grace to all his chosen ones. But (2) Grace puts a man in a new kingdom. It draws a man out of Satan's kingdom, and makes him a king, who before was a subject. The man was led captive by sin and Satan at their pleasure. He served his own corrupt lusts and the prince of this world. Sin reigneth in his mortal body, whatever his passion and corruption did put him to, he could have no bridle, but as a horse went on to the battle. And ye may see daily that there is scarce one of an hundred that is master of himself. He is a servant of sin, but

grace makes him a priest and a king, Rev. i. 6, chap. v. 8, 10. He can now command himself. Sin reigned before unto death, but now grace reigns through righteousness unto eternal life, Rom. v. 20, 21. And O! but this victory over a man's self is more than a man's conquering a strong city. This victory is more than all the triumphs and trophies of the world's conquerors. For they could not conquer themselves, the little world, but were slaves to their own lusts. Some men talk of great spirits that can bear no injury. Nay, but such a spirit is the basest spirit. The noble spirit is that spirit which can despise these things, and be above them. Grace puts men upon a throne of eminence above the world. The Spirit of God makes a man of a noble spirit. (3) Grace translates a man from Satan's kingdom to God, and makes him a subject, a free born subject, of God or Christ's kingdom, and therefore Christ is the "King of saints," Rev. xv. 3. Our Lord and Saviour hath an "everlasting kingdom," 2 Pet. i. 11. We were subjects of the powers of darkness, but grace makes the translation into the kingdom of God's own dear Son, Col. i. 13. Now what an unspeakable privilege is this, to be one of Christ's subjects, who is our dear Saviour and King! Surely we must all be great courtiers. David, the great king of Israel, had this for his chief dignity, his style of honour, "the servant of the Lord," as kings use to write down themselves; and this was his title, "servant of God." Paul gloried much in this, "Paul, an apostle and servant of Jesus Christ." And surely all the families of heaven and earth may think it their highest honour to get liberty to bow their knees to Jesus, the "King of kings, and Lord of lords," the first-born of God's creation. The converted man is turned from the power of Satan to God. Mark but the emphasis of these two terms. Mark the whence or from,—that it is from Satan, the great destroyer of mankind, the first transgressor and deceiver. And how great is his power, tyranny, and dominion! He had us all in chains reserved for the day of judgment. But to what a happy change grace turns us, *from* him! But the term *to*, which is more admirable, it is to God, to Christ, to true religion, to God himself most High. And O! but this must be a more wonderful and excellent change than our conversion from darkness to light, from hell to heaven. These are but shadows of this glorious conversion. (4) Grace makes a man likewise a "partaker of the divine nature," 2 Pet. i. 4. This is the image and glory of God. This is the imitation and resemblance of God's spotless holiness and purity, "Be ye holy, as I am holy," 1 Pet. i. 15, 16. Every creature hath some dark characters of God. Some things speak his power, some things his wisdom, but this he hath called his own image. And so the Christian is more like unto God than all the world beside. This is the magnifying of a man, and making him but "a little lower than the angels," Psal. viii. 3, 4. Therefore God loves grace better than all the creation. Holiness is a great beauty, and God requires to be worshipped in the beauties of it. Albeit grace be often clouded with infirmities, and sometimes is reckoned despicable, because of the vessel it is in, yet it is precious as the finest gold, and more precious than any rubies. It is like gold in ashes, not the less excellent in itself, though it appear not so. But sin is the devil's image and likeness, and therefore Satan is called the father of sinners. "Ye are of your father the devil, and the lusts of your father ye will do." O but sin hath an ugly shape! It is the only spot in the face of the creation which God's soul abhors. For he loves righteousness, and hates iniquity, Psal. xlv. 6, 7. But there is one thing more, (5) That may commend grace to all your hearts. Grace is the way to glory. It gives title and right to, or at least declares it. It is inseparably joined with it. Grace is glory in the bud, and glory is the flower of grace, grace is young glory, and glory is old grace. Without holiness it is impossible to see God's face in peace. No man can come unto heaven without grace. Glorification is the first link of the chain, Rom. viii. 30. But sanctification must intervene first. No unclean thing can enter into heaven, but he that gives grace, gives glory, Psal. lxxxiv. 11. Heaven cannot receive many of you, because ye have not holiness. But it may commend holiness unto you, that it ministers an abundant entrance "into the everlasting kingdom of our Lord and Saviour Jesus Christ." As much as eternity is beyond the poor span of your time, so much is grace and holiness, whereon depends your everlasting condition, preferable to all things of this present vain world. O! but the children of men have many vain pursuits of the creature, that when it is had is nothing and vanity. Ye labour to secure an inch of your being, and to have contentment here in this half day, and never look beyond it to many millions of ages, when ye are to continue. Your honour, your pleasure, your gain, your credit, many such things like these can have no influence on the next world. These cannot go through death with you. Only grace and holiness, begun here, are consummated in glory, and make the poor man, that was miserable for a moment, eternally happy.

SERMON XVII.

Matth. vi. 33.—"But seek ye first the kingdom of God, and his righteousness, and all these things shall be added unto you."

The perfection even of the most upright creature, speaks always some imperfection in comparison of God, who is most perfect. The heavens, the sun and moon, in respect of lower things here, how glorious do they appear, and without spot! But behold, they are not clean in God's sight! How far are the angels above us who dwell in clay! They appear to be a pure mass of light and holiness, yet even these glorious beings cannot behold this light without covering their faces. These God may charge with folly. "God is light," saith the apostle, 1 John i. 5. This is his peculiar glory, for "in him there is no darkness at all." Is there any thing more excellent and divine than to seek God, and find him, and enjoy him? Yet even that holds forth the emptiness of the creature in its own bosom, that cannot be satiated within, but must come forth to seek happiness. Nay, even the greatest perfection of the creature speaks out the creature's own self indigence most, because its happiness is the removal from itself unto another, even unto God the fountain of life.

Now the enjoyment of this "kingdom of God" mentioned in the text, holds forth man's own insufficiency for well being within himself. But seeking this kingdom declares a double want, a want of it altogether. Not only hath he it not in himself, but not at all, and so must go out and seek it. God is blessed in himself, and self sufficient, and all sufficient to others. Without is nothing but what has flowed from his inexhausted fulness within, so that, though he should stop the conduit, by withdrawing his influence, and make all the creatures to evanish as a brook, or a shadow, he should be equally in himself blessed. "Darkness and light are both alike to thee," says David in another sense, Psal. cxxxix. 11, 12. And indeed they are all one in this sense, that he is no more perfected and bettered, when all the innumerable company of angels, and the spirits of just men made perfect, follow him with an eternal song, nor[496] before the mountains and hills were, when nothing was brought forth. Many thousand more worlds would add nothing to him, nor diminish anything from him. It is not so with man, he is bounded and limited, he cannot have well being in his own breast. He was indeed created with it in the enjoyment of God, which was his happiness, so that he had it not to seek, but to keep, he had it not to follow after, but to hold it still fast. But now, alas! he hath lost that, and become miserable. Once all Adam's posterity were void of happiness. By catching at a present shadow of pleasure, and satisfaction to his senses, he lost this excellent substance of blessedness in communion with God. Now, how shall this be recovered again? How shall this pearl of great price be found?

Certainly we must agree upon two principles, and according to them walk, ere we come within reach of this. It is a great question that is of more moment than all the debates among men,—how shall man's ruin be made up, and the treasure be found? If ye think it concerns you, I pray you hearken to this, and condescend[497] upon these two grounds, that the question may be right stated. One is, we have all lost happiness, fallen from the top of our excellency into the lowest dungeon of misery. We are cast down from heaven to hell. There needs not much to persuade you of the truth of this in general. But alas! who ponders it in their hearts? And until ye think more seriously upon it, ye will never be serious in the search for reparation of it. All of you by your daily experience find that ye are miserable creatures. Ye have no satisfaction nor contentment.

Ye are compassed about with many infirmities and griefs. But this is but an appendix of your misery. All the calamities of this life are but a consequent, a little stream of that boundless ocean of misery that is yet insensible to you. Therefore enter into your own hearts, and consider what Adam once was, and what ye now are, nay, what ye will all quickly be, if God prevent it not. We are born heirs of wrath and hell. It is not only the infinite loss of that blessed sight of his face for evermore, which an eternal enjoyment of creature pleasures could not compensate the want of, one hour; but it is the kingdom of darkness, and the devil that we are all born to inherit. Let this then once take root in your heart, that ye are in extreme misery, and that a remedy must be provided, else ye must perish. Now when this principle is established, ye must agree upon this also. "But out of myself I must go. Blessedness I must have. It is not in me. While I look in, there is nothing but all kind of emptiness, and, which is worse, all kind of misery. Not only the common lot of creatures (that none is sufficient to its own well being) is incident to me, but I have lost that being which I had in another, which was my well being, and do now possess, or shall shortly possess, all misery." Now, are ye settled upon these two? I am not happy, I must go out of myself to find it. It is not in me, in my flesh dwells no good thing, in my spirit and flesh both, is nothing good. Ask then this great question, Whither shall I go? What shall I do to find it? All men know they must seek it. But Christ tells where they shall seek it, and whither they shall go. The word of the gospel is for this very purpose to answer this question. If we were sensible that we had lost happiness, certainly we would be earnest in this question, where shall it be recovered? What shall I seek after? And no answer would satisfy but the gospel itself, that directs unto the very fountain of life, and holds "forth the kingdom of God" as the true happiness of men to be sought. "Seek ye first," says Christ, "the kingdom of God," and the righteousness thereof. Here only is a solid answer. Seek me, for I am eternal life, I am the life and the light of men. Oh! that your souls answered, with David, "Thy face, Lord, I will seek." Peter had sought and found, and thought himself well, so that he answers Christ with great vehemency, when he said unto his disciples, "Will ye also leave me?" Peter saith, Leave thee, Lord, "to whom should we go but unto thee, for thou hast the words of eternal life? And we believe and are sure, that thou art the Christ, the Son of the living God," John vi. 66, &c. It were all the absurdity in the world to leave thee, or to go to any other thing for life itself. Shall not death be found, if I leave life? It were madness not to seek thee, but what shall it be called to leave thee, when I have found and tasted thee to be so good? Every man misses happiness and justification within himself, and so is upon the search after it. But is it not strange, that all the experiences of nations and generations conjoined in one, cannot hold forth even a probable way of attaining it? Gather them all in one, the sum and result is, "We have heard the fame thereof with our ears," but "it is hid from the eyes of all living," as we read more fully, and should apply, what Job said of wisdom, to the true happiness of man, Job xxviii. 12, to the end of that chapter. Certainly there is some fundamental and common mistake among men. They know not what was once man's happiness, and so it is impossible they can seek the right remedy. Look upon us all, what do we seek after? It is some present thing, some bodily and temporal thing, that men apprehend their happiness lies in, and so whether they attain it or not, or being attained, it doth not answer our expectation, and thus still are we disappointed, and our base scent becomes a vain pursuit, whether we overtake it or not. Every man proposes this within himself as the principle of his life and conversation, what shall I seek after? What shall I spend most of my time and affections upon, to drive at? And alas! all men, save those whose eyes the Spirit openeth, err in the very foundation. One man propones honour to himself, another pleasure, and a third riches, and the most part seek all of them, some accommodation and satisfaction in a present world. And almost every man conceives he would be blessed, if he had that which he wants, and sees another have.

Now while men's designs are thus established, all must be wrong. The ship is gone forth, but it will never land on the coast of happiness. And thus we see men seek many things. They are divided among many thoughts and cares, because no one thing is found that can satisfy, and so we have put ourselves upon an endless journey to go through all the creatures. Neither one nor all together have what we want, and neither one nor all can be had or possessed with assurance, though we had it. But the gospel comes to lay a right foundation, and frame a right principle within us. "Seek ye first the kingdom of God." Here is the principal design that should be driven at and if men would make it, and follow it, O how should they be satisfied with the fulness of that kingdom, the vast dimensions of it, the incorruptibleness of it!

Now there is one of two you must fall upon, either many things, or one thing. All that a man can seek after is here ranked. On the one side is many things, "all these things," that is, food, raiment, honour, pleasure, and such like, that concern the body, or men's condition here in this world, and these things a man hath need of, verses 31 and 32, "Therefore take no thought, saying, What shall we eat? or, what shall we drink? or, wherewithal shall we be clothed? (for after all these things do the Gentiles seek) for your heavenly Father knoweth that ye have need of these things." Nay, there is but one thing that is set up against all these many things, namely, "the kingdom of God and his righteousness." Now without all controversy the more unity be, there will be the more satisfaction. If all other things be equal, it is a kind of torment to have so many doors to go to for help. If a man could have all in one, he would think many things a great vexation and burden. If any one thing had in it as much as to answer all our necessities, that one thing would be of great price, beyond many things, having but so much virtue among them all. I shall suppose then, that there were real satisfaction and happiness to be found in the affluence and conjunction of all created things here, that there was some creature that could answer every necessity of men, yet, I say, would ye not exchange all that variety and multitude, if ye could find one thing that did all that to the full, that so many did but no more? Then certainly ye would choose a variety in one thing beyond the scattered satisfaction in many things. But when it is not to be found in all these things, and though it were, yet all these are not consistent together, then of necessity we must make another search. I say then, in the name of Jesus Christ, that if ye seek satisfaction in this present world, ye shall be disappointed. Ye may be all your days sowing and ploughing, but ye shall not see the harvest. Ye shall never reap the fruit of your labour, but in the end of your days shall be fools, and see yourselves to have been so, when ye thought yourselves wise. I shall also suppose that ye have attained what ye have with so much vexation toiled for, that ye had your barns and coffers full, that all the varieties of human delights were still attending you, that ye were set upon a throne of eminency above others, and in a word, that ye had all that your soul desired, so that no room was left empty for more desire, and no more grief entered into your hearts. Are ye blessed for all that? No certainly, if ye do but consider that with all ye may lose your own souls, and that quickly, and that your spirits must remove out of that palace of pleasure and delight into eternal torment, and then count, are ye blessed or not? What gained ye? It is madness to reckon upon this life, it is so inconsiderable when compared with eternity. A kingdom, what is it, when a man shall be deprived for evermore of the kingdom of God, and inhabit the kingdom of darkness under the king of terrors? Do ye think a stageplayer a happy man that for an hour hath so much mirth and attendance, and for all his lifetime is kept in prison without the least drop of these comforts? Will not such a man's momentary satisfaction make hell more unsatisfying, and add grounds of bitterness to his cup? For it is misery to have been happy.

Nay, but this is a fancied supposal. All this, how small soever it be, was never, and never shall be, within the reach of any living. Ye may reckon beforehand, and lay down two things as demonstrated by scripture and all men's experience. One is,—all is vanity and vexation of spirit under the sun. All that ye can attain by your endeavours for an age, and by sweating and toiling, will not give you one hour's satisfaction, without some want, some vexation, either in wanting or possessing. Nay, though you had all, it could not give you satisfaction. The soul could not feed upon these things. They would be like silver and gold, which could not save a starving man, or nourish him as meat and drink doth. A man cannot be happy in a marble palace, for the soul is created with an infinite capacity to receive God, and all the world will not fill his room. Another is,—that it is impossible for you to attain all these things. One thing is inconsistent with another, and your necessity requires both. Now then, how shall ye be satisfied when they cannot meet? I think, then, the spirits of the most part of us do not rise very high to seek great things in this world, we are in such a lot among men. I mean that we have not great expectation of wealth, pleasures, honours, or such like. Oh then so much the more take heed to this, and see what ye resolve to seek after! Ye do not expect much satisfaction here. Then I pray you hearken to this one thing, seek the kingdom of God.

This kingdom of heaven and righteousness are equivalent unto, nay they exceedingly surpass, all the scattered perfections and goodness among these many things, or all things that God hath promised to add to them in the text. Why should I say equivalent? Alas, there is no comparison. "For I reckon (says Paul, Rom. viii. 18, 19) that the sufferings of this present time are not worthy to be compared with the glory that shall be revealed in us. For the earnest expectation of the creature waiteth for the manifestation of the sons of God." What this kingdom is in itself, is beyond our conception, but all these things which God will add thereunto, are to be considered only as an appendix to it. Is not heaven an excellent kingdom? All that ye are now toiling about, and taking thought for, these, "all these things" (as a consequent to itself), food and raiment, and such like, "shall be given you" as your heavenly Father judges fit. "For godliness (says the apostle, 1 Tim. iv. 8), is profitable unto all things having the promise of this life," as well as of "the life to come." I think then, if all men would but rationally examine this business, they would be forced to cry out against the folly and madness of too many men, who have their portion only in this life, Psal. xvii. 14. What is it ye seek? Ye flee from godliness as your great enemy. Ye think religion an adversary to this life, and the pleasures of it. Nay, but it is a huge mistake, for it hath the promise of this life, and that which is to come. Ye cannot abide to have Christ's kingdom within you. Ye will not have him to rule over you. Ye will not renounce self, and your own righteousness. But consider,

O men, that here is that which ye should seek after. Here is wealth, and honour, and long life, and pleasures at God's right hand for evermore. Ye seek many things first, and ye will not seek this one thing needful, Luke x. 41, 42. But here is the way to get what ye seek more certainly and solidly, "Seek first the kingdom of God and his righteousness," and all these other things will come of will. Ye need not seek them, for your heavenly Father knows best what ye need. Behold what a satisfying portion this kingdom is. When the pitch and height of men's attainments in this world is but a consectary, an appendicle of it, what must this kingdom be in itself, when all these things follow as attendants? Here then is one thing, worth all, and more than all, even Jesus Christ, who is all in all, Col. iii. 10, 11. Ye speak of many kingdoms, nay, but here is one kingdom, the kingdom of grace and glory, that hath in it eminently all that is scattered among all things. It unites us to Jesus Christ, "in whom all the fulness of the Godhead dwells, and ye are complete in him, who is the head of all principality and power," Col. ii. 9, 10. In his house is fatness, and ye shall be satisfied with this, and drink of these rivers of everlasting pleasures that are at his right hand, Psal. xxxvi. 8, 9, xvi. 11. When the pious Psalmist was over-charged with the very forethought and apprehension of this, he says, "How excellent is thy loving kindness, O God! therefore the children of men put their trust under the shadow of thy wings," Psal. xxxvi. 7. "O how great is thy goodness, which thou hast laid up for them that fear thee, which thou hast wrought for them that trust in thee," Psal. xxxi. 19, 20. When the sight of it afar off, and the taste of it in this wilderness, is of so much virtue, what shall the drinking of that wellhead be, when the soul shall be drowned in it?

As these things are divided,—on the one side, many things, and on the other, one kingdom more worth than all, so are men divided accordingly. On the one hand are the nations and Gentiles, on the other a poor handful. Ye my disciples, "Seek ye," says Christ, "first the kingdom of God, and his righteousness, and all these things," what ye shall eat, and what ye shall drink, or wherewithal ye shall be clothed, "shall be added." For after all these things the Gentiles seek, and your Father knoweth that ye have need of them. "Fear not, little flock, for it is your Father's good pleasure to give you the kingdom," Luke xii. 29, 31. Now this division hath been always in the world. "For many say, (Psal. iv. 6, 7), Who will show us any good?" But they who have their affections gathered in one channel toward one thing, are as it were but one man. But, Lord, "lift thou up the light of thy countenance upon us, thou hast put gladness in my heart more than in the time that their corn and wine increased." Here then is even the course of the world, the way of the multitude. They have their way scattered, their gain lies in many arts. Many things they must seek, because they forsake the one thing necessary. When they forsake the one fountain of living water, they must dig up, and hew out to themselves many broken cisterns, that can hold no water, no one to help another. This is even proclaimed by the conversation of a great part of the world. Do ye not declare this, by your eager pursuit of this world, and the things of it, and your careful thoughts of it, that ye have no mind[498] of eternity, or the kingdom to come? Ye seek nothing but things here, and these do not descend after you. Be persuaded, I beseech you, be persuaded of this, that when ye have your hearts below, that ye are no better, the most part of you, than pagans. Ye have this pretence, that it is necessary to live and follow some calling. It is true indeed. But is it not more necessary to live for ever after death than for a moment? Godliness will not prejudge this life or thy calling, but ye seek after these things, as if ye were to live eternally in this vain world. Ye could toil no more, take no more thought for a million of ages, than ye do now for the morrow. This prejudges and shuts out all thoughts of heaven or hell. Ye are called to a kingdom. This is offered unto you. Will ye be so mad as to refuse it, and embrace the dunghill, and scrape it still together? We declare unto you in his name, who is truth itself, that if ye will be persuaded to be Christians indeed, ye shall have these outward things ye have need of, without care and anxiety, which now ye are tormented for. And for superfluities, what need ye care for them? A reasonable man should despise them, and much more a Christian. If ye would not be as pagans without the church, ye must be sober in these things, mortified and dead unto them. There shall be no real difference between thee and a heathen, in the day of appearing before Christ's tribunal, O Christian, except thou hast denied and despised this world, and sought principally the things that are above. Is Christianity no more, I pray you, but a name? Ye would all be called Christians. Why will ye not be so indeed? For the name will never advantage you, but in the day of judgment it shall be the greatest accession and weight unto your guiltiness, and also to your judgment. Ye would all now be accounted Christians, but if ye be not so in truth, and in deed, the day will come that ye shall wish from your soul ye had wanted the name also, and had lived among these Gentiles and pagans whose conversation ye did follow. For it shall be more tolerable for the covetous worldly pagan in that day, than the covetous Christian.

Oh that ye were once persuaded that there is an inconsistency in them, who seek these many things, and this one kingdom. "But seek ye first the kingdom of God, and his righteousness," in opposition to the Gentiles seeking of many things. Ye may seek the world, but if ye seek it, seek it as if ye sought it not, if ye use it use it as if ye used it not, or use the world as those who do not abuse it, knowing that the fashion thereof passes away. Certainly ye cannot with all seek grace and glory, 1 Cor. ii. 29, 32. Therefore Christ says to enforce his exhortation, (Matth. vi. 24) "No man can serve two masters, for either he will hate the one, and love the other, or else he will hold to the one, and despise the other; ye cannot serve God and mammon." I fear many of you conceive that this belongs not to you. Those who are not naturally covetous and greedy, who are not still in anxiety and perplexity about the things of the world, will possibly conceive themselves free. Nay, but look upon the division that Christ makes. Was there not many a heathen man among the nations, as free of that covetousness noted among men? Were there not as gallant spirits among them, that cared as little for riches as any of us,—nay, men every way of a more smooth and blameless carriage than the most part of us are? Yet behold the construction that Christ puts on them, "after all these things do the nations seek." I think many of them have declaimed more against the baseness of covetous spirits,[499] than many Christian preachers, and in the very practice of it have outstripped the most part of the Christian world. Yet in the scripture sense, even all these who have cried down the world, are but lovers of it, and of themselves too. How can this be? It is certain every man is composed of desires and breathings after some thing without himself. Some men's desires are more shallow and low than others. One man hath honour in admiration, and may despise riches. Another follows his pleasures and may neglect both these. Nay, possibly a man may be moderate in all these things, so that none can challenge him, and yet he is but a lover of the world. It is the master he serves, and the idol he worshippeth, because no man wants one, or many idols, something to take up his affection and desires. Now though such a man seems moderate in these, in comparison of others whose hearts run more after them, yet, because there is no other thing, that does take up his heart so much as these, he is but in Christ's account among the heathen nations. Some of you are not in great expectations, ye have but mean projects, ye seem content with few things, ye are not vexing yourselves as others do, but let the world come and go as it pleases, without much disquiet. This, I say, may be the temper of some natural spirits, yet I ask such of you, is there any thing else ye seek more after, or spend more time and thought upon, and what is that? Is there any other thing ye are more taken up with, than your present ease and accommodation in this life? No certainly, ye cannot say so, however your projects be mean and low, yet they are confined within time and things present, and the kingdom of grace and glory comes not much in your mind. Then, I say, thou art but a lover of the world. Mammon is thy god. Thou seekest not the kingdom of heaven, and shalt not obtain it. For that which the nations seek after is thy predominant.

Will ye then, I beseech you, gather in your hearts to consider this. Is it a light matter we speak of, life or death? Doth it not concern you as much as you are worth? Therefore consider it as seriously as if you were going hence to be no more. Many of you will not grant worldly mindedness a sin. When ye make it a god, and sacrifice unto it, ye fancy that ye are seeking heaven. I pray you do not deceive your souls. Give them as good measure as ye would do your bodies in any thing. Would ye say ye were seeking after any thing, I suppose to find such a friend to speak to, would ye, I say, think that ye earnestly desired to see that friend, and sought him, if ye did all the day take up your time with other petty business that might be done at any time? How can ye imagine ye seek not the world but heaven, when, if ye would look back upon the current and stream, both of your affections and endeavours, ye would find they have run this way toward your present ease and satisfaction? Ye do not give one entire hour to the thought of Jesus Christ and his kingdom, it may be, in a whole week.

Are ye then seekers of the kingdom? If ye did but examine one day how it is spent, ye might pass a judgment upon your whole life. Do ye seek that first which is fewest times in your thoughts, and least in your affections, and hath least of your time bestowed on it? Alas, do not flatter yourselves. That ye seek first which is often in your mind, which uses to stir up your joy or grief, or desire most. It is this present world only, and this present world is your portion. Ye shall lose the kingdom of heaven by seeking to make the world sure. As for the children of God, ye who will be his disciples, (to such he speaks here,) it becomes not you to be like the heathens. Ye ought, most of all, to adorn your holy profession, your high calling to a kingdom above. If then ye seek these things below, as if ye sought them not, ye ought to make religion your main business, else ye are not indeed religious. If Christianity take not up a man, he hath not the thing, but the name. "Seek first," that is, chiefly, principally, and above all, "the kingdom of God and his righteousness." Nay, this is more strange, it is a first that hath no second. Seek this first, so as if ye sought nothing else, and all things necessary here shall be superadded to the seeking and finding of this kingdom.

This is that which I would have engraven on all our hearts, that there is a necessity of making Christianity our calling and trade, our business and employment, else we must renounce it. It will take our whole man, our whole time, not spare hours, and by thoughts. Ye have a great task to accomplish, a great journey to make. If ye give not all diligence to add to your faith, virtue, knowledge, temperance, patience, godliness, brotherly kindness, and charity, ye are certainly blind, and see not afar off, and have not been purged from your old sins, 2 Pet. i. 5-11. This imports that those who make not religion their great comprehensive study, do neither know eternity, nor see into it. Oh, how may this word strike into the hearts of many Christians, and pierce as a sword! Is our lazy, indifferent, and cold service at some appointed hours, "all diligence"? Or, is it diligence at all? Is there not more diligence and fervour in other things than this, to add grace to grace? Who is covetous of such a game? Are not many more desirous of adding lands and houses to their lands and houses, and money to their stock, than to add to their faith virtue? &c. Who among you is enlarging his desires, as the grave, after conformity to Jesus Christ, and the righteousness of his kingdom, that this treasure of grace may abound? Alas, we are poor mean Christians, because we are negligent! For "the hand of the diligent maketh rich," Prov. x. 4. But we become poor in grace, because we deal with a slack hand. Is there any great thing that is attainable without much pains and sweating? *Difficilia quæ pulchra.*[500]

Think ye to come to a kingdom by sleeping through some custom of godliness? "Seest thou a man diligent in his business? that man shall stand before kings, he shall not stand before mean men," Prov. xxii. 29. This advances him to be a courtier. And is not this business of Christianity more considerable to be diligent about when it advances a man into the court of heaven, into his presence in whose favour is life, and whose loving kindness is better than life? And not only so, but if ye be diligent here ye shall obtain a kingdom. "Seek first the kingdom of God." "The hand of the diligent shall bear rule but the slothful shall be under tribute," Prov. xii. 24. If ye make this your business, and spend your spirits in it, ye shall be kings and priests with God in the kingdom above, that may suffer many partakers without division or emulation. It is he that overcomes, that shall have the new name, the white raiment, the crown of life, and all the glorious things which are promised to them that overcome in the second and third chapters of the Revelation. O what glad tidings are these! This is the gospel of peace. This is the joyful sound that proclaims unto us so great, so excellent things as a kingdom, the kingdom of God, an everlasting kingdom like God, a kingdom glorious as he is, a kingdom suitable to his royal Majesty, and the magnificence of his palace above. Are we called into this by the gospel, and would ye know what is the sum thereof? It is this. Ho! every one that will have great things, ho! every one that will be a king to God, and to bear rule over kings in the great day, come, here it is, overcome yourselves here in the Lamb that hath overcome, follow Jesus the captain of your salvation, who for the joy and glory which was set before him, despised all the glory of this world, and the pains and shame of the cross, Heb. xii. 1, 2. "Why do ye spend your money for that which is not bread, and your labour for that which satisfieth not?" Isa. lv. 1, 2, 3. All ye toil about, what is it? Children's fancies. Such houses and kingdoms as they build in the sand. Why spend ye your time and labour upon earthly things that are at an end? Here is a kingdom worthy of all men's thoughts, and affections, and time. The diligent shall have it. Gird up the loins of your mind, and seek it as the one thing needful. Many of you desire this kingdom, but alas! these are sluggard's wishes, ye have fainting desires after it. Your desires consume and waste you. But ye put not forth your hand, and so ye have nothing. "The soul of the sluggard desireth and hath nothing, but the soul of the diligent shall be made fat," Prov. xiii. 4. Do ye see any growing Christian, but he that is much in the exercise of godliness, and very honest in it? See ye any fat souls, but diligent souls? Our barrenness and leanness hath negligence written upon it. Do ye not wonder that we are not fat and flourishing, as palms and cedars in the courts of our God? Certainly it is no wonder. Is it not a wonder that our sleeping away secure, keeps so much as the leaves of a profession upon us? Therefore Christians, let this be your name, Seekers, but seekers of what? Not of any new religion, but of the good old kingdom of God, proponed to us in the gospel. And remember that the seeker must seek diligently, if he think that which he seeks worthy of finding. "He that comes to God must believe that he is, and that he is the rewarder of them that diligently seek him," Heb. xi. 6. Your seeking will proclaim your estimation of what ye seek. It will be written on it, what your desires are. Many men's unfrequent and lazy prayers have this written upon them in legible characters, I care not whether God grant or not. Diligence speaks affection, and affection principles[501] diligence. And if ye be seekers, ye must be so still, till ye find, and have no more want. When ye have done all, ye must stand, Eph. vi. 10, 16. When ye have found all, ye must seek. Ye do but find in part, because the kingdom of God is but coming in the glory and perfection of it. Nay, I believe the more ye find, the more ye will seek, because tasting what this kingdom is, can best engage the affection and resolution after it. Seeking is an exercise suitable to a Christian in this state of pilgrimage. Enjoyment is for his own country, heaven. And shall not the bitterness and pains of seeking, sweeten the enjoyment of this kingdom when it is found? This will endear it and make it precious. Yet it needs no supereminent and accessory sweetness, it is so satisfactory in itself. Christians, remember your name. When you have attained all, still seek more. For there is more to be found here than ye have yet found. It is sitting down on our attainments that makes us barren and lean Christians. Desires and diligence are the vital sap of a Christian. Enlarge once your desires as the grave, that never says I have enough. And ye have good warrant so to do, because that which ye are allowed to desire is without bounds and measure. It is inexhaustible, and when once desires have emptied the soul, and made it capable of such a great kingdom, then let your study be henceforth to fill up that void with this kingdom. Let your diligence come up to desires, and at length ye shall be what ye would be, ye shall find what ye sought.

SERMON XVIII.

Matt. vi. 33.—"But seek ye first the kingdom of God," &c.

O "seekest thou great things for thyself," says God to Baruch, (Jer. xlv. 5) "seek them not." How then doth he command us in the text to seek a kingdom? Is not this a great thing? Certainly it is greater than those great things he would not have Baruch to seek after, and yet he charges us to seek after it. In every kind of creatures there is some difference, some greater, some lesser, some higher, some lower; so there are some men far above others in knowledge, understanding, strength, and such like. Yet such is the order God hath made, that the lowest angel is above the highest man, so that in comparison of these, the greatest man is but a mean worm, a despisable nothing. Among things created, some are greater, some lesser. "When I consider the heavens, the work of thy fingers," says David, "the moon and stars which thou hast ordained: What is man, that thou art mindful of him? and the son of man that thou visitest him?" Psal. viii. 3, 4. But when all these are compared with God, then the difference of greater and lesser disappears. In the night there are different lights, the moon and stars, "and one star," says Paul, "differeth from another in glory." Some are of the first, some of the second, and most of them the third magnitude. Nay, but let the sun arise—and all these are alike, they are all darkness when compared with the sun's brightness. What then are angels and men to God, who is a light inaccessible and full of glory, whom no eye hath seen or can see? "All nations before him are as nothing, yea, they are counted to him less than nothing, and vanity," Isa. xl. 12-19; 1 Tim. vi. 15, 16. The sun himself shines not before him, and the moon gives not her light. Now is it not so proportionably here? If we stay within the sphere of temporal and worldly things, some are great, some small, some things of greater, some things of less consequence, greater or smaller in their appearance to us, and in men's fancies. But if we go further and look into eternity, then certainly all these will appear small and inconsiderable. This earth seems very spacious, and huge in quantity unto us who dwell upon it. We discern mountains and valleys, sea and land, and do make many divisions of it. But if one man were above where the sun is, and looked down upon the earth, he would consider it but as one point almost invisible, that had no proportion to the vast dimensions of heaven. Even so it is here, while men abide within their own orb, their natural understanding, and do compare time only with time, and temporal things with temporal, riches with poverty, honour with disgrace, pleasure with pain, learning with ignorance, strength with weakness, pleasant lands and goodly houses with wildernesses and wild deserts where none do well. It is no wonder, I think, that those who compare themselves with some that commend themselves, are not wise, 2 Cor. x. 12, 13. There is but one perfect pattern they should look to, if they would not be deceived. While ye stay your thoughts within these bounds, ye apprehend in yourselves great odds between one thing and another. But if once the Spirit of God enlightened your eyes, and made you to see far off, if ye were elevated above your own station, to the watch-tower of the holy scriptures, to behold off[502] these, by the prospect of saving faith, things that are afar off, such as heaven and hell, eternity, salvation and condemnation, O how would all these differences in a present world evanish out of sight, in the presence of these vast and infinite things! Food and raiment are great things to the most part of men, therefore do they toil so much about them, and take so much thought for them, how to feed, and how to be clothed, how to have a full and delicate table, and fine clothes! Again, many others apprehend some greatness and eminency in honour and respect among men; others in pleasure and satisfaction to their senses, even as a beast would judge. Others apprehend some worth and excellence in great possessions, in silver and gold beside them, and have a kind of complacency in these. But if once this kingdom of God entered into your heart, if ye saw the worth of it, the vast dimensions of it, the pleasure, honour, and profit of it, then certainly all other things would appear to be mean and low, not worth a thought beforehand. Advantage and disadvantage would be all one to you. Honour and dishonour, evil report and good report, pleasure and pain, would have no distance from one another; this gain, this honour, this pleasure of the kingdom of God, would so overmaster them, so outshine them.

Nay, I may say, if ye but knew your immortal souls, or your own worth beyond the rest of the creatures, such as silver, gold, lands, houses, &c., I am confident ye would fall in your esteem of them. They would appear but low, base things in regard of the soul. Suppose even this world came in competition, (the gain of it now seems great gain,) but I pray you, if ye laid all that world in the balance with your soul, what would weigh most? Christ holds it forth to a rational man, to judge of it; "What shall it profit a man, if he shall gain the whole world, and lose his own soul, or be cast away?" Would ye account yourselves gainers, when ye have lost yourselves? Matt. xvi. 26; Luke ix. 25. Is not a man better than meat? Are not your souls more precious than the finest gold? When you lose your souls, whose shall these be? "What shall a man give in exchange for his soul?" And if there be no one more to possess or use, what profit is it? This then that we have in hand is one thing of greatest moment and concernment in the world. Let me then beseech you to weigh these things in the balance of the sanctuary,—your souls, and this world, the kingdom of God, and many temporal things, such as food and raiment. Ye never enter into the comparison of these things in your mind. If ye did, would ye not see to which side the balance would turn? Therefore we would have you look upon these words of our Saviour, which are the just balance of the sanctuary. Behold how the question is stated, how the comparison goeth. It is not whether I shall want food and raiment, and other necessary things here, or the kingdom of God hereafter? It is not thus cast—in the one balance, the present life and its accommodations, in the other, the life to come and God's kingdom. Indeed if it were so, without all controversy this kingdom would carry it. I say, if there were an inconsistency supposed between a life here, and a life hereafter, suppose no man can be godly, except he be miserable, poor, naked, afflicted, extremely indigent, yet I say the balance thus casten, would be clear to all men that judged aright. Would not eternity weigh down time? Would not an immortal soul weigh down a mortal body? What proportion would the raiment of wool, or gold, or silk have to the white and clean linen, the robes of righteousness, the robes of saints, and to the crown of glory that fadeth not away? What proportion would our perishing pleasures have to the rivers of pleasures, pure, unmixed, undefiled pleasures at God's right hand for evermore? Would ye thus rate this present span, inch, and shadow of time, if ye considered the endless endurance of eternity? I am sure reason itself might be appealed unto, though faith were not to judge.

Though it would hold well enough so, yet our Lord Jesus Christ states the controversy otherwise, and holds out another balance, that it may be the more convincing and clear, if it were possible even, to overcome natural consciences with the light of it. And it is this, in the one hand you may see food and raiment, things that belong to this life; and, on the other hand, you may behold the kingdom of God, and his righteousness, grace, and glory; and, besides that, even all these other things that ye did see in the other hand, food, raiment, &c., "all these things shall be added."

Wisdom, in the Proverbs, uses such a device to catch poor, foolish, and simple men: "Happy," says Solomon, "is the man that findeth wisdom, and the man that getteth understanding. For the merchandise thereof is better than the merchandise of silver, and the gain thereof than fine gold. She is more precious than rubies: and all the things thou canst desire are not to be compared unto her." Here is the weight of wisdom in itself. See how ponderous it is of itself; so heavy that it may weigh down all that come within the compass of desire, and certainly its compass is infinite. But, he adds, "Length of days are in her right hand, and in her left hand riches and honour. Her ways are ways of pleasantness, and all her paths are peace. She is a tree of life to them that lay hold upon her." She is a tree of life in herself, though she had no accession of other things, "and happy is every one who retaineth her," Prov. iii. 13-19.

Now, O men, if ye will not be allured with the beauty and excellency of the princess, wisdom herself, then, I pray you, look what follows her. That which now ye are pursuing after with much labour and pains, and all in vain too, is here in her train. Look how the comparison is stated. Christ Jesus would catch us with a holy guile, and, if it had success, O! it would be a blessed guile to us. Ye have large and airy apprehensions of temporal things, which ye call needful, and ye cannot behold eternal things. Ye know not the worth of this kingdom. Ye conceive that godliness is prejudicial unto you in this life, that the kingdom of grace will make you miserable here; and that ye cannot endure. Ah, be not mistaken, come and look again. If godliness itself will not allure you, if the kingdom itself will not weigh with you, then, I pray you, consider what an appendix, what a consectary these have. Consider that the sum is added to the principal, which ye so much seek after. But ye refuse the principal, the kingdom. Ye have not right thoughts of godliness, "for godliness is profitable unto all things, having the promise of the life that now is, and that which is to come," 1 Tim. iv. 8. Now, is not this "a faithful saying?" If ye believe it so to be, is it not "worthy of all acceptation?"

Ye may have things necessary here, food and raiment. And if ye seek more, if ye will be rich, and will have superfluities, then ye shall fall into many temptations, snares, and hurtful lusts, which shall drown you in perdition, 1 Tim. vi. 8-11. Nature and reason might check such exorbitances, for nature is content with few things. Therefore believe that "godliness with contentment is great gain." Ye are now only seeking temporal gain, but that is neither great gain, nor gain at all, when ye lose your soul. For that is an irrecoverable and incomparable loss. Ye may have these outward things, God's blessing, and peace with them, and heaven too if ye choose this kingdom before all things, and above all things. But if ye give these other things the pre-eminence, it is uncertain if ye will get what ye seek, and ye shall certainly be eternal losers beside. If there were no more but this kingdom alone, it might weigh all down. If heaven and earth were laid in a balance, would not heaven, if it were ponderous according to its magnitude, weigh down the earth exceedingly out of sight? Would it not evanish as a point? Even so, though this kingdom of grace and glory were alone, in opposition to all these things that ye take thought for, it would weigh them down eternally. Look what the weight of glory was to Paul, when he says, 2 Cor. iv. 17, "For our light affliction, which is but for a moment, worketh for us a far more exceeding and eternal weight of glory, while we look not at the things which are seen, but at the things which are not seen, for the things which are seen are temporal, but the things which are not seen are eternal." The weight of glory is eternal, and far exceeds any thing temporal. The one scale of the balance goes up, as it were, eternally out of sight, out of thought, the one goes up for lightness and vanity, and the other goeth down, for weight and solidity, out of sight, and out of the thought and imagination. If ye looked upon these things which are invisible and eternal, as Paul did, it would be so with you also.

But when withal the earth and its fulness is in the scale with God's kingdom and righteousness, will not these, with that accession, weigh down the earth alone? Is it food and raiment that ye seek? Then I say, food and raiment is on this kingdom's side also. And ye shall be more sure of these things, because ye have God's promise for them. The wicked have not his word and promise for prosperity, even not so much as to answer their necessities, but only they may sometimes prosper in the world, in his providence. But God's people shall have him engaged in their need for their temporal being here in this world. "O fear the Lord, ye his saints, for there is no want to them that fear him. The young lions do lack and suffer hunger, but they that seek the Lord shall not want any good thing," Psal. xxxiv. 9, 10. Godliness hath the promise of this life. Now, then, ye are more assured of temporal things by these means than any monarch can be. The world's stability depends only upon a command. But your food and raiment here is grounded upon a promise, and though heaven and earth should fail and pass away, yet not one jot of truth shall fail. God indeed may change his command if he pleases, but not his promises. Now, then, let all the world judge, come and see this balance, how on the one hand are food, raiment, and all things needful for this present life, on the other hand, these same thing necessary for our bodies, and well being here, and that more solidly and sweetly flowing from God's love, grounded on a promise,—I think this weighs down already, if we should say no more. But then behold what more is on his right hand. There is a kingdom of God beside, an eternal kingdom, and this weighs down eternally. All this world is but an accession and addition to it. The promises of this life are not your portion and inheritance, they are but superadded to your portion, so then we have as much beside, an inheritance incorruptible and undefiled, as the world have for their inheritance, yea, and more sure and more sweet beside. We might with reverence change that verse which Paul has on this consideration, "If we had hope only in this life, we were of all men most miserable," 1 Cor. xv. 19. He speaks thus because of afflictions and persecutions. But on this consideration we might say, If we have hope in Christ only in this life, we were *not* of all men most miserable, but most blessed, because we have all these things added to us, without toil and vexation, without care and anxiety, by divine promise and providence, with God's blessing and favour, what the world takes thought for, rendeth their hearts for, toils their bodies for, and yet are not sure of success, or if they get them, they get a curse with them.

Now when the balance is thus presented, what is your choice? What will ye seek after? Will ye seek this present world, and lose the kingdom of heaven? Or will ye choose to "seek first the kingdom of God and his righteousness," and then ye shall have in this world what is good for you? The choice is soon made in men's judgments. Ye dare not any of you deny, but it ought thus to be. But who seriously ponders these things till their minds affect their hearts? Who will sit down to meditate upon them, and pass a resolute and well grounded choice upon deliberation? Remember what Christ says, "No man can serve two masters." Ye may indeed have both these things, and the kingdom. But ye cannot seek them both, they are not so consistent. "But seek first the kingdom of God," and then all these things shall be given you.

Now there is no more need of any second seeking. For "all these things shall be added" as an accessory to the first. O see then, ye whose projects and thoughts are towards present things,—ye spend the prime and flower of your affections, and time upon them,—ye cannot also seek the kingdom of heaven. Unless ye seek them as if ye sought them not, ye cannot seek this blessed kingdom. If ye seek not this kingdom as the one thing necessary, and your seeking proclaim that ye account it so, ye do not seek it aright. If ye be careful and troubled about many things, ye proclaim that ye do not think there is but one thing needful, ye do not, like Mary, choose the good part which shall not be taken from you, Luke x. 41, 42. If ye would abandon the distracting care of the world, and let all your anxiety and care vent itself here upon the kingdom of God, all these things would be added besides the kingdom itself. "Seek the kingdom of God *and his righteousness*." I conceive this is added to make us understand the better what it is, and what is the way to it. The kingdom of God is the kingdom of grace, in which he rules in us by his Spirit. For Jesus Christ is come for this end, and made grace to superabound over the abounding of sin, that as sin reigned unto death, so grace might reign through righteousness unto eternal life by Jesus Christ our Lord (Rom. v. 21), that as sin had a throne in us, so grace might have a throne, and subject the whole man, rendered obedient to that rule of righteousness that he here holds forth in his word. But this kingdom of God also includes the kingdom of glory, wherein these who overcome this world by faith in the Son of God, reign as kings set upon thrones with God the Father of all. Now because the most part, when they heard of the kingdom of God, dreamed of nothing but a state of happiness in heaven, and passed over the way to it, which is holiness, and they thought not upon the kingdom of grace, which is preparatory unto, and disposes us for the kingdom of glory, therefore Christ exhorts us also to seek his righteousness, opposite to the righteousness of the scribes and Pharisees, who satisfied themselves with a mere walk before men. This was man's righteousness but not God's. This righteousness may be also opposed to the rags of our own righteousness, that we seek to cover ourselves with, Isa. lxiv. 6. The apostle says of the Jews, Rom. x. 3, 4, "For they being ignorant of God's righteousness, and going about to establish their own righteousness, have not submitted themselves to the righteousness of God. For Christ is the end of the law for righteousness to every one that believeth."

Now here is the business, and I would have you to conceive it right. The gospel calls you to a kingdom. This is certainly more than all earthly kingdoms. But how shall ye come to it? Not at the nearest hand, not *per saltum*.[503] No, believe it, ye must come and enter this way, before ye compass the end, and the way to this kingdom is by another kingdom, namely righteousness. It is the kingdom of grace within us, and the fruit of it is this. Deny thyself, and follow me, Matt. xvi. 24-26. Overcome yourselves, and your corrupt lusts, and ye shall be more than conquerors. Kingdoms are gotten by conquest. But here is the greatest conquest and triumph in the world, for a man to overcome himself. He that rules himself and his own spirit, is greater than he that taketh a city, Prov. xvi. 32. Other conquerors but overcome men like themselves, and yet are overcome by themselves, and their own passions, and so are but slaves indeed. But if ye deny yourselves, and resign yourselves to Jesus Christ, ye shall be more than conquerors, Rom. viii. 37. This then is the kingdom ye must seek first, and it is the first step to the throne of glory. If ye would have a throne after this life, you must have a throne of grace in your hearts. "If the Son shall make you free, then shall ye be free indeed." They truly are kings who are most subject to God above themselves, and free from the bonds of creatures. This is the glorious liberty of the children of God, to have liberty from him to make sin a captive. It is a righteous kingdom, a kingdom of righteousness. Therefore ye must here study righteousness and holiness, "for the grace of God that hath appeared to all men, and bringeth salvation, teacheth us, that denying all ungodliness, and worldly lusts, we should live soberly, righteously, and godly in this present world looking for the blessed hope, and the glorious appearing of the great God, and our Saviour Jesus Christ," &c. Tit. ii. 11, &c. All men love the salvation it brings. But do ye love the lessons it teaches you? Ye would all be glad to have that blessed hope, and obtain the salvation which the saints look for, when Christ shall appear again in glory. But how few learn and practise what the gospel teacheth, to mortify and deny your corrupt lusts, and live daily in the practice of sobriety, equity, and piety! O if this were engraven upon your hearts, that ye might study to do that in this present world, which this precious grace and gospel teaches us to do in it! Know ye not, brethren, that all your pains in seeking heaven, are not about heaven itself immediately, but the way to it, which is holiness? Without this, no man shall see the Lord, ye need not seek the kingdom of glory, hope for it, and look for it. But seek grace and righteousness in this world, and if ye obtain them, ye have not much to do, but to look for the blessed hope and Christ's glorious appearance to judgment. For if ye have sought and got grace here, Christ will come with grace and glory at the day of his revelation. Will ye consider that ye are redeemed by Christ? But from what is it? From hell only, and eternal death only? No, no, for we are redeemed from all iniquity, as well as the curse of the law and the wrath to come, Matt. i. 21, Tit. ii. 14. This deliverance from sin is the greater and best half of our redemption. Consider also to what ye are redeemed. Is it to happiness and glory only? No certainly, but unto grace also. For Christ "gave himself for us, that he might purify us unto himself a peculiar people, zealous of good works." These things should ministers teach and exhort, and above all things press them upon men's consciences. We are redeemed from all our enemies to serve God without fear, in holiness and righteousness all the days of our life, Luke i. 74, 75. Yea, glory is not glory, except it be complete grace, so we must call the kingdom of glory. If ye believed that it was nigh you, ye would look then for the perfection of grace. And will ye not love the beginning of it here?

But this is not all. There is yet more here to comfort us. Seek the righteousness of God. There is a righteousness of God by faith, manifested in the gospel for lost sinners, who have nothing to cover them. Now I say ye must so seek inherent grace, as ye may not make it your covering, and the only foundation of your confidence. Sinners, the thing which ye first seek and find, is to be clothed with God's righteousness, that he may see no iniquity within you, and then let it be your daily study henceforth to be adorned and made all glorious within, with grace and holiness. Ye must first renounce all your own righteousness, and then be clothed with the robes of God's righteousness, ye must still renounce it, that grace may appear as the gift of God, and not yours; as his beauty, not your ornament. If ye be imperfect in your own righteousness, comfort yourselves in the righteousness of God made yours by faith, that worketh by love and purifies your hearts, for, says the apostle, Gal. ii. 16, 17,

Though we are not justified by the works of the law, but by the faith of Christ, yet we must keep ourselves from every wicked thing, and perfect holiness in the fear of God, for if while we seek to be justified by Christ, and we ourselves be found sinners, impenitent and impure, is therefore Christ the minister of sin? God forbid.

SERMON XIX.

Matt. vi. 33.—"Seek first the kingdom of God," &c.

It may seem strange, that when so great things are allowed, and so small things are denied, that we do not seek them. The kingdom of God and his righteousness are great things indeed, great not only in themselves, but greater in comparison of us. The things of this world, even great events, are but poor, petty, and inconsiderable matters, when compared with these. Yet he graciously allows a larger measure of these great things relating to his kingdom and righteousness, than of those lesser things he hath promised to give his people, and he commands us to seek after these greatest things. "Seek first the kingdom of God, and his righteousness, and all these things shall be added unto you."

This indeed is most suitable to his Majesty, and to us also. It is most becoming his loyal Majesty when he is to declare his magnificence, and to vent his love, to give such high and eminent expressions of it. A kingdom is a fit expression of a king's love and good will. Kings cannot give empires, unless they unking themselves. But Christ is the "King of kings," and hath prepared a kingdom for them that love him. It is a glorious declaration of God's excellent name, that he is good to all, kind even to the evil and unthankful. His tender mercies are over all his works. The whole earth is full of his riches, and the wretched posterity of Adam have the largest share of his goodness, even since the first defection from him. Nay, but there are other things prepared and laid up for them that seek him, O how great is that goodness! How excellent is that loving kindness! Psal.

xxxi. 19, 20, Psal. xxxvi. 5, 10. These things have not yet entered into the heart of men to consider. If ye could speak the mind of it, then the tongue could express it. If ye could apprehend the wonders of it, then the heart could conceive it, but this the scripture denies, Isa. lxiv. 4. "For since the beginning of the world, men have not heard nor perceived by the ear, neither hath the eye seen, O God, besides thee, what he hath prepared for him that waiteth for him," or as Paul writes, "Eye hath not seen, nor ear heard neither have entered into the heart of man, the things which God hath prepared for them that love him. But God hath revealed them unto us by his Spirit, who searcheth all things, even the deep things of God," &c., 1 Cor. ii. 7-14. Is not a kingdom a gift suitable to such a Giver? And is not this kingdom of God every way like himself? These things are prepared by Christ, and there is no more to do, but to give to him that asks, and he that seeks shall find. This righteousness, divine and human, is it not wholly of God's finding out? Is it so glorious, so excellent, as to hide the greatest spots of the creation from his spotless eyes? For even hell itself is naked before him, and destruction hath no covering, even the heavens are not pure in his sight, he chargeth his angels with folly, Job xxvi. 6, chap. iv. 17, 18, 19, chap. xv. 14-17. When all the creatures could not procure the salvation of sinful men, when the depth said, it is not in me, and the sea said, it is not with me, and the heavens and heights said so too,—even angels could not redeem us,—the redemption of the soul was so precious, it would have ceased for ever, if divine wisdom had not found it out, and almighty power brought it to pass. "Sacrifice and offering thou wouldest not, but a body hast thou prepared for me. Lo, I come, in the volume of the book it is written of me, I delight to do thy will, O my God, yea thy law is within my heart," Psal. xl. 6, 7, 8, Heb. x. 5-11. All this was with God, and he knew the way thereof. Christ framed this royal robe of his righteousness, by suffering and death, which may cover all our nakedness. He came and sought the human nature with all its infirmities. He became in all things like unto us, sin only excepted. On him God laid our iniquities. For he himself "bare our sins in his own body," when he was slain upon the cross or tree, "that we, being dead unto sin, might live unto righteousness," 1 Pet. ii. 24, 2 Cor. v. 21. Behold what a wonder! Iniquities, and our iniquities, laid upon the immaculate Lamb, Jesus Christ. Our Redeemer hid his divinity, his holiness, and his innocence, as with a vail and covering from the eyes of God's awful justice. He smites the Shepherd, his beloved Son, as he did the rebel creature. It pleased the Father to bruise him and put him to grief, when his soul was made an offering for sin, Isa. liii. 4-11, Zech. xiii. 7. Justice did not look through the covering to his innocence, but reckoned and numbered him among transgressors, when he bore the punishment of our sins, and made an atonement for them, Isa. liii. 11, 12, Gal. iii. 13, 14.

Now hence it is that the righteousness of Jesus Christ, which he learned in the days of his flesh, and purchased by his death, is prepared for us, to put on. "Who soever will, let him come and take it." Empty yourselves, stripped naked of all kind of coverings but sin and unworthiness, that which God's holy eye cannot behold, and seek Christ's righteousness to adorn and cover you. Behold it shall hide all your sins and abominations, of whatsoever nature and degree, from the pure and unspotted eyes of God's justice, which are as a flaming fire, to consume what it cannot look upon without abhorrence. Put on this righteousness of God, and justice shall not draw by the covering, to look under it. It shall look upon the sinner as a righteous man on the slave of Satan as a child of God, on the heir of hell as the heir of heaven, if he sincerely repent of, and forsake his sins, believe in Christ and obey his gospel. "Behold all things are new, and all things are of God, who hath reconciled the world unto himself by Jesus Christ," &c., 2 Cor. v. 17-19, Col. i. 19-24. Christ was no worse dealt with for our sins, than we shall be well dealt with for his righteousness. This is the gift of God. And is it not worthy to be sought? Is it not a gift worthy of him to give? Is it not also suitable for us to ask? "If thou knewest the gift of God, and who it is that saith to thee, Give me to drink, thou wouldst have asked of him, and he would have given thee living water," &c. John iv. 10-15. So say I to you, if ye knew the gift of God, what this kingdom is, what this righteousness is, and who is appointed by God to be the treasure house of all fulness, to be communicated to us, ye would certainly ask of him the water of life. Ye would surely seek this kingdom of God and his righteousness. He doth not value other things. God only hath these things offered in the gospel, in choice of many, therefore are they laid up for some few, whom he makes his peculiar treasure and jewels, Mal. iii. 17, Exod. xix. 5, 6. If ye knew a monarch that was a possessor of all this habitable world, and was about to express his singular affection towards some persons, if his kingdom or the half or whole of it was not sufficient, to be a token of it, but he had found out some other thing, and laid it up for them, and distributed the kingdom, the lands and cities among others, certainly ye would think that behoved to be some strange thing of great price. If the Lord was pleased to give you abundance of all things here, make you all great, rich, and honourable persons, then many would seek no other expression of his love. They would think he did well enough to them. But alas! what is it all? He esteems it so little that he often casts it to swine, the profane and wicked world. He fills their belly with his hid treasure, Psal. xvii. 14. He makes his sun to shine, and his rain to fall on the evil and the good, Matt. v. 45. It is a demonstration that it is but a base thing, when it is so common, I mean, in comparison of the portion of his saints. For though these worldly things are good in themselves, yet they are not precious, they are not pearls. Would he cast pearls before dogs and swine? The honourable man's brutishness and ignorance of God may demonstrate to you he cares not for it. "The Most High ruleth in the kingdom of men, and giveth it to whomsoever he will," and sometimes "setteth up over it the basest of men," Dan iv. 13-18. If God loved riches well, do ye think he would give them so liberally, and heap them up upon some base covetous wretches? Surely no. But here is the precious thing that is laid up and treasured. The world and its gain seems great, and big in your eyes, ye cannot imagine more, nor wish for more. But alas! how low and base spirits have ye! It is but as the dunghill that the swine feed on, or the husks which the prodigal desired to feed his belly with, when he began to be in want, Luke xv. 13-17. So are all men's worldly pleasures, preferments, and profits. But here are some particular things, that only deserve to be called good, namely, "the kingdom of God and his righteousness." And when God had searched the whole world, (to speak with reverence of his glorious Majesty, who needs not inquire into secret things,) when he had looked through all the works of his hand, he sets these apart from all the rest, to be given to the men whom the King shall honour. This kingdom is the substance and accomplishment of heaven's eternal counsel and purpose of grace, which was given in Christ before the world, and it is the end of the Son's redemption of a sinful world, and his intercession for them at God's right hand. "Father," says he, (John xvii. 24), "I will that those whom thou hast given me, be with me where I am, that they may behold the glory which thou hast given me," and for other things he makes them as the stones of the field.

Now I say, as this kingdom of God and his righteousness are suitable expressions of his love, according to his magnificence, so they are also suited to our condition and necessities. No question but he would permit us to seek great things in this world, if these things were really great and good, and if they did become such great immortal spirits as we have. Your souls are above all these things. But this kingdom, and this only, is above the soul. Now then, if ye go out to seek these earthly things, ye must go down from the throne of eminency that God hath set your souls upon by creation, and abuse your spirits by stooping to the very dust of your feet, to embrace these things, and, which is worse, ye put yourselves out of that high throne of dignity that ye are exalted to by Christ's redemption, which we may call a second creation. Jesus declared by the infinite ransom he gave, when he offered himself a sacrifice without spot to God, (Heb. ix. 14) and laid down his life for us, what the worth of your souls was. "None of them," saith the Psalmist, "can by any means redeem his brother, nor give to God a ransom for him, for the redemption of their soul is precious, and it ceaseth for ever," Psal. xlix. 6-10. Call and assemble all the creatures in heaven and earth, summon gold, silver, precious stones, houses, cities, kingdoms, places of trust and dignity, great learning and parts, and every other thing ye can imagine, let them all convene in a parliament, and consult how men shall be ransomed. All of them combined together, though they make one purse, cannot do it. They cannot pay the least farthing. The Lord Jesus Christ then stepped in here, "Lo, I come,"—I give the body thou gave me, my life for theirs, "I delight to do thy will, thy law is in my heart."

Are your souls then exalted to such great dignity? Is such a price set upon them, and will ye spend them, for that which could not pay the price for them, "for that which profiteth not?" Ye must go out of yourselves to seek happiness. Then I pray you, go not downward. It is not there, but misery is there. And by going down to the creatures, ye have found it, and cannot lose it to this day. But the kingdom of God is the only thing above. Go up to it. "Seek these things that are above," Col. iii. 1-4. "If then ye be risen with Christ," through the faith of God's operation, "set your affection on things above, where Christ sitteth at God's right hand, and not on things on the earth." These things are but great in your apprehension. If they are at all great indeed, it is only in evil. If then ye seek great things for yourselves, ye may find evil things, ye shall certainly find such evil things as shall drown you in everlasting destruction. "They that will be rich" (in worldly things), who lay up treasures for themselves, and are not rich towards God, "fall into temptation, and a snare, and into many foolish and hurtful lusts which drown men in perdition. For the love of money is the root of all evil, which while some coveted after, they have erred from the faith, and pierced themselves through with many sorrows," 1 Tim. vi. 9, 10. Great things in this world are not always good. To seek them, makes them certainly evil and hurtful. It is not so hurtful to have them, though very dangerous, but it is hurtful, yea, present ruin to seek them. But here is a kingdom that is great, and great in goodness, every way answerable to our necessities. This is the kingdom we should seek above all things.

We would therefore beseech you to be wanters in yourselves, and seekers in Christ, and seekers ye cannot be till ye be wanters, and finders ye cannot be except ye seek in Jesus all satisfaction and remedy of your necessity. This is even the very nature of a Christian, his chief exercise and employment. What then is a Christian's principal study, his great business, his important calling, and what is his success in it? He is a seeker by his employment, or calling here, and he shall certainly find what he asks. But what puts him to seeking? The discovery of his own emptiness, and God's fulness. Therefore study these things most, if ye would be Christians in truth and in deed. It is these two that ye must still pass between, if ye keep them not both in your view at once, ye cannot well perceive any of them, either comfortably, humbly, or profitably.

This is even the sum of Christianity. Look what ye want in yourselves, and make up that in God. Discover your own emptiness and fill it up with God's fulness. "The liberal soul shall be made fat, and he that watereth, shall be watered also himself," Prov. xi. 25. Be not niggards here. Be liberally minded, both in seeking and receiving, so shall ye please him best who counts it his glory to give. "The instruments of the churl are evil, but the liberal deviseth liberal things, and by liberal things he shall stand," Isa. xxxil. 7, 8. Seek answerable to your own necessity, and God's all sufficiency, and know no other rule or measure.

Now, Christians, this is your calling and employment here, to be seekers of God's kingdom and righteousness. But shall we come speed? Yes certainly. It is so far put out of question here, that it needs not be expressed. "Seek first the kingdom of God, and all these things shall be" superadded to you. He thinks it needless to say, *and ye shall find the kingdom of God, and his righteousness*, for it is supposed as a thing unquestionable, and he adds these words, "and all these things shall be added to you," to answer the faithlessness of these who could not credit him in temporal things, though they had concredited[504] to him their immortal souls. Ye do not doubt, then, but ye shall have the kingdom of heaven. Ye do indeed seek it. Many by seeking kingdoms lose here—by seeking to make them more sure, they lose the hold they have. Many by aspiring to greater things, lose these things they have, and themselves too. But here is the man that is only sure of success,—the man that may reckon upon his advantage before he take pains, if indeed he resolves to take pains for it. This one thing is made sure, eternal life, if ye lay hold on it here by faith, and quit your hold of present things that end in death, Rom. vi. 21. We may well submit to the uncertainty of all other things, as David, who held himself well satisfied with the everlasting covenant God had made with him, which was well ordered in all things and sure, 2 Sam. xxiii. 5. Though the kingdom and house go, it matters not, if he keep this fast. If he take not away his loving kindness, this is all my comfort, my joy, and my desire. Comfort yourselves with this, amidst the manifold calamities and revolutions of times. Ye see no man can promise himself immunity, or freedom from common judgments. Here ye have no continuing city. Why then do ye not seek one to come, and comfort yourselves in the hope of it? Your rights and heritable securities will not secure your lands and riches for any considerable time. Therefore seek an eternal and sure inheritance, sure mercies. Seek that which ye cannot miss, and having found, cannot lose. Nothing here can you expect either to find, or keep, until ye have found it.

But besides all this, there is an accession to the inheritance. All needful things shall be added, ye shall want "no good thing," Psal. lxxxiv. 11. Will not all this double gain and advantage recompense, yea, overcome all the labours of seeking? Shall it not drive away the remembrance of them? Here then is the most compendious and comprehensive way to have your desires in this life granted, to get your necessities supplied. "Seek first the kingdom of God" and ye shall have them. But if ye seek these things and not heaven, ye shall want this kingdom. I think then it is all the folly and madness in the world, not to take this way, for it is the way to be blessed here and hereafter. And if we choose any other way, it brings no satisfaction here, and it brings eternal misery hereafter. If ye would be well in this world, seek heaven. Do not think that ye should have heaven, or seek God's kingdom from this sordid principle, that ye shall have all worldly things given you, which God pleaseth to bestow. For now man can seek the kingdom of heaven aright, but he that seeks it for itself. Yet if they were no more to proclaim the madness of men, this would sufficiently suffice, all they can desire or expect is promised with the kingdom, and yet they will not seek it.

SERMON XX.

1 Pet. iv. 7.—"But the end of all things is at hand, be ye therefore sober and watch unto prayer."

If ye would ask what ye should do till Christ come again, or what should be your exercise and employment in this old age of the world, here ye have it in a word, "be sober, and watch unto prayer." When Christ was to go away to his Father, and leave his disciples in this world, as he left them not orphans, or comfortless, without the Comforter, so neither left he them without counsel and direction. The word he left to them was, "Take heed, watch and pray," Mark xiii. 33. In this chapter, Peter is mindful of his Lord's directions, as Paul also was, 1 Thess. v. 6. The substance of this chapter is to exhort Christians to a holy conversation, suitable to their high calling. He presses mortification in general, from that which should be of greatest force with a believer's heart,—the strongest and most convincing reason in the world,—union with Christ crucified, even as Paul does, Rom. vi. And then, in the 3d and 4th verses, he argues from their former conversation, ye have sinned enough already, all the rest of your time is over little[505] to consecrate to God, according then as ye have advanced Satan's kingdom while under it, so advance Christ's kingdom when it comes to you, and take that noble revenge upon yourselves and sins, so as to bring them both captive to the obedience of Christ. And although the world may think it strange ye walk not with them, yet so much the rather ought ye to aspire after a disconformity to the world. Be then ambitious of being singular in the world. Ye would lay down such a conclusion as this, I am a stranger, and will walk as a stranger. And ye need not think yourselves miserable to be out of so much company, and to be alone. No, if ye knew what was to come upon them, ye would get you out from among them, lest ye be partakers of their plagues. The day of the Lord is coming, and the world must give an account to the Judge of all flesh. Ye may endure their mockings, and all the hard measure which ye get her, for it shall be recompensed unto them. And your lot is the same that other saints had, who now sleep in the Lord. The gospel was preached unto them, and they had the same fruit of it before God, and got everlasting life by it, yet they were judged in the world as well as you, and were counted base and contemptible. Now, in this verse, he comes to particular exhortations from the former reasons. This text hath two parts. I: An exhortation to some special duties, which are so conjoined in this form of speech that they seem all but one duty. "Prayer" is the duty, and sobriety and watchfulness are means to it. II: There is a reason given, because "the end of all things is at hand." So, then, ye have here the posture the world is in, and the posture a Christian should be in. This is the world's old age. It is declining, albeit it seem a fair and beautiful thing in the eyes of them who know no better, and unto them who are of yesterday, and know nothing. It looks as if it had been created yesterday, yet the truth is, and a believer knows, it is near the grave. Gray hairs are here and there upon it, though many know it not, and Jesus the Lord is at hand to put an end to it. Now, what should be your condition in the meantime? What should immortal souls do, that are to remain for ever, and outlive this habitable world? How should they be employed? The spirit and soul is to endure longer than the man's possessions, goods, honour, and place. How, then, should ye look upon these things? Here it is. Be sober in the use of all things. Use the world as if ye used it not, watch unto prayer. Ye are encompassed about with manifold temptations. Therefore watch, and be as men on their way waiting for the Bridegroom. The bride's exercise, since Christ hath ascended unto heaven, should be to say, "Lord Jesus come quickly."

In discoursing upon this subject, I: We shall speak of these three parts of a Christians duty severally. II: Consider how they help one another, and so jointly speak of them. And then, III: Of the reason and motive to them all, and how it enforces such an exercise. As to be the first of these, we observe, that sobriety is a duty becoming every Christian, that is united unto Jesus Christ, and is separated by God's holy calling from the rest of the world. I add these two considerations because of the preceding verse. For in the first and second verses he lays down an excellent ground of all kind of mortification, viz. the believer's union with Christ crucified. Jesus Christ suffered and died for us, as a Common Person, to sustain the guilt of our sins. He died as a Cautioner and Undertaker for us and as our Head and King, and we by virtue of that, are obliged to crucify sin also. In verses 3d and 4th, the other consideration is set down. There ought to be a vast difference between a believer now, and before his conversion. He should not be the same man, but as Paul, say, "I am crucified with Christ, nevertheless I live, yet not I, but Christ liveth in me." Gal. ii. 20. He should be separated from the world, that all the world may wonder at him, and think it strange to see his conversation. Now I conceive this exhortation is gathered from both these, and the word of reference *therefore* relates to the preceding verse, as well as his reason in the words now read. Now therefore be sober. This sobriety is not limited to meat, drink or apparel, the object of it is more comprehensive in scripture. It uses sometimes to be expressed singly, without making mention of any particular matter, evidently importing, that sobriety ought to be in all things. That which we ought to be sober in is certainly the "all things spoken of in the reason of sobriety, whose end is at hand." They are most distinctly expressed 1 John ii. 15-17, "All that is in the world, the lust of the flesh, the lust of the eye, and the pride of life," all that perishes is not of the Father, but of the world, that is, the world which wicked men frame to themselves. Here then is a large commentary on "all things." Therefore whatever is in the world is the matter of sobriety. Whatever comes under the senses calls for sobriety. Whatever comes under the object of the mind is the matter of sobriety. Nay, whatever is corruptible and perishing, or whatever the last day of the Lord a coming shall put an end to, in all these, there must be sobriety exercised. There is a threefold sobriety: 1. Sobriety in the mind, or sober mindedness, Rom. xii. 3. We ought not to think more highly of ourselves than we ought to think, "but to think soberly," 1 Cor. iv. 6, 7, Tit. ii. 6, Rom. xi. 20, 1 Cor. vii. 2. Sobriety of mind is that excellent lesson that Christ Jesus both taught and practised in his humble state. "Learn of me, for I am meek and lowly in heart," Matt. xi. 29. Humility is not like Peter, who said, "Depart from me, for I am sinful man, O Lord," "Lord, thou shalt never wash my feet." But humility is rather like Mary, that sat down at Christ's feet, and washed them with tears. Sobriety of mind does not undervalue God's gifts and graces, neither doth it overvalue them. It thinks of itself according to the measure of grace freely given, (Rom. xii. 3) and sobriety looks on all its own gifts, and ornaments, as not its own but another's, as free gifts, and therefore it puffs not up a man against his neighbour, though he should see a gift given beyond his neighbour. High mindedness is like the high bending of a string of an instrument, which easily breaks in two pieces. Sobriety walks with a low sail, and creeps through under the wind, but the high mind is like the cedar, that moves with the wind, and falls when the bowing twig stands still. Some will think the aspiring of the spirit a sign of a better spirit than the humble mind, and so look down upon others. But oh, if they walk safely, they will walk humbly with God.

2. There is also sobriety in the affections when they are moderate. The objects of this world which come under the affections, are either sinful and unlawful or in themselves lawful and allowable. Now sobriety towards the first kind is simple abstinence, towards the second moderation. The rule of the first is, "Abstain from fleshly lusts which war against the mind" (1 Pet. ii. 11), and, as it was said in another sense, "Touch not, taste not, handle not." "Have no fellowship with the unfruitful works of darkness," Eph. v. 11. As a man who would be clean should not touch pitch, and he who would not be burnt should not carry coals in his bosom, so ought the child of God, who walked formerly in the lusts of ignorance, after the custom of this world, to abstain from all appearance of evil (1 Thess. v. 22.), not only from sin itself, but from all the occasions of it, and inducements unto it, all that which hath any appearance of evil. There is no measure of moderation here, a man must not think to give his lusts part, and Christ part. No, he must have all or none. Ye should have no quarters with sin, ye should be out of speaking terms with it. The least motion of the affections and heart that way, is insobriety, and inordinate affections. 3. But sobriety in things lawful is moderation, when the spirit is kept within bounds, Col. iii. 1, 2. And the rule of this is that which

Paul prescribes, 1 Cor. vii. 29, "Use the world as not abusing it," knowing that the fashion of the world doth pass away. Love this world as if ye loved it not. Every thing hath too much of the heart, and Jesus Christ would have his royal palace his peculiar place here. He may have suitable affections to God's dispensations in this world, (for the Christian wants none of his senses,) yet he ought not to be "greatly moved," as David speaks, Psal. lxii. 2. Now we consider this in three things, (1) In seeking of any thing; (2) In enjoying of any thing; (3) In losing or wanting any thing. That rule of Paul's may be applied to all the three, he should seek the world as if he sought it not. He should enjoy the world as if he enjoyed it not. He should want or lose the world as if he lost it not. This sobriety makes him want, in abundance, and abound, in want,—to have nothing, and yet possess all things. All our time and pains and affections are spent out upon these, and turn about on these three points. Desire, attended with care and anxiety, goes out to fetch in any thing that the mind fancies. When the soul hath gotten its desire, it delights and rejoices in it, and when it is frustrated, disappointed, or crossed, it grieves and torments itself. If ye find a Christian sober in these, you find his pulse beat well. (1) Ye should then seek the world or any thing, as if ye sought it not. We are given to idolize the creatures, and dig broken cisterns, and forsake the fountain of living waters, to seek the creature as if it were God, and the strength of affections uses to be spent on it. Men have big and large apprehensions of the things of this world, and are like foolish children amazed with pictures and dreams. Fancy busks[506] up and adorns the object with all things suitable, and thus the poor soul is put in expectation of some thing, and stretcheth out itself, to the utmost of its ability, to purchase that, which being had will not satisfy. The world promises fair to deluded minds that know no better. But the child of God must be sober here. He ought to have a low estimation of all created things, and conclude all under vanity and vexation of spirit, Luke x. 41, 42. Sobriety so seeks, that it can want, because it seeks a better thing that it cannot miss. But the poor worldling seeks this world as his only thing, and if he want it, what hath he more? He must have it, or else he hath nothing. The child of God should seek as a rich man that is satisfied, and needs no more, so that he cares not whether he obtain or not. The worldlings seek it as their portion, their heart and affections are on it, but he seeks it not as his portion, but as an accessory to his inheritance, Matt, vi. 33. Again we observe, (2.) That the good man uses the world, and enjoys it, as if he enjoyed it not. When riches increase, he sets not his heart on them. He is dead to the world, and crucified to it. It is but an unpleasant thing to him, and he to it. He can be refreshed with his meat more than another, because he sees God and his love in it, yet he hath it not as his portion. He is not excessive in gladness for any dispensation cast in the balance, one kind of dispensation or another. That which would make another man think he was half in heaven, or half in hell, it will not add much moment and weight to such a spirit. It is but like the casting in of a feather in a great balance, that will scarcely incline it to either side. (3) He loses or wants[507] the world, as if he lost it not. That which would break another man's heart, sobriety will make him go light under, and not be much disquieted for any thing. Why, what is the matter of it? Can it trouble his peace or access to God? Can his portion be removed? What, then, should ail him, for the light of God's countenance is more recompense than all the world? Proceed we now to apply this in some uses.

Use I. It discovers unto the most part of men how little they are advanced in Christianity. Many are insober in the use of the world, and what must their affections be? The works of darkness, that become not the children of God nor the children of the day, are yet common in the visible church. Insobriety in many is palpable, and written on their forehead. That beastly sin of drunkenness abounds in many congregations. But II. We would even convince the Lord's own children of great short coming in this duty. Although your carriage before men might pass free of censure of insobriety, yet O! how many things will God put such a construction on! There are many saints that cannot walk soberly in the use of this world. They spend their time upon it, and this is insobriety. Scarce can prayer and communion with God get an hour in the day from their calling, and when ye have to spend, insobriety is written upon many passages of your behaviour. Your meat, and drink, and clothing, should declare that ye are waiting for a better inheritance. But O! how are your affections wedded unto this present world! The current and stream of many of your thoughts go this way, what shall I eat or drink, or what shall I put on for clothing? And ye spend your spirits in projecting, and in following out your projects. There are some evident demonstrations of insobriety in the affections. For, (1) Most of your thoughts run upon temporal things and certainly if your hearts were not in this world, your minds would follow your hearts. Christians, too many amongst you spend whole days, and never any object enters into your minds but one thing of the world after another. Your minds are highways for the travellers of this world to come through. It may be ye will steal an hour, or half an hour for prayer, but the rest of your conversation is not in heaven, but void of God. According as every hour furnishes new opportunities, so are your minds here, Phil. iii. 20. And meditation upon spiritual things, that is the nerves and sinews of religion, that is a rare thing. If your affections were not more upon this world than upon Christ Jesus, would not our Saviour be uppermost in your thoughts? Would not Christ interrupt your thoughts of the world? Would not heaven come in the midst of your business, and get a spare look and ejaculation? The world uses to interrupt your thoughts of God, and the mind is given to wander in prayer. But put you upon something temporal, ye can fix your heart as long as you please, and never wander. David was not so. He awaked, and was still with God. He meditates upon him in the night watches. He remembers him day and night, (Psal. lxiii. 8) and this made him a lively Christian. But, (2) If ye be seeking any thing, ye seek it so, as insobriety is stamped upon it. Your seeking of the world is prejudicial to your seeking of God, and takes away much time for prayer. Ye will be so eager in the pursuit of a momentary passing vanity, as ever ye were in the seeking of God, Col. iii. 1, 2. Care and anxiety comes in to be your provision, and ye put not prayer in the place of it, to make your requests known unto God. Ye seek it as if it were your portion and inheritance, surely this is insobriety. (3) Look upon your affections toward present enjoyments, and are ye sober? Ye can delight in these things, and take the sweetness of them, but the consolations of God are a small thing to you. Any thing adds to your joy and lifts you up. Albeit ye be not in good terms with God, yet ye can take your pleasure in the world. Ye see not a worm and moth in your pleasures, ye are not afraid to fill your belly with honey. Some think themselves made up when they get such a lot. But saints, are ye sober when such a thing changes your condition? O but the children of God look upon this world as David did in his fretting condition, (Psal. xxxviii.) and in his prosperous condition, Psal. xxx. Ye sit down and say, "My mountain stands strong, and I shall never be moved." Ye have more delight in your outward lot than ever ye had in Jesus Christ. But, (4) When any outward thing goes cross to your mind, then your insobriety appears. The taking[508] of a sad and cross dispensation will evidence how ye sought the world. The taking away of a friend or idol, will declare ye idolized it. As the saints have too longing desires for the things of this world, and look upon them as the paradise of God, not as Paul did, who thought the world a dead thing, so remove any thing that ye enjoy, and your joy is taken from you. Give you something for which you pray, your sorrow is away, and ye can no more mourn for sin; and take something away, and your joy is gone, ye cannot delight in God. Ye vex and disquiet yourselves in vain, and are weighed down with it. Are ye not then under the feet of this present world, when it tramples upon you? Are ye not servants unto it, when your condition altereth and changeth according to the nod of outward things? Ye may know what puts you up and down that commands you, and this is not sobriety. Ye are drunk with the creature. The child of God should be like mount Zion, that can never be moved. Therefore,

III. We would exhort all the saints to study more sobriety in this world. We need no more exhortation than what Paul gives, 1 Cor. vii. 29. It is a strange language, saints, "Set not your affections upon the things of this earth, but on the things which are above," Col. iii. 1, 2. "Love not the world, nor the things of the world," &c., 1 John ii. 15-17. Ye ought to study such a walk abstracted from this world, that ye might be as strangers at home, as sojourners in your own country. The child of God should sit down in his own family among his children, as if he were abroad, and he ought to be abroad, as if he were at home. Wherefore your life is called a pilgrimage, and ye strangers. Engage not much your heart to any thing of this world. Take but a standing drink and be gone, ye may not lay down your staff and burden, that his may bear you right. (1) Consider that insobriety is idolatry. Insobriety puts the creature in God's place, and sobriety puts all things in their own place. When a man's heart or affections are set on any thing, that is his idol and his master, and Christ says, "Ye cannot serve God and mammon," (Matt. vi. 24) these two masters. Sure the worldling thinks not that he serves his riches, yet Christ puts that construction upon his loving them well, Christ calls any thing that is a man's master his god. Now, any thing that the heart goes after is a man's master. That which commands a man's affections commands the whole man, for the affections are the man's master, and they command the man. If ye knew this, ye would be afraid of spending your hearts upon vanity; ye put that vanity in the place of Jesus Christ, and so your heart is a temple of idols, and the great gospel promise (Ezek. xxxvi. 25, 26) hath not gotten place in you. The due place of the creature is to be subservient to the Lord its Maker, to be only the footstool, that he may have the throne. True insobriety puts the creature upon the throne, and worships it. (2) Insobriety or love to the world hinders the love of God, as much as is added to the one, is taken from the other, 1 John ii. 15. If the love of the world have one gram weight of allowance more than Christ speaks of, that is incompatible with the love of the Father. The creature will suffer a parting of affection, and will be content with a share, like the harlot and false mother that would be content with the divided child; but God must have all or none, and will not share with the creature. Ye may find it by experience when your hearts have been much set upon any thing in this world, Christ Jesus has not been so pleasant to you, ye have not so much delight in him. Affection must run in the channel, or it is but weak, if once ye divide the streams. The love of the world makes the heart carnal, it is the defilement of the whole soul, and a weight that easily besets us, that it cannot mount up in a cloud of divine affection to Jesus. Can the needle go to two contrary points both at once? Can it move to the north and the south at the same time? Such an opposition is there between the Father, and the things of the world. If then ye turn your face on the creature, ye must turn your back upon God. Think not, Christians, to keep love entire to God, and to set your affections on the world. Solomon's backsliding had this false principle, he thought to retain his integrity, and his wisdom should abide with him, though he would try folly and madness, Eccles. vii. 23. But did he not grow more foolish? Did he retain his wisdom? Many have come down from their excellence by this presumption. (3) Insobriety is the world's sin. It is the sin of the days of your ignorance, when ye walked after the lusts of the Gentiles, and it is a shame for a child of God to be so. This duty[509] is opposed to their former walking, verses 3d and 4th. There should be a great distance between you and the world, that ye may seem men of diverse countries. Though ye dwell in one city or in one house, ye ought so to walk as men may think it strange, as it may be, a wonder in the world. O but few Christians give the worldly men occasion to speak of them for holiness, few give them any ground for wondering at and mocking their conversation! Your conversation is so like theirs, that they need not think any thing in it strange. Is it not a shame, saints, to be like pagans? Christ uses such an argument with his disciples to dissuade them from carnal carefulness, Matt. vi. 32. Sobriety is a work of the day becoming a child of light, as Paul observes, 1 Thess. v. 4-9, importing as much as if it were a shame for the Christian to be found much in love with the world, as it is for a man to be drunk at nine in the morning and staggering in the streets. There ought to be as great a difference between you and the world, as there is between day and night, light and darkness. Since the true light hath shined, to discover a more excellent happiness than the world can give, and since it hath concluded all under vanity, ye are not answerable to your holy calling to have it in any higher estimation. Consider also, (4) That the world is not your portion. Your life consists not in what you enjoy, your inheritance is above, reserved in the heavens for you. Therefore be sober. If ye believed this, that one day ye shall put on white robes, and be clothed with immortality, would ye so pursue after the world? It is the world's portion, and let them who know no better seek it as their god, and love it as their inheritance; but fie upon believers, that have a hope laid up in heaven, and fixed as an anchor within the vail. Should ye cause your portion to be evil spoken of, by your groping so much after this present world? If ye walked right ye should torment the world, and oblige them to be convinced that ye seek a city to come, and that ye despise all their enjoyments. But, (5) Insobriety becomes not a reasonable soul and is very unbeseeming a Christian, even so is it to every man. Are ye not better, says Christ, than many sparrows? Is not the life more than meat? Matt. vi. 25, Luke xii. 23, 24. So we may say, Is not the soul better than the perishing creature? O it is the disgrace and debasement of an immortal spirit to be put under the feet of a piece of clay, to be subjected to vanity, and to the poor perishing things of the world. If a man but knew himself, and his natural prerogative above the creatures, let be[510] his Christian privileges, he would despise the world, and think all that is in it not a satisfying portion for his spirit. He would count it a great disparagement to lodge upon this side of infiniteness and divine fulness. Would ye not think it a base thing to see a king's son sitting down among beggars, and puddling in the filth of the city? God made man to have lordship and pre-eminence over the creatures, and his spirit shall outlive all these things he sees, and looks to, and what a dishonour must it be to spend an immortal spirit on vanity, to have no eye beyond the span of time? As Christ said, "What hath a man gained, if he lose his own soul?" What gain ye in this world, though all things should befall you according to your contentment, what gain ye, since ye prostitute an immortal soul unto the service of the world, and have made it, to the prince of the world and all things, a servant and slave?

SERMON XXI.

1 Pet. iv. 7.—"And watch unto prayer."

"Watch." A Christian should watch. A Christian is a watchman by office. This duty of watchfulness is frequently commanded and commended in scripture, Matt. xxiv. 42, Mark xiii. 33, 1 Cor. xvi. 13, Eph. vi. 18, 1 Pet. v. 8, Col. iv. 2; Luke xii. 37. David did wait as they that did watch for the morning light. The ministers of the gospel are styled watchmen in scripture and every Christian should be to himself as a minister is to his flock, he should watch over himself. This imports the Christian's condition in this world, and expresses his exercise in it. Watching is a military posture, and insinuates the Christian's case in this world. He is compassed about with enemies, and therefore he must be a soldier, 2 Tim. ii. 3. "Thou therefore endure hardness, as a good soldier of Jesus Christ." The Christian hath a warfare to accomplish in this world, and therefore the church here is militant, and in heaven triumphant, 1 Tim. i. 18. Every Christian should war a good warfare, holding faith and a good conscience. What is the reason that when Christ triumphed upon the cross, and conquered all his enemies, and is ascended on high, that he hath not made all believers conquerors? Is the man that sits with Christ in heavenly places, (Eph. ii. 6) and he who was dead with Christ, and also risen with him, is he yet a soldier, when Christ hath overcome, and gotten the crown? And the believer, hath he not the victory that Christ obtained? Why then is he put to fight any more? Hath not Christ completely done it? Yes indeed, Christ hath overcome by his own strength, (Col. ii. 15) and is now on high, yet he will have the poor pieces of contemptible clay to overcome the Archangel,[511] the immortal spirits. It was not so much for the prince Gabriel,[512] the messenger of the covenant, the King of saints, to overcome his own creature, but he hath drawn out a battle and warfare to all his followers, that, in the strength of their victory in him already past, they may be made more than conquerors, and that there may be a perpetual song of triumph and victory in heaven, he hath made the saints strong, and hath made the strong weak. He hath set the poor with princes, and the kings on the dunghill. The Christian's heart and grace are like a besieged city, that is blocked up upon every hand, there are enemies without, and false friends within. Its party is great principalities and powers, &c. (Eph. vi. 12) and these go about continually to spy a breach. In the city, what strength can do, what policy can do, will not be wanting. All things of the world besiege the heart, and every sense is a port to let the enemy in. All a man's negotiation and trading in the world, is as dangerous as the proclaiming a public market in a town, for the country, while the enemy is about it. There is a desperate wicked heart within, that hath deceived many thousands, and would surrender the city upon any occasion. Here are fleshly lusts which war against the soul, (1 Pet. ii. 11) temptation to sin, and to unbelief. There is a heart within that can conceive and bring forth sin, and needs no temptation, a heart within that can seduce temptation itself, but it follows the tempter and when to all that a foreign power is added, Oh then, who can stand? Christ himself was tempted, but Satan found nothing in him, and had nothing in him, but when Satan comes he finds all in us, and we are like powder to conceive flame. We can even tempt ourselves, as well as be tempted by another. The Christian keeps a house that the enemy surrounds, and if he sleep he will enter, he is here a pilgrim, and is not yet come home, yet he hath a foul and dangerous way to go through. He is like a servant that his lord hath left, and given provision to, and is to come home when he pleases, Mark xiii. 33, Matt. xxiv. 32. If his master find him sleeping, woe to him. This is his case. What then should his exercise and posture be? He should be a watchman. (1) Watching is opposed to security and sleeping, Matt. xxiv. 42, Mark xii. 33. He must keep his eyes open, or else he is gone, (1 Pet. v. 8) be vigilant, lest the devil attack him. The sluggard's destruction comes as an armed man, because of his "little sleep" and slumber, Prov. vi. 10, and Prov. xx. 13. Security is the Christian's night, when he ceases from his labour, and the adversary does with him according to his pleasure. But the Christian is in a better condition when he is wrestling with temptation, and getting sore blows. When he is at peace and dwells securely, as the people of Laish, he troubles himself with nothing, but dreams over his days, but that is a decaying condition. (2) To watch, is to observe all things, 1 Sam. iv. 13, Luke vi. 7. This is a special point of the watchman's duty, to let nothing pass by without observation, whatever object would come in, to ask at it from whence, and whither. The heart is a highway side that all things travel through. If the Christian then be not exact in this to know what comes in, and what is its errand, he may be surprised or he know. He should observe all the motions of the enemy, and be well acquainted with all the subtleties of temptations. He must know his own spirit, or his thoughts, he should also observe all the Lord's motions and dealings with his spirit. It concerns him also to know what is his enemy or friend. Therefore the Christian should get upon the watch tower of the word, and look through the prospect[513] of faith round about him, that he may know what his spiritual condition is. But, (3) The watchman gives warning while it is seasonable, and the enemy far off. He raises the alarm, and all must be in readiness. So ought ye to be. Come to Jesus Christ with all ye observe, inform the Captain of your salvation whose soldiers you are. It is best dealing with temptation far off, and resisting the first motions of sin, for when it comes near hand, it gets many friends within, and it is the watchman's part not to give his judgment of what he sees, but to report only. Do not ye sit down to pass the sentence on any thing, whether it be good or evil, sin or not, but come unto Jesus, and let him speak, for oftentimes we reason according to flesh and blood. (4) There must be no interruption in this watching. He must give diligent heed to it, Mark xiii. 33, 1 Thess. v. 6. It is a very laborious exercise for a Christian to watch, all his senses will be exercised by it. He must look up, and that steadfastly, he must stand, and when he hath done all, to stand. When he hath overcome he must yet watch, lest he enter into temptation. He is in greater hazard after victory than before, Ezra vi. 13. He must watch when he is come out of one temptation lest he enter into another. The greatest disadvantage that armies have gotten hath been after some victory, when they were secure. Therefore we ought to give all diligence, and love not sleep, lest we come into poverty.

From what hath been said, (1) We see how few are in a warlike posture against Satan. Many serve under Satan's colours, and the strong man keeps the house. They watch not against him, but for him, they fight for him, and not against him. Do not many Christians, in profession, even watch for their sin, how to encompass what they would be at? Many wait on all advantages to get their own heart's desires, they watch against God's word, to hold out conviction. These are the children of darkness, in whom the devil reigns. We also observe from this, (2) That even the children of God are seldom found watching. There is much woful security among them and this is the universal complaint, who of you walks as if you were among enemies? Ye walk as if ye were in a peaceable city without gates, as the people of Laish, who dwelt securely. Ye have no friend in all the world, and yet what unspeakable negligence and sleeping is there among you? The flesh is so weak, that ye cannot watch but one hour for Christ. And O! but the intermission of one hour's watching hath brought down many strong ones. This made a breach upon David that could hardly be made up for ever again. From the words, (3) We observe, that prayer is a part of a good Christian's exercise. We may be ashamed to speak or hear of this duty. It is true, indeed, our religion is all compendized in this duty. Yet this duty is so little in practice, that our religion must be but little. We would, then, speak somewhat of prayer, and observe,

1. That it is the distinguishing character of a Christian in scripture. The child of God, and the man that calls upon God's name, is all one and the same thing. The wicked man's name is one that calls not upon God, nor seeks him, but the godly call upon their Maker, Acts ix. 11, 1 Cor. i. 2. All the saints in scripture have been praying men. The wicked, or natural man, is not an indigent man, he wants nothing, and therefore seeks nothing from God, but the Christian is one who hath nothing in himself, a beggar by birth, one that is cast out into the open field, and he is still seeking to make up his losses. Praying and wanting goes hand in hand together. Prayer then is the first breathing of the new man. What sign of life would ye know him by? Motion is an infallible sign of life and this is the motion of the new creature. Prayer is the stirring of the soul, and going out of

itself for bread, it is the sucking of the breasts of consolation. Grace turns a man's face God-ward and Christ-ward. 2. Prayer is the pouring out of an indigent man's heart in God's bosom. It is the emptying of the soul, and the landing of it on God's lee shore, Psal. cii. 2, 1 Sam. i. 10, Psal. cxlii. 2, &c. When a pious heart is overwhelmed and sore disquieted, it prays. Prayer emptieth the vessel, and brings the soul above the water again. It is a present ease in the time of trouble. Care and anxiety of spirit plunge the soul over the ears, but prayer brings it again unto dry land, Phil. iv. 6. Care burns and drowns a man's requests, but prayer makes them known to God in every circumstance of life. Therefore prayer is called a "making known our requests unto God," and "the lifting up of our souls unto God," Psal. xxv. 1, 2. But, 3. Prayer is the provision of a soul, for it is sufficient to do that which carefulness and thoughtfulness undertake to do, and effectuate not, Phil. iv. 6. Prayer does all a man's business. He lives by prayer, as Paul lived by Christ living in him, &c. Gal. ii. 20. He lived the natural life of a Christian by faith. So David says, "I gave myself unto prayer," he opposes this unto all that his enemies do against him. Not only doth it ease the spirit of the present burden, but prayer does all his business, because it puts it over into a better hand, viz., the hand of him who cares for us, 1 Pet. v. 6. It is like a child who is under his father's tutory,[514] and he does nothing himself, but all is done for him, and he needs to do no more but ask, and have, to seek, and find, to knock, and it shall be opened unto him. Prayer hath the promise of all spiritual and valuable blessings, and the promise is true. 4. Prayer speaks a life of indigence and dependence in the creature, and also speaks out the attributes of God, for the supply of all our need, sovereignty, bounty, and good will in God. It is the travelling of the poor creature between his own emptiness and God's all sufficient fulness. It acknowledges that he hath nothing, and that God hath all things he can desire to make him happy. Prayer is an act of homage and subjection to our Creator, and it is also an act of love and reverence, for prayer looks upon God, as a Lord, a Father, and a Master. 5. Prayer is the pulse of a Christian, and here ye may find him. If he be vigorous and frequent here, he is well, a decay in this is a woful symptom of a dangerous and dwining[515] condition. This is the fountain of the spirit of life, and the Spirit's breath. For the Spirit helps our infirmities with groans which cannot be uttered, (Rom. viii. 26, 27) and according as the Spirit of God dwells in a man, in so far is he a good Christian. If, then, ye would ask how ye should walk here, and thrive in true Christianity, we would only say this, pray fervently and without ceasing. Pray and prosper, and daily be strong, and the Lord shall be with you. He will never fail nor forsake you. Again, consider, 6. That prayer is not so much a duty as a privilege, and if saints knew this, prayer would not so often be a burden unto them. Is there any privilege like this? For prayer is an admission into the secrets of God, it is an emptying of the heart into his bosom. It is a great part of our correspondence with heaven. It is a swift messenger sent thither, that never comes back with ill news. It never returns empty, but accomplishes its intent. Prayer is as it were speaking with God face to face, as a man speaks to his friend, and is it not an honourable privilege, that believers are admitted to him, and may boldly come to him under all their necessities, and have such a sympathizing friend as Jesus? What is wonderful in scripture is, that God hath put that honour upon prayer to be instrumental in obtaining the greatest blessings. Did not the Lord, at the prayer of Moses, dry up the Red sea? Did he not, at the prayer of Elias, withhold and give rain? Did not the prayer of Joshua make the sun to stand still, till he had vanquished his enemies? Wherefore was all this? Could he not have done it unasked? Certainly, but the Lord would put that honour and respect upon prayer in all ages, that it might be a demonstration to all ages and generations, how ready and propense[516] God was to hear prayer. Nay, to speak with reverence, God will submit his own omnipotence to prayer. Command, ask of me, and command me, says the high and holy One, Isa. xlv. 11. O but "the effectual fervent prayer" of the righteous avails much, 1 James v. 16. It does a man's business, and upon less expenses; it gives a reward in the hand, and the hope of the things sought. Withal, prayer is like Jacob's getting that within doors, without much toil, which careful Esau goes about all the fields for, and toils all day to obtain. Prayer is the most compendious way of remedy of all things else. It always makes up losses either of the same kind, or better; for if the loss be temporal, if the want be bodily, prayer makes it up with access unto God. It pays in gold. If it give not the same coin, yet it is better.

We have spoken something of prayer for this end, that your hearts may fall in love with it. It is the property of a sincere upright man, that he calls always upon God, whereas the hypocrite will not always do it. Count, then, yourselves as much Christians as ye find of the spirit of prayer and supplication in you; for those that call not on God, their portion is very terrible. God will pour out his wrath upon them. God's face is set against such as do not pray. And I believe the multitude of this visible kirk have this brand upon their face, they call not upon God. God hath taken this character to himself, "the hearer of prayer," and those who mock at it, their judgment hasteneth, their damnation slumbereth not.

SERMON XXII.

1 Pet. iv. 7.—"Be ye therefore sober, and watch unto prayer."

We now come to consider the coherence and connexion these duties have one to another. *First,* Prayer is the principal part of the Christian's employment, and sobriety and watchfulness are subordinate to it. "Be sober, and watch unto prayer." (1.) Prayer is such a tender thing that there is necessity of dieting the spirit unto it. That prayer may be in good health, a man must keep a diet and be sober, sobriety conduces so much to its well-being, and insobriety makes prayer fail. Prayer respects a wholesome Christian at his best estate. (2.) Because prayer that is well in itself must have much divine affection in it, that may be the wings of it to rise upon, the oil that may keep the flame, James v. 16. Now insobriety is the moth of divine affection. The love of this world eats out the love of God and spiritual things; as much as the one goes up the other goes down, like the contrary points, 1 John ii. 15. Vehement desires would be a cloud of incense to carry the petition up unto heaven; but the love of this world scatters it, pours water upon the heart, and makes it neither to conceive heat nor flame. To be carnally minded is death, both here and hereafter, Rom. viii. 5-7. It is death to duties, it kills the spiritual life of the soul. Insobriety is carnal-mindedness, and minding of the flesh, so that a man hath no more taste of Jesus Christ than the white of an egg. It quite distempers his taste, and makes that only savoury which is like itself, and all other things bitter. But, (3.) Prayer must have hope in it. For how shall a man pray if he hope not to come speed? If he maintain not a lively hope, he will cool in his petitions. Insobriety is not consistent with hope to the end, 1 Pet. i. 17. He that would hope to the end must lift up his garments that hang side, and take a lick[517] of every thing by the way; he must not let them hang down, but gird up his affections with the girdle of truth and sobriety. We observe, (4.) That prayer must come out of a pure heart, and God must be worshipped in spirit and in truth, John iv. 23, 24; 2 Tim. ii. 22. Insobriety makes an unclean heart; the lusts of the flesh, and the love of the world defile the spirit, and makes it to send forth impure streams. (5.) There cannot be lodging for the Spirit where there is much love to the world. This grieves the Spirit, and makes him depart from us, and so a man is best to express his own groans, or to have none at all, which is worse. Where the Spirit of the Lord is there is liberty, and the Spirit must have a clean house; ye must touch no unclean thing, if you would have God to receive you into the holy adoption of his children. (6.) Prayer cannot thrive where faith is not in a good condition. For faith purifies the heart which sends out prayer, 1 Tim. i. 6; Acts xv. 9; 2 Tim. ii. 22; and O! but insobriety makes an ill conscience; and faith and a good conscience scarce sail in one bottom.[518] Both fall and stand together. How then can the soul look that Holy One in the face whose eyes are pure, and cannot look upon iniquity but with abhorrence? how can it look upon his holiness, when it hath been going a-whoring after the world, and forsaking the fountain of living waters? In a word, the heart that is not dead to this present world, will neither pray much nor well; for the heart is otherwise taken up, hath not many wants to spread before God, nor room for spiritual things. The creature gives him no leave to come to God. O but communion with God is a tender thing, and subject to many alterations and changes of weather! A little more mirth than is needful will indispose us for prayer. A little more sadness than is within bounds will also indispose us for this duty. Carefulness and anxiety cannot pray. Therefore it concerns all the saints to keep their hearts with all diligence, to keep themselves unspotted from the world. If ye would keep yourselves in speaking terms with God, ye must not entertain the creature too much. Any excess in your affections will divert the current of them, that they shall not run towards God. And next, ye see a solid reason why ye are so little in prayer, and keep not a praying temper, because ye are too liberal and lavish of your affections upon the world. Christians, how can ye pray, when your affections are upon the things of the earth? Will ye seek heavenly things, or care much for communion with God, when a present world is so much in your eye? Prayer must be wersh[519] and unsavoury when the world is sweet; and religion turns a compliment, when your hearts are here. Prayer is a special point of your conversation in heaven, and the love of this world keeps your hearts beneath heaven. Your treasure is here, and your hearts can be nowhere else willingly. Ye must then be mortified to the world before ye can pray aright. But we would likewise consider,

Secondly, That sobriety is a great furtherance to watching, and therefore they are usually joined together, 1 Pet. v. 8; 1. Thess. v. 6-9. This is clear. For if a man be not sober, but drink too much of the creature's sweetness, or bitterness, till he lose his feet, he cannot watch, and the enemy will make invasion when he sleeps. Sobriety is the mother of security. A surfeit of any thing indisposes the body for any action. When the mind goes without the bounds of moderation, and stretches its Christian liberty beyond the bounds of edification, it cannot hold waking, a little sleep and slumber overtakes, till poverty and destruction come like an armed man. (2.) When a man hath drunk to excess of the creature and hath his heart engaged to it, he is in an incapacity to discern a friend from an enemy; whatever comes in with his predominant or idol will get fair quarters; though it may be, it will betray him. The love of the world when it stands centry at a man's heart, will keep out true friends. It will hold out Jesus Christ and spiritual things, all that seems to come in contrary terms with itself, and will let in the enemy that will destroy the soul. (3.) Insobriety entangles a man with the snares of the world, and so he cannot be a good soldier of Jesus. I think the conjunction here is expressed more fully, 2 Tim. ii. 2-4. The good soldier of Jesus Christ that wars a good warfare, must not entangle himself with the affairs of this life. He must be sober in the use of all things, or else he cannot be faithful to his master; he will be about his own business when he should be watching. He will not only labour to please the Captain of his salvation, Jesus, but he has many other things to please besides: and if any of his too kind friends come to speak with him, he will leave his duty and go apart with them, the watchman's office will take him up nothing beside. But the insober man cannot give himself wholly to it. Because his idols cry upon him, he will prefer his pleasures before his credit and honesty. Therefore, as ye would not expose your souls and all ye have, to the will of temptation, be sober. The devil hath gotten his will of a man that he can force to lie down with the creature, and sleep in its bosom. If once Satan can gild up the world in your eyes, and represent it amiable, and cause high and big apprehensions of it, O, ye are in the greatest hazard from the world of being overcome wholly by it! That was the temptation Satan sought to prevail with Christ by, but he found nothing in him. If the devil hath taken thee up to a mountain to see the glory of the world, and make you fancy a pleasant life here-away,[520] take heed of it, for ye will drink drunk,[521] and forget yourselves, and will not discern between good and evil.

Thirdly. Prayer must be watched unto. We must not only pray, but continue "instant in prayer," Rom. xii. 12. We must "continue in prayer, and watch in the same with thanksgiving," Col. iv. 2. It is a strange expression, and familiar in scripture, Eph. vi. 18. O what a strange word is it! It is either very needless, or else imports the unspeakable necessity of prayer. "Praying always," what needed more? But we must pray with all manner of "prayer and supplication in the Spirit;" and more yet, "watching thereunto;" and to express the superlative degree of the necessity of prayer, he adds "with all perseverance." Since the words at the first view do speak infinitely more than we practise, let many a Christian express their own practice and set it down beside this verse, and blush and be ashamed. The most part of you behoved to speak thus, I pray sometimes morning and evening, when I have nothing to do. And is this praying always, and watching thereunto with all perseverance? To watch unto prayer we conceive speaks these things.

I. To observe all opportunities, occasions, and advantages of prayer,—to be glad of getting any occasion to sit down and pray. It is to seek out occasions and to be waiting for them. Too many use to excuse themselves easily that their other employments take them up, and they think on this account they may omit prayer with a good conscience, as ministers, busied about their calling, and at their book, think it no omission that they pray not often. But alas, is this watching unto prayer? Ye should be as men lying in wait upon some good opportunity to take hold of it. Prayer would hinder no business of that kind, but much further it. Prayer would be the compendious way of it. Ye used not to be challenged when ye get not a commodity[522] to pray; but do ye seek opportunity when it is not offered? Do ye look after a retiring place, and withdraw from company, when ye cannot pray with company? This were indeed watching unto prayer. But watching unto prayer will make men sometimes uncivil (so to speak, that which it may be would be called uncivility). It will be a very pressing necessity that will draw away the time of prayer, no compliment should hinder you to go to it. If ye got a corner alone, that would invite a man that watches unto prayer. He even seeks it when he finds it not offering itself. The watcher unto prayer will steal much of his time from others, and other employments, and he will not spend time unnecessarily.

II. To watch unto prayer is to accept willingly of all occasions and opportunities offered. O! if such a man find a corner, but it will be seasonable and sweet unto him. If he have nothing to do, and knows not how to pass his time, then he conceives he is called to prayer, and to keep communion with God. But how many opportunities have ye, and what advantage make ye of them? Ye have time and place convenient, all the day or much of it, and yet ye content yourselves with an ordinary set diet. Sure this is not watching. Watching unto prayer would make all emergent occasions welcome, ye would not have any impulse of the Spirit and motion to pray, but ye would follow it, and be led by the Spirit to your duty. Ye would not hear of any rare passage of providence, or any of God's dispensations towards yourselves, and other saints, but you would think it a good call to pray and make the right use and improvement of it.

III. To watch unto prayer is to observe all the impediments of prayer, all the enemies of that precious thing prayer, that ye ought to keep as the apple of your eye. Whatever ye find by experience prejudicial unto prayer, mark that. What indisposes the spirit and makes it carnal, mark that. What fills you with confusion and astonishment, and what hinders the liberty of your delighting in God, and rejoicing in his promises, mark that; and set yourselves against these. O but many Christians find liberal discoursing, and much mirth, prejudicial to the Spirit's temper, and yet who watches against it?

IV. Watch over your hearts that ye may keep a praying temper, and be still in speaking terms with God. And if ye would still keep a praying temper, 1. Be frequent and often in the meditation of God. Keep yourselves in his presence, as before him, that ye may walk under the sight of his eye, Psal. cxix. 168; Psal. cxxxix. 1-7. Stealing out of God's sight makes the heart bold to sin. The temper of the heart is but like the heat of iron, that keeps not when it is out of the fire, or like the melting of wax. If ye be out of God's sight your hearts will close. But, 2. Let no object come through your mind without examination of it. Let not your heart be a highway for all. If a good motion enter, entertain it, and let it not die out. Give it up to God, that he may cherish it. 3. Repel not any motion of the Spirit, but entertain it. There are three things ye would watch over, as, (1.) Yourselves, your own hearts, Prov. iv. 23, &c. ye must keep your heart, and it keeps all. (2.) Watch over your duty, Luke viii. 18. (3.) The time of Christ's coming, his second coming to judgment, Matt.

xxiv. 42; Mark xiii. 33. So did David wait and watch till the Lord should return, Psal. cxxx. 5, 6. So did Job wait all the days of his appointed time, till his change came. Now, Christians, where are ye? Is not your practice your shame? It is one among a thousand professors that can be noted for much praying. Who among you can get this commendation that the Holy Ghost gives to Anna, she served God with fasting and prayer night and day? Your morning and evening are the limits of your duty, and it is almost an heresy to go beyond that. Is there any tender well-doing Christian in scripture, but he prayed much? This made David so exemplary, and hath not Jesus Christ gone before you, (Heb. v. 7.) to lead the way? O! but Christ's praying so often in the days of his flesh, and making supplication with strong cries, is a crying witness against the sloth of Christians in this generation. Both people and pastor, how should ye be ashamed? Hath Jesus prayed so long and often, and should not the poor followers, indigent beggars, be all in supplication? The Christian should name himself as David did, "I gave myself to prayer." Many a man sits down to his employment and prays not much, because he hath gifts and abilities. But so did not Christ, who was able to save, yet he prayed and went about the Father's work with dependence upon him. And O that ministers would seek all from heaven immediately, and people seek it from heaven also! Think ye that the Spirit will take twice a-day for praying always, and set times for watching thereunto? No, no, we think there is little of this practised in this generation.

Now we come to the reason that is added in the text, "the end of all things is at hand;" that is, the day of the Lord is at hand. Christ Jesus, who was once here offered for sins, shall again appear without sin, unto salvation, unto them who look and wait for his appearance; and he shall put an end to all these things, either to themselves, by consuming them, or to the use of them. All that ye now dote upon is perishing, and it is not far hence that ye shall see the world in a flame, and all that ye spend your spirits on; and Jesus Christ shall bring salvation to his own saints, therefore be sober and watch. But how is it that the end is said to be at hand? Are not many generations passed since this word was spoken? It is almost two thousand years since, and yet Peter spake of it, and Christ spake of this day, as at hand. Sure it must be nearer us now than it was then. The day of the Lord is at hand: I. Because if we would count years as God doth, we would call the world but of one week's standing, for God counts a thousand years as but one day, 2 Pet. iii. 8, 9. The world thinks he is slack concerning his promise, and asks, "Where is the promise of his coming?" But believers, think not ye so, reckon years according to the duration of the Ancient of days, and by faith see the Lord's day at your hand, as it were to-morrow still. But, II. It is not without special reason that the New Testament speaks of all the time from Christ's coming to the end, as the last time, as it were but one age or generation immediately preceding the great day, as if the day of judgment were to be, or this generation of the earth would pass. It is of great use to us, because the Lord would have believers in the last age of the world come to some great pitch of mortification and deadness to the world, and hope of immortality, than has been come to before. He would have them be as men waiting for the Bridegroom, and this their exercise,—every one in his generation standing with his loins girded, and his shoes put on ready for the journey, and his lamp in his hand, Luke xii. 37; Mark xiii.; Matt. xxv. He would have all walking as if the day of judgment were to-morrow, as if the King of saints were now entering into the city, and all believers should go out to meet him as their King bringing salvation.

This then is the posture of the world, all things are near run, the fashion of this world passes away, 1 Cor. vii. 29: and the same exhortation is here pressed. This then, I say, is the state all things ye see are in, it is their old age. The creation now is an old rotten house, that is all dropping through, and leaning to the one side. The creature is now subject to vanity and groaning, Rom. viii. 21, 22. The day is not far hence, that this habitable world must be consumed, and O! but many a man's god and idol will then be burnt to ashes. 2 Pet. iii. 10-12, "The heavens shall pass away with a great noise," &c. God hath suffered men to live long in this world, that they might come to repentance, and he hath kept it so long for the elect's sake. If it had not been for them, the world should not be unburied till six hours at night;[523] but when he hath gathered in all the election, then shall an end be put to all the administrations of kingdoms, all governments, all nations. Think ye that God had so much respect to the world, or to the kings of it? No, he would put an end to all the kingdoms of the world, and never let them make their testament, if the elect were completed. If Christ were completed, there would be no marrying or giving in marriage, no more food and raiment, no more laws and government, all your fair lands and buildings must go to the fire. Now ask the question that Peter asks, "Seeing all things shall be dissolved, what manner of conversation ought ye to have?" And here it is answered, "Be sober, and watch unto prayer." Ask at Paul, and he will tell you, (1 Cor. vii. 29, 30, 31.) "The time is short," what remains then, but that he that marries be as they who marry not, they that weep as they that wept not, &c. So then here is the duty of those who look for Christ's second coming; Christ hath left it with you till he come again, and put an end to all things: "be ye sober and vigilant." But consider what strength this reason hath to enforce this exercise, and how suitable this duty is to them who look for Christ's second coming. 1. In relation to sobriety it hath a twofold force; for, (1.) It is all the absurdity of the world, that ye should so eagerly pursue perishing vanities; that ye should fall in love with the old decrepit world that is groaning under vanity, and very near consumption. The day is coming that the soul shall see all these things destroyed to ashes, and what will it then think of this idol? This is the thing I lost my soul for, and it is gone. And O how tormenting a thing will it be to the conscience! How have I been put by heaven for a thing of nought, for a vanity! Be sober, for the world cannot be a portion to an immortal spirit. Your spirit is immortal, and will continue after these things are gone, and it will outlive this world. Your goods and good name, your pleasures and profits, your lands and rents, all will have an end, and your spirit shall continue after them. Why then will ye choose that for your portion that will take wings and flee from you, or you will leave it? When ye see all burnt up, where then will your god and your portion be? (2.) Christian believers, ye have another portion; for Christ, who comes to put an end to these things, shall appear in glory, and ye shall appear with him in glory. He shall come with salvation to you, Heb. ix. 28; Col. iii. 4. Your life shall appear with him. Your inheritance is above. That sweet Saviour that came unto this world for saving lost sinners, shall come again, and will not think himself complete without you, and till he have all his members at his right hand. And therefore, saints, be sober. While ye are in this world, ye need not any other thing in the interim but the hope of eternal life, to keep your hearts, and hold them up. O but ye will think yourselves well come to it ere it be long. Ye may laugh at the poor, blind, demented[524] worldlings, who are standing in slippery places, and like children catching a shadow, or labouring to comprehend the wind in their fists. They are but dreaming that they eat and drink, and behold when the great day of awakening comes at the resurrection, they find their souls empty, though while they lived they blessed their own souls, and men blessed them also. Your inheritance is above, and what need ye more that have such a hope? May ye not purify yourselves as he is pure, and purge your hearts from all corruptions, and use this world as strangers, in your passage through it, that owns nothing as their own? Ye have no propriety[525] here, and therefore ye may the better live as strangers. But, 2. In relation to watching; Christ Jesus is coming, and is near, therefore watch. This Christ himself presses earnestly: Be as men that wait for the coming of their Lord, since he is not far off. Therefore, Christians, ye ought to be upon your feet, and not sit down with the creature. Ye should entertain this hope of his coming, and comfort yourselves by it, and be kept at your duty by it. I may say, there is nothing that is less known among Christians. Christ and his apostles often pressed it, as it seems he would have it the one ever running duty, through all generations. Ye ought then to be ready for Christ's coming, and not be found sleeping. 3. In relation to prayer; for if the end of all things is at hand, and Christ will soon come again, then the Spirit's exercise, and the bride's should be, "Come, Lord Jesus, come quickly." Pray Christ back again, and say, Why tarry his chariot wheels? Pray him back with salvation, and hasten his return by prayer. He hath left such a dependent condition, left such an employment for us, as speaks dependence and necessity. This is the time of promises, and we ought to pray for their accomplishment. In heaven there will be no prayer, for prayer shall be swallowed up in praise, faith in vision, and hope in possession. But prayer is a duty suitable to the time, and to the Christian's minority, to his banishment and sojourning. Dream not of an eternity here-away. Learn wisdom to number your days, and apply your hearts to religious wisdom; and if ye die thus, ye may rejoice that so many of the number are passed, and cannot return again.

FOOTNOTES

244. [A celebrated English preacher, who was cotemporary with Binning makes a similar remark: "No question but those that have been so bold as to deny that there was a God have sometimes been much afraid they have been in error, and have at last suspected there was a God, when some sudden prodigy hath presented itself to them and roused their fears. And whatsoever sentiments they might have in their blinding prosperity, they have had other kind of notions in them in their stormy afflictions, and like Jonah's mariners, have been ready to cry to him for help, whom they disdained to own so much as in being, while they swam in their pleasures. The thoughts of a Deity cannot be extinguished, but they will revive and rush upon a man at least under some sharp affliction. Amazing judgments will make them question their own apprehensions." (Charnock's Works, vol. 1, p. 42 Lond. 1682). An ancient historian relates, concerning Caligula the Emperor of Rome, whose licentiousness knew no bounds, and who professed the utmost contempt for the gods of his country, that, when it thundered, he was accustomed from fear of the gods he derided, to shut his eyes, cover his head, and even conceal himself under a bed.—Suet. in Calig. cap. 51 Seneca de Ira, lib. i, cap. 16.—*Ed.*]

245. [That is, place or station.—*Ed.*]

246. [That is, judge.—*Ed.*]

247. [That is, to sue for.—*Ed.*]

248. [Many of the speeches and actions of Philip, who was the father of Alexander the Great, are worthy of being remembered. A collection of his most memorable sayings has been made by Erasmus, in his Apothegmata Opus (pp. 268-279, Lutetiæ 154). The conduct of Philip, in many respects however, was very unlike that of a wise and virtuous prince. Like mankind in general, though he was reminded daily of this, he too often forgot that he was mortal.—*Ed.*]

249. [There is no fact, connected with the history of former times, which can be more easily proved than this that religious sacrifices were prevalent throughout every part of the Gentile world. Animals, which were deemed suitable for sacrifice by one nation, might be considered improper for such a purpose by another. But in the most remote countries victims of one kind or another, and not unfrequently human victims were seen bleeding on the altars of superstition, and with the death of these, the idea of substitution, or of presenting life for life, was almost invariably connected. When sacrificing her victim, Ovid makes his votaress exclaim—"I like heart for heart, I beseech thee, take entrails for entrails. We give to thee this life for a better one"—

Cor pro corde, precor, pro obras sumite fibras.
Hanc animam vobis pro meliore damus
Fast lib. vi. v. 161

But "as Kennicot observes from Delaney, whatever practice has obtained universally in the world, must have obtained from some dictate of *reason*, or some demand of *nature*, or some principle of *interest*, or else from some powerful influence or injunction of some Being of universal authority. Now the practice of animal sacrifice did not obtain from *reason*, for no reasonable notions of God could teach men that he could delight in blood, or in the fat of slain beasts. Nor will any man say, that we have any natural *instinct* to gratify, in spilling the blood of an innocent creature. Nor could there be any temptation from appetite to do this in those ages, when the whole sacrifice was consumed by fire; or when, if it was not, yet men wholly abstained from flesh; and consequently this practice did not owe its origin to any principle of *interest.* Nay, so far from any thing of this, that the destruction of innocent and useful creatures is evidently *against nature*, *against reason*, and *against interest*, and therefore must be founded in an authority, whose influence was as powerful as the practice was universal and that could be none but the authority of God, the sovereign of the world; or of Adam, the founder of the human race. If it be said of Adam, the question still remains, what motive determined him to the practice? It could not be nature, reason, or interest, as has been already shown, it must therefore have been the authority of his Sovereign, and had Adam enjoined it to his posterity, it is not to be imagined that they would have obeyed him in so extraordinary and expensive a rite, from any other motive than the command of God. If it be urged, that superstitions prevail unaccountably in the world, it may be answered, that all superstition has its origin in true religion; all superstition is an abuse; and all abuse supposes a right and proper use. And if this be the case in superstitious practices that are of lesser moment and extent, what shall be said of a practice existing through all ages, and pervading every nation?—See Kennic, Two Diss. pp. 210, 211 and Rev. Exam. Diss. 8 p. 85-89." Magee on the Atonement, vol. ii. part i. pp. 27-29.—*Ed.*]

250. [That is, restrain.—*Ed.*]

251. [See note page 96.]

252. [Lucius Cinna was the grandson of Pompey the Great. It was through the intercession of Livia, the wife of Augustus, that Cinna was pardoned. "Do" said she to Augustus, "what physicians are accustomed to do, who, when the remedies they have employed do not succeed, try others which are entirely different. You have done no good by severity—Try now the effect of clemency. Forgive Lucius Cinna. Now that he has been discovered, he cannot injure you, but he can advance your reputation"—Seneca de Clem. lib. i.—*Ed.*]

253. [Language of this description was in common use with the Antinomians of the time, as may be seen in Edwards' Gangræna (Part First, p. 22, Lond. 1646). Gataker's Antinomiania Discovered and Confuted, (pp.

18, 19, Lond. 1652) and other similar works written about this period.—*Ed.*]

254. [How inconsistent is this maxim of Machiavel with the semblance even of Christian integrity! Pascal, however, has supplied us with ample proofs not only from the books of the Jesuits but from their public Theses, that they hold it to be perfectly justifiable to calumniate their enemies or to charge them with crimes of which they know them to be innocent. He declares that this doctrine is so generally received by them (si constante,) that should a man dare to oppose it, he would be treated by them as a fool,—Les Provinciales tome troisieme quinzieme lettre.—*Ed.*]

255. [The philosophy of Aristotle was called architectonica (αϱχιτεϰτονιϰη), *pertaining to building*, from αϱχος *a leader*, and τεϰτην an *artificer*), as if every kind of knowledge had been rendered subservient to it.—*Ed.*]

256. [That is, arts or sciences.—*Ed.*]

257. [The Records of the Presbytery of Glasgow show, that this Fast was appointed by the commission of the General Assembly. "The commissioun of the Generall Assemblie, upone the 25 day of June 1650 did emit ane seasonable warning concerning the present dangeris and dewties unto all the memberis of the kirk. To draw neir to God, to murne for thair ayin iniquiteis, and for all the synnes, prophanitie, and bakslydinges of the land, to studie to mak peace with God in Cryst Jesus, to searche and try our wayis and to return speedilie to the Lord, and to lift up our hartis with our handis to God in the heavines, that he may spair and save his pepill, that thai be not a prey to the enymie," &c. (Nicol's Diary of Public Transactions in Scotland, p. 17. Printed by Bannatyne Club, Edin. 1836). On the 28th of June, a copy of this warning was presented to the Scottish parliament, who thanked the commission of the General Assembly for it, and requested them to delay the printing of it for a few days, that it might be accompanied with a Declaration from them suited to the existing crisis (Sir James Balfour's Annals of Scotland, vol. iv. p. 63.). When the Presbytery of Glasgow met on the 31st of July, 1650, "the brethrene that wer present declaired that yei had keepit the fast, that yei had read the warning"

(Presb. Rec). See also Lamont's Diary, 7th July 1650. The appointment of Fasts to be observed on the Lord's day, was at a subsequent period disapproved of by the Church of Scotland. "Albeit by the treatise of fasting emitted by the Assembly 25 December, 1565, the Sundays were appointed for some fasts as being for the greater ease of the people, and since by the last act of Assembly 1646, a fast is appointed on the Sabbath next except one preceding the then following General Assembly, yet seeing the work to be performed on the first day of the week is, by divine institution, already determined, we ought to set about it exactly, which we all acknowledge to be a thanksgiving and not a fast. Extraordinary duties are not to interfere with the ordinary, nor is one duty to shuffle out another. If either should be allowed, it would look somewhat like the reverse of redeeming the time, for thereby diligence is rather diminished than doubled in the service of God."—Overtures of the General Assembly, 1705.—*Ed.*]

258. ["The abstinence is commanded to be from Saterday at eight of the clock at night, till Sonday eftir the exercise at eftir noone, that is, after five of the clock. And then onlie bread and drink to be used, and that with great sobrietie, that the bodie craving necessarie food, the soul may be provoked earnestly to crave of God, that which it most neideth, that is mercie for our former unthankfulnes, and the assistance of his holie spirit in tyme to cum." (*The Ourdoure and Doctrine of the General Fast, set down by John Knox, and John Craig, at the Appoyntment of the Assemblie in the year 1565, Apud. Dunlop's Confessions*, vol. ii. p. 686.) This Order was afterwards observed in all the fasts appointed by the General Assembly. (Id. p. 699.)—*Ed.*]

259. [That is, "Nor does God please all, when he sends rain."—*Ed.*]

260. [That is, parts.—*Ed.*]

261. [The army of the Commonwealth was now on its march towards Scotland, under the command of Cromwell, who had been appointed by the English parliament captain general of their forces. But the hopes of the people of Scotland had been revived by the arrival of Charles II. from Breda, about a fortnight before this, who, at the mouth of the river Spey, before he landed, had signed the national covenant, and also the solemn league and covenant, though the commission appointed to receive his subscription appear, on too good grounds, to have suspected his sincerity (Sir Edward Walker's Hist. Disc., p. 158. Life of Rev. J. Livingston, written by himself, p. 51. Glasg. 1754.) A letter, addressed by Charles to the Committee of Estates, immediately after the battle of Dunbar, and dated Perth, 12 September, 1650, contains the following passage: "Wee cannot but acknowledge that the stroke and tryall is very harde to be borne, and would be impossible for us and you, in humane strength, but in the Lord's wee are bold and confident, whoe hath always defended this ancient kingdome, and transmitted the governement of it upon us from so many worthy predecessors, whoe in the lyke difficulties have not fainted, and they had only the honor and civill liberties of the land to defend, but wee have with your religion, the gospel, and the covenant, *against which Hell shall not prevaile*, much lesse a number of sectains stirred up by it. Wee acknowledge, that what hath befallen is just from God for our sinns, and those of our house, and the whole land, and all the families in it, have lykewise helped to pull downe the judgement, and to kindle this fierce wrath. Wee shall strive to be humbled, that the Lord may be appeased, and that he may returne to the thousands of his people, and *comfort us according to the days wee have beene afflicted, and the yeares that wee have seene.* You are going, you sat, upon the deuites, for returne of the afflicted land, (you do well to do soe,) and to try the instrumentall causes and occasions of the disaster and surpressal. Looke not too much upon second causes, the pryme and originall, and only cause, is God's just displeasure: for the causes of defeats in armys, they are harder to be found out than in any other of the actions of men, a word, a sound, the mooving or remooving of any body or squadron, may be, and have beane, the causes of the losse of battles, and how often have pannicke feares seazed upon them, that never any ground or resone could be given for? Lay not the fault upon this or that, coming doune, or not staing upon a ground of advantage, or upon this person or the other. That is the worst way of all, for nothing devided nor discord can stand or prosper, but leaste of all ane army; any thing of that kinde is the sodaine ruine of it. Upon any other constitution it will not worke so soone. Therefore wee intreete and charge you, as ye feare God, love his cause in your hands, have affection to your countrie, or respect to us, that you will remember, you are brethren in a covenant, and that you now stand up and joyne together as one man for religion, your countrie, your wives, children, liberties, and us, as your predecessors have done in their difficulties in their generations. Wee shall as willingly as any of them be ready to hazarde our lyfe (nay to lay it down) with you for God, the covenant, and the honor and freedom of this hitherto unconquered kyngdome, with any handful you have together, or when it shall be thought convenient." (Thurloe's State Papers, vol. i. p. 163.) The gross hypocrisy of Charles, in putting his name to a letter containing sentiments like these, and thus exciting false expectations in the minds of his credulous subjects, must be apparent to all who are acquainted with his subsequent history.—*Ed.*]

262. [The narrative of Hume presents an affecting posture of the cruelties perpetrated at the time of the Irish insurrection and massacre. (Hist. of Eng. vol. iv. pp. 361-366, Lond. 1825). It is said that "200,000 Protestants in two months space, were murdered, and many by exquisite torments, and many more were despoiled of all their worldly fortunes." (May's Brevary, p. 33. First printed in the year 1655. Reprinted London 1813). For several years after this period, Ireland was laid waste by contending armies and by the wild rage of the native inhabitants.—*Ed.*]

263. [A reference to this passage may be seen in the Life of the Author prefixed to the Work.—*Ed.*]

264. [That is, compensated.—*Ed.*]

265. [When the national covenant was first subscribed by King James and his household, and by persons of all ranks, in the year 1581, a number of Jesuits and popish priests had unexpectedly made their appearance in the country. Various dispensations from the Pope likewise had been intercepted, whereby the Catholics were permitted to *promise, swear, subscribe, and do what else should be required of them, so as in mind they continued firm, and did use their diligence to advance in secret the Roman faith.* These dispensations, says Archbishop Spotswood, "being showed to the king, he caused his minister, Mr John Craig, form a short confession of faith, wherein all the corruptions of Rome, as well in doctrine as outward rites, were particularly abjured and a clause inserted (because of these dispensations) by which the subscribers did call God to witness that in their minds and hearts they did fully agree to the said confession, and did not feign or dissemble in any sort. This confession [or covenant] the king, for an example to others, did publicly swear and subscribe; the like was done by the whole council and court." (Hist. of Ch. of Scotland, pp. 308, 309). By an ordinance of council and at the desire of the General Assembly, the national covenant, along with a Bond for the maintenance of the true religion, and the safety of the king's person and government, was again subscribed by persons of all ranks in the year 1590. This Bond had been previously entered into and signed by his majesty, and various men of rank and station in the kingdom, in anticipation of the threatened Spanish invasion, and as a counter association to the Holy League, which had been formed by the most powerful popish princes in Europe with a view to extirpate the reformed religion. When the national covenant was renewed in 1638, and once more subscribed by all classes of the community, the Bond which accompanied it was altered to suit the circumstances of the times. It expressed a solemn determination on the part of those who subscribed it to aim at "a personal reformation," as well as a resolution to withhold their sanction from the late innovations in religion, "till they be tried and allowed in free Assemblies, and in Parliaments." These are the words—"And because we cannot look for a blessing from God upon our proceedings, except with our profession and subscription we join such a life and conversation as beseemeth Christians who have renewed their covenant with God. We therefore faithfully promise for ourselves, our followers, and all others under us, both in public, and in our particular families and personal carriage, to endeavour to keep ourselves within the bounds of Christian liberty, and to be good examples to others of all godliness, soberness, and righteousness, and of every duty we owe to God and man" (Dunlop's Confessions vol. II., p. 136.). The following corresponding clause is contained in the Solemn

League and Covenant, which was ratified by the parliaments both of England and Scotland, and subscribed generally by the people of both kingdoms in 1643, and renewed in Scotland in 1648.—"And because these kingdoms are guilty of many sins and provocations against God, and his Son Jesus Christ, as is too manifest by our present distresses and dangers, the fruits thereof, we profess and declare before God and the world, our unfeigned desire to be humbled for our own sins, and for the sins of these kingdoms, especially that we have not, as we ought, valued the inestimable benefit of the gospel; that we have not laboured for the purity and power thereof, and that we have not endeavoured to receive Christ in our hearts, nor to walk worthy of him in our lives, which are the causes of other sins and transgressions so much abounding among us, and our true and unfeigned purpose, desire, and endeavour for ourselves, and all others under our power and charge, both in public and in private, in all duties we owe to God and to man, to amend our lives, and each one to go before another in the example of a real reformation, that the Lord may turn away his wrath and heavy indignation, and establish these churches and kingdoms in truth and peace."—*Ed.*]

266. [Nemo repente fuit turpissimus—Juv. Sat. II. v. 83.]

267. [Num. xxiii. 21.—*Ed.*]

268. [Jer. l. 20.—*Ed.*]

269. ["About the time of the first renewing of the covenant, there was a sensible change to the better in men's carriage and conversation, most of all those who joined in opposing the defection not only reforming themselves from common and gross sins such as drunkenness, uncleanness, swearing, profaning the Lord's day, slighting of the ordinances, self seeking, covetousness, oppression, &c., but giving themselves to the duties of religion and righteousness, such as sobriety, edifying discourse, chaste behaviour, hallowing of the Lord's day, diligent seeking of the Lord in secret and in their families, attending on the preaching of the word as often as opportunity is offered, liberality, love, charity one toward another, a public spirit and zeal for God. But all these things are now decayed in many and they are again grown as ill if not worse than before." Causes of the Lord's Wrath against Scotland. pp. 48, 49. Printed in the year 1653.—*Ed.*]

270. [Much less.—*Ed.*]

271. [An inference unfavourable to the religious character of the countrymen of Binning, has been too hastily drawn from this and some other passages in his works. (Orme's Mem. of Dr. Owen, p. 129). The late Dr M'Crie observed, that this was like "the attempts of popish writers to prove the *Reformation* a *Deformation*, by culling quotations from the sermons of such Protestant preachers as inveighed most freely against prevailing vices." (Christ. Inst. vol. xx. p. 624). In the "Representation, Propositions, and Protestations," however, "of divers Ministers, Elders, and Professors," printed in the year 1652, and probably about the time this sermon was preached, it is affirmed, that the religious aspect of the country had undergone an unhappy change, in the course of the two preceding years. "If we look back," it is said, p. 3 "to that which we have already attained of the work of Reformation, (notwithstanding our short-coming in the power and practice of godliness,) what purity was there of worship, what soundness of doctrine, unity of faithful pastors, order and authority of assemblies, what endeavours for promoting the power of godliness, for purging of the ministry, judicatories and armies, and for employing such in places of power and trust as were of constant integrity and good affection to the cause, and of blameless conversation? And again, if we consider how in place of these, within these two years, have succeeded, for unity, division, for order, confusion, for purity of worship, outward contempt; for the power of godliness, atheism and profaneness; for purging of the ministry, judicatories and armies, sinful mixtures; for zeal, lukewarmness and toleration,—it is too palpable that we are far gone on in the way of declining, having lost much of that which we had attained, and that which remains being ready to die."—*Ed.*]

272. [The author and the other protesters disapproved not only of the proceedings of the civil and ecclesiastical judicatures, but of the composition of these courts, after the act of classes had been rescinded on the 30th of May, 1651. In consequence of the repeal of this act,

they who, on account of what was in the language of the times called malignancy, had formerly been excluded from their places in the Scottish parliament, were allowed to take possession of their seats, by signing a bond, the terms of which the parliament prescribed. This the protesters considered to be wrong as a matter both of policy and principle. They likewise declared the assembly, which in July, 1651, met at St. Andrews, and afterwards adjourned to Dundee, and also that which was held in Edinburgh, in July, 1652, to be "unlawful and corrupt," adding, that "although with the renewing of the national covenant, and with the casting out of prelates, and the corruptions introduced by them, the Lord was graciously pleased to give repentance to not a few who were involved in that defection; yet, since that time, there hath always remained a corrupt party of insufficient, scandalous, and ill-affected ministers in the kirk, enemies to the power of godliness, and obstructors to the work of reformation, . . . that party perceiving that they were not able to endure trial in a time of reformation and purging, began the last year to lift up their heads, and speak a language of their own," &c. (Representation, ut supra, pp. 11, 12). The protesters, moreover, are found complaining at this period, "how gracious and well qualified elders are removed and kept out from church judicatories, and ignorant and profane persons brought in, and more endeavoured to be brought in in their room, how gifted and gracious young men are debarred from entering into the ministry, and a door is opened to others, whereof some are loose and profane, and many are ignorant and strangers to the work of the Lord upon their own hearts."—Letter from Protesters, subscribed in the name of many ministers, &c. met at Edinburgh, 17th of March 1653, by Mr. Andrew Cant, p. 6. See what is said in reply to this, in "The Assertor's Answer," printed in the same year, p. 18.—*Ed.*]

273. [Acknowledge.—*Ed.*]

274. [See note, *page 126.*—*Ed.*]

275. [Recognise.—*Ed.*]

276. [That is, genius or ingenuity (from *ingenium*, Lat.) "But gif corporall doth be commoun to all. Why will ye jeoparde to lois eternall life to eschap that which neither ryche nor pure, neither wise nor ignorant, proud of stomoke nor febill of corage, and finally, no earthlie creature by no craft or engine of man, did ever avoid?" Letter of John Knox from Dieppe.—*Ed.*]

277. [That is, "He who cries up his descent boasts of that which is another's."—*Ed.*]

278. [Much less.—*Ed.*]

279. [This is a literal translation of a Greek proverb which is quoted by Aulus Gellius (Noct. Att. lib. xiii. cap. 17) and which has been rendered into Latin thus:—*Multa cadunt inter calicem labrumque supremum.—Ed.*]

280. [Diod. Sic. Bibl. lib. i. p. 68.

Venit ad occasum, mun lique extrema Sesostris,
Et Pharios currus regum cervicibus egit.
Lucan lib. x. ver. 276.
The farthest west our great Sesostris saw,
Whilst captive kings did his proud chariot draw.
May's Translation.

Sesostris was so much affected and humbled, by the delicate appeal of the enslaved monarch, that he immediately commanded him, and the other unhappy kings who were harnessed to his car, to be removed from it.—Theophylact Hist. Maurit. lib. vi. chap. ii. Joan Tzetz. Hist. Chibad. iii. 69.—*Ed.*]

281. [See note *page 98.—Ed.*]

282. [Hear, O heavens and give ear, O earth. ver. 2.—*Ed.*]

283. [Regret, or accusation.—*Ed.*]

284. [Agreeably to the course of discipline in former ages, (Hooker's Eccl. Pol. vol. iii. p. 15,) they who had been convicted of any gross crime were required by the First Book of Discipline, (chap. ix.) and by subsequent enactments of the Church of Scotland, to confess their sin in the hearing of the whole congregation. The same thing was required of delinquents by the canons of the Church of England. Dr. Grey, in his Impartial Examination of Neale's History of the Puritans, (App. pp. 62-68,) has, from original documents which were in his own possession, furnished us with various forms, according to which, towards the end of the sixteenth century, offenders were appointed to make their confession, in different parts of England, in their respective parish-churches. The dues which, in cases of scandal, were exacted by the ecclesiastical courts of Scotland, were imposed and defined by acts of parliament. Power to levy these was given to justices of the peace, who were frequently members of the kirk session, or parochial consistory of their district. In the year 1648, the General Assembly "recommended to every congregation, to make use of the 9th act of the parliament 1645, at Perth, for having magistrates and justices in every congregation." (Rec. of Kirk of Scot. p. 511, Edn. 1839.) It was in this way, it would seem, or from elders acting both in a civil and in an ecclesiastical capacity, that the practice of exacting fines by kirk sessions arose and was continued. "You object that our church sessions did exact fines. But if you consider, that these fines, which you mention, are particularly imposed and determined by statute, and thereby appointed to be applied to pious uses, and therefore the demanding and uplifting thereof only, as well for the more summary and effectual restraint of sin, as for the end whereto they are destined, is in use to be exercised by kirk sessions, or rather by their officers and beadles in deficiency of the magistrate, this your scruple must quickly cease." "The True Non-Conformist," p. 55, printed abroad in the year 1671.—*Ed.*]

285. [See Note, *page 375.—Ed.*]

286. [This passage is quoted in the Life of the Author.—*Ed.*]

287. [That is, the persons who prescribe or appoint it.—*Ed.*]

288. ["The longer I live in the world the less fond am I of that divinity that stand upon quirks and subtilties. What should drive us upon determining whether faith or repentance goes first? What valuable ends or purposes in religion can it serve to promote? What edification can it give to an audience to dispute learnedly about a point of this nature? . . . I cannot but heartily approve what Mr Robert Blair, an eminent light of this church now in glory, said upon the question in hand. He told his people from the pulpit, that it was a very needless one. 'Tis just (said he,) as if you should ask me, when we are to walk, which foot should we lift first. If we should walk to purpose we must make use of both limbs; and so despatched the thorny question. I wish we may all imitate the wisdom of that great and good man. Is it not sufficient for us to declare that both are necessary, without determining the nice point of priority and posterority?" (Essay on Gospel and Legal Preaching, by a Minister of the Church of Scotland, pp. 22, 23. Edin. 1723.) "Mr. Robert Blair, born in Irvine, was first a Regent in the College of Glasgow, at which time he was licensed to preach the gospel, and was from the beginning zealous for truth and piety." (Livingston's Memorable Characteristics, p. 73) Mr. Blair died in 1666 in the 73d year of his age. (See Memoirs of the Life of Mr. Robert Blair, the first part written by himself, p. 128, Edin. 1754.) Mr. James Durham, Minister of the High Church of Glasgow, a short time before his death, intrusted to him the publication of his "Dying Man's Testament to the Church of Scotland, or a Treatise concerning Scandal," to which Mr. Blair wrote a preface. Principal Baillie gives this account of Blair, "Truly, I bear that man record that in all his English voyages, in many passages of the Assembly, private and public, he contributed as much to the pacifying of our differences as any, and much more than many." Journals and Letters, vol. i. p. 306.—*Ed.*]

289. [Or, sin itself.—*Ed.*]

290. [That is, *power* of persuasion.—*Ed.*]

291. [This is the word in the first Edition. It would seem to have been substituted for *arrive.*—*Ed.*]

292. [That is, unless you please.—*Ed.*]

293. [A proverb, which signifies that conscience does not deceive, and that its testimony is as overwhelming as that of a thousand witnesses—*Quintil Inst Orator* lib. v. chap. xi.—*Ed.*]

294. [That is, not to will.—*Ed.*]

295. [See Note, *page 96*. *Si vis cadem semper vella, vera oportet velis.*—"If you are desirous to have always similar wishes, it is necessary that you should wish for things that are proper." *Senec. Epist.* xcv.—*Ed.*]

296. [That is, laid open or explained.—*Ed.*]

297. [Dispone is a Scots law expression. It signifies to convey a right or property to another.—*Ed.*]

298. See:

Non bene conveniunt, nec in una sede morantur,
Majestus et amor.
Ovid. Met. lib. ii. v. 846.—*Ed.*]

299. [The name Immanuel ונמע לא signifies, *God with us.* Immelanu עמאל ונא signifies, *we with God.—Ed.*]

300. [The Goel (גאל), or nearest kinsman, was, by the Mosaic law, entitled not only to redeem a forfeited inheritance, but to avenge the blood of any of the family, by slaying the murderer, if he found him out of a city of refuge. He was therefore called the redeemer, or "avenger of blood," Josh. xx. 3.—*Ed.*]

301. [The word λυτϱον denotes the price of redemption, or that which is given to purchase the freedom of those who are in a state of captivity. "Even as the Son of man came not to be ministered to but to minister, and to give his life a ransom (λυτϱον) for many" (Matt. xx. 28, Mark x. 45). αντιλυτϱον is but once used in the New Testament. Its gratification is a counter-price, or the ransom that is paid when the life or person of one is given for that of another. "For there is but one God and one mediator between God and men, the man Christ Jesus, who gave himself a ransom (αντιλυτϱον) for all," 1 Tim. ii. 5, 6. Vide Leigh's Critica Sacra.—*Ed.*]

302. [That is, proposed.—*Ed.*]

303. [That is, however.—*Ed.*]

304. [Verse 6.—*Ed.*]

305. [That is, place it upon God or charge him with it.—*Ed.*]

306. [That is, adorned itself.—*Ed.*]

307. [*Scottice* for *than.—Ed.*]

308. [There is some obscurity in this sentence. The sentiment that is expressed, however, seems to be this:—*Much love to a particular object makes the act of seeking or praying for it to be loved more.—Ed.*]

309. [That is, an earnest (*arrha* Lat.).—*Ed.*]

310. [Yule is a name that is still applied to Christmas, in the Northern parts of England as well as in Scotland. "This name was originally given to the great annual feast celebrated among the northern nations, at the time of the winter solstice in honour of the sun. Hence Odin was denominated Julvatter, or the *Father of Yule*." (Jamieson's Etymological Dictionary of the Scottish language.) "He praised God that he was born in such a time, as in the time of the light of the gospel—to such a place as to be king of such a kirk, the sincerest kirk of the world. The kirk of Geneva keep Pasch and *Yule*; what have they for them? They have no institution. As for our neighbour kirk in England their service is an evil sad mass in English, they want nothing of the mass but the liftings." (Speech of King James VI, to the Central Assembly of the Church of Scotland, at Edinburgh, August 1590. Calderwood's Hist. of the Ch. of Scot. p. 206.) What is called the birch or "birk in Yule even'" was probably the *Yule clog*. On Christmas eve at no very remote period, the *Yule clog*, which was a large shapeless piece of wood, selected for the purpose, was dragged by a number of persons bearing in their hand large candles, and placed by them on the fire where it was to be burned in compliance with an ancient superstitious custom. Our author may refer to this practice or perhaps he had simply in view the old proverb, "He's as bare as the birk at Yule."—Henderson's Scottish Proverbs, p. 47. Edin. 1832.—*Ed.*]

311. [The records of the kirk session of the parish of Govan, during the incumbency of the author, after having been lost for many years, were fortunately recovered not long ago. These show the great strictness of the ecclesiastical discipline of those days. There were not fewer than twenty-two elders in the kirk session. Each of these had a ward or district assigned to him, of which it was his duty to take a particular superintendence. It was hardly possible, therefore, that any irregularity of which a parishioner was guilty could be concealed, and consequently, what is recorded in the register is to be regarded, not as a specimen, but as the gross amount of the immorality of the parish. Some may affect to ridicule the severe notice that was taken of particular instances of misconduct. But the cognizance that was taken of such things is a proof of the high tone of moral and religious feeling that prevailed at that time among the office bearers of the church. Individuals, we find, were brought before the kirk session, on account of family and domestic feuds, for quarrelling with their neighbours, for solitary instances of drunkenness, and of the use of profane language, for carrying water on the Lord's day, for sleeping in church, for resorting to taverns on the Sabbath, for calumny, and for neglecting the education of their children, &c. They who were convicted of such offences, were sometimes rebuked in private by an elder, and at other times by the minister in the presence of the eldership. It was only in the case of graver offences, the number of which was comparatively small, that a reproof was administered in the presence of the congregation.—*Ed.*]

312. [In the "Causes of the Lord's Wrath against Scotland, agreed upon by the Commission of the General Assembly," 1650, "Backsliding and defection from the covenants and our solemn vows and engagements," is specified (p. 46) to be "one of the greatest and most comprehensive and provoking sins in the land." *Printed in the year 1653.—Ed.*]

313. [This is the language of a man who did not use "at any time flattering words," or utter to his people "smooth things." From what he says here, however, and in some other sermons, and from corresponding evidence which might be adduced, we are forced to conclude that the well-known description which Kirkton has given of the state of religion in Scotland in those days, (Hist. of Ch. of Scot. pp. 48, 54, 64) must be too highly coloured. The presence of a large military force and a state of civil warfare could not but be prejudicial, in various ways, to the religion and morality of a country. I am perfectly aware that the authority of Lord Clarendon, Bishop Burnet, Milton, and others, may be brought forward to prove that the parliamentary soldiers were kept under the strictest discipline, and were remarkable for their grave deportment. But I know likewise that the characters of not a few of those soldiers are seriously affected by the offensive details of the ecclesiastical records of the parish with which Binning was connected.—*Ed.*]

314. [See Note, *p. 368.—Ed.*]

315. [Or together.—*Ed.*]

316. [That is, explain.—*Ed.*]

317. [Coldly or indifferently.—*Ed.*]

318. [Languishing.—*Ed.*]

319. ["Upon Sunday, the 27th of February [1642], a declaration was read out of the old town pulpit [Aberdeen] by our minister, Mr William Strahan, showing the state of the Protestants in Ireland, and how their wives and bairns were miserably banished, and forced to flee into the west parts of Scotland for refuge, and the land not able to sustain them. It was found expedient that ilk parish within the kingdom should receive a collection of ilk man's charity for their help and support, whereupon was collected of this poor parish fourscore pounds." (Spalding's "History of the Troubles in Scotland," vol. i. p. 34. Aberdeen, 1792.) "As a body, the presbyterians [in Ireland] suffered less by the ravages of the rebellion than any other class. The more influential of their ministers, and the principal part of their gentry, had previously retired to Scotland to escape the tyranny of Strafford and the severities of the bishops and were thus providentially preserved." (Dr. Reid's "History of the Presbyterian Church in Ireland," vol. i, p. 339.) After the execution of Charles I, an oath called the *Engagement*, was framed by the English parliament, requiring all persons to be "faithful to the commonwealth of England as now established, without a king or house of lords." The Irish ministers refused to take this oath. The republicans were irritated by this refusal, and by the loyalty of the ministers, who publicly preached against them. They therefore imprisoned some of the ministers, while others fled to the woods, and some to Scotland. At length, at a council of war held at Carrickfergus in March, 1651, a formal act of banishment from the kingdom was passed against them. "Those that staid in the country, though they could not exercise their ministry orderly as formerly, and though their stipends were sequestered, yet they, changing their apparel to the habit of countrymen, travelled in their own parishes frequently, and sometimes in other places, taking what opportunities they could to preach in the fields, or in barns and glens, and were seldom in their own houses. They persuaded the people to constancy in the received doctrines, in opposition to the wild heresies which were then spreading, and reminding them of their duty to their lawful magistrates, the king and parliament, in opposition to the usurption of the times, and in their public prayers always mentioning

the lawful magistrate. This continued throughout the summer of 1651, at which time there was diligent search made anew for them. Some were again taken, others fled, and those who were taken were imprisoned first, for a time, in Carrickfergus, in lodgings where they quartered; and thereafter, Colonel Venables not gaining any ground upon them, they were sent to Scotland." Adair's MS. apud Dr. Reid's Hist. vol. ii. p. 246-248. See also a narrative of the sufferings of the Irish Presbyterians, for their religion and loyalty, in the "Sample of Jet-Black Calumny," p. 214.—*Ed.*]

320. [What is perhaps meant is, it *swelleth* much.—*Ed.*]

321. [That is, *that can lay claim to the favour of his Saviour even when his Saviour turns away his face from him.—Ed.*]

322. [What is here said would seem to fix the date of this sermon. It appears to have been preached before the battle of Dunbar.—*Ed.*]

323. [That is, strongly.—*Ed.*]

324. [That is, his utmost.—*Ed.*]

325. [It is evident from this, and similar references to recent events, that the Case of Conscience must have been written in the early part of the year 1651. The proceedings of the commission of the General Assembly, from July 1650 to July 1661, fill a large MS volume of more than 400 pages. These proceedings have never been printed, with the exception of certain detached papers, which are found engrossed in the controversial pamphlets and journals of the times.—Peterkin's "Records of the Kirk of Scotland," p. 592.—*Ed.*]

326. ["The Gen. Assembly itself at Edinburgh, in July thereafter, did, upon the 19 of that moneth, publish a Declaration, in which they give warning concerning Malignants thus:—'We exhort all those who are in publick trust in ye comitee of Estates, or otherwise, not only to take good head of their private walking that it be suitable to the Gospel of Jesus Christ, and of their families and followers, that they bee void of offence, but also be straight in the cause and covenant, and not to seek themselves, nor befriend any who have been enemies to the Lord's work, self-seeking, and conniving at, and complying with, and pleading for Malignants, having been publick sins that have been often complained of; and we wish to God yr were no cause to complain of these things still, notwithstanding of the solemne confession of them, and ingadging against them. God forbid that any mocke the Lord. He is a severe avenger of all such things, and there is the more reason at this time not to own Malignants, because it is ordinary with men so to be taken with the sense of the dangers such is before them as not to look back to that which is behind hem. There may be inclinations in some to employ these men, and make use of them, that we may be strengthened in this and in our neighbour land, but God hath hitherto cursed all such counsels, and blasted such resolutions, and if we shall again fall into this sin, as our guilt shal be so much the greater by reasone of many promises and ingadgments to the contrair, so we may expect ane heavier judgment from the Lord upon it. Let us keep the Lord's way, and though we be few and weake, the Lord shall be with us, and make us to prosper and prevail. They are not fit for the work of God, and for the glorious dispensations of his more than ordinary works of power and providence in these times, who cannot beleive nor act any thing beyonde what sense and reasone can make clear unto them from the beginning unto ye end of their undertakings. Former experiences and present straits call upon us that we should act and follow our deutie in such a way as may magnify the Lord, and make it known to others that we may live by Faith.'—'The Waters of Sihor,' or the Lands Defectione, By Mr. James Guthrie, Minister of Stirling," Wodrow MSS vol. xvii. p. 41, in Bib. Ad.—*Ed.*]

327. ["At Stirlinge, the 12 of Septem. 1650. A shorte declaration and warninge to all the congregations of the Kirk of Scotland, from the commissioners of the General Assembly.

"Albeit the Lord quhosse judgments are unsearchable, and quhosse wayes past finding out, has brought the land werey low wnder the hand of ane prewaillinge enemey, yet must we not forbeare to declair the mynd of God, nor vthers refusse to hearken thereto. It wer superfluous to give answer to the maney calumnies and reproches that are blazed abroad, for albeit in every thing we cannot justify the conducte of the armey, yet we hold it our deutie to desyre every one not to beleive groundless reports, bot rather to eye the Lord, and looke vpe to the hand that smytts them. And therfor, in the first place, we exhort and warne all the inhabitants of the land, to searche out ther iniquities, and to be deeplie humbled before the Lord, that he may turn away his wraith from us. The Lord hath wounded us and chasteissed us sore, wiche sayes that our iniquities are muche, and that our sins are increessed. It concerneth the King to mourne for all the grivous provocations of his father's housse, and for all his auen guiltiness, and to consider if he hes come to the covenant, and joined himselve to the Lord, upone politicke interests, for gaining a croune to himselve rather then to advance religione and righteousness, that it is iniquitie quhilk God will not forgett excepte it be speedilie repented offe. It concerns our nobles and judges to consider wither ther carriadge in publicke matters be straight and equall, or rather savoring of seeking themselves and the thinges of this worlde, and how they walke in ther families, and in ther privat conversations. There is in maney a grate deall of perversenes and incorrigiblenes in regard of forsaking some and performing some deuties, notwithstanding publecke confessions and engagements, and this cannot bot heighlie provock the Lord. And it concerneth the officers of the armey, especially thesse quho are cheiffe among them, to weight weell quhat the Lord hes against them, and to repent of ther diffidence and carnall way of acting and undervaluing of God's people. And ministers have also neid to searche themselves concerning ther faithfullness to be sound, for wiche God is angrie, doutles even amongest thesse is muche negligence. Albeit the Lord hes suffred that armey of perfideous and blasphemous sectaries to prevaill. Yet God forbid that the land should complay with him, quhatever may be the plauseable and faire carriage of some of that enimey, yet doubtless there is ane levin of error and hypocrassy amongest them wich all the lovers of treuth wold decern and avoyd. As the Lord hes trayed the stability and integritie of his people in the land heirtofore, by the prevailing of malignants, so doeth he now tray them by the prevailing of sectaries, and wee trust they will thinke it ther deutie and commendatione to prove staidfast against them als weill as the other.

"3. Nather wold men be lesse cairfull and active to opposse the enimey, then they have beine in opposeing malignants heirtofor, our religione, lives, liberties and estaits, are als muche in hazard now as ever, all the ordinances of Jesus Christ in the land are in danger, and the foundatione lyke to be overturnid by thesse men quho are oblidged, by the band of the covenant, to mantiene all thesse and it wer a grate guiltines to ly doune and complay, and crutche under the burden of the strange impositions that they will lay upon us, and as men without head, to suffer our land to be brought in bondage and ourselves to be robbed of all thesse things quhilk are most precious and deire to us. If wee should doe so, the Lord wold be angrie with us, and our posterity could not bot curss us.

"4. We would not think that all danger from the malignants is now gone, seeing that ther is a grate maney suche in the land, quho still retein ther former principales, therfor we wolde, with als muche watchfullnes and tendernes now as ever, avoyde ther snars, and beware of complayance and conjunctione with them, and take head, that under a pretence of doing for the king and kingdome they gett not power and strenth unto ther handes, for advanceing and promoveing ther old malignant desseinges. Doubtles our saftie is in holding fast our former principales, and keeping a straighte faithe, without declyning to the right hand ore to the lefte.

"5. It concernes all the inhabitants of the land to bewarre of murmuring and complaning against God's dispensations, and questioning the treuthe and goodnes of our causse or quarreling with God, or blaming or casting off the covenant, becausse of aney thing that hath befallin them, that wer a grate iniquitie not to be pardoned. Lett us beare the indignatione of the Lord patientlie, becausse wee have sinned against him, untill he plead our causse and execut judgment for us, he will bring us fourthe to the light, and we shall behold his righteousnes."—Sir James Balfour's Annales, vol. iv. pp. 98-102.—*Ed.*]

328. ["Causes of a soleme publicke humiliatione upone the defait of the army, to be keepit throughout all the congregations of the Kirk of Scotland.

"Albeit soleme publicke humiliations hes beine muche slighted, and gone about in a formall way by maney in this land, so that it is not one of the least of our provocations that we have drawn neire to God with our mouthes and keepit our heartes fare from him, for wich the Lord hath turned the wisdome of the wysse unto foollishnes, and the strenthe of the strong men unto weaknes, yet seing it is a dutie that hath oftin provin comfortable to uswards, God doeth new call us in a speciall way by a singular peice of dispensatione, and knowing that all quho are acquainted with God in the land will make conscience of it, wee conceave it expedient that the quhole land be humbled for the causses following.

"1. The continued ignorance and profanitie of the bodie of the land, and the obstinacey and incorrigiblenes of maney, notwithstanding of all the caires that God hath takin upon us by his word, and by his workes of mercy and judgement, to teache us in the knowledge of his name, and to refraine us from the eivell of our wayes.

"2. The manifest provocations of the kinges housse wiche we feare are not throughlie repented off, nor forsaken by him to this day, togidder with the crooked and precipitant wayes that wer takin by sundrie of our statesmen for caring the trettey with the king.

"3. The bringing home with the king a grate maney malignants, and indevoring to keepe some of them about him, and maney of them in the kingdome, notwithstanding of publicke resolutions to the contrarey.

"4. The not purging of the kinges familie from malignant and profane men, and the constituting of the samen of weill affected and godlie persons, albeit it hathe beine oftin pressed upone the parliament and comittee of Estaits, undertaking and promessed to be performed by them.

"5. The leveing of a most malignant and profaine guard of horsse to be aboute the king, quho having beine sent for to be purgit aboute 2 dayes before the defaite, were suffred to be and feight in our armey.

"6. The exceiding grate slaknes of maney and aversnes and untowardnes of some in the cheiffe judicatories of the kingdome and in the armey, in guid motione and publick deuties, especially in thesse thinges that concerne the purging of judicatories and the armey from malignant and scandalous persons, and filling all places of powre and trust with men of knowen integritie and trust, and of a blamles and Christiane conversatione, togider with grate inclinations to keepe and bring in malignants to the judicatories and to the armey, as if the land could not be gydit and defendit without thesse, and grate repyning and craying out against all that is done to the contrarie, and studding to make the same ineffectual.

"7. The exceiding grate diffidence of some of the cheiffe leaders of our armey, and others amongest us quho thought wee could not be saved bot by ane numerous armey, who quhen wee have gottin many thousands togider, wold not hazard to acte aney thing, notwithstanding that God offred faire opportunities and advantages, and fitted the spiritts of the souldiers for ther deutie, for carnall confidence that was in maney of the armey, to the dispysing of the enimey and promising victorie to themselves without eying of God.

"8. The lousnes, insolencie and oppressione, of maney in the armey, and the litle or no caire that was taken by maney to preserve the corne, by wich it hath come to passe that verey much of the food of the poore people of the land have beine neidlesly destroyed, and quhile wee even remember this, we wishe that the prophanitie and oppressione of sundrie of oure officers and souldiers in Ingland, quhen we were fighting for the assistance of the parliament of that kingdome, may not be forgottin, because it was matter of stumbling in that land, so it is lyke it is ane of the causses of the sore indignatione now manifested against us by the hands of thesse men.

"9. Our grate unthankfullnes for former mercies and deliverances, and even for maney tokins of the Lords favor and goodness towards our present armey quhile they wer togider, and the grate impatience of spirit that was to be seine in maney thesse weekes past, quhilk made them limitt the Lord, and to compleine and weerie of his delaying of ane deliverance.

"10. The enving and eyeing of the kings intrest and quarrell by maney, without subordinatione to religione and the liberties and saveties of this kingdomes.

"11. The carnall selve seiking and crooked way of sundrie in our judicatories and armies, quho make ther employments and places rather ane matter of intrest and gain and preferment to themselves then of advancing religione and righteousness in the land.

"12. The not putting difference betwix thesse that fear God, and thesse that fear him not, for our services, our companie, our employments, bot acompting all men alike, maney times preferring thesse quho have nothing of God in them.

"13. The exceiding grate negligence that is in grate ones, and maney others, in performing the deuties in ther families notwithstanding of our former soleme acknowledgment of the samen; as also, our neglecte of the deuties of mutuall edificatione, and grate unfruitfullness and barrennes that is to be seene amongest all sorts of persons; togider with the following of deutie with a grate deall of mixture of carnall affections and fleschly wisdome wich grives the Spirit of God, and takes away muche of the beutie of the Lords image from our judicatories.

"As we wold be humbled for thesse thinges, so wold wee also intreat the Lord that he wold sanctifie this affliction to his people that they nather dispysse his chestisings, nor faint quhen they are rebukit of him, bot that they may beare his indignatione patiently, and cleive steadfestly to the treuthe, and the covenants, and the causse of God without yeilding to the power of the enimey, or receaving ther errors, or complaying ather with them on the one hand, ore malignants on the other, and that the Lord wold poure out of his Spirit upon the people, that ther spiritts may be raissed unto ther deutie, and that they may be filled and furnished of God with wisdome and resolutione to acte against their enimies for the honor of God, ther awen preservatione; and that the Lord wold not suffer them to be tempted above that whiche they are able to beare, bot that he wold break the yoke of ther oppressors from off ther neckes, and give them salvatione and deliverance; earnestly to intreat the Lord in private and in publicke that he wold preserve with us the ordinances of Jesus Christe, the kingdom, the kings ma[ties] persone, the ministrie, from the power of ther enimies, quho seekes the destruction of all."—Id. pp. 102-107.—*Ed.*]

329. [See the Acts of the Parliaments of Scotland, Anno 1650, xxx Novembris, vol. vi. p. 544.—*Ed.*]

330. ["About this time the king's head was filled by some unhappy men about him, especially Dr. Fraser [who was the king's physician] and Henry Seymour, with many extreme fears. After the affront at Leith, they had raised suspicions in his mind, which, upon the defeat at Dunbar, were increased, but by the separate rising in the west brought near to the head of a design to break the treaty with him, and agree upon his expences with Cromwell. Upon these motions the malignants in the north stept in, and by the forenamed persons began a correspondence for the raising of the north for his present service, under the conduct of Middleton. So many noblemen were on this unhappy enterprise. Crawford was given out for its head and contriver, albeit be professed to me his opposition to it. Lauderdale knew of it; but he has said so far to me, that I believe him he opposed it to his power. However, the thing was so foolishly laid, and the king, by the counsels of those about him, was so various in giving order for that rising, sometimes commanding and then countermanding to rise, that all the party was put in a confusion; yet, by the information of these foresaid fools, the king being put in fear, that Lorn, going timely to bury a soldier, was drawing together his regiment to lay hands on him, contrary to his

former resolutions, he took horse with some two or three, as if it had been to go a hawking, but crossed Tay, and stayed not till he came to Clowe in Angus. By the way he repented of the journey, and meeting with Lauderdale at Diddup, and Balcarras coming from Dundee by accident, was almost persuaded by them to return, yet by Diddup and Buchan he was kept in Clowe. But when he came to that miserably-accommodated house, and in place of the great promised forces, he saw nothing but a small company of Highlanders, he presently sent for Robert Montgomery, who was near with his regiment, and without more ado, did willingly return, exceedingly confounded and dejected for that ill-advised start. When it was first blazed abroad, it filled all good men with great grief, and to my own heart it brought one of the most sensible sorrows that in all nay life I had felt. Yet his quick return of his own accord, and his readiness to give all satisfaction for that failure, and his kind receiving by the committee of states, among whom he ever sat after his return (though never before) turned our grief suddenly into joy, his absence not lasting above two full days. Yet all men were not so soon satisfied.

"Sundry of them who had been on the plot, fearing a discovery and punishment, flew to arms; Lewis Gordon, Ogilvie, Athol, and others, under Middleton's command, putting out a number of fair pretexts for their rising. This might have destroyed all; yet, by God's mercy, all was quickly quieted. D. Leslie, with all his horse, marched towards them; the king wrote earnestly to them to lay down. The committee of estates sent a fair act of indemnity, and so without more ado they went home."—Baillie's Letters, vol. ii. p. 356.

Middleton, like the Marquis of Montrose, had been at one time a covenanter. After the Restoration, he was appointed to open the Scottish parliament, as his Majesty's commissioner. But this did not prevent him from taking part in the debate, when the Act Rescissory, by which the presbyterian form of church polity was completely destroyed, was under consideration. Mr. David Dickson, along with some others, was delegated by the presbytery of Edinburgh to present to the Earl of Middleton a petition upon this subject. Middleton told Mr. Dickson "he was mistaken if he thought to terrify him with papers,—he was no coward." Mr. Dickson dryly replied, "They knew well he was no coward ever since the bridge of Dee." This was a skirmish which took place on the 19th of June, 1638, in which Middleton had displayed great zeal for the covenant, in opposition to Charles I. He took no notice of Mr. Dickson's sarcastic remark.—Kirkton's "History of the Church of Scotland," p. 118.—*Ed.*]

331. [This was the "Acte of Pardon and Indemnitie, granted by the King and Comittee of Estaites to the Northerne Rebells, 26 October, 1650, and proclaimed at the mercat crosse of Perth, the 29th ditto, by Rosse Heraulde, A.L." See Balfour's Annales, vol. iv. p. 132.—*Ed.*]

332. [He refers to "The Northerne Band and Othe of Engagement sent by Mideltone to L. Generall David Lesley, 26th of October, 1650." Middleton and the other subscribers of the Bond promise and swear that they "shall manteine the trew religione, as it is established in Scotland; the covenant, league and covenant, the Kings Majesties persone, prerogative, gratnes and authoritie; the previllidges of parliament and freedome of the subjects."—Id. p. 129.—*Ed.*]

333. [See the Acts of the Parliaments of Scotland, ut supra.—*Ed.*]

334. [The reader will find a very interesting account of the negociations at Breda, in "A Brief Historical Relation of the Life of Mr. John Livingston, Minister at Ancrum in Scotland, and last at Rotterdam in Holland," who was one of the commissioners sent from Scotland to Breda (pp. 39-52. Glasgow, 1754). Dr. Cook, who quotes from the MS., does not seem to have been aware that the Life of Livingston was ever printed. See his "History of the Church of Scotland," vol. iii. p. 177, *note*.—*Ed.*]

335. ["Immediately after the Scots army had marched in to England to the parliament's assistance, did the King commissionate Montrose to raise a war in Scotland, by which he made account either to oblige the covenanters to recall their army out of England, or at least to make that nation smart for their boldness. And this indeed he did effectually, for landing in the West Highlands, with a party of bloody Irish papists, who had been but a little before clashed in the cruel massacre of the innocent protestants he overran the whole country and beat the covenanters forces in six bloody conflicts. His war, I believe, was the most cruel in the world." (Kirkton's History, p. 43) "Montrose's History is written in good Latin (supposed to be by Bishop Wishart), but with as little truth as most in the world." Id. p. 122.—*Ed.*]

336. [Sir James Turner and Colonel Urrey were sent to the west of Scotland with their respective regiments, in 1648 to overawe and reduce to obedience, those who were averse to Hamilton's Engagement. (Guthry's Memoirs, p. 272 second edition). This service seems to have been perfectly congenial to the habits and taste of Sir James Turner, who appears, says Sir Walter Scott, ("Tales of a Grandfather," vol. ii. p. 211. Edin. 1829), by the account he gives of himself in his Memoirs to have been an unscrupulous plunderer, and other authorities describe him as a fierce and dissolute character. On coming to Glasgow, the way he took, as he himself tells us with considerable *gusto*, "to make the hardest headed Covenanter in the toune to forsake the kirk and side with the Parliament," was to quarter on suspected persons "two or three troopers and halfe a dozen musketeers." In the same heartless strain he proceeds to say—"Finding my Glasgow men groune prettie tame, I tenderd them a short paper, which whoever signed I promisd, sould be presentlie easd of all quartering." It was nothing but a submission to all orders of Parliament, agreeable to the Covenant. This paper was afterward, by some merrie men christend Turner's Covenant. (Memoirs of his own Life and Times by Sir James Turner, pp. 53, 54 printed at Edinburgh, by the Bannatyne Club, in 1829). As he was deprived of his rank by the Act of Classes in 1649, Sir James Turner was one of those pretended penitents, of whom according to Bishop Burnet, "all churches were full" after the passing of the Public Resolutions. (Memoires of the Duke of Hamilton, p. 425.) "Martii 12, 1651. The qlk day was given in ane lettre from the comission of the kirk, the tenour whereof follows,—Reverende and loving brethrene, having received a petition how general adjutant James Turner, acknowledgeing verie humblie his sin, in ye great accession he had to that unlawful engadgement against England, and partcularlie his impious carriage in your citie by perturbing divine service, he seems to be verie sensible of his former miscarriage. We however still continue him under conference wt presbyteries hear. Bot if we shall find him in a condition to mak publik satisfaction, we desire to know of you, if he can com and staye there wt safetie, and without danger from the enemie, that he may satisfie in ye kirk of Glasgow, which we thinke the most convenient place for removing the scandal, that if he can be secur, he may be appoynted to com to you, and if not, we may tak such other course as shall be thought most convenient. We have no more to say, bot commending you in all thingis to ye Lordis direction, we remain your loving brethrene the comissioners of ye generall assemblie. Perth, 13 Feb 1651. Sic subscribitur, Mr. Robert Douglas, Moderator." (Records of the Presbytery of Glasgow.)

What Principal Baillie says of the oppressive conduct of Sir James Turner at Glasgow, during the time of the Engagement, is this—"Some regiments of horse and foot were sent to our town, with orders to quarter on no other but the magistrates, council, session, and their lovers. These orders were executed with rigour. On the most religious people of our town, huge burdens did fall. On some 10, on some 20, on others 30 soldiers and more, did quarter, who, beside meat and drink, wine, and good cheer, and whatever they called for, did exact cruelly their daily pay, and much more. In ten days, they cost a few honest but mean people, 40,000 lb., besides plundering of those whom necessity forced to flee from their houses." Letters and Journals, vol. ii. p. 294.—*Ed.*]

337. ["Stirling, 27 Sept, 1650: The comittee of Estaits considering the necessarey devine lying upone them in prosecutione of the acte of parliament and according to the frequent and serious remonstrances of the commissione of the churche for purging of the kings familey of all profaine, scandalous, malignant, and disaffected persons, and that it be constituted of such as are pious, and well affected to the cause and covenant qwho have not opposed the same by ther counsells and actions. And lykewayes considering the grate offence hes beine taken that the persons after nominated have not removed from courte nor departed out of the kingdome respectively, and having taken also into consideratione the report of the sub comittee, appoynted to think on the purging of the kings familey doth heirby therfor ordaine and command, The French Marques of Villaneuffe, The Earle of Cleveland, Lord Wentworthe his son, Viscount Grandeson, Lord Volmett, Lord Withringtone, Robert Long, Secretarey, Sr Edward Walker, Garter, Mr. Progers, Groome of His Maties Bed chamber, Master Lane, Master Marche, Colonell Darcey, Mr. Antoney Jacksone, Major Jacksone, Colonell Loes, Master Oder, Under Secretary Lord St. Paule, Sr Philipe Musgrave, Sr Faithful Fortskew, Sr Timothey Featherstons, L Coll Meutis, Collonell Carbraithe, to depart the courte within 24 houres, and to remove out of the kingdome within 20 dayes after intunatione, and Doctor Fraser and Sr George Melveill to withdraw from the court within 24 houres." (Sir James Balfour's Annales of Scotland, vol. iv. pp. 109, 110). Sir Edward Walker, whose name is included in the above list, says, "Money being ordered for my transportation, which I never got I was connived at for about three months, and therein had the opportunity to collect and write my observations of the Affairs as they then stood. Yet upon Friday the 4th of October, I was, by Sir James Balfour, lion king of arms, commanded from court, which I presently obeyed, and about a month after imbarqued for Holland, where I resided several years after." (Historical Discourses. Contents folio. Lond. 1705.) The circumstances in which this zealous royalist was placed, together with his national prejudices, may account for his extreme credulity, in believing that the clergy of Scotland, after the battle of Dunbar, offered up such impious prayers as he has ascribed to them. (Id. p. 182) It was not to be expected that Mr. Hume would neglect the opportunity which was thus afforded him of covering with ridicule the Scottish covenanters. (See Hume's Account of the Battle of Dunbar.) Rapin vindicates the conduct of the Estates, in inquiring the removal from about the person of the king, of some of his friends and attendants' men he says, "whose principles and maxims were directly opposite to the interests of Scotland and who were the kingdoms reputed enemies." Hist. of Eng. vol. ii. p. 581. Lond. 1833—*Ed.*]

338. ["At the nod of a prince."—*Ed.*]

339. [That is, "He says, I say, he denies, I deny." It is the parasite Gnatho that is referred to. Terence makes the shameless sycophant proclaim his own infamy—

Quicquid dicunt, laudo, id rursum si negant, laudo id quoque
Negat quis? Nego. Ait? Aio.—*Eunuchi* Act ii. Sc. ii.
"Whatever they say, I applaud. If again they deny that, I applaud that too. Does any one deny a thing? I deny it. Does he affirm it? I affirm it."—*Ed.*]

340. [That is, the characteristics.—*Ed.*]

341. [For an account of the origin, progress, and unsuccessful issue of Hamilton's Engagement or the Unlawful Engagement, as it was also called, the reader may consult Stevenson's History of the Church and State of Scotland, book iv. chapter x., Cook's History of the Church of Scotland, vol. iii. p. 149.—*Ed.*]

342. [Old MS.—*Ed.*]

343. ["Pearth Novemb. 29, 1650—The Comrs. of the Gen. Assemb. considering the great sin and offence these men are guilty of, who have had accessione to the late Rebellione in ye north, therefore they doe appoint that all these persons that were actually in arms at the late rebellione, and all such as subscribed the Bond and Declaratione emited by them to be suspended from the communione till the nixt Gen. Assemb. to which there are hereby refered for further censure, and for all others that had any accessione by counsel or otherwise, to that rebellione, or to the King's withdrawing from his Counsell, refers to Presbytries to try diligently in their severall bounds these persons and the degree of their guiltiness and to report the same, with the evidences and proofs thereof, to the nixt meeting of this Commissione." A. Ker.—"The Waters of Sihor." Wodrow MSS., vol. xvii. pp. 44-45.—*Ed.*]

344. [James, Marquis of Montrose. After his forfeiture by the Scottish parliament he was usually styled in their Act and proclamations *James*

Graham, and sometimes *James Graham, late Earl of Montrose.* Bishop Guthry says (Memoirs, p. 175) that it was considered a proof of malignancy to distinguish him and the Earl of Auly by their titles. In a letter to Principal Baillie, 19th March 1649, Mr. Spang mentions that he was admitted to an audience by the Prince of Orange at the Hague. Something was said by the Prince, which led Mr. Spang to suspect he alluded to Montrose. "I hoped," says Mr. Spang, "his Highness did not mean of that man, whose apostasy, perjuries, and unheard of cruelty, had made him so odious, in all our country, that they could not hear of his name." He presently gave me to understand he meant not him or any such, for by the comportment of our Scottish noblemen at court now, he perceives how odious *James Graham* must be at home, for they will not salute or speak to him, nay, not look where they think he is, and this I have observed with my own eyes. Baillie's Letters and Journals, vol. ii. p. 323.—*Ed.*]

345. [On the 14th of December 1650, an answer was returned to Parliament, "be the commissioners of the general assemblie to the quære, given in to thame be the estattis of parliament, anent the persones to be admitted to ryse in armes, and joyne with the forces of the kingdome, and in what capacitie, for defence thereoff aganes the armie of sectaries, &c." (Acts of the Parliaments of Scotland, vol. vi. p. 554.) The Answer of the Commission, after a declaration that it is the duty of parliament to use all necessary and lawful means for the defence of the land, and a description of the enfeebled state of the kingdom, contains the following exposition of their views. "In this case of so great and evident necessity, we cannot be against the raising of all fencible persons in the land, and permitting them to fight against this enemy for defence of the kingdom, excepting such as are excommunicate, forfaulted, notoriously profane or flagitious, and such as have been from the beginning, and continue still, or are at this time, obstinate and professed enemies, and opposers of the Covenant and cause of God; and for the capacity of acting, that the Estates of Parliament ought to have, as we hope they will have special care, that in this so general concurrence of all the people of the kingdom, none be put in such trust or power as may be prejudicial to the cause of God, and that such Officers as are of known integrity and affection to the cause, and particularly such as have suffered in our former armies may be taken special notice of."—"A True Representation of the Rise, &c. of the Present Division in the Church of Scotland," pp. 10, 11. London, 1657. "The Answer of the Commission of the General Assemblie to the Quæree Propounded to them from the Parliament," pp. 2, 3. Aberdeen, Printed by James Brown, 1651.—*Ed.*]

346. ["*Act of Leavie*: At Perth, the twentie third day of December, one thousand six hundred and fiftie yeiris, the Kingis Majestie and Estaits of parliament, being verie sensibill of the dangerous and distressed conditione of this kingdome, and most desyrious, according to the law of God and nature, in discharge of there public trust, to use all lawful and necessarie means for the saiftie and defence of religione, his Majesties persone and royal authoritie, laws and liberties of the kingdome, aganis an armie of sectaries, who most unjustlie and perfidiouslie, contrarie to the solemne league and covenant and treaties, have invaded, and are by all actis of hostilitie destroying the same, Thairfore hes statute and ordained that all fensible men, within the sherrefdomes of Fyiff, and Kinross, Clakmanan, Stirling, Dumbartane, Argyll, Boott, Perth, Forfar, Kincardine, Aberdeine, Bamff, Murray, Nairne, Inverness, Ross, Sutherland, Cromartie, Caitnes, and Orknay, cum to an randevouze in the severall divisions of ilk schyre respective, to be set doun and appoyntit be the comitties of war in ilk schyre, according to the number of the regimentis efter specifit. The haill hertofore noblemen, gentlemen, and utheris to burt and landwartly frenteris, woodsetteris, and all other fensible men, betwixt thriescore and sixteine, with all there horses fitt for service, and their haill armes for horsemen and footmen (except such as are excommunicate, forfeited, notoriouslie profane or flagitious, and such as have beene from the beginning, and continew still, or are at this tyme, obstinat and professed enemies and opposeris of the covenant and caus of God). Out of the quhilk haill number of fensible persones, in ilk division, all such as are vigorous and able men for war are heirby appoynted to be drawin out, and put in Regimentis, as is efter specifit, with there best horses and arms, so many as are serviceable horses, and the rest on foot, with their best armes, twa part musquettis and third part pickis, and all with swords. The horsemen to be armed with pistollis, hulsteris or syidpistollis, and launces," &c., &c.—"Acts of the Parliaments of Scotland," vol. vi, pp. 560-562.—*Ed.*]

347. [This disastrous attack was made by the forces in the west, from whom had proceeded, what was called the Western Remonstrance, which had been condemned both by the Committee of Estates, and the Commission of the church. ("Causes of the Lord's Wrath in Scotland," p. 60, printed in the year 1660). "Befoir this feight at Hammilton, Collonell Ker inquyred the judgement of his inferior officers the night befoir, quhat thai thocht of the caice of effaires, as they then stood, and schewed thame that he wold joyne with nane quho wes not for the Remonstrance, nor yit with those quho wold not declyne the Stait,—I meane the committee of Estait as it then stood." (Nicol's "Diary of Transactions in Scotland," p. 37) The following letter from Cromwell describing the defeat at Hamilton, is interesting in itself as well as on account of the writer. "Sir, I have now sent you the results of some treaties amongst the enemy, which came to my hand this day. The Major General, and Commissary-Generall Whaley marched a few days ago towards Glasgow, and the enemy attempted his quarters in Hamilton, and entred the town, but by the blessing of God, by a very gracious hand of Providence, without the losse of 6 men, as I hear of, he beat them out, kild about 100, took also about the same number, amongst which are some prisoners of quality, and near 100 horse (as I am informed), the Major Gen. being in the chase of them, to whom also I have since sent the addition of a fresh party. Col. Kerre (as my messenger this night tells me) is taken, his Lieutenant-Col. and one that was sometimes Major to Collonel Straughan, and Keires Captain Lieutenant. The whole party is shattered, and give me leave to say it, if God had not brought them upon us, we might have marched 3000 horse to death, and not have lighted on them, and truly it was a strange Providence brought them upon him. For I marched from Edenburgh on the north side of Cloid, appointed the Major-General to march from Peebles to Hamilton, on the south side of Cloid. I came thither by the time expected, tarried the remainder of the day, and untill neer 7 o'clock the next morning, apprehending the Major-Gen. would not come by reason of the waters. I being retreated, the enemy took encouragement, marched all that night, and came upon the Major-General's quarters about two houres before day, where it pleased the Lord to order as you have heard.

"The Major-Gen. and Commissary Gen. (as he sent me word) were still gone on in the prosecution of them, and saith, that except 150 horse in one body, he heares they are fled by 16 or 18 in a company, all the country over. Robin Montgomery was come out of Sterling, with 4 or 5 regiments of horse and dragoons, but was put to a stand when he heard of the issue of this businesse. Straughan and some other officers had quitted some 3 weeks or a month before this businesse, so that Ker commanded this whole party in chief.

"It is given out that the malignants will be all (almost) received and rise unanimously and expeditiously. I can assure you, that those that serve you here, find more satisfaction in having to deale with men of this stamp, then others, and it is our comfort that the Lord hath hitherto made it the matter of our prayers, and of our endeavours (if it might have been the will of God), to have had a Christian understanding between those that feare God in this land, and ourselves, and yet we hope it hath not been carryed on with a willing failing of our duty to those that trust us, and I am persuaded the Lord hath looked favourably upon our sincerity herein, and will still doo so, and upon you also whilst you make the interest of God's people yours. Those religious people of Scotland, that fall in this cause, we cannot but pitty and mourne for them, and we pray that all good men may do so too. Indeed there is at this time a very great distraction, and mighty workings of God upon the hearts of divers, both ministers and people, much of it tending to the justification of your cause. And although some are as bitter and as bad as ever, making it their businesse to shuffle hypocritically with their consciences and the covenant, to make it lawfull to joyne with malignants, which now they do (as well as they might long before) having taken in the head of them, yet truly others are startled at it, and some have been constrained by the work of God upon their consciences, to make sad and solemn accusations of themselves, and lamentations in the face of their supream authority, charging themselves as guilty of the blood shed in this warre, by having a hand in the treaty at Breda, and by bringing the king in amongst them. This lately did a Lord of the Session, and withdrew, and lately Mr. James Leviston, a man as highly esteemed as any for piety and learning, who was a Commissioner for the Kirk at the said treaty, charged himselfe with the guilt of the blood of this war, before their assembly, and withdrew from them, and is retired to his own house. It will be very necessary to encourage victuallers to come to us, that you take off customes and excise from all things brought hither for the use of the army. I beg your prayers, and rest your humble servant, *O. Cromwell.* Edinburgh, 4 Dec. 1660."—Sev. Proc. in Parl. Dec. 12 to 19, apud Cromwelliana, pp. 94, 95.—*Ed.*]

348. [That is, "How much changed from that assembly which was formerly!" (Quantum mutatus ab illo Hectore, qui, &c. *Virg. Æneid*, lib. ii. ver. 274.)—*Ed.*]

349. ["Ult. July, 1648. Post Meridian Sep. xxi. *A Declaration of the General Assembly concerning the present dangers of Religion and especially the unlawful engagement in War, against the kingdom of England.* Together with many necessary exhortations and directions to all the Members of the Kirk of Scotland." Records of the Kirk of Scotland, pp. 498-505. Edited by A. Peterkin.—*Ed.*]

350. [At a meeting of the Committee of Estates, on the 6th of January, 1651,—"Rege Presente. The letter from the Presbytery of Stirling to the Commission of the Generall Assembly, still disclaiming the kings intereste, and the unity of all the subjects of the land to assist their countrey against the comon enimey, redd, with the Commission of the Generall Assemblies ansuer therto, redd lykwayes approvin and ordained to be published and printed." (Balfour's Annales, vol. iv. p. 235). The Commission of the Assembly complained, that the letter of the Ministers of the Presbytery of Stirling, which was printed at

Edinburgh 165l, had prefixed to it "the false and odious title of *A Remonstrance of the Presbtytery of Stirling against the present conjunction with the malignant partie.*" ("Answer of the Commission," &c. dated Perth, 6 Jan. 1651 p. 19. Printed at Aberdeen, 1651). What Binning now advances is in vindication of the Letter of the Presbytery of Stirling and in reply to the Answer of the Commission. Mr. James Guthrie, and Mr. David Bennet, Ministers at Stirling, were charged by the committee of Estates with training this Letter, and summoned to appear before them, at Perth, on the 19th of February, 1651, to answer for their conduct.—"Acts of Parl., vol. vi. p. 578."—*Ed.*]

351. ["And first, we shall desyre every one seriously to consider the case and condition wherein the kingdome is engaged and standeth at this tyme, that now we are not upon an engagement of invasive warre but upon necessary defence against a forraign enemy, who hath not only injustly invaded us, but also (through the holy permissive providence of God) slaine many of our brethren with the sword, subdued a great part of the land, is oppressing the people of God therein, and following his injust designes and intentions against the rest of the kingdome, that in this case, in the ordinary way of providence, according to which men must act, unlesse they would be guilty of tempting God, there is need of, and ought to be employed against the enemy, such a competency of power as is required in right and warrantable prudencie, and may be had, not being of itself sinful. This certainly is mans duety, whatever God, out of his soveraignity, hath done, or may doe in the case of want, or disproportion of meanes."—Answer of the Commission, ut supra, p. 6.—*Ed.*]

352. ["In such parts of the kingdome, as are yet free from the oppression of the enemy, and so out of which any men can be raised, there is not a possibility to get such a competencie of power, unlesse there be a more generall calling foorth of the body of the people than hath been before, this as it is most certain in itselfe, so it is most apparent, and evident unto all, that doe understand these parts of the kingdome. And whereas faithfull and honest men in the State, well acquainted with the severall shares of that part of the kingdome, have publickly declared that when all shall be brought together, that can be called foorth of these parts, according to publick resolution, there will scarce be a competent power against the power of the enemy, we cannot but much wonder, if any, not so acquainted therewith, shall hold the contrary, and not give credit to the declaration of honest and faithfull men, especially in authority, the matter being such, as in the immediate knowledge thereof dependeth on sense, and, as to those that have not that knowledge, pertaineth to humane faith, which giveth credit to the testimony *testium idoneorum* of competent witnesses such as these are whom we have designed."—Id. pp. 6, 7.—*Ed.*]

353. ["We need say no more unlesse there were some show of proofe to the contrary. Yet we shall say somewhat particularly to one place that which is said in the case of Amaziah's associating with and taking to him the Israelits for help in his just defence, (2 Chron. xxv. 7: 'O king let not the army of Israel goe with thee for the Lord is not with Israel even with all the house of Ephraim,') as being mainly urged and as it seems most to stick with some in the present businesse to which sundry things may be answered, which clear the present businesse from the force thereof. 1. The Israelits were idolaters, and forreiners not so in our case, in either respect. But it is alledged that the reason why Amaziah is disswaded from taking their assistance is because God was not with them, and therefore the same reason having place in manie of these, whom the present resolution comprehendeth, the disswasion hath the same force against them. Therefore 2. God's not being with them may be either conceived and understood, in regard of the estate of grace and reconciliation with God but how-so ever that with many of them God was not in this regard, yet the reason cannot be alledged in this sense because then it would follow by the argument, that we might not take the help of any man out of the estate of grace, for our just and necessary defence, which none will admit, or it may be understood of God's assistance and prospering providence simply. But neither can it be taken thus, because it is certain and clear that God was often with them in this sense in their own cause and quarrells. Therefore it must needs be conceived, in regard of their profession, and religion, which was corrupt and idolatrous. Now the reason thus understood hath not place in our businesse. 3. Yet doe we not find that Amaziah is commanded to exclude any of the subjects of his own kingdom, from acting in that defence, or reproved for not doing of it notwithstanding many of them no doubt were naughty and corrupt in their way, 2 Kings xiv."—Answer of the Commission, p. 12.—*Ed.*]

354. [That is, "chiefly." The strict signification of *ut plurimum* is, *as much as possible.*—*Ed.*]

355. ["At the bar of conscience."—*Ed.*]

356. ["Doeth our mentioning onlie the kingdome in that resolution, import a separation of the kingdome, and the cause in the quarrell against our enemie? Or what logick can draw out such a consequence out of it? Wee do think that the kingdome being in danger by this enemie, the cause also is in danger, and the defending of the kingdome will be the defending of the cause also. And we trust no instruments shall bee employed for the defence of the kingdom to the prejudice of the cause."—Answer of the Commission, ut supra, p. 19.—*Ed.*]

357. ["In point of fact."—*Ed.*]

358. ["On that very account."—*Ed.*]

359. [Bishop Hall quaintly remarks, that "No devil is so dangerous as the religious devil." "Suppose the ends of this Engagement to be good, (which they are not,) yet the meanes and ways of prosecution are unlawful, because there is not an equall avoiding of rocks on both hands, but a joyning with malignants to suppresse sectaries, a joyning hands with a black devill to beat a white devill. They are bad physicians who would so cure one disease as to breed another as evil or worse." ("A Declaration of the Gen. Assembly concerning the present dangers of Religion." Rec. of the Kirk of Scotland, p. 501.) In the year 1649 the Scottish parliament passed an "Act against Consulters with Devils and Familiar Spirits," &c. (Acts of the Parl. of Scot. vol. vi. p. 359.) It was supposed that the power of some of these was employed in particular instances for the benefit of mankind. They were therefore distinguished from the others in the same way that white witches or persons who used charms and incantations for curing diseases, &c. were distinguished, but not in the eye of the law, from black witches, or those who practised their art for the purposes of mischief. (Whitelock's "Memorials," p. 550. See also Sir Walter Scott's "Tales of a Grandfather," vol. ii. p. 117.) If we look to the strange confessions of many of the unfortunate creatures who were condemned to suffer death for witchcraft in those days, without adverting to the cruel means that were often resorted to with a view to extort from them such confessions, the credulity of the age will not appear to have been so extraordinary as it has been represented. It is impossible not to admire the singular discretion of Dr. Grey, Rector of Houghton Conquest when speaking on this subject: "Nothing," says he, "more plainly discovers the iniquity of those times than the great numbers of people executed in England and Scotland for witches, *if they were guilty*, or the barbarous superstition of the times, *if they were innocent*, which is the more probable."—"Impartial Examination of the Fourth Volume of Mr. Daniel Neal's History of the Puritans," p. 96, Lond. 1739.—*Ed.*]

360. [That is, openly persisting. See "The Answer of the Commission to the Presbytery of Stirling," p. 11.—*Ed.*]

361. [See "The Nullity of the Pretended Assembly at Saint Andrews and Dundee," &c., p. 312. Printed in the year 1652. As many had been under age when the Solemn League and Covenant was first sworn the Commission of the General Assembly ordained it to be renewed by their Act, October 6, 1648, joining to it the "Solemn Acknowledgment of Public sins and Breaches of the Covenant, and a Solemn Engagement to all the Duties contained therein."—*Ed.*]

362. ["We desire it may be remembered that in the beginning of these troubles, anno 1638, when as there were then standing laws in this kingdom, which are not yet repealed to this day, discharging all subjects from rysing in armes, without the kings expresse warrant and command, yet the subjects of this kingdome perceiving themselves in danger to be destroyed by forraign invasion, did fynd these lawes no wayes to bynd up their hands from taking armes, for their just defence and selfe preservation,—these lawes, in the intention of the lawgiver, being made for the preservation of the kingdom and not for the destruction of it.—" Answer of the Commission, pp. 13, 14.—*Ed.*]

363. [See "The Waters of Sihor, or the Lands Defectione," Wodrow MSS. vol. xvii. pp. 39-41, in Bib. Ad. Peterkin's "Rec. of the Kirk of Scotland," pp. 619-620.—*Ed.*]

364. [See Note, *page 96*.—*Ed.*]

365. [That is, "every where and at all times like himself and the same."—*Ed.*]

366. [We learn from Principal Baillie, ("Letters and Journals," vol. ii. p. 363,) that Binning had identified himself with the Association of the West, which was required to dissolve itself, by an Act of the Scottish parliament, passed 28th Decem., 1650.—*Ed.*]

367. [Or, general officers.—*Ed.*]

368. [The *first* or *principal proposition* in the preceding syllogism.—*Ed.*]

369. [(Minor probatur,) that is, *the second proposition* in the preceding syllogism. It will be perceived that the arguments of the author are constructed according to the rules of the Aristotelian logic. A familiar acquaintance with this mode of reasoning continued to be cultivated, at this time, by all who wished to excel in public disputations (Professor Jardine's "Outlines of Philosophical Education in the University of Glasgow," p. 12. Glas. 1825). In the Westminster Assembly, the different speakers often presented their opinions under the form of syllogisms, which were impugned and defended by employing the usual terms and technical formalities of the dialectic art.—See Lightfoot's "Journal of the Proceedings of the Assembly of Divines." Works, vol. xiii. pp. 123, 157, 203-205, &c.—*Ed.*]

370. [Aiming at.—*Ed.*]

371. [Mr. Robert Ramsay, Principal of the University, reminded the Presbytery of Glasgow at their first meeting in June, 1651, "that Mr. Hew Binnen had expresslie protested that it was not lawfull for us to pray for ye succeese of the armie, as it was constitute, and becaus of those who now have power in the same. And farther, the said Mr. Hew Binnen, when notice was taken of these words repeated them over and over agane, and avowed, he wold pray for a blessing to them, yt

is, that yet might be converted, but, that he could not pray for success to them as yet are now constitute."—"Records of the Presbytery of Glasgow."—*Ed.*]

372. [Or shudder.—*Ed.*]

373. [For the Instructions given by the Scottish parliament to the Commissioners who went to Breda see "Acts of the Parliament of Scotland," vol. vi. pp. 513, 514. A copy of the Treaty itself agreed upon by his Majesty Charles II and the Scottish Commissioners and afterwards ratified by parliament, will be found in Thurloe's State Papers, vol. i. pp. 147, 148.—*Ed.*]

374. [That is, "who, because they are wise, are ignorant of that which they know." (Tu pol, si sapis quod scis, nescis. Terent Eun. iv. 4, 54.)—*Ed.*]

375. [That is, *lively* or *distinct* characters.—*Ed.*]

376. ["A fisherman is made wise by a bite." A Greek proverb, the original of this (ὁ ἅλσευς πληγες νους φυσες) has been preserved in a fragment of Sophocles, Erasmi Adagiorum Chil. Quat. p. 41. Coloniæ 1612. Scholiastes Græci In Sophoc. Tom. iii. p. 602. Argentorati 1788.—*Ed.*]

377. ["Another consequence of this defeat [at Dunbar] was, that every one blamed the other, the one side for purging out too many who might have been of service against the enemy, and these again blamed their opposites for being too remiss, and not well enough purged."—Memoirs of the Life of the Rev. Robert Blair, p. 113. Edin. 1755.—*Ed.*]

378. [Answer of the Commission, *ut supra*, p. 8.—*Ed.*]

379. [P. 178 Edin. 1649.—*Ed.*]

380. [Or as a general principle.—*Ed.*]

381. [In opposition to what is here affirmed it is stated in the pamphlet entitled, "A True Representation of the Present Division in the Church of Scotland," (p. 15.) that the Scottish Reformers did not look upon their conjunction with the Duke of Chatelherault and his followers, "as a cause of that sad stroak, as some would make the world believe, from Mr. Knoxes Sermon at Sterlin. For in the heads of that Sermon, printed in the History of the Church of Scotland, p. 217 *Edit. Edinburgh*, 1644, in 4to, there is no mention of any such thing but only of their carnal confidence, that possibly they had not sincerely repented of their former opposition, and that they who were late come in were made to feel in their own hearts, how bitter a cup they had made others to drink before them. Nor doth he (as our Brethren's tenets now lead them) presse them to purge out such as were lately admitted, but doth only presse repentance upon all of them."—Dr. M'Crie presents his readers with an analysis of this sermon of the "great Apostle of the Scots," as he was called by Beza.—See "Life of Knox," pp. 192, 193, sixth edit.—*Ed.*]

382. [See *page 495* of this edition.—*Ed.*]

383. ["The safety of the people" is "the highest law."—*Ed.*]

384. ["The very heathens had a notion of the unlawfulnesse of confederacies with wicked men. For as Victorinus Strigelius on 2 Chron. 25, noteth out of Æschylus his tragedy, intituled *Seven to Thebe*, Amphiaraus a wise vertuous man was therefore swallowed up in the earth, with seven men, and seven horses, because he had associat himself with Tydeus, Capaneus and other impious commanders marching to the siege of Thebe." ("Gillespie's Miscel. Quest.," p. 178.) Æschylus makes Eteocles give the following description of the character of Amphiaraus, and foretell his destiny.—("Septem cont Thebas," ver. 597.)

"Nothing worse
In whate'er cause than impious fellowship,
Nothing of good is reap'd for when the field
Is sown with wrong the ripened fruit is death
So this seer
Of temper'd wisdom, of unsullied honour,
Just, good, and pious, and a mighty prophet,
In despite to his better judgment join'd
With men of impious daring, bent to tread
The long, irremeable way, with them
Shall, if high Jove assist us, be dragg'd down
To joint perdition."—*Potter.*

Regarded simply as a poetical fiction, the account which Statius has given of the fate of Amphiaraus is particularly striking and beautiful—(Thebald. lib. vii. ver. 815-823)—*Ed.*]

385. ["A Hypothetical Proposition is one which asserts not absolutely, but under an hypothesis indicated by a conjunction. An hypothetical syllogism is one on which the reasoning depends on such a proposition."—Whately's "Elements of Logic," p. 388.—*Ed.*]

386. ["For he who gives life gives the things which are necessary to life."—Cic. De Offic. lib. cap. 4.—*Ed.*]

387. [The MS. in my possession which will be afterwards described has no part of this third answer. In place of it I find the following passage: "And though there had been disproportion of numbers betwixt us and the enemy, yet we cannot but still say, it had been a way much better beseeming the people of God, and in which there should have been much more peace and consort, to have had to do our duty with such a disproportion, than to have taken in the malignant party for making it up."—*Ed.*]

388. [Than with.—*Ed.*]

389. [Dirge, or some such word is wanting here.—*Ed.*]

390. [That is, put them in mind.—*Ed.*]

391. [The remaining part of the Section is not contained in either of the two preceding editions of the "Case of Conscience," but is taken from a MS. in the handwriting of the period with the use of which I have been favoured by my friend David Laing, Esq., Secretary to the Bannatyne Club. This MS. terminates with Section IV.—*Ed.*]

392. [Mr. George Gillespie, who was the son of Mr. John Gillespie, Minister of Kirkaldy, was at this time one of the Ministers of Edinburgh, but he had gone to Kirkaldy for the benefit of his health. He was one of the Commissioners from the Church of Scotland, to the Westminster Assembly. In his letters from London, Principal Baillie, who was also one of the Scottish Commissioners, speaks of his youthful colleague in terms of high admiration. "Of a truth," he says, respecting him, in a letter dated March 26, 1644, "there is no man whose parts in a public dispute I do so admire. He has studied so accurately all the points ever yet came to our assembly, he has gotten so ready, so assured, so solid a way of public debating, that, however there be in the assembly divers very excellent men, yet in my poor judgment, there is not one who speaks more rationally and to the point, than that brave youth has done ever." ("Letters and Journals," vol. l. p. 451. See also, pp. 407, 419, 431.) Gillespie's "Treatise of Miscellany Questions," which was published after his death, in 1649, contains a chapter entitled, "Another most useful Case of Conscience discussed and resolved, concerning associations and confederacies with idolaters, infidels, heretics, or any other known enemies of truth and godliness" (pp. 169-193.) This, it will be observed is, with very little variation, the title of the Tractate of Binning. It is probable, that they who first undertook the publication of Binning's MS. were led to adopt this title from the similarity of the views, as well as the identity of the subjects of the two authors. When the Commission of the church met at Perth, in December, 1650, for the purpose of considering the *query* of the parliament as to the persons who ought, or ought not, in present circumstances to be employed, in the defence of the country,—it was not likely that the published opinions of Gillespie upon such a subject would be overlooked. But says Baillie, when giving an account of this meeting, "The question was alleged to be altered from that which Mr. Gillespie writes of."—"Letters and Journals," vol. ii. p. 365.—*Ed.*]

393. [The name of "M. F. Carmichael" is attached to a warrant, which is dated Sept. 1, 1651, and bears to be subscribed by certain commissioners of the church, authorizing George Ogilvy of Harras, to deliver up to Lord Balcarres, the Registers of the Kirk that were in his house (Reg. of Deeds, 6 March, 1701. Dr. M'Crie's Mem. of Veitch and Brysson, Append. p. 525.) There can be little doubt that these were the original records of the church, which were produced and identified at the meeting of the General Assembly at Glasgow, in the year 1638. (Id. p. 497. "Rec. of the Kirk," vol. l. pp. 22-24, Edited by A. Peterkin.) It is boldly asserted by Gordon, parson of Rothiemay, that the old authentic records of the Assemblies were at that time in the hands of Archbishop Spottiswood, who had carried them with him, he says, to London, though he more cautiously adds, in a *nota*, "It is *very uncertaine* if the registers presented wer the principalls, or if only copyes." ("History of Scots Affairs," vol. i. pp. 146, 147. Aberdeen. Printed for the Spalding Club, 1841.) Keith tells us in what way these records afterwards came into the possession of Mr. Archibald Campbell, a Scottish non-juring clergyman residing in London, by whom they were most unjustifiably detained from the Church after the Revolution, and subsequently gifted to Sion College, the governors of which being expressly restricted from permitting them to pass out of their custody. ("Hist. of the Aff. of Church and State in Scot.," p. 497.) After some delay on the part of the governors, the long concealed records, bound up in three volumes, and embracing the whole period between 1560 and 1616, were given up by them for inspection, in the year 1834, to the Select Committee of the House of Commons on Church Patronage. ("Minutes of Evidence," pp. 126, 355, 374.) Dr. Lee, one of the witnesses before the Committee, declared, after examining them, he was quite certain that they were "authentic records." (Id. p. 450). The loss of such invaluable archives, soon after this, which now appears to be placed beyond all doubt, in consequence of the destruction of the House of Commons by fire, is much to be deplored.—*Ed.*]

394. [At the Restoration, Mr. Moncrieff was ejected from his parish, for the part he had acted in framing or sanctioning the "Remonstrance," and the "Causes of the Lord's wrath," which was engenuously confessed by him ("Acts of the Parliaments of Scotland," vol. vii. p. 367.) Wodrow has collected various particulars regarding the life, character, and subsequent sufferings, for conscience' sake, of this pious and useful minister. ("Hist. of the Suff. of the Ch. of Scot.", vol. i. pp. 197-200.) As he was persecuted, during the Usurpation, for persisting in praying publicly for the king, he had thus the singular misfortune of being punished both for his loyalty and his supposed disloyalty. Mr. Moncrieff has had a niche assigned to him by Howie among the *Scots Worthies*. (pp. 411-415. Dumfries, 1835.) Mr. James Guthrie, Minister at Stirling, who was imprisoned at the same time with his friend, Mr. Moncrieff, and afterwards executed, was accused at his trial of compiling "the

Remonstrance." This he denied, affirming he could prove, by hundreds of witnesses, that he was at Stirling at the time, many miles distant.—See his Defences, "Acts of the Parl. of Scot.," vol. vii. Append. p. 37.—*Ed.*]

395. [The parliament of Scotland passed the *Act of Classes* on the 23d of January, 1649. It was entitled an Act "for purging the Judicatories, and other places of Public trust." Those whom it declared to be incapable of sitting in parliament, or of holding any civil or military appointment, were divided into four classes. The disqualification of such as, on account of their supposed greater criminality, were placed in the first class, was to continue for life, that of the second class for ten years; that of the third class for five years; and that of the fourth class for one year only, provided they gave previously sufficient evidence of their penitence.—"Acts of the Parl. of Scots," vol. vi. p. 352.—*Ed.*]

396. ["After the woful rout at Dunbar, in the first meeting at Stirling, it was openly and vehemently pressed to have David Lesly laid aside, as long before was designed, but covertly by the chief purgers of the times. The man himself did as much press as any to have liberty to demit his charge, being covered with shame and discouragement for his late unhappiness, and irritated with Mr. James Guthrie's publick invectives against him from the pulpit. The most of the committee of estates, and commission of the kirk, would have been content to let him go; but finding no man tolerably able to supply his place, and the greatest part of the remaining officers of horse and foot peremptory to lay down, if he continued not; and after all trials finding no maladministration on him to count of, but the removal of the army from the hill the night before the rout, which yet was a consequence of the committee's order, contrary to his mind, to stop the enemy's retreat, and for that end to storm Broxmouth house as soon as possible. On these considerations the state, unanimously did with all earnestness entreat him to keep still his charge against this order, my Lord Wariston, and, as I suppose Sir John Cheesly, did enter their dissent. I am sure Mr. James Guthrie did his, at which, as a great impertinency, many were offended. Col. Strachan offered to lay down his charge, being unwilling more to be commanded by D. Lesly. Some more inclined to do so, but all were quieted by this expedient."—Baillie's Letters, vol. ii. p. 350.—*Ed.*]

397. [The religious zeal of Binning, his patriotism, and his dread of arbitrary power were, it is clear, stronger than his loyalty. Sir Edward Walker, however, vouches for the loyalty, at this period, of the Scottish nation in general. "For the disposition of the people," he says, (Hist. Disc. p. 194) "they are generally for the king and his government, being most under the notion of Malignants and Engagers, about 100 of 120 noblemen being in that condition. Most of the Gentry are very loyal, and in a manner all the common people." Binning's language respecting Charles II. at the time of passing the Public Resolutions, appears to have startled his co-presbyter, Principal Baillie, who writes thus in a letter which was first designed for his friend Mr. Dickson, but afterwards sent to Mr. Spang at Campvere.—"Mr. Patrick [Gillespie] and Mr. James Guthrie, wherever they came, uttered their passion. I heard one who had married Mr. Patrick's sister's daughter report to Mr. Douglas, that Mr. Hugh Binning, with Mr. Patrick, in Kirkaldy, had spoke like a distracted man, saying to Mr. Douglas's own wife, and the young man himself, and his mother-in-law, Mr. Patrick's sister, 'that the commission of the kirk would approve nothing that was right; that a hypocrite ought not to reign over us; that we ought to treat with Cromwell and give him security not to trouble England with a king; and whoever marred this treaty, the blood of the slain in this quarrel should be on their heads.' Strange words if true."—Letters, vol. ii. p. 363. The ungrateful, impolitic, and barbarous treatment which his Scottish subjects received from Charles II. after the Restoration, must be held to be a proof of the sagacity at least of Binning, and a justification of the suspicion with which he and some of the other Protesters regarded him. It is not unlikely that, in their case, the strong appeal to the fears of the English and Scottish presbyterians, as the supposed friends of monarchy, contained in Milton's "Tenure of Kings and Magistrates," which was published but two years before this, had not failed altogether of its effect.—*Ed.*]

398. [I have not been able to discover to what "old translation" the author alludes. But Wilcox puts the same interpretation, that he does, upon the ninth verse of this chapter. "*Sinne*, (viz. which the wicked and ungodly men commit, and they know one of them by another,) *maketh fools to agree*, (viz. one of them with another: q.d. their partaking in wickednesse joineth the wicked's minds, one of them towards another;) *but among the righteous*, (i.e. good and holy people,) *that which is acceptable* (viz. before God and good men) *maketh agreement* (viz. among themselves: q.d. good things onlie tie good men's minds together)." *A Short yet Sound Commentarie Written on that Worthie Work called the Proverbs of Salomon.* London, 1624.—*Ed.*]

399. [The Estates, or parliament.—*Ed.*]

400. [That is, notorious or manifest.—*Ed.*]

401. [In the margin of the authorized version the verse is translated thus "A great man grieveth all and he hireth the fool, he hireth also transgressors."—*Ed.*]

402. [That is, violent blowing. *Cairding* however, is not unlikely the proper word, a *caird* being in Scotland the name of a tinker.—*Ed.*]

403. ["Although you expel nature by violence, she will still return."—*Per. Epist.* lib. i. ep. 10. ver. 24.—*Ed.*]

404. [Having burst, as it were, its floodgates.—*Ed.*]

405. [That is, more.—*Ed.*]

406. [That is, a deficiency.—*Ed.*]

407. [Gen. xxx. 11.—*Ed.*]

408. [Vide Cic. de Offic. lib. iii. cap. 33.—*Ed.*]

409. [Or mines.—*Ed.*]

410. [Or, unsuitable.—*Ed.*]

411. ["Charity does not inflict punishment because an offence has been committed, but lest an offence should be committed."—*Ed.*]

412. ["He that is not inclined to-day will be more inclined to-morrow." This is reversing the saying of the poet—
Qui non est hodie, cras minus aptus erit
Ovid, Remed. Amor. ver. 94.—*Ed.*]

413. ["She does not see what is in the bag behind her."

Sed non videmus manticæ quod in tergo est.
Catul. Carm. xxii. ver. 21.

There is an allusion here to one of the fables of Æsop. Jupiter, says Aesop, placed two bags upon men. The one, which contained their own faults, he put upon their back, and the other, which was filled with the faults of others, he suspended from their neck, upon their breast. In this way, we cannot see our own misdeeds, but, perceiving those of others, we censure them freely. Phæd. Fab. Æsop, lib. iv. fab. 10.—*Ed.*]

414. [These are terms (locus inventionis *the place or topic of invention*, and medium, *the argument or middle term of a syllogism*) which, belonging to the dialectic art, were employed by the school-men. All the arts and sciences have certain general subjects connected with them which presuppose particular facts, axioms, and rules. These general subjects, being used in the *invention* of arguments, were called topics or common places. "They were so called by Aristotle, as if they were the seats from which arguments were to be brought forth." (Sic appellatæ ab Aristotele sunt hæ quasi sedes e quibus argumenta promuntur). Cic. Top. cap. ii.—*Ed.*]

415. [We grant and solicit in our turn this indulgence. Hor. De Art. poet. ver. 11.—*Ed.*]

416. [Or, condescendence.—*Ed.*]

417. [Or, without its begetting love.—*Ed.*]

418. [Overlook it.—*Ed.*]

419. [Most.—*Ed.*]

420. [The word *homo* (man) has been supposed to be derived from *humus* (the ground) because man sprang from the earth. Quintillian's objection to this derivation of the word is that all other animals have the same origin. (quasi vero non omnibus animal bus eadem origo. Instit. Orator lib. i, cap. 6) Such an objection however has but little force. For though, according to the account which Moses gives of the creation, the earth at the command of God, not only brought forth man, but other creatures, (Gen. i. 24) man alone was called *Adam* מדא because he was formed of the dust of the *ground*, (האדמה) Gen. ii. 7.—Joseph, Antiq. lib. i, cap. 1.—*Ed.*]

421. [That is, "humble beings."—*Ed.*]

422. [See note *page 168*.—*Ed.*]

423. [Humility is "the seasoning of the virtues," as well as "the garb." Cicero represents suavity of speech and manners to be the seasoning of friendship (condimentum amicitiæ). De Amicitia, cap. 18.—*Ed.*]

424. [That is, "an ornament and covering."—*Ed.*]

425. [Crede mihi, bene qui latuit, bene vixit; et intra
Fortunam debet quisque manere suam.
"Believe me, he who has not attracted the notice of the world has lived well, and every one ought to keep within his own proper sphere." Ovid Trist. lib. iii. eleg. iv, ver. 25.—*Ed.*]

426. ["He who falls on a smooth surface, (yet this rarely happens,) falls in such a way that he can rise again from the ground he has touched." Ovid, ut supra, ver. 17.—*Ed.*]

427. [A relation of the principal circumstances in Binning's life follows.—*Ed.*]

428. [That is, he will not refuse.—*Ed.*]

429. [Parcel.—*Ed.*]

430. [Such a disburdening of former offences.—*Ed.*]

431. [Inclination.—*Ed.*]

432. [De Agricola filios suos docente. Æsop. Fab. p. 98. Oxon. 1653.—*Ed.*]

433. [Subdue.—*Ed.*]

434. [Such a wonder.—*Ed.*]

435. [Violent inclination.—*Ed.*]

436. [That is, truths of little value.—*Ed.*]

437. [In the Scottish universities, they were said to have *laureated*, who had a decree conferred upon them, as they were "crowned with laurel leaves." Ev. Un. Com. vol. i. p. 153. Lond. 1837.—*Ed.*]

438. [These are the generous sentiments of an enlightened Christian. They would lead us to infer that the author's views, as a Protester, had been

modified somewhat before he died or that he had never taken such high ground, as some others on this score.—*Ed.*]

439. [Or, *while we, on the other hand.—Ed.*]

440. [See note, *page 168.—Ed.*]

441. [Perhaps it should be *at least, less.—Ed.*]

442. [The word *mystery* seems to be used here in the sense of *energy*. It is sometimes spelt by Scottish writers *mister* and *myster*, and signifies an art or calling, being derived from the old French word *mestier*, a trade. When employed to denote something above human intelligence, it has a different origin (being formed from μυστηριον, a secret).—*Ed.*]

443. [Exonerate, or unburthen.—*Ed.*]

444. [Or harness.—*Ed.*]

445. [Senec. Ep. 107. See note, *page 76.—Ed.*]

446. [We are not, "of our own authority."—*Ed.*]

447. [That is, weight or force.—*Ed.*]

448. [That is, *the honour* not *a load* or *a load of honour.—Ed.*]

449. [Confined.—*Ed.*]

450. [See note, *page 115.—Ed.*]

451. [The friendly salutation which the steward of Joseph addressed to his master's brethren, when they went a second time to Egypt to purchase corn, was (מכל מולש Shalom leikoum) "Peace be to you." After the lapse of so many ages, it is interesting to know that this still continues to be, with little variation, the common salutation of friends in the East. Salam aleikoum, "Peace be with you," is immediately acknowledged by a similar greeting, Aliekoum salam, "To you be peace."—*Ed.*]

452. [To sit an offer is, not to accept it.—*Ed.*]

453. [Reception.—*Ed.*]

454. [The heathen mythologists represented the Sirens to be three in number, and described them as effecting the destruction of mariners, by luring them from their course with their singing.

—They the hearts
Enchant of all, who on their coast arrive
The wretch, who unforewarn'd approaching, hears
The Sirens' voice, his wife and little ones

Ne'er fly to gratulate his glad return;
But him the Sirens sitting in the meads
Charm with mellifluous song, although he see
Bones heap'd around them, and the mouldering skins
Of hapless men, whose bodies have decay'd.
Hom. Od. lib. xii. v. 39. Cowper's Translation.]

455. [That is, one tune from another.—*Ed.*]
456. [Or gifts of nature.—*Ed.*]
457. [See note, *page 595.*—*Ed.*]
458. [In the ancient Scottish dialect as in this instance, *always* is frequently synonymous with *although*, *however*, *notwithstanding.*—*Ed.*]
459. [That is, coldly.—*Ed.*]
460. [Natural.—*Ed.*]
461. [Fallen out or quarrelled.—*Ed.*]
462. [Some words are omitted here, which may be supplied thus:—though *they* said *this*, they perverted God's meaning of the law, &c.—*Ed.*]
463. [Serves the purpose.—*Ed.*]
464. [Imperfect attempts.—*Ed.*]
465. [A Scottish forensic word corresponding to *Surety.*—*Ed.*]
466. [Acknowledge this.—*Ed.*]
467. [A name formerly given to bankrupts in Scotland.—See Act. James VI. par. 23, cap. 18.—*Ed.*]
468. [Attending the church.—*Ed.*]
469. [Aim at.—*Ed.*]
470. [Near the command.—*Ed.*]
471. [A belief in the prevalence of witchcraft at this time seems to have pervaded all ranks and classes. An Act of Parliament was passed against it on the 1st of February, 1649.—*Ed.*]
472. [Portal, or gate.—*Ed.*]
473. [Exempted.—*Ed.*]
474. [The illustration of the second proposition found in the text, "There is a faith feigned, and a faith unfeigned, a true and a false faith," (p. 602) is omitted. We may conclude that this was the subject of a separate sermon, which has been lost.—*Ed.*]

475. [Deposes or testifies.—*Ed.*]
476. [That is, foresee or anticipate.—*Ed.*]
477. [Charges, or accusations.—*Ed.*]
478. [Than.—*Ed.*]
479. [Gates.—*Ed.*]
480. [Remove.—*Ed.*]
481. [Always.—*Ed.*]
482. [A proverbial expression signifying food and raiment.—*Ed.*]
483. [Much less.—*Ed.*]
484. [The sect of *Seekers* hold that there are not at this time, neither have been for many ages past any true ministers or ambassadors of Christ. (Gillespie's Miscellany Questions, p. 1. Edinburgh, 1649.) A few years before this, Laurence Clarkson, a *Seeker*, published a pamphlet entitled "The Pilgrimage of Saints." Edwards, in his Gangræna (Part I, p. 24, Part II, p. 6. London, 1646) refers to it for an account of the opinion of the Seekers. Clarkson declared that in these days there ought to be no churches built, no sacraments administered, that the saints as pilgrims, wander here as in a temple filled with smoke, not being able to find religion, and that, on this account, waiting for a church and for the coming of the Spirit as the apostles did, they ought to seek knowledge of any passenger, of any opinion or tenet whatsoever.—*Ed.*]
485. [See note *page 607*.—*Ed.*]
486. [Kindred alliance.—*Ed.*]
487. [Or, in the third place.—*Ed.*]
488. [Notwithstanding.—*Ed.*]
489. [A cold desire.—*Ed.*]
490. [That is a glimmering or slight degree of desire.—*Ed.*]
491. [This was the exclamation of Archimedes the celebrated geometrician of Syracuse, (ευρηκα, ευρηκα), after discovering, when in the bath, a method of detecting the quantity of alloy, which a fraudulent artisan had mixed with the gold of Hiero's crown. (Plut. Mor. et Phil. Op. p. 1094.) An exclamation somewhat similar was uttered by Cicero, when, searching for the tomb of Archimedes in the neighbourhood of Syracuse he at length perceived it covered with thorns and brambles

(Cic. Tusc. Quest lib. v. cap 23.) But if they had cause to be delighted, much more surely had Philip the apostle reason to be so when addressing Nathanael, he cried out in ecstasy—We have found him of whom Moses in the law and the prophets did write, Jesus of Nazareth, the son of Joseph! John i. 45.—*Ed.*]

492. [In the present world.—*Ed.*]

493. [Specify or enumerate.—*Ed.*]

494. [Acknowledging.—*Ed.*]

495. [Path or way.—*Ed.*]

496. [Than.—*Ed.*]

497. [Fix upon.—*Ed.*]

498. [That is, no thought of eternity.—*Ed.*]

499. [Quid non mortalia pectora cogis
Auri sacra fames?
Virg. Æneid, lib. iii. ver. 56.
"O sacred hunger of pernicious gold!
What bands of faith can impious lucre hold?"
Dryden's Translation.
Nihil enim est fam angusti animi, tamque parvi, quam amare divitias nihil honestius, magnifi entrusque, quam pecuniam contemnere, si non habeas si habeas, ad beneficentiam liberalitem que conferre. "There is no surer characteristic of a narrow and little mind than to love riches, nothing more amiable and noble than to despise money if you possess it not—if you possess it, to be beneficent and liberal in the use of it." Cic. De Offic. lib. i. cap. 20.—*Ed.*]

500. [That is, "It is difficult things that are admired."—*Ed.*]

501. [Excites.—*Ed.*]

502. [From these, as from mount Pisgah.—*Ed.*]

503. [That is, not "by a leap."—*Ed.*]

504. [Intrusted.—*Ed.*]

505. [Too little.—*Ed.*]

506. [That is, bedecks.—*Ed.*]

507. [That is, has no interest in the world.—*Ed.*]

508. [That is, *the way in which you will take or receive.*—*Ed.*]

509. [That is, the duty of sobriety.—*Ed.*]

510. [Much more.—*Ed.*]

511. [It must be perceived that the reading ought to be "overcome *like* the Archangel."—*Ed.*]

512. [It is no less obvious that for "the prince Gabriel" we ought to read, *the prince Michael.* See Dan. x. 13, 21; Jude 9; Rev. xii. 7.—*Ed.*]

513. [That is, the prospective glass.—*Ed.*]

514. [Or tutelage.—*Ed.*]

515. [Declining.—*Ed.*]

516. [That is, disposed. The word, though now obsolete, is found in Hooker.—*Ed.*]

517. [That is, that hang *low*, and take a *sweep* of every thing by the way.—*Ed.*]

518. [A single word appears to have dropped out here, the absence of which materially changes the meaning of the author, and makes him contradict himself. The sentence, it is conceived, ought to run thus:—faith and a good conscience scarce sail *but* in one bottom, that is, *in one ship.*—*Ed.*]

519. [That is, insipid.—*Ed.*]

520. [Upon the earth.—*Ed.*]

521. ["It is hard to find many who are not tipplers or common drunkards, or will *drink drunk* on occasions and with company." Causes of the Lord's Wrath, p. 17. printed in the year 1653.—*Ed.*]

522. [That is, a convenient time or place.—*Ed.*]

523. [Or, till the evening.—*Ed.*]

524. [That is, *insane* worldlings.—*Ed.*]

525. [Property.—*Ed.*]

END

Lightning Source UK Ltd.
Milton Keynes UK
UKHW020420301220
376108UK00003B/212

9 781375 003759